Antiquity Papers 1

LANDSCAPES FROM ANTIQUITY

edited by

Simon Stoddart

Antiquity Publications Ltd

Cambridge 2000

ANTIQUITY, the archaeological journal founded in 1927, covers a wide sweep of the modern development of archaeology. This is the first of a planned series of volumes which will take selected articles from ANTIQUITY, from the great range of archaeological thought and practice of the nearly 75 years which cover the professional recognition of the discipline. Our intention is to set the original articles within a modern context, but, as always with ANTIQUITY, to add a personal perspective.

One personal perspective is the choice of articles. Over 250 articles covering over 2500 pages have been published broadly on the theme of landscape. 24 articles covering some 250 pages have been selected for this volume. Lack of space has necessitated the exclusion of many articles among the more populated landscape themes. A principal aim has been to illustrate the breadth of the subject.

The articles have all been reproduced in the modern format of ANTIQUITY, occasionally dropping some of the illustrations (e.g. Zammit 1928) and making some corrections (e.g. Barker 1988). The personalized introductions by the editor introduced by Glyn Daniel have been replaced by longer introductions to set context and outline subsequent developments. All articles and illustrations were originally published in ANTIQUITY. The references include the full bibliographic reference of each article. The cover illustration was published in ANTIQUITY by Piggott (1965: 170, figure 3) as an example of superb draughtsmanship.

I should like to thank the authors for allowing their articles to be reprinted. I should like to thank Anne Chippindale and Libby Peachey for all their hard work in the production process.

Published in the United Kingdom in 2000 by Antiquity Publications Ltd
New Hall, Cambridge CB3 0DF

ISBN 0-9539762-0-3

Printed and bound in the United Kingdom by Short Run Press Ltd, Exeter

LANDSCAPES FROM ANTIQUITY

Contents

Introduction
by SIMON STODDART

THE THEME of landscape is embedded deep in the origins of archaeology as a discipline, many years before the foundation of ANTIQUITY in 1927. These more distant origins of the landscape archaeology in the Romantic Movement are, nevertheless, covered in its pages (Piggott 1937). The early landscape articles in ANTIQUITY on contemporary research (Section 1) record the emerging systematization of landscape studies in the 1920s. Ordered landscapes — trackways, fieldsystems (FIGURE 1) — were recognized in increasing numbers by techniques such as aerial photography (Section 2) and detailed ground survey. Concurrently, steps were taken to prove and differentiate their antiquity. Pattern became increasingly chronologically ordered.

The editor of ANTIQUITY has always had a powerful influence on the shape of the journal, but he (and most recently she) has always drawn on the most exciting and relevant of current research. Consequently, the frequency and content of landscape in ANTIQUITY provides an illuminating commentary on the definition and prominence of the theme *landscape* in archaeological research (TABLE 1). In the time of the first editor (1927–1957) Crawford, there was a rich variety of approaches to landscape which included, but was not dominated by aerial photography. Many of the classics of aerial photography (e.g. Woodbury, Durrington Walls and Woodhenge) were illustrated, but there was a wider range of landscapes from regions and themes as separated as the classical world and Maori hillforts. One area of investigation is perhaps unexpected. There was significant study of modern 'ethnographic' landscapes in the *celtic* fringe, drawing on ethnohistory to deepen understanding of long-lasting landscape practices.

The period of the second editor (1958–1986), Glyn Daniel, although also a geographer, had much less variety. The only systematic presence of landscape was provided between 1964 and 1980 by the regular inclusion of aerial photographic reconnaissance by the Cambridge 'plane of St Joseph and comparable continental European coverage (Section 2). One explanation may be that an interregnum existed between the excitement and novelty of the Ordnance Survey/Royal Commission surveys under Crawford (which of course continued in their own volumes and as reviews in ANTIQUITY) and a new and varied investigation of landscape, employing changed methodologies. For instance, it was only in 1977 that the first results of the second generation of a new wave of surveys from the Mediterranean world were reported in ANTIQUITY (Barker 1977). Two distinct strands of the British tradition of survey were thus integrated in its pages.

The third editor of ANTIQUITY, Christopher Chippindale (1987–1997), brought a major expansion and proliferation of landscape approaches which reflected the changed conception of the subject. The many and varied strands of landscape study were once again presented alongside one another in the pages of ANTIQUITY. Physical (Section 5) , industrial (Section 6), contested (Section 7) and experienced (Section 8) landscapes are the themes chosen here, but many others such as political (e.g. Ralston 1988), colonial (e.g. Young 1987), agrarian (e.g. Allen & Lewison 1987) and military (e.g. Dobinson *et al.* 1997) landscapes could equally have been chosen. These are the new generation of interpretative themes which have emerged from the classificatory structures of field monuments. These monuments had formed such a central part of the early British tradition of

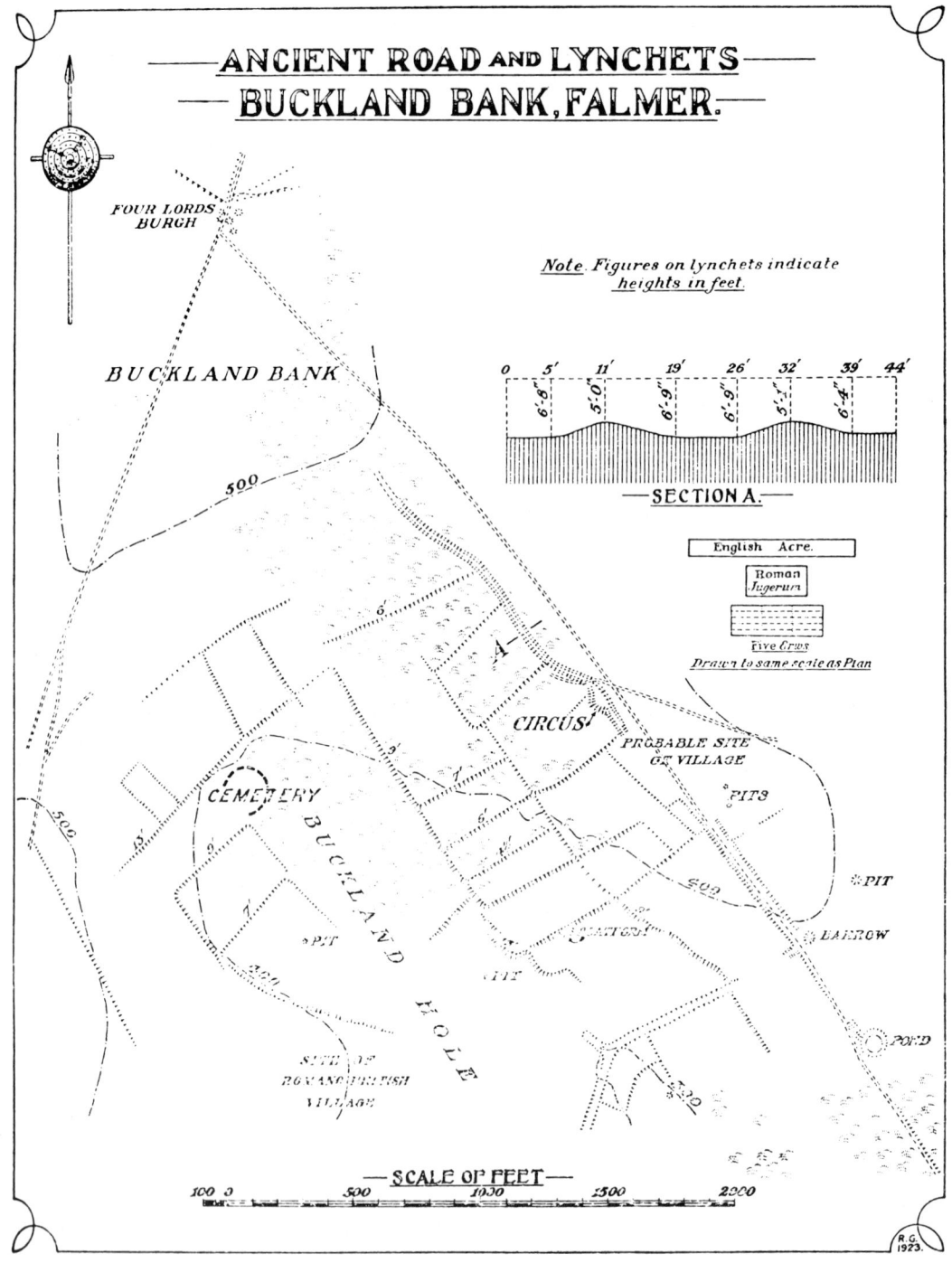

FIGURE 1. *This fine drawing embellished with an appropriately stylized North sign is a good illustration of the systematization of knowledge of the prehistoric landscapes of England recorded in* ANTIQUITY. *(Holleyman 1935: 451).*

landscape, strongly assisted by both an aerial perspective and a strong topographical understanding. Furthermore, the increasing sophistication of the method of survey (Section 3) was registered in a series of articles (e.g. Bintliff & Snodgrass 1988a; Schofield 1989). A comparable rate and range of landscape articles has continued under the present editors (1998–2000) who are active landscape archaeologists themselves. The coverage has included a special section on the archaeology of landscapes.

editor	aerial photography	landscape (including aerial photography)	total pages
Crawford	1·5%	7·8%	11,616
Daniel	2·6%	4·2%	8736
Chippindale	0·4%	9·5 %	10,387
Malone	0·3 %	11 %	3006
All editors	1·3%	7·7%	33,745

TABLE 1. *The proportion of space devoted to aerial photography and landscape in the pages of* ANTIQUITY.

Landscapes in archaeology

The term 'landscape' appears to have been adopted as a painterly term from Dutch in the 16th century (Schama 1995: 10). In the intervening centuries, landscape has become a theme common to many modern disciplines. Art, architecture, anthropology and history are developing specialist interests (Appleton 1996; Hirsch & O'Hanlon 1995; Schama 1995; Spirn 1998). It is central to two academic subjects: archaeology and geography. Both these disciplines share an unresolved tension between the human and physical landscape where balance is difficult to attain (Cosgrove & Daniels 1988). Of these, archaeology provides the most developed exploration of time and space, and, to its great strength (although sometimes considered its great weakness) it draws on a great diversity of definitions and insights. To be provocative, archaeology has a privileged access to landscape through time depth. It needs to be clarified for some geographers that this time depth requires archaeological knowledge to understand the underlying assumptions and sampling issues (Stoddart 1999).

Landscape, conceived broadly, is central to archaeological study. Many archaeologists have correctly emphasized the centrality of material culture for archaeology (Childe 1956; Clarke 1968). However, even material culture, recognized as a central focus, must have context in order to allow engagement and effective interpretation. Landscape, variously measured, is simply that very context in which objects are found, and from which meaning can be sought.

Two authors — Kent Flannery (1976) and David Clarke (1972) — have been immensely influential in their studies of landscape, as in other fields. The studies of the Early Mesoamerican Village and the Glastonbury Lake Village respectively share one common and influential sense of landscape even if some other inherent assumptions of the 1970s may now be criticized. These two studies have demonstrated the interlinkage of different spatial dimensions of the archaeological landscape, and given indications of the richness of approaches to exploring those dimensions. A similar concept of the many-layered landscape is favoured here. The interconnected and many-layered approach to

author	natural landscape	cultural landscape	
Commissioned by: Wagstaff (1987)	Palaeoecology of erosion Prehistoric subsistence	Economic Industry Power	
Crandell (1993)		Confronting Staging Cloistering Elevating Bewildering Offering a prospect Picturesque Democratic Perceptive	time ↓
Schama (1995)		Wood Water Rock	
Ashmore & Knapp (1999)		Constructed *vs* Conceptual = Ideational Memory Identity Social order Transformation	
Muir (1999)		Mind Politics and power Evaluation Symbolism Aesthetics Place	

TABLE 2. *Some classifications of landscape approach.*

landscape is now commonly favoured in archaeology and history (Schackel 1993). Johnson (1996) has noted parallel trends at the different scales of landscape and domestic space, effectively different scales of landscape, and Hall has emphasized the mutual interdependence of global and the local (Hall 2000: 78). A broadly similar framework even survives in studies that are explicitly testing the accepted approach to fieldwork (Bender *et al.* 1997). One section (Section 4) in this volume is devoted to landscapes where these layers have been uncovered by integrated, intensive and repeated archaeological research: Wessex, the Fenlands of East Anglia and Italy.

Current researchers have added many new exploratory models to the anthropological and geographical which tended to guide scholars (and indeed Flannery and Clarke) in the 1960s and 1970s. The 1990s have especially witnessed a plethora of volumes of the theme of landscape where agreement on a conceptual scheme or a landscape definition is difficult to achieve (Wagstaff 1987; Townsend 1992; Bender 1993a; Bradley 1993;

Tilley 1994; Bradley 1998; Bruck & Goodman 1999; Carmichael *et al.* 1994; Ucko & Layton 1999; Ashmore & Knapp 1999; Muir 1999). A survey of some of their typologies of landscape (and some from other disciplines (Crandell 1993; Schama 1995)) is sufficient to show the variety (TABLE 2). The most convincing approaches attempt to involve both the natural and the cultural. Individuals may have different views of landscape, but are still affected by its physical form and have to define practical ways to survive and thrive in any given landscape.

In spite of this variety there are some common trends. Outside strictly environmental approaches to landscape, there is a general move from a stress on the natural to an emphasis on the variously defined cultural landscape. There are extremes. From the post-modern perspective, landscape is no longer a palimpsest, or series of superimposed layers, which can be recovered but 'a flickering text displayed on the word processor screen whose meaning can be created, extended, altered, elaborated and finally obliterated by the merest touch of a button' (Daniels & Cosgrove 1988: 8). It is possible to down play the flickering qualities of landscape and engage with the 'veins of myth and memory that lies beneath the surface' (Schama 1995: 14), but what most historians such as Schama fail to recognize is the importance of pre-textual landscapes in developing those 'veins of myth and memory'. A fully articulated approach requires archaeology and recognizes the full depth of history in the creation of landscape without sacrificing the importance of the environmental setting (Bradley 2000).

Some continue to recognize the importance of the natural as well as cultural landscape. Some do not. Many of those who do not, hope to avoid the problem by attacking the dichotomy of natural and cultural, claiming that one is dissolved into the other. On the other hand, the landscape is generally given an active rather than passive role, now working more on the minds than the stomachs of the individuals who walk over its topography. The most judicious approaches acknowledge that there is an interrelationship between the symbolic and the practical which avoids the current polemics of dichotomy (Brück & Goodman 1999: 10). The symbolic is neither some ideological superstructure nor a governing agent.

Amongst field archaeologists there are also methodological trends. Settlement archaeology has been replaced by a study of the continuity and discontinuity of landscape, and this has had important consequences in the methodology of landscape reconstruction (Section 3). In many British-based theory-orientated approaches, there has been a tendency to concentrate on monuments, the visible continuities of an historic landscape. This approach, bedded in the problems of Wessex prehistory, ignores the more subtle nuances of landscape which are required for a complete reconstruction. In the Mediterranean world particularly, a balance of monument and less apparent 'land use' is being achieved, drawing on a sophisticated range of material culture, including texts where and when they are relevant. Archaeologists in general are now beginning to address not just the issues of field archaeology, but also the necessary theoretical adjustments which accompany the redefinition of the settlement and the intervening space (Brück & Goodman 1999: 11).

1 Early studies of landscapes

THE BRITISH TRADITION of landscape studies is long-standing. It is pre-eminently a geographical tradition. The first editor of ANTIQUITY, himself a geographer, engaged a large number of distinguished contributors who laid the foundations of a type of landscape study which continues today in the journal of *Landscape History*, through the work of the Ordnance Survey, the Royal Commissions and in many regional studies recognized by geographers (Muir 1999: xiii). As Everson (1999: xi–xii) writes of Christopher Taylor's contribution, this represents a curiosity about all aspects of the landscape brought together as a coherent story. It is this vision of landscape that has been heavily critiqued as 'a huge Heath Robinson apparatus* within which human beings have the metaphysical status of ghosts in the machine' (Thomas 1993: 25–6). As we will see this is not a fair assessment, even if they failed to cite continental European philosophers. The strength and weakness of the approach lie in its empirical detail.

Themistocles Zammit was the father of Maltese archaeology. He brought system and professionalism to the study of the Maltese past. His main achievements were the products of excavation and material culture, but the ANTIQUITY article on the cart-ruts of Malta demonstrates his landscape interests. These signs of intensive land-use on the Maltese islands have been much studied in more recent times (Hughes 1999; Grima 2000: 37–41), but Zammit had already succinctly exposed the problem in 1928. He covered the dating and the purpose of the trackways, making a highly plausible case that they were caused by the need to replace earth on the eroded slopes behind terraces. In this interpretation he avoided the temptation of attributing the tracks to the movement of stone for the construction of the famous prehistoric temples when the evidence failed to support this idea. Instead he identified terracing as a second, even more pervasive phase of construction in the Maltese islands, and linked the tracks to their maintenance. The only progress since the time of Zammit has been to undertake extensive survey, employing aerial photographs similar to those used by Zammit to illustrate his article (Gracie 1954; Parker & Rubinstein 1984; Ventura & Tanti 1994), giving better statistical sense of the their distribution. Gracie (1954), in a second ANTIQUITY publication, suggests that a large proportion of the tracks follow contours or lead to promontories, but since this is based on a local study it may not be the general pattern. Recent work (Brudenell pers. comm.) at Mtarfa has suggested that these ruts may at least in part be locally dated to the Phoenician period, although many are now covered by modern building. The characteristics of these trackways across the eroded islands are illustrative of an early understanding of the nature of landscape. Cart-ruts collectively form a classic palimpsest, the material record of repeated activity across the landscape from prehistoric times until the classical period. It is probable that all the local evidence for dating the cart-ruts to the Bronze Age (Trump 1998), Phoenician (Brudenell pers. comm.) and Classical periods (Bonanno 1997: 72) is correct, pointing to a spate of earth-moving and quarrying activity that was not repeated again until the time of the Knights of St John.

---

*   A reference to a cartoonist famous for his depiction of clumsy mechanical apparatus.

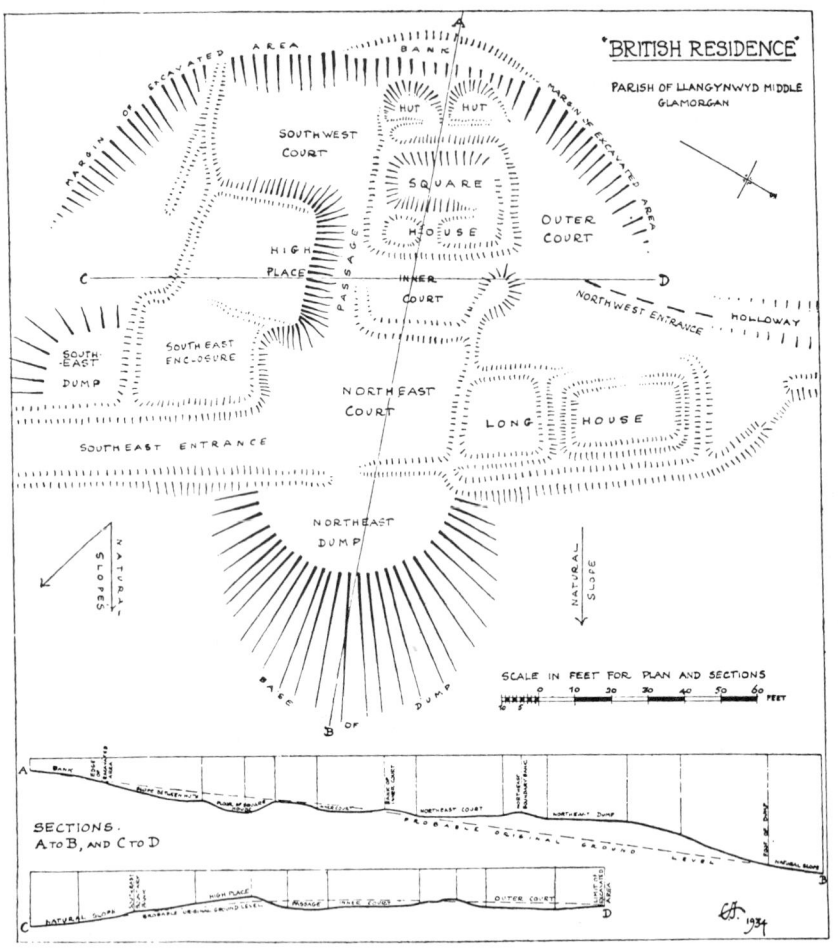

FIGURE 1. *Fox worked with his wife, herself a distinguished archaeologist (Fox 2000), on many projects. One field survey was of the Margam Mountain in Glamorgan. This sketch and profiles of the Residence is a fine example of field records from their joint article in* ANTIQUITY *(Fox & Fox 1934: 410)*

Sir Cyril Fox was, together with O.G.S. Crawford, one of the major influences on landscape archaeology in Britain (FIGURE 1). Two books were fundamental. *The archaeology of the Cambridge region* (Fox 1923) was one of the first doctoral dissertations in archaeology, written while he was at Magdalene College, Cambridge. It presented a series of period distribution maps set against an environmental landscape of fens and uplands. This same distinction between highland and lowland was written large in his later book, *The personality of Britain* (Fox 1952). The ANTIQUITY article on dykes, one of five papers he wrote for the journal, was written shortly after *The archaeology of the Cambridge region*. In the dykes article we detect the same emphasis on the physical environment: 'the changes . . . in the appearance of the country are determined by alterations in the soil and subsoil'. However, the analysis goes much further than a simple relationship between distribution of archaeological features and environmental zones. Although the dykes in turn are related to these physical traits, he employs terms which stressed 'visual control', identified canalized movement of individuals, and, furthermore, made conscious attempts to enter the 'mind' of the builder or builders and fit them within their social and political context. The landscape is interpreted. There are more than the seeds here of a sophisticated cultural analysis whose language is scarcely dated. A primary concern is, it is true, to define space (distribution) and time (dating by selective excavation). In this he built explicitly on the work of Pitt-Rivers and corrected the Iron Age date he had earlier hypothesized (Fox 1923: 90) when faced by new excavated data, indicating the post-Roman period. The effectiveness of Fox's analysis is demonstrated by the fact that more recent fieldwork on the same dykes (Malim 2000) has scarcely affected conclusions, adding some refinement of dating and placing the dykes in relationship to major trackways.

E.C. Curwen is a representative of the strong regional tradition of archaeology in Britain. Curwen was best known for his contribution to archaeology of the county of Sussex (Curwen 1929) where he was a major force in the development of local archaeology. In ANTIQUITY, he frequently wrote on prehistoric agriculture (Curwen 1927; 1928; 1930), enriched with wonderful draftsmanship (FIGURE 2), but he also contributed to the study of British landscape ethnography. Both Fox (1937; Fox & Fox 1934) and Curwen sought out 'primitive' agricultural conditions within the British Isles to further understanding of ancient landscapes. Curwen's study of the Hebrides focused on the Black Houses of Lewis that 'perfectly fit the wild landscape of the islands' at a time when social reform was rehousing their occupants in 'red-brick

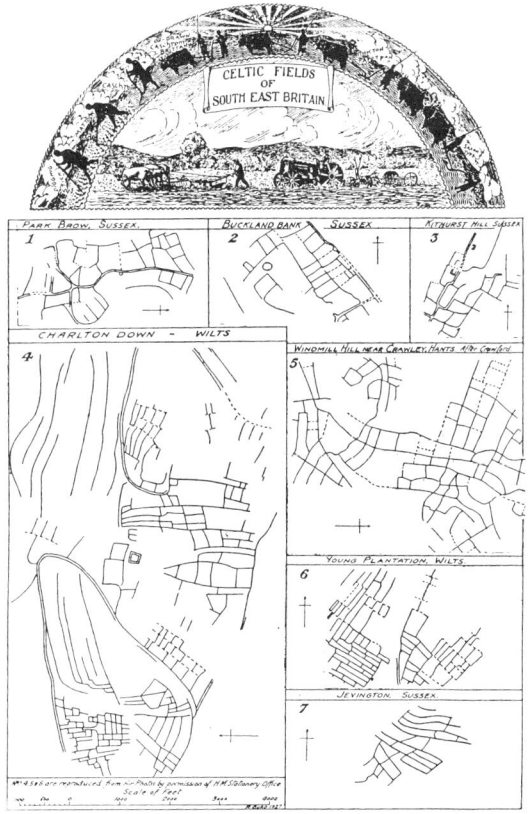

FIGURE 2. *Curwen's landscape drawings reveal considerable command of detail, as well as the luxury of embellishment with scenes of early agriculture. These scenes of prehistoric Celtic fields of southeast Britain and the evolution of the plough were published as part of his study of prehistoric agriculture in Britain published in the first volume of ANTIQUITY (Curwen 1927: 276).*

Council-Houses'.* Curwen is already arguing for preservation of these vestiges of an ancient landscape in 1938. The further focus of the article is on the *shieling*, a temporary shelter situated in remote parts of the landscape. Material culture — characterized as another primitive survival — is integrated within this spatial pattern. Throughout Curwen combines direct observation with ethnohistory to provide a complete account of what would now be called social practice, even if it is shrouded by concepts of the 'survival of the primitive', 'culture lag', 'backward races of the tropics' and 'woman's work' which are now politically unacceptable as terminology. However, once stripped of that language, the whole approach has aspects of more enduring value. Here is an almost ethno-

---

* Council houses in Britain are built by the state.

graphic access to the material culture of landscape, drawing on personal obervation and earlier accounts. The theme is epitomized by the combination of a black house and Dun Carloway broch in one picture (Curwen, this volume: FIGURE 8): the continuity of prehistory or the *longue durée* before the term had been defined.

Figures such as Hoskins (1955) are often credited with the understanding of the English landscape, but his publications were later than figures such as Fox, Curwen and Crawford. Furthermore, he chose to play down the fundamental prehistoric phase of development. Like many historians he would have been well advised to have read AN-TIQUITY, where this importance was beginning to emerge. It is only in the second edition of his volume, *The making of the English landscape* (Hoskins 1977), that he came to the conclusion that 'everything is older than we think' in a radically prehistoric sense.

Alexander Hogg was by training an engineer which gave his passion for archaeology the professionalism of the surveyor (Briggs 1981). It was only in 1949, 22 years after graduation, that he moved from a lectureship in engineering at Cambridge to his first archaeological post in the Royal Commission for Wales. As with Fox, Wales was an important focus of both career and research. The ANTIQUITY paper reprinted here predates this professional appointment by six years. In later years Hogg was synonymous with hill-fort studies. In this paper there is a classic combination of distribution map and typological classification to lay the ground-work for analytical understanding of the landscape. The problem was and continues to be dating, with the relative lack of material culture present on these sites. Hogg's outdated interpretation of the rectilinear enclosures as the product of migrations from the continent partly derives from this difficulty. Nevertheless, without these achievements the more interpretative phases of landscape archaeology would not have been possible. The ANTIQUITY paper was the product of research which opened up the importance of pre-Roman settlement in the northeast of Britain, away from the concentration of research on Wessex and the southeast. Publicity of this resource, perhaps in part in response to the invitation at the head of the reprinted article, led to the excavation of the well-preserved earthworks and a deeper understanding of the varied landscapes of Iron Age Britain (Burgess 1984; Bevan 1999) so that today it is one of the 13 (out of 72) regions where there is a reasonable framework of understanding (Haselgrove n.d.).

These early approaches appear, at first sight, to be mere distribution maps. The distribution map has been characterized as stripped of cultural meaning, providing simply a sequence of synchronic snapshots (Bruck & Goodman 1999: 7–8). Allowing for the fact that these early studies are concentrating on the systematization of time and space, there is some effort by the authors reprinted here to go beyond the constraints of ordered chronology. They belonged to a humanistic world before the impact of the New Archaeology and had interests in reconstructing a rounded and not simply environmental vision of landscape. They also mark the foundations of a powerful tradition of British landscape archaeology which had its impact not only on archaeology, but also on geographers (Roberts 1996).

Prehistoric Cart-tracks in Malta
by **T. ZAMMIT**

ANTIQUITY 2 (5), 1928

ONE of the problems that students of Maltese archaeology have to face is the meaning of the numerous cart-tracks furrowing most of the barren rock-surfaces. These tracks are scarce on Gozo and non-existent on the islands of Comino and Filfola.

They consist of pairs of parallel grooves running for long distances on the hard coralline limestone patches, now straight and now curved as if avoiding an obstacle or having to change their direction. The grooves are mostly v-shaped, usually from 10 to 20 inches wide (25–50 cm) on the surface, and about 4 inches (10 cm) at the bottom. Between the two grooves, measured at the middle part, the distance is nearly always 4 feet 6 inches (1.37m). Naturally the depth of the grooves varies with the lie of the ground; if there is a strong tilt sideways, one of the grooves is shallow whilst the other is very deep. Grooves over one foot deep are very common. The carts that ran over these roads had an axle-tree about four and a half feet long and the wheels had to be very high to move freely in the grooves. The modern country carts of Malta have an axle 5 feet (1·53 m) long and a diameter of 5 feet 3 inches (1·60 m) (FIGURE 1).

FIGURE 1. *Modern cart-tracks, Malta.*

I do not think that there can be much doubt as to the kind of vehicle used on this track: they were, very probably, strong heavy carts with solid wooden wheels without a metallic tyre. It has been suggested that some kind of sledge with strong runners may have been used instead, but when one is familiar with the sharp curves frequently met with along these tracks the idea of a sledge is abandoned, as no runner could be made to glide at all under such conditions.

If no account is taken of the long time required to wear out the hard coralline limestone to the actual depth of some of the grooves, it seems hard to believe that a wooden wheel could cause such erosion, but time explains the difficult task. The grooves are triangular in section and very smooth. Of course pebbles and sand between wheel and groove would act as an abrasive and help the erosion. The grooves caused by modern wheels, fitted with iron tyres, are differently shaped from the smooth prehistoric ones; they are rectangular in section and the wobbling of the wheel abrades the sides and wears them away rapidly and irregularly. These grooves appear therefore wide and straight-walled and are at once recognized by the most superficial observer.

These cart-tracks, for no other name can be given to them, are to be met with on practically every stretch of barren land on the slope or on the top of a hill. They are sometimes seen to run in single pairs wending their way over hill and dale but more often they run in groups, crossed occasionally by other tracks coming from a different direction (FIGURE 2). In some cases their number is so great that one wonders how many carts had been detailed to carry on this heavy traffic. A group of ten pairs of ruts run close to each other on the sloping surface of the hilly ground to the east of Nadur tower in the Benjemma district. They cross the main road at the end of the slope and may be followed in a southern direction to the west of Tas-Salib road towards Ghemieri. Another numerous group of these ruts covers the undulating ground of the same district to the south-east. The uneven surface is furrowed deeply by over twelve pairs of cart-tracks. They are far deeper ruts than those in the group just mentioned, but they are less striking to the observer because they cannot be seen on a long stretch of ground like the others, as they disappear here and there under modern fields and boundary walls.

One gets an impressive sight to the south of the Boschetto gardens, where the barren slope running towards the Inquisitor's Palace and the Tal Ghalia plateau is furrowed by seven parallel groups of ruts covering the surface like so many railroads built by a modern engineer.

On closely observing these primitive roads one is impressed by the fact that the grooves run by the side of a narrow strip of rock which cannot be called a path on account of its rough, clumpy, uneven surface. It is unthinkable that the carts were hauled by hoofed animals, for no such animals could drag heavily laden carts over such roads and survive after a hundred yards of such toil. It is further observed that no signs whatever of the wearing of the rock by hoofs striking against it for hundreds of years is to be perceived.

There are many cases when an old cart-track has been used in later times by modern carts drawn by horses, mules or donkeys. In these cases the worn condition of the path between the ruts is obvious. At distances corresponding to the steps of the animals, notches and furrows are formed by the continuous pounding of the animals' hoofs, and where the rock is not very hard the path is broken, and from a ridge it becomes hollow to such an extent as to become difficult and even dangerous to use. These practical considerations lead to the conclusion that the carts destined to move over these rough paths

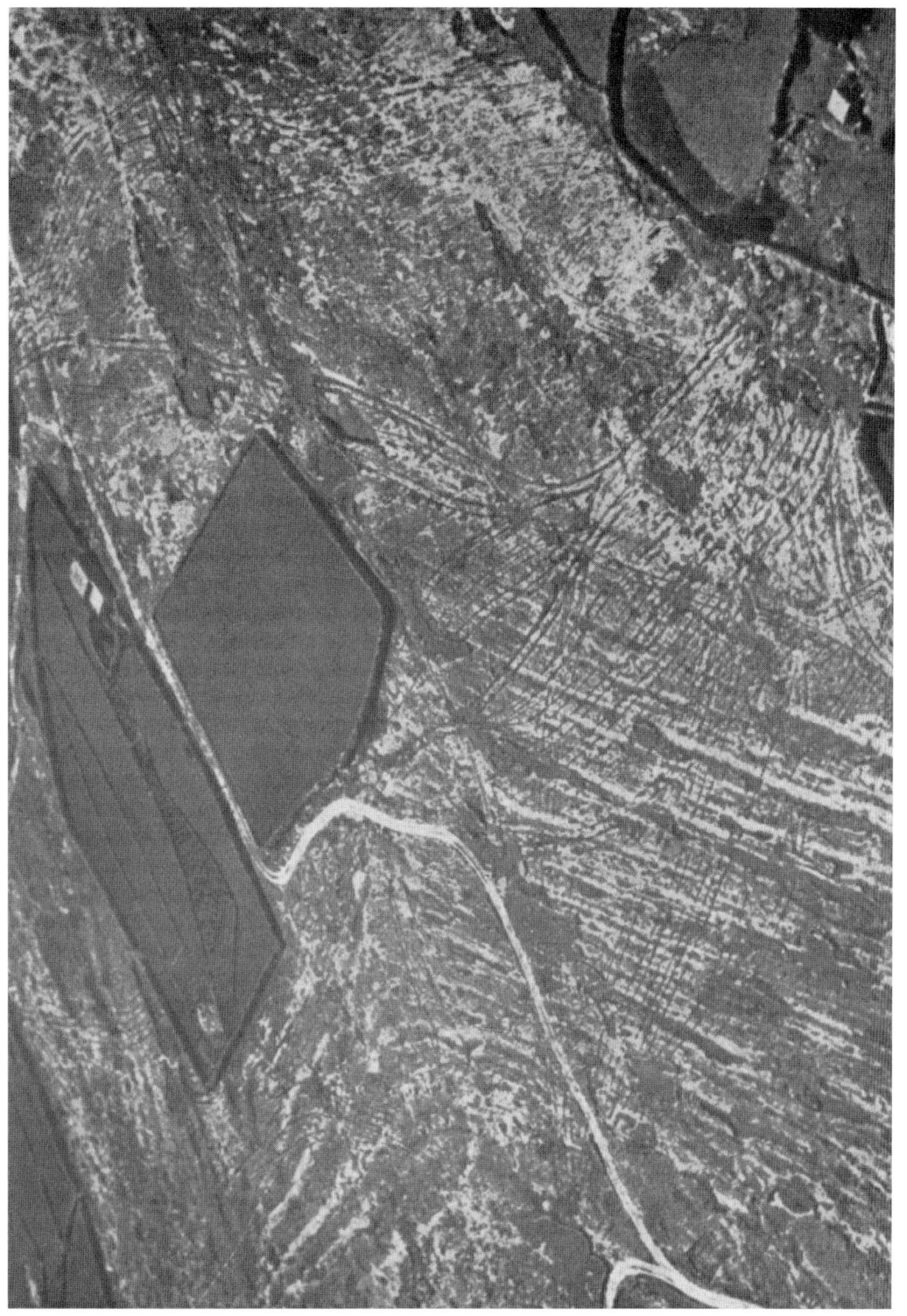

FIGURE 2. *Cart-tracks, Malta: seen from the air.*

FIGURE 3. *Cart-tracks intercepted by shaft of prehistoric rock-cut tomb at Mtarfa, Malta.*

were dragged or pushed by human power. It was team work, most probably very laborious, but surely more adequate to cope with the sudden changes of gradient, the sharp curves of the ruts, and the hundred and one obstacles encountered on the rock roughened for ages by natural agencies.

The question next arises as to how these tracks began and how it was possible for the numerous vehicles to keep on the same tracks before they had become sufficiently deep.

One may imagine the rocky ground being originally covered with soft loam on a level surface; it is easy then to believe that the first carts left a notch in the ground that could be seen by the carts that followed afterwards. In time the rut deepened, the rock was attacked, and in due course grooved deeper and deeper by the passage of the wheels. It is, however, difficult to account for the tracks on sloping ground where a soft loam was not likely to exist. Under these circumstances a cart could never follow the identical track of the one that went before it in an open country, unless helped to do so either by special posts or other guides, or by notching the first tracks. The capable and energetic people who built the megalithic monuments and who conducted the enormous traffic on the roads under discussion, certainly would not shirk the preliminary work of cutting the necessary notches to initiate roads which they required as essential for their welfare. It is evident that on the whole the cart-tracks were started by human labour, to be deepened later on by use. Definite signs of carefully laid sets of cart-tracks are seen on different sites of the island. At Minsia on the St. Julian's heights, between Sliema and Birkirkara, we have a system of shunting which cannot in any way be attributed to mere accident. On this table-land one pair comes straight from a northern direction whilst

FIGURE 4. *Ancient cart-tracks at Mtarfa, Malta*

another pair enters the same ground from the south. About the middle of the ground one of the pairs deviates gradually to the left and the other to the right, and after describing a curve each pair joins the main ruts on the opposite side to that from which it started. The two pairs of ruts cross each other before joining the main trunk, so that two carts moving from opposite directions are free to continue their course by shunting on to the side track.

The disintegration of cliffs and their cleavage — with detachment of the parts that break off, the cutting of rock whilst quarrying stones for building purposes, and covering large tracts of rock surface with soil to make fields, caused many cart-tracks to disappear in part or altogether. This, naturally, led to great confusion in the attempt to determine the course of the tracks, and induced many people to believe that the cart-tracks existed when these islands were connected with a continent and consequently were not meant for local traffic. Independently of the fact that these islands could not have been inhabited by an industrial population at the end of the last ice-age when the separation from the continents took place, the assertion that some of the ruts disappear on the seashore in the direction of the sea has never been proved in any way.

There is only one case where a pair of ruts appears to enter the sea and that is in the bay of St. George at Birzebbugia. These cart-tracks skirt the bay and plunge into the water in a western direction, that is they follow the bend of the bay landwards, hugging the shore. They probably appear once more on the other side of the bay, now covered with silt and with field soil further to the south-west. This disappearance of the cart-tracks into the water is certainly due to the subsidence of the soil long after the tracks were formed, for a number of bell-shaped pits that once studded the shore of the bay are to be seen at the bottom of the sea. In any case, the cart-tracks are not directed towards the open sea and can never prove that they were meant to run beyond the present shores of the island.

Ruts appear in some cases to run at right angles to the cliffs to the south-west of the island. These cliffs are miles away from the seashore. They are made of the coralline limestone and, having a layer of clay under them, cleave off easily on the free side. Large loose masses of rock break away and slide down the side.

At Mtahleb, a pair of cart-tracks appear to end at the edge of such a cliff, but looking down the side at that point one can see the cart-ruts in a direction nearly parallel to the cliff on the detached mass. The tracks, therefore, were broken just at the point when they were changing their direction, that is when about to follow the bend of the cliff. Other cart-ruts in the same locality move in a line with the cliff for a considerable distance.

If some imaginative persons have believed that the cart-ruts were in use in Palaeolithic ages, others went to the other extreme and attributed them to the historical period of the Roman occupation of these islands and even to a later time. Although it is very difficult to assign a date to these signs of human activity, there are some positive data which help us to affirm that the cart-tracks existed long before the Roman occupation of these islands, that is before 200 BC.

Every student of our local archaeology is aware that from time immemorial, the natives of these islands used to bury their dead in rock-cut tombs. Most of these tombs resemble the well known Sydonian tombs of Phoenicia proper, which may be taken to have come in use during the Phoenician occupation. These rock-cut tombs consist of a shaft, the depth of which varies considerably, and a funeral chamber at the bottom cut in one of the sides of the shaft.

On the Mtarfa plateau to the west of the Military Hospital there are numerous rock-tombs of this description in a good state of preservation. Not far from the main road leading to the hospital, the shaft of one of these rock-tombs is found to have been dug out across a very fine pair of cart-tracks (FIGURES 3 & 4), a clear indication that when the rock-tomb was cut the cart-tracks were no longer in use and therefore cut much earlier than the tomb itself. Similar cases are to be met with in the Falka district on the way to Sebbieh, at Benjemma, and on other open spaces.

From the foregoing considerations it is certain that the cart-tracks were intended for local purposes and are the signs of great activity of the native population extending for long periods of time. What remains to be found out is the approximate date when such considerable activity showed itself, and what was the material transported so persistently along these primitive roads. Superficial observers have often stated that in view of the existence of numerous megalithic buildings in the islands the Neolithic people required these roads to cart the large blocks of stone from the quarries to the site of the proposed monuments. This would be a plausible argument had cart-tracks been found close to the megalithic buildings, but unfortunately these primitive tracks are never found in their vicinity. They occur only on the flat top of hilly districts, or deeply furrowing the sides of the hills from the valleys and ravines at their feet to the highest table-land. The carting of stones, large or small, is out of the question, as stone is found everywhere and when required for ordinary use could be cut on the spot. It is evident that the material transported was abundant at particular places and badly lacking in others where its value was far greater than the labour required to get it there. By elimination the only

FIGURE 5. *Ancient cart-tracks, Malta.*

precious material to the primitive man was the field soil, capable of growing his food and making his life possible in a barren land such as we have reason to believe Malta was in the Neolithic period.

Walking across the country, one is struck at once by the number of terraced fields along scarped, ragged hills, ensconced in odd corners, and stretching on the table-lands on which soil could not form and collect by natural means. A little thought brings a clear conviction that the terracing on the slopes of the hills is not the result of natural agencies. Even if soil formed in fissures, nooks, and corners of crumbling hill-sides, it would have a downward movement in the course of ages. Wind and rain would, in a comparatively short time, move the sandy soil and wash it as far down as it would go.

When the energetic Neolithic population cast their lot on these islands they could not, in the course of time, be satisfied with the tilling of the soil collected in the valleys and the ravines; when the population increased, the food supply had to be augmented as a scanty soil cannot support a growing population.

Nobody can doubt the enormous activity of a people who covered the island with megalithic monuments, and as this people had to live at the same time that it quarried stones and erected buildings, part of their energy was surely employed to increase the number of fields and their area. The fields in the valley could not satisfy their increasing numbers and they had to aim higher, and try to carry up some of the surplus soil stored for centuries in the ravines, and by their united effort reclaim the wild land. Here was therefore work of the greatest magnitude to occupy thousands of people for ages. The sloping hills did not deter them from their task, carts were devised and constructed, and the precious soil found its way higher and higher on the barren hills. This huge work of a large and peaceful society has never been adequately appreciated, although it must have been greater than the result apparent to us. Walking along the high table-lands in Malta, one is at once struck by the existence of extensive rubble walls, high and very well constructed, that once enclosed fertile soil but now stand abandoned with nothing beyond them but barren rock. Nobody would dream of building high walls to enclose an empty space, yet such walls are abundant on the extensive rocky surface to the south of Boschetto, towards the Tal Ghalia plateau, at Benjemma, and practically on every top of a hilly ground.

Far more fields existed in Neolithic days than those in use at present, but in the course of centuries those which for some reasons were not properly attended to were slowly but surely washed away by rain and deposited once more in the valleys from which they had been removed.

The farmers on these high lands had not only to provide the soil but, with incessant toil, had to keep the red earth where it was spread with infinite labour. Yet the great effort of the Neolithic population is hardly recognized by their offspring who are apt, now and then, to admire their megalithic monuments, but give no thought to the greater performance of turning the rocky hills into arable land.

Mr Sidney Freeman suggests that another very precious element might have been carted along the furrowed slopes, and that is water. Malta has always been a dry country and the few springs that gush out of the rocks are only found on low ground, certainly below the lower coralline limestone. In the absence of tanks, water had, certainly, to be carried up from the valleys below and this must have been another necessary but arduous task of the Neolithic farmer.

It was also essential that water should be carried to the shores of the harbours which had no springs in the vicinity. Ships must have called often at Malta, judging by foreign stones such as flint, obsidian, and lava, which are not to be found locally, and yet freely met with in all Neolithic and Bronze Age stations. The cart-tracks seen on the shore of St. George at Birzebbugia may have been detailed for the water service, for near that harbour no water is to be found except what was probably stored in the 35 pits cut along the shore, close to the sea.

This is the tale revealed by the modest cart-tracks that are seen to wind their way from valleys and ravines up the craggy slopes of hills.

I have often watched the deep winding grooves that, from the Kligha valley, reach by slow degrees and devious ways the first slopes of the Kallilia hill, to the north of the Mtarfa heights; as soon as the cart-tracks are firmly established on the hard rocky ground they proceed straight up to attain the first heights of the Benjemma hills, the Nadur ridge. At this point other cart-tracks may be seen to reach the table-land from the south-east and the south-west. Along these paths millions of cart-loads of earth found their way, ready to fertilize those barren rocks which in many points are again being denuded by natural agencies.

Seen in this light the huge buildings of Hajar-Kim, Mnaidra and Tarxien must pale before the fertile terraces of Benjemma, Naxxar, Wardia, Dweira, Mgar, splendid monuments of the will and the energy of a people who, determined to make the most of the rocky land on which Providence had cast them, with the most primitive tools covered the land with fertile soil, and raised the finest buildings of their type in existence to the Divinity that helped them in their difficult enterprise.

Dykes
by CYRIL FOX
ANTIQUITY 3 (9), 1929

DYKES have been described as travelling, running or linear earthworks. All these terms express their essential character, that of a bank, usually of earth but occasionally of loose stone, extending for a considerable distance across country. The existence of a bank presupposes an adjacent ditch from which its material was derived, and the descriptive term Ditch is as common as Dyke in the nomenclature of linear earthworks. Both terms have indeed a common origin.

Dykes vary greatly in structural character and in length; but however marked such differences may be, they possess at least one characteristic which permits them to be analyzed and discussed as a group; their ends rest on natural obstacles, and, where natural obstacles calculated to prevent the movement of men or animals occur in their course, they are discontinuous. Thus if they are political (tribal or racial) boundaries, they are present only in areas which men (and flocks and herds) inhabited or could inhabit, or across which they passed or could pass; if they are military works they exist only where passage to armed and organized bodies of men with their impedimenta was reasonably possible.*

It will be observed that the feature which characterizes dykes is equally applicable to the defences of promontory forts, whose ends rest on slopes difficult to scale, or inaccessible cliffs. Though borderline examples occur which might be classed either as defences of promontory forts or as linear earthworks, the distinction is clear. A dyke bars the approach to an extensive tract of country; the defences of a promontory fort protect a limited area — a few acres at most. It will be observed that the distinction is not an arbitrary one; in the one case the inhabitants of a district combine to delimit or protect their countryside, in the other a community provides defences for its settlement site, or constructs for itself a refuge. Different social organizations and concepts seem to be involved.

The essential feature of linear earthworks referred to above is in some cases immediately apparent, but in others it can only be elucidated after close and prolonged scrutiny; a few travelling earthworks in other respects typical fail to yield the necessary evidence: they end 'in the air'. These difficulties are mainly due to two causes: destruction by man the agriculturist, and changes wrought by the same agency in the character and aspect of the countryside.

These points may usefully be illustrated by reference to a well-known group of linear earthworks, the Cambridgeshire dykes, or ditches as they are locally called. The map (FIGURE 1) shows the series the ditches are roughly parallel one to the other, the direction being NW–SE. They are four in number: (1) Bran Ditch (2) Brent Ditch (3) Fleam

---

* There are, of course, a number of minor banks and ditches to which the above definition does not apply. Some of these are probably the boundaries of prehistoric settlements; some delimit agricultural land from moor — or down — land; others define medieval parks, or coppices; such are not considered in this paper.
† A fifth dyke, Black Ditches, to the north of the Devil's Ditch, should perhaps be regarded as part of the system (see p. 21).

Ditch (4) Devil's Ditch.[†] All, it will be observed, at their NW ends rest on, or are close to, rivers — the Cam or its tributaries — but in respect of none is there any evidence on the ordinary map which provides a reason for the position of the SE termination.

A traveller proceeding south-eastward from the neighbourhood of Cambridge crosses a tract of upland of moderate elevation, some six miles wide; the country is very open, pastoral and agricultural, bare of villages. If he continues to walk in the same direction a slight change in character manifests itself; a plateau country some 300 feet above sea-level is reached, the fields are smaller, and hedgerow trees and woods more frequent. Hereabouts he will find that each of the Ditches has its westward termination: some fade away into a hedge bank, others, the Devil's Ditch in particular, end abruptly.

The changes observed by our traveller in the appearance of the country are determined by alterations in the soil and subsoil. The plateau is covered with glacial drift — boulder clay; the more open country has a chalk subsoil, and was originally down-land, though the ancient covering of chalk turf has nearly everywhere been destroyed. On the map the limits of the clay are outlined, the outline being based on the drift map of the Geological Survey. The presence of clay connotes oak forest and dense, brambly and thorny undergrowth, practically impassable. If, now, the SE terminations of the ditches be examined on the map, it is seen that they coincide with the margins of the ancient forest. Each of the valley-ward terminations, moreover, if not actually resting on a river, is related to a definite water obstacle:- Bran Ditch ends in a mere, now drained; Brent Ditch in a marshy field whence a strong spring still flows.

Thus in the Cambridgeshire Ditches we have admirable examples of the essential character of travelling earthworks; they are barriers drawn across open country, from one natural obstacle to another. Reference has been made to the discontinuity of travelling earthworks where areas difficult for man to cross are on its line; the Fleam Ditch provides an example of this in the long gap between the two existing halves. This area, now pasture land, was in early times a mere, and its limits are clearly defined on the Geological Survey map by the peaty deposits which form its floor.

The special fascination which the linear earthwork has for the field worker is here revealed. The survey of a work of this class vividly brings home to the student a forgotten England; an island mainly covered by forest, whose valleys were swamps in which the rivers followed devious and changing courses. Belts of gravel by streams and rivers, sandy heaths, chalk down-lands, limestone ridges, and, in the west and north, the ancient rocks which form the mountainous backbone of the country, were either open or sparsely forested and suitable in great measure for man's dwelling places, his primitive agriculture, his traffic, and the sustenance of his flock and herds. Human activity in southern Britain was thus, geographically speaking, strictly limited and movement was canalized — restricted for the most part to definite routes, the position and extent of which were determined by the geological structure of the country.

The greater Cambridgeshire Ditches, the Devil's and the Fleam, still dominate the landscapes they cross,[*] but others afford examples of the destruction wrought by agricultural operations, and reveal the means open to the archaeologist for the recovery of such when apparently lost. Parish boundaries fix the line of the Bran Ditch, which has been almost entirely flattened out; once the line is approximately known changes in the colour of the soil on the line of the bank, or a wave in the ground on the line of the ditch,

---

* Apart from a doubtful extension of the Fleam, shown on the map by broken lines, recently revealed by air-photography.

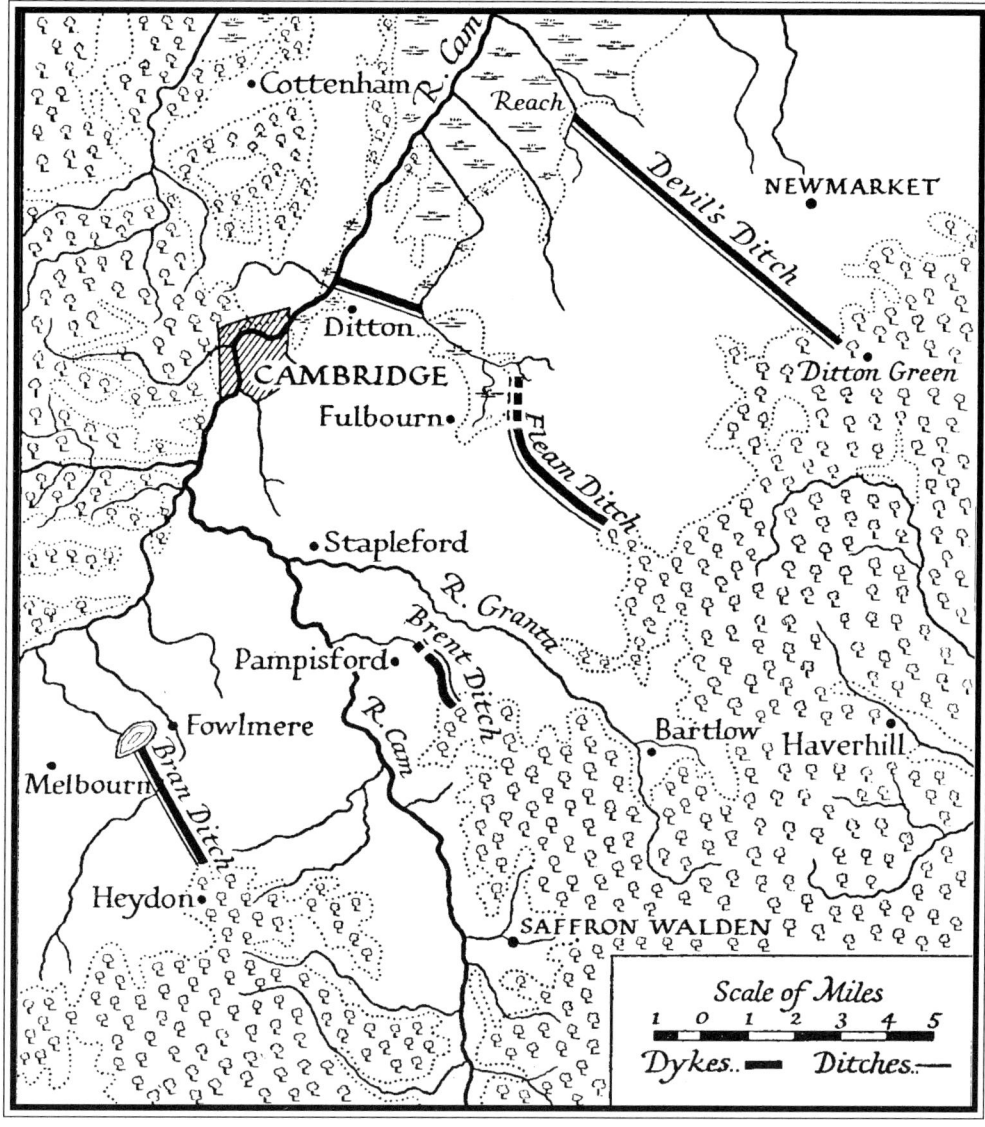

FIGURE 1. *The Cambridgeshire dykes in relation to forest, fen, river and downland.*

serve to fix its exact position. The complete elimination, indeed, of a large travelling earthwork has rarely if ever occurred. Sometimes a dyke, from its nature a well-drained ridge, forms a convenient grassy track or even a modern metalled road. In the latter case the persistent and strongly marked elevation of the metalling above the surface of the adjacent fields reveals the existence of the older work. The northwestern end of the Fleam Ditch, between mere and river, has been put to use in this fashion. The Cambridgeshire series of dykes, so typical in most respects, provides one anomaly, an earthwork apparently ending 'in the air'. The earthwork known as the Black Ditches — which is sited on open heath country, some miles to the north of the main group — appears to terminate before any trace of the heavy clays of the plateau are reached, and I am uncertain whether it is destroyed or incomplete (see FIGURE 9).

All early fortification in earth presents a ditch facing the enemy with a bank on the inner side, this bank being constructed of material taken mainly from the ditch. Linear earthworks are usually of this character, and it may be taken as certain that whether a dyke be a political boundary or a military work, the main ditch faces the countryside foreign, or hostile, as the case might be, to the builders. Thus the ditches of Cambridgeshire, considered as a series, were built by a people living in Norfolk and north Suffolk as a boundary to separate them from, or as a barrier against, folk living to the south-west. The belt of chalk country between the fens and the forest which the ditches traverse is, indeed, as is well known, one of the more important prehistoric and early historic highways of Britain, providing a dry and well-drained route across open country from the Thames — and beyond — to Norfolk, and thus linking up the Salisbury Plain area, the one-time economic centre of southern Britain, with East Anglia. Many of the dykes of this country bestride traffic lines in a similar manner.

At some date within the dyke-building period or periods conditions in the Cambridge area were reversed, and the interesting little earthwork known as the Brent Ditch, aligned from marsh to forest where the chalk belt is narrowest, has its ditch on the opposite side, facing north; and, as if to confirm this structure as the work of a people whose home country lay to the southward, the dyke is aligned along the crest of the slope overlooking a lateral valley of the Cam river-system, affording wide visual control of the downland to the northward.

Visual control was indeed, it would appear, of primary importance to the designers of linear earthworks. The writer is engaged, at the moment, on the survey of Offa's Dyke, the greatest of all linear earthworks in Britain, reputed to cover the greater part of the distance of 120 miles separating the Dee estuary near Prestatyn in the north, from the junction of the Wye and Severn below Chepstow in the south. Its course is shown on a map (FIGURE 2); the survey for which I am responsible has, however, only been carried out from the Dee to the neighbourhood of Montgomery, and I hope to show that it is less incomplete in its southern half than it appears to be at present.

This great work is laid out with remarkable skill in country of varied relief, across lowland and highland, almost invariably in such a manner as to take advantage of westward-facing slopes; the ditch — with rare exceptions due to local conditions — is on the west side, and the structure clearly was designed by a man of military genius and exceptional engineering skill. FIGURES 3 and 4 illustrate the selection and utilization of favourable ground by the makers of this earthwork, FIGURE 6 the profile of bank and ditch.

The greater dykes such as that of Offa present problems to the field archaeologist similar to those with which the student of the topography of Roman roads is faced, and call for a similar technique of elucidation. When the method by which the course of a dyke is laid out is grasped, one is in touch with the mind of the builder, and is armed with knowledge which is vitally important if the trace be temporarily lost, as not infrequently happens. Again and again in following Offa's Dyke from the Dee to Montgomeryshire I have found that the builder adopted the same methods in dealing with obstacles of like type, and I was able to foresee, when studying (for example) a transverse valley ahead of the detailed survey of the dyke, what lines of approach would commend themselves to him. He always sought lateral re-entrants when crossing a broad valley, following the re-entrants down, or up, their western-facing slopes. The mode of utilization of rivers as the boundary when these are aligned approximately in the required direction, again, is identical in the valleys of the Dee (FIGURE 5) and of the Severn. In my opinion no method of dealing with the problem of the greater dykes, other than this, will enable us to determine whether they are the work of one mind, created as

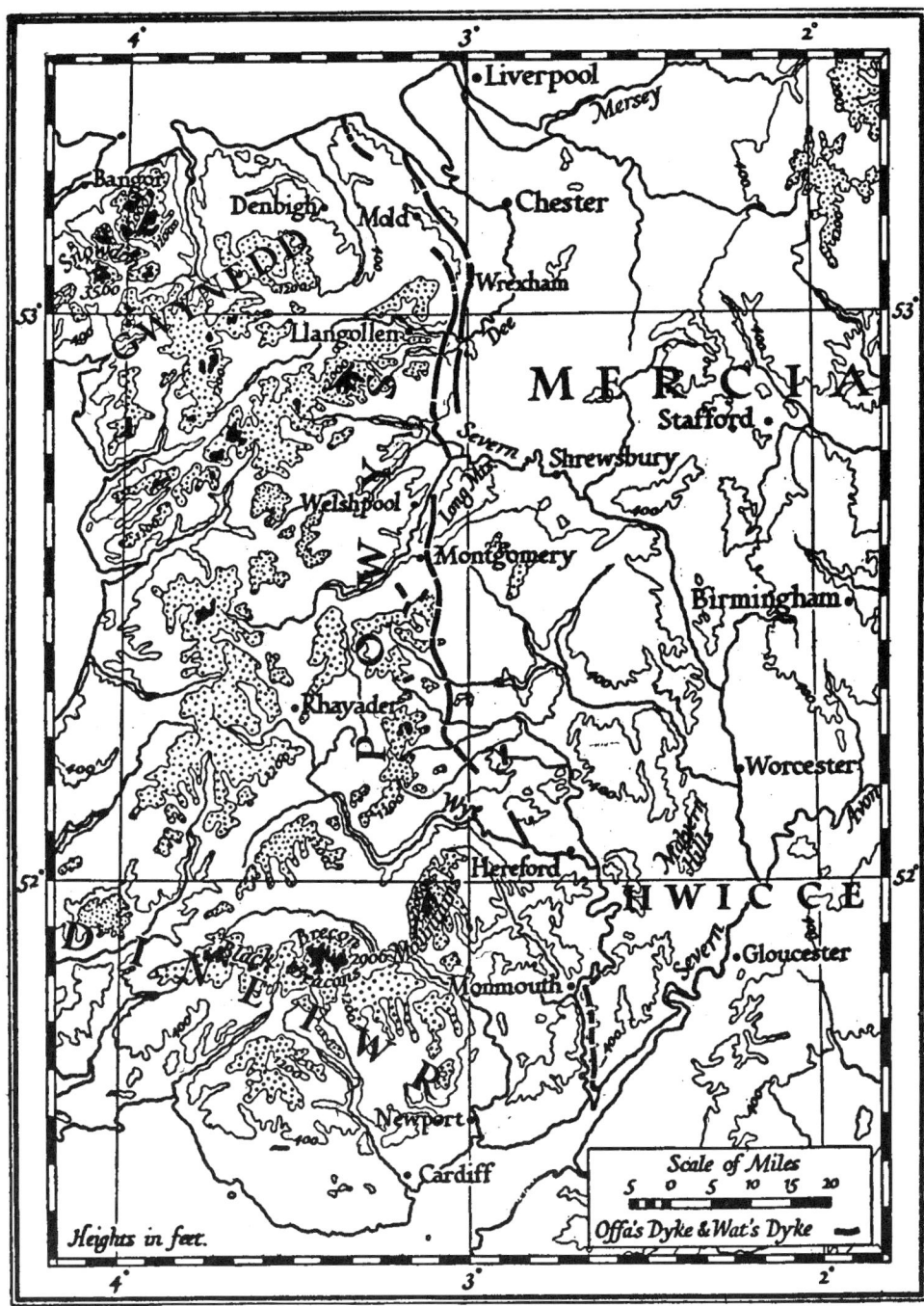

FIGURE 2. *Offa's Dyke: the course from the estuary of the Dee to the estuary of the Severn. A subsidiary work, Wat's Dyke, SW of Chester, is also shown.*

an entity for a given purpose, or whether they developed piece-meal and were linked up in the last phase of their evolution. I regard Offa's Dyke, so far as I have studied it, as the product of one mind and the work of one generation of men.

FIGURE 3. *Offa's Dyke crossing a hill top, and aligned on the western edge of the flattened crest: Brymbo Hill, Denbighshire. (From* Archaeologia Cambrensis.*)*

FIGURES 4a & 4b. *Offa's Dyke (indicated by arrows) on a crest line: Treuddyn Parish, Flintshire. (From* Archaeologia Cambrensis).

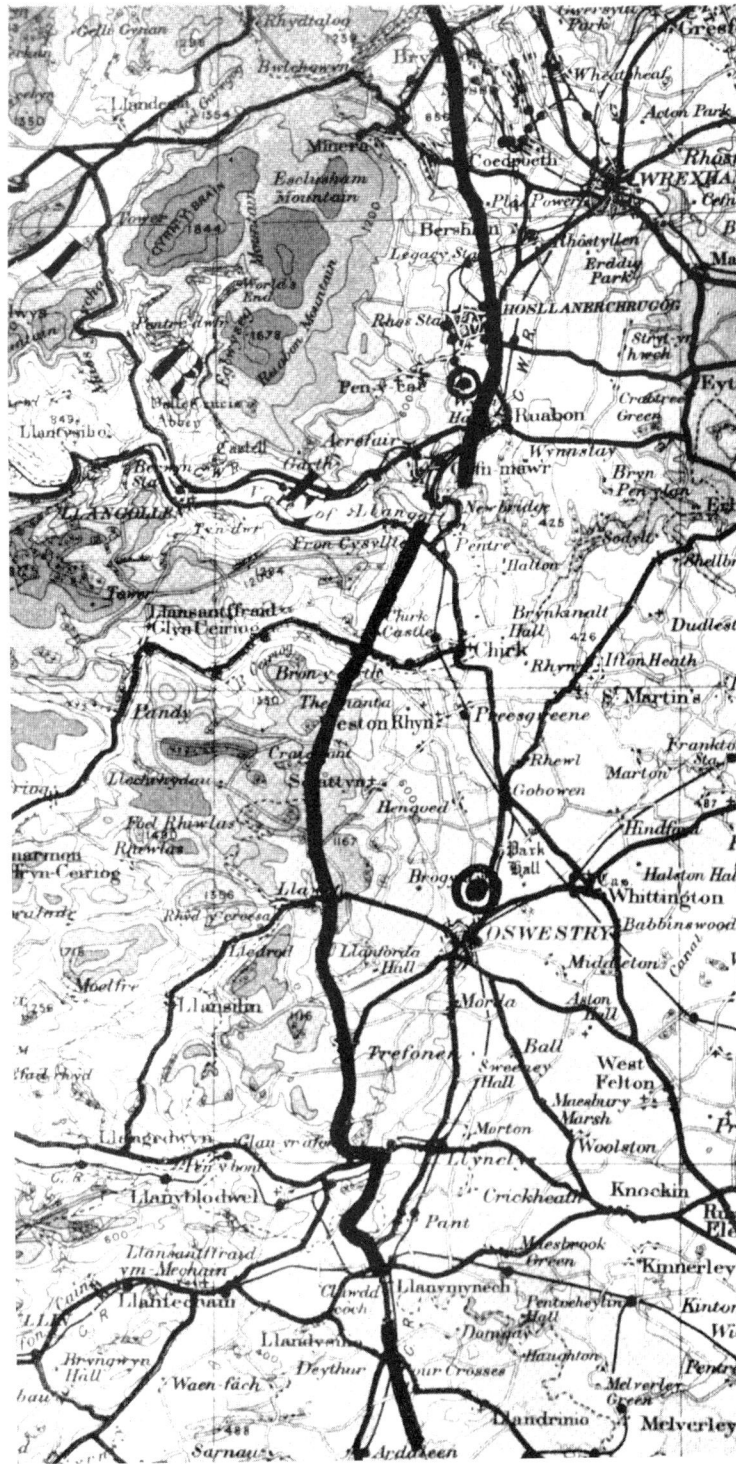

FIGURE 5. *The course of Offa's Dyke in Denbighshire and Shropshire. Two hill-forts are shown: Y Gardden, SW of Wrexham, and 'Old Oswestry'. (From Archaeologia Cambrensis.)*

FIGURE 6. *Offa's Dyke: a typical view near Montgomery.*

Another feature of great interest presented by linear earthworks is direct alignment. It is to be expected that the builders should try to save labour by avoiding unnecessary bends and curves, but it is surprising to find with what skill dykes have been laid out on stretches of undulating or mountainous country, deviating but a few yards from absolute directness, for mile after mile. FIGURE 5 is an example of this; Offa's dyke in a 22-mile stretch across Denbighshire and Shropshire is laid out on three great alignments 8, 7·5 and 12 miles in length, over hills up to a thousand feet in height and across deep trough valleys. On the northern, and the central, of these stretches the maximal deviations from the straight line are 280 yards and 300 yards. As will be seen from the map, the third stretch is equally direct, apart from a limited area where the extreme boldness of the relief necessitated wide detours.

In some cases alignment, from point to point, is absolutely direct. Of this directness the simplest and noblest example is afforded by the Devil's Ditch. Five miles of the ditch are in the same straight line, but each end is slightly deflected. If the ditch be studied on

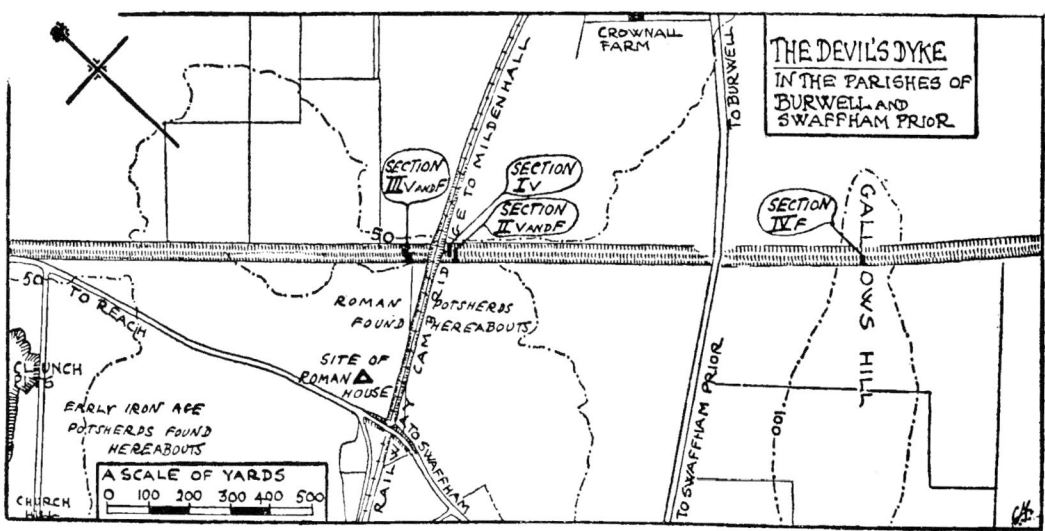

FIGURE 7. *Devil's Dyke. Map of Gallows hill sector showing change of alignment on the hill top, and sites of excavation. (From the* Cambridge Antiquarian Society's Communications.*)*

FIGURE 8. *Devil's Dyke, looking NW from Gallows Hill. (From the* Cambridge Antiquarian Society's Communications.*)*

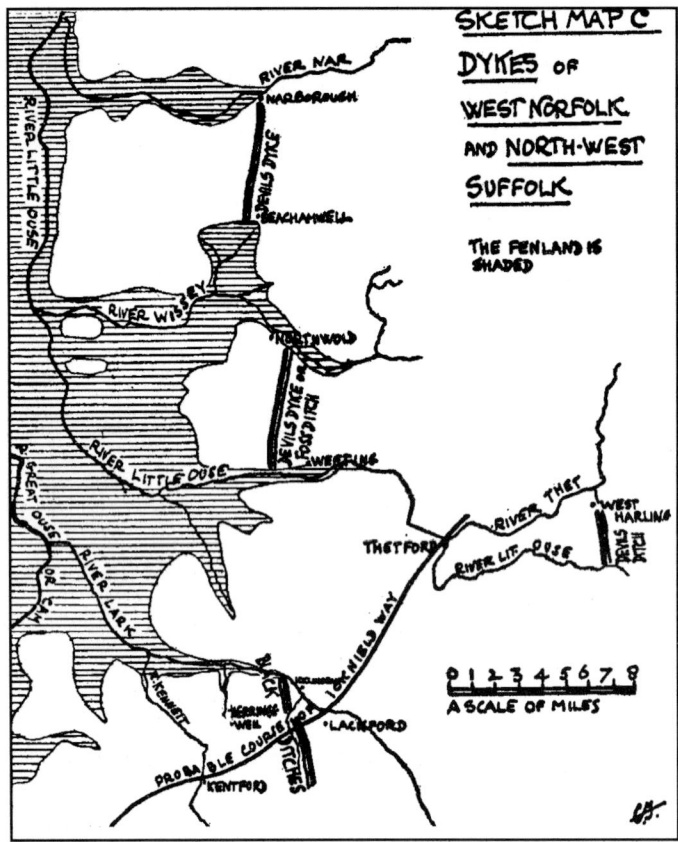

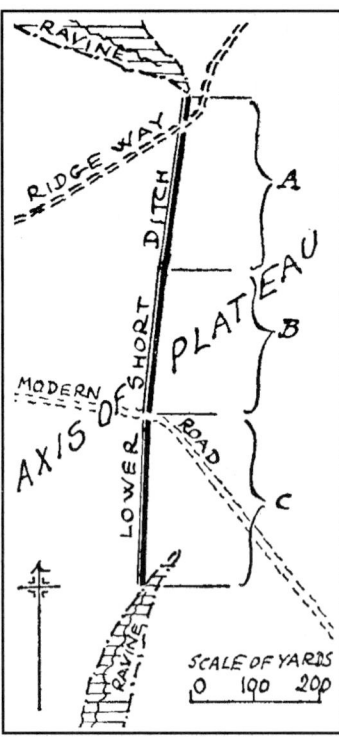

FIGURE 9a. *A cross-ridge dyke: the lower short ditch across the Kerry Hill Ridgeway, Montgomery. Aligned in 3 straight stretches as indicated by the letters A B C.*

FIGURE 9. *The dykes of West Norfolk and Suffolk. (From Fox 1923.)*

the ground it is observed that the 5-mile stretch is visible from either end, Gallows Hill and Stetchworth Hall, and could thus be accurately plotted. From the crest lines which terminated the main stretch, new and equally direct alignments were laid, on the one side to the fen, on the other side to the forest, approximately but not absolutely in line with the central portion of the work. FIGURE 7 shows the change in direction on Gallows Hill, while the photograph (FIGURE 8), is taken from Gallows Hill looking westward towards the fen termination at Reach; it shows the directness, and also the magnificent scale of the Ditch.* This enormous work, thus carried out with absolute precision, reminds one forcibly of Roman genius and Roman energy, and we are brought face to face with the question, what is the age of linear earthworks such as this? Two possibilities present themselves; either they belong to a variety of periods, being constructed at times when, cultural development having reached a certain standard, the occasion for great works of this class was manifest, or they represent the constructive activity of one period only, when dyke building was in fashion. The extent of the problem may briefly be referred to. In addition to the great systems already discussed, there is Wansdyke which, facing north, extends from near the Bristol Channel (Maesbury in Somerset) by Bath and

* Hereabouts the scarp, from crest of rampart to floor of ditch, measures 60 feet.

Savernake Forest to Inkpen in Berkshire, a distance of 60 miles, and covers south-western Britain against attacks launched from the Cotswolds, the upper Thames valley and the Berkshire uplands. With Wansdyke, Bokerley Dyke, a much smaller work (4 miles long) on its eastern flank, is probably to be associated; and it is relevant here to mention that Offa's Dyke has a parallel and apparently subsidiary construction, Wat's Dyke, at its northern end. North of the Cambridgeshire series, moreover, a pair of dykes barring access to extensive tracts environed by fen, and facing east, are to be seen. These latter are illustrated in FIGURE 9. In Cleveland, Yorkshire, on the Welsh borders in Montgomeryshire, Radnorshire and Shropshire (near Offa's Dyke), and in many other counties, are ramparts, usually short, called cross-ridge dykes these form barriers across ancient ridgeways, their terminals resting on ravines, steep slopes or the sources of streams on either side of the ridges. An example from Montgomeryshire is figured (FIGURE 9a). Grim's Dyke in Buckinghamshire, a work the extent of which is not yet fully explored, but which is at least 16 miles long, offers many problems, structural and functional. The Devil's Dyke near Andover, a shorter work, bestrides the Harroway; while Comb Bank, Dorset, crosses the upland traffic routes between Dorchester and Blandford. In Ponter's Ball east of Glastonbury, and in New Ditch in Butleigh Wood, Somerset, fen to fen earthworks comparable in character with the East Anglian series are met with. The ends of Grim's Dyke, Oxfordshire, rest on a river; it appears to extend from the Thames at Mongewell to the Thames at Henley, a distance of over 9 miles. These examples, selected mainly from the southern counties, illustrate the importance of linear earthworks to topographer and archaeologist, and their variety.[1] We have to deal with structures varying in length from a few hundred yards to well nigh a hundred miles. In size extreme differences occur, the smaller works being of the scale of a hedgebank, the larger, such as the Devil's Ditch, occupying a belt of ground over 40 yards across, and having even today after the wastage of centuries a rampart the crest of which is over 15 feet above the natural ground level, and 30 feet above the bottom of the ditch. The scale of this work is, perhaps, best brought home to a modern mind by the fact that the *breadth* of the area thus — for a distance of seven miles — transformed from a level flat into a high rampart and deep ditch, is equivalent to that of the widest of our new arterial roads, with its footpaths and grass verges.

Dykes differ in character as well as in size. Sometimes the bank is built up with material taken from both sides, more frequently the ditch is on one side only. They are usually single; but some of the smaller (cross-ridge) dykes have double or even treble banks and ditches like the defences of a hill fort. Parallell banks facing outwards, enclosing and protecting a ribbon of land, or a trackway, are known to occur. Variations in scale and structure occur not only between one dyke and another but also in different parts of the same earthwork. FIGURES 10 and 11 for example, represent profiles of Offa's Dyke. FIGURE 10 shows the normal features of the earthwork, a high bank with a broad and deep ditch on the western side; such profiles are possible only on practically level ground. FIGURE 11 shows how the normal mode of construction was modified on steep slopes, the bank being constructed entirely from material taken from the upper (eastern) side. A double-ditched profile is shown on the same figure; here Offa's Dyke crosses marshy ground and it was doubtless difficult to obtain sufficient material from the wet land on the west side; the men were probably working up to their waists in water. Much of the soil of which the bank is composed was taken, therefore, from the other side, and we have an earthwork symmetrical in profile.

To return to the question of date. The determination by excavation of the date of dykes and ditches is more difficult perhaps than in the case of any other class of earth-

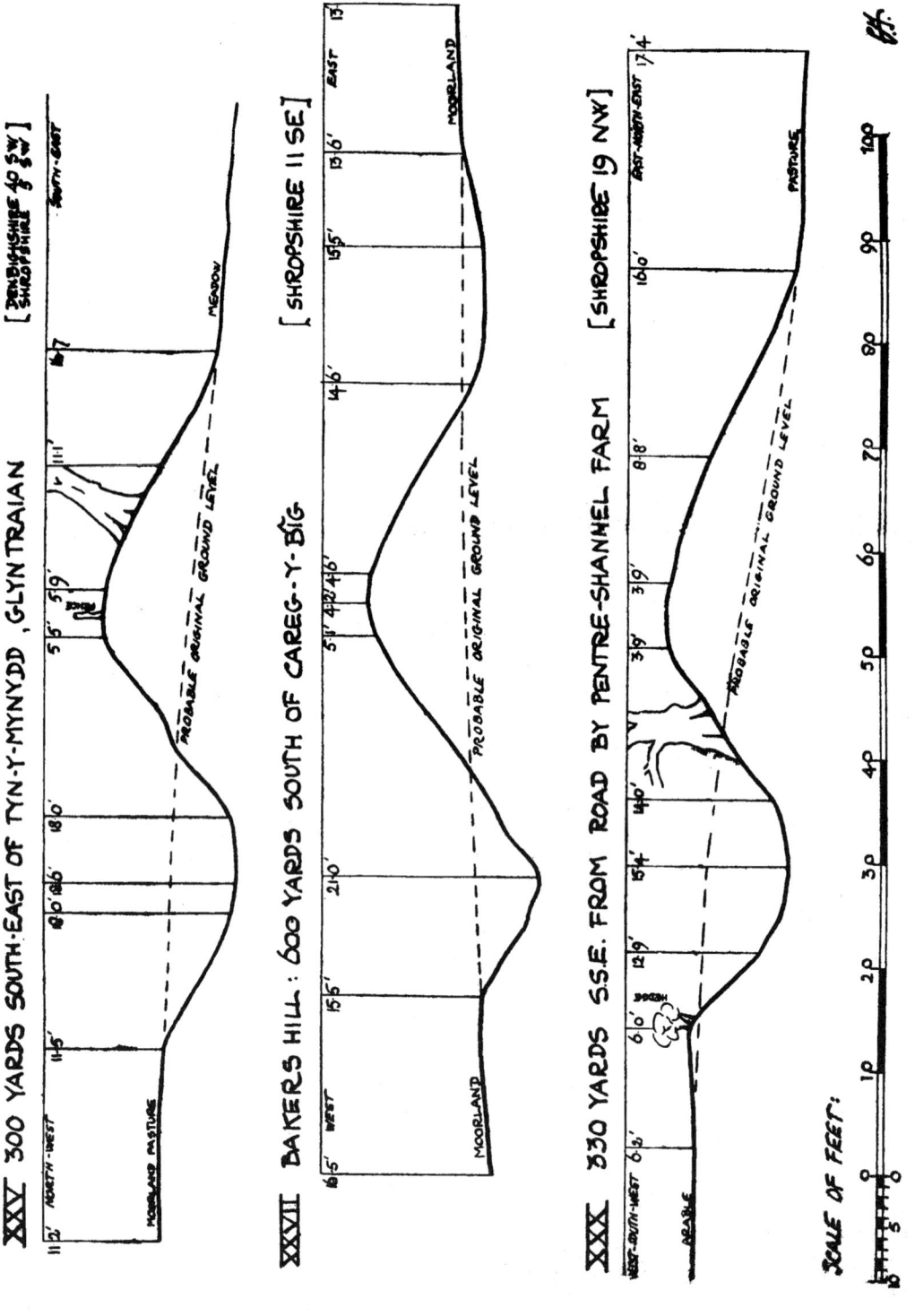

FIGURE 10. *Offa's Dyke: profiles on Denbighshire-Shropshire border and in Shropshire.*

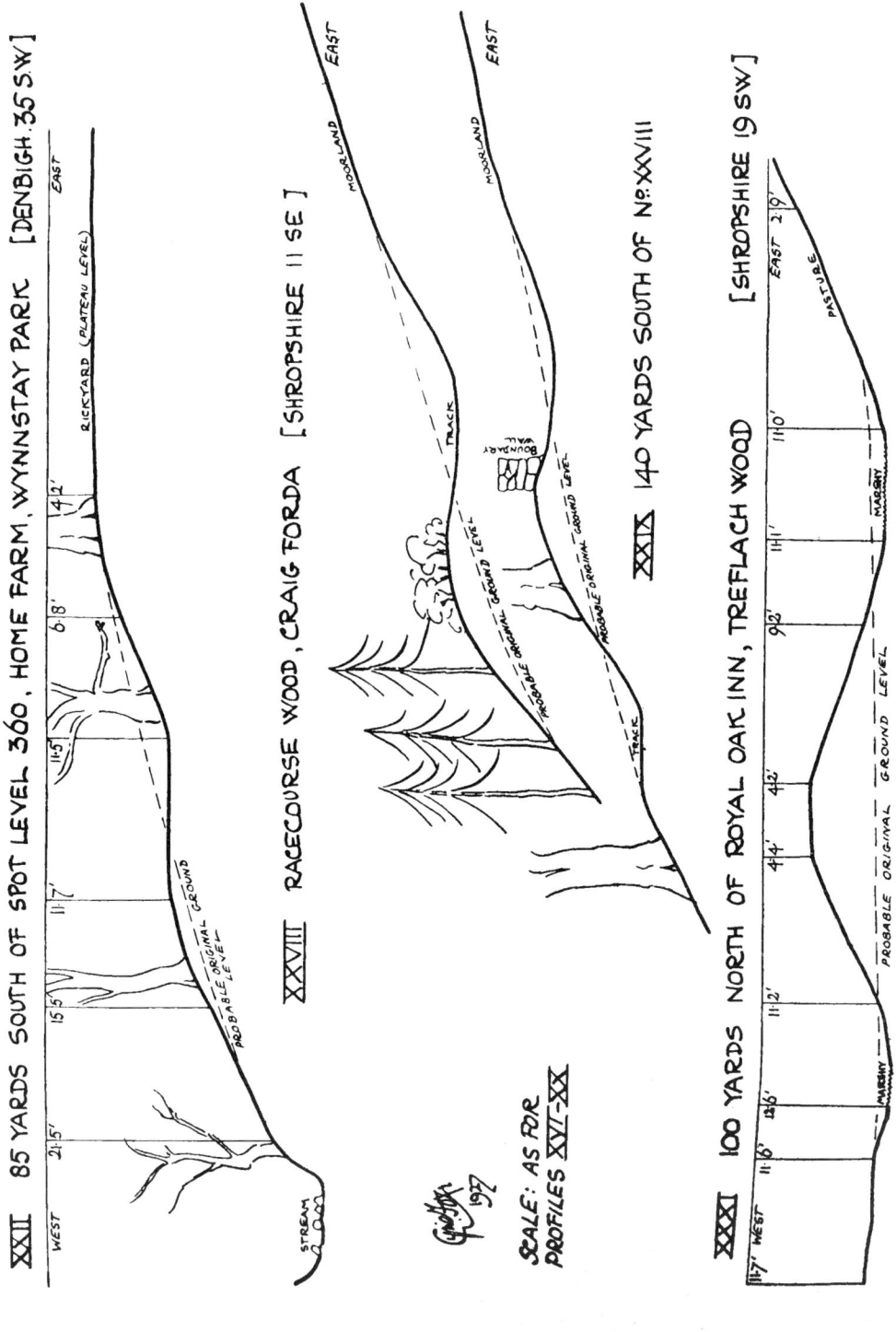

FIGURE 11. *Offa's Dyke: profiles in Denbighshire and Shropshire.*

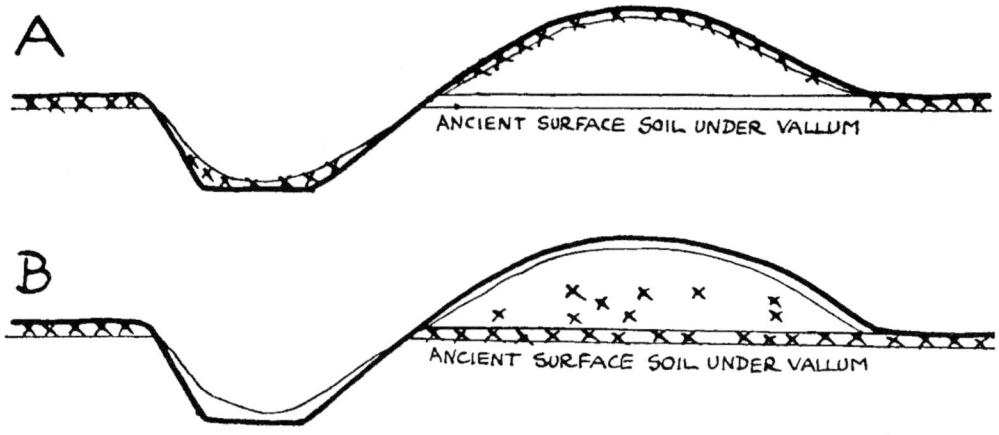

FIGURE 12. *Diagram showing the theoretical position of Roman objects (shown by XXX) in relation to (A) a Pre-Roman earthwork, and (B) a later earthwork.*

work, because their use was in the nature of things, intermittent and probably of rare occurrence. On some parts of Offa's Dyke it is possible that no man save shepherd and hunter trod for centuries after its construction, and human activity in relation to other dykes was confined in most cases, I suspect, to the crossing points — now difficult to identify.* Hence the chances of finding, by haphazard excavation of the ditch or bank, material traces of the culture of the builders, are remote. The problem was successfully tackled by Pitt-Rivers who, realizing the difficulties, concluded that the abundance of Roman remains in and near settlements of that period offered the best chance of arriving at an approximate date for linear earthworks. Such earthworks must be either pre-Roman, or later; and the relation between the rampart and ditch of such a dyke and the artefacts found therein and on the ribbon of ground which it traverses, ought to reveal its age to the careful investigator. The principle on which conclusions must be based is simplicity itself; a linear earthwork cannot be earlier than the date of the latest object found in or under its rampart, provided that the rampart has not been disturbed since erection. The diagram (FIGURE 12) illustrates, by way of example, the theoretical position of Roman objects in relation to a pre-Roman and to a later earthwork respectively. If the dyke be pre-Roman, objects of Roman date may be expected to occur *in* the ditch and *on* (but not in or under) the rampart; if of later construction, then Roman objects should be found, not *in* the ditch or *on* the rampart, but *in* the rampart and *in* the ancient surface soil thereunder.

Pitt-Rivers carried out excavations in Bokerly and Wansdyke, which are described in volume III of his *Excavations.* His section across Bokerly Dyke near Woodyates shows that the bank at the point excavated was constructed after the time of Claudius Gothicus, 269–270 AD, while another undisturbed sector of the rampart yielded coins extending from Gallienus to Honorius. Thus the dyke hereabouts was built at the very end of, or

---

* There is reason to suppose that the continuity of the Cambridgeshire ditches was unbroken by road-gaps. Travellers along the Icknield Way probably crossed, under surveillance, a wooden gangway. In the case of other dykes the differentiation between original and later crossing-points should be demonstrable by excavation; in respect to the original openings a causeway of undisturbed subsoil should be present on the line of the ditch; in the case of later gaps cut by road-maker or farmer, the ditch would be filled in — 'made ground'.

later than, the Roman occupation. Sections through Wansdyke at similarly suitable points provided similarly cogent — though less precise — evidence of date, fragments of Samian pottery having been found in the ancient surface soil covered up by the rampart.

The writer, adopting Pitt-Rivers' methods, has attempted to determine the limiting dates of the other greater systems; the Cambridgeshire ditches and Offa's Dyke. In Cambridgeshire the Fleam and the Devil's Ditches were chosen in succession for investigation; the Fleam yielded Roman material under the undisturbed bank in two places, as well as interesting evidence that the construction of the work was intermitted for periods probably considerable (illustrated by FIGURE 13). The Devil's Ditch, examined in the neighbourhood of a Roman house, yielded numerous Roman sherds from various points in and under the rampart (FIGURE 15). The character of such finds is shown in FIGURE 14 they illustrate one important point in connexion with investigations of linear earthworks. It is that the intrinsic value of the finds thus laboriously obtained is likely to be nil. On the other hand, the historical value of these trifling fragments, in so far as they provide evidence of date, can hardly be over estimated.

When one considers how exhaustive an effort was involved in the construction, by a partially developed and imperfectly organized community, of such works, and how profoundly their presence must, for generations, have influenced the economic, military and political development of the communities whose boundaries they formed, one can realize how important it is, if we are to recreate the history of England in the periods when historical record is minimal or absent, to determine the period of their construction and use.

I next turned my attention to Offa's Dyke, which is attributed by Asser, King Alfred's bishop of Sherborne, a Welshman who wrote within a hundred years of Offa's death, to this great king of Mercia, who reigned from 757 to 796. Few points along its line are known to offer any likelihood of the finding of Roman remains in relation to the structure; one of these points is Ffrith in Flintshire. Here a section made in 1926 showed that the bank of the dyke covered Roman material and contained Roman rubbish — potsherds, nails etc. (FIGURE 14).

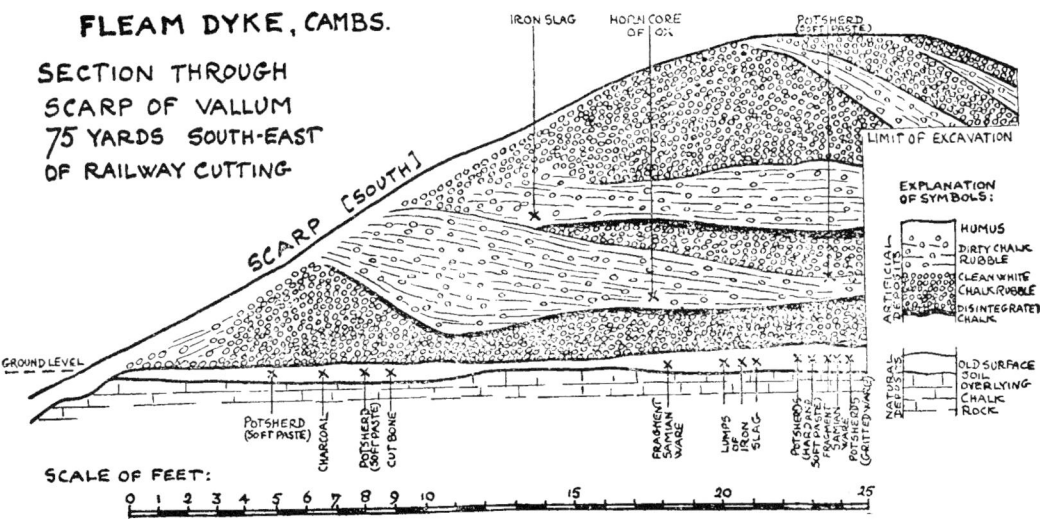

FIGURE 13. *Fleam Dyke, Cambs. Section through scarp of vallum. (From the* Cambridge Antiquarian Society's Communications.*)*

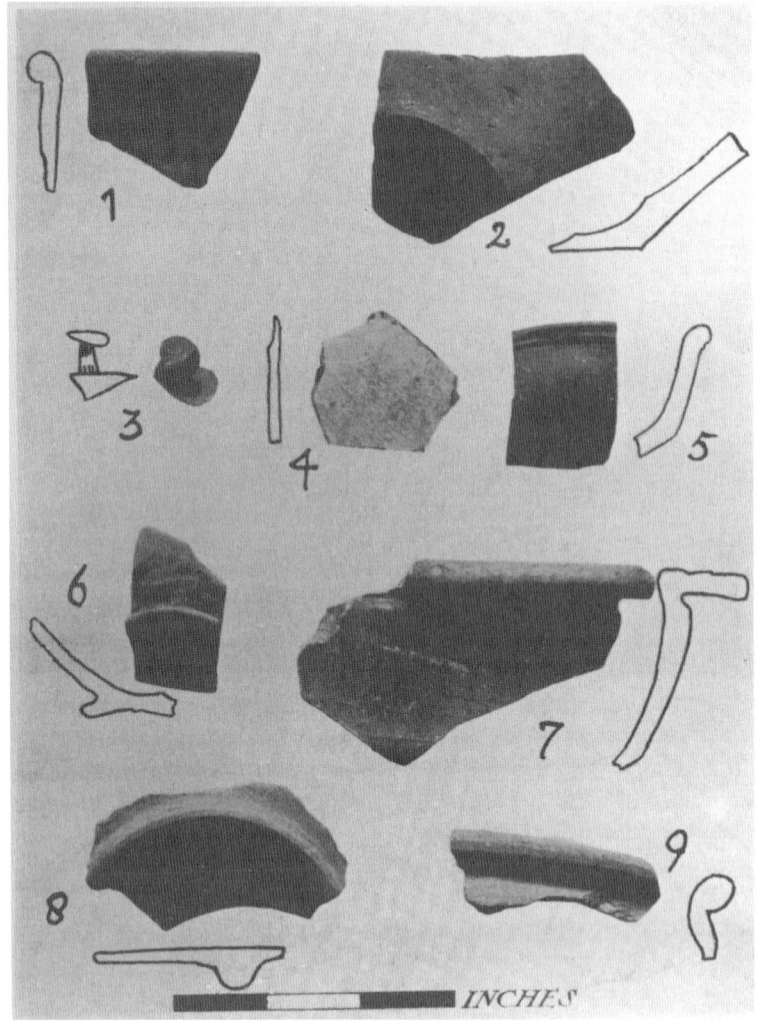

FIGURE 14. *Offa's Dyke: Roman pottery, etc. found in and under the vallum at Ffrith, Flintshire. (From Archaeologia Cambrensis.)*

Investigation of the three great dyke-systems thus proves that they are not, in the sections examined, pre-Roman. Offa's Dyke (so far as it has been studied), and the more important members of the Cambridgeshire series are certainly individually homogeneous, and in the case of each the date ascertained for any one portion may safely be regarded as the date of the whole work. There is nothing in the known history of the Roman period to justify the attribution of any of the three systems to the period of Roman rule. For their attribution to the Dark Ages we have direct evidence from two sources; one the ascription of Offa's Dyke to the 8th century in a document of the 9th; the other a recent excavation of Bran Ditch, Cambridgeshire, by Mr. T. C. Lethbridge, F.S.A., which has revealed under the remains of the bank Anglian burials presumably of the Pagan period, 450–650 AD.[2] The date of Bokerly Dyke, it will have been observed, was by direct evidence pushed so close to the end of the Roman period as to make it practically certain that this also was a work of the Dark Ages.

Since then the greater dykes may be regarded as post-Roman, is it probable that all dykes in southern Britain are of this period? One widely prevalent detail of construction

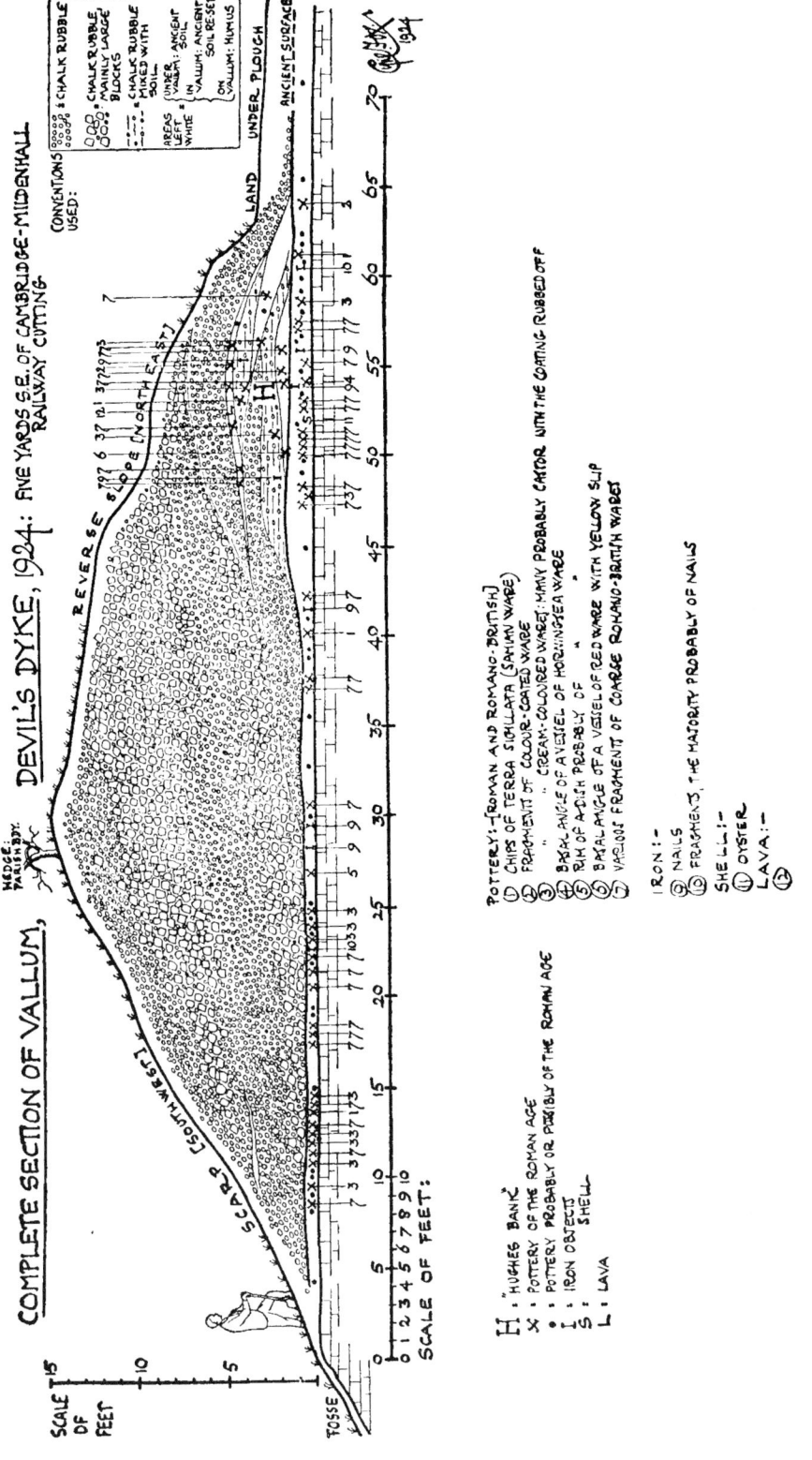

FIGURE 15. *Devil's Dyke: section through the vallum. (From the Cambridge Antiquarian Society's Communications.)*

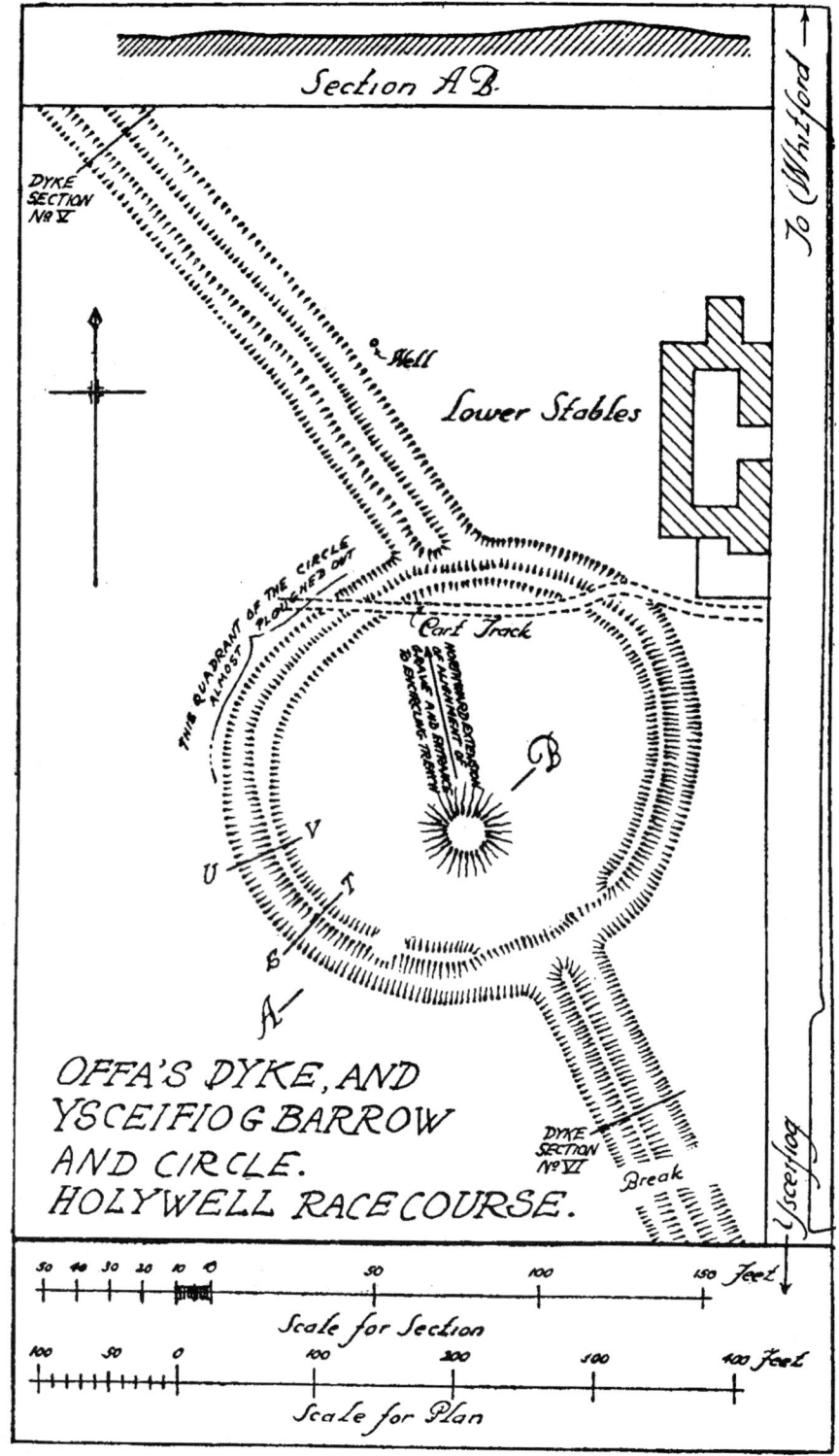

FIGURE 16. *Offa's Dyke and Ysceifiog Barrow and Circle.*

— direct alignment — tends to suggest this. There is a Roman character about such a mode, to which known work of the pre-Roman period offers no parallel. Thus I am inclined to believe that we shall ultimately arrive at the conclusion that practically the whole of our native dyke systems, large and small, belong to one period, and that the Dark Ages. We have only to consider for a moment the historical background to find a reason for this — a reason which emphasizes its probability. In north Britain there were erected by the Romans two barriers with sea-protected flanks, the Antonine Vallum and Hadrian's Wall. The existence of the latter at least must have been known to all dwellers in Roman Britain, and since by its aid the native population was protected against the attacks of the northern tribes, it must have learnt to appreciate the value of such constructions. Again, the Germanic tribes on the Continent must have become familiar, through direct contact or tradition, with the *limes* between the Rhine and the Danube; and they themselves in the Augustan age created linear earthworks[3] It is only to be expected, therefore, that this method of defence should have been utilized in England by Britons and by Saxons alike.

Boundary or defensive dykes are, in the nature of things, likely to be constructed by higher civilizations in contact with lower. They define the limits of law and order as against lawlessness and anarchy. Our greater dykes appear to afford excellent illustrations of this; in the south-west Romanized Britons, it is reasonable to suggest, attempted to secure the shattered elements of their civilization from the Saxon raiders by means of Wansdyke and Bokerly Dyke; in Cambridgeshire the East Anglians of the 7th century, comparatively civilized as a result of contact with the continental culture of the Franks, defended themselves against the still pagan and probably barbarous Mercians of the interior; in the west again, the Mercians, a century or two later, turned to protect the civilization which they by this time had gained or evolved, from the wild highlander of the Welsh border.

The dominance of purely military ideas and requirements in the siting of dykes has been emphasized in this article; in their alignment considerations other than the dominant one seem normally to be in abeyance. There is, however, no doubt that in the past, when frontier lines were to be drawn, political considerations had weight. A curious instance occurs in the case of the Devil's Ditch. Before excavation was undertaken, I was working on the Early Iron Age in the Cambridge region, and in analyzing the distribution of coins found that the countryside crossed by the dyke separated the Cambridge region into two districts in which coins of the Iceni on the one hand, and of the Catuvellauni and the southern tribes generally on the other, were commonly found. The results were as follows:-

North of the Devil's Ditch: Icenian coins 249, others 4.
South of the Devil's Ditch: Icenian coins 6, others 186.

It is not surprising that the conclusion was drawn in 1922[4] that the dyke might be of pre-Roman origin designed to control and limit trade and intercourse between neighbouring Celtic tribes. It is now seen to be probable that the barrier when erected — presumably by the East Anglians of the 7th century — followed a political frontier of very old standing, the significance of which neither the Roman domination nor the Saxon conquest had destroyed.

In the case of Offa's Dyke again the exceptions to the rule that the alignment selected was, from the military point of view, favourable to the lowland power, are so outstanding that I was in last year's report[5] forced to the conclusion that 'the alignment of the dyke in general may not represent, as I have been disposed to hold, the free choice of a conquering race, but a boundary defined by treaty or by agreement between the men of the hills and the men of the lowlands. The latter, one would say, although clearly the dominant partners in the arrangement, did not have matters all their own way'. If, for example, the map (FIGURE 5) be referred to, it will be seen that the exclusion of the Y Gardden fort and the dominating spur on which it is situated must have been to the disadvantage of the builders of the dyke. Another example illustrating the influence of considerations other than military, of a very different order, is also provided by Offa's Dyke. In Flintshire the dyke is frequently aligned on tumuli which provide convenient sighting points in this somewhat featureless country. One such barrow, in Ysceifiog parish, is surrounded by a small, circular bank and ditch of very slight relief, at the edge of which the dyke stops short, commencing again on the other side (FIGURE 16). So similar and unexpected a break in the continuity of the earthwork suggested that the burial mound might be a contemporary construction with a sacred enclosure round it; its investigation was evidently desirable. The barrow was completely excavated in 1926 and revealed a primary burial of the Early Bronze Age with a secondary cremation interment of the middle phase of the Age. Thus at a date some 2500 years later than the creation of this burial place and some 2000 years later than its last employment as a place of interment, the site seems to have possessed sanctity; at all events the builders of Offa's Dyke, whether Mercians or Welshmen impressed as labourers for the task, did not trespass on the enclosure.

Acknowledgement. The Editor desires to acknowledge the courtesy of the Cambrian Archaeological Association, the Cambridge Antiquarian Society, and the Cambridge University Press in lending blocks to illustrate this paper.

References.
1   I am indebted to the Editor of ANTIQUITY for additions to my list. Those interested in the subject will find references
        to others in Allcroft's *Earthwork of England,* pp. 494–522.
2   Mr Letbbridge's report will appear in the *Camb. Antiq. Soc. Comm.*
3   Tacitus, *Annals,* II. 19.
4   Fox, *Arch. Camb. Reg.,* p.90.
5   *Archaeologia Cambrensis* 1928, p. 103.

The Hebrides: a Cultural Backwater
by E. CECIL CURWEN
ANTIQUITY 12 (47), 1938

IN our efforts to reconstruct the life of vanished peoples and cultures we often find ourselves making comparisons with the implements and customs of modern primitive peoples. This practice seems, with due safeguards, reasonably sound, for similar cultural conditions may produce similar cultural phenomena. Our comparative material is usually sought among the backward races of the tropics, less frequently in parts of Europe that are off the beaten track; but it is not generally realized that we have in Britain itself a populous region which, owing to its remoteness, did not emerge from the Iron Age until the end of last century. By 'the Iron Age' we mean that simple state of culture that is found in peasant communities in southern Britain between, say, 500 BC and AD 1000, extending in a variable degree into the Middle Ages. This stage of cultural development is distinguished from more advanced stages by the prevalence of self-supporting communities which are necessitated by difficulty of communications, and in this respect the culture of the Hebrides as late as the middle of the nineteenth century was more like that of the pre-Roman Iron Age in southern England than any succeeding phase.

Before the invention of the steam and internal combustion engines communication between the Hebrides and the mainland, and between different parts of the Hebrides, was difficult and dangerous, and the people produced little that could attract traders to undergo the hazards of such voyages. Consequently little was imported, and in the villages everything that was needed had to be produced on the spot just as was the case in pre-Roman England.*

During the present century, and especially since the War, communications have been immeasurably improved by the introduction of motor-boats and motor-cars, and by the making up of the island roads. Little, therefore, now remains to be seen of the functioning of the self-supporting village-community, unless it be the primitive dwellings known as 'black houses', and the shielings.

'Black Houses'
The term 'black house' is a translation of the Gaelic *tigh dubh*, and is applied to the primitive dwellings which may still be seen in large numbers — though not always in their pristine form — in the island of Lewis, and less frequently elsewhere. In their original form they have neither window nor chimney, but have a hearth with a peat-fire in the middle of the floor, the smoke from which finds its way out mainly through the door, and sometimes to a small extent through a hole in the thatch of the roof. A second opening was usually left in the thatch to admit light, and this is nowadays generally furnished with a pane of glass. Many 'black houses' have undergone alterations in the course of time, whereby windows have been cut into the walls, hearths have been moved

---

* This is a general statement, and does not necessarily apply to the households of the chiefs and landed proprietors. Even today, of the 30,000 (odd) inhabitants of Lewis and Harris, the majority have probably never seen a train.

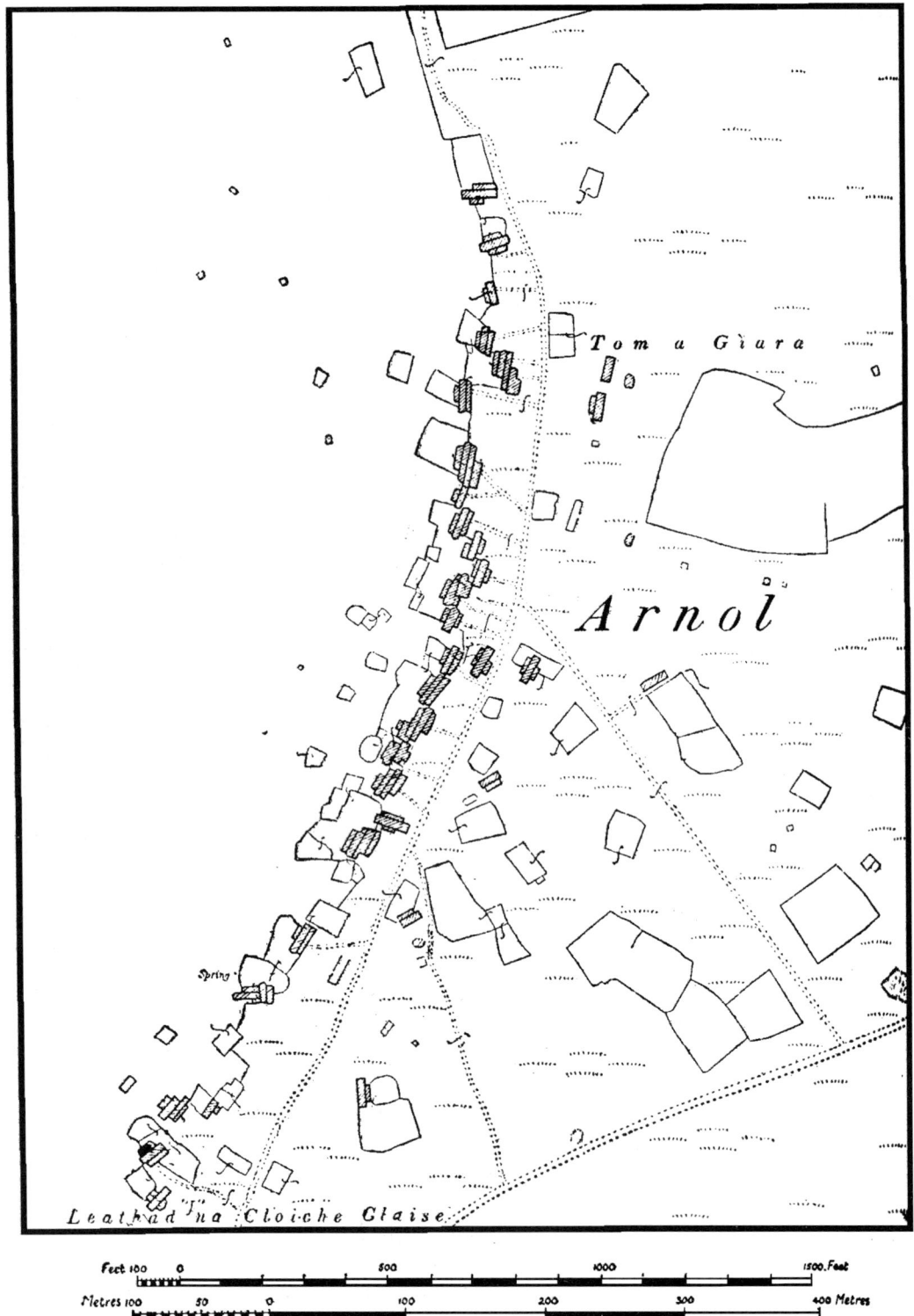

FIGURE 1. *Arnol: a typical village of 'Black Houses' in West Lewis (1897). (Reproduced by permission of the Ordnance Survey and the Controller of H.M. Stationery Office.)*

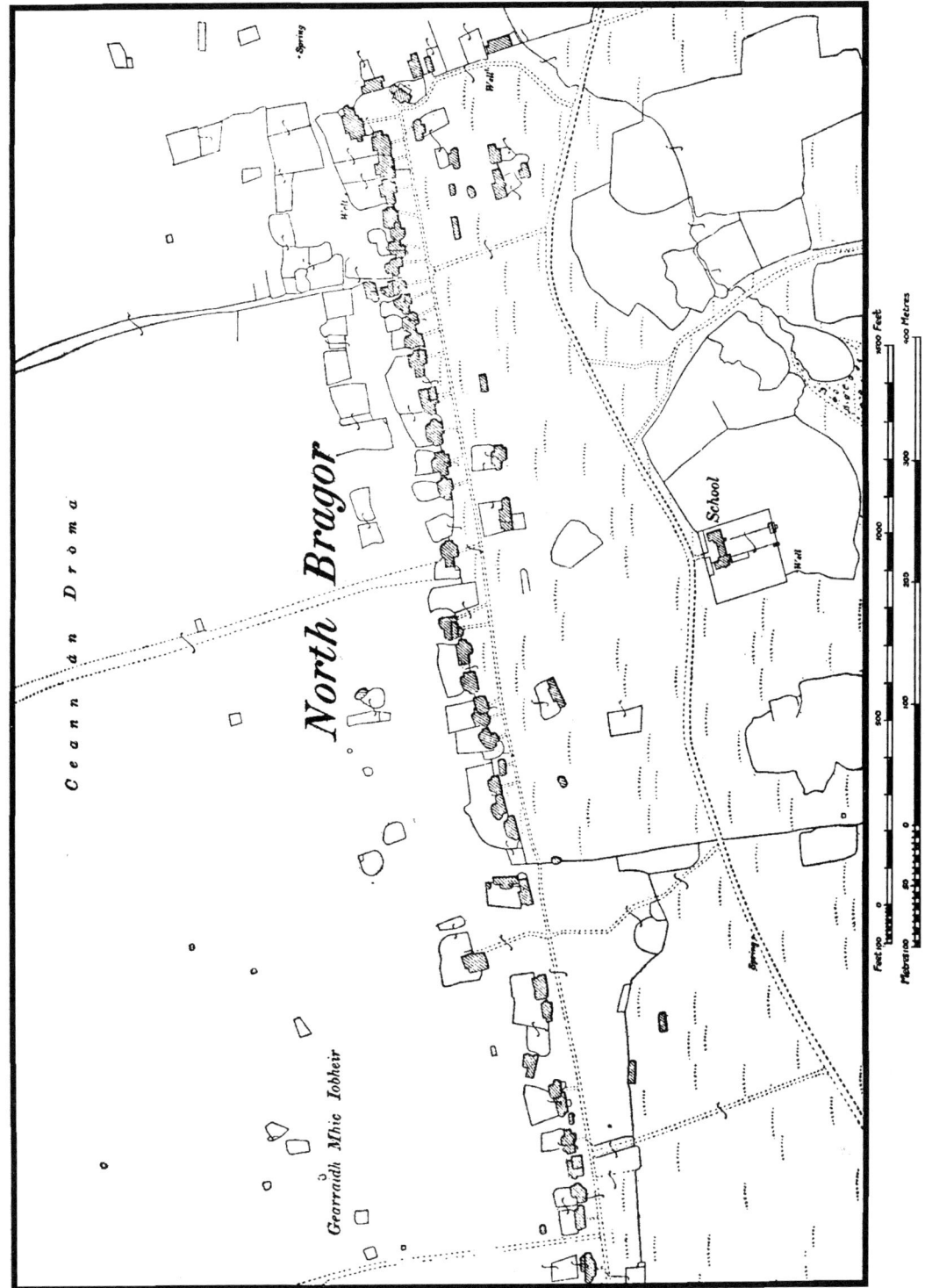

FIGURE 2. *North Bragor: a typical village of 'black houses' in West Lewis (1897). (Reproduced by permission of the Ordnance Survey and the Controller of H.M. Stationery Office.)*

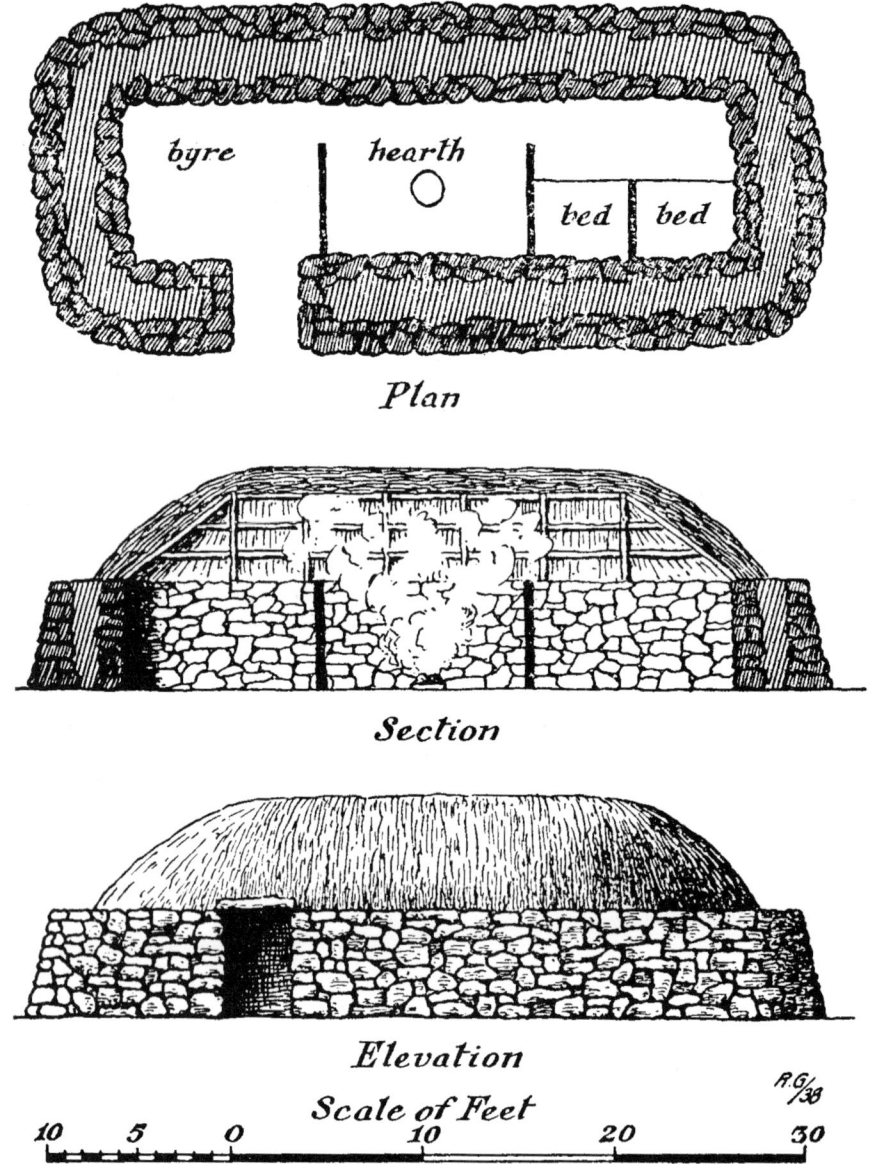

FIGURE 3. *Plan, section and elevation of typical 'black house' e.g. in Skye.*

so as to abut on a newly built stone partition wall, or on an end-wall, and chimneys have been added. In a house of this latter type that the writer entered in Barvas (Lewis) a young mother rocked her baby in an ancient wooden cradle of a kind only found in folk-museums elsewhere.

'Black houses have as a rule a simple elongated plan, about 30 to 60 ft. long externally, by about 20 ft. wide. The walls, which stand about 6 ft. high, are usually double, being built of dry stone without mortar, the space between the double walls being filled with turf or small stones to render them weather proof (FIGURE 3). The whole wall may be as much as 5 ft. thick at the base, often thinning to about 3·5 ft thick at the top. In the older houses the corners are rounded externally, and the stones may be more or less undressed boulders; in more recent examples the corners are often square, and the stones are dressed to fit neatly together. The roof is supported by couples, made either of branches or of any procurable pieces of wood, and these rest on the *inner* facing of the double wall, so that it is usually possible to walk round the top of the wall outside the edge of the roof, there being no projecting eaves. The covering is of thatch, loosely laid on, and held in place by heather-ropes from which numbers of biggish stones are suspended all round the building to prevent the thatch being blown away by the wild winter winds. For the same reason there are no projecting eaves, as already mentioned, and the whole contour of the roof is a rounded ridge of hipped form, without gables, and without square edges. Nowadays heather-ropes tend to be replaced by fishing-nets or even by wire netting.

The interior of such a house is generally divided by rough wooden partitions into three apartments. At one end is the cow-byre into which the outer door leads; this door, which stands the full height of the wall, and is generally provided with a thin flat stone for a lintel, is placed near the end of one of the long walls of the house. From the cow-byre one passes through a rough wooden partition into the living-room where one sees a peat fire burning in the middle of the clay floor, and a kettle hanging over it by a chain from the roof. It is an interesting point that the fire is never allowed to go out, summer or winter, day or night; it is smoored over with peat-ash in the evening and keeps in sufficiently to be revived in the morning; complete extinction would be extremely unlucky. Even in the 'black house' which is preserved as a local museum by the Scottish National Trust at Callernish (Lewis) the fire is said not to have been allowed to go out for a hundred years. The peat-smoke, which, unlike wood-smoke, is not irritating to the eyes or lungs, finds its way out principally through the cow-byre and the outer door — and to a negligible extent through any hole which may have been left for it in the thatch of the roof. One of the results of this arrangement is that the rafters and thatch become coated with a sticky, sooty fur which was formerly valued as a manure for the fields and was carefully collected for this purpose whenever the thatch was renewed.

Round the walls of the living-room are chests, settles, a dresser, and perhaps a spinning-wheel — all rather old and elegant pieces of furniture. Through a door in the second partition lies the sleeping apartment, one side of which is occupied by two wooden-framed beds in cupboard-like recesses occupying the whole of one wall between the partition and the end-wall of the house. Each bed is perhaps 5 ft. wide and 5 or 6 ft. long, and they lie foot to foot, being separated by a wooden partition between the two bed-recesses. Each of the two inhabited apartments will nowadays be lit by a pane of glass let into the lower part of the thatch of the roof.

Such is a general description of one of the usual types of 'black house', excluding the more recent modifications to which many have been subjected, and it is based largely on specimens visited by the writer in Skye in 1920 and 1934.* The occupants of these remarkably picturesque old houses — proud, reserved Gaels — are unfortunately exceedingly sensitive about what they consider to be evidence of their poverty, and they are intensely resentful of anything resembling curiosity on the part of a 'Sassenach'. It is therefore seldom possible to gain entry to a 'black house' without much diplomacy and the greatest tact; a personal introduction by another local inhabitant is nearly always necessary. The people are also very camera-shy, so that it was something of a triumph to

*In the case of one house at Woodend, near Portree, the present occupant could account for its past occupants for 200 years. The house is obviously an old one and less carefully built than most, but has been recently modified internally.

be able to obtain a photograph of an interior with central fireplace in the village of Arnol in Lewis in 1937 (FIGURE 4).

A more complex type of 'black house' is characteristic of the island of Lewis, particularly the west coast, where some of the best examples may be seen at Arnol (FIGURE 5); here they are still extremely common, though few can have escaped undergoing some modification since they were described by Capt. Thomas in 1867.[1] The general type of construction is the same as that just described, but the house may consist of two, three, or even four[2] long structures of unequal length, lying parallel to one another so that share the intervening long walls in common, but each covered with a separate ridge roof (FIGURE. 7). The rain that falls in the trough between adjacent roofs percolates down through the thick wall upon which they rest, no attempt being made to carry the water

FIGURE 4. *Interior of 'black house', Arnol, showing central fireplace (Photograph E. Cecil Curwen, 1937.)*

FIGURE 5. *The village of Arnol in Lewis. Several of these 'black houses' must have been built since the map of 1897 (FIGURE 1) was published.*

FIGURE 6. *Old and new houses in Arnol, Lewis. (Photograph E. Cecil Curwen, 1937.)*

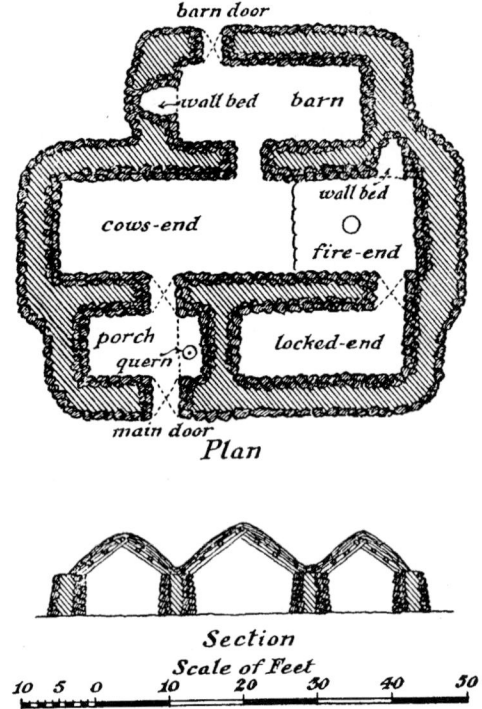

barn door

wall bed   barn

cows-end

wall bed

○

fire-end

porch
quern

locked-end

main door
Plan

Section
Scale of Feet
10 5 0   10   20   30   40   50

FIGURE 7. *Plan and section of a typical 'black house' in Lewis. (Plan after Thomas.)*

off by guttering. After all, what matters damp in a dry-stone wall which has neither plaster nor paper to cover it within, and when the air is kept warm and dry by the ever-burning fire?

When the house consists of three parallel structures in this way, the central one is generally the longest, widest and highest, and forms the main chamber of the house, the other two forming a porch and a barn respectively. The porch accommodated a quern on a fixed table on one side of the entrance,[3] and provided room for stalling a horse on the other side. The main chamber might be from 30 to 50 ft. long internally, and 12 to 14 ft. wide, and consisted in Capt. Thomas's time of two parts separated from one another only by a step and not by a partition of any kind. The larger part — about two-thirds of the whole — formed the cow-byre, while the smaller part formed the domestic quarters of the household and had a fire in the middle of the floor, as usual. As the long axis of these houses generally lies at right angles to the contours of the ground there may be a considerable fall in level between the upper and lower ends of the house. The byre is always at the lower end and anyone entering the house from the porch would have to pass through the byre to reach the domestic end, the floor of the latter being raised by a step about a foot above that of the byre. The animals would be tethered round the walls of the byre, and as the floor was cleared only once a year the accumulation of manure might in the course of the year raise it well above the level of the domestic end. And yet the approach to the latter lay of necessity through the byre, because it was better so than that the animals should be taken in and out through the 'living room'. The end-wall of the byre usually has a wide gap in it, about 6 or 7 ft. wide; this is kept blocked with a wall of turves which can be taken down for the annual cleaning of the byre floor.

Capt. Thomas thus describes the domestic end of such a house as he saw it in 1867:-

> Externally there is no smoke-hole nor window; but the purpose of both is served by two holes, about a foot square, in and at the bottom of the thatch . . . the custom arises from the desire to keep in the smoke until it fills and saturates the vault of the roof. . . . If the sun is shining brightly, these cottages appear on entering to be quite dark, until the eyes become accustomed to the dim light within. . . . The fire, which never goes out, is about the middle of the floor; on the right hand side is a bench of wood, stone or turf, on which the men sit; on the opposite side the women perform their domestic duties. Tables and chairs are almost unknown; but the evidently modern luxury of bedsteads and a dresser are quite usual. I am not sure of the date of their introduction; but they cannot have been long in use, from the former scarcity of wood, at least of planks. Behind the dresser is the calves' location, because it is near the fire; and the cows are tethered in winter along the wall. . . . A door

opposite the entrance door admits to the barn, which is also commonly the sleeping-place of the grown-up young people[4]

Though Capt. Thomas says that in his day there was a prejudice against shutting the cows out from a view of the fire, it is doubtful whether this has survived the pressure of Ministry of Health regulations; consequently it is probable that all such houses have in more recent times been provided with wooden partitions between the byre and the domestic quarters.

The *crûb,* or wall-bed, was becoming obsolete in Capt. Thomas's time, though he was acquainted with people who had used them. It consisted of a recess in the thickness of the wall, raised about 2 ft. above floor level. At the mouth it might be 2·5ft. wide and 3 ft. high, and it would extend into the wall to a depth of 5 or 6 ft., becoming narrower and lower as it went; it was roofed with flag-stones. The would-be sleeper introduced himself feet foremost into this recess, sometimes with the help of a rope hanging from above — no mean achievement, one would think — and lay with his head at the opening. In the oldest houses in Lewis, Capt. Thomas says, there was usually a *crûb* in the wall opposite to the hearth, 'and where there was one on each side of the fire, the house was considered to be well supplied. If there were more in the family than these beds would hold, they lay in a corner upon the floor, railed in by a plank on edge. Occasionally the second *crûb* was in the barn. . . . An old lady of my acquaintance, when a girl, was on a visit, where the servant girl used to carry her to her sleeping-place in the wall (which, in this instance, was at the cows' end of the house), that she might not soil her feet by walking among the cattle.[5]

'Black houses' are nowadays confined to the more northerly of the Western Isles, and are not now found on the mainland. Those of Orkney and Shetland, though closely related to those of the Hebrides, show certain differences, such as a stricter rectangularity of plan (avoiding rounded corners), and the possession of gables and single walls.

Recently a Danish architect, Aage Roussell,[6] has demonstrated the Scandinavian affinities of these primitive 'long houses' of which the typical feature is that the family occupies one end, while the other end forms the byre. This was the characteristic plan of the Scandinavian houses of the Iron Age and Viking period, as evidenced by very many examples in Norway, Sweden and Denmark, some of which have been amply described by Professor Gudmund Hatt in ANTIQUITY.[7] Allowing for the difference of material — wood and clay — some of the houses of the Roman Iron Age in Jutland seem to be an almost exact counterpart to those Hebridean 'black houses' which consist of a single long building. Other examples are known in large numbers from southwest Norway and from Sweden. The recent discovery of the remains of a Viking house at Jarlshof in Orkney provides another striking parallel to the 'black houses', including such a feature as the double stone wall with earthen core.[8] The type of house which consists of two or more Lewis and in the Orkneys and Shetlands, and certain analogies are parallel chambers, each with separate ridge-roofs, is found both in Lewis and the Orkneys and Shetlands, and certain analogies are available from Iceland.[9]

To judge from the accounts of 18th-century travellers, such as Pennant and Boswell in 1772–3, 'black houses' of some such form as those described above were still the normal dwellings throughout the Western Isles from Rum northwards.[10] Further south in Islay Pennant illustrates a somewhat similar dwelling with central hearth, but having windows and gables.[11]

In the remote island of St. Kilda the old 'black houses' were almost all replaced by a more modern type of cottage between 1829 and 1843. An entertaining description of the old houses is given by the Rev. Neil Mackenzie, who was minister of St. Kilda at that time.[12] After describing the thatch and the use of the soot on it for manuring the barley, he says: 'The furniture consisted of an iron pot or two; a chest or two; a wooden dish called *buta* and another called *cuman;* a straw vessel like a large flat-bottomed beehive called *loban* ; an iron lamp called *cruisgean;* a quern, and a few old barrels, some of them hooped by a rope made of a kind of ground willow twisted. The cattle occupied the division next the door, and it was not cleaned out till spring. At the other end lived the family, and there all the ashes, dirty water, and still worse, was spread out over the floor, and covered from time to time with layers of dry peat dust. Before the time for removal for use in spring the mixture was often higher than the side walls, so that a visit to a sick parishioner was quite an adventure. Owing to the thickness of the wall the door of the house was at the end of a low tunnel. Before the door, and extending part of the way into the tunnel, was a hole into which was thrown all the birds not used for food, the refuse of the others, and such like abominations. As the doorway was not more than 5 ft. high, you had to make your way past this in a stooping position, till at the end of the tunnel you reached the door. If it was spring-time, on passing the door you had to climb up among the cattle, which got excited from the presence of a stranger, the barking of dogs, and the shouting of your friends above. Amidst great excitement you got helped along, and hoisted over the 'fallan' [*i.e.,* the low stone partition between byre and living quarters]. Now you had to creep along on hands and feet, as it was only near the centre of the house that you could even sit upright. In this way you arrived at the edge of the steep slope above the bed opening [*i.e.,* a *crûb,* or recess in the thickness of the wall], down which you went head foremost, nothing visible above but your legs, while you spoke and prayed with the sick'.

Martin, in his descriptions of the Western Isles and of St. Kilda in particular (in 1697), does not say much about 'black houses', because to him, a native of Skye, they were too ordinary to be worth more than a passing mention.[13]

Houses built of turf (*i.e.* peat) are not common now, except as shielings, but they can be very stable and durable. Mr Crawford has photographed a fine example by Loch Eynort in South Uist, built in 1914. and showing the careful laying of the turves in herringbone fashion* (FIGURE 10). Houses of turf were more commonly met with on the mainland in the 18th century: Boswell describes one consisting of three rooms, lined with wattle, in Glen Moriston, and another consisting of byre, dwelling room and sleeping room near Loch Ness[14]; others mention oval turf houses — apparently not shielings — in Argyllshire,[15] Lochaber,[16] Sutherlandshire[17] and even on Deeside, near Ballater.[18] Turf shielings are still common in Lewis, as will be seen below.

The survival of 'black houses' to the present day in Lewis and elsewhere should not in any way be looked upon as a stigma upon their occupants. The latter are extremely sensitive about them, and envy those of their neighbours who, with the help of a Government loan, have built for themselves modern two-storey cottages. The social reformer rejoices at this change which is gradually but surely altering the face of the islands, and he comforts himself with the thought that in a few years 'black houses' will be no more. With social reform there will be universal sympathy, but one cannot help regretting the light-hearted way in which these ancient and picturesque dwellings, that so perfectly fit the wild landscape of the islands, are being eliminated in favour of houses that stand gaunt, stark and unsympathetic on the local sky-line. It is as when in England old thatched, timbered cottages are replaced by red-brick Council-houses of the severest and most

---

* For a knowledge of this, and for much other valuable information, Mr Crawford is indebted to Mrs Margaret Campbell, of Barra, whom he wishes to thank for her generous help.

FIGURE 8. *Dun Carloway, Lewis, broch with inhabited 'black house' in foreground. (Photograph O.G.S. Crawford, 1936.)*

FIGURE 9. *'Black house' at Bragor, Lewis. (Photograph O.G.S. Crawford, 1936.)*

blatant pattern; here an effective protest is generally made, but there not one voice seems to be raised in favour of those unique dwellings which within a very few years will have vanished for ever.

It is not that anyone wishes to perpetuate a standard of life in which human beings live herded with cattle, and without light or air. And yet from these despised 'black houses' has issued as fine a race of men as ever came from any kind of house in England — men who have distinguished themselves in public life in Scotland and throughout the Empire. It is only since the comparatively recent introduction of tuberculosis to the islands by returning emigrants that the 'black houses' have become unhealthy. In the 17th and 18th centuries centenarians appear to have been commoner on the islands than they are now, even attaining ages of 140 or more.[19]

Is it too much to hope that, even if 'black houses' cannot be modernized to satisfy the requirements of hygiene, some specimens may be preserved entire with their furniture, before it be too late? One such is preserved at Callernish in Lewis by the Scottish National Trust, and this contains the nucleus of a folk-museum. This house is not, however, furnished as it was when it was occupied, except that the peat-fire has not been allowed to go out, it is said, for a hundred years. The place ought obviously to be fully furnished in the original manner, each exhibit being displayed in its natural setting, and several more such houses might well be so preserved in different parts.

Shielings

Lewis is now the only part of Britain in which the villagers still repair to the moors with their cattle during the summer — between seed-time and harvest — and live an idyllic life in the shielings. This custom is still widely followed in Norway and Switzerland, and it was formerly observed on the mainland of Scotland, and in the north of England

FIGURE 10. *'Black house' built of peat, L. Eynort, S. Uist. (Photograph O.G.S. Crawford 1936.)*

— as witness the numerous place-names incorporating the word 'shiel 'or 'shield'. We know from Boswell and Pennant that shielings were in use even as far east as Aberdeen-shire round about 1770,[20] but of their character nothing is said.

A shieling (Gad. *gearraidh,* pronounced 'garry'; or *airidh,* pronounced 'ah-ry', to rhyme with 'starry') consists of a group of more or less permanent huts, to which the same population return every summer. It may be situated in an extremely remote part of the moors, many miles from any kind of track, and all the furniture required has to be carried thither. Skene gives a vivid picture of the departure for the summer shieling.

> 'Having finished their tillage, the people go early in June to the hill-grazing with their flocks. This is a busy day in the town-land. . . . The different families bring their herds together and drive them away. The sheep lead, the cattle go next . . . and the horses follow. The men carry burdens of sticks, heather-ropes, spades, and other things needed to repair their summer huts. The women carry bedding, meal, dairy and cooking utensils. Round below their waists is a thick woollen cord or leathern strap, underneath which their skirts are drawn up to enable them to walk easily over the moors. . . . Women knit their stockings, sing their songs, talk and walk as free and erect as if there were no burdens on their backs. . . . When the grazing ground has been reached and the burdens are laid down, the huts are repaired outwardly and inwardly, the fires are rekindled, and food is prepared. . . . Having seen to their cattle . . .the people repair to their removing feast . . . the chief thing being a cheese. . . Here they remain making butter and cheese till the corn is ripe for shearing, when they and their cattle return home'.[21]

Once more we are indebted to Captain Thomas for the fullest information we possess regarding the shielings of last century in Lewis and Harris.[22] His observations were made in 1857–66, and his second-hand information went back to the beginning of that century. In his time the huts were either timber-roofed, with stone walls (*airidh)* or round 'beehive' huts, built and roofed entirely with dry stones on the principle of the corbelled arch, and covered externally with turf and grass. These latter were called *both,* plur. *bothan* (pronounced 'bo', 'bo-un'), a loan-word from the Norse, akin to our 'booth'. Thomas visited over forty specimens of these beehive huts, mainly in the parish of Uig in Lewis, about half of which number he found to be still inhabited as shielings. He says that they were valued by their occupants more than the timber-roofed structures, partly on account of the scarcity of timber, and its liability to be dislodged in winter gales. In most cases their origin went back beyond living memory; but an example on Cnoc Dubh, Ceann Thulabhig, near Garrynahine (one of the very few still trace-

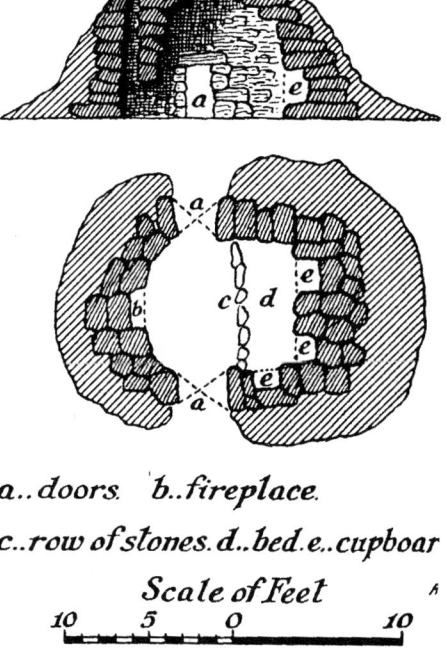

a..doors.   b..fireplace.

c..row of stones. d..bed. e..cupboar

Scale of Feet

10   5   O   10

FIGURE 11. *Plan and section of beehive hut, Cnoc Dubh, Ceann Thulabhig. (After Thomas. Cf. FIGURE 12.)*

FIGURE 12. *Beehive shieling, Cnoc Dubh, Lewis, (cf. FIGURE 11) inhabited in 1866. (Photograph E. Cecil Curwen, 1937.)*

able today; see FIGURES 11 and 12) was said to have been built by the grandfather of a man still living in 1866, *viz.,* probably about 1776. This one was still occupied in 1866.

In general these huts had dimensions somewhat as follows: diameter, external, 12–18 ft., internal 6–8 ft., height, external, 9 ft., internal, 6 ft. The chamber was usually round or oval, occasionally rectangular. They had either one or two doors, about 2.5 ft. high, and generally some small recesses or aumbreys in the wall for storing things. Some had wall-beds *(crûb)* like the 'black houses', and all had a smoke-hole at the apex of the dome, except the one at Cnoc Dubh, which is furnished with a recessed fireplace and chimney in the wall (FIGURE 11). The huts with only one door, and those with wall-beds, are probably the oldest; the practice of having two doors seemed to Thomas to be a more recent device by which one or other door could be blocked with turves, according to the direction of the wind, thus better controlling the draught for the fire and thereby the elimination of smoke. When there are two doors they are opposite one another, but a line joining them divides the interior of the hut into two unequal parts; the smaller contained the peat fire on the floor, while the larger was filled with hay or rushes to serve as a bed for two or even three persons. Between this bed and the fire was a 'bench' consisting of a row of stones covered with turf placed right across the hut, and on this the occupants could sit during the day (FIGURE 11). A longish stone could be drawn in and out of the wall for the purpose of hanging a pot over the fire. The furniture did not as a rule exceed the following: a blanket, an iron pot, a basin, a spoon, a bag of meal, and some utensils for the milk; not many years previously these last consisted of hand-made pottery vessels.

FIGURE 13. *Sketch of model of group of three behive shieling-huts at Bairn-Gail, Near Morsgail, Lewis, occupied till shortly before 1885. (Model in Pitt Rivers Museum, Farnham, Dorset.)*

Some of these beehive huts stood singly, or in a group, like those at Fidigidh Iochdrach in a remote part of the Uig mountains, which Thomas found still occupied in 1858. Others consisted of two or more interconnecting chambers, one of which served as a dairy. Dr Mitchell's[23] description of his first experience of finding such a structure inhabited (in 1866) is worth quoting:

> We found one of these beehive houses [near Kinloch Resort] actually tenanted, and the family happened to be at home. It consisted of three young women. . . . None of them could speak English . . . they invited us into the *bo'h*, and hospitably treated us to milk. . . I do not think I ever came upon a scene which more surprised me.... By the side of a burn which flowed through a little grassy glen. . . we saw two small round hive-like hillocks, not much higher than a man, joined together, and covered with grass and weeds. Out of the top of one of them a column of smoke slowly rose, and at its base there was a hole about three feet high and two feet wide, which seemed to lead into the interior of the hillock. . . . There was no one, however, actually in the *bo'h*, the three girls, when we came in sight, being seated on a knoll by the burn-side, but it was really in the inside of these two green hillocks that they slept, and cooked their food, and carried on their work. . .

Another group of three conjoined and intercommunicating huts of this type, situated at Bairn-Gail, near Morsgail (Lewis), was inhabited up to a short while before 1885 (FIGURE 13).[24] These (to judge from the model preserved in the Pitt Rivers Museum at Farnham, Dorset) were provided with horn-like projections to shelter the entrances from the wind. Capt. Thomas also described the ruins of several other such huts and hut-complexes on the northern shore of Loch Resort, near the headland of Aird Mhor (FIGURES 15–18). These consist of two or four chambers apiece, except one, known as Gearraidh na h'Airde

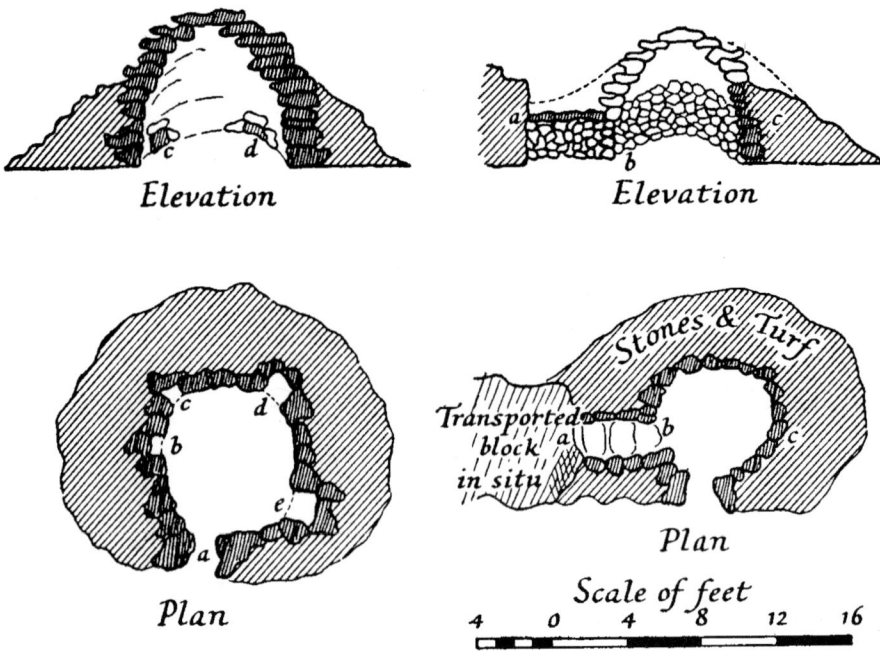

FIGURE 14. *Plans and sections of two beehive huts near L. Meavig, Harris (after Thomas).*

Moire (FIGURE 18), which had no less than twelve beehive chambers arranged in four suites, the members of each suite communicating with one another by means of passages about 2·5 ft. high. At the time of Thomas's visit two of the chambers were still complete, but collapsed as a result of his explorations. He found nothing but ashes and the shells of edible molluscs in great quantity, but was able to learn that this shieling was occupied as recently as 1823 by four families, the then tenant of the neighbouring farm of Aird Bheag having lived in it as a boy for eight successive summers.

The development of the modern shieling hut *(airidh)* seems to be traceable to the chimneyed *both* already referred to at Cnoc Dubh near Garrynahine (FIGURES 11 and 12). The interior of this beehive hut is more or less rectangular, and measures 8 ft. by 7 ft. It has two doors facing one another, each about 2·5 ft. high, on either side of a recessed fireplace, with chimney. The other half of the hut was shut off by a low bench of stones and turf which faced the fire; this bench has now gone.

The next stage of development seems to be represented by an oval stone hut called Airidh a' Chnoic Ghuirm (no imitated pronunciation could do justice to this name), near the road between Garrynahine and the head of Little Loch Roag. The rectangular interior chamber is here expanded to about 12 ft. long, with the result that a beehive stone roof is no longer possible. The fireplace is at one end, the two low doors, 3·5 to 4 ft. high, face each other on either side of it, and the bench faces the fire as before. The hut is oval externally, with walls sloping inwards, to be crowned by a low wooden roof covered with turves. This hut had not long been abandoned when the writer visited it in 1937, because the somewhat flimsy roof was still almost intact, and flakes of newspaper were still adhering to its under-surface.

The modern shieling hut seems to be a further development from this last, and is best seen in those shielings which lie not far from the roads which traverse the island. These huts are built of large blocks of peat owing to the scarcity of loose stones. They are rectangular in plan, having internal dimensions perhaps 15 or 20 ft. long by about 9ft. wide. The long walls are about 4 ft. high and 2·5 ft. thick; the end walls form gables, 7 or 8 ft. high, one of which is constructed of stone and contains a fireplace and some kind of chimney. Again we have two doors, facing one another, in the long walls near the chimney end, and one of them is always blocked with turf, according to the direction of the wind, both being so blocked at night. The modern way of dealing with the roofing problem, which has always been a dominant factor in the past, is practical if unromantic. The proximity of these shielings to the road makes it possible for a quantity of miscellaneous furniture, including the roof, to be brought out to the shieling by motor-lorry, and taken away again at the end of the season. Such a roof is constructed of planks, boards and bits of corrugated iron, the whole being covered with a tarpaulin, and lined inside with flowery wall-paper, or even newspaper. The papering may also extend to cover the inner faces of the turf walls. The interior is made cosy with iron bedsteads, feather-beds, cupboards, dressers, chairs, and hangings of all kinds, and even in these degenerate days no visitor is allowed to go away without at least a large glass of creamy milk.

The turf walls are so solid that they neither yield nor quiver when pushed, and the hut, when unroofed, keeps in good repair throughout the long and stormy winter.

Beehive huts have for some time been disused as shielings, but, on the authority of Skene,[25] they were still inhabited as lately as 1880. They constitute a remarkable survival of a form of dry stone construction — corbelled vaulting — that was introduced to western Europe by the megalith-builders, and has survived throughout prehistoric times in those western regions which were most affected by them. Thus we find them in Ireland in connexion with early monastic foundations, in Orkney in such prehistoric villages as Skara Brae and Jarlshof, in the brochs, souterraines and 'earth-houses' of the north and west coasts, and in such Iron Age sites in Cornwall as Chysauster and Bosporthennis. Recent examples of this type of construction have been noted in the Hebrides, particularly in Lewis, Harris and the St. Kilda group[26]; in Anglesey and Holyhead, in Cornwall at Fernacre Farm on Bodmin Moor, and in various parts of France — notably near Clermont in Puy-de-Dôme, and in Vaucluse and Basses-Alpes.[27]

Taking the combined picture of the 'black houses' and the beehive shielings, we can readily agree with Prof. Gordon Childe's view that the 19th century culture of the Hebrides was but a survival of that of the prehistoric village of Skara Brae in the Orkneys,[28] modified by the blending of Norse influences.

Other primitive survivals

We have so far been considering only the architectural aspects of this cultural backwater in the far northwest of Britain. But there are many other features of daily life which help to complete the picture, and these must receive brief mention.

(i) Hand made pottery.

The first and most significant is the survival of hand-made pottery in Lewis down to about

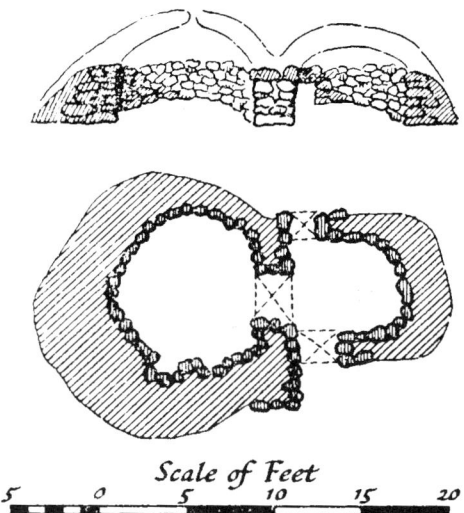

FIGURE 15. *Plan and section of beehive hut near Aird Mhor, Lewis. (After Thomas.)*

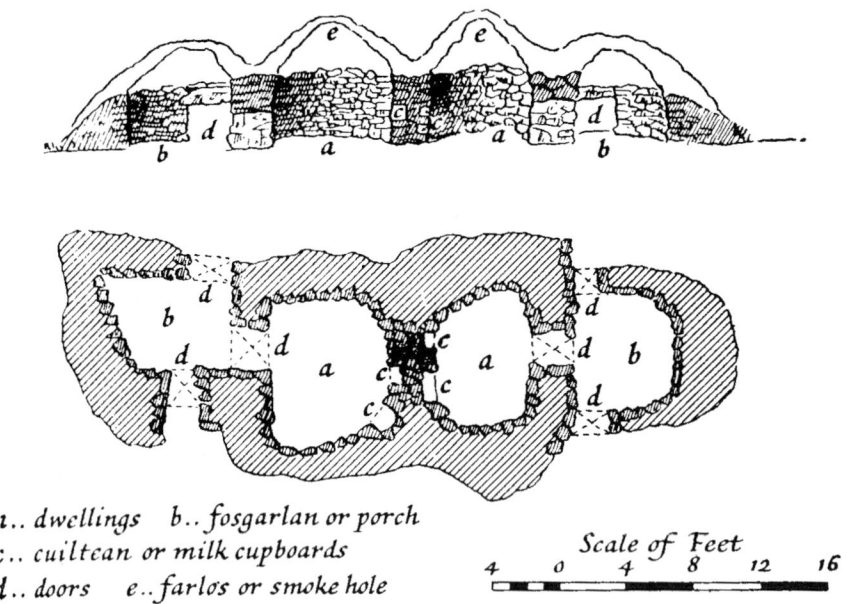

a.. dwellings   b.. fosgarlan or porch
c.. cuiltean or milk cupboards
d.. doors   e.. farlos or smoke hole

Scale of Feet
4   0   4   8   12   16

FIGURE 16. *Plan and section of group of beehive huts near Aird Mhor, Lewis (After Thomas.)*

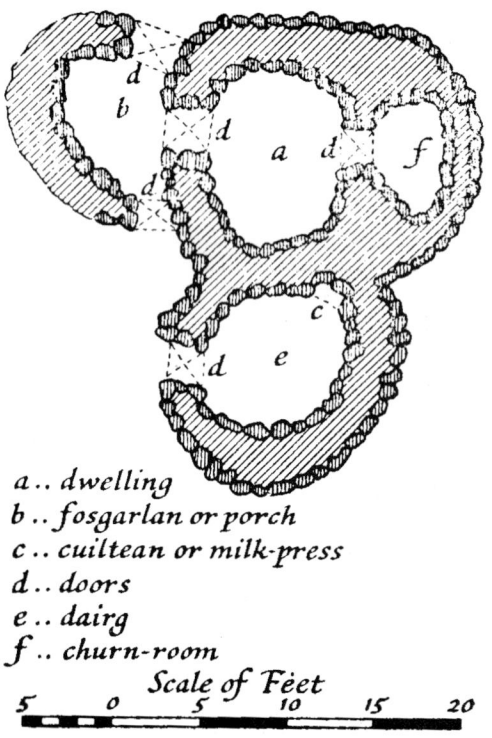

a.. dwelling
b.. fosgarlan or porch
c.. cuiltean or milk-press
d.. doors
e.. dairg
f.. churn-room

Scale of Feet
5   0   5   10   15   20

FIGURE 17. *Plan of beehive hut group near Aird Mhor, Lewis. (after Thomas).*

the end of last century. Before the dawn of the 'Enamel Age' comparatively little Staffordshire earthenware and crockery found its way as far as the wild west coast of Lewis, with the result that the people there continued to depend very largely on making their own pots by hand on the domestic hearth in the true 'prehistoric' tradition, and without the use of a potter's wheel. These vessels were last made at Barvas in Lewis, and the writer met a middle-aged woman at Uig (Skye) in 1920, who in her younger days used to make these 'craggans', as they are called, in Barvas (FIGURE 19). In 1697 Martin remarked on the fine red clay in Lewis, and on the pottery made from it by local women for boiling meat or preserving ale; he also says that in the island of Tiree ale was preserved in large earthen vessels, and its quality improved by plunging into it red-hot stones.[29] But the fullest description we have is that of Dr Arthur Mitchell, who in 1863 found a stone-breaker sitting at the roadside not far from Barvas, and eating his dinner out of a little handmade pot closely resembling a Saxon cinerary urn.[30] He was able to study the manufacture of these vessels, and has left us the following description of this piece of 'woman's work':

> 'The clay she used underwent no careful or special preparation. She chose the best she could get, and picked out of it the larger stones, leaving the sand and the finer gravel which it contained. With her hands alone she gave to the clay its desired shape. She had no aid from anything of the nature of a potter's wheel. In making the smaller craggans, with narrow necks, she used a stick with a curve on it to give form to the inside. All that her fingers could reach was done with them. Having shaped the craggan, she let it stand for a day to dry, then took it to the fire in the centre of the floor of her hut, filled it with burning peats, and built burning peats all round it. When sufficiently baked, she withdrew it from the fire, emptied the ashes out, and then poured slowly into it and over it about a pint of milk, in order to make it less porous'

Dr Mitchell adds that in Lewis these vessels were usually unornamented, but that such ornamentation as did occasionally occur was composed of straight lines made with a pointed stick, cord, or thumb-nail. He also quotes a similar description of the making of craggans in Tiree at the same period, and says that as late as the early 19th century this hand-made pottery was common all over the Hebrides and was not unknown in the villages on the west side of the mainland.

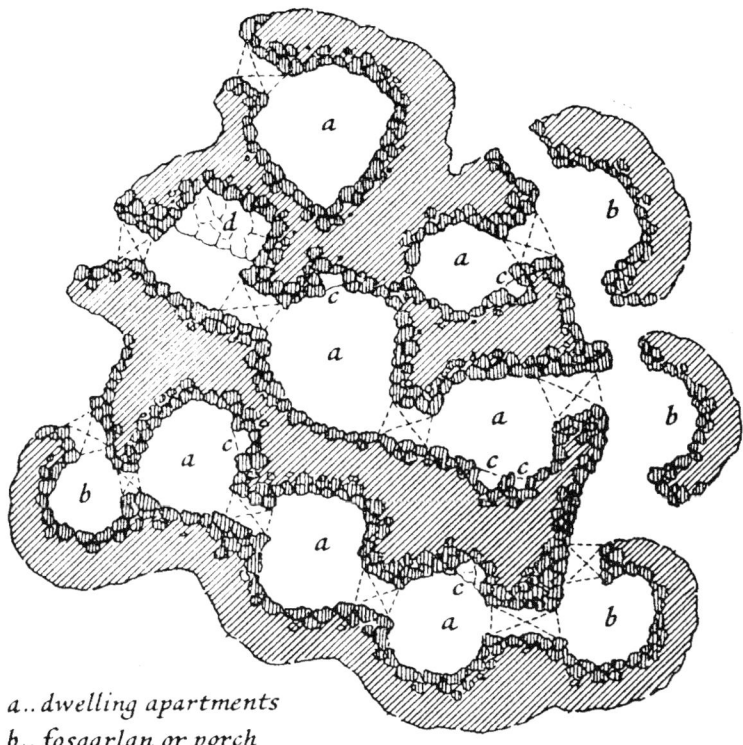

a.. dwelling apartments
b.. fosgarlan or porch
c.. cuiltean or milk cupboards
d.. stone bench or bed-place

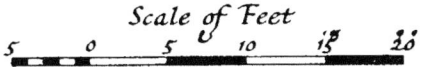

Scale of Feet

FIGURE 18. *Plan of complex group of beehive huts, Bothan Gearraidh Na H'Airde Moire (after Thomas).*

FIGURE 19. *Hand-made 'Craggan', Lewis, probably mid-nineteenth century. Note vertical stroked decoration. (Height about 9 inches).*

A quaint feature of the Barvas pottery is that it latterly began to 'show Staffordshire influence' — if one may adapt a phrase from the pre-historians. This consisted in the production of crude imitations of tea-pots, tea-cups, sugar-basins, etc., in the local unglazed fabric, and it was a featurewhich heralded the complete extinction of thismarkable survival (FIGURE 20). With a branch of Woolworth's established in Stornoway it is not altogether surprising that in 1937 the writer failed to trace a single specimen of Barvas ware in the island — apart from what was already in the Callernish Museum.

(2) Pot-boilers

Dr Mitchell even saw water boiled in pots by dropping in a heated stone, one or two stones being kept constantly in the fire for this purpose. The stones, which weighed from two to five pounds, soon cracked and fell to pieces, and frequently needed to be replaced.[31]

(3) Spindle and whorl.

Spindle-whorls — small perforated balls or discs of clay or stone — are found in nearly every excavation of a prehistoric dwelling-site, but their use in spinning did not finally die out till about the year 1900 in the more remote parts of Scotland. The whorl fitted on to the lower part of the tapering wooden spindle in order to give it momentum in spinning, and this formed the most primitive device for the purpose (FIGURE 21). It is widely distributed throughout the world, and has been used from the earliest times down to the

FIGURE 20. *Hand-made Lewis pottery showing 'Staffordshire influence'.*

present. Pennant records that in 1769 he found that about £1600 worth of yarn was annually sold out of Breadalbane, most of it being spun 'with rocks', *i.e.,* with distaff and spindle, and he adds: 'Their Lord gives among them annually a great number of spinning-wheels, which will soon cause the disuse of the rock'. One great advantage of 'the rock' was that it could be used by the women while they tended their cattle on the hills.[32] By about 1864–6 Dr Mitchell records that he had observed the spindle and whorl in use in many of the more remote parts of Scotland besides the Hebrides, Orkney and Shetland — namely in the counties of Ross, Sutherland, and Inverness, and the district of Galloway,[33] and in 1880 it was still in common use among the herring fishers of the west coast of Scotland.[34] Today it is the spinning wheel which is used, but even this is suffering from the effects of machine production and distribution.

The whorl itself was sometimes replaced by a potato, or by an expanded end on the wooden spindle. Consequently the absence of a whorl of clay or stone does not necessarily imply that no spindle was used.

(4) Querns and water-mills.

Querns, or hand-mills, remained in common use in the Hebrides down to quite recent times, and did not disappear from Lewis till about the time of the War. The writer has recently met more than one Lewis woman of about fifty who used to labour at the quern in her younger days, and a photograph of a quern in full working order, taken in a cottage in Foula (Shetland) in 1902, appeared in a recent number of ANTIQUITY.[35]

Besides querns, small water-mills are found in some of the is-lands, notably on the west coast of Lewis. One village may possess four or five such mills, placed at short intervals along the banks of the local stream. These mills are of distinctive Norwegian type, and their wooden counterparts are very numerous in Norway today. They are found in those islands which once belonged to Norway or Den-mark, viz., the Shetlands, Orkneys and Hebrides. Their distinguish-ing characteristic is a small water-wheel with a vertical shaft and horizontal blades ; the shaft passes up through the floor and through the lower mill-stone, and acts directly on the upper mill-stone, with-out any gearing. There is no mill-pond, but the water is carried off from the river by means of an aqueduct and delivered through a chute on to the blades of the wheel.

The Lewis water-mills differ architecturally from those of Shet-land,[36] in that they are constructed like the 'black houses'; they are small oval buildings built across the aqueduct, with sloping walls of dry stones, and a low, rounded thatched or turfed roof. The last of such mills to work in Lewis is at Shawbost on the west coast, and it is the only one that still retains most of its roof and its wooden parts in easily restorable condition (1937). It would be a shame if such a unique building were allowed to decay unheeded; can no one be found to re-store and preserve this sole surviving specimen before it be too late ?

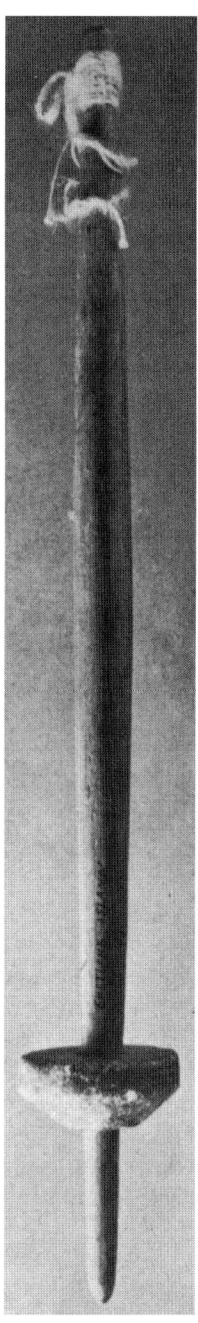

FIGURE 21. *Modern spindle and whorl from Shetland. (length 10 inches). (Photograph E. Cecil Curwen.)*

(5) *Agriculture.*

The run-rig system of agriculture — a form of open-field cultivation — was practised throughout the islands, as in most other parts, until a comparatively recent period. The chief crops are oats, barley and potatoes. Though the plough was known in the Hebrides in the 17th century — for Martin describes its use in North Uist[37] — it was little used on account of the nature of the ground, which is hilly, rocky and boggy. The cultivations took the form of mounded-up ridges, from 5 to 10 ft. wide, and from 20 ft. to 100 yds. or more in length, the longer ridges curving and forking irregularly. The purpose of the ridging was partly to promote drainage, and partly to facilitate manuring with sea-weed, for the soil dug from the ditches was piled up on top of the sea-weed to form the ridges. For this purpose the *caschrom,* or foot-plough, an improved form of digging-stick, was in general use throughout the western Highlands and Islands at the end of the 18th century,[38] and is still occasionally seen in Skye.[39] Of late years it has been superseded by the gardening fork, but it is still a curious sight to see in Lewis, for instance, little patches of oats, perhaps no more than 10 or 15 ft. in length and breadth. These ridges are by some curious perversity called 'lazy-beds' (Gaelic *feannag).*

Harrows were drawn by hand, and were like large wooden rakes, with one or two rows of teeth and a third row of pieces of heather to smooth out the soil.[40] This implement recalls the large wooden rakes found in the Danish peat-bogs, and suggests yet another link with Scandinavia.[41]

Reaping is still done with a sickle in Lewis, but in some parts the crop was simply pulled up by the roots. It was then dried in 'kilns', which in their form recall the corn-drying furnaces found in some Romano-British settlements in southern Britain.[42] After drying it might be 'graddan'd' by rapidly burning off the husks and beating the ears with a stick so that the grains fell out in a roasted but not a charred condition — a kind of combined threshing and 'parching' operation.[43] In Shetland corn was roasted by rolling hot stones among it as late as Mitchell's time.[44] It was then ready for the quern.[45]

(6) Miscellaneous.

There seems no end to the survivals of primitive customs and beliefs in the Highlands and Islands, about which much can be learnt from such books, among others, as those cited in this paper. As illustrating the retarded permeability of this part of Sir Cyril Fox's 'Highland Zone' to influences from the 'Lowland Zone', we may mention a few general tendencies. In the more remote islands the Gaelic language still holds its own against English, which is regarded very much as a foreign tongue, in spite of its compulsory study in schools; in the villages children of pre-school age and the older folk, especially the women have no English at all. Then there was the late survival of the tribal system of government down to the break-up of the Clans in 1746, together with the persistence of a distinctive form of dress and primitive weapons; the broadsword and target were normal at Culloden in 1746, and as late as 1665 an army of Camerons and Macgregors included 300 archers in their preparations to resist an attack by the Macintoshes and Macphersons.[46] Martin also says that in 1697 the people of Lewis were dexterous at archery.[47] Furthermore, in addition to a wealth of highly significant superstitions and folk-lore there have not been lacking occasional instances of frankly pagan practices such as sacrifices and libations to Celtic deities as late as the 17th century — practises which the Church had some difficulty in stamping out. One may instance the annual libation of ale to a sea-god Shony at Eoropie in Lewis, with a view to gaining more sea-weed for manuring the fields — a curious fertility rite which was not discontinued till

1665[48]; also the sacrifice of a bull annually to 'Mourie his devilans' in an island in Loch Maree as late as 1678[49]; and, finally, the placing of a female fertility figure on the wall of the 16th century tower of Rodil Church (Harris) in circumstances which indicate beyond all reasonable doubt that the figure is contemporary with its setting.[50]

Among individual points of interest one may instance the use of short oval coracles on the river Spey in 1769, covered with hide, and only 4 ft. long by 3 ft. wide, managed by a one-handed paddle[51]; and a curious case of trephining of the living human skull, mentioned by Martin,[52] who states that an illiterate empiric, Neil Beaton, established a great reputation for himself as a physician in Skye in the 17th century, and that to cure a severe headache 'he had the boldness to cut a piece out of a woman's skull broader than half a crown, and by this restored her to perfect health'.

The observations and information set forth in this paper illustrate the extraordinary culture-lag which has existed, even in so small a region as Britain, between the Lowland Zone and the more remote parts of the Highland Zone, due partly to the difficulty of communications, and partly to an inherent conservatism. If we had visited Lewis even fifty years ago, we should have been able to study the life and manners of a Celtic-speaking race emerging from roughly the same state of culture as the Celtic people of the pre-Roman Iron Age in Wessex. Today this culture-lag is being eliminated by the uniformity which results from air-travel, radio and the Ministries of Health and Agriculture — unifying forces which were unknown of old.

The writer wishes to express his indebtedness to Mr Crawford for placing at his disposal the data he had collected on this subject, and also the photographs he had taken in the Outer Hebrides.

NOTE by O.G.S.C.

The use of kilns for corn-drying goes back, in the west, at least to the 6th century. The kiln was called in Latin *canaba;* there was one at Iona (Reeves, *Adamnan,* 1857, 88). Its use is described in the Life of St. Cainnech as being 'ad spicas siccandas et triturandas'; and it is stated there that the members of his *familia,* not having a *canaba,* were obliged to thresh their corn 'super nudum pavimentum in campo'. In the Life of St. Ciaran is mentioned a 'rota de virgis contexta plena spicis igni supposita, ut siccarentur ad triturandum secundum morem occidentalium, id est, Britaniae et Hyberniae'. Both these saints were Irish contemporaries of St. Columba, their lives are preserved in forms which suggest little alteration from the original prototype, which in the case of St. Ciaran was probably composed not later than the 9th century (J. F. Kenney, *Sources,* I, 1929, 379, 394). If Dr Curwen's suggestion is correct[53] — that the Wessex hypocausts were corn-drying kilns — then these modern Hebridean kilns can be linked, through the Dark Ages, with the prehistoric Iron Age culture of southern Britain and his main thesis receives striking confirmation.

References

1   *Proc. Soc. Ant. Scot.,* 1870, VII, 153–60.
2   I have only seen one instance of a house consisting of as many as four parallel chambers; this is in the township of Fivepenny Borve, and is illustrated in a recent photo by Aage Roussell in his *Norse Building Customs in the Scottish Islands* (1934), 13, Fig. 3 ('Mealahost').
3   For the arrangement of the quern see ANTIQUITY, 1937, XI, 144–5, Fig. 39 and pl.III in; Arthur Mitchell, *The Past in the Present* (1880), 33–8.
4   *Proc. Soc. Ant. Scot.,* 1870, VII, 155–6.

5 *Ibid.* 159.

6 Aage Roussell, *Norse Building Customs in the Scottish Isles* (London, 1934)

7 ANTIQUITY, 1937, XI, 162–73.

8 *Proc. Soc. Ant. Scot.,* 1935, LXIX, 265–88.

9 *Proc. Soc. Ant. Scot.,* 1873, X, 156.

10 Thos. Pennant, *A Tour in Scotland* (3rd edn. 1774), II, 277; *Boswell's Journal of a Tour to the Hebrides* (Heinemann, 1936), 137–8.

11 Pennant, *op. cit.,* II, 229 and pls. XV, XVI.

12 *Proc. Soc. Ant. Scot.,* 1905, XXXIX, 401–2.

13 M. Martin, *A Description of the Western Isles of Scotland,* apud Pinkerton's *Voyages and Travels,* 1809, III, 667.

14 *Boswell's Journal,* 99–101, 103.

15 *Proc. Soc. Ant. Scot.,* 1905, XXXIX, 508–9 (anonymous journal of 1791–2).

16 Pennant, *op. cit.,* 1, 209.

17 *Ibid.* II, 315.

18 *Ibid.* I, 117.

19 *Cf.* Martin, 649; Pennant, II, 214.

20 *Boswell's Journal,* 107 (Glen Moriston); Pennant, I, 108 (near Glen Tilt).

21 W. F. Skene, *Celtic Scotland* (1880), III, 385–8.

22 *Proc. Soc. Ant. Scot.,* 1862, III, 127–44; 1870, VII, 161–4. See also Dr Arthur Mitchell, *The Past in the Present* (1880), 58–72 ; Skene, *Celtic Scotland(1880),* III, 387–8.

23 A. Mitchell, *op. cit.,* 58–9.

24 Skene, *op. cit.,* III, 388, states that beehive huts were still inhabited in 1880.

25 Skene, *op. cit.,* III, 388.

26 Martin (late 17th cent.) says that he saw over 500 small huts of this type in St. Kilda, and about 40 in the neighbouring Borera, used for drying fish and preserving birds'-eggs *(Voyage to St. Kilda, apud* Pinkerton's *Voyages and Travels,* III, 708, 721).

27 Pierre Fournier, 'Les ouvrages de pierre sèche des cultivateurs d'Auvergne', *L'Auvergne littéraire,* 1933, no. 68; also *Bull. de la Soc. préhist. franc.,* 1921, XVIII, 338–57.

28 V. Gordon Childe, *Skara Brae* (1931), 182–4.

29 Martin, *loc. cit.* 575, 660.

30 Mitchell, *op. cit.* 25–32, 45–7, 236–7.

31 Mitchell, *op. cit.* 121–2. (The sand-dunes of Glenluce are thickly strewn with cracked and broken pebbles, which can only have got there by human agency. The adjacent 'floors' contain fragments of beaker pottery, thus suggesting that the practice here described endured for perhaps three millennia.— O.G.S.C.).

32 Pennant, *op. cit.* 1, 92–3.

33 Mitchell, *op. cit.* 1–9.

34 *Proc. Soc. Ant. Scot.,* 1880, XV, 148–51.

35 ANTIQUITY, 1937, XI, pl. III, f. p. 136, and Fig. 39. For a general account of Scottish querns in the late 19th century see Mitchell, *op. cit.* 33–8.

36 For an account of similar mills in Shetland see Mitchell, *op. cit.* 39–43.

37 Martin, *loc. cit.* 592.

38 *Stat. Acc. Scotland,* 1793, VI, 288–9; Pennant, II, 288; Boswell, 282.

39 ANTIQUITY, 1927, I, pl. i, f. p. 261; 1932, VI, 404–5.

40 Martin, *loc. cit.* 575, 705; Pennant, II, 288.

41 ANTIQUITY, 1938, XII, 147.

42 Aage Roussell, *op. cit.* 48, 60–2; *Antiq. Journ.* 1933, XIII, 121–5. See also note at end of this article.

43 Described by Martin, *loc. cit.* 639; Pennant, II, 280–1.

44 Mitchell, *op. cit.* 46.

45 For the effects of drying and roasting before grinding see ANTIQUITY, 1938, xii, 151–2.

46 Pennant, I, 191, 362.

47 Martin, *loc. cit.* 579.

48 *Ibid.* 583–4.

49 Mitchell, *op. cit.* 271–4. This book contains a great deal of further information on kindred topics.

50 *Anc. Mon. Comm. Inventory, Outer Hebrides,* Rodil Church, Harris.

51 Pennant, I, 270.

52 Martin, *loc. cit.* 637.

53 The suggestion was Prof. Gowland's ; see *Archaeologia,* LXXI, 151–8. Corn-drying kilns seem to have been a product of Roman culture in western Europe; they are mentioned by Ovid in two passages *Fasti,* II, 519–26; vi, 313–4. As far as I know they do not occur in Britain before the latter part of the Roman period, though it is likely that previous to their introduction corn was dried on the domestic hearth as in Denmark (see ANTIQUITY, 1938, XII, 151–2). Boswell saw corn dried in the living-room in Raasay (*op. cit.,* 138).—E.C.C.

Native Settlements of Northumberland
by A.H.A. HOGG
ANTIQUITY 17 (67), 1943

TO most archaeologists Northumberland is noted chiefly for its remains of Roman military engineering, but the interest of these and the care with which they have been studied have diverted attention from the less spectacular relics of the native population. It is seldom realized that the county still contains traces of about 400 of their forts, farms, and villages, together with about 100 destroyed sites the positions of which are known more or less certainly from place-names or other sources. The purpose of this paper is to give some account of these settlements. They are of interest in themselves, but they are also potentially important as comparative material, especially in relation to the archaeology of Ireland, the South of Scotland, and Western England. They are generally in good preservation, and the fairly frequent occurrence of Roman relics provides a better prospect of establishing some sort of chronology than in more remote areas.

The records of previous work show how little has been done. Explorers have no doubt been discouraged by the paucity of relics, but this is itself partly due to the lack of excavation. Only one site[9], and that a very small one, has been completely examined, and it is probable that all the labour ever expended on native sites in Northumberland does not much exceed that devoted each year to the examination of prehistoric remains in such areas as Sussex or Wiltshire. It may not be out of place here to suggest that the sites are of a type particularly well suited to investigation by small parties of volunteers, including of course an experienced excavator, but employing no hired labour. There is no lack of sites awaiting excavation, and it is hoped that this article may attract more workers to these remains. The views here put forward are tentative only, and must be regarded as subject to considerable revision in the light of future investigation.

The native culture in Northumberland

It is convenient to discuss the native culture without reference to chronology or to the different types of structure which occur in the area. The resulting picture can be regarded as representing the state of the majority of the inhabitants during the Roman period, but the apparent uniformity may well be due merely to lack of excavation.

What is now Northumberland seems to have formed the southern part of the territory of the Votadini, a tribe whose main centre was near the estuary of the Forth. Traprain Law, if not actually their 'capital', must have been one of their most important towns, and some idea of their culture in its most advanced form can be derived from the excavation reports relating to that site[11].

The Northumbrian area, however, was far less prosperous. The main occupation of the inhabitants was the breeding of cattle, their herds being mostly of a type of small ox. Sheep were also kept but they were not so numerous. The excavations at Corbridge[12] give a ratio of seven oxen to one sheep and the remains found at Gunnar Peak[4] agree well with this. The horse was also domesticated but was not very common. The food supply may have been supplemented by hunting, but traces of animals other than ox and sheep are scarce.

The only evidence for agriculture is the presence of rotary and saddle querns. A few of these occur in almost every settlement, but their number is not sufficiently great to suggest extensive cultivation and there is no satisfactory evidence at present for early field-systems. The cultivation-terraces which are such a striking feature of the Cheviots seem everywhere to be later than the native sites, and the small irregular stone-walled enclosures which sometimes occur, and which show some resemblance to the Celtic fields of Southern England, are generally associated with the sites of what are probably medieval farms.

Spindle whorls are sometimes found, but they are so uncommon in this district that it seems unlikely that the thread produced would be sufficient for weaving, although some evidence for the manufacture of textiles was found at Traprain Law. Carts were used in this area, as the iron band for a wheel-hub was found at Gunnar Peak[4]. Pottery, although plentiful at Traprain Law, is rare on Northumbrian sites. The native ware is extremely coarse, resembling that of the late Bronze Age cinerary urns, but much inferior in quality[10]. It varies from a half to one inch in thickness and it is not uncommon to find 'grits' an inch across in the ware. The types in use included large bucket-shaped pots and roughly hemispherical bowls with either simple roll or flat rims, but very little material is available. The cultural and chronological implications of this material will be discussed later. Roman pottery, generally of the second century, is also found, and when this was available the native ware seems to have been less used. Frequently no pottery at all is found on a site, and indeed few relics of any kind. Much of the equipment used must have been of wood. Rough stone discs of various sizes were probably used as covers both for pots and for wooden tubs.

Personal ornaments are uncommon. Brooches[4,9] of types manufactured at Traprain Law and elsewhere are sometimes found and fragments of glass armlets[2,9] also occur. At Yevering Bell[2] armlets of a rounded triangular section were found, said to be of 'oak', but probably of lignite.

Apart from cattle rearing and agriculture there is little evidence for any activity which could form a basis for commerce. The large number of quern stones found at Farhill Crags (8, p. 137, 55° 36' 05" N; 1° 47' 45" W) suggests that there was a factory there. It seems reasonable to suppose also that iron-working was carried on in the area as iron tools are fairly common, but direct evidence for this is unsatisfactory. Isolated lumps of 'slag' have been recorded from three sites, but the only specimen analysed proved to be natural[4], being derived from the Whin Sill.

Types of settlement

Before discussing the distribution of the settlements it will be convenient to describe briefly the types into which they may be divided. This classification is preliminary only, and the identification of the types on the distribution map is based largely on the 6-inch to the mile Ordnance Survey, so that some revision may become necessary as a result of further field work.

Some curvilinear sites appear irregular on the 6-inch map, and cannot be fitted into any particular group without a detailed survey. These are shown on the distribution map as Unclassified Curvilinear sites.

It seems likely that the main basis of the classification is sound, in particular the distinction between rectilinear and curvilinear sites, but further investigation will almost certainly enable sub-groups to be identified within those discussed here. Some indication will be given below of the probable nature of these sub-groups.

There does not seem to be any significance in the material of which the ramparts are constructed. This is sometimes stone, sometimes earth with a stone revetment, sometimes apparently earth only, and it is probable that the material used depends only on what is available in the neighbourhood. Similarly the presence or absence of ditches depends largely on the ease with which the ground can be excavated.

Classification

Contour and hill forts.

These are not common in the area and the smaller sites may perhaps be more nearly related to the multiple ring forts. Only Yevering Bell (13 acres) has any claim to be considered a 'town', as no other site exceeds 6 acres in internal area.

Ring forts and small enclosures.

This group includes remains of very diverse types. The most impressive are the 'multiple ring forts' in which a small central area, seldom of more than 2 acres, is surrounded by two or three strong ramparts. The plan is usually circular but the builders did not hesitate to adapt their fortifications to some extent to the shape of the ground, and oval forts of an obviously related type occur. These are not distinguished on the distribution-map. Without field work and excavation it is impossible to say whether the differences, between oval, circular, and nearly circular plans, are of any significance. The entrances, however, may give more information of chronological value. They are of two types, but information as to their relative distribution must also await further field work. The simplest is a straight passage leading through the ramparts, but a more interesting type is that in which it is necessary to make a double right angle turn to enter. In Northumberland the turn is usually first right then left, but the other direction also occurs. Some of the forts have two entrances.

A multiple ring fort is here illustrated by the plan of Greaves Ash (FIGURE 1) which shows a zig-zag entrance of the type described. Attention may also be drawn to the double facing which appears in the inner dry stone wall, a method of construction not uncommon in the area. From other points of view the plan is not wholly typical as the great number of hut sites is unusual, but it was selected deliberately as an illustration of the spread of a settlement beyond its original limits. The more usual arrangement where huts are visible is to find a relatively small number distributed round the central space close to the rampart.

The single ramparted enclosures range from large fortified sites related to the multiple ring forts to small unfortified farmsteads. From their appearance on the 6-inch map it is not possible to classify them accurately, and some of the single rings should probably be shown on the map as small enclosures. Hartside Hill (FIGURE 1) may be considered typical, and Mr Richmond has recently shown[13] how the description of St. Cuthbert's hermitage on Farne Island would apply to many of these small farmsteads in the Cheviots. An enclosure of rather unusual type is that at Ingram Hill (FIGURE 1) where the huts are rectangular and mostly attached to the enclosing wall. Excavation showed that this site was preceded by one enclosed within a wooden palisade[10].

Related sites. As mentioned above, the builders of the multiple ring forts did not adhere slavishly to the circular form, and when a promontory or cliff could aid defence the form of the work was modified. The ramparts are often sufficiently distinctive to indicate the connexion. Middle Dean (FIGURE 1) represents a site of this type. It has a zig-zag entrance

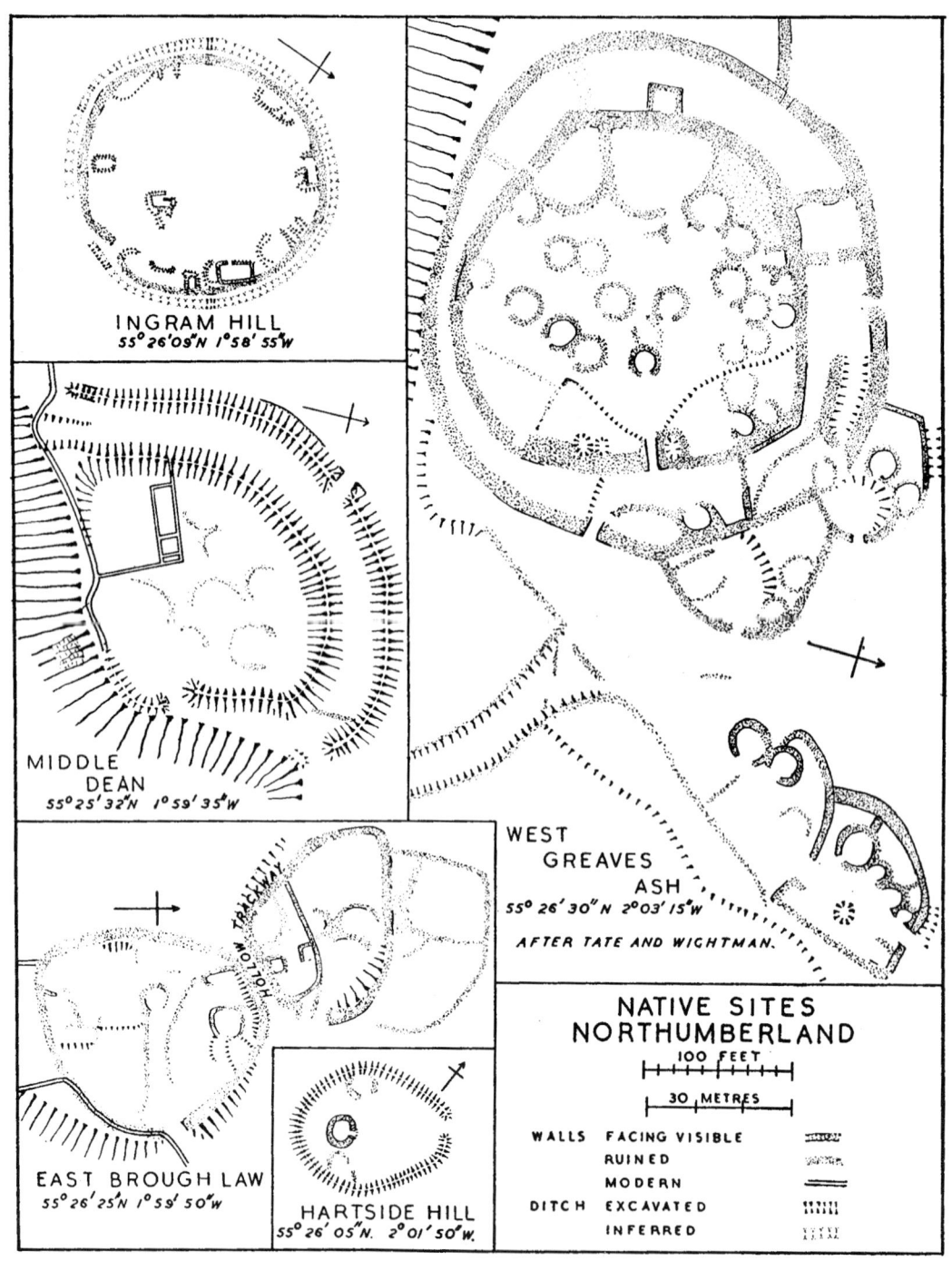

INGRAM HILL
55°26'09"N 1°58'55"W

MIDDLE
DEAN
55°25'32"N 1°59'35"W

WEST
GREAVES
ASH
55°26'30"N 2°03'15"W

AFTER TATE AND WIGHTMAN.

EAST BROUGH LAW
55°26'25"N 1°59'50"W

HARTSIDE HILL
55°26'05"N 2°01'50"W.

NATIVE SITES
NORTHUMBERLAND
100 FEET
30 METRES

WALLS	FACING VISIBLE	
	RUINED	
	MODERN	
DITCH	EXCAVATED	
	INFERRED	

FIGURE 1.

and two ramparts of earth with stone revetting, with a level area between. It seems probable that the wide space between the ramparts was intended to enclose cattle, which would provide an additional protection against attack. The way in which cattle could assist the defence is indicated by the following quotation from a modern African source[14]

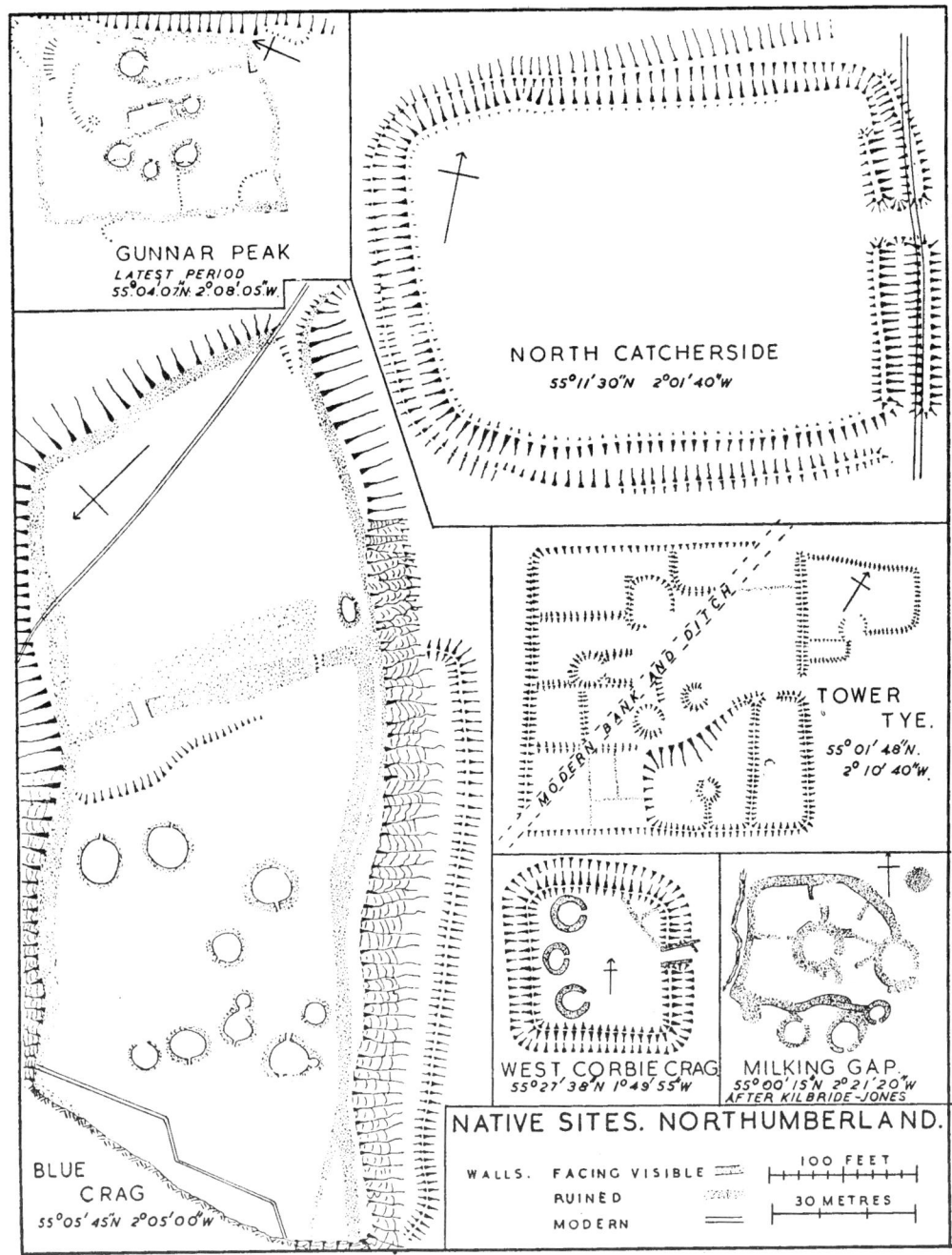

FIGURE 2.

— 'When night came we made a double *boma* of thorns: Bwana Y and the rest of us in the middle and a mass of cattle outside so that the Lumbwa could not rush us in the dark. The Lumbwa tried to get at us once in the dark; they put their shields on the thorns of the fence and got among the cattle, but a sentry saw them and fired, the cattle stampeded and knocked over the Lumbwa and they did not attack again'.

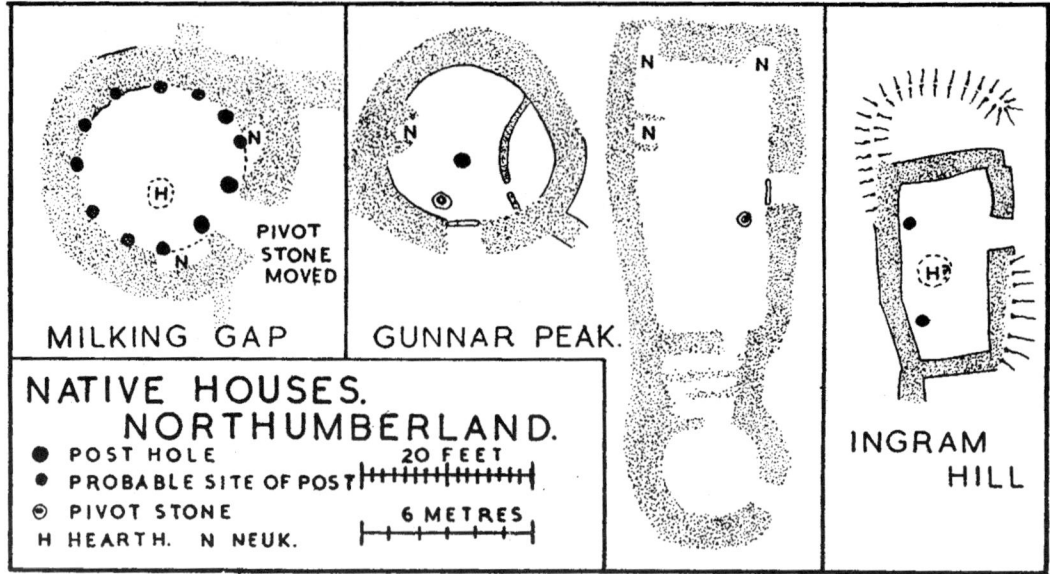

FIGURE 3.

Rectilinear sites (FIGURE 2).

This class again contains a number of different subgroups, ranging from the relatively large and strongly embanked works such as North Catcherside to simple enclosures such as Gunnar Peak or Milking Gap. So far as the present evidence goes, however, the sites seem generally to belong to about the same period and culture. The significance of the different strengths and sizes will not become clear without further research. Some of the earthworks classified under this heading may be Roman and others may be medieval, but it is probable that most are native.

The largest type is represented by North Catcherside. The interior of this site has been ploughed and no huts remain, but the evidence of other enclosures such as Quarry House, Thockrington[5], suggests that the usual arrangement consisted of a straight track leading from the entrance across the enclosure with a row of circular huts on either side. At Quarry House the surrounding area is flat and marshy and North Catcherside is situated at the end of a low ridge with a marshy valley on either side. The entrance is towards the end of the ridge.

Some of the small rectangular sites are also relatively strongly walled, as at West Corbie Crag, which may be compared in everything except its shape and the size of its ramparts with the small enclosure on Hartside Hill, but most have only a slight wall. There is a fairly continuous gradation from the almost perfectly rectangular plan, through irregular sites such as Milking Gap, to the curvilinear enclosure, but the intermediate types of plan are not common and most of the works can be assigned with certainty to one group or the other.

Villages.

A few villages show signs of deliberate planning, such as the rectilinear site of Tower Tye (FIGURE 2). But most are irregular collections of small egg-shaped enclosures and huts. They are not as common as the more regular walled sites and occur usually near the multiple ring forts. East Brough Law (FIGURE 1) is an example. This and two or three other similar villages seem to be associated with the strong fort of Brough Law (55° 26' 28" N, 2° 00' 08" W) nearby and there is a similar grouping round Middle Dean. Villages are most frequent in the Cheviot foot-hills.

Isolated huts.
Isolated huts do occur, but the recorded examples are not numerous and have not been marked on the map. Their rarity is probably due to their inconspicuousness in the field and the ease with which they can be destroyed.

House types (FIGURE 3).
The excavated houses are not sufficiently numerous to permit detailed classification. Almost every site excavated has produced a different type. They frequently contain a pivot-stone for the door and small extensions arranged to screen the entrance have been noted on several sites.

The most usual form is the simple circular hut sometimes with an internal partition as in the example from Gunnar Peak. Another common type is that formed by a ring of palisading. Examples of this have been noted at Witchy Neuk, at Gunnar Peak, and perhaps at Ingram Hill, and traces are still visible on the surface at Brough Law. No plans are given here as none is available on a sufficiently large scale. Milking Gap produced examples of an interesting type of hut which does not seem yet to have been paralleled on other sites. All the houses there showed a similar arrangement of posts; that illustrated had also a rough drain formed by a circular trench filled with rubble beneath the hut floor.

Rectangular huts which can be definitely assigned to the native culture are not common. At Gunnar Peak a single rectangular building was associated with the circular houses and seems to have formed part of a complex house containing three rooms, one circular.

A similar but smaller house of two rooms was excavated at the curious site of Ingram Hill. It seems to have had a pent-house roof supported by two posts only. The stonework of the walls can never have been of great height but the walling seems to have been completed with earth. No pivot-stone was found in this house and no relics of occupation.

Associated large enclosures.
Although no indications are known of early cultivation, some of the multiple ring forts have associated with them extensive systems of enclosures, presumably of use in connexion with cattle keeping. Lordenshaws Camp[21] (55° 17' 15" N, 1° 54' 50" W), and the Ringses, Doddington Moor (55° 35' 20" N, 1° 58' 40" W), show these features. The character of these enclosures is very similar to those at Y Bwlwarcau[15] in Glamorganshire. Details of the layout differ in each case. Slightly hollowed roads, often deliberately revetted with stone, are associated with these and other sites.

Burials.
Small cairns are associated with many sites. Few have been excavated and only that at Gunnar Peak has produced human remains, but the survival of bone is unlikely in the acid soils usual in the area, and it seems fairly certain that these cairns were in fact the burial places of the inhabitants of the adjacent settlements. They may be compared with those in the cairn cemeteries recently excavated at Hirwaun in Glamorganshire[16]. But no 'scoop graves' have yet been noted, and the cairns seem seldom to be grouped in

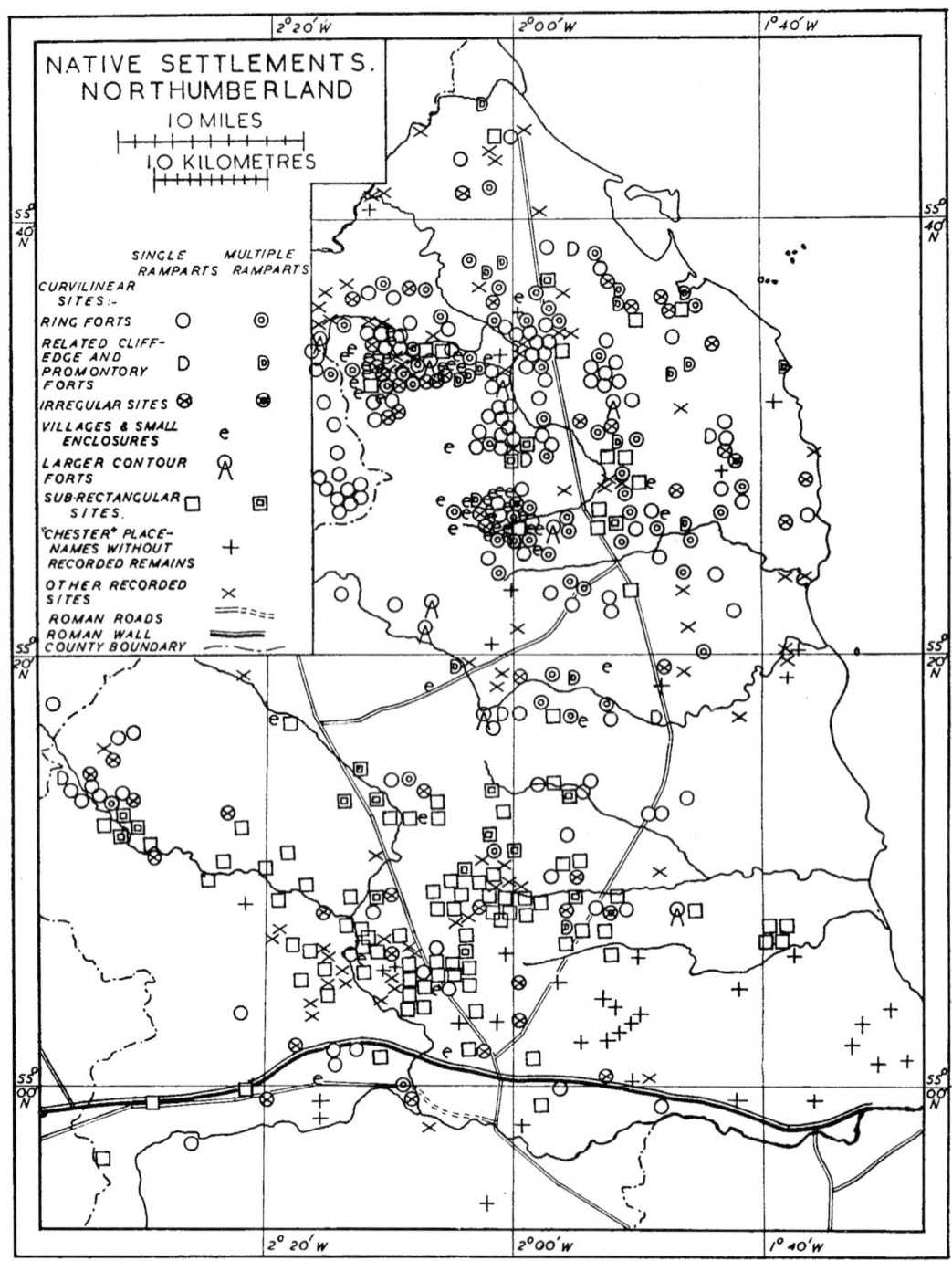

FIGURE 4.

cemeteries. These small mounds are very plentiful on the high ground near Brough Law and Middle Dean, but search will reveal them near almost any native site, and even scattered over the high moorland far from any traces of occupation.

Distribution (Map, FIGURE 4).

The map is intended to show the general distribution of settlements, rather than that of individual types. The most striking feature is the way in which the South Tyne forms a boundary to the distribution of the sites. The change is so definite and abrupt that there seems strong reason to suppose that the river actually formed the southern boundary of the Votadini.

The map also shows that the upper parts of small river valleys were favoured areas for settlement, and the concentrated occupation of the area round Yevering Bell stands out clearly. How far the occupation extended over the lower ground is not certain, as cultivation has been intensive, but the distribution of 'chester' place-names suggests that many other sites must have been destroyed, leaving not even that evidence for their existence.

In the other direction, the high moorland, above the 1000 foot-contour, was almost uninhabited, but must have been used extensively for grazing.

A third point brought out by the map is the limited distribution of the rectilinear earthworks.[21] It will be seen that they are almost confined to the southern part of the county. A possible explanation of this is discussed below, when dealing with cultural relationships outside Northumberland.

Cultural connexions outside Northumberland

Some of the settlement types found in the district are not sufficiently distinctive to justify an attempt to find parallels elsewhere, but three deserve further discussion.

Small enclosures.

The small oval enclosure or isolated farmstead seems to be less common and widely distributed than would be expected in view of its simplicity. The unimpressive character of the remains may have caused them to escape notice but their apparent rarity renders one possible parallel interesting. The general arrangement and the dimensions of the late Bronze Age enclosures on Plumpton Plain[17] show considerable similarity to the Northumbrian farmsteads. This may be accidental, but in view of the character of the culture associated with the Northumbrian sites it is probably significant. Some of the undecorated pottery from Plumpton Plain shows a strong resemblance to the ware found in Northumberland, but no early cultivations are recorded in the North.

Rectilinear earthworks.

These raise a more difficult question. They show a striking resemblance to the *viereckschanzen*[18] of the district around the upper Rhine and its tributaries. This alone would not necessarily be significant, as rectilinear sites might reasonably be expected in any area subject to Roman influence. But other evidence also points to a connexion. It may be summarized as follows.

About AD 140, settlers were transferred from Britain to the Rhaetian frontier, near the sources of the Rhine and Danube. The evidence of brooches suggests that they came from the Votadinian area[19], although it does not exclude districts further north and west. This transfer is probably to be associated with the reorganization of the frontier under Lollius Urbicus, involving the construction of the Antonine Wall.

Rhaetian pikemen — *Raeti gaesati* — have left epigraphic evidence for their presence (*c*. AD160), at or near Aesica[20], Risingham (early 3rd century), and Jedburgh[21].

The *viereckschanzen* occur in an area which includes at least part of Rhaetia. Their full distribution is unknown. They appear to date from the 1st or 2nd century BC to the 1st century AD. The Northumbrian rectilinear sites are most numerous in a limited area between the North Tyne and the upper Pont, although outlying examples occur else-where. This limited distribution must surely imply that the majority of the earthworks can be referred to some particular group of settlers. And it seems noteworthy also that this area could be controlled by the garrison at Risingham. The slender evidence available suggests a date in the middle of the 2nd century for the Northumbrian sites.

Considered singly, none of these items is of much account. And together they provide evidence which falls far short of that required for proof. But it is justifiable to suggest a tentative hypothesis. It seems probable that the British settlers on the Rhaetian frontier were transferred from the area north of Hadrian's Wall. In this connexion the scattered human remains found at Gunnar Peak in associations earlier than the rectilinear enclosure may be mentioned. The cleared area may then have been resettled with Rhaetians and others from the area within which *viereckschanzen* occur. Such a settlement would provide a compact body of men who for their own safety would probably support the Roman power, as it seems unlikely that they would be on friendly terms with the natives.

This transfer of population would, on this hypothesis, have taken place about AD 140–150. At this time, the area north of Hadrian's Wall was well within Roman territory. But from AD 155 onwards various disturbances threatened the safety of the frontier districts. It seems reasonable to associate with these dangers the appearance of the *Raeti Gaesati*, who can be regarded as a body of irregulars raised from among the alien settlers to meet the new dangers which threatened their farms and villages. Such irregulars would naturally be under Roman military control, and would not necessarily operate only in the actual area covered by their settlements.

It must be emphasized that this is merely a tentative hypothesis. The evidence in its favour is slight and circumstantial. It must be admitted also that apart from the earthworks themselves no object has been found which shows any connexion with the upper Rhine, although this objection loses weight when the scarcity of objects of any kind from these sites is realized.

But this group of sites can be explained with almost equal plausibility as representing the resettlement by the Votadini themselves of an area cleared in connexion with some phase of Roman frontier policy, the rectilinear form of the sites being due to Roman influence. In any case some of the rectilinear sites must probably be assigned to this last cause. And sub-rectangular enclosures dating from the Bronze Age occur in Wessex[22].

How much truth is contained in either of these hypotheses can only be decided by further extensive excavation and field-work, the necessity for which is again emphasized by the uncertainty surrounding this question.

Multiple ring forts.

These are probably the most interesting of the types found in Northumberland. They deserve extensive and detailed study, but can only be discussed briefly here. Their plan is very distinctive and they have a curiously limited distribution which has not been fully worked out. In Great Britain they seem to occur only in Cornwall, in a belt near the Scottish border, and occasionally in Pembrokeshire. In Ireland however they are extremely numerous. Leeds derives Chun Castle[23], a typical Cornish example,* from the *Citanias* of northwest Spain, but these latter are much larger sites.

---

* The sub-rectangular enclosures which form such a striking feature of the interior in all published plans were shown in the second report to be secondary. The original habitations were simple round huts.

Date.

In discussing the date of the sites it will be convenient to start with the evidence for occupation during the Roman period. This is not plentiful. Milking Gap (9) is the only site the occupation of which can be assigned to a definite time interval (AD 120–180). Roman fragments (2nd century) have also been found at Gunnar Peak[4] Quarry House[5] (Samian ware), Witchy Neuk[8] (3rd century), and Carry House[3]. The rectangular house-plan may probably also be attributed to Roman influence.

For earlier periods evidence from relics is almost absent, but at Yevering Bell[2] the excavators found fragments of bracelets, said to be of oak but probably of fossil wood, with a rounded triangular section. This is a rare type and similar bracelets from other sites are discussed by Hencken[24] and are shown to belong to a late Bronze Age culture associated also with pottery apparently related to that from Northumberland. Their absolute date is unknown. There is further evidence for a prolonged occupation of many sites in the remains themselves. Two or three periods of construction are often visible.

The multiple ring forts have not been dated in this area. If the typology suggested by Cornish and Irish examples is any guide the zig-zag entrance should be early, as it is found at Chun (3rd–2nd century BC), but the ring fort type had a long life. Garranes[25] belonged to the 5th century and Cahercommaun[26] appears to be a related structure of the 9th century.

Conclusions

It is dangerous to generalize about the tangle of cultures which covers the western and northern parts of these islands. Structures such as the multiple ring forts, the earth-houses, and the courtyard houses, to name only a few, usurp by their numerical superiority the place taken by pottery and small objects in the south. A distinctive type of structure is as much a cultural element as a type of pot, and if sufficiently numerous can provide as much information concerning chronology or population movements. Until a detailed analysis of each individual type has been undertaken attempts at a general synthesis are premature, but it seems likely that the approximate coincidence of the distribution of multiple ring forts and flat-rimmed pottery with the area which was little influenced by the Iron Age cultures[27] is significant.

As several writers have suggested, in this area the culture of the Late Bronze Age may have survived up to Roman times and later. There seems no need to postulate any Iron Age invasion to account for the bulk of the pottery and other relics, but it is reasonably certain that further work will make it possible to distinguish various groups within the 'late Bronze Age survival' area. But to attempt such a study would be outside the scope of this paper.

Acknowledgements. The writer is greatly indebted to Mr I. A. Richmond for his kindness in reading the draft of this paper, and for valuable criticisms and suggestions, and to Dr W. Fisher Cassie and Miss N. Henderson for help with the surveys.

Excavation reports
1   GREAVES ASH, 55° 26' 30" N, 2° 03' 15" W. *Berwicks. N.C.* 1856–62, pp. 294–316.
2   YEVERING BELL, 55° 33' 30" N, 2° 06' 50" W. *Berwicks. N.C.* 1856–62, pp. 431–53.
3   CARRY HOUSE, 55° 06' 25" N, 2° 12' 20" W. *Arch.,* 1880, XLV, 355–74.
4   GUNNAR PEAK, 55° 04' 07" N, 2° 08' 05" W. *A. Ael.* 1885, ser. 2, X, 12–37; 1942 ser. 4, XX, 155–73.
5   QUARRY HOUSE, 55° 06' 38" N, 2° 03' 10" W. *A. Ael.* 1887, ser. 2, XII, 155. *PSANewcas,* 1887, ser. 2, II, 337. (Samian found).

6   BLUE CRAG, 55° 05' 45" N, 2° 05' 00" W. *PSANewcas,* 1925, ser. 4, II, 23–24; 138–43.

7   OLD BEWICK, 55° 29' 15" N, 1° 52' 50" W. *PSANewcas,* 1934, ser. 4, VI, 252–6.

8   WITCHY NEUK, 55° 17' 17" N, 2° 01' 45" W. *A. Ael.* 1939, ser. 4, XVI, 129–39.

9   MILKING GAP, 55° 00' 15" N, 2° 21' 20" W. *A. Ael.* 1938, ser. 4, XV, 303–50.

10 INGRAM HILL, 55° 26' 09" N, 1° 58' 56" W. *A. Ael.* 1942, ser. 4, XX, 110–33. Including a report on the native pottery.

Other references

11 *PSA Scot.* XLIX, 139; L, 64; LIV, 54; LV, 153; LVI, 189; LVII, 180; LVIII, 241; LXXIV, 48.

12 *A. Ael.* 1911, ser. 3, VII, 260–67.

13 ANTIQUITY, 1941, XV, 88.

14 M. Perham: *Ten Africans* (Faber 1936), p. 102.

15 ANTIQUITY, 1934, VIII, 395–413.

16 *Arch. Cambs.,* 1942, pp. 77–92.

17 *Proc. Preh. Soc.,* 1935, I, 16–59.

18 Déchelette's *Manuel,* V, 275–80; ANTIQUITY, 1928, II, 50-55.

19 *Archaeologia,* 1930, LXXX, 37–58.

20 Eph. Epig., 1191, *A. Ael.* 1909, ser. 3, V, 158.

21 *Northumberland County History,* XV, 96, 135.

22 *Proc. Preh. Soc.,* 1942, VIII, 48–61.

23 *Archaeologia,* 1927, LXXVI, 205–40; 193 I, LXXXI, 33–42.

24 *Proc. R. Irish Acad.,* 1942, XLVII, sect. C, no. 1.

25 *Proc. R. Irish Acad.,* 1942, XLVII, sect. C, no. 2.

26 *Roy. Soc. Antiquaries. Ireland,* 1938, extra vol.

27 Fox, *Personality of Britain* (3rd ed.) figs. 5, IIa, IIb; Childe, *Preh. Comm.,* fig. 83.

2 The impact of aerial photography

CRAWFORD, the first editor of ANTIQUITY, was instrumental in illustrating the importance of aerial photography for the understanding of landscape, and it was the one landscape theme that his successor, Glyn Daniel, continued with equal enthusiasm. From1964 until 1980, Dr Kenneth St Joseph, Director of Aerial Photography at Cambridge, was given one plate and 500 words in each issue (Daniel 1986: 232–3), until specialist journals (e.g. *Aerial Archaeology*, founded in 1977) took over. Crawford invited many others to demonstrate the effectiveness of aerial photography in the pages of ANTIQUITY. Historically the inspiration had come from desert regions where Crawford himself was a pioneer with French aviators such as Poidebard (Kennedy & Riley 1990). There are striking aerial images from Arabia (FIGURE 1), the Transjordan desert, Northern Ireland, the Fayum depression (Egypt), Mesoamerica, Central and Southern Italy and Thailand. Crawford, himself, may be famous for *Wessex from the air* (Crawford & Keiller 1928), but he also took his technique further afield. In the last paragraph of the 1929 note he prophesied the impact of aerial photography on the lowlands of Scotland. In a pencilled note in the margin of the archival edition of the ANTIQUITY volume, he recorded his success in achieving this potential, itself published in Antiquity some 10 years later (Crawford 1939).

The 1929 note by Crawford conveys the excitement of an important moment in British landscape archaeology. It records the discovery and heralds the realization of the importance of one of the key sites of British prehistory. Little Woodbury had been noted by Crawford in 1924, but it was the brilliant photography of Pilot Officer Jonas in May 1929 which uncovered its interior detail and to whom Crawford awards the real discovery. The distinctive horned enclosure had an extreme clarity under drought conditions, particular crops and soils. This same site was excavated by Bersu, who made the term Little Woodbury synonymous with a new conception of Iron Age settlement. A skilful use of open-area excavation (although undertaken in strips) transformed the 'hut depressions' of Crawford into posthole structures (Bersu 1938; 1940; Evans 1989). Aerial photography has the capacity to record landscape detail, but once integrated with other archaeological investigation, the clarity is greatly enhanced.

The articles from Germany and France witness the similar transformations of knowledge taking place after the war in continental Europe, and now extended east into central Europe (Gojda 1993; Bewley *et al.* 1996). The impact on archaeological knowledge has been impressive, but has consistently been followed by a period of reassessment of its representativity. In all these cases, it is once again the integrated research approach to the landscape which is the most successful. Only in this way can a valid understanding be obtained.

The *Grabgärten* (generally boundary-ditched enclosures for graves) appear in impressive concentrations, but as Wightman (1970: 211–12) makes clear are related to where soils and crops are favourable to aerial photography. Some sites have received more detailed subsurface investigation following their discovery by aerial photography (Decker 1968; Wightman 1970; Roymans 1990: 220–28), generally assigning them to the Late La Tène or Roman period. In particular, Wederath has been studied in some detail (Haffner 1989), producing some 2300 graves from the last century BC until the 4th century AD.

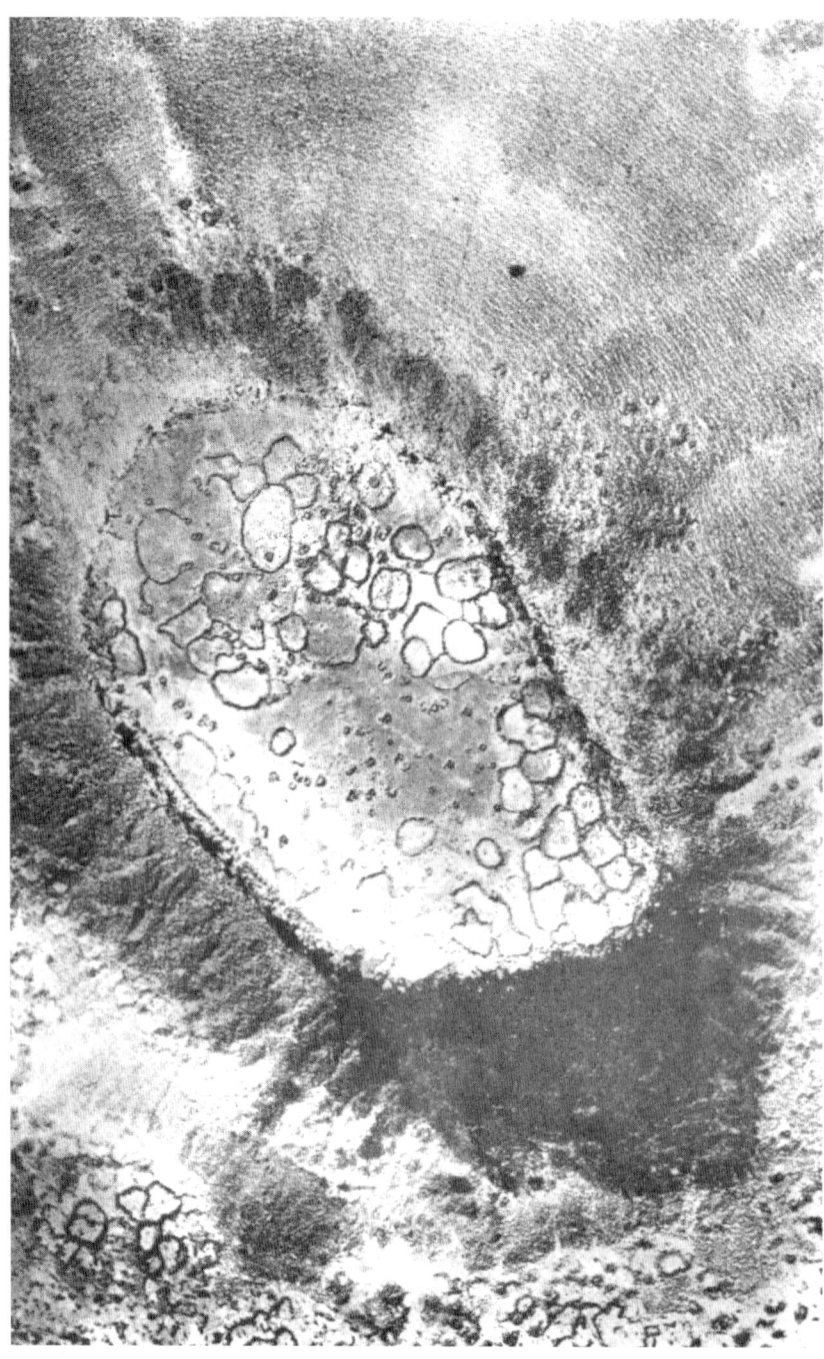

FIGURE 1. *This aerial photograph of a hillfort in the basalt country of 'Arabia' has almost an artistic quality (Maitland 1927: plate II, opposite p. 201).*

This cemetery appears to have been attached to a Gallo-Roman *vicus*, raising interesting questions of the relationship to settlement, not yet fully solved. As a rule, the rectangular *Grabgärten* contained clusters of cremations and appear to have been introduced in the very late La Tène period. Other investigations have revealed a variability of ditched enclosure that is not immediately detectable from the air. There is a whole range in size and form of enclosure from those used for burial (*Grabgärten*) (10–20 m across, generally in groups) to the *Viereckschanzen* (40+ m across, more often isolated), employed for

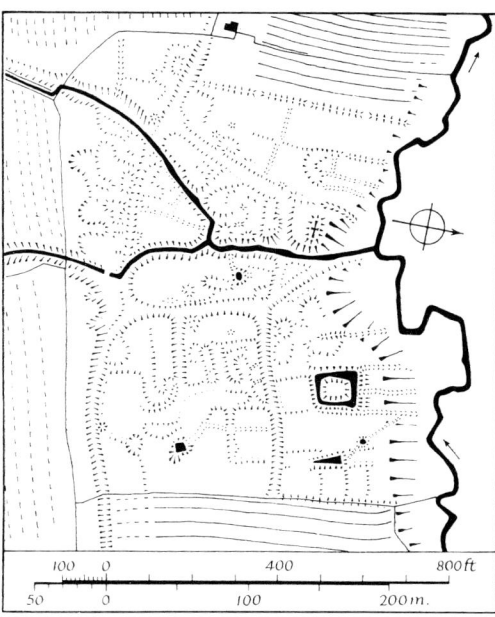

FIGURE 2. *The aerial photograph and transferred plan of the Deserted Medieval Village from North Marefield Leicestershire, illustrate very effectively the high quality of many of the aerial photographs and the ability to transfer information into a plan format. (St Joseph 1967: 217 & plate XXIV).*

ritual (Wightman 1970; Büchsenschütz & Olivier 1989). Further work is required to investigate the complete landscape.

Aerial photography on the plains of northern France brought a revolution in the understanding of Iron Age and Roman landscapes. It was a window of opportunity at a time of agricultural intensification, in an extensive open agricultural area. The article of 1964 covers all periods but focuses on the period between the centuries immediately BC and AD. In spite of this focus, it makes the important point that Palaeolithic landscapes and World War battlefields are as amenable to interrogation as other periods. In the conditions of northern France, winter flying for soil marks proved particularly effective. However, Agache makes clear the limitations of aerial photography, the dependence on soil types, the need for repeated flights and the importance of integrated excavation. The subsequent publications have become some of the classics of aerial photography (Agache 1978; 1999; Agache & Bréart 1975). The result is the knowledge of a dense and articulated occupation of a landscape that was previously considered empty. A density of more than 1 villa per 10 sq. km was established (Greene 1986: 116–17). Wightman (1995: 119–23) took this further and offered insight into population levels, suggesting a rural population (outside towns and villages) of 15 people per sq. km. At the same time she expressed caution about the reconstruction of demography, particularly on the basis of the highly visible villas alone.

The opportunity given by Glyn Daniel to Dr St Joseph to publish regularly in ANTIQUITY publicized a wealth of interesting discoveries. These cover all periods and types of site, often clearly interpreted by a line drawing to guide the eye, or by explanations of the varied impact of crops and soils: cursus, ring ditch, enclosed settlement, deserted medieval village (DMV) (FIGURE 2), Roman villa and high medieval building. A large number of these were subsequently collected together in well-illustrated volumes which investigate the prehistory and history of Britain from the air (Norman & St Joseph 1969; Beresford & St Joseph 1979; Frere & St. Joseph 1983; Darvill 1996) The 41st of the series of aerial photographic reports in Antiquity is chosen here for reprinting since it placed Crawford in perspective and provided a commentary on the value of aerial photography from a 1976 perspective, including explanations for the domination of Wessex. The illustrated photo shows extraordinary detail, extracted after a repeated visit (the first visit was also recorded in ANTIQUITY (St Joseph 1972)), placing a settlement in its landscape context of surrounding field systems. Aerial photography, although sometimes threatened by financial stringency, has come of age with major archives (Hampton 1972) and sophisticated techniques of recording and classification (Edis *et al.* 1989; Wilson 1982). The Cambridge archive, which provided many of the photographs in the pages of ANTIQUITY, is currently being transformed into a digital format which will make the resource even more available and flexible in its use. The aerial photographers represented here already had a good understanding of the impact and yet the limitations of aerial photography. These limitations have now been effectively assessed in detailed (Palmer 1984) and more specific studies (Evans 2000) which suggest the on-going need for aerial photographic recording and complementary landscape techniques as shown in the following sections. A surfeit of evidence does not indicate a complete sample. In spite of these recognized limitations, the impact of aerial photography has been crucial. As those interested in more interpretive approaches to landscape acknowledge, this rich ground shows the fundamental importance of the meticulous collection of data (Tilley 1996: 162).

Woodbury:
two marvellous air-photographs
by O.G.S. CRAWFORD

ANTIQUITY 3 (12), 1929

THE PLATES (FIGURES 1 & 2) represent the culminating point of archaeological air-photography. They were taken by Pilot Officer Jonas, R.A.F., between 11 and 12 o'clock on the 16th of May 1929, using a K.2 filter. The sites lie half a mile apart on the hill called Woodbury, less than a mile south of Salisbury Cathedral, between the Blandford and Bournemouth roads. Woodbury is three miles south of the aerodrome at Old Sarum, from which they were taken and where I found them when taking over obsolete negatives on behalf of the Ordnance Survey (where they now are). They were taken during pin-pointing, as part of the ordinary routine of training; but that these particular sites were selected for practice is due to the keenness of the photographic section at Old Sarum, which has been closely associated with the development of this branch of air-photography from its birth. (It was the Old Sarum section that obtained many of the first archaeological air-photographs ever taken, including those of the Stonehenge Avenue, in 1921, and of the Celtic fields round Winchester, in 1922.) Regarded merely as photographs, from a technical standpoint the negatives are as nearly perfect as possible. The wonderful definition of the crop-marks is probably due partly to the use of a K.2 filter, partly to the dry spell during the first half of 1929.

The larger of the two enclosures (FIGURE 1) is Woodbury, which I discovered in 1924 (*Wessex from the Air,* plate viii, page 80); but this is a far better representation of it. Not only does the black band of the surrounding ditch come out very distinctly but the interior of the camp is seen to be covered with black spots and lines. The black spots are of two kinds, large and small; the large blobs are doubtless the sites of huts; they are mostly circular, and some are surrounded by a faint narrow black line, representing possibly a drainage ditch. The small black spots must represent small pits and post-holes, serving doubtless many different purposes. On the western side a rectangular enclosure may be faintly discerned. In the middle of the north side is a large dark blur (corresponding to a shallow depression on the ground). The entrance may have been here, and if so the dark line leading northeastwards from it across a field of wheat may be a prehistoric hollow track-way — it is in any case plainly contemporary with the camp, where it ends.

Just outside, on the southwest near the road and between the two ricks, is a beautiful little double circle. It is too small, apparently, for a disc-barrow, and must remain a puzzle till it is excavated — an easy task.

The larger (central) portion of the interior was under barley when this photograph was taken. The field on the west (where the ditch disappears) was under grass, and that on the east under wheat. Note that barley registers far better than wheat, and grass not at all. The field on the north also contained wheat; its lighter colour may perhaps be due to later sowing.

I visited the site on 13 October. There was nothing whatever to be seen except on the western side, where the broad shallow depression of the ditch is plainly visible. Here too the remains of the white chalk rampart can also be seen, though far less plainly than

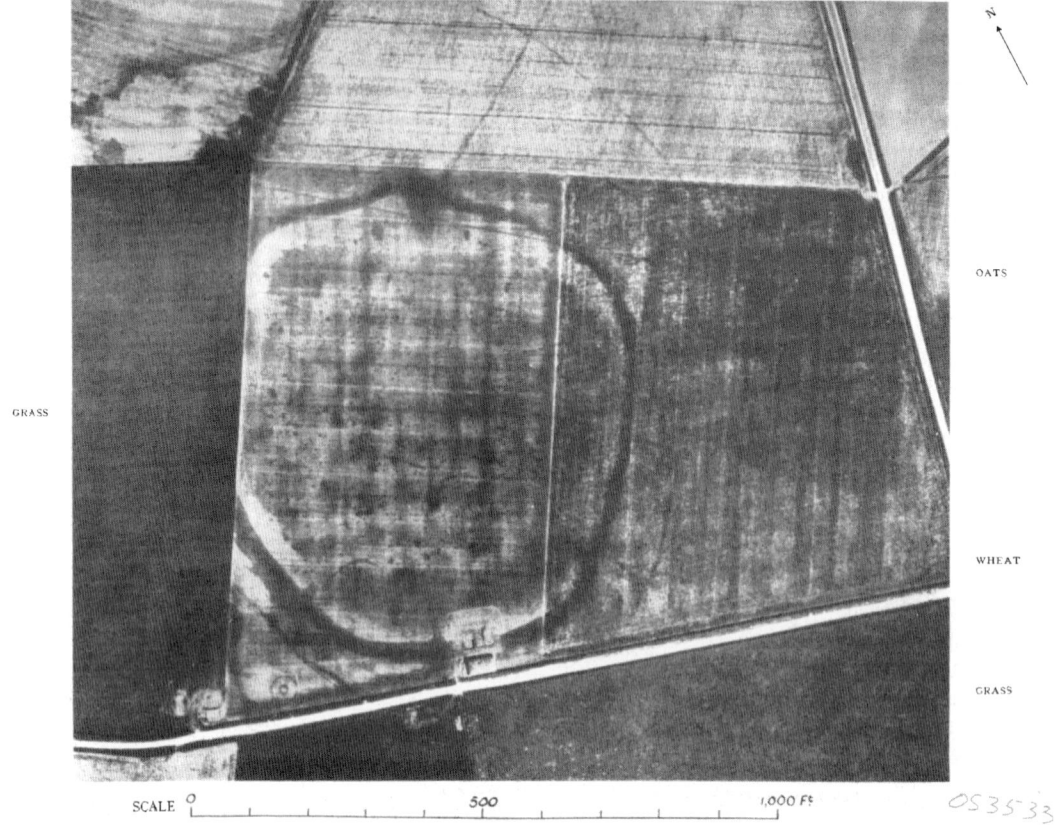

FIGURE 1. *Woodbury, south of Salisbury, Wilts: taken between 11 and 12 o'clock, 16 May 1929 (R.A.F., Old Sarum).*

on the photograph. There seems to have been an outer rampart also here, and it is just the place where one would expect it. There were hints of such on the air-photograph I took; but the western field both then and subsequently (in 1928 when some other R.A.F. photos were taken) has unfortunately been planted with an unsympathetic crop.

The whole of the interior is covered with pot-boilers, and I found part of the base of a pot of New Forest ware. One would naturally attribute the construction of the camp to the people of the Iron Age, but there is no evidence one way or the other.

The discovery of Woodbury in 1924 was a pure accident. At the same time I observed, about half a mile to the east, a *smaller enclosure* with a slighter ditch. It was, however, much less striking, and we did not photograph it. It is merely recorded in *Wessex from the Air* (pp. 80–1). The magnificent photograph (FIGURE 2) presents it, therefore, as virtually a new discovery. The honours are divided between Old Sarum on the one hand and a crop of barley and oats, starved by drought, on the other. The enclosure itself consists of an irregular, very plainly marked black line, continuous except at a point on the northeast, where a gap, about 62 feet wide, represents the entrance. From near by diverge two curious narrow horns, like the antennae of some giant insect. But the most striking feature of the photograph is the fact that it shows a mass of black spots within the enclosure. These occur nowhere else and are without any doubt the vestiges of permanent habitation. They consist, as before, of a number of small dots and some

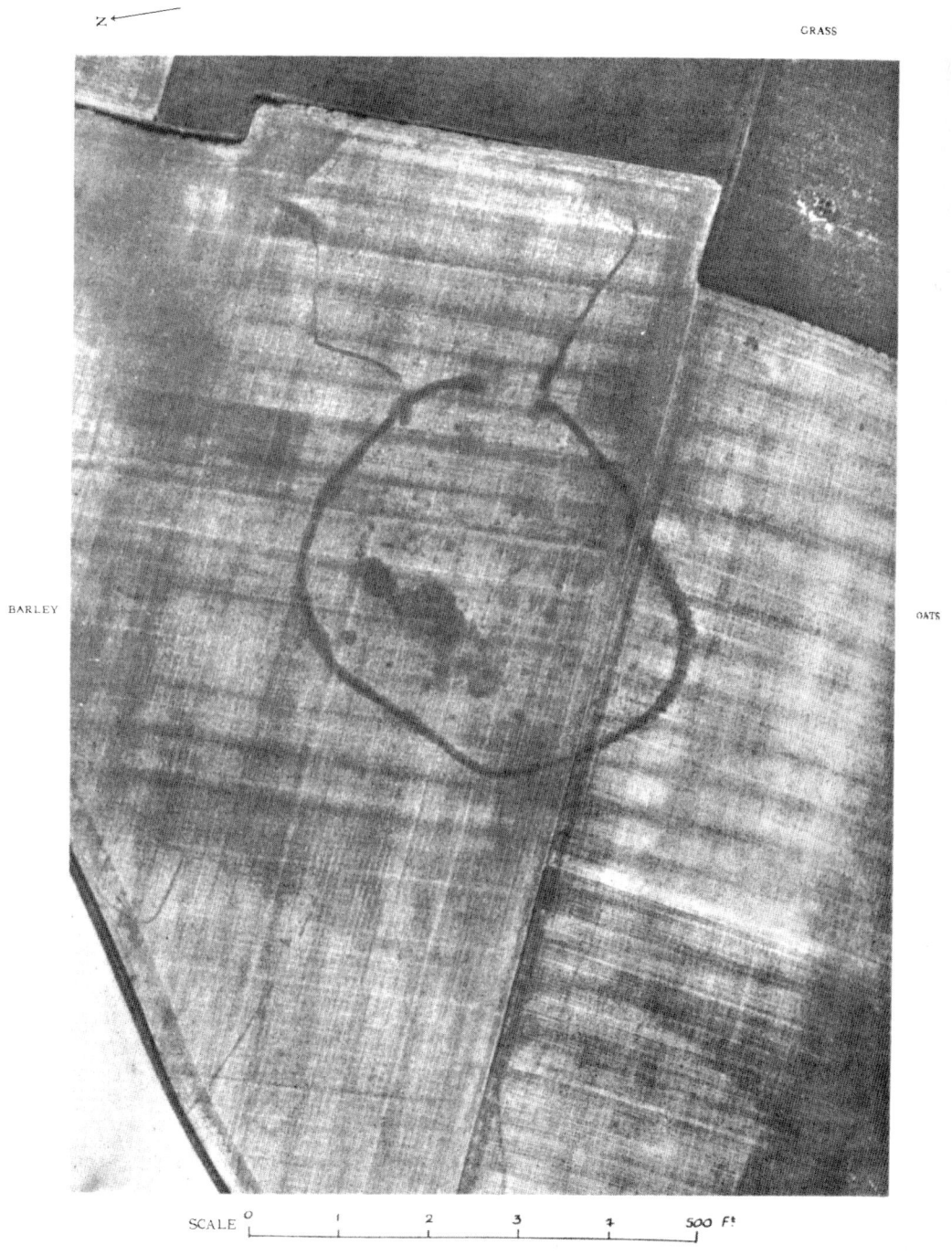

SCALE

FIGURE 2. *Enclosure near Woodbury, Wilts: taken between 11 and 12 o'clock, 16 May 1929 (R.A.F., Old Sarum).*

larger blobs. The latter, however, are here strung loosely together, forming a group. One may reasonably infer that they represent the site of the main group of huts.

The absence of pits and hut-depressions outside the enclosure is very striking — more so than on the other photograph, though also to be observed there. This is the first time that air-photography has proved capable of recording by means of crop-marks the presence of these prehistoric hut-sites; and it shows that, given favourable conditions, we may hope for great things in the future. The bulk of the area of the enclosure, as well as the 'antennae' and the sites about to be described, was under barley which, *on certain soils*,[1] is thus proved to be a better 'developer' than oats, wheat or grass. We may expect to find similar dots and blobs amongst the many air-photographs stored at the Ordnance Survey, now that we know from this instance that they can be relied upon. Many such settlements may have existed in the open, without a protecting bank and ditch round them.

A small segment of the enclosure encroaches upon a field of oats on the south. Here the ditch seems wider. It is of irregular width throughout, expanding in places for a short distance; the two ends at the entrance are also slightly expanded.

At the time of my visit the whole area was covered with stubble. I could not even see anything on the ground to enable me to identify the site of the enclosure or its contained markings. The farmer whom I met on the spot, with some of the labourers, told me, however, that they knew the 'ring' well and had regarded it as the relics of some former field-enclosure. They could see it in the spring. The area is covered with pot boilers.

Outside, in the NW corner of the plate, is a small four-sided enclosure. The ditch was evidently very narrow, since the black line, though quite distinct, is much fainter. The two eastern angles (of the enclosure) are sharp and the other two are rounded. There is a gap in the north side, and two black spots set close together within the area. Southwest of it a smaller rectangle is just discernible; it is divided into two unequal halves. It suggests some sort of a building. The dark line beyond is an old hollow field-track, still in use and aiming at Britford.

I have not, in the above brief account, exhausted the many points of interest revealed by these remarkable photographs. (I have not, for instance, said much about the wandering lines that can be seen; one of them runs directly from Woodbury to the smaller enclosure). They are valuable not only in themselves but for what they foretell. They are the heralds of innumerable queer resurrections. They assure us that no site, however flattened out, is really lost to knowledge. Scotsmen in particular will welcome their message; for certain lowland regions, such as the Vale of Strathmore and the coastal plain near Edinburgh, where oats and barley predominate, are admirably suited to this method. Not only will many of General Roy's Roman camps come back to life, but others doubtless will be discovered, particularly along the line of the known Roman roads. One can imagine no more fascinating pursuit for the owner of a private aeroplane.

[I fulfilled this prophecy myself, with Geoffrey Allington as
pilot, in June 1939; see ANTIQUITY *xiii, 1939*
but I had forgotten it long ago & have only come across it
again today, 9 November 1940. O.G.S.C.]

Annotation in pencil in archive volume.

---

1   But not on all; see ANTIQUITY, I, 469 (The big circles near Dorchester, Oxon.).

Iron Age square enclosures in Rhineland
by **K.V. DECKER & I. SCOLLAR**

ANTIQUITY 36 (143), 1962

BANKED AND DITCHED rectangular burial enclosures, called 'Grabgärten' (grave garden, literally) by the local folk, are found frequently in the southern Rhineland, with distribution centred on the southeast Eifel, the Rhine–Moselle junction and the northern part of the Hunsrück mountains. All examples known to us up to the time of writing are plotted on the map (FIGURE 1).

Within these enclosures are found incineration burials, either in urns, pits or stone cists made of schist slabs, or simply a scatter of bones in a pit. In some cases post holes which have been found may belong, by analogy with finds in Champagne, to mortuary houses, cult stelae or the like. Chronologically, the enclosures in the Rhineland fall partly in the late La Tène period, but the majority are early Roman Imperial in date. Inasmuch as the origin of these enclosures, due to the paucity of data, is still unclear, it is not possible to comment on that aspect of the question.

In the fifties of the last [19th] century attention was paid to these earthworks for the first time by von Cohausen, though he misinterpreted them as Roman fortifications.[1] Half a century later, R. Bodewig recognized that the 'Grabgärten' which he excavated in the Koblenz municipal forest were flat graves, and he contrasted them with the round barrows which often accompanied them. He considered them to be the individual family burial plots of the Treveri, a view which the present writers support.[2]

The first scientific study of a 'Grabgärten' was made twenty years later by the Bonn museum, a site at Hambuch Kreis Cochem.[3] Additional 'Grabgärten' were subsequently published by F. Oelmann and J. Hagen in the *Bonner Jahrbucher*.[4] Further impetus to the study was given by the museum's excavations at Mayen, Kreis Mayen, Kerben Kreis Mayen, Kärlich and Mülheim, Kreis Koblenz.[5] Since the second war field work and aerial photography have considerably increased the number of known sites. Over a hundred examples have been found in the flying seasons of 1960–61, for they constitute the most frequently encountered archaeological air site in their distribution area.

Enclosures similar to those in the Rhineland have been reported from Champagne (Yonne and Maine), northeast England (Yorkshire) and a number are said to exist in the Low Countries, Westphalia and even southwest Slovakia.[6] The reader is referred to a recent work by I.M. Stead for a general survey of these monuments in western Europe as a whole.[7]

It is generally thought that the origins of these enclosures are to be sought in the early Iron Age and that there are connexions with older ring ditch barrow rites, and, in addition, Italian parallels have been drawn.[8] Post holes which may have been from mortuary houses as well as space for cult stelae and the like show that the 'Grabgärten' in some cases may have served temporarily as a sacred enclosure for a mortuary cult or for memorial services.[9] In this connexion, the numerous rectangular enclosures which are found in southern Germany may be cited which, as parallels from France show, are to be considered as sacred areas.[10]

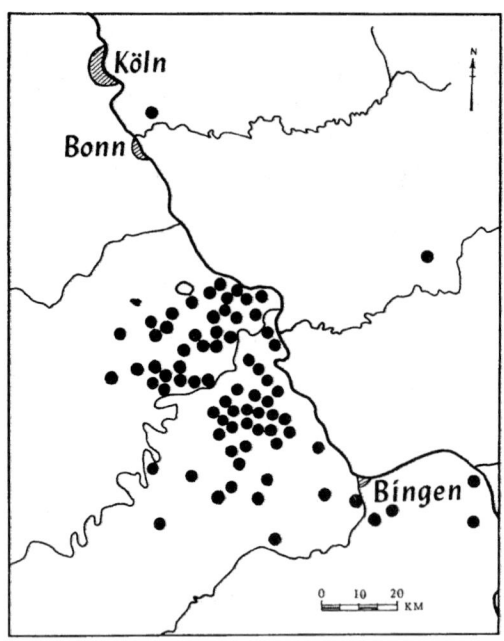

FIGURE 1.

Chronologically, the monuments of this type in the Rhineland seem to belong to the late Iron Age or to the early Imperial period, as far as the limited excavation material allows one to say.[11] There are various opinions on the possibility that the rectangular walled burial enclosures of the middle Imperial period are a continuation of the 'Grabgärten' rite.[12] It is interesting to note that several of the excavated 'Grabgärten' appear to have been reused for late Roman inhumation burials.[13]

The enclosures are usually perfectly square, with the sides varying from 10 to 40 m. When excavated, the ditches are for the most part triangular in section, often with a rounded lower apex (Miesenheim, Kreis Mayen, unpublished; Hambuch, Kreis Cochem; Andernach, Kreis Mayen). The low banks may lie either inside or outside of the ditch and a well preserved example of the latter type is shown in the air photograph (FIGURE 2a). The banks may rise to as much as one metre in height in preserved examples like that at Hambuch. The upper width of the enclosure ditch varies between 2 and 6 m and the depth is between 0·8 and 1·5 m. Most of the 'Grabgärten' are ploughed out and cannot be assigned with certainty to any type inasmuch as only the ditch survives, but often the aerial photograph, such as the example here (FIGURE 2b) enables one to determine the position of the bank. Topographically, the enclosures were preferably placed just below the crest of a steep slope (FIGURES 2b & 3a).

'Grabgärten' may appear singly, but more often they turn up in groups of up to eight, sometimes linked up (FIGURE 3b).[14] Often they form part of a group with round barrows.* A series of them lies on the edge or even partly within round barrow fields of the Hallstatt and early La Tène periods.[15] In examples known at Wederath, Kreis Bernkastel, Kärlich, Kreis Koblenz and Miesenheim, Kreis Mayen, they lie surrounded by large Roman incineration cemeteries.[16]

The enclosures in the Rhineland can be classified roughly into three types for convenience:

A: Banked and ditched enclosures with level or slightly raised interiors.[17]

B: Banked and ditched enclosures with noticeably raised interiors or with perhaps a small barrow inside them.[18]

C: Ditch-enclosed rectangular barrows.[19]

It is not known if these types have chronological or cultural significance for too few survive intact to obtain an adequate idea of their geographical distribution or content within the whole assemblage.

Within the enclosure are one or more incineration burials. The ditches often contain further incinerations. These incinerations are deposited either in urns, left in the burning pits or placed in stone cists made of slabs of the local schist (Koblenzer Stadtwald;

---

*   Koblenzer Stadtwald; Sohrschied, Kreis Simmern; Mayen Stadtwald 'Distrikt Greueler Kopf'.

a

b

FIGURE 2a. *Oberfell, Kreis St Goar, Co-ordinates 33.91.75; 55.69.65.*
    2b. Moselkern, Kreis Mayen, Co-ordinates 25.98.33; 55.61.48.

a

b

FIGURE 3a. *Heyweiler, Kreis St Goar, Co-ordinates 26.04.36; 55.55.23.*
3b. *Briedel, Kreis Zell, Co-ordinates 25.89.40; 55.38.52.*

Miesenheim, Kreis Mayen; Hambuch Kreis Cochem). At Hambuch, the foundations of some sort of funeral monument were found in enclosure four. At Kruft, Kreis Mayen, the rectangular ditch enclosed a cist made of the local tuffa and containing, besides the usual incineration, an assortment of pots which presumably once contained grave offerings.[20] Often the incinerations are outlined with a circle of small stones (Koblenzer Stadtwald). Post holes were found inside the enclosure at Hambuch but they cannot be joined up in a coherent pattern. In the Koblenz municipal forest, at the place called 'am Stösschen' the remains of a charred wooden mass were found in an excavated 'Grabgärten'.[21]

The 'Grabgärten' of the Rhineland, because of their compact distribution, large number and interesting international connexions are a group of monuments which seriously merit a detailed study and excavation campaign which we hope will soon be carried out.

Notes

1   *Bonner Jahrbucher* 26, 1858, 7 ff.
2   *Westdeutsche Zeitschrift,* 19, 1900, 32 ff. and 58.
3   *B.J.,* 128, 1923, 136; 130, 1925, 316; (133) 1928: 260; 134 (1929): 143.
4   *B.J.,* 134, 1929, 134, 149, 151; 133, 1928, 263, 270; 132, 1927, 274; 135, 1930, 180.
5   *B.J.,* 140–141, 1936, 433 f. and 492; 143–144, 1938–39, 423 ff. with a summary of the then known 'Grabgärten' by W. Haberey; *B.J.,* 145, 1940, 322; 146, 1941, 337; *Nachrichten Blatt für Deutsche Vorzeit,* 17, 1941, 121.
6   *Bulletin de la Société Archéologique Champenoise,* 24, nr. 3–4, 1930, 85 ff.; *Gallia,* 7, 1949, 116; 12, 1954, 516 f.; *Revue Archéologique de l'Est et Centre-Est,* 5, 1954, 71 ff.; *Germania,* 39, 1961, 196 ff.; *Nassauische Annalen,* 44, 1916–17, 186; *Westfälische Forschungen,* 1, 1938, pl. 16; 3, 1940, 189, no. 13; *Germania,* 22, 1938, 93; *Benadik, Vlček, Ambros, Keltische Gräberfelder der Südwestslowakei,* p. 15, 23, 28, and figs. 3, 6, 7.
7   I.M. Stead, 'A Distinctive Form of La Tène Barrow in Eastern Yorkshire and on the Continent.' *Ant. J.,* XLI, 1961, 44ff.
8   *B.J.,* 148, 1948, 114; *Germania,* 14, 1930, 26ff.
9   *Neue Ausgrabungen in Deutschland,* 1958, 213.
10 *Ibid.*
11 E.g. late La Tène: *Mainzer Zeitschrift,* 24–25, 1929–30, 125 ff.; 54, 1959, 47 ff.; early Imperial: *B.J.,* 143–144, 1938–39, 423 ff.; 145, 1940, 337 ff.
12 *Germania,* 14, 1930, 26 ff.
13 Kärlich, Kreis Koblenz, 'Flur 15' unpublished; *Gallia,* 5, 1947, 445 f.; *Gallia,* 7, 1949, 116, fig. 4.
14 For example, *B.J.,* 18, 1852, 33 ff.; 148, 1948, 82.
15 *B.J.,* 148, 1948, 82; Buch, Kreis Simmern, unpublished; W. Dehn, *Katalog Kreuznach,* 1941, II, 99.
16 *Germania,* 39, 1961, 196 ff., pl. 35, fig. 1; *B.J.,* 145, 1940, 322; 146, 1941, 337; Miesenheim, Kreis Mayen, Distrikt Hinter Zantermann, unpublished, and we thank Dr J. Röder for telling us about it.
17 *W.Z.,* 19, 1900, 38; *ibid.,* 32 ff., 34; *B.J.,* 140–141, 1936, 433 f.
18 Dehn, *Katalog Kreuznach,* 1941, II, 100.
19 *B.J.,* 142, 1937, 287.
20 Kruft, Kreis Mayen near the housing estate behind the village school, according to information from Dr J. Röder.
21 *W.Z.,* 19, 1900, 32 ff.

Aerial reconnaissance in Picardy
by R. AGACHE
ANTIQUITY 38 (150), 1964

ALTHOUGH French archaeologists such as Père Poidebard in Syria, and Colonel Baradez in North Africa, have been using air photography very successfully for a long time in sub-desert regions overseas, this has not been so in Metropolitan France. In fact it was a mere ten years ago — a considerable time after systematic air photography had been going on in England — that French research workers began to use air photography, and even then as individual efforts each in his own region. In almost all cases they used, like the author, the aircraft of local aero-clubs, and small non-professional cameras, usually the simple 24 x 36 mm. models. That these individual efforts have been far from negligible became more widely apparent in Paris, in August 1963, at the conference on, and exhibition of, air photography organized by M. Raymond Chevallier (ANTIQUITY 1963: 296), under the auspices of the Ecole Pratique des Hautes Etudes of the Sorbonne where he has recently inaugurated the first university course in photo-interpretation in France.[1]

J. Bradford was the first to report that he had discovered, in the North of France, crop-sites on the air photographs taken in the last war.[2] In 1960, I published the first photographs of crop-sites of the region, taken at low altitude in the Spring of 1960.[3] Nevertheless it must be remembered that it was more than 300 years ago that archaeologists on the ground noticed that the differential growth of cereal crops could reveal buried archaeological features.[4]

Two aerial surveys of the region were made in 1938 and 1939 by the Institut Géographique de l'Armée, now the Institut Géographique National (I.G.N.). But no archaeologist was called upon to examine the photographs, most of which were of excellent quality. It is true that these were not taken for archaeological reasons, and no attention therefore was paid to the conditions especially favourable for this purpose, and the scale (1:20,000–1:25,000) was too small. However, on some of them, ploughed-out features were remarkably clear, particularly around Abbeville on the 1939 survey. For example, on photograph no. 125 the shape of the great camp outside the *oppidum* of Liercourt/Erondelle can be seen perfectly; nos. 44 and 45 show equally clearly the circles situated around and beside the barrows of Port-le-Grand; other protohistoric circles are well seen near Abbeville and de Vauchelles (nos. 20 and 36). Unfortunately the numerous sorties flown over the region during the last war were studied only for military purposes.

At the request of M. Aufrère, then Directeur régional des Antiquités préhistoriques, I undertook, in April 1960, several air surveys of Picardy, with two objects in mind: the first was to get photographs of sites already known, and second and more important, to reveal remains which had been levelled to the ground and so far unsuspected.*

In June 1961, J.K.S. St Joseph also flew sorties over this region, with excellent results, as readers of ANTIQUITY will know.[7] More recently M. Vasselle, a Gallo-Roman

* I must record my gratitude to M. Aufrère and M. Will (Directeur régional des Antiquités historiques) and to the Direction de l'Architecture (Ministère d'Etat aux Affaires Culturelles) for putting funds for this task at my disposal.

specialist, has also taken some good air pictures, particularly in the valleys of the Avre and Noye rivers.

Palaeolithic sites

Aerial photography of the classic Palaeolithic sites of the Somme valley has made it possible to get an overall picture of the actual state of these famous sites, now almost entirely built over. These 'photographic plans' were far from being useless because they give a more precise and detailed picture than any map or cadastral plan. It was possible on these photographs to locate occasional pieces of land which had been neither excavated nor built on, where after a small test excavation it might be urgent to schedule a particular piece for archaeological purposes.

At Abbeville, all that is left it seems are the gardens of the co-operative milk centre. At Menchecourt, on the other hand, near the old excavations at Leraille and Gauchy, which in the last century yielded abundant pleistocene fauna, a number of open fields look interesting. The next job was to make a number of test excavations here to get certain parcels of land reserved for later excavation. As for the type-site of Saint-Acheul, nothing is left to preserve except one zone of the middle terraces (near the NE border of the original workings at Bultel-Tellier where a small section has already been scheduled), and a narrow band of the high terrace to the north-west of the rue Edmond Rostand. It should be mentioned in passing that air photographs yield important evidence for the study of recent geology. Photographs taken in the crisp light of winter throw into relief deposits of tufa which rise a little above the general level of the marshland. It is known that this geologically recent tufa is formed by springs and seepages gradually depositing their lime content whenever the water rises to the surface. The distribution of such tufa is important, for these deposits are extremely rich in Neolithic, and even more in protohistoric, remains. Other features picked out on air photographs include ancient coastlines clearly visible behind the present-day coast (FIGURE 1a); the siliceous soils of these former coastlines are more water-holding than the surrounding lands and thus present a different agricultural pattern. Similarly, photographs taken from a very low altitude during a period of drought (beginning of June 1962) reveal very distinctive polygonal soil patterns. Sections in gravel pits show important evidence of frost action; the pebbles are sometimes raised up vertically, the effect extending to a depth of $2^{1}/_{2}$ and even 3 metres (FIGURE 2). The aerial survey cast new light on some Palaeolithic sites. On the beach at Ault-Onival[8] for example, a large number of enormous Levalloisian nuclei was found, similar to those of the earlier Levalloisian of the low terraces of the Somme near Amiens. On the rocky fore-shore, the pieces are very broken up, but more widely dispersed. At the level of the low tides at Onival and the very low tides at Ault, I collected unbroken worked flints with no traces of wear, associated with a molar of *elephas primigenius*. All these had been dislodged by the storms from a coomb-rock from which numerous flints had been split off by frost action. From an aeroplane, it at once became obvious that this coomb-rock corresponds to an ancient cliff-line, set at an angle to the modern sea-bank, but an exact continuation of the dead cliff, still visible from Brutelles to Onival.

Neolithic sites

In many cases the aerial survey of known Neolithic sites has not revealed any new facts, but the characteristic positions of the centres for extracting and knapping flints stand out clearly. They were all situated just on the edges of the plateaux. At Troussencourt, surveys made in flat lighting conditions show well the position of small depressions corresponding to the falling in of the sides of some flint shafts. As for the very small soil-

a

b

FIGURE 1a. *Le Crotoy at the mouth of the Somme: Pleistocene shoreline. Protohistoric circles and polygonal soil patterns visible in cultivated fields at the beginning of June 1962. Ground checks showed violent frost action; see FIGURE 2b. 1b. Northern side of Amiens: the circle is protohistoric; the straight lines remain from the siege works of 1597; the zig-zag lines are trenches from the last war. (Photos R. Agache, Ministère de la Culture.)*

marks which reveal the positions of these shafts, these are more easily seen on the ground, or from the top of a tall ladder, than from an aircraft; at Hardivilliers-Troussencourt, small dark stains in the middle of white chalky fields give their presence away. At Hallencourt, on the contrary, they show up as light marks, for the Neolithic mine-workings had to cut through a bed of limon to reach the chalk. At Ayencourtle-Monchel, where there is a rare example of Neolithic extraction of primary material from clay-with-flints, the site of the workings is betrayed only by a mass of flint-chip debris, brought to the surface by deep ploughing and visible only on the ground.

Bronze and Iron Age sites
The most striking results of this aerial survey have, however, been the discovery of ditches of the protohistoric period. During the first two years my efforts were directed entirely to cultivated land in the spring. The season of 1960, having been so dry, produced the best conditions and therefore the best results in that year. However this procedure was not followed without inconvenience; only certain crops are good indicators of crop-marks, the more so when the season is too damp as in 1963, when very few crop-marks were visible; and lastly the source of errors is considerable and is increased by the difficulty of an immediate ground-check, as farmers do not look kindly on anyone trampling down their growing crops.

It is for some of these reasons that I am particularly grateful to M. Raymond Chevallier, who advised me to make winter surveys; these have proved extraordinarily fruitful. Above all it was the 'damp-marks' which gave the most striking results. Unfortunately, although these signs are of the greatest clarity, they appear for only a very brief time. The optimum conditions occur when a very sudden improvement in the weather follows a long period of rain at the end of the winter (FIGURES 3 & 4). The ground dries superficially in places and produces extraordinary contrasts in regions of bare soil, particularly when they have been rolled or tamped down; these contrasts are less visible in recently harrowed or ploughed fields. In studying crop-marks it is necessary to make a number of flights to collect enough data for one region. The comparison between crop-marks and damp-marks of a protohistoric site always shows that the damp-marks are much more precise. On chalky soils, protohistoric remains keep their humidity for a longer time; after the ground dries out, they appear as dark marks on a white background (FIGURES 3 & 4). The smallest of the ditches or trenches are easily discernible. Also, in fallow fields, the risk of confusion is reduced to the minimum. Early in the survey it was possible to distinguish recent terraces from older ones: in chalky soils, modern trenches appear white,[9] like open wounds, for they have been filled up again very quickly with the materials of excavation; on the other hand, the protohistoric ditches have generally been filled in gradually by a trickling process, and are usually vegetation-covered. Often, too, the latter are rich in organic matter and sometimes in ash, and take on a darker hue. From the air can be distinguished other marks in the soil such as threshing floors, manure heaps, burnt clearings. . . . On the other hand, when the ground is covered with crops, not only are these signs invisible but also the double process of sowing and fertilizing, as well as old and recent terracing, show up in the same way — undifferentiated — by the more vigorous growth of the vegetation. Then, only by ground examination of the form of these plant-growth anomalies can one distinguish one from the other. And so, inspection of uncultivated ground is a considerable advantage, as it can be carried out immediately. Any doubts can be soon settled by quick sondage and the collection of samples.

a

b

FIGURE 2. *Le Crotoy (Somme).* a *Former coastline. The polygonal soil pattern is clearly seen after the surface soil has been stripped by bulldozing.* b *Coastal strip showing profound frost action. The pebbles are aligned vertically, the effect extending to 2¹/₂ and even 3 m. The adjacent beds are horizontal. (Photos R. Agache, Ministère de la Culture.)*

In April 1963, an air survey of the Picardy plateau after a rainy period showed that the superficial variation in water-holding properties made it equally possible to distinguish ditches dug in 'rich' soils as in argilo-limon soils. But now the colours were reversed; the latter appeared in white on a black background, for they dried out more quickly than when dug in rich 'fat' soils. Thus one may hope that in ensuing years the

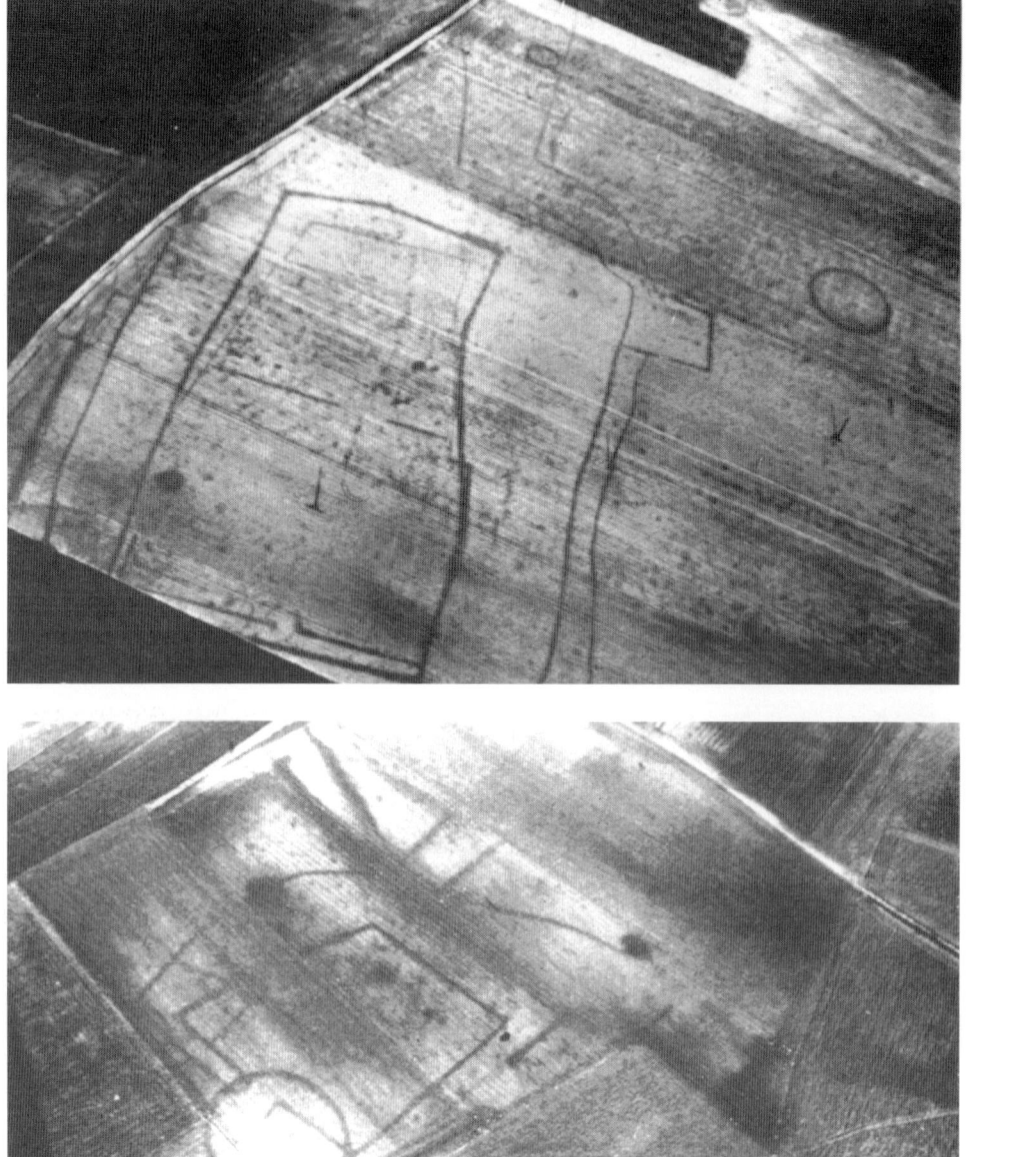

a

b

FIGURE 3a. *Erondelle (Somme): ploughed-out enclosure discovered in cereal fields in June 1960, but not seen so clearly before as here in bare soil after a very wet period in March 1963.*
3b. *Neufmoulin, known locally as 'le Mont d'Evangile', in January 1964: a very clear picture of protohistoric ditches showing up as damp-marks. (Photos R. Agache, Ministère de la Culture.)*

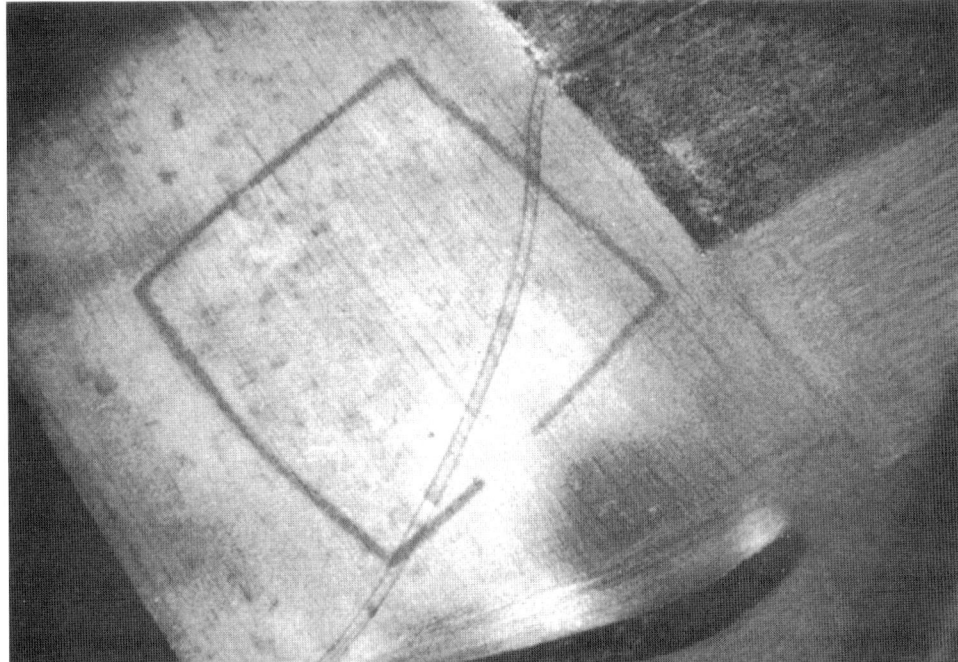

a

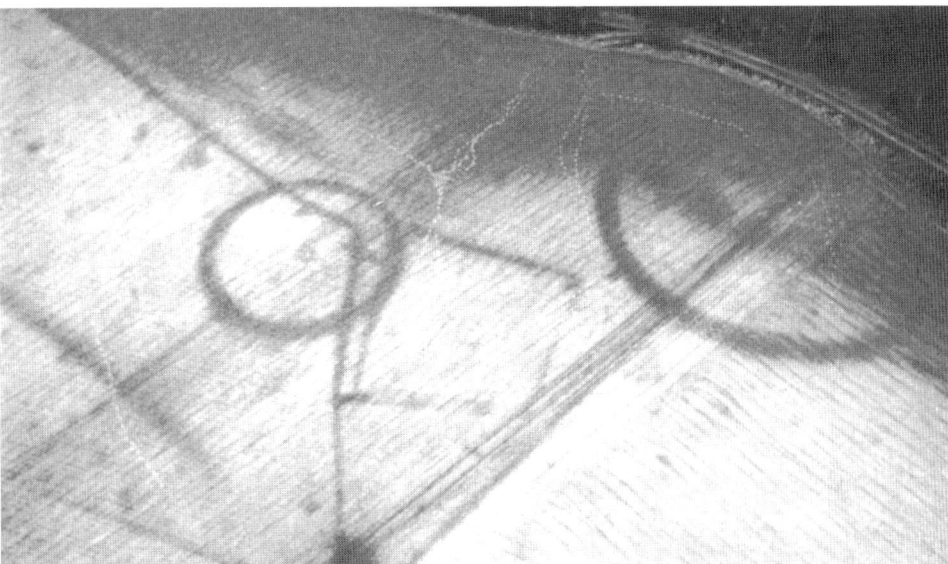

b

FIGURE 4a. *Vauchelles (Somme) near Abbeville: square enclosure showing clearly the passage of a tractor. 4b. Drucat (Somme): damp-marks in the soil at dawn on the first day after a rainy period. The little white spots are the footsteps of the author, who waited on the ground until the soil contrasts were very clearly marked before taking the air photograph. (Photos R. Agache, Ministère de la Culture.)*

Picardy plateau may be effectively prospected when the limon is as much as 10 or 12 m. thick. But for the moment, it is true to say that the distribution map of protohistoric sites discovered from the air is primarily a map of areas that lend themselves to aerial prospection.

In Picardy, as in most other regions, circular structures are by far the most numerous. Among these, many must be all that remains of tumuli which have been completely ploughed out; elsewhere, around tumuli that can still be seen, air photographs bring to light circles, sometimes two or even three concentric circles, such as for example at Noyelles-sur-Mer (the *tombelles* of Saint-Ouen and Port-le-Grand).

The small square enclosures, generally of the La Tène III period, also have a ritual and funerary character. There are many fewer of these in Picardy than there are in the Maine and the Yonne. They peter out almost entirely towards the lower Somme, but are relatively numerous, especially downstream, in the region of Picquigny, Quesnoy-les-Airaines and Flixecourt.

Larger enclosures, irregularly shaped, which seem to represent animal enclosures, are fairly numerous; particularly so in a large area around Quesnoy-les-Airaines.

The large rectangular enclosures, in most cases square, are in all probability more recent. Some may be Gallo-Roman farms. Their distribution is quite distinctive. They are comparatively common to the south-west of Amiens, to the north-east of Abbeville, and in the vicinity of Ponthoile-Romaine and Noyelles-sur-Mer. In the region south of Liercourt-Erondelle and near Picquigny, Aillysur-Somme, Mont Caubert, Vers, St Riquier, Prouzel and Chaussoy, are many examples of both types. Sometimes indeed they are joined together as at Cagny or Condé-Folie.

Hillforts

The survey of the magnificent *oppida* of the Somme[10] did not reveal anything new inside them except at La Chaussée-Tirancourt where, as Dr St Joseph noticed, there are traces of a smaller and older hillfort inside. Outside I photographed two quadrangular enclosures.[11] At the *oppidum* of Mont Caubert, near Abbeville, there are rectangular traces on the southern side. At L'Etoile, in the winter, there clearly appeared a track leading from it, bordered by two ditches, towards Amiens, but which fairly rapidly petered out. By contrast, on the high land to the south of the Somme, air photographs revealed in places a long and very broad trackway completely unknown before. The line of this trackway is often broken because it is made up of a succession of zig-zag rectilinear stretches. It could be an important Roman strategic way. It leaves Amiens, and, clinging all the time to the plateau, runs westward to end in the important group of earthworks at Liercourt/Erondelle.

Alongside the *oppidum* of Liercourt a series of earthworks has come to light. The most important is a Roman camp of 15 hectares. It is immediately outside the *oppidum* and joined to it.[12] Dr St Joseph has discussed this structure.[13] Many subdivisions and a great many filled-in ditches can be seen inside, as well as a small quadrilateral enclosure at the south-west corner near an entrance way. In some places it is delimited by two parallel ditches. Trial sections showed that the outer ditch had a V-profile, while the inner 'ditch' which was very shallow, was flat-bottomed with traces of ruts leading to a specially well-defended entrance in the SE corner of the *oppidum*. In the make-up of the ditches Roman sherds are fairly common, and native Gaulish pottery very common, as well as a great many freshly chipped flints. It seems likely that the Romans occupied the *oppidum* and established this camp outside for their auxiliary troops. That would explain why the enormous Gaulish mound was built just opposite the camp, the better to oversee it.

Roman sites

On the hills overlooking the valleys of the Noye more Roman camps have been picked up on air photographs near Breteuil (perhaps on the site of ancient Bratuspantium) and at Folleville.[14] They are also quite visible on some Institut Géographique National photographs.[15] At Folleville the camp is nearly square, containing an area of 15 hectares. It is bounded by two parallel ditches, shown by sondage to be of V-profile. Outside the south-west corner tangled lines correspond probably to advance defence works. From the east of the camp very long straight lines emerge which look like access routes, such as those observed leading to the entrenchments of Mont Catelet, where one ends at an entrance protected by a *tutulus* (FIGURE 5a). There is a similar entrance to the east of Folleville camp (FIGURE 5b).

I have discovered other traces of camps all along the Roman roads from Pierregot and to Festel. In the latter case, the in-filled ditch is very wide (nearly 8 m.) and very deep (nearly 3 m.). At the bottom was a coin struck at Trier at the beginning of the 4th century. It would appear that we are dealing with a *burgus* of the Late Empire, set up to ensure the safety of this highly important Roman road from Lugdunum (Lyon) to Gesoriacum (possibly Boulogne) via Samarobriva (Amiens).

Research into Roman buildings has been much less fruitful and, quite often, the air views of *villa* sites already known has shown nothing. But a large number of Gallo-Roman rectangular constructions has come to light, notably at Pont-Rémy, Pissy, Louvrechy, Picquigny, Allonville, Cottenchy, Chirmont, Paillart, Esquennoy, Thory, Pendé, Tilloy and Mons-en-Chaussée. Even more interesting is a number of important *vici* at Remiencourt, Andainville and Lahoussoye. Near Remiencourt, a little temple has been revealed after very deep ploughing had taken place. In the region south of Breteuil, important Roman monuments rased by agriculture are, however, clearly visible even on the small-scale photographs of the I.G.N. (theatres, temples, altars, etc.).

Medieval and later sites

It is impossible to go much further without mention of the countless medieval structures observed on air cover. The comparison between these photographs and ancient drawings and engravings is often surprising and shows to what extent the rural countryside has been shaped by historical events, and guards numerous secrets rooted in the past. It would be very useful to publish side by side these old plans and the modern photographs as M.W. Beresford and J.K.S. St Joseph have done so well in England.[16] But, in Picardy, a special place would have to be given to the countless traces of the interminable wars which have ravaged the province in the course of two thousand years. The scars left by the wars of 1870–1, 1914–8, and 1939–45 are without number, above all those of the Second World War. Some of the German military bases, the vast reinforced concrete installations of the 'Atlantic Wall', and particularly the launching ramps of the V1 missiles and their storehouses: some of these have been so heavily bombarded that the peasants have given up any attempt to bring them under cultivation again.

Finally, mention must be made of the curious 'rediscovery' by air of the military works of the siege of Amiens by Henry IV of France in 1597. The Spaniards took the town by surprise. Henry took this very much to heart and he sallied forth himself at the head of his army to re-take Amiens. The siege marks an important date in military his-

a

b

FIGURE 5a. *Mont Catelet near the source of the Noye. A discovery of double ditches defending the entrance of the side next the plateau: a remarkable growth of cereals, grown on poor chalk land, shows up as dark bands in the ditches. (The white strip is fresh plough.) Note the somewhat unusual* tutulus *protecting the entrance. 5b. Folleville (Somme): Roman camp discovered by air photography. Note the* tutulus *protecting the entrance near the wood. (Photos R. Agache, Ministère de la Culture.)*

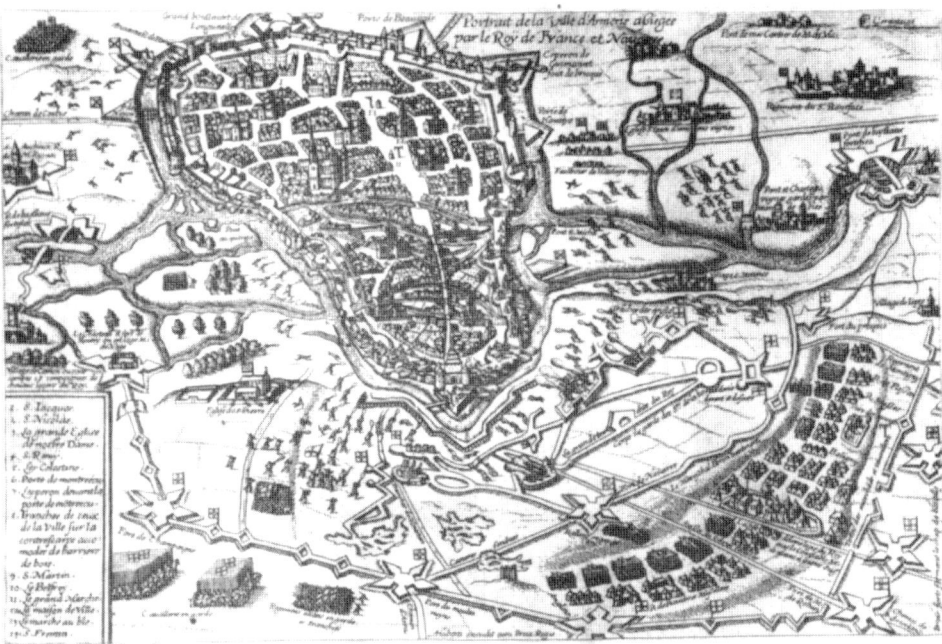

a

b

FIGURE 6a. *Old drawing of the siege of Amiens by Henry IV in 1597. 6b. Rediscovery by air of the completely destroyed bastions of the time of the siege of Amiens. (Photos R. Agache, Ministère de la Culture.)*

tory for the chain of redoubts, breastworks and ramparts was unequalled in extent before that time. Many contemporary engravings remain as witness to these feats (FIGURE 6a), but no traces have been found of the many little earthen forts, now square, now lozenge-shaped or even pentagonal. But, not only have these completely rased bastions been found on air photographs, taken at suitable moments of lighting, and not only has the air survey confirmed the general accuracy of the old drawings, but also they have provided many complementary pieces of information about the small defensive works which were totally unknown before (FIGURE 6a). On bare soil, in winter, an interesting palimpsest of many remains can be discerned: protohistoric circles, military works of Henry IV, and trenches of the last war (FIGURE 6b).

Conclusions

Such, briefly, are some of the first results of the air survey of Picardy. If one compares a distribution map of protohistoric remains discovered in this way with one of the sites known before, the first impression is at once apparent: for certain zones (for example the region of Breteuil, Liercourt, Noyelles-sur-Mer and Port-le-Grand) where abundant remains have long been known, air photography has confirmed the facts, but also has made the distribution even more precise; in other regions (Vauchelles, Crécy, for example, and above all a very large area around Quesnoy-les-Airaines), air photography has revealed a great number of protohistoric remains which had not previously received any attention. While being well aware, however, of the immense possibilities of air photography, one would do well also to be aware of its limitations. As Dr St Joseph rightly pointed out,[17] the distribution map which I published in 1962 corresponds closely to a distribution map of loess.[18] But I do not believe that one should draw very precise conclusions as to the distribution of population at that time. If the protohistoric sites brought to light by air photography are nearly all situated on the chalky edges of the plateaux,[19] it is that the natures of these soils lend themselves best to revealing to the air camera the 'ghost' remains of ditches, banks, etc.; on these poor soils very marked contrasts are seen between undisturbed and disturbed ground both in cultivated and in open land. This is not sufficient evidence upon which to conclude that the rest of the countryside was practically uninhabited. Besides, chance finds on the Picardy plateau are by no means rare and on the valley bottoms they have been numerous: these are both areas where the air camera has failed to reveal anything, for the zones which have not been dug for peat have not been cultivated and are enveloped in bulrushes and brushwood. It is, however, curious to observe that protohistoric structures seem clearly less frequent on air photographs in the Pas-de-Calais, even on the chalky slopes of the Canche and Authie valleys. But it is too soon to draw many conclusions here; several years of widely ranging air survey must be undertaken before these problems can be fully understood. Indeed, only methodical excavation will solve the identity of some sites.

Lastly, it must be urged upon my countrymen that the necessity for full-scale air photography of France is a matter of urgency. We are witnesses to an agricultural revolution which will have grave consequences for archaeology. The use of heavy tractors is a grave danger. Before the last war 20 cm. was the deepest that a plough would dig. Now they are ploughing as deeply as 40 or even 50 cm. And so, every year, countless burial grounds and habitation sites are destroyed, unperceived by the new-style farmer perched high on the seat of his mechanical tractor. On the other hand the creation of enormous new fields is in the process of disfiguring the countryside. The systematic destruction of hedges, clumps of trees and above all of topsoil carries in its wake disastrous soil-erosion. This is why one of the essential aims of air photographic research must be to isolate the most important archaeological sites and get them scheduled or protected against the depredations of modern agricultural and industrial progress for future generations to study.

References

1   Cf. *Archéologie aérienne et Techniques complémentaires.* (Illustrated catalogue of the exhibition 4 July–9 November 1963. Paris: Institut Pédagogique National. The papers given at this conference are in the press.)

2   J. Bradford, *Ancient Landscapes: studies in field archaeology* (London, 1957).

3   *Bull. Soc. Préhist. du Nord,* 3, October 1960.

4   Louvet, *Histoire du Païs de Beauvaisis,* 1631, p. 24, reads: 'quand cette grande campagne est ensemencée en bled, on y reconnoit encore le compassement et les endrois des rües ou le bled est plus petit qu'es lieux ou les maisons étoient bâties. . .'

6/5   These researches are the subject of a special number of *Bull. Soc. Préhist. du Nord,* 5, October 1962.

7   J.K.S. St Joseph, 'Aerial Reconnaissance in Northern France', ANTIQUITY, 1962, 279–86.

8   In July 1961, Dr Mariette showed a remarkable series of worked flints to the Colloque international des Préhistoriens et quaternaristes septentrionaux de Calais.

9   In some cases, however, a dark line of damp is present but is encircled with white.

10   *Revue du Nord,* 176, 1962, 319–38; R.E.M. Wheeler and K.M. Richardson, *The Hill Forts of Northern France (Society of Antiquaries Research Report,* XIX, 1957).

11   *Bull. Soc. Préhist. du Nord,* 3, 1960, 31.

12   J.K.S. St Joseph, loc. cit. pl. XL *(a)* is a good photograph of the southern zone.

13   *Revue du Nord,* loc. cit., 326. More information obtained in winter flying since then has to be added to this plan.

14   *Bull. Soc. Préhist. Française,* LIX, 1962, 257–66.

15   Cf. I.G.N. photos in *Bull. Soc. Française de Photogrammétrie,* 5, 1962, 21–2.

16   M.W. Beresford and J.K.S. St Joseph, *Medieval England on Aerial Survey* (Cambridge, 1958).

17   J.K.S. St Joseph, loc. cit., 283.

18   *Bull. Soc. Fr. de Photogrammétrie,* 5, 1962, 16.

19   As well as on quaternary deposits of gravel such as ancient coastlines.

Air reconnaissance: recent results, 41
by J.K. ST JOSEPH & D.R. WILSON
ANTIQUITY 50 (1976): 237–9

FIFTY years ago was for O.G.S. Crawford a time of great activity. His pioneer aerial reconnaissance of Wessex in conjunction with Alexander Keiller had taken place in the summer of 1924, and his report, with all the fieldwork that entailed, was in active preparation. *Wessex from the air* was published in 1928, and at the same time Crawford was assembling material for two *Ordnance Survey Professional Papers* published in 1928 and 1929. Nearly all the illustrations were vertical photographs, but while those in *Wessex from the air* had been taken specially for the purpose, most of the plates in the *Professional Papers* were photographs taken by the Royal Air Force and Crawford was to draw on the same source for a number of the air photographs that illustrated the early issues of ANTIQUITY beginning in 1927. Most of these photographs are of earthworks or of soil marks, and it is of interest to compare the illustrations in *Wessex from the air* with those in the *Professional Papers.* The first, being taken under carefully chosen conditions, having regard to the subject to be photographed, are on the whole the better in quality and more revealing in detail; the second, often chosen from runs of vertical photographs, demonstrate very well the value of such routine survey for archaeology in that they often revealed features previously quite unsuspected. A good example of this appears in the mapping of the so-called 'Celtic fields' over a considerable area of Hampshire: these are not only illustrated photographically but recorded on two folding plans at a 6-in scale, included at the end of *Professional Paper* 7 (Crawford, 1928). Meanwhile, popular attention was drawn to this new technique of reconnaissance by articles in the London *Observer* in 1923, on Celtic fields, and on the Stonehenge Avenue, while about this same time the *Illustrated London News* published vertical aerial photographs of such famous sites as Pompeii and Ur. A dramatic demonstration of the contribution that the new technique could make to Roman archaeology came a little later with the publication in 1929, in ANTIQUITY, of a photograph, taken by the Royal Air Force, of the Roman site at Caistor by Norwich, revealing for the first time the streets and buildings of a buried town in unexpected detail. This was amongst the first photographs, receiving wide publicity, to demonstrate the extraordinary sensitivity of certain cultivated crops to differences in the soil where they are growing.

Crawford had already gained great experience as a field archaeologist before the opportunity came for him to turn his attention to air photography. Before there was any opportunity for flying, he had noted the effect of oblique lighting in picking out earthworks by reason of the shadows they cast, and he has recorded how before flying was at all common he used to discuss with Dr Williams-Freeman, apropos of earthworks in Hampshire, the possibilities of an 'overhead view'. However, to obtain the maximum information from air photographs requires knowledge of the terrain, its geology and soils, and familiarity with comparable sites elsewhere, while for the air observer there is no substitute for the experience that can be gained only by scrutinizing the ground surface from a convenient height, usually a few thousand feet. It was his skill in fieldwork and his early appreciation of the importance of studying the impact of man on a landscape in widely

FIGURE 1. *Settlement and 'Celtic fields', S of Wonston, Hants., SU 471372 Scale 1:5000. 18 April 1972 (N is to the right).*

differing aspects, as seen in his first book *The Andover district* (1922),[1] together with his war-time flying experience as an observer in the Royal Flying Corps, that enabled Crawford to exploit aerial reconnaissance for archaeological research when opportunity came after the end of the war of 1914–18. The first writer well remembers too his infectious enthusiasm, particularly in describing sites previously unrecorded, as for example on the occasion of his aerial reconnaissance of south Scotland in 1939, while a good many letters in his characteristic style, written while he was engaged on fieldwork, survive to show his interest in many different aspects of whatever part of the country he happened to be studying.

That nearly all the early air photographs of archaeological sites were taken over Wessex was no chance, for nowhere else in southern England are there so many well preserved earthworks free of masking vegetation, while the chalk of Salisbury Plain afforded very suitable ground for the military airfields of the time. Many of the official photographs upon which Crawford was able to draw were taken by the School of Army Co-operation, then stationed at Old Sarum. Amongst this early material, photographs of large and well preserved hillforts perhaps have pride of place, if only for the reason that the entirely new point of view introduced by air photography could demonstrate the whole circuit of the defences in a way that could never be achieved on the ground. However, the defences of many hillforts were visibly upstanding, and the sites were already familiar as features of the landscape. Crawford himself was perhaps most intrigued with the remains of early agriculture. One of the six sections of *Wessex from the air* (pp. 124–69) is devoted to 'ancient fields', illustrated in eleven plates, one of them a vertical photograph of the remarkable Celtic fields on Bathampton Down; and Crawford returned to the same topic in 'Air survey and archaeology' (1928). There, the most remarkable photograph on this theme was the picture of 'Celtic fields' on Windmill Hill, Hampshire, seen as soil marks in early May, and similar photographs provided the information for the two pioneer maps of 'Celtic fields' included at the end of the volume. Crawford had also shown that air photographs could bring a fresh understanding of the relationship between 'Celtic fields' and other earthworks, for example, the hillforts on Bathampton Down (Somerset) and at Ogbury (Wiltshire) and the curious enclosure known as Soldiers Ring, in Hampshire, where the fields are demonstrably earlier than the enclosure. If hillforts and remains of ancient agriculture were thus firmly recognized as outstanding elements in the cultural landscape of Wessex, the question of prehistoric settlements, whether of family or larger groups, remained for the most part relatively unnoticed. Pitt-Rivers's excavations of the settlement sites on Cranborne Chase were a model of their kind (Pitt-Rivers, 1887–8), but it was some time before air reconnaissance was to give any idea of the variety and extent of these settlement sites, and even now singularly few photographs showing settlements in relation to 'Celtic fields' have been published. Crawford was indeed aware of the problem, and on his map of the 'Celtic field' system in central Hampshire, the sites of three 'Celtic villages' are marked, though with no details as to plan. One of the first such settlements that yielded photographs showing its position in relation to ancient fields was that on Gussage Hill, Dorset, where very clear soil marks were visible some thirty years ago after a first ploughing of the site. Considerably fuller understanding of the ancient agricultural systems of Dorset is now possible as a result of the Royal Commission's survey of the monuments of that county (RCHM, 1970–5).

---

1   *Man and his past* was published in 1921, but *The Andover district,* though not published till 1922, was written as a thesis for the Diploma in Geography at Oxford in 1910.

FIGURE 1 is a vertical photograph of a prehistoric, possibly Iron-Age, settlement in immediate relation to a system of 'Celtic fields'. The site, which lies south of Wonston (Hampshire) at the point SU 471372, has already been illustrated in these Notes (St Joseph, 1972), but the soil marks seen here, evidently photographed soon after the field had been ploughed, give a much clearer picture than has been available hitherto. In the main enclosure there is a suggestion of pennanular or ring-marks, perhaps for timbers to hold the wooden uprights of huts, or gulleys dug round such huts. A number of more or less circular dark marks 10–15 m in diameter are likely to represent 'working-hollows'. There is a certain evident resemblance to sites recorded at Pimperne (ST 892097) and on Gussage Hill (ST 992141) in Dorset. Even more interesting is the fact that this site immediately adjoins an extensive system of 'Celtic fields'. The boundary of the system comes within a very short distance of the south (left-hand) side of the settlement (FIGURE 1), and traces of the familiar banks outlining a number of fields appear beyond it.

Other photographs show that the 'Celtic fields' extend far to east and west. Amidst the fields, not far south of the settlement, there are marks suggestive of a round barrow and a long barrow in positions of which account may have been taken when the fields were laid out. The edge of the system of fields is no more than 15 m or 20 m from the outer ditch of the settlement. A dark line runs between the two: if this is a trench or ditch, there may be an opportunity here for digging to test their relationship. This particular site lies within the area of Crawford's 'Celtic field-system in central Hampshire' (1928, map), some 700 m W of West Stoke Farm, near the centre of the upper margin of his map, but evidently neither the settlement nor the immediately adjoining 'Celtic fields' were visible on photographs available in 1926. Indeed, only by photography repeated over years, and at different times of year, can a record of so extensive an agricultural system as these 'Celtic fields' approach reasonable completeness.

References

CRAWFORD, O.G.S. 1922. *The Andover district.*
    1928. Air survey and archaeology, OS. *Prof. Pap., 7.*
CRAWFORD, O.G.S. and KEILLER, A. 1928. *Wessex from the air.*
PITT-RIVERS, A. 1887–8. *Excavations on Cranborne Chase,* vols. I–II.
ST JOSEPH, J.K. 1972. Air reconnaissance: recent results, 28, *Antiquity,* XLVI, 224–6, Pl. XXXVId.
ROYAL COMMISSION on HISTORICAL MONUMENTS, *Inventory of Dorset* II–V, (1970–75).

3 Survey method and analysis

Surface survey technique has developed dramatically in sophistication over the last few decades. Flexible research designs have developed to recover spatial data. Methodologies have been enhanced and relatively accessible computerized techniques (loosely grouped under Geographical Information Systems (GIS)) have been adopted to work with large quantities of new data. These are the two themes illustrated here by selections from the pages of ANTIQUITY.

Much has been written on the appropriate methodology of survey since the 1970s (Parsons 1972; Ammerman 1981; Cherry 1983; Cambi & Terrenato 1994). The main debates have taken place in the Mediterranean and the United States. The British tradition (encountered in the first section) and the *Siedlungsarcheologie* tradition of continental Europe have, with some exceptions (Shennan 1985; Gaffney *et al.* 1985), been less concerned with these issues, concentrating on the accumulated record of landscape information. In Mediterranean and American survey, with offshoots in Africa (Foley 1981), several debates have predominated: intensive *vs* extensive survey, continuous *vs* discrete coverage and the definition of the region under study. The general trend has been towards increasingly intensive survey of smaller regions, particularly in Greece, where there has been some convergence of approach between some Anglo-American practitioners (Bintliff & Snodgrass 1985; Cherry *et al.* 1991). Other surveys have adopted a more pragmatic approach to the areas covered, although sharing trends towards increasing intensity (Jameson *et al.* 1994; Mee & Forbes 1997). A second important trend has been towards more continuous coverage of landscapes, critically assessing the concept of the 'site' and replacing the site with studies of varying densities of land use (Foley 1981; Bintliff & Snodgrass 1988b). Finally, the sources of inaccuracy in the surface record have been of increasing concern. To control for this a series of measures including geomorphological study, analysis of visibility and quantification of observer error have been increasingly included in most surveys (e.g. Hodder & Malone 1984; Shennan 1985).

The article by Schofield addresses one particular question: the representativity of material found on the surface during survey. The issue of representativity is an especially apposite question for the fragile material studied: early medieval pottery. In this context he defines 'major factors responsible for shaping a surface pottery question': quantity in circulation, quality, landscape taphonomy, use and discard, intensity of collection and agricultural processes. Schofield concludes that the control of negative results is to be achieved by intensity of collection and complementary approaches of geophysics, documentary study, and, where funds allow, subsurface investigation. Site formation processes are identified as key. Further work by Schofield (1990) has aimed to make a more precise definition of the problem and similar issues have been addressed by one of the Populus Project (funded by the EU) volumes addressing the archaeology of the Mediterranean landscape (Francovich & Patterson 2000). Ultimately greater integration with sampled subsurface structures will have to be implemented as the principal solution in deciding whether a single sherd represents a dense concentration or a land-use activity such as manuring. With other materials, such as lithics, Schofield (1987) comes to the conclusion that the relative robustness of the artefacts requires a remodelling of our conception of domesticity in the Neolithic. More work still needs to be undertaken on the consequences of differences in the representativity of material culture on the surface.

Geographical Information Systems (GIS) allow the analytical comparison of layers of mapped data: topography, geology, pedology, hydrology and archaeological evidence itself. There is now an established record of archaeological application, making many of the standard studies of 1960s landscape studies routine and rapid, *once* the data are collected and arranged in a number of standard formats (Allen *et. al.* 1990; Gaffney & Stančič 1991; Lock & Stančič 1995; Gillings *et al.* 1999). However, GIS has not always kept pace with the move towards the study of a continuous landscape discussed above. It often continues to employ a concept of individual sites or monuments (Gaffney & van Leusen 1995). Furthermore, the strong presence of physical information and the availability of standard routines at the touch of a button have led to an emphasis on environmental determinism and a corresponding absence of attention to the cultural dimensions of landscape (including time). These restrictions of GIS-based approaches have been much criticized (Gaffney & van Leusen 1995; Wansleeben & Verhart 1997). Solutions developed to counter this trend have tended to concentrate on vision as an important constituent of any cultural landscape. Cumulative viewsheds (Wheatley 1995) and contrasts between accessibility and visibility (Belcher *et al.* 1999) have received some attention, but it must be debated whether GIS can yet serve the purpose of many new theoretical approaches (Section 7). The problems have been raised but not yet solved (Witcher 1999).

The article by Llobera represents one of a number of attempts to achieve a more humanistic use of GIS. Whereas many practitioners have concentrated on methodological issues, Llobera attempts to bridge the divide between the latest social theory and computerized techniques. He defined topographic characteristics of human interest and then mapped them in his study area. To this he added the highly human concern of visibility. The article has recently been critiqued by Webster (1999) in the pages of ANTIQUITY. The ultimate problem is that a GIS package standardizes and generalizes the individuality inherent in much modern social theory. In defense of Llobera, standardization can at least be expressed more explicitly in a GIS context than in many of the 'ethnographic' archaeological accounts undertaken in some of the new theoretical studies of landscape. GIS requires explicit statements of assumptions which cannot be so readily concealed under layers of elaborate literary language. At best ambiguity and vagueness can be banished. At worst, the conclusions are mechanical and unexciting, leading to reductionism. Not all work is explicit about the sample and the representativity of information.

Understanding early medieval pottery distributions

by A.J. SCHOFIELD

ANTIQUITY 63 (240), 1989

THE QUANTITY and quality of early medieval pottery recovered by surface collection is sufficiently variable that many archaeologists are reluctant to accept isolated finds as anything more than 'background noise', preferring instead to examine the more visible elements defined by regional survey. But should isolated finds, recovered through systematic collection, really be regarded as 'rubbish data' in the light of recent debate concerning off-site scatters in other periods (e.g. Foley 1981; Bintliff & Snodgrass 1988; Schofield 1987)? It is towards this question that the paper is directed.

Three questions arise:

1. Why are there regional variations in the quantity of pottery visible on the field surface?
2. Are we justified in our tendency to focus attention more on pottery concentrations than on isolated finds?
3. How might the 'rubbish data', the isolated finds recovered by systematic collection, be made both useful and usable?

In order to tackle these questions we need to establish a fuller understanding of what early medieval (i.e. pre-Conquest) pottery distributions represent in terms both of the quantity of pottery recovered and of its distribution within the landscape. The use of results from excavation is seen as a key factor in this respect and a valid 'control' for surface investigations.

Causes of variation in surface distributions

A number of well-documented factors determine the quantity of early medieval pottery recovered by surface collection: the amount of pottery in circulation; the nature of the pottery; landscape taphonomy; use and discard behaviour; the scale and intensity of collection and agricultural activity. These will be considered in two sections, looking first at visibility and second at formation processes and the collection strategy.

The survival and visibility of pottery

Three factors influence the survival and visibility of pottery:

The amount of pottery in circulation

Millett (1987; 1991) has suggested that total pottery supply and differential access to pottery supply are both period- and regionally-defined. For example, Vince (1988) has demonstrated that the Welsh Marches and West Midlands managed without pottery from after AD 400 until six centuries later. Yet in the East Midlands, large amounts of pottery were in circulation during these centuries. Similarly, access to pottery supplies could vary between settlements within a region, according to the nature of the exchange system in operation and/or local communications and the wealth, status and independence of individual communities. For example, pottery distributed from a production centre by river or coastal trade routes may follow a pattern of directional trading. Settlements located in a position to take advantage of such communication routes, will be more likely to receive larger quantities of pottery from such centres of production than sites in a less advantageous setting. If settlements in less privileged trading positions were more independent, home-based production may generate equally large amounts of pottery but of a different quality and life-expectancy. If the pottery is both more available and of lower quality, more is likely to be used, broken and finally discarded.

The production of Ipswich Ware and the pottery collections from East Anglia may present an example of directional trading. Production was centred on the *wic* at Ipswich between the 7th and 9th centuries AD (Smedley & Owles 1963), while the distribution of finds appears to follow a pattern throughout East Anglia based on rivers and the coast (Dunmore *et al.* 1975). At Hay Green, Terrington St Clement, Norfolk, Rogerson & Silvester (1986: 320) collected 999 sherds from an area of 7 ha, a total of 143 sherds per ha despite the site being over 80 km from Ipswich. While other factors may be partly responsible for such a high recovery, proximity to a river system and thus a possible trade link with the production centre, is considered a major influence in this case. West Stow, on the other hand, appears closer to the production centre (*c.* 50 km) yet is situated on a river system *not* connected with the East Suffolk coast. In this case the total number of Ipswich Ware sherds was only 381 from an excavated area of 1·8 ha, substantially less than the figure from Hay Green, although in the case of West Stow, Ipswich Ware only appeared in the later phases of occupation (West 1985: 137). If we attempt to compare the figures in terms of the number likely to appear on the surface of ploughed fields at any one time (see below), the recovery rate of Ipswich Ware sherds across the site at West Stow would appear as 9·5 per ha, assuming intensive collection. Furthermore, as most of the Ipswich Ware occurred in a cultural layer covering the entire site, a general scatter rather than discrete concentrations would result. In the case of Hay Green the figure is 143 sherds. It is also worth noting that numerous other sites in Norfolk have produced similarly high figures (e.g. Wade Martins 1980a).

At West Stow the quantity of other wares, most likely home-produced, is substantial; West provides a figure of 53,189 sherds from the excavated area of 1·8 ha (1985: 128). If 90% of the pottery was within the plough soil (after Gingell & Schadla Hall 1981) and if 5% of that total was recovered by surface collection (see below) the corresponding quantity from surface survey would be 2411, or 1330 sherds per ha. Either West Stow was exceptional in the quantity of pottery it produced or some other factor is at work. Other sites with home or local production have produced nothing like this quantity. At Cowdery's Down, for example, only 146 abraded and chronologically undiagnostic sherds were recovered (Millett & James 1983: 255), while at Chalton only 30 sherds were recorded.

Millett's suggestion that production will vary both in time and space has major implications for understanding the apparent discrepancy between the recovery of pottery in East Anglia and the south of England. Indeed he suggests that limited or no access to pottery may explain why so few early medieval settlements have been recovered by surface collection in this area (1991).

Finally, political factors may also influence access and supply. Millett (1987: 106) notes the difference between ceramic assemblages from forts of Hadrian's Wall in the 2nd century AD and those from contemporary farmsteads in the region. The forts, with access to a Romanized exchange network, received large quantities of factory-made pottery from a wide geographical area. The farmsteads rarely have more than a handful of sherds.

The quality of pottery
The grass-tempered ware of the early medieval period is soft and friable, as is pottery from the Neolithic and Iron Age. Much Roman pottery as well as Ipswich Ware and the home-produced pottery from West Stow is hard and well-fired. In survey it is often the case that blanks usually associated with the Neolithic, Iron Age and early medieval periods correspond to the poor quality pottery being produced at that time. A comparison of Roman and early medieval pottery recovered by surface collection in the south of England certainly suggests this to be the case. The East Hampshire survey, for example, produced 233 Romano-British sherds and three possible early medieval sherds (Shennan 1985: 81; Oake & Shennan 1985: 89); The Maddle Farm survey produced Romano-British sherd densities of up to 50 per ha while only five early medieval sherds were found (Gaffney & Tingle 1989: 209, 245). The same applies within a site. At the early medieval settlement at Bishopstone, Sussex (Bell 1977: 197) fabric 1, a hard sandy ware, comprised 311 of the 328 sherds from structure XLVIII and 84·5% of the total collection; fabrics 2 and 3 were of inferior quality and less numerous. Is this the result of differential survival, or was the better-quality pottery used more intensively?

Experiments by Reynolds (1982) have produced clear indications of pottery fragmentation, possibly by as much as 60% over 10 years, and common sense suggests that natural agents such as frost will break up the less well-fired material more readily. Indeed, by a process of soaking, freezing and defrosting, Swain (1988) subjected sherds to the equivalent of between 3·75 and 7·50 years of weathering (assuming between 20 and 40 frosts per year). The results, though limited, have major implications; for example, the main factor determining survival was the fabric type, some Iron Age sherds surviving better than others, and medieval and Roman surviving better than Neolithic.

Both this and the experiments being conducted at the Butzer Farm Project (Reynolds 1982; 1989) are important to understanding regional variations in pottery density. More such studies are needed if results are to be fully integrated into the interpretation of regional survey. It might be possible to suggest, for example, that fabric x will survive 10 times better than fabric y, providing a comparative yardstick against which to assess the quantity recovered. Ultimately a full catalogue of the survival rates of pottery types and fabric groups should be compiled for this purpose.

Landscape taphonomy
The landscape itself is a major factor affecting visibility and recovery, especially the intensity and type of modern farming. But survival is irrelevant in this context if the material is not *visible* to standard methods of prospection. In the south of England, for example, colluviation has masked medieval occupation beneath a significant depth of soil, thereby making it invisible to surface investigations. In the middle Avon valley, west Hampshire, Smith (n.d.) observed Victorian pottery beneath 0·2 m of colluvium (i.e. the depth of ploughsoil), while at Kiln Combe, East Sussex, Drewett & Freke (1982) record the structural remains of medieval farmsteads buried by up to 0·5 m of colluvium.

At the opposite end of the scale, 'packing' of pottery within the ploughsoil will be reflected on the surface. Where a thinner ploughsoil exists and where occupation levels have been integrated into the ploughsoil (e.g. a downland hilltop), density of pottery within it may be exaggerated. The principle also works the other way. Thinner soils may reflect land which has been intensively farmed, and therefore where pottery is more likely to have been destroyed by fragmentation (Reynolds 1982).

Formation processes and the collection strategy

Formation processes refer to those factors which create a pottery assemblage within the cultural system. Here they concern the distribution of pottery within settlements or the surrounding area, i.e. both on- and off-site material. How is each produced and in what proportions? What types of activity are represented in an off-site scatter and are they of sufficient intensity to be represented on the surface, despite all destructive processes listed above? Can we offer at least an educated guess as to whether a surface concentration represents habitation, discard or manuring? Three aspects need to be considered: a) what is the 'life-story' of a sherd in an early medieval settlement, and where does it end up? b) how does the collection strategy control the character of the distribution? c) how far do environmental conditions affect artefact distributions in terms of location and the relationship with sub-surface remains?

Use and discard behaviour

This aspect, prominent in prehistoric archaeology, is still untapped for the medieval period (but see Brown 1988: 123). Yet, as Brown suggests, disposal patterns can identify areas of specialized activity within the house or village, and could relate them spatially. Similarly, discard behaviour could indicate the economic status of households; the more rubbish produced, the more they owned (Brown 1988: 121).

Early medieval pottery may derive from three main contexts: rubbish disposal, occupation, and manuring. The extent to which each is represented by surface collection may only be estimated in the light of figures from excavation. It is on this basis that the following models are suggested:

Hypothesis

There exists in early medieval rural settlements, a tendency towards formal rubbish disposal in specified zones away from the domestic unit (FIGURE 1b). The zones may be in rubbish pits and/or ditches (in which the majority of pottery would be disposed), on dumps or middens, for example at Maxey (Crowther 1983) and implied by the absence of pits and the small number of ditches in the early medieval settlement at Cowdery's Down (Millett & James), and/or through manuring. Evidence for this model stems from sites such as Chalton, from which excavation of domestic units produced only 30 sherds (Addyman et al. 1972), from Wicken Bonhunt (Wade 1974: 89) and Meonstoke (Hughes pers. comm.), where the bulk of early medieval settlement lay outside the main pottery concentrations, and from the excavation of areas around St Neots. In this case only pits and ditches were recorded, but nevertheless produced a far greater sherd density than for those sites listed above (Addyman 1969). Indeed Addyman (1969: 77) further suggested that boundary ditches functioned as 'sporadic dumping grounds' for many years, while rubbish pits were only open for a few weeks. Similarly, the Middle Saxon ditches at North Elmham contained large quantities of domestic refuse while rubbish pits were rare (Wade Martins 1980b: 119). By this model the majority of surface finds would represent rubbish disposal areas, with a minority representing manuring and only a very small proportion of material remains suggestive of occupation areas (for an example of formal discard in a post-medieval context, see Mytum 1988). A notable exception might be settlements containing a predominance of sunken-featured buildings. Where the floor was raised above an open space and pottery was used in the building, breakage would result in accidental loss and/or deliberate discard beneath the floor. An alternative suggestion, particularly relevant at Cowdery's Down where floors were apparently well-made (Millett pers. comm.), concerns the re-use of sunken-featured buildings as rubbish pits. Excavation would produce a random distribution of artefacts within the structure, while surface collection would produce localized high-density scatters similar to those representative of pits. At West Stow, West (1985: 118) has observed, 'the lower fill (of the sunken-featured buildings) often contained considerable quantities of pottery, objects and animal bones, usually distributed in a haphazard way'.

Null hypothesis

Rubbish disposal was a random process occurring in general zones in and around the settlement unit (FIGURE 1a), intensity of discard tending to decline with distance from the centre of occupation. Surface remains should appear as a general pottery distribution without obvious breaks separating on-site activity, pit clusters and manuring activity.

The results of excavation suggest the hypothesis to be upheld; greater densities of pottery occur in the pits and ditches surrounding domestic units rather than in the occupation areas themselves. Where pottery does occur in large proportions associated with structures and habitation (as may be argued for West Stow, above), high pottery production rates may be suggested as a possible explanation, while loss and discard beneath the floors of sunken-featured buildings or their re-use as rubbish pits are alternative suggestions.

Human activity will tend to be represented by early medieval pottery in the following proportions (expressed as total quantity in circulation within a settlement):

> rubbish disposal > manuring > habitation

However through surface collection the concentration of less pottery within the smaller area taken up by habitation would produce a higher density than the larger quantity covering several hectares resulting from manure spreading. Expressed in terms of density per unit area, the following proportions apply:

> rubbish disposal > habitation > manuring

Intensity of collection

This leads into a further point. 'Site' and 'settlement' are two terms widely used in the description and presentation of survey results, yet their usefulness depends on the intensity of collection. 'Sites' at one scale might be easy to define; delimiting a settlement on a 1:50,000 map should be fairly straightforward. Yet with surface collection, finding the edge may be more difficult; when does the off-site background scatter become the 'site'?

With early medieval settlement the problem has already been partly defined. Most pottery from surface collection will be representative of formal discard activities within the settlement unit; much lower proportions will be indicative of habitation itself. But the extent to which this may be recognized will depend largely on the intensity of collection. Let us illustrate this question with two hypothetical examples (FIGURE 2).

In the first case, fields were investigated by line-walking at 15-m intervals (FIGURE 2a). One scatter of early medieval pottery was encountered within field X, and a distinction drawn, by density alone, between 'off-site' and 'on-site' areas. A concentration is defined although the three types of activity from which pottery scatters result could not be distinguished.

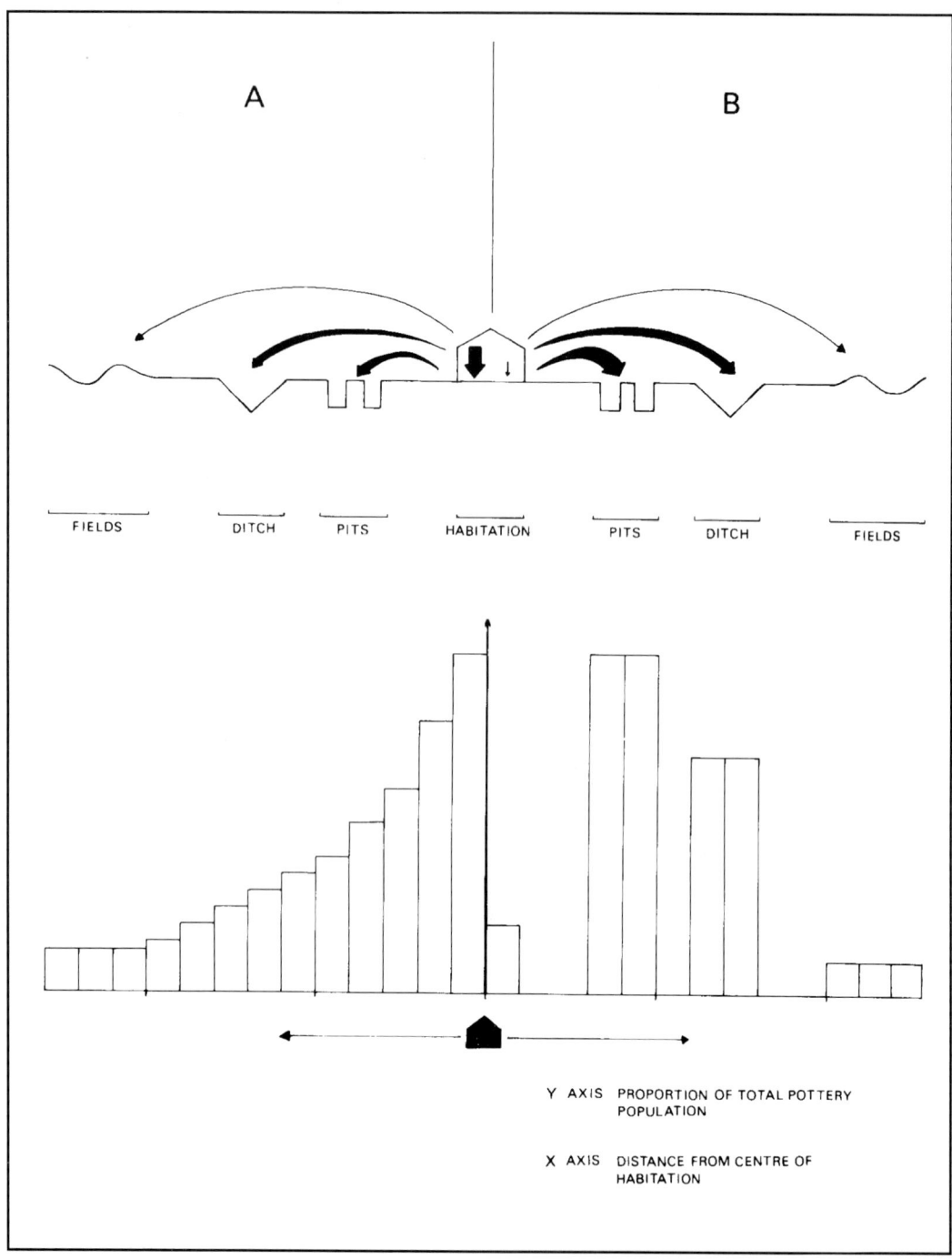

FIGURE 1a. *Pattern resulting from random pottery dispersal within the settlement unit. Quantity will show a tendency to decline with distance from the centre of habitation outwards.*
1b. *Pattern resulting from structured deposition. Discard will be targeted towards specific areas with the result that high density will occur in discrete zones away from the nodes of habitation.*

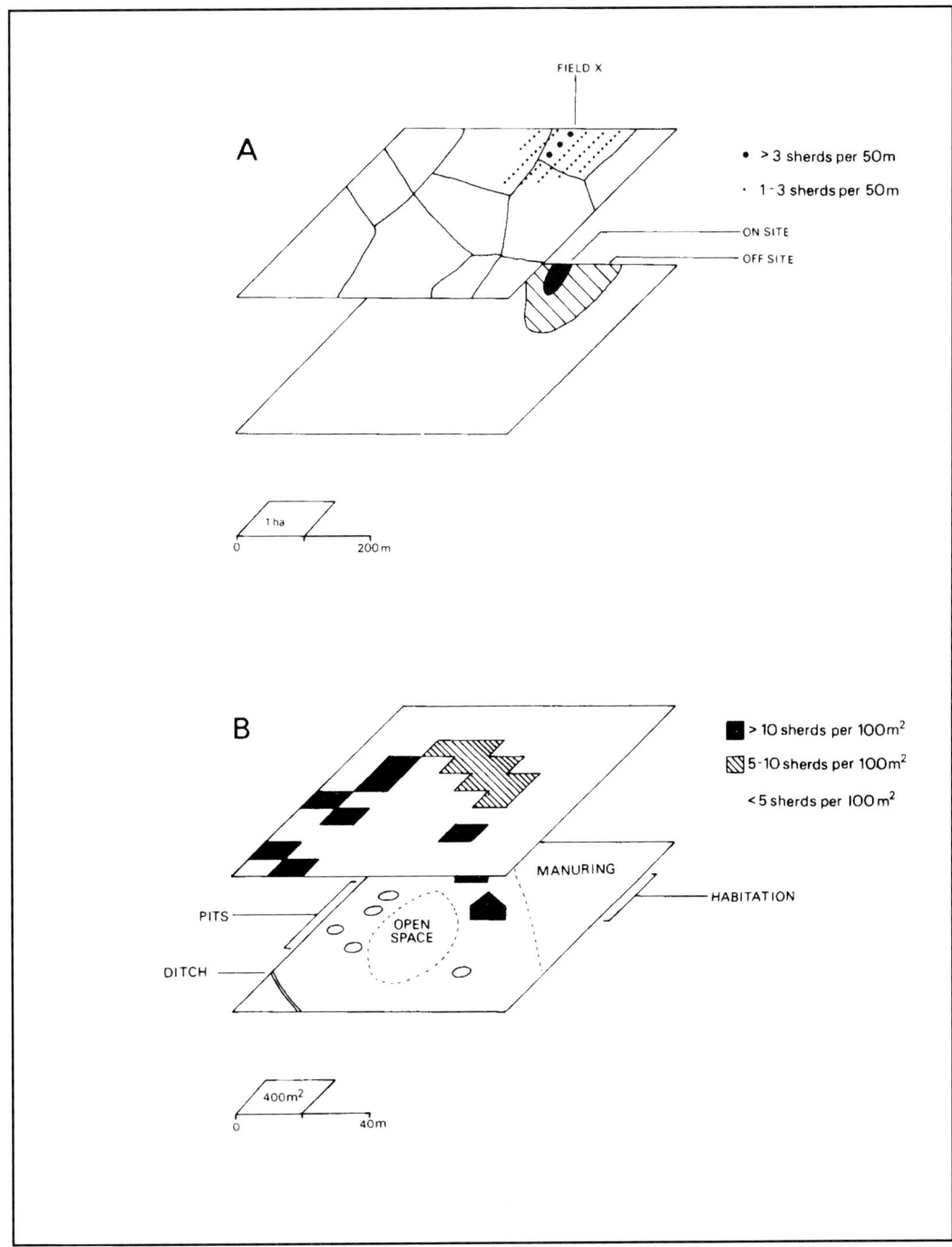

FIGURE 2a. *Example of pottery distribution resulting from extensive regional survey. The top plate represents the archaeological distribution (the observation) and the bottom plate the type of reconstruction which may result (the interpretation).*

2b. *Example of pottery distribution resulting from area-intensive survey (field X from* FIGURE 2a). *The two plates are designed as before. Note the levels of interpretation possible under varying levels of observation.*

In a second hypothetical example, field X was investigated by a 10-m grid (FIGURE 2b). In this case three density scales were created to distinguish high (on-site discard), medium (on-site habitation) and low (off-site manuring). An additional density scale was introduced for this level of investigation as the greater spatial control provided by a 10-m grid allows actual patterns of occupation to be defined. Again it is proportions that are important, although comparison may be drawn between FIGURE 2b, the distributions presented by Williamson (1988: figure 7·2) and that projected for the hypothesis presented above (FIGURE 1b). Similarities at this scale are valid as the levels of enquiry are comparable.

Advantages can be seen in both methods of investigation. The former provides a general view of occupation and landscape evolution in which areas that were a focus of attention in specific periods may be outlined, at least where the pottery is chronologically reliable. Intensive collection is a more major undertaking, but worthwhile. The additional spatial information provided by gridded collection could reflect environmental processes (Boismier & Reilly 1988) or indicate the structure of an underlying settlement. Where much pottery is in circulation or has survived this is surely a profitable exercise.

Agricultural processes
Other factors may determine the final distribution of pottery on the surface. Of great significance is lateral displacement, both on slopes and flat surfaces.

Plough-zone experiments conducted in England (Clark & Schofield 1991; Reynolds 1989), Italy (Ammerman 1985) and North America (Lewarch 1979; Odell & Cowan 1987) suggest that lateral displacement occurs on flat surfaces and that movement will be cumulative. The actual distances involved are often limited, and the idea of a 'rocking motion' caused by seasonal variation in ploughing supports this. Experiments by Allen (forthcoming) on slopes of the Sussex Downs showed that, once fluvial energy is significant enough to move small objects, pottery displays the greatest tendency to movement of all classes of artefact. Boismier & Reilly (1988: 224) make the same point in plotting the distribution of modern pottery from Fair Oak, Hampshire against topography. Immediately apparent are a concentration at the top of the slope and a lesser concentration at the bottom. The thinner soil (and thus higher artefact density per unit soil) may account for the major concentration being upslope, while soil creep, as suggested by Allen (1991), would account for the 'spillage' at the bottom.

Discussion: the future for 'rubbish data'
These are the major factors responsible for shaping a surface pottery distribution. Does that imply that isolated finds represent such 'rubbish data' that attention should be focused on the more pronounced concentrations? And how can we further enhance our ability to understand surface distributions? Can 'rubbish data' be converted into useful and usable information?

To illustrate the potential importance of isolated finds (in this case single sherds), the results of excavations in southern and eastern England were compared with plough-zone experiments. Gingell & Schadla Hall (1981) suggest that 90% of a sub-soil assemblage disturbed by ploughing will appear in the ploughsoil. Experiments, conducted by Ammerman (1985), Lewarch (1979), Odell & Cowan (1987), and Clark & Schofield (1991) under very different environmental conditions, produced a consistent score of around 5% for the proportion of the ploughsoil assemblage visible on the surface. And 20% of that 5% figure is recovered by line-walking at 15-m intervals. Applying these figures in

site	observed pottery total	expected no. in ploughsoil	expected no. on surface	expected no. recovered by line-walking (15 m)
West Stow	53,570	48,213	2,411	409
Maxey	270	243	12	2
Cowdery's Down	146	131	7	1
Chalton	30	27	1	0

TABLE 1. *The results of selected excavations in southern England when compared with plough-zone experiments. Note that the expected number of sherds recovered by line-walking is for an area approximating to that of the excavated unit.*

relation to selected excavations in southern England gives the results presented in TA-BLE 1.

West Stow clearly stands out, readily identifiable as a major and important pottery concentration (West 1985). From Maxey, however, an early medieval settlement from which 270 sherds were derived (Addyman 1964: 47), only two sherds might be recorded by extensive collection. For Cowdery's Down, from which 146 abraded and chronologi-cally undiagnostic sherds were recovered (Millett & James 1983: 255), only one sherd might be recorded. From Chalton the chance of recovering a single sherd would be 1 in 5, assuming collection at 15-m intervals over an area of 450 sq. m (after Addyman *et al.* 1972). Yet surface collection prior to excavation at Chalton did produce quantities of pottery greater than the expected value. This may have been for three reasons: collection over a wider area; collection from areas corresponding to zones of off-site rubbish dis-posal; and collection under ideal conditions (after plough soil had been washed by rain) and on more than one occasion (Cunliffe 1972: 2).

As Williamson has observed (1985: 52), a tiny rate of recovery poses considerable problems for the interpretation of negative results from fieldwalking. One sherd may represent a settlement or it may result from manuring activity. In the East Hampshire survey only three possible early medieval sherds were recovered by line walking (Oake & Shennan 1985: 89) while Williamson's (1985) survey in East Anglia recovered by in-tensive collection between 4 and 6 sherds, which were considered representative of early medieval occupation. So are individual sherds 'rubbish data'? As long as they remain individual sherds without any understanding of context, yes they are; they are both unusable and unreliable. It is impossible to say what a single sherd means, except that it *might* be another Chalton or Cowdery's Down.

To answer these questions, research must focus on the specific question concerning early medieval settlement, both at a regional scale and in terms of individual locations. Where a pottery scatter is encountered, more intensive collection could attain greater spatial control over the distribution. Other prospection methods can be employed, soil phosphate analysis for example (Faull & Smith 1980), magnetometer survey (Hinchliffe 1986) or small test-pit excavations combined with geophysical prospection (see Schofield (1991) for an example of such an approach employed on post-medieval pottery distribu-tions). Place-name evidence may be considered as may the distribution of other finds classes such as burnt stone, animal bone etc. Each approach can be applied at a variety of scales, either for site location or site delimitation (Heron & Gaffney 1987: 74). But most important, we need to know how behaviour was organized within the sites themselves. Was rubbish disposal a structured process, or was garbage scattered wherever convenient?

The chances are that 'rubbish data' will prove significant if further investigated. In the majority of cases, however, this will prove impossible. It may be too costly in the case of research projects; there may not be time in rescue and evaluation work. The danger, then, might be that important settlements (the Chaltons and Maxeys of this land) might be ignored at the expense of other sites which appeared more visible purely by the 'luck of the landscape', for example better qualities for the preservation of pottery, or because the region as a whole maintained higher levels of pottery circulation or produced pottery of higher survivability. The situation might then arise where settlement X yielded large quantities of surface pottery but produced no structural remains, while settlement Y yielded one surface sherd and spectacular sub-surface archaeology.

The Society for Medieval Archaeology (1987) recently recommended to HBMC (English Heritage) that:

1   the entire landscape should be investigated, not merely fragmented parts of it;
2   minor rural settlements are insufficiently understood, and
3   the classification of artefacts is not the end of their study.

On the first two points a selection of all known surface scatters, irrespective of size or density, should be further investigated by methods such as those described above. To enhance our understanding of those scatters the third recommendation must be upheld with a particular emphasis towards site-formation processes.

This is the time to decide what early medieval pottery distributions represent and which, if any, are worth further investigation. To ignore surface artefact distributions would be disastrous; to investigate and thus select only the 'best' examples would distort the archaeological map and ignore a substantial literature dealing with the reasons why regional variations, both in quality and quantity, arise. Single sherds may be 'rubbish data' in one region, but not necessarily in another. Let us therefore ensure that, in the case of surface distributions, it is cultural and environmental aspects of the early medieval landscape that determine which examples are further investigated, not simply the density of sherds visible on the surface.

Acknowledgements. I am grateful to Duncan Brown, Tim Darvill, David Hinton, Mike Hughes, Martin Millett and Martin Oake for commenting on earlier drafts of this paper. All views expressed are however my own.

References

ADDYMAN, P. 1964. A Dark Age settlement at Maxey, Northamptonshire, *Medieval Archaeology* 8: 20–73.
    1969. Late Saxon settlements in the St Neots area, *Proceedings of the Cambridge Antiquarian Society* 62: 59–93.
ADDYMAN, P., D. LEIGH & M.F. HUGHES. 1972. Anglo-Saxon houses at Chalton, Hampshire, *Medieval Archaeology* 16: 13–32.
ALLEN, M.J. 1991. Analysing the landscape: a geographical approach to archaeological problems, in Schofield (ed.): 39–57.
AMMERMAN, A.J. 1985. Ploughzone experiments in Calabria, Italy, *Journal of Field Archaeology* 12: 33–40.
BELL, M. 1977. The Anglo-Saxon period, in M. Bell, Excavations at Bishopstone, Sussex, *Sussex Archaeological Collections* 115: 193–241.
BINTLIFF, J. & A. SNODGRASS. 1988. Off-site pottery distributions: a regional and interregional perspective, *Current Anthropology* 29: 506–13.
BOISMIER, W.A. & P. REILLY. 1988. Expanding the role of computer graphics in the analysis of survey data, in C.L.N. Ruggles & S.P.Q. Rahtz (ed.), *Computer and quantitative methods in archaeology 1987*: 221–5. Oxford: British Archaeological Reports. International series 393.
BROWN, D.H. 1988. Finds in medieval archaeology, *Scottish Archaeological Review* 5: 120–4.
CLARK, R.H. & A.J. SCHOFIELD. 1991. By experiment and calibration: an integrated approach to archaeology of the ploughsoil, in Schofield (ed.): 93–105.
CROWTHER, D.R. 1983. Old landsurfaces and modern ploughsoil: implications of recent work at Maxey, Cambs., *Scottish Archaeological Review* 2: 31–44.

CUNLIFFE, B. 1972. Saxon and medieval settlement pattern in the region of Chalton, Hants., *Medieval Archaeology* 16: 1–12.

DREWETT, P. & D. FREKE. 1982. The medieval farm, in P. Drewett, *The archaeology of Bullock Down, Eastbourne, East Sussex: the development of a landscape*: 143–92. Lewes: Sussex Archaeological Society Monograph 1.

DUNMORE, S., V. GRAY, T. LOADER & K. WADE. 1975. The origin and development of Ipswich: an interim report, *East Anglian Archaeology* 1: 57–67.

FAULL, M.L. & R.T. SMITH. 1980. Phosphate analysis and three possible Dark Age sites in Yorkshire, *Landscape Archaeology* 2: 21–38.

FOLEY, R. 1981. A model of regional archaeological structure, *Proceedings of the Prehistoric Society* 47: 1–17.

GAFFNEY, V. & M. TINGLE. 1989. *The Maddle Farm Project: an integrated survey of Prehistoric and Roman landscapes on the Berkshire Downs.* Oxford: British Archaeological Reports. British series 200.

GINGELL, C. & R.T. SCHADLA HALL. 1980. Excavations at Bishops Cannings Down, 1976, in J. Hinchliffe & R.T. Schadla Hall (ed.), *The past under the plough*: 109–13. London: HMSO. DoE Occasional publications 3.

HERON, C.P. & C.F. GAFFNEY. 1987. Archaeogeophysics and the site: ohm sweet ohm, in C.F. Gaffney & V.L. Gaffney (ed.), *Pragmatic archaeology: theory in crisis*: 71–81. Oxford: British Archaeological Reports. British series 167.

HINCHLIFFE, J. 1986. An early medieval settlement at Cowage Farm, Foxley, near Malmesbury, *Archaeological Journal* 143: 240–259.

LEWARCH, D.E. 1979. Effects of tillage on artefact patterning: a preliminary assessment, in M.J. O'Brien & R.E. Warren (ed.), *Cannon Reservoir Human Ecology Project: a regional approach to cultural continuity and change*: 101–49. Lincoln: University of Nebraska, Division of Archaeological Research. Technical Report 79–14.

MILLETT, M.J. 1987. A question of time? aspects of the future of pottery studies, *Bulletin of the Institute of Archaeology* 24: 99–108.

1991. Pottery: population or supply patterns? the Ager Tarraconensis approach, in G. Barker (ed.), *Roman agrarian structure: archaeological survey in the Mediterranean*: 18–26. Rome: British School at Rome. Supplementary publication.

MILLETT, M.J. & S. JAMES. 1983. Excavations at Cowdery's Down, Hampshire, 1978–1981, *Archaeological Journal* 140: 151–279.

MYTUM, H. 1988. The Clydach Valley: a 19th century landscape, *Archaeology Today* 9: 33–7.

OAKE, M. & S. SHENNAN. 1985. The Saxon and medieval periods, in S. Shennan, *Experiments in the collection and analysis of archaeological survey data: the East Hampshire survey*: 89–104. Sheffield: Sheffield University Press.

ODELL, G.H. & F. COWAN. 1987. Estimating tillage effects on artefact distributions, *American Antiquity* 52: 456–84.

REYNOLDS, P.J. 1982. The ploughzone, in *Festschrift zum 100 jahrigen jubiläum der abteilung vorgeschichte der Naturhistorischen Gesellschaft Nürnberg*: 315–40. Nürnberg.

1989. Sherd movement in the ploughzone, *British Archaeology* 13: 24–7.

ROGERSON, A. & R.J. SILVESTER. 1986. Middle Saxon occupation at Hay Green, Terrington St Clement, *Norfolk Archaeology* 39: 320–2.

SCHOFIELD, A.J. 1987. Putting lithics to the test: non-site analysis and the Neolithic settlement of southern England, *Oxford Journal of Archaeology* 6: 269–86.

(Ed.). 1991. *Interpreting artefact scatters.* Oxford: Oxbow.

Forthcoming. Archaeological fieldwork 1988: the results of test-pit excavations and geophysical prospection south of Quarter Wall, *Annual Report of the Lundy Field Society* 39.

SMEDLEY, N. & E. OWLES. 1963. Some Suffolk kilns: IV Saxon kilns in Cox Lane, Ipswich, 1961, *Proceedings of the Suffolk Institute of Archaeology and History* 29: 304–35.

SMITH, R.W. n.d. Ploughzone formation processes and some suggestions for recording broken and buried landscapes. Paper given at TAG, 1984, Cambridge.

SOCIETY FOR MEDIEVAL ARCHAEOLOGY. 1987. Recommendations by the Society for Medieval Archaeology to the Historic Buildings and Monuments Commission for England, *Medieval Archaeology* 31: 1–12.

SWAIN, H. 1988. Pottery survival in the field: some initial results of experiments in frost shattering, *Scottish Archaeological Review* 5: 87–9.

VINCE, A. 1988. Did they use pottery in the Welsh Marches and the West Midlands between the 5th and 12th centuries AD?, in A. Burl (ed.), *From Roman town to Norman castle: essays in honour of Philip Barker*: 40–55. Birmingham: University of Birmingham, Department of Extra Mural Studies.

WADE, K. 1974. Whither Anglo-Saxon settlement archaeology?, in T. Rowley (ed.), *Anglo-Saxon settlement and landscape*: 87–92. Oxford: British Archaeological Reports. British series 6.

WADE MARTINS, P. 1980a. Fieldwork and excavation on village sites in Launditch Hundred, Norfolk, *East Anglian Archaeology* 10.

1980b. Excavations in North Elmham Park, 1967–72, *East Anglian Archaeology* 9.

WEST, S. 1985. West Stow: the Anglo-Saxon village, *East Anglian Archaeology* 24.

WILLIAMSON, T. 1985. Sites in the landscape: approaches to the post-Roman settlement of south-eastern England, *Archaeological Review from Cambridge* 4: 51–64.

1988. Settlement chronology and regional land-use: the evidence for the claylands of East Anglia, in D. Hooke (ed.), *Anglo-Saxon settlements*: 153–75. Oxford: Basil Blackwell.

Exploring the topography of mind:
GIS, social space and archaeology
by **MARCOS LLOBERA**
ANTIQUITY 70 (260), 1996

THE STUDY of human space in past archaeological research rested on strong empirical methodologies. However, the theoretical premises underlying these models were often very weak including a strong *reductionism* and *normative* elements. Current landscape (regional) archaeology works incorporate sophisticated accounts of how spaces/places are created and their impact on the individual but lack formal methodology. Some preliminary thoughts are included here on the way GIS may be used (in a more humanistic way) in order to close the gap between method and theory. Some of these ideas are explored using an example from the Wessex linear ditches study (Bradley *et al.* 1994).

This paper aims to show the potential of Geographic Information Systems (GIS) in the light of current anthropological approaches to landscape. It follows from an attempt to break free from the environmental determinism dominating GIS applications in archaeology. Emphasis is placed here on GIS as a heuristic tool. The difference between this work, illustrative of the author's present research, and previous ones undertaken in GIS is the focus on forms of practice (Bourdieu 1991), which has not yet been explored *via* an information system. These are explored by reference to the nature and spatial location of activities and the possible use of topographical features as perceived on the landscape.

In working towards this aim, it was necessary first to investigate the source of determinism found in GIS studies. So far, this effort has resulted in the description of the first steps towards a methodology for landscape archaeology that combines an interpretative (hermeneutic) approach with a more empirical study.

Determinism in past GIS applications

In the past few years, discussion about the limitations of GIS in archaeology has centred around the deterministic nature, mainly environmental, present in all GIS applications. Often this determinism has been implicit rather than explicit. In one view this characteristic is a simple consequence of the type of data fed into an information system, of which GIS is a special type, and the limitations of data representation and manipulation; as a consequence this limitation cannot be surpassed or avoided. There are others who resist accepting this handicap (see discussion by Gaffney & van Leusen 1995). Unfortunately, no one has yet produced any solid alternative, and their suggestions favour a highly problematic area in anthropology: cognition (Zubrow 1994). I believe that GIS *can* be employed to look at human practices and meanings *via* a new approach inspired by notions from sociology, geography, anthropology and of course archaeology.

According to Gaffney & van Leusen (1995), determinism in GIS applications is due to the emphasis put on environmental data as directly obtained from existing maps; however this information has no inherent deterministic property. This misapprehension, commonly found among critics of GIS, follows when confusing the terms *environmental* and *determinism*. An archaeological study which incorporates environmental information is not condemned to determinism (or *vice versa*). Determinism is the product of our interpretation as reflected though the way we use our information.

Thus, the determinism present in GIS applications has a more subtle origin. It is in this sense that it is worth learning about the assumptions surrounding the definition and implementation of those techniques from which many of the GIS procedures employed in archaeology have derived. These originated in geography and were later adopted by archaeologists: e.g. Clarke 1972; Hodder & Orton 1976.

An important aspect, if not the most important one, underlying GIS techniques is their reference to an abstract, *singular* space, inert and empty, devoid of meaning and agency. Space is a medium in which human beings play out their activities. The assumption of abstract space is well illustrated by the heavy emphasis placed on the use of distribution maps in traditional spatial analysis. Most formal techniques require the study area to be represented in a bird's-eye perspective, on to which imaginary Cartesian co-ordinates with a *fixed origin* are overlaid, so it appears detached from the individual. Spatial models are simplified versions of the distributions of some entity (household, city, religious centre, density scatter, etc.) recognized as an element of a larger system (Haggett 1971). This stress on systems in spatial models is probably the result of their development within a western historical context in which the study of institutions, groups and systems rather than individuals takes priority (Lefebvre 1994). Often, elements of geometry, economy and other disciplines are employed in the way of *thiessen polygons*, *nearest-neighbour analysis*, *site-catchment analysis*, and so forth. Ultimately, the intention has been to compare between the spatial characteristics of different regions by attending to the interplay of recognized systems, the establishment of an order or ranking and the recognition of hierarchies.

This perspective has influenced approaches to archaeological, as well as geographical, study-areas, influencing researchers to view landscapes in a synthetic way, quite removed from the way an individual experiences his/her surroundings (Thomas 1993b). In *Locational analysis in human geography* (1971), Haggett alluded to the confusion surrounding the concept of landscape; sometimes as being 'the general appearance of a section of the earth's visible surface' (see also Cosgrove 1989) while at other times as a synonym for the word *region* (Haggett 1971:11). The notion of landscape as a region loses what I consider to be a key element: *perspective*, not only visual perspective, but the general idea of locating the centre of reference in a *mobile* individual's body rather than at a fixed point in our study area. The removal of the notion of individual perspective resultant from this view is reinforced by the use of distribution maps and the reductionism of human apatiality to sites; traditional spatial analysis by means of distribution maps favours conclusions that refer mainly to a removed reality. This outlook has been carried through to GIS in archaeology, where map-layers have been employed in the same fashion as paper distribution maps. While I am not discarding the advantages of using distribution maps, my aim is to point out that GIS can incorporate new ways of studying landscapes. However, current GIS/archaeology users are trying to overcome GIS limitations by improving their methods — how do we represent 'cultural' information? how much weight do we attach to it? how do we quantify it? — rather than re-assessing their theoretical stance to represent and conceptualize space.

New approaches in landscape archaeology
The concept of landscape considered here is borrowed from Ingold's article 'The temporality of landscape' (1993):

> In short, the landscape is the world as it is known to those who dwell therein, who inhabit its places and journey along the paths connecting them.

This and similar concepts have been employed by several archaeologists — Barrett (1994); Thomas (1993a; 1993b); Tilley (1993; 1994); Gosden (1994); Bradley *et al.* (1994). Within its simplicity, it combines several ideas from anthropology (Bourdieu 1977; 1991), sociology (Giddens 1984), geography (Pred 1986) and from a growing interest in how mobile communities understand landscape (see Ingold 1986). Attention is shifted towards *practices* (activities) (Bourdieu 1977; 1991), occurring in the landscape: their nature, their characteristics, their location, how they change through time, how their distribution attaches meaning to certain spaces (localities or set of localities), the importance of how and why they are carried out, and who carries them out. The importance of the spatial and temporal characteristics of practices as integral to the process of reproduction and transformation of social relations is acknowledged. Space, or spaces, are no longer passive media but active agents. While practices leave their spatial–temporal imprint on the landscape, those same practices are 'informed' by the already existing spatial order; the landscape fills up with spaces/places possessing various meanings and connotations. The focus of attention reverts back to the individual as the importance of a larger spatial unit, the landscape, is recognized as essential to understanding the socialization of an individual.

However, one of the difficulties associated with this approach is the lack of formal methodology. Tilley (1994), makes several references to the local topography surrounding the sites and the relation of the sites to landscape features; he includes comments about the movement of people through the landscape. Most of his conclusions follow field observations and no attempt is made to ascertain whether these comments would also apply to other locales in the landscape, rather than only to the sites studied. One of the ways in which this limitation could be overcome is by the GIS capability of producing new map layers with indexes derived from exploring the relation between a locale and its surrounding. At this point, it is appropriate to introduce two concepts (Giddens' *structures* and Gibson's *affordances*) that will help understand how GIS can be used to study landscape.

Structures and affordances

$$\text{structures} = \text{rules} \ (\approx \text{Bourdieu's } habitus) + \text{resources}$$

Structures, as the equation describes, are constituted by resources and rules. Resources are material ones, although sometimes others, such as the allocation of time or the use of ideas (Hodder 1987: 142), can be considered. The term 'rule' is somewhat misleading, for *Giddens' rules* do not determine an individual's behaviour in a mechanical sense, but must be understood in relation to Bourdieu's concept of *habitus* (1977). They are a set of dispositions, ultimately based on the material conditions of existence, that 'direct' or 'inform' an individual's practices tending to reproduce what constitutes 'common sense'. Since the conditions of existence are in constant dynamism and the *biography*, or *life-path* (Pred 1986) of each individual varies, an individual's actions always (consciously or unconsciously) include an element of social transformation which may be larger than the one of social reproduction. While human history is full of deliberate activities, the end product is far from intended (Giddens 1984).

Gibson's affordances, as described by Ingold (1992: 46), 'are properties of the real environment as directly perceived by an agent in the context of practical action'. In the

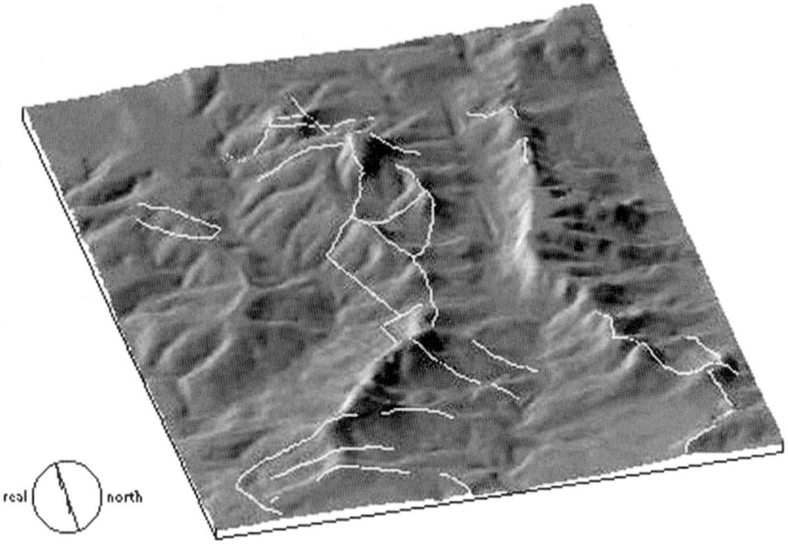

FIGURE 1. *The Wessex Linear Ditches in Salisbury Plain (as derived from Bradley* et al. *1994). The northwest corner of the territory must be dismissed as it was not possible to obtain contour values.*

following context, I will use 'environment' to refer to Gibson's 'potential environment' (Gibson 1986: 8), full of affordances, and 'practical action' to refer to any type of activity.

Affordances, although 'in a sense objective, real, and physical', can only be understood in relation to the subject (Gibson 1986: 129), in our case the individual. This is better understood through Gibson's use of the concept of *niche,* as a set of affordances referring 'more to *how* an animal lives than to *where* it lives [*habitat*].' *Niche* is just one among the infinite affordances that the environment (as we usually understand it) can offer, only becoming meaningful in relation to a kind of animal.

Thus the nexus between *structures* (*habitus* + resources) and *affordances* is made through the concept of practice: individuals sharing similar *structures* produce and reproduce similar practices, and consequently share similar *affordances. Affordances* are, therefore, integral to the *habitus* of a group. With the link between affordances, structuration (Giddens 1984) and theory of practice (Bourdieu 1979) established it is possible to explore how mechanisms of social reproduction and transformation play a role in an individual's environment. Ultimately, affordances may be associated with the organization of power and domination, as power relations are acted and re-enacted within *structures.*

From an archaeological point of view, the existence of particular affordances may be explored via GIS by relating the distribution of different material evidence with some characteristic (morphological, visual, etc.) for a location, as defined from the perspective of an individual at that location. This is one of the ways in which we might consider a more humanistic use of GIS. However, GIS may also be used to help define practices and to understand their nature by considering the local characteristics of a landscape. Clarity is ultimately achieved in this way, as a natural consequence of using an information system that forces the researcher to state things clearly and with no ambiguity.

The Wessex linear ditches study

A study by Bradley *et al.* (1994) of the Wessex linear ditches, Salisbury Plain, on the chalk downs of Southern England (FIGURE 1), offers instructive challenges to a GIS study.

The information used here comes out of that publication; the digital terrain model, or DTM, was created from the topographic map included in the publication after determining values for missing contours.

The Wessex linear ditches are associated with the Late Bronze Age (LBA) period, but no evidence indicates whether they were created through several stages or all at the same time. In this study they are considered contemporaneous, since at some stage during the end of the LBA, they were all present on the landscape. That period is characterized by being an open environment, dominated mainly by grassland; this is important given the emphasis put on the visible aspect of the ditches.

Bradley *et al.* emphasize that the Wessex linear ditches were territorial markers. This is supported, quite loosely, by the distribution of coarse-ware pottery and field observations. Bradley *et al.* maintain that the linear ditches, at least some, were meant to be seen *within* the territories they define. Consequently, an individual *outside* a territory would not have been able, or was not supposed, to see the linear ditches of a neighbouring territory.

In their work, Bradley *et al.* (1994: 138) refer to the apparent relation between the topography and the linear ditches, an observation relevant to the concept of affordances. Linear ditches may have been laid out to create spatial divisions (territories?), amongst those who inhabited Salisbury Plain, which may have been reproduced over a period of time through different activities. The layout may have exploited a particular relationship/s between the ditches and the topography. But before exploring this possibility using GIS, it is necessary to state more precisely, for the sake of the computer, what it is meant by the linear ditches being related to the topography.

At this point one is confronted with a series of difficulties: the complexity and vagueness inherent in many concepts used to describe spatiality; the difficulties in 'translating' spatial concepts into GIS; the large number of possible 'translations'. Initial ways of thinking about a concept, and its spatial manifestation, are often reassessed as they become almost impossible, or at least not practical, to translate into GIS easily. On some occasions, a concept may be modelled in an easier way if a change of perspective is adopted. Eventually, the result will be a compromise between our 'intuitive idea' and that which is allowed by the capabilities of the program (i.e. the way spatial data is structured within the program) and the system used.

After studying FIGURE 2a, the proposal that linear ditches may be 'related' to topography was 'translated' into another idea, that linear ditches conform to changes in the aspect of the terrain. This relatively broad idea includes the placing of linear ditches on hills, hills being among those places where the terrain changes aspect.

The relation between the linear ditches and those locations where the terrain changes in orientation is considered in order to see whether local changes in the orientation of terrain (aspect) influence changes in the orientation of the linear ditches. To explore this notion, we could extract from the Salisbury Plain DTM those locations where the terrain changes its aspect and check whether these coincide with those locations where the linear ditches change their bearing. This would only give us a qualitative yes/no. It is more informative to find the distance between both types of location — the near-by places where the terrain changes aspect and the places where the ditches change orientation. If these locations are distant from each other, this would suggest that changes in the orientation of the linear ditches are not related to changes in the aspect of the terrain, and are not conforming to the topography.

The emphasis is on changes in the horizontal plane, in the aspect and bearing of the ditches, rather than on changes in the vertical one, i.e. changes in the slope. Changes in

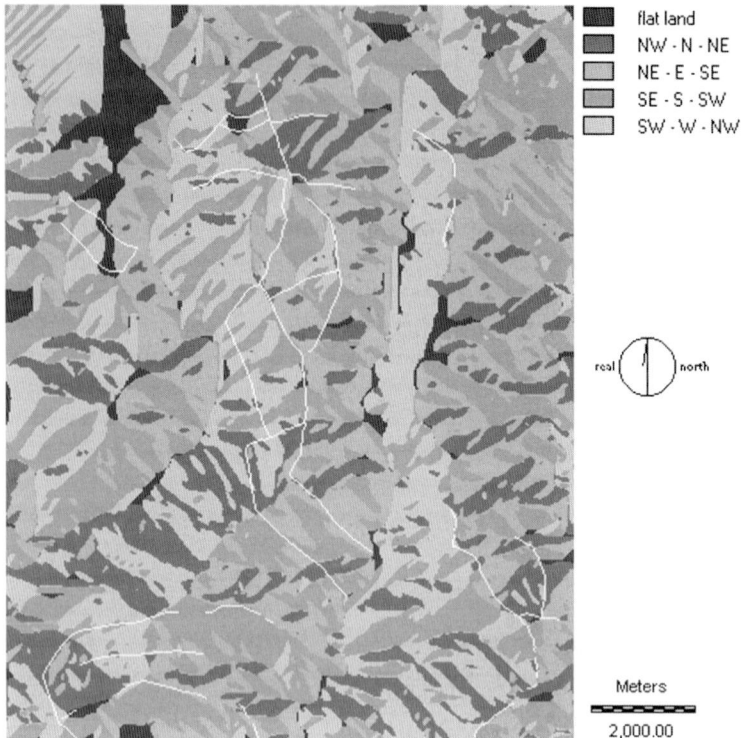

FIGURE 2a.
*Reclassified aspect
for Salisbury Plain.*

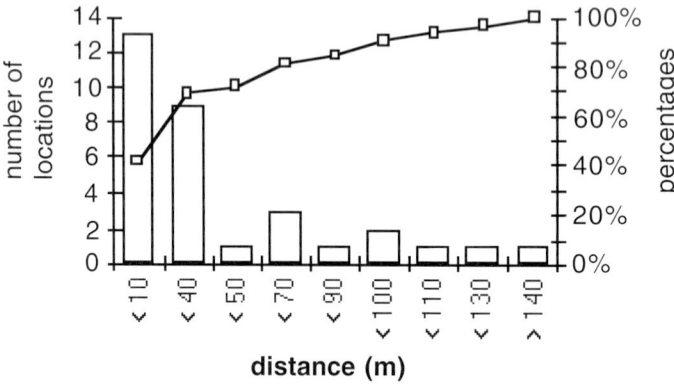

FIGURE 2b. *Distance
between locations
where the ditches
change orientation
and locations where
the local terrain
changes orientation
(aspect).*

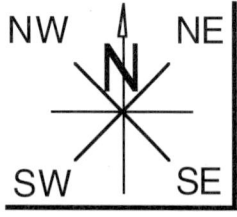

FIGURE 2c. *The aspect for the Salisbury Plain was classified into
four quadrangles.*

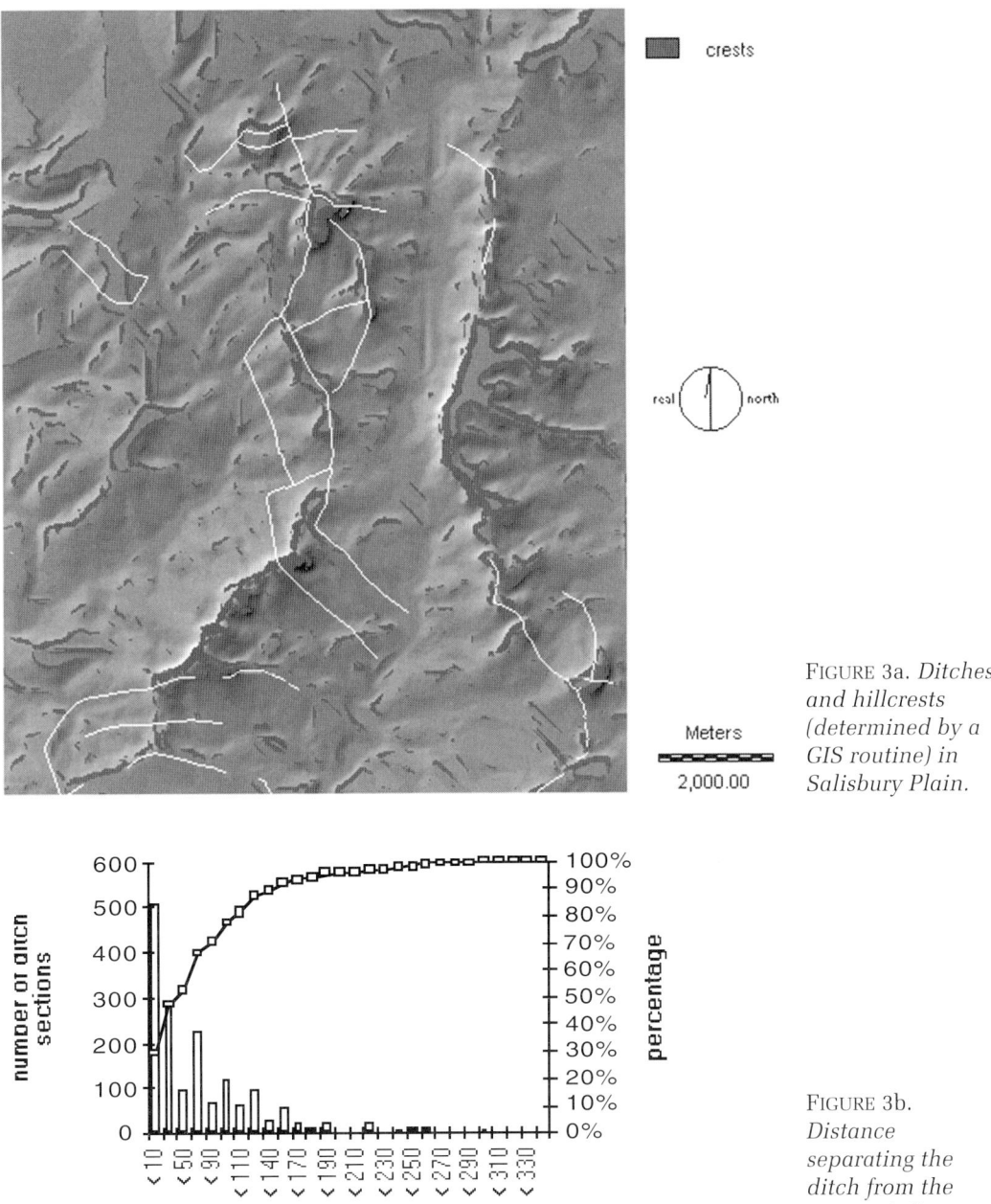

FIGURE 3a. *Ditches and hillcrests (determined by a GIS routine) in Salisbury Plain.*

FIGURE 3b. *Distance separating the ditch from the nearest hillcrest.*

altitude throughout Salisbury Plain are relatively slight. And no evidence hints at the existence of territories, or areas of a particular significance, within different altitude ranges.

FIGURE 2b shows the results after considering 32 (all) locations where the linear ditches change their orientation from one quadrangle to another (see FIGURE 2c).

41% of changes in ditch orientation are within less than 10 m of changes in aspect, 70% within less than 40 m. Its seems the orientation of linear ditches was influenced by

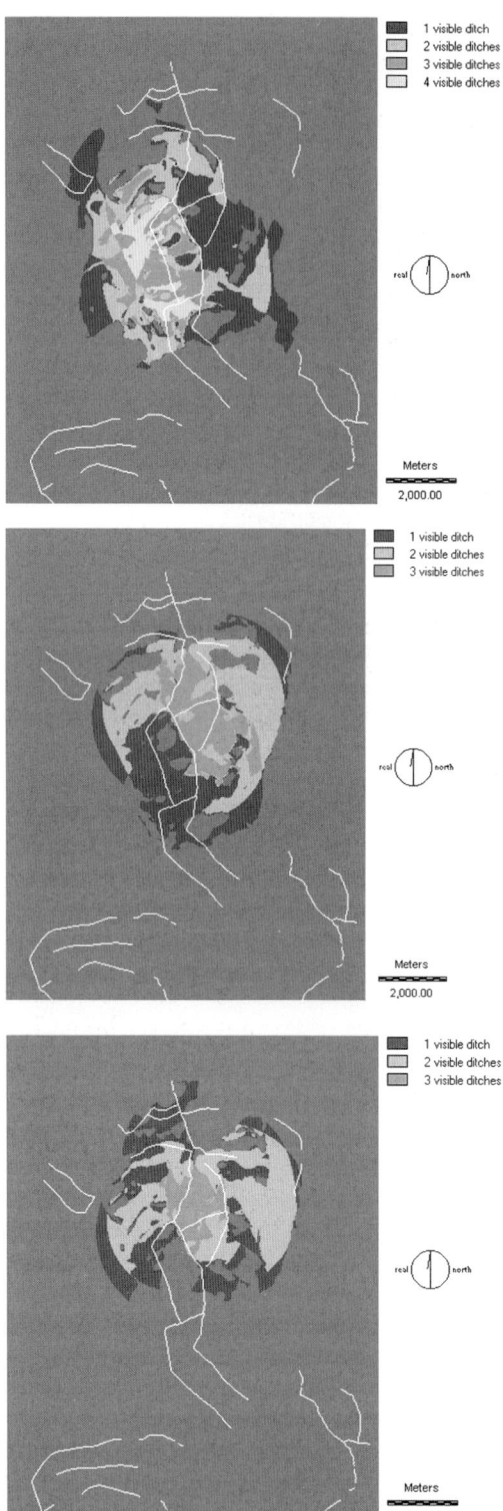

the local orientation of the terrain; the ditch-builders were taking advantage of morphologic properties of the topography.

The relationship between linear ditches and hillcrests (FIGURE 3a) was also studied. Hillcrests may be important, as they represent locations where the landscape subdivides naturally. Questions like: how close are the ditches from the nearby hillcrests? were they laid directly on top of the hillcrests?, are relevant to obtain an insight into the characteristics of the territory defined.

FIGURE 3b shows that 30% of the linear ditches are 10 m or less from hillcrests; we need to go as far as 40 m away to get a figure of 53%, followed by 67% at 60 m or less.

Next, three areas 'enclosed' by linear ditches were selected in order to study the relationship between the locations within the 'enclosed' areas and the linear ditches that circumscribe them (see FIGURE 4). In two of the three cases (those defined by the group of ditches 1957, 1963 and 1982 and by ditches 1982, 1959 and 1983, see Bradley *et al.* 1994: 28) we find that an individual walking within the 'enclosed' territory would have been able to keep visual contact with most of the boundaries (linear ditches). In the third case (defined by ditches 1971 and 1959), this would not be the case. In some areas within this 'enclosed' territory, visual contact with the boundaries (linear ditches) is reduced to one side. Moreover, visual contact may not be established with the side nearest to the viewer (see FIGURE 5a).

FIGURE 4a. *Visibility of the ditches within the territory defined by ditches 1971 and 1959.*

4b. *Visibility of the ditches within the territory defined by ditches 1982, 1983 and 1959.*

4c. *Visibility of the ditches within the territory defined by ditches 1957, 1982 and 1963.*

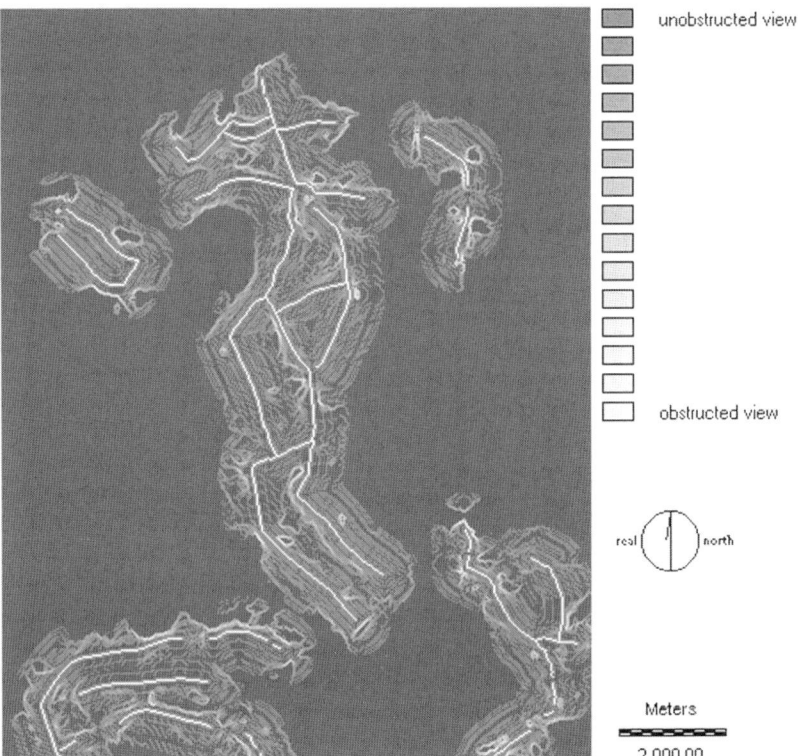

unobstructed view

obstructed view

real north

FIGURE 5a. *Gradient view. Visibility patterns associated with the ditches.*

Meters

2,000.00

Finally, FIGURE 5a shows the 'gradient view' from the linear ditches. Several steps were employed to derive this image. The *viewshed*, visible area from a certain view-point, for different radii was calculated (from 50 m to 650 m with an interval of 50 m) taking as viewpoints the entire linear ditch system and the viewer's head height set at 1·60 m above ground-level. All of the *viewsheds*, one for each radius, were then added together creating a *cumulative viewshed* (Wheatley 1995: 171), not shown here. The purpose was to investigate whether a similar amount of territory could be seen on each side of the linear ditches. FIGURE 2b suggests that this is not the case given the distance between the linear ditches and the hillcrests; in that case, linear ditches were perhaps meant to be seen only from one side. That would support Bradley's view of the linear ditches as territorial markers meant to be seen from *within* a territory, provided this characteristic held for other lines-of-sight originating within the territory.

To clarify this point an additional step was taken, the creation of the *gradient view*, which represents the degree of change along the *cumulative viewshed*. The meaning of this gradient is explained in FIGURE 5b.

In FIGURE 5b, we see what would be the value of the gradient if the view of the terrain on one side of a ditch was obstructed, in this case by the topography (right). Although the radius for the *viewshed* is augmented, the visible area increases very little or not at all. Higher gradient values correspond to areas that can be considered as *visibility barriers* where the extension of consecutive *viewsheds* are close to each other rather than evenly spaced, as they are on the left.

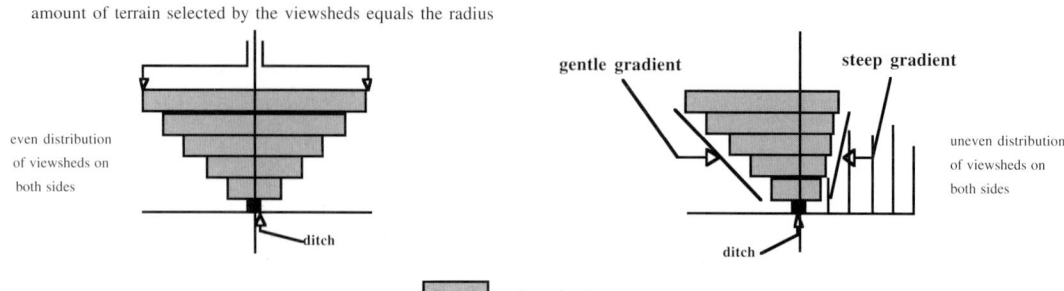

FIGURE 5b. *Making of the gradient view.*
Left: *Unobstructed accumulation of viewshed.*   Right: *Obstructed accumulation of viewsheds.*

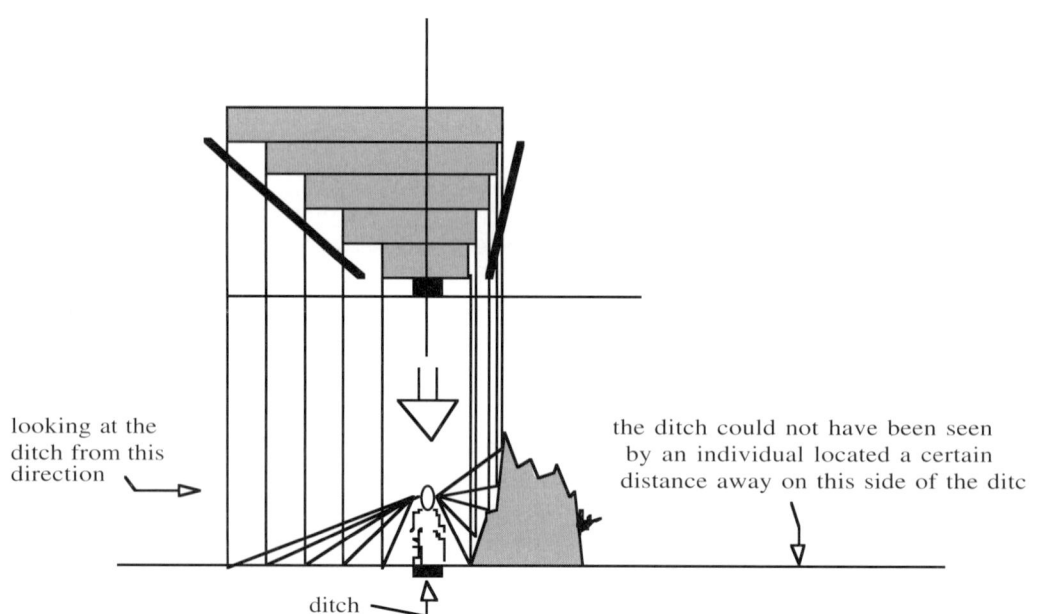

FIGURE 5c. *Interpreting the gradient view.*

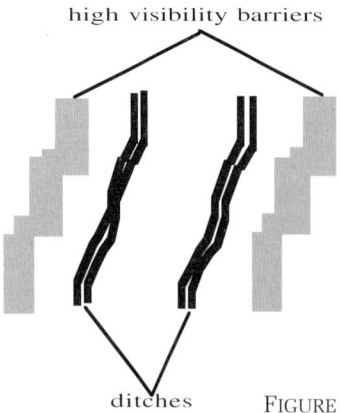

FIGURE 5d. *Hypothetical scenario for a visually closed (*inward*) territory.*

Several interesting conclusions can be drawn from FIGURE 5a The shape of several visibility barriers seems to closely follow that of linear ditches, allowing us to speculate about the direction from which the linear ditches were meant to be seen (see FIGURE 5c).

Careful examination of FIGURE 5a reveals that the linear ditches did not define 'enclosed' territories on the basis of visibility. If that was the objective we would have expected to find some cases similar to that of FIGURE 5d, examine FIGURE 5a. It looks more likely that the linear ditches were initially meant to define 'linearities', splitting the land into two sides (an east/west dichotomy seems a prime candidate). In this sense, it would be interesting to find out whether the distribution of coarse-ware pottery found by Bradley *et al.* (1994: 87) is explicable in terms of 'linearities' rather than territories. Bradley *et al.* see it correlated with the demarcation of territories defined by the ditches; however, no discussion on their concept of territoriality is included.

At this point, we may ask: is there any pattern in the visual aspects associated with the ditches (FIGURE 5a)?. Visibility patterns emerging from the relation between the topography and the linear ditches may have defined a set of spatial precepts, shared as part of a *habitus* reproduced every day (e.g. pottery production) and affecting, ultimately, modes of social behaviour. So far, we can only state that the linear ditches seem to have emphasized, and/or taken advantage of, a 'threshold effect' in the natural topography: the visual field of an individual drops substantially shortly after the linear ditches. These 'thresholds' would have partitioned the landscape into distinct spaces to which some kind of tenure may have been associated. These spaces, although distinct, were not exclusive given that, at least visually, the ditches were not defining enclosed spaces. People would have been free to wander in and out, their visibility unconstrained (except towards some ditches). This seems corroborated by the pottery distribution (Bradley *et al.* 1994: 85). One could argue that the topography of the area did not allow the creation of territories that were closed in the visual sense, so the ditches could only define partially enclosed territories. Yet, if the ditches *were* meant to segregate space, why can some of the ditches (e.g. ditches 1971, 1959) only be seen from a reduced area within the 'enclosed' territory they define? As it is, an individual would stumble upon them, rather than keep track of them by sight. If the linear ditches were territorial boundaries, they were not meant to create an sense of enclosure.

So it seems unlikely that, using Raymond's words (1994: 87), the 'focus of space' was 'inward' in character. It would more likely have been *segmented*. Space was not *boxed* all around; it was *compartmentalized*. This way of describing the spaces defined by the linear ditches conveys a higher level of cohesion.

All of these elements point towards space being sub-divided for organizational purposes, the ditches become informative markers, similar to today's milestones, other than control-related. The idea of territoriality as a knowledge tool has already been put forward by Ingold for hunting–gathering groups (1986) which demarcate their territoriality with respect to places and/or tracks, making no effort to establish and maintain formal boundaries. Knowledge about the territory is a factor used to distinguish between insiders and outsiders: whenever outsiders acknowledge their entrance into someone's else territory, they gain access to partial information on that territory. The Wessex linear ditches may have been used for information-related purposes, but it is unlikely that the distinction between insider and outsider would have been made. In addition, and contrary to hunter–gatherers, more effort would have been put into defining territories as a consequence of the economy that was most likely practised in the area: animal husbandry and farming.

Concluding remarks

All these ideas are based on the images created (see previous figures), and they are tentative as they depend on few data, mainly, the location of the linear ditches and the surrounding topography. Their value resides in their showing the potential of GIS to explore processes in a landscape. The possibilities for improvement and including other aspects are really endless: the location of the banks, the distance between areas with high visibility barriers and ditches, the distribution of different types of artefacts, especially pottery, the distribution of artefacts from different time-periods compared and contrasted, natural communication ways in relation to other evidence, and so on. We are limited by the amount and nature of the information provided by the survey. The larger our database, the larger the number of possible explorations — each subject to the limitations and errors associated with our data and computer procedures (e.g. *viewshed*, see Fisher 1993).

This article began with the determinism dominating GIS/archaeology applications, determinism not inherent to GIS but in the concepts and methods used to study the spatiality of human existence.

Rather than trying to incorporate the 'less-quantifiable' information, the more 'cultural' elements into GIS (as it has been coined by GIS users), this author proposes to use GIS as a heuristic, to explore processes, concepts and notions defined within a larger landscape framework as it is perceived from an individual's perspective. Emphasis is put on the study of the spatial dimension of practices (activities), possible relation between perceptual elements of a landscape and social aspects, the importance of movement, and so on.

The ideas developed here conform with Tilley's opening remarks in *A phenomenology of landscape* (1994). In spite of not having complete information about the 'skin' of the earth's surface, without being able to reconstruct the exact nature of landforms and vegetation of the ancient time-period/s, we can still use, to a certain extend, the 'bones' of the landscape as we know it by geology and topography.

The example uses GIS to explore *affordances* in the landscape derived from an individual's perspective within it. These characteristics are real in the context of our modelled landscape, for they are measurable properties, calculated by the computer as a combination of angles and distances which produce an index. The derivation of similar characteristics may be inspired in other disciplines, such as landscape architecture, planning and civil engineering, where their importance is generally accepted for a contemporary western society. Equivalent characteristics in cultural landscape for ancient or contemporary non-western societies could be explored in a similar way. The fact that these characteristics are highlighted in the landscape does not guarantee or directly imply that they were perceived and/or used by people. This can only be confirmed by reference to other evidence coming from a wider context.

I hope to have shown with this article, that GIS may be used by archaeologists and anthropologists to study landscape; it is in this sense that we are beginning to explore its possibilities within an anthropological context.

Acknowledgements. I would like to acknowledge the advice and ideas given by several people: Alice Gorman, John Mitchell and Gary Lock. I also want to thank Derek Roe in the Donald Baden-Powell Quaternary Research Centre for allowing me to use its facilities. Finally, I would like to acknowledge the support and encouragement, among heaps of advice and patience, given by Chris Gosden, without whom this article would have never seen the light. Finally, I would like to say that I am responsible for any erroneous data and bogus information that might be present in this article.

References

BARRETT, J.C. 1994. *Fragments from Antiquity — an archaeology of social life in Britain, 2900–1200 BC.* Oxford: Blackwell.

BOURDIEU, P. 1977. *Outline of theory of practice.* Cambridge: Cambridge University Press.

1990. *The logic of practice.* Cambridge: Polity Press.

BRADLEY, R., F. CRIADO BOADO & R. FÁBREGAS VALCARCE. 1994. Rock art research as landscape archaeology: a pilot-study in Galicia, northwest Spain, *World Archaeology* 25(3): 374–91.

BRADLEY, R., R. ENTWHISTLE & F. RAYMOND. 1994. *Prehistoric land divisions on Salisbury Plain: the work of the Wessex Linear Ditches Project.* London: English Heritage. Archaeological Report 2.

CLARKE, D. (ed.) 1972. *Models in archaeology.* London: Methuen.

COSGROVE, D. 1989. Geography is everywhere: culture and symbolism in human landscapes, in D. Gregory & R. Walford (ed.), *Horizons in human geography*: 118–35. Basingstoke: Macmillan.

FISHER, P.F. 1993. Algorithm and implementation uncertainty in viewshed analysis, *International Journal of Geographical Systems* 7(4): 331–47.

GAFFNEY, V. & M. VAN LEUSEN. 1995. GIS, environment determinism and archeology: a parallel text, in Lock & Stancic (ed.): 367–82.

GOSDEN, C. 1994. *Social being and time.* Oxford: Blackwell.

GIBSON, J.J. 1986. *The ecological approach to visual perception.* London: Erlbaum, Hillsdale.

GIDDENS, A. 1984. *The constitution of society.* Cambridge: Polity Press.

HAGGETT, P. 1971. *Locational models in human geography.* London: Edward Arnold.

HODDER, I. 1987. converging traditions: the search for symbolic meanings in archaeology and geography, in J.M. Wagstaff (ed.): *Landscape and culture*: 134–45. Oxford: Blackwell.

HODDER, I. & C. ORTON. 1976. *Spatial analysis in archaeology.* Cambridge: Cambridge University Press.

INGOLD, T. 1986. *The appropriation of nature — essays on human ecology and social relations.* Manchester: Manchester University Press.

1992. Perception of the environment, in E. Croll & D. Parkin (ed.), *Bush Base: Forest Farm — culture, environment and development*: 39–56. London: Routledge.

1993. The temporality of the landscape, *World Archaeology* 25(2): 152–74.

LEFEBVRE, H. 1991. *The production of space.* Oxford: Blackwell.

LOCK, G. & Z. STANCIC (ed.). 1995. *GIS in archaeology: a European perspective.* London: Taylor & Francis.

PRED, A. 1986. *Place, practice and structure: social and spatial transformation in southern Sweden.* Cambridge: Polity Press.

THOMAS, J. 1993a. The hermeneutics of megalithic space, in Tilley (ed.): 73–98.

1993b. The politics of vision and the archaeologies of landscape, in B. Bender (ed.), *Landscape: politics and perspectives*: 19–48. Oxford: Berg.

TILLEY, C. (ed.) 1993. *Interpretative archaeology.* Oxford: Berg.

1994. *A phenomenology of landscape.* Oxford: Berg.

WHEATLEY, D. 1995. Cumulative viewshed analysis: a GIS-based method for investigating intervisibility, and its archaeology application, in Lock & Stancic (ed.): 171–86.

ZUBROW, E. B.W. 1994. Knowledge representation and archaeology: a cognitive example using GIS, in C. Renfrew & E.B.W. Zubrow (ed.), *The ancient mind: elements of cognitive archaeology*: 107–18. Cambridge: Cambridge University Press.

4 Integrated landscape archaeology

The most effective landscape studies are often the most costly in time, manpower and interdisciplinary integration of the different methods at the disposal of the landscape archaeologist. No surface study of the landscape, however sophisticated the methodology, can substitute for the interlinkage of surface and subsurface remains. Pragmatic claims have been made (under a regime of restricted excavation permits) for the interdisciplinary efficacy and effectiveness of self-contained surface survey in Greece (Cherry 1983), but it is only in landscape studies where there has been effective investment in environmental reconstruction, surface survey *and* excavation that a more effective landscape understanding can be achieved (Barrett *et al.* 1991; Malone & Stoddart 1994; Barker 1985a; 1985b; Kennedy 1996).

Three landscape regions have been selected here where this interlinkage is being achieved and which are well represented in ANTIQUITY. In two (Italy and Wessex), there has been a long history of study of monuments (largely of the dead) which has now been replaced by a more sophisticated, integrated study. In the case of the Fens of East Anglia, a seemingly flat and undistinguished landscape has been proven to be full of subtlety and distinction. Other regions could have been selected from ANTIQUITY to illustrate these changes, but these three regions illustrate both some of the current trends and the diversity of European human landscapes.

Wessex is probably one of the most intensively studied areas of Britain, and has been particularly well represented in the pages of ANTIQUITY. The two articles presented here represent two important developments in the 1980s and 1990s which have enhanced this region's status of immense importance in prehistory. Firstly, surface survey has been added to the repertoire of information available for study. Major clusters of prehistoric monuments such as Stonehenge (Richards 1990; Cleal *et al.* 1995), Avebury (Malone 1989; Ucko *et al.* 1991; Evans *et al.* 1993; Whittle 1997; Whittle *et al.* 1999; Gillings *et al.* 2000) and the Dorset cursus (Barrett *et al.* 1991) have been the subject of archive reassessments and re-invigorated fieldwork campaigns which have given a new pattern to the landscape. Secondly, the richness of the data source has attracted a wide body of interpretation using the latest body of theory (Thomas 1991: 145–51; 162–75; Bender 1992; Barrett 1994; Tilley 1994; Cunliffe & Renfrew 1997). Good data attract a plethora of alternative theories.

The two articles on Wessex printed here fall into this bipartite refreshing of the Wessex landscape. The study of lithic scatters in the Avebury landscape reminds archaeologists that this is not simply a landscape of prominent monuments. A combination of flint scatters and molluscan environmental information (Evans *et al.* 1993) give a sense of the wider land use against which the monuments can be set. Until recently, it was thought that intensive agriculture and the fragility of prehistoric pottery has militated against the survival of other evidence, but a combination of aerial photography, geophysics and excavation is showing that much more of the landscape is still to be discovered (Gillings *et al.* 2000). Furthermore, alluvial deposits in the valley bottoms conceal not only environmental evidence of Neolithic clearance, but extensive archaeological evidence covered over by eroded sediments (Evans *et al.* 1993). Nevertheless, there is still much debate over the nature of settlement in Neolithic of Wessex, particularly focused on the degree of sedentary behaviour and the nature of domesticity (Pollard 1999). Most work in the Avebury area is still focused on the better-preserved monuments which have attracted researchers for generations (Whittle 1997; Whittle *et al.* 1999).

The most successful interpretations integrate these component parts with a powerful understanding of ethnography and potent theory. The second published article is a good example of this recipe. This particular recipe is deeply embedded in the physical properties of material culture, in this case stone, wood, water and fire, providing a rich metaphorical layering. The proposed formula — living wood and dead stone — is, however, strongly dependent on the natural qualities of any given landscape. Other Neolithic monumental landscapes as far-flung as Orkney and Malta lacked the natural vegetation to sustain this formula. The rich message of the memory or ancestry of landscape was immediately critiqued (Barrett & Fewster 1998; Whittle 1998) as resting too strongly on one analogy, creating too static a landscape reconstruction. Parker Pearson & Ramilisonina (1998b) responded that the analogy only provided the comparison; the interpretation rose or fell on the basis of the archaeological evidence. Once again the critical importance of the effective use of good data is emphasized.

The Fens of East Anglia provide a very different landscape where the monument typology of Wessex transfers with difficulty (Last 1999). They comprise the largest area of uninterrupted wetland in England (Coles & Hall 1998: 1–10). Apparently flat, small changes in topography are very significant. It is, furthermore, a 'dynamic and changing landscape', once dominated by the sea (2000 BC), then dominated by peat (1000 BC), subsequently drained, and now perhaps threatened by rising sea levels. The evidence for the interplay of environmental change and human response, well preserved in this environment, has been studied by a fruitful combination of archaeologists, geographers and other scientists. This has been a long period of study which started systematically with Fox (1923), continued with the Fenland Research Committee founded in 1932 (including the distinguished figures of the botanist Harry Godwin and the prehistorian Grahame Clark) and was considerably assisted by aerial photography (Riley 1945; reprinted here). The Riley article demonstrated the great potential of the aerial view and how the photographs could be successfully transcribed into settlement patterns.

By the 1970s the national importance of the area was well established. A Fenland Research Officer (David Hall) had been appointed in 1976 to undertake systematic survey which by 1988 had covered 60% of the 400,000 hectares, revealing some 2500 ancient sites (Hall & Coles 1994). Knowledge of the fens, particularly in some periods such as the Iron Age, has been radically transformed. In the last decade of the 20th century, as the 'silicon fen' phenomenon of the Cambridge region has expanded, work has concentrated on evaluation, rescue, management and formation of research priorities (Coles & Hall 1998; 1997, reprinted here). Brown & Glazebrook (2000) have taken this a step further by systematically identifying themes which will advance knowledge for individual periods: gaps in knowledge, the potential of the resource and research topics.

The changing knowledge of Italian landscapes has both similarities with and differences from that of Britain. The first landscape considered here, the Tavoliere plain, was, like the Fens of East Anglia, an apparently flat landscape with little archaeological evidence until the arrival of aerial photography. The impact of the aerial photography was, as Riley recalls through Poidebard's words (Riley 1992: 291), one of the creative aspects of the Second World War. In Italy it is to John Bradford that we owe the discovery of the extensive ditched villages of the Tavoliere plain, as well as later Daunian (Iron Age) and

Roman farmsteads, often revealing a detail similar to some of the most famous shots of Wessex (see above). Before the disruption of his research through ill health, Bradford had set up an Apulia project and ably presented the potential in papers principally published in ANTIQUITY (e.g. Bradford & Williams-Hunt 1946, reprinted here; Bradford 1949; 1950) and in his book *Ancient landscapes* (Bradford 1957). Sadly, it was left to other British and Italian scholars to explore the full potential of this rich landscape through excavation, environmental reconstruction and the mapping of roads (Alvisi 1970; Tiné 1983; Jones 1987), and the publication of these results is not yet completed. The results of these excavations show that internal features survive within the ditched compounds with cobbling, daub floors and other features on sites such as Passo di Corvo (Tiné 1983), Ripatetta (Tozzi & Verola 1990) and Lagnano da Piede (Mallory 1984–7).

Central Italy was, until the 1970s, known only for its ruined cities and more extensively excavated monuments to the dead. The work of Bradford (1947) stimulated a new approach to the landscape by Ward-Perkins and other members of the British School at Rome. The territories of cities as well as their cemeteries were uncovered in a readable landscape history (Potter 1979), that is itself being currently updated (Patterson *et al.* 2000). The article of Barker (1988, reprinted here) comes at a mid stage in this process of presenting a new vision of landscape, after some of the first global studies of settlement (Guidi 1985; Stoddart 1987) and agriculture, but before later studies which have benefited from many more surveys by Italian scholars (Spivey & Stoddart 1990; Rendeli 1993; Barker & Rasmussen 1998). There is now a much more detailed knowledge of key parts of the landscape. Rural survey is available for the hinterlands of the major city of Cerveteri (Enei 1993) as well as Veii and Tuscania. The internal layouts of Tarquinia (Mandolesi 1999), Vulci (Pacciarelli 1991), Veii and Cerveteri have now been successfully surveyed and partly excavated, providing new evidence for the crucial phases of state formation at the turn of the 2nd and 1st millennia BC. All the major cities appear to have been founded as small settlements by the time of the late Bronze Age. Finally, the first evidence of rural settlement is being published from sites such as Podere Tartucchino (Perkins & Attolini 1992). In this central Italian landscape there is the immense potential of combining rich artefactual evidence and settlement survey, allowing *subsequent* comparison with the textual evidence, setting cities in context and addressing the dynamics of hierarchical power after the onset of the state (Stoddart 1990; Riva & Stoddart 1996).

Neolithic settlement patterns at Avebury, Wiltshire

by **ROBIN HOLGATE**

Antiquity 61 (232), 1987

THE GROUP of later Neolithic ceremonial monuments at Avebury (Wiltshire) — including the megalithic henge and avenues and the mound of Silbury — are among the most famous and impressive prehistoric sites in Britain. Their significance and their relationship to earlier monuments at Avebury, such as the Windmill Hill causewayed enclosure and the West Kennet long barrow, has often been discussed. What has been missing from such accounts, however, was any consideration of domestic sites, as until recently there was simply no evidence available.

Although structural remains on Neolithic domestic sites do survive under exceptional circumstances, for example at Lismore Fields, Buxton (Garton 1987), the continuous history of cultivation and the natural solution of the fertile chalkland soils over 5000 years have largely removed all but the deepest-lying features such as ditches and pits, and incorporated artefacts once associated with the Neolithic land surface within the ploughsoil horizon. While pits have occasionally been encountered during construction work or by the excavation of later period sites, these discoveries give only sporadic indications of domestic activity. Nor does the usually friable Neolithic pottery survive long enough in the ploughsoil to give a representative picture of the extent of settlement. One element, however, is sufficiently durable to preserve a representative pattern of domestic activity: the flintwork.

It has long been known that large quantities of flint artefacts could be collected from ploughed land in this area, and amateur flint enthusiasts such as the Rev. H.G.O. Kendall, Rector of Winterbourne Bassett and the discoverer of the Windmill Hill enclosure, and A.D. Passmore, an antique dealer from Swindon, amassed large quantities of this material earlier this century. Their collections are now in the Alexander Keiller Museum, Avebury and the Ashmolean Museum, Oxford respectively. Both Kendall and Passmore kept accounts of sites where they found large quantities of flints, and it is possible to identify the locations of most of these concentrations. It is apparent from their records and by studying their collections that they attempted to retrieve all humanly struck flints (as Kendall (1921: 520) put it, 'from the rudes upward') from the sites they investigated, and that these sites yielded not only large quantities of material but also a variety of implement types.

Valuable as these indications are, their record is still inadequate for serious use in the study of Neolithic settlement patterns. They give no information about field conditions or collection methods, nor of the precise areas searched and the kinds of negative observations that are necessary to reconstruct the distribution of material across the landscape. In order to provide this kind of information a survey was undertaken by the writer and Julian Thomas, of the University of Sheffield, in autumn 1983. Transects spaced at 50-m intervals and orientated on grid north were walked; the flints found along each 1-m wide transect were picked up and bagged in 50 m collection units. The flints from the survey have been deposited at the Alexander Keiller Museum, Avebury.

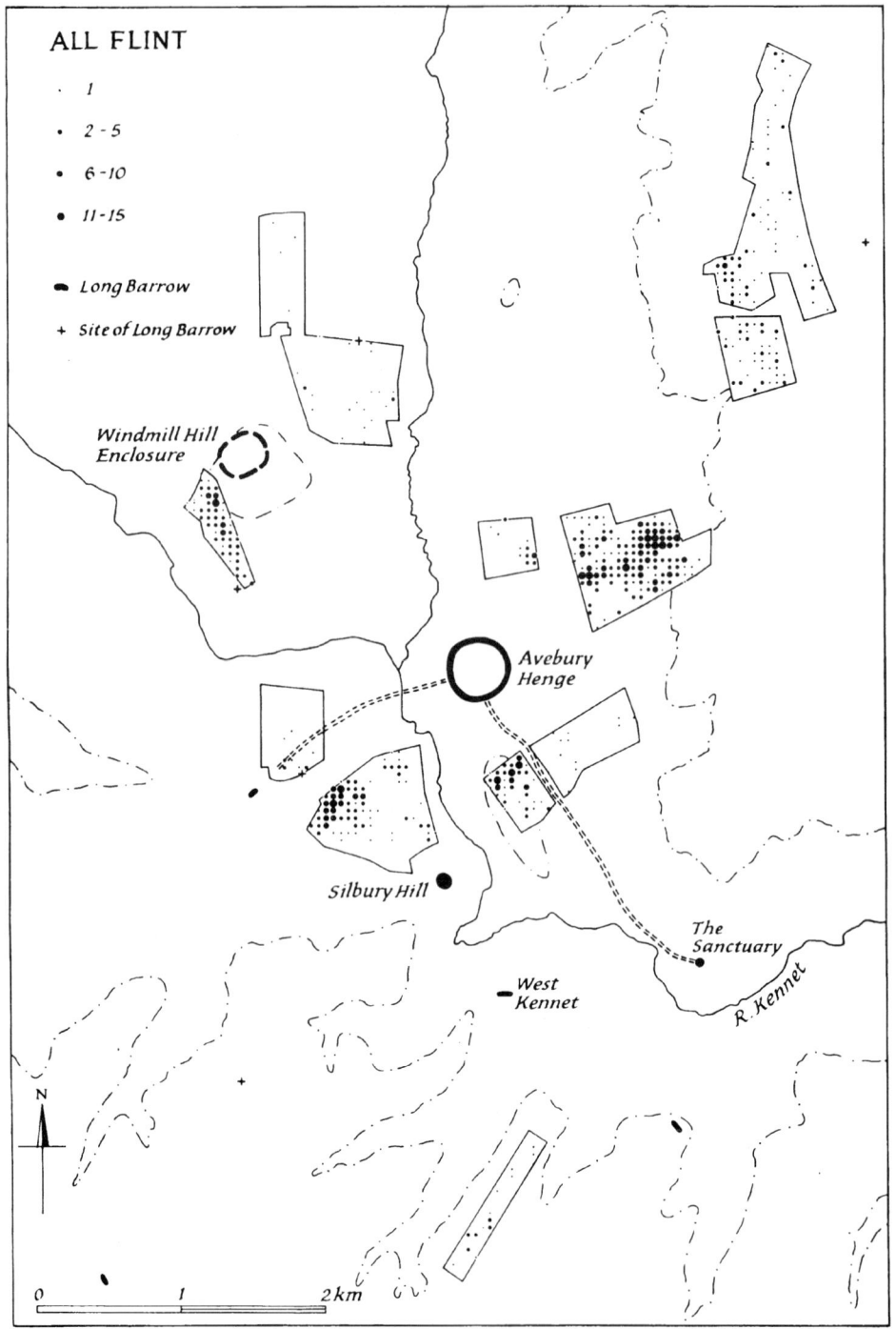

FIGURE 1. *Distribution of all humanly-struck flint recovered during the survey. The flint scatters on the SW slope of Windmill Hill and NE of Avebury are mainly later Neolithic in date and contain a variety of implements; those to the S of Avebury are probably Bronze Age and contain few implements.*

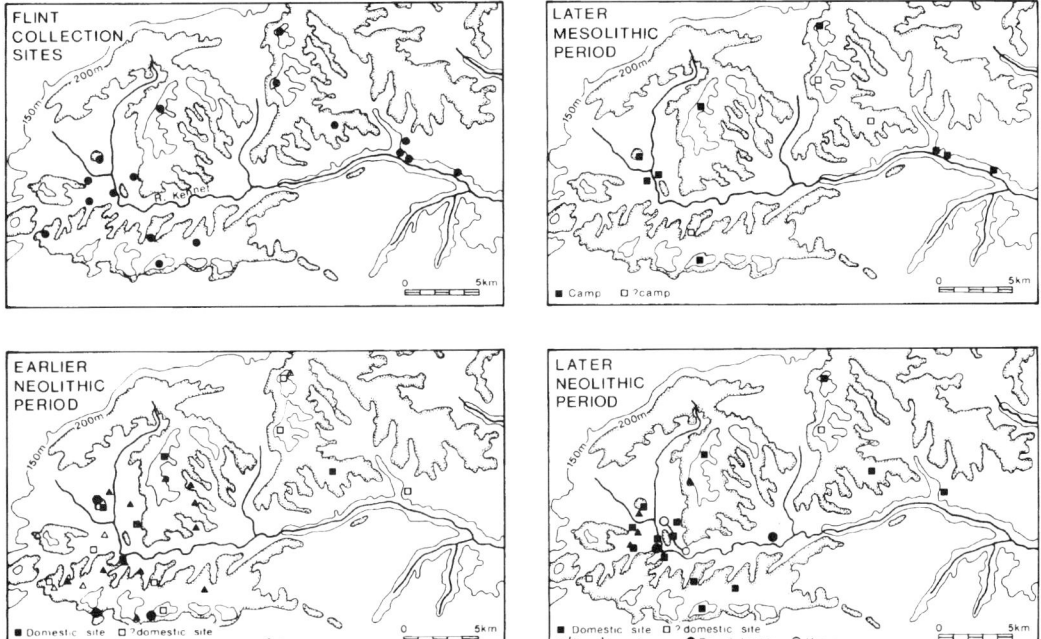

FIGURE 2. *Location of the major flint scatters discovered by flint collectors in the early 20th century, along with the location of Mesolithic camps and both earlier and later Neolithic domestic sites and monuments in the Avebury area.*

A full report on this work is in preparation for publication in the *Wiltshire Archaeological and Natural History Magazine*; but it is already possible to answer some of the most important questions which prompted this work, and to indicate that the history of the monuments must be set in a more comprehensive picture of domestic activity in this region.

The distribution of all the flint recovered during the survey is plotted in FIGURE 1. It is evident that an almost continuous low-density scatter of flints exists all around Avebury; the blank areas largely correspond with colluvial deposits lining the floors of dry valleys or the area north of Windmill Hill. Most of the flintwork consists of hard hammer-struck flakes which are characteristic of the later Neolithic period or Bronze Age. Two of the richest sites noted by Kendall and Passmore were on the southern slope of Windmill Hill and at the foot of the Downs immediately east of Avebury. These can be identified in part with two of the dense flint scatters evident from our survey (FIGURE 1). Since the samples collected by Kendall and Passmore were the result of sustained visits over several years, it can be stated with confidence that not only do these represent substantial accumulations of material, but they contain the wide range of implements (scrapers, knives, piercers, fabricators, arrowheads, axe fragments, etc.) characteristic of a variety of activities. In the Neolithic period, flintwork was likely to have been disposed of carefully in pits or on middens (cf. Crowther *et al.* 1985: 65), as the sharp edges on freshly worked flints could have caused harm to both animals and people if left lying around. By analogy with the settlement residues of present-day agrarian societies who use stone tools, dense flint scatters which produce a variety of implements are best interpreted as domestic sites.

Some contrasts in spatial pattern between earlier and later Neolithic material can also be identified, using diagnostic artefacts such as arrowheads and the different technologies employed in flake production — broadly speaking, the difference between producing blades from carefully prepared cores worked largely with soft hammers in the earlier Neolithic period and the production of flakes from rough cores using hard hammers in the later Neolithic period (Holgate 1988). Earlier Neolithic domestic sites occupied small areas and were located on the upper slopes of the Downs, often on clay-with-flints deposits (FIGURE 2). Causewayed enclosures, built within woodland clearings (Evans 1971: 66), were situated on the downland scarp at the periphery of the main settled area. Contemporary domestic sites have yet to be located in northeast Wiltshire beyond this block of downland. In the later Neolithic period a new range of monuments, along with a number of domestic sites, became established on lower valley slopes (FIGURE 2). Some of these domestic sites cover areas of up to 1 sq. km and probably represent permanently occupied farmsteads practising an 'infield-outfield' mixed farming strategy (Holgate 1988).

The valleyward expansion of settlement in the Avebury area during the later Neolithic period is part of a more widespread colonization of lower-lying areas in southern Britain (Holgate 1988). The general characteristics of the Avebury pattern can thus be compared, for instance, with the extensive later Neolithic occupation of the gravel terraces of the upper Thames (Holgate 1985), although each area has its own pattern in relation both to flint sources and the specific features of earlier settlement. This expansion in settlement also corresponds with the evident contrast between the location of causewayed enclosures and henges. While much more work is required to define these patterns in detail, it is now possible to complement the evidence of ceremonial sites such as those at Avebury with the remains of the equally extensive, though visually less impressive, domestic sites. Only by considering both classes of evidence can Neolithic society be understood.

Acknowledgements. I am grateful to Dr Andrew Sherratt for commenting on a draft of this note and for encouraging me to make use of the Passmore material.

References

CROWTHER, D., C. FRENCH & F. PRYOR. 1985. Approaching the Fens the flexible way, in C. Haselgrove, M. Millett & I. Smith (ed.), *Archaeology from the ploughsoil: studies in the collection and interpretation of field survey data*: 59–76. Sheffield: University of Sheffield Department of Archaeology and Prehistory.

EVANS, J.G. 1971. Habitat change on the calcareous soils of Britain: the impact of Neolithic man, in D.D.A. Simpson (ed.), *Economy and settlement in Neolithic and early bronze age Britain and Europe*: 27–73. Leicester: Leicester University Press.

GARTON, D. 1987. Buxton, *Current Archaeology* 103: 250–53.

HOLGATE, R. 1985. Neolithic settlement in the Upper Thames, *Current Archaeology* 95: 374–5.

1988. A review of Neolithic domestic activity in southern Britain, in J. Barrett & I. Kinnes (ed.), *The archaeology of context*: 104–12. Sheffield: University of Sheffield Department of Archaeology and Prehistory.

KENDALL, H.G.O. 1921. Scraper-core industries in north Wiltshire, *Proceedings of the Prehistoric Society of East Anglia* 3: 515–41.

Stonehenge for the ancestors: the stones pass on the message

by M. PARKER PEARSON & RAMILISONINA

ANTIQUITY 72 (1998): 308–26

MEGALITHIC stone monument construction in Madagascar has close associations with the honouring of the ancestors. Through the use of probability, piecemeal and relational analogies, and a consideration of the materiality of stone, a case can be made for certain structuring principles linking the ancestors with stone and the living with wood which can be found, in their own specific manifestations, to be relevant to historical and contemporary Madagascar and to Late Neolithic Britain. As a result Stonehenge can be interpreted as belonging to the ancestors, a stone version for the dead of the timber circles used for ceremonials by the living. By extension, Avebury and many other stone monuments of this period can be understood as built for the ancestors in parallel to the wooden monuments constructed for the living.

Introduction

That most enigmatic monument on Salisbury Plain continues to resist our attempts at understanding whilst, at the same time, it provides fertile ground for countless speculations and theories from all corners of archaeology's broad church. It has been conceived of as an astronomical observatory, a computer, and a centre of earth energies amongst many other interpretations (Hawkins 1966; Hoyle 1966; Chippindale 1983; Chippindale *et al.* 1990). All of these notions are grounded in some way or another in our own British and western 20th-century concerns and imaginings of Late Neolithic and Early Bronze Age society, as a distorted mirror of the present (Ruggles 1997). There have been attempts to draw on the knowledge of monumental architecture in traditional societies in other parts of the world, such as Colin Renfrew's use of Polynesian analogies of chiefdom organization to explain the conditions which gave rise to Stonehenge's construction (1973). With the full publication of excavations at Stonehenge (Cleal *et al.* 1995) and the publication of other volumes on the monument (Cunliffe & Renfrew 1997; Bender 1998), we should now be in the best position to think about the meanings embodied in the megalithic architecture of Stonehenge and associated monuments in Wessex (Barrett 1997). We may well be able to say much about *how* the monument was erected (Startin & Bradley 1981; Richards & Whitby 1997) but there is no satisfactory overall view as to *why* it was built.

The perspectives of indigenous scholars on their colonial and pre-colonial pasts have been a welcome and significant development in recent years (e.g. Gathercole & Lowenthal 1989; Layton 1989a; 1989b), yet there has been little opportunity for such commentary on the archaeological remains of the European heritage. At the 1986 World Archaeological Congress in Southampton, there was a relatively informal move to do so with Edward Matenga from Zimbabwe providing an alternative view of the Avebury monuments. Such an approach has also been possible through the preparation of a television documentary on Stonehenge in which both of us participated (FIGURE 1). Not only have we been working together on issues of monumentality in Madagascar since

FIGURE 1. *Ramilisonina at Stonehenge during filming. (Photo M. Parker Pearson.)*

1991 but Ramilisonina has lived his life in communities which regularly erect standing stones and which have a complex knowledge and understanding of stone's symbolism and significance.[1]

Ethnographic analogy: wood and stone

Analogy can be considered to work in four different ways: as formal or piecemeal analogy; as cross-cultural generalization; as relational analogy between structuring principles in different societies; and as analogies of materiality, appreciating the physical tangibilities of the world as experienced. Each *schema* has its contribution to make in developing an appreciation as to what is the most appropriate understanding of monumental stone architecture in Late Neolithic/Early Bronze Age Britain.

Formal analogies between present-day societies and the remains from the past are generally predicated on the notion that precise parallels can be drawn between the two. As a result, these types of analogy are often limited to relatively simple observations. In this particular case there is a formal analogy between contemporary Madagascar and Neolithic Britain in the erection of standing stones by both societies. Throughout Madagascar, stones, known as *vatolahy* ('man stones'), are erected in many places in many different circumstances. These *vatolahy* are explicitly identified with ancestors. Despite the occurrence of standing stones in both societies, the problems of extending this formal analogy are self-evident: Madagascar cannot be conceived of as a society parallel to that which existed in Britain over 4000 years ago. There is, of course, no monument in Madagascar which provides a direct comparison for Stonehenge. We cannot take any single Malagasy social context, such as the belief that the hardness of stone constitutes the essence of men as opposed to women, and present it as the mirror image of prehistoric Wessex. And yet the power of analogy opens avenues of new understanding, enabling us to explore the articulation of links between stone and ancestors, and perhaps uncover the expression of such links in the megalithic architecture of Britain.

We employ cross-cultural generalizations as a means of assessing the likelihood of certain aspects of social organization being shared between different cultural contexts. We may define these generalizations as probability analogies since they work on the principle that, if a certain relationship is found amongst most traditional societies today, then there is a probability that this relationship probably obtained in most societies in the past. A related approach can be termed the 'social typology analogy'. An example of

---

1   Ramilisonina is Bezanozano and many of the observations and sayings used in the text derive from this ethnic grouping.

this is Renfrew's use of social evolutionary typologies for characterising Late Neolithic Wessex as a chiefdom on the basis of matching certain archaeologically visible traits with a list of social traits which are deemed indicative of ethnographically documented chiefdoms (Renfrew 1973; Service 1962; Sahlins & Service 1960; Earle 1991). Criticized for its 'catch-all' definitions (Whittle 1997a: 147), the chiefdom model is not particularly pertinent to this investigation since monumentality in Madagascar is not restricted to 'chiefdom' societies; indeed, in the southern lands of Androy, megalithic funerary architecture only commenced after the collapse of chiefly authority (Parker Pearson *et al.* 1996).

Cross-cultural generalization is relevant in one area, that of the social significance of ancestors, a phenomenon found in many societies. Formal worship of ancestors is a feature of many societies, primarily in East Asia (Watson & Rawski 1988; Ahern 1973; Chidester 1990: 125–36). Lehmann & Myers claim that a universal belief in the immortality of the dead exists in all cultures whilst Steadman, Palmer & Tilley have revised Swanson's results to argue that ancestor worship is a universal aspect of religion (Lehmann & Myers 1993; Steadman *et al.* 1996: 63–4; Swanson 1964). They include ghosts, spirits and ancestral totems as ancestors and define worship broadly as reverence or respect and cast doubt on the conclusion of Swanson's cross-cultural study that, in 24 out of 50 societies, dead ancestors do not influence the living (Steadman *et al.* 1996). Although we might question the merits of defining ancestor worship so loosely and also retain a scepticism of both the sample size and the ethnographic basis of such knowledge, Steadman *et al.*'s study highlights the power of tradition in kinship-based societies in which 'the way of the ancestors' provides an unquestioned authority and truth. The role of the ancestors is very marked throughout the many ethnic groups within Madagascar (Mack 1986). Cross-cultural generalization thus suggests that the people of Late Neolithic Wessex would have engaged in particular relationships with their ancestral dead.

We may consider a relational analogy as that which links different manifestations through a common structuring principle. Hodder's work on the notion of pollution and purity in structuring relationships between men and women shows how different material outcomes stem from the same underlying ideas in Moro and Mesakin Nuba society, and in British Gypsy society (1982). Hodder is never clear as to whether his structuring principles have cross-cultural universal validity; if so, then it is hard to see exactly how his notion of relational analogy differs from the laws of human behaviour presupposed by the probability analogy. It is better to assume that structuring principles are not universal and to work on the assumption that we require a certain level of inter-contextual analysis in order to establish whether they are relevant for the purposes of analogy. In this particular case, looking at Madagascar and prehistoric Wessex, we have standing stones as the main formal analogy. We know from cross-cultural generalizations that ancestors are an intrinsic part of the social world in many kinship-based societies. In Madagascar, the ancestors are associated with standing stones in an intimate relationship with complex meanings. If we take this entwined co-presence of stones and ancestors to be a structuring principle, we can examine its different manifestations in the Later Neolithic and Bronze Age as compared to Madagascar. The manifestations will be specific to each cultural context and what is required for the relational analogy to work is a demonstration that the archaeological facts of Neolithic Wessex can be read acceptably in terms of the structuring principle of stones and ancestors. In other words, we need to construct a hermeneutic bridge between the analogy and the data. Another structuring principle might be the concept of worship of the sun and the moon, linked with ancestors, made visible through monumental constructions. We are now able to explore prehistoric Wessex for itself rather than placing Madagascar's known present and recent past lock, stock and barrel into the long-forgotten past of Britain.

There is a further reason why we consider this relational analogy of stone for the ancestors, explored below, as more than just a plausible 'just-so' story. Whilst the meanings of things can be arbitrary and open to continuous reinterpretation, the physical properties of materials such as stone, wood, water and fire are such that they resist certain interpretations and understandings and invite others. In such cases, their materiality may be a significant element of their metaphorical associations. In comparison to wood, stone has physical properties of durability, hardness, solidity and weight, the latter implying unity in the physical labour of moving a large stone. In terms of materiality, as opposed to linguistics, the sign is not arbitrary. Stone's durability and enduring nature places it at a different temporal level to the lifetimes of wood or people. Monuments of stone transcend the transience inherent in more perishable materials such as vegetal matter and wood.[2] They express the eternal in material form. This concern with materiality has been recently raised in the context of the British Neolithic and Bronze Age (Richards 1996; Tilley 1996: 168; Whittle 1997b: 152) and Whittle has even suggested that stone may have stood metaphorically for the ancestors at the time of Stonehenge (1997b: 152). This is a relationship which we can now consider in more detail through the examination of the use of stone in Madagascar.

Madagascar: ancestors and stones

Madagascar is twice the size of the British Isles. Subsistence practices vary enormously from wet rice cultivation in the central highlands and on the north and east coasts, to hunting and gathering in the forests of central southern Madagascar, to dry agriculture in the west, to semi-nomadic pastoralism in the arid south and southwest. There is also considerable diversity in political histories, from the formation of the Merina and Betsileo states in the highlands in the 17th and 18th centuries to the replacement of chiefdom societies by egalitarian yet hierarchical (in terms of clan organization) communities in Androy in the south.[3] Whilst Malagasy language and certain broad conceptions about house organization and orientation, cattle symbolism and economy, and ancestral respect are shared, Madagascar is a cultural mosaic of regional and ethnic interpretations and reworkings of these central themes. In spite of ecological and social organizational differences, the many ethnic groups in Madagascar are united in sharing cultural practices centred on elaborate funerals, monumental funerary architecture, and recognition of the power of the ancestors. It is the island of the ancestors (Mack 1986).

The significance and use of standing stones

Stone has been a fundamental component of tombs in the highlands since the 14th century AD (Lebras 1971; Joussaume & Raharijaona 1985: 540) though stone tombs have only

---

2   We also need to bear in mind that, as we shall see, wood can stand in for stone in certain contexts. Equally, earth can also be considered as durable and enduring; in Madagascar, for example, it is sacred like stone.

3   The Tandroy, the inhabitants of Androy, have a fiercely egalitarian ethos yet the structuring of asymmetrical marriage alliance relations between wife-givers and wife-takers produces a series of hierarchical relationships between the different clans and between lineages within the clans. For societies of this type, the simple distinction between egalitarian and ranked is not sufficient to describe their social structure.

FIGURE 2. *A standing stone (*vatolahy*) in the highland region of Betsileo country. (Photo M. Parker Pearson.)*

been constructed in areas such as Androy since the mid 19th century (Parker Pearson 1992; Parker Pearson *et al.* 1996). Traditionally, houses in the highlands were constructed of wood and other perishable materials. They were never built out of stone since this was reserved solely for the housing and commemoration of the dead. Similarly, in Imerina (the dominant kingdom in the highlands) soil was considered to have sacred properties and, though it belonged to the king, even he could not build his house out of it. This material symbolism began to change in the 1870s in the highlands when Welsh Protestant missionaries encouraged the building of houses in brick and stone. Today the distinction between wooden houses and stone tombs is still strongly maintained by the Tandroy in the region of Androy.

Standing stones are known as *vatolahy* ('man stones') and are erected for many reasons (FIGURE 2). Traditionally, stone is reserved for the dead in the form of tombs and commemorative standing stones but the extent and nature of the association of standing stones with the dead varies from region to region.[4] For highland groups such as the Bezanozano, a *vatolahy* may represent a deceased individual or group of dead (Ndema 1973: 168–74). The stone is put up after death to commemorate a man whose body has not returned to his ancestral tomb or, alternatively, to celebrate a well-known individual who is buried in his ancestral tomb. Very occasionally a gifted wise woman will be similarly commemorated though normally all women, and men under 30 years, are excluded from this honour. Among the Tanosy of the southeast, the *vatolahy* are erected at a short distance from hidden forest tombs. For the Tandroy, they are incorporated in the tombs of men at the east and west ends except when they are erected in isolation as

FIGURE 3. *A Tandroy tomb with* vatolahy *at its east and west ends. (Photo M. Parker Pearson.)*

cenotaphs to men or as the result of ancestral visitation in dreams (FIGURE 3). Standing stones are also used to mark the boundaries of different groups' territories, or to deflect the malign influence of a tomb whose position with respect to a house or village might affect the living. In Imerina stone came to have a legitimatory purpose in inaugurating and underwriting the establishment of state power in the 18th century. The great king Andrianampoinimerina's succession to power was established, in part, through his procession to three sacred stones in 1787 (Kus & Raharijaona in press). Kings erected stones as a mark to show that they had passed that way. Standing stones were used to mark important events such as the winning or losing of a battle. Within the kingdom of Imerina, royal palaces and residences were linked by lines of standing stones along which messages would pass; a runner would wait at each stone to pass on the message.

The association of stone with the passing on of messages has a deeper, polysemous meaning, expressed in one of the many metaphorical proverbs: *vato namelan-kafatra* ('the stone passes on the message'). The commemorative stone is a text which informs about the person remembered. It is also the nexus of communications and exchanges between living and ancestors. Requests for supernatural help can be made to the ancestor at his stone. If the request is followed by good luck, the living leave gifts at the stone

---

4   In certain regions where stones are not available, the hardest of woods are used for standing 'stones' (*vatolahy hazo*; 'wooden man stones'). The tree named *ambora* is used for symbolic stones in eastern Madagascar by groups such as the Betsimisaraka, the Bezanozano, the Tsimihety and the Antembahoaka, where it is, like stone, reserved for the ancestors.

for the benevolent ancestor. In Bezanozano and Betsimisaraka country *vatolahy* are occasionally wrapped in white *lamba* (shawls) in response to communications from the ancestor to the living. Standing stones may also bring good fortune or grant wishes in other ways, by touching them for example. The asking of the ancestors' blessing prior to ceremonies of circumcision, marriage and *famadihana* (secondary burial) may also be directed to a standing stone or tomb though it is more normally requested from the living elders. The stone's passing on of messages also refers to the position of the elders who are metaphorically like stones, passing on the messages of the ancestors to the young. This links to a further metaphor in which human growth, especially that of males, is a process of hardening.[5] Babies are soft and fluid, like water, and dead infants are excluded from the ancestral tomb. Male circumcision is a significant stage in men's process of hardening, culminating in death when, as ancestors, people become hard, resistant and eternal. Tombs must also be hard, coherent and dry. If the tomb becomes unsound and is breached, its integrity is threatened by the entry of water and damp: if the ancestors become wet, their *angatra* ('ghosts') cry out. Finally, stone is not only eternal but it is also binding: *izay mitambatra vato fa izay misaraka fasika; fa ny firaisana no hery* ('as stone we are united but as sand we are separated; there is strength in togetherness'). *Vatolahy* actually embody this concept in the very activity of their quarrying, moving and erection since many people are required to act together in unison.

In summary, stone has a number of important associations which are mobilized slightly differently among the various ethnic groups of Madagascar and which have become modified in different ways through time. Yet there are certain coherent themes which have endured for over 500 years across the mosaic of the many ethnicities. These are the association of stone with the ancestors (for tombs and standing stones), the metaphorical hardening of the living to become like stone, the eternal durability of stone, and the unity symbolized by stone and mobilized in its erection.

Ancestors in Madagascar
Ancestors continue to inhabit the world of the living, though predominantly within their tombs or at the *vatolahy*. They are one of four sets of entities which may be found in most parts of Madagascar: *Zanahary* (the creator), *Andriamanitra* (God — a recent Christian concept), the *razana* (the ancestors), and other invisible spirits such as *Vazimba* (the original inhabitants of Madagascar), *kalanoro* and *zazavavy-ndrano*. Spirit possession is a feature of life in Madagascar and the living may be possessed by the spirit of an ancestor as well as by the other supernatural forces. Spirits inhabit the trees, the hills, the grass, the earth and the animals — all is sacred. Before breaking the ground for use as a rice paddy, prayers to the spirits are necessary for permission to be given.[6]

Places where the ancestors may be contacted, other than at the tombs and *vatolahy*, are located within three spatial scales: the house, the village and the territory. The northeast corner of the house, the *jorofirariazana*, where the sun rises, is the corner of the ancestors. The ancestors may be approached in the northeast corner only during the

---

5   Certain hardwoods, the *valanirana* and the *arahara*, are also linked to the process of masculine and ancestral hardening. A song containing the words *arahara tsy zanakazo dilony avy* ('the arahara is not a baby wood but is always hard') is sung at Antembahoaka circumcision ceremonies and at Bezanozano funerals, emphasising the hardening of both men and the dead. *Teza*, the hardwood beneath the sapwood, has similar connotations (Bloch 1995a; 1995b).

6   For groups that practice *tavy* (slash and burn), such as the Betsimisaraka, the spirits' permission is required before forest clearance. The summits of hills are, however, never cleared and these remain as domains of those spirits.

morning when the sun is in that direction, except in the afternoon of the day before a *famadihana* when the dead are requested to be present for the next day. In many regions, villages have sacred places at their centre, marked by a small stone, a bush or a pointed post, where the ancestors can be approached, thanked and sacrificed to. At the territorial level of large lineages or clans, ceremonial gatherings are held around a pointed wooden post (or occasionally a tomb or *vatolahy*) on level, high ground.

Concepts of the relationship between living and ancestors also involve the sun and moon, and the circularity that they embody in their shapes and in their movement. Life is conceived of as a circle from birth to ancestorhood (*mihodinkodina ny fiainana* ('life turns in a circle')) whilst the earth is considered as round and as turning in a circle. Respect for the elders is summarized in the title of grandparents: they are *masoandro amambolana* ('the sun and the moon') and should be respected in the same way as we respect the sun and the moon and their movements. Both sun and moon are important for the timing of ceremonial activities. Circumcision is held during the full moon while house-building and inauguration take place during the new moon. Marriages should never be performed during the 'dead' moon. *Famadihana* in the highlands are held between July and early October, centring on the lunar months of August and September, whereas the Tandroy forbid any activities concerned with the dead during the lunar month of September. Dancing and singing should be conducted *fari-bolana* ('round like the moon') and the direction of dancing is always sunwise (anti-clockwise since the turning of the sun is in the opposite direction in the southern hemisphere).

Stonehenge as a ceremonial circle of the ancestors

Alasdair Whittle's recent discussion of the meaning of Stonehenge (1997b) utilizes the example of the Zafimaniry of central Madagascar to emphasize the properties of wood as a metaphor for people and ancestral bones (1997b: 152) though he does not pursue the Zafimaniry's linking of stone with the ancestors (Bloch 1995a; 1995b). However, this is a theme which he develops separately, concluding that circular sites of this type, including the stones themselves, were connected with spirits, ancestors and the dead (1997b: 163). Whittle's observations on the possible meanings of Stonehenge are perhaps the most perceptive yet but they do not go far enough in spelling out the specific metaphorical associations embodied by Stonehenge, especially in relation to its wooden counterparts at Durrington Walls and Woodhenge (FIGURE 4).

The recent programme of radiocarbon dating of material from Stonehenge has resulted in a reconsideration of its overall chronology and phasing. It is currently divided into three phases (Cleal *et al.* 1995): Phase 1 (2950–2900 BC) is the construction of a circular ring of posts (known as the Aubrey Holes) within a circular earthwork, consisting of a bank and external ditch, with openings to the south and northeast. These orientations have been tentatively associated with symbolism of the rising moon (Ruggles 1997: 225). In Phase 2 (2900–2400 BC) a large number of wooden posts were erected in the interior and at the northeast entrance. Towards the end of this phase, cremation burials were placed throughout the monument. Phase 3 (2550–1600 BC) is the period of stone construction and building of the avenue. The earliest of these stone phases is a semi-circle of Welsh bluestones[7] brought from southwest Wales and the Preseli mountains (sub-phase 3i). This was dismantled and replaced by the sarsen circle and the five sets of trilithons (sub-phase 3ii), possibly with a setting of bluestones (sub-phase 3iii). The bluestones were again dismantled and set up as a bluestone circle within the sarsen circle and as a bluestone oval within the trilithons (sub-phase 3iv). An arc of these bluestones was removed to form the bluestone horseshoe (sub-phase 3v). Finally, two concentric circles of stoneholes (the Y and Z holes) were dug outside the sarsen circle but they were never filled (sub-phase 3vi).

Four radiocarbon dates from the sarsen stoneholes suggest that the sarsens were erected around 2400 BC (Allen & Bayliss 1995: 524–5), several centuries earlier than had previously been thought. The significance of this is that the major stone-building period at Stonehenge was broadly contemporary with the construction of large timber post circles within the henge enclosures at Woodhenge (*c.* 2500–2000 BC) and Durrington Walls (*c.* 2500–2100 BC) (Cunnington 1929; Wainwright & Longworth 1971). Archaeological opinion is divided as to whether these concentric circles of timber posts were roofed or simply lintelled (see Musson 1971; Parker Pearson 1993: figure 58; Gibson 1994) but the large diameter of the timber circle recently detected by magnetometry at Stanton Drew in Somerset precludes the likelihood of roofing. Whether these timber circles were roofed or not, their quantities of associated finds, especially pig bones and Grooved Ware pottery, from within the post circles and from the midden areas outside them are indicative of considerable activity, involving feasting and structured deposition (Richards & Thomas 1984).

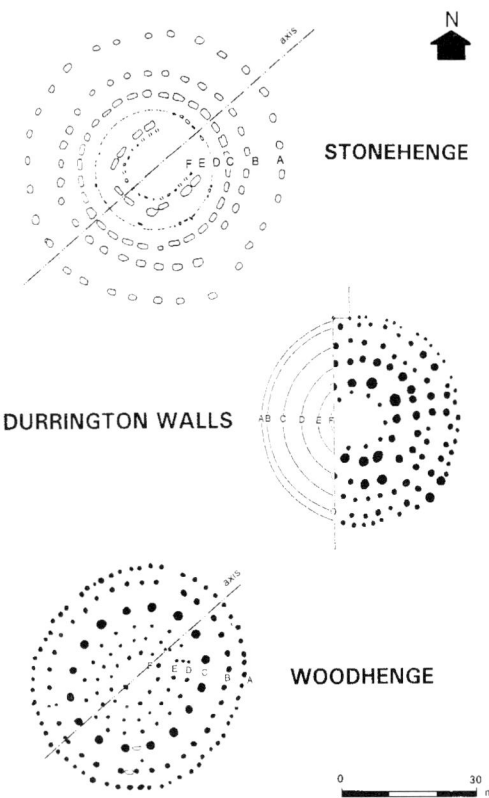

FIGURE 4. *Ground plans of Stonehenge (sub-phase 3vi), Durrington Walls Southern Circle and Woodhenge. (From Darvill 1997, courtesy of the British Academy.)*

There continues to be much speculation about the timber circles' purpose since they are monumental in size and massively bigger than the insubstantial remains of the few Late Neolithic houses, constructed with organic materials, which have been found in southern Britain. The presence of many thousands of relatively unfragmented pig bones within these monumental timber circles has been interpreted as evidence of an élite or a priestly caste (Wainwright 1989; MacKie 1977) though many other interpretations are possible. What is particularly important here is the relationship between the timber circles and the stone circle of Stonehenge (Darvill 1997: 189–91).[8] The structural features which link Stonehenge to the Durrington and Woodhenge timber monuments are: the six concentric rings (if we include the Y and Z holes at Stonehenge); the use of both the circle and the oval (both incorporated into the same monument at Stonehenge), the similar sizes (between 39 m and 53 m), and the solstice sunrise axes (midsummer at Stonehenge

---

7   'Bluestone' is used here as a catch-all term for all of the Welsh rocks at Stonehenge, including not only the dolerites, rhyolite, and volcanic ash or tuff but also the sandstone rocks.

8   Coneybury henge should also be mentioned here. Lying about a mile southeast of Stonehenge, it is a small oval-ditched enclosure containing a circle of posts, inside which is a circle of pits which held either stones or posts (Richards 1990: 123–58; 1991: 89–96). Despite the many stakeholes and two large pits, the quantities of Grooved Ware and other refuse were slight. Coneybury henge dates to *c.* 2750 BC and, prior to its abandonment, can be compared to Stonehenge in Phase 2.

FIGURE 5. *Mortice and tenon and tongue and groove jointing at Stonehenge. (From Atkinson 1987: 16, courtesy of English Heritage.)*

and Woodhenge and possibly midwinter at the Southern Circle at Durrington Walls).

It has been noted for some time that the dressing of the Stonehenge stones, the provision of mortices and tenons,[9] and the use of tongue and groove joints for the lintels in the sarsen circle are reminiscent of techniques of woodworking (Atkinson 1979: 39; Gibson 1994: 211; FIGURE 5). Although the postholes of the Durrington and Woodhenge timber circles provide no indication whether these posts were similarly dressed with rectangular sections above ground, there appears to have been an intention to dress and erect the Stonehenge stones as if they were wooden. If stone was the medium associated with the ancestors (or simply the spirit world) then Stonehenge can be understood as a 'ceremonial circle' used and occupied by the ancestors (and/or spirits) in the same way that the timber circles were 'ceremonial circles' used and occupied by the living. The distinction can be followed up in three ways.

Firstly, Stonehenge's isolation and invisibility from Durrington Walls and Woodhenge, where three timber circles are known and other circular features are inferred (David & Payne 1997: 91–4), suggests a spatial dislocation such that the ancestors occupied the same world as the living but were given their own distinct place within it (FIGURE 6). The two monument complexes, though separate, may have been complementary. Both are linked by the flow of the River Avon, since Stonehenge's avenue leads down to the river and Durrington Walls' main entrance faces directly onto it. Whilst further work is needed to establish whether there was an avenue leading from Durrington Walls to the river, there is evidence throughout Britain of a strong association in this period of henge monuments with rivers and streams (Richards 1996).

Secondly, the quantities of rubbish at Stonehenge are far fewer than those from the timber circles. The Stonehenge finds assemblage includes sherds from only a few vessels and about 1000 animal bones. The 11 sherds of Grooved Ware and 229 Beaker sherds, most of them small, suggest that deposition was limited. Although we must bear in mind the inadequate retrieval methods of the early excavations and the limited depositional contexts for bones and pottery, the 3675 pieces of bluestone, 2173 pieces of sarsen and 1285 pieces of flint from the excavations suggest that the retrieved quantities of pot and bone are indicative of their restricted deposition. At Durrington Walls, the 5861 sherds of Grooved Ware and 71 Beaker sherds, and the 8500 animal bones attest to a different scale of deposition, interpreted as the remains of feasting (Wainwright & Longworth 1971: 189–90). About half of this material came from the Southern Circle and its environs. There were smaller but still significant quantities from the Northern Circle and from Woodhenge (Wainwright & Longworth 1971: 188; Cunnington 1929; Pollard 1995). The material record from Stonehenge presents us with two possibilities. Either little ceramic or faunal rubbish was discarded here or the monument was kept clean, with the refuse being deposited outside the earthwork in some place as yet unlocated. The latter

9   Technically these are ball and socket joints (Alex Gibson pers. comm.).

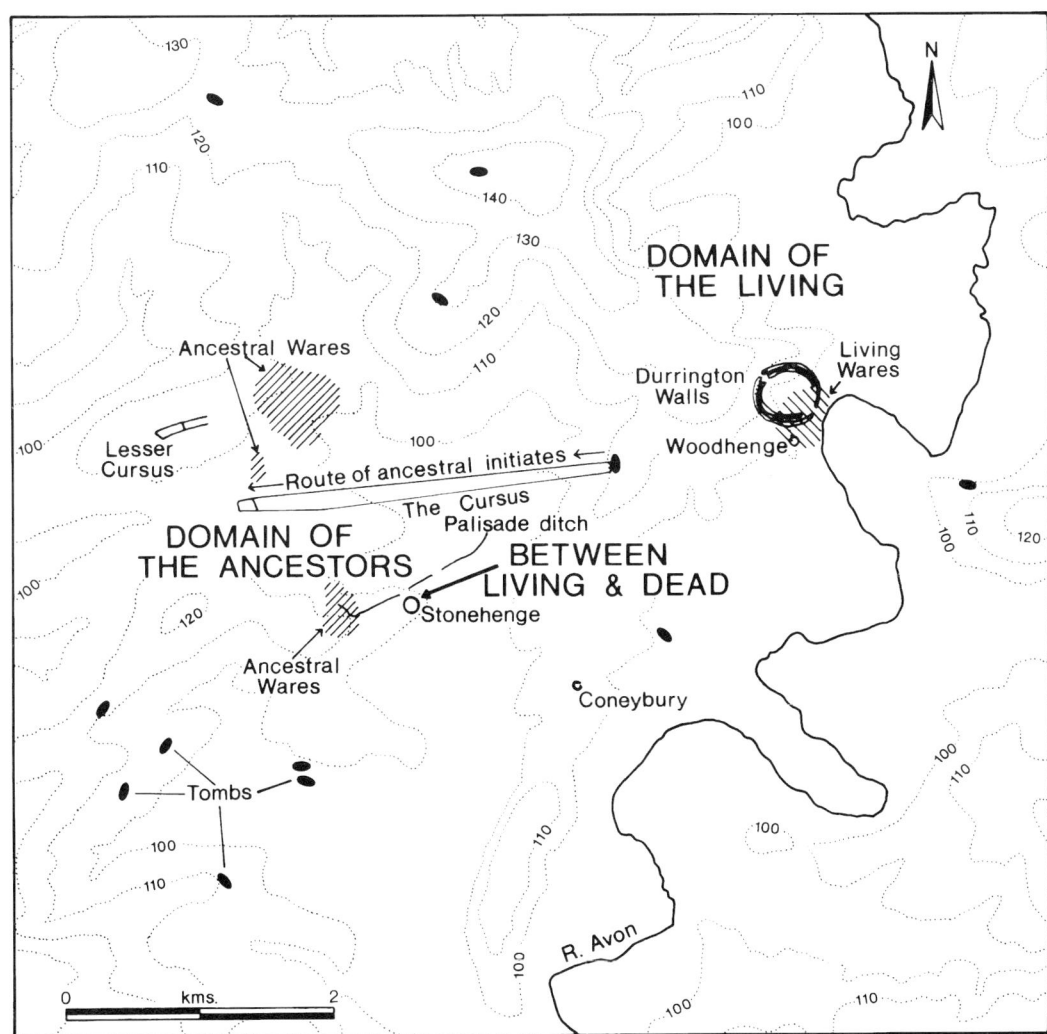

FIGURE 6. *Interpretation of the Middle to Late Neolithic landscape around Stonehenge in phases 1–2. (Adapted from from Cleal* et al. *1995: figures 252–4, drawn by Colin Merrony.)*

interpretation is less likely, given the many thousands of pieces of stone and flint recovered during excavation. The lack of ceramic and faunal debris suggests that this ceremonial place of the ancestors was probably never the scene of feasting by the living.

Thirdly, there is an unusual visual relationship between Stonehenge and the Early Bronze Age (*c.* 2200–1700 BC) round burial mounds in its vicinity (FIGURE 7). Although this part of Salisbury Plain contains one of the densest and largest groups of round barrows in Britain, only about 20 are located within Stonehenge's 'envelope of visibility' (Cleal *et al.* 1995: figure 21). The most impressive round barrow cemeteries, on Normanton Down, King Barrow Ridge and the Cursus, are all located so as to be just visible from Stonehenge, placed at the limits of visibility. The remainder, numbering several hundred, are placed so as to lie further outside this area of visibility from Stonehenge. This 'envelope of visibility' from Stonehenge provides a zone which was largely free of the physical remains of the Early Bronze Age dead except at its margins which we may

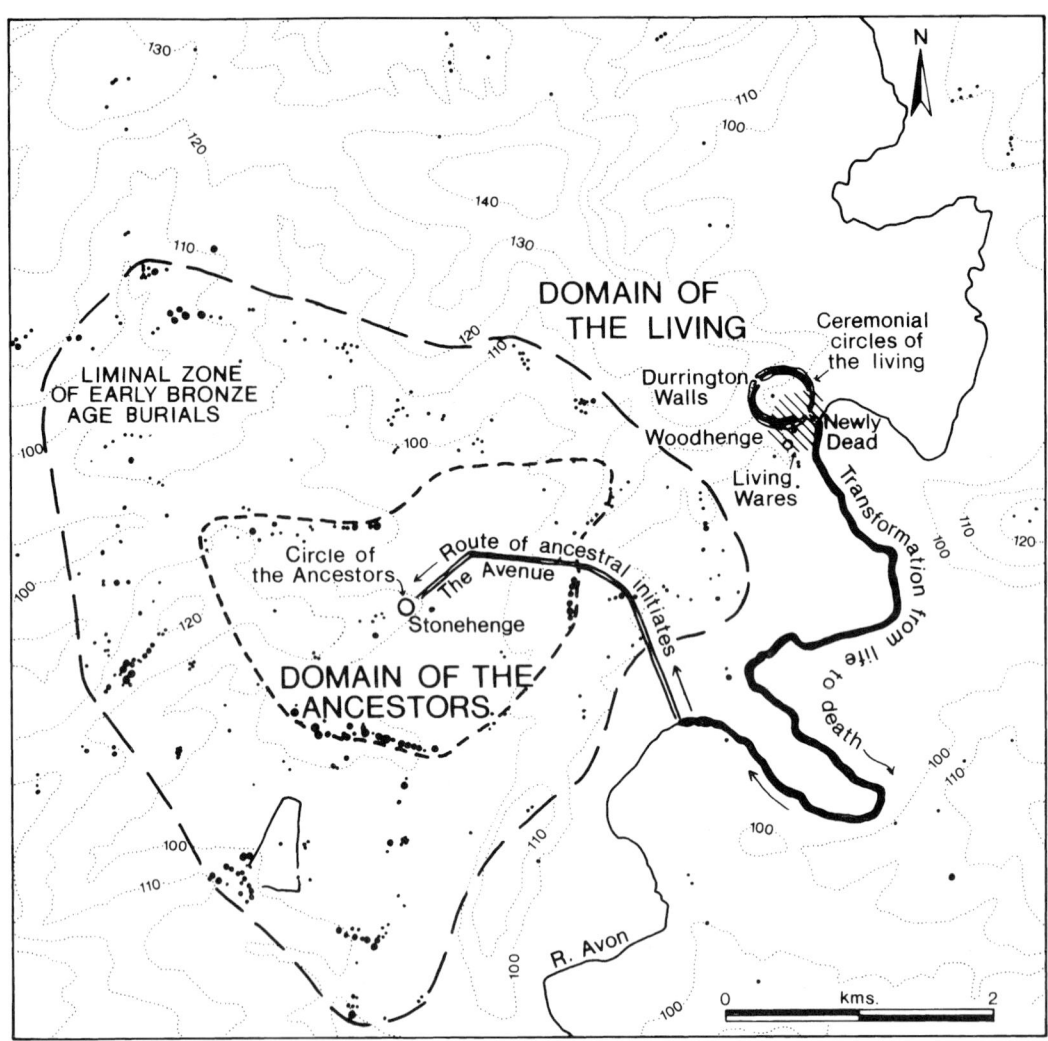

FIGURE 7. *Interpretation of the Late Neolithic to Early Bronze Age landscape around Stonehenge in phase 3. (Adapted from from Cleal* et al. *1995: figures 21, 254–5, drawn by Colin Merrony.)*

interpret as liminal zones between the landscape of the living and the landscape of the ancestors. The world of the ancestors was thus a physical domain, a place which, for over 500 years after the Late Neolithic, was separate from the places where the physical remains of the dead were put.[10] It was also cut off from the domain of the living by a liminal circular zone containing the corporeal remains of the Early Bronze Age dead (Woodward & Woodward 1996).

---

10   Whilst some of the Beaker burials around Stonehenge date to the later 3rd millennium BC, we have little idea about the placing of the remains of the dead during the time when Grooved Ware was in use. The associations with water raise the possibility that corpses, defleshed skeletons or cremated bones were disposed of in rivers (Richards 1996). The encroachment into the ancestors' domain by round barrows may have happened towards the end of the Early Bronze Age, judging by the presence of a Collared Urn in the barrow immediately east of Stonehenge.

The living will have visited Stonehenge, no doubt, at certain moments to meet the ancestors, to communicate directly with them. Yet, outside the moments of building, the monument and its immediate surroundings were probably left largely alone. In other words, in terms of human action, little or nothing happened within Stonehenge in Phase 3 other than its various periods of construction work.[11] Once built, its inhabitants were the spirits of the ancestors, using it for incorporeal feasting ceremonies and calendrical rituals which mirrored those corporeal ceremonies held by the living in the timber circles of the region, specifically at Durrington Walls.

Avebury, the West Kennet enclosures and beyond

It is difficult to talk of Stonehenge without mentioning Avebury and, if our notion has any validity, then it should be equally applicable here. Avebury is a large earthen henge with four entrances, within which is a large stone circle containing two adjacent stone circles associated with unusual stone edifices; the 'Cove' in the north circle and the 'Obelisk' in the south circle (Smith 1965; Malone 1989: figure 85). Running southeast out of the south-southwest entrance of the henge is the West Kennet avenue, a double row of standing stones which culminates over 2 kilometres away at the Sanctuary, a round building which was constructed in both timber and stone (Cunnington 1931).[12] Radiocarbon dates suggest two phases of ditch-digging between c. 3490–3280 and 3150–2630 BC (Pitts & Whittle 1992). The dating of the erection of the stones rests on two dates, c. 2840–2590 and 2510–2230 BC (Pitts & Whittle 1992) which Whittle rationalizes as falling within the period c. 2800–2400 BC (1997a: 140). Though no radiocarbon dates are available for the Sanctuary, it is considered to be broadly contemporary (Pollard 1992: 213).

One of the most exciting discoveries near Avebury in recent years has been the complex of palisade enclosures at West Kennet, dated to c. 2400–2000 BC (Whittle 1997a). Here we find a modified and smaller version of Avebury but created in wood rather than in stone (FIGURE 8). There is only a short stretch visible of an outer palisade[13] to match the outer stone ring at Avebury but otherwise the adjacent circles, the southeast-running avenue and the Sanctuary are all replicated. Spatially and structurally, the south circle at Avebury can be matched with Palisade Enclosure 1 at West Kennet, the north circle with Palisade Enclosure 2, the West Kennet avenue with Outer Radial Ditch 1 (though the latter is shorter and appears to have only the southern side), and the Sanctuary with Structure 4 (Whittle 1997a: figure 28). The Avebury Cove and the stone arrangements in the south circle may equate to the simple concentric post circles such as Structures 1, 2 and 3. Although excavations of the West Kennet complex were limited in extent, over 5000 animal bones and large quantities of Grooved Ware indicate large-scale feasting within the enclosures.[14]

---

11   The living, or certain persons amongst them, may have accompanied the ancestral spirits or come to meet them at particular moments but they would have needed no razor wire to keep them outside the circle and to either side of the avenue. As we will see below, a similar situation can be envisaged at Avebury where Keiller noticed slight depressions in the chalk bedrock running along either side of the West Kennet avenue (Ucko et al. 1991: 189), and where a gap in the standing stones on the southwest side of the avenue was used for the offering of stones, flint and stone-tempered pottery (Smith 1965: 210–12).

12   A second avenue, the Beckhampton avenue, was thought to have led out of the west-southwest entrance of the henge but geophysical survey has failed to reveal any certain trace of it (Ucko et al. 1991: 199).

13   This is visible in one aerial photograph (Whittle 1997a: figure 26) as a 150-m long crop-mark which appears to be a wide ditch containing large, widely spaced post-holes. Unfortunately it has not yet been investigated.

14   The animal bones are, like other timber circle assemblages, dominated by pig. More peculiarly there is a strong preponderance of right-side portions.

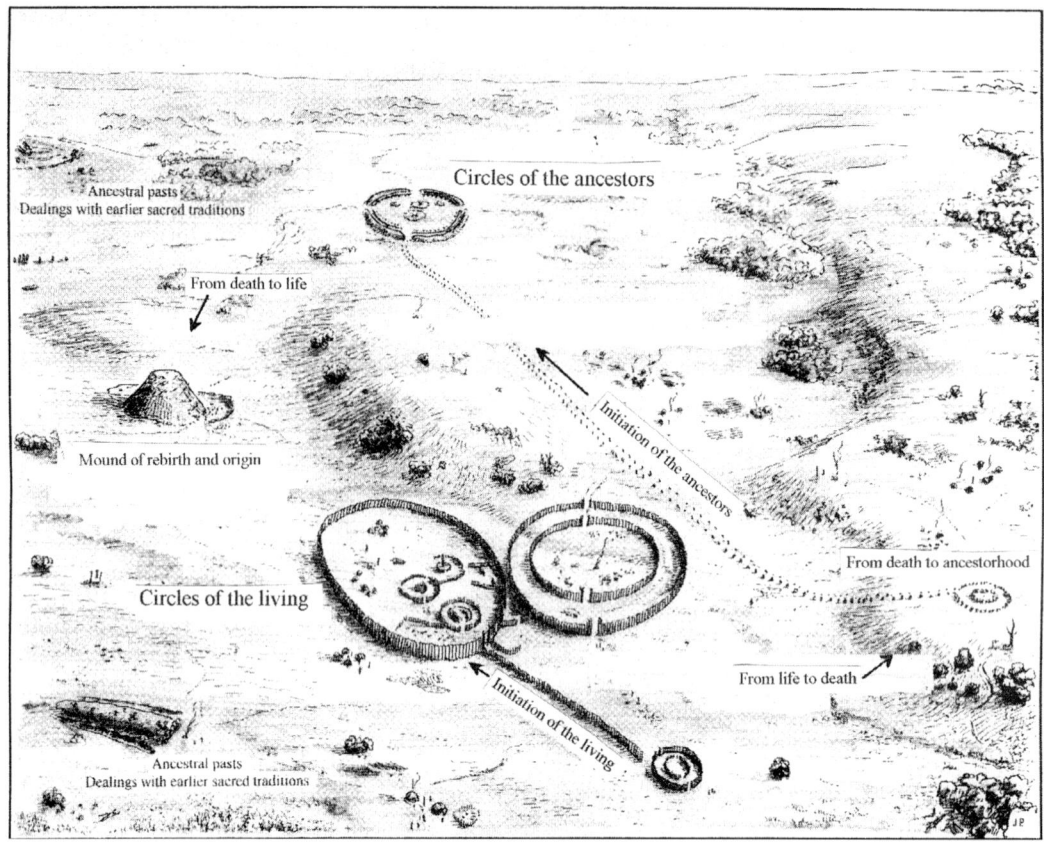

FIGURE 8. *A reconstruction of the parallel stone and timber monuments at Avebury and West Kennet. (Adapted from the drawing by Josh Pollard from Whittle 1997a: figure 87.)*

Not only does the Avebury–West Kennet evidence replicate the spatial segregation of the ancestors' stone-built space from the timber domain of the living but it also provides a set of relationships similar to those for the Stonehenge–Durrington monuments. The paired circles at Avebury and West Kennet are not intervisible; both sites have a close association with water; and the distribution of round barrows is markedly sparse within a 1-km radius of Avebury yet it lies within another major concentration of barrows.[15] We know relatively little about the interior of Avebury henge except that there is a dearth of pottery and animal bones that might be construed as feasting debris (Barclay *et al.* 1995: 113). Cunnington's extensive excavations of the Sanctuary produced little more than 80 sherds of Grooved Ware and a small assemblage of animal bones, though Pollard advises that surface accumulations could have been substantial (1992: 221). The

---

15   As Colin Richards has indicated (1996), water is very significant for the placing of henges. At Avebury the entry point (the Sanctuary) to the 'henge' of the ancestors lies downstream from the palisade enclosures, the 'henge' of the living, just as the beginning of the Stonehenge avenue is similarly located with respect to Durrington Walls. However, Avebury has a potentially unique monument in the form of Silbury Hill, which intercepts passage upstream from the palisade enclosures to Avebury henge (FIGURE 8). In terms of the flow of water and spiritual procession in a counter-clockwise direction, Silbury Hill marks the transition point where death turns to life, a monument of renewal and rebirth as Whittle has suggested on other grounds (1997a: 151). Its links with rebirth were also noted by Dames (1976).

geometric arrangement of post-holes and standing stones at the Sanctuary raises the possibility that wood and stone may have been in contemporary use here although it might also have begun as a timber monument and finished as a stone one (Pollard 1992). If the former is the case then we have the possibility that the Sanctuary was constructed as a place where the worlds of the living and the dead coincided, perhaps where the physical remains of the Late Neolithic dead were put, possibly immediately northwest of the Sanctuary, prior to the initiate ancestors' path up the avenue to Avebury.[16] If the latter then the Sanctuary is one of a small number of sites where wooden monuments were replaced in stone during the Later Neolithic (Pollard 1992: 218–19; Gibson 1994: 205).

If stone constructions are for the dead as opposed to timber for the living, we can use this principle to begin to understand transformations in the use of ceremonial sites over time. Timber structures which become 'lithicized' in later reworkings may be revealing in their material form a shift in their role in the social universe. We might interpret these sites as removed from the realm of the living into the realm of the ancestors as they were remodelled schematically in stone. The West Kennet enclosures, which appear to be later than the Avebury circles, may never have reached this stage of 'lithicization', of being transferred from the realm of the living to the realm of the dead. This was presumably because the ancestors' ceremonial site at Avebury was already in place. Likewise, the timber circles within Durrington Walls were never 'lithicized'. Stonehenge itself went through this wood-to-stone transformation between its Phases 2 and 3, significantly when it was used as a place of burial. It was precisely during this transition, and at no other time, that Stonehenge was used as a cemetery.[17] Other timber circles, such as Woodhenge and Mount Pleasant at Dorchester (Wainwright 1979), appear to have been replaced by token markers in stone. Mount Pleasant can also be regarded as potentially forming a wood–stone pair in that the timber circle (Site IV) is located adjacent to an unusual enclosure at Flagstones (Smith *et al.* 1997). The latter is, like Stonehenge's Phase 1, perfectly circular and, in contrast to Mount Pleasant, contains very few artefacts. Irregular hollows within the interior may have held stones.

The configuration of Later Neolithic stone and timber monuments in Wessex was undoubtedly different to those in other regions of Britain, yet there is a possibility that the same structuring principle of stone for the ancestors was in use throughout the British Isles, albeit expressed through regional variants. For example, the change from wood to stone can be seen to have occurred in Scotland. On sites at Machrie Moor, Arran (Haggarty 1991), at Moncrieffe (Stewart 1985), Temple Wood, Argyll (Scott 1988–89), Cairnpapple (Piggott 1947–48), probably Balfarg (Mercer 1981) and Croft Moraig on Tayside (Piggott & Simpson 1971), excavations of stone rings have revealed that they replaced timber predecessors. Precisely why some wooden monuments were lithicized and others were not is not clear but we might assume that the conferring of ancestral status was something which was largely dependent on local human agency and regional variation. The Wessex pattern of wood-and-stone paired

16   Burl (1979: 127) records an observation in 1678 by Dr Robert Toupe, the physician who sought out human bones to grind into medicinal powder, about human remains near the Sanctuary '. . . soe close by one another that scul toucheth scul . . . I really believe the whole plaine, on that even ground, is full of dead bodies', and another by John Aubrey: 'About 80 yards from this monument, in an exact plain round it, there were some years ago great quantities of human bones and skeletons dug up.'
17   The Beaker burial in Stonehenge's outer ditch (Evans 1984) now looks, in this new light, suspiciously like a clandestine killing (rather than a sacrifice *pace* Gibson 1994: 187). He was shot in the back and, other than the arrows that killed him, is accompanied only by a wristguard.

monuments appears to be very different to this southern and eastern Scottish example of stone-for-timber replacement.[18]

Within the Neolithic context of southern Britain we may broadly equate the use of large stones with the architecture of the ancestors, in contrast to the wooden and organic structures inhabited and used by the living.[19] The previous direct association of most Early Neolithic stone monuments with human remains, as in chambered tombs such as West Kennet, Wayland's Smithy and the Cotswold–Severn group in particular, provides us with some understanding of the contexts wherein the dead were associated with stone, a point also noted by Whittle (1997b: 163). Our general inability to locate the remains of the vast majority of the dead in the Late Neolithic presents a problem as to how that relationship between ancestors and stone might be conclusively demonstrated. Yet the prior associations between ancestors and stone provide a series of preconditions for the Late Neolithic: specific manifestations had changed, such as different means of disposal, yet there will have been threads of continuity in the more significant structuring principles of material life. Houses for the living continued to be built out of perishable materials and thus stone remained reserved for those transcendental aspects of the world associated with the ancestors. With the exception of treeless Orkney, stone was generally not incorporated into dwellings until the Middle Bronze Age. Yet not all Neolithic mortuary structures incorporate stones since many are built in regions where large stones are simply not available. In such circumstances we might expect similar solutions to those found in the stone-free regions of Madagascar where the hardest woods are substituted for stone. We should also remember that regional adoption of stone as a medium of the ancestors will have happened at different times and rates, by recalling the chronological variations in adopting raised stones as metaphors for the ancestors in different regions of Madagascar, with a 500-year gap between its adoption in Imerina and in Androy for instance.

Implications for the future

There are many avenues which the Madagascar analogy opens up. If stone was the material of the ancestors then our understanding of its modification for rock-art (Bradley 1997), its context in cave and rock-shelter burials (Chamberlain 1996) and its quarrying and shaping for stone axes (Edmonds 1995) takes on a new dimension. Equally the use of stone temper in pottery such as Peterborough Ware had ancestral associations different from Grooved Ware pots tempered with shell, grog or other materials.[20] The perfectly circular forms of Stonehenge 1 and Flagstones, along with the timber circles and Stone-

18   The henge at Marden in Wiltshire (Wainwright *et al.* 1971) contains a modest timber circle but there is no adjacent stone monument. We can only surmise that the ancestors of those celebrating at Marden were in residence at Stonehenge or Avebury.

19   It would also appear that, in the Earlier Neolithic, earth (or chalk) dug from the ground also had a certain degree of metaphorical equivalence with stone, being other materials associated with the ancestors, utilized in long-barrow construction. The ancestral significance of earth and chalk appears to have diminished in the Later Neolithic whereas that of stone was emphasized.

20   In this respect, we should rename Peterborough Ware and other Later Neolithic impressed wares, generally tempered with flint, chert, sandstone and quartz (Cleal 1995: 187–90), as 'ancestor ware'; pottery made for interactions specifically with the ancestors. Gibson (1995: 29) has noted that the quartz tempering probably had a deep significance whilst Thomas has recognized Peterborough Ware's contextual associations with the ancestral dead (1991: 92) and with continuity from the distant past (1991: 98). Peterborough Ware dominates the small assemblage from Avebury and the sherd scatter immediately west of Stonehenge. The large scatters of this pottery either side of the west end of the Stonehenge cursus lead us, additionally, to infer that this and other cursuses were built as pathways of initiation for the ancestors.

henge 3, are specifically features which are first found in the Late Neolithic; perfect circles are found in nature in the form of the sun and moon, the human eye[21] and ripples in still water. We would suggest that the former are more likely metaphors for the circular monuments since their correlations with solar and lunar movements are broadly accepted. Although there are no such round monuments today in Madagascar,[22] metaphors link the sun, moon and earth with respect for the ancestors and with the timing of rites of passage and other ceremonials.

The constitution of the Late Neolithic cosmological universe is also something which we can begin to explore. We are not dealing with ancestor worship as such. Our proposed model places the community of ancestors in an incorporeal world which they inhabit in a human fashion, a world parallel to the corporeal world inhabited by the living. Given existing interpretations of the timber circles as ceremonial centres, involving feasting — presumably calendrical celebration and sacrifice — and given the scarcity of bones and sherds at the stone circles, we suggest that the ancestors too were feasting and celebrating in their own intangible parallel world. This model suggests the presence of a third entity — an object of worship by all humans, living and dead. This 'third party' may have been a creator similar to the Malagasy's *Zanahary* but the architectural concern with precise circularity suggests that this transcendental entity was manifested in the heavenly bodies of the sun and the moon. We may invest Late Neolithic society, then, with at least two axes of transcendence, between the living and the ancestors and between people, both living and dead, and the object of their worship.

This interpretation of stone monuments as being for, or belonging to, the ancestors throughout much of Britain during this period may cause us to question Renfrew's model of chiefdom evolution in which Stonehenge is the central place of a confederacy of powerful chiefdoms in southern Britain (1973). As we have seen from Madagascar, the putting-up of stones for the ancestors is something which is found in states, chiefdoms and relatively egalitarian communities. There is no doubt that the size of the Avebury and Stonehenge stones is greater than those erected anywhere in Madagascar and that the sustained construction of these Late Neolithic composite monuments hints at a very high level of co-operation. We might heed the Malagasy metaphorical associations between stone and unity.

With the re-dating of the Stonehenge sarsens to *c.* 2400 BC, the gold-rich barrow burials of Bush Barrow, the Normanton Down cemetery and others in Britain now date to the sub-phases after the stones had been erected. With these probable 'chiefly' burials no longer dating to the relevant time frame, the copious barrow burial record of the later part of the 3rd millennium BC (associated with the Beaker period) reveals no certain social differences between individuals which might be indicative of a ranked society. Even the Beaker burials in the Cursus barrows immediately north of Stonehenge contain no exceptional collections of grave goods nor reveal any outstanding expenditure of effort in funerary rituals. Although small single items of gold occasionally appear in Beaker burials throughout Britain, these are not sufficient to indicate a chiefdom society. In fact, the funerary record of this period is far more akin to that found today amongst the competitive egalitarian Tandroy where women and children are the bread-winners whilst men are free to take part in monument construction. It may well be that the mobilization of labour for monument building in the Late Neolithic was orchestrated not by

---

21   In Malagasy the sun is *masoandro* ('the eye of the day').
22   Though tombs attributed to the Vazimba, the earliest inhabitants, are small circles of stones, hence the saying *mitangorongorona tahaky ny Vazimba* ('to be grouped tightly in a circle like Vazimba').

secular chiefs but by charismatic spiritual leaders and ritual specialists. In this respect, Whittle draws attention to the building of an enormous mound by the Nuer of eastern Africa in the 1890s (Whittle 1997a: 148–9). In a strongly egalitarian society, a charismatic war leader and prophet was able to mobilize the community in the construction of a great mound to bury all the bad things associated with smallpox and rinderpest (Whittle 1997a: 148–9; Evans-Pritchard 1956; Johnson 1994). What we might call egalitarian or even egalitarian yet hierarchical societies are capable of united mobilization to construct large monuments. What matters most is not the attainment of a certain level of social evolutionary complexity but the strength of the motivation and the ideology which drive people from their own volition to construct the world in new ways and build cosmic order on earth.

Finally, Stonehenge retains some of its mysteries. Why was it constructed where it is? Why were the Welsh bluestones brought all the way from the Preselis? We can suggest some possible answers. Associations between people and land in Madagascar are very strong[23] and links are maintained across hundreds of miles with the *tanin'drazan* ('land of the ancestors') in both rice-cultivating and cattle pastoralist regions. Perhaps the Preseli mountains were the place of origin for the founding ancestors of the people who built Stonehenge. Thus the ancestors from that place, embodied as stones, were fetched and physically incorporated into the landscape of Wessex, the new homeland. By the time that Stonehenge 1 was constructed, around 3000 BC, this part of Wessex had been the focus for much monumental activity in the form of long barrows and the Cursus. Yet Allen's synthesis of the remarkable post-holes beneath the carpark at Stonehenge establishes that they were constructed to hold *c.* 0·75-m diameter pine-tree trunks in the Early Mesolithic, *c.* 8500–7000 BC, about three or four millennia before even the earliest Neolithic monuments in Britain (Allen 1995; 1997). There is the possibility that more such post-holes may lie within Stonehenge Bottom, to the north of the monument, perhaps forming a ceremonial focus of some sort. Transmission of oral traditions over so many millennia is extremely unlikely but the post voids were visible as pits when Stonehenge was constructed, as indicated by their Late Neolithic/Early Bronze Age tertiary fill (Allen 1995: 51).[24] Thus there is the possibility that these unusually ancient diggings into the land were recognized as the work of human agency belonging to a time remote from the Neolithic. In this connection, Stonehenge Bottom is unusual in being an apparently empty space lying at the centre of one of the most densely constructed ceremonial landscapes in prehistoric northern Europe. This apparent absence of features may relate not only to the 'dead zone' set apart for the ancestors but perhaps also to as yet undiscovered pre-Neolithic structures.

Conclusion

The complex metaphorical associations between ancestors and stones in different parts of Madagascar incorporate, or are linked to, structuring principles of hardness increasing with age. These are especially associated with men, with stone as a symbol of eternity and unity, and stone (and certain hardwoods) thus being reserved for the ancestors, and which signify the sun and moon and their links with elders and with rites of passage. We can use cross-cultural or probability analogies to indicate that all traditional societies place significance on the ancestors and their role in the world of the living.

23   *Tsy tany mandeha fa olon' belona* ('it is not land which moves but people').
24   This might seem highly improbable but we should remember that negative features from 5000 years ago can still be seen clearly on the surface, such as ditch fills at Knap Hill amongst others.

Secondly, there is a formal analogy with Madagascar, where stones are linked to ancestors. Thirdly, relational analogies enable us to identify the structuring principles which work in both societies but to different ends. For example, the same principle can generate stones as identifiable individual ancestors in Madagascar and stones as ancestral replacements of timber in Britain, even though each outcome may be unknown in the other country. Finally, this relational analogy can be strengthened by reference to ideas about the materiality of stone as a durable and permanent marker, in contrast to the changing nature of wood, emphasizing the eternal as opposed to the transitory.

Whereas the Madagascar case-study provides a basic analogy, it also helps to highlight specific and important differences with Neolithic Wessex. These include the identification of individual *vatolahy* with individual ancestors, as opposed to the Neolithic collective stone monuments which gave the ancestors a place in which to dwell and celebrate. In Madagascar the bones of the ancestors are carefully kept in the visible stone tombs where they reside, whilst in Wessex the remains of the Late Neolithic dead were disposed of and leave little trace. The ancestors appear to have inhabited places largely separate from those where their physical remains ended up.

The efficacy of any persuasive analogy is that it not only explains the context under investigation but also opens up understanding of associated contexts. In this case, we have explained Stonehenge as a ceremonial circle built for the exclusive use of the ancestors. As a result, it appears that other stone monuments and their wooden counterparts, such as Avebury and the West Kennet enclosures, can be similarly understood as parallel ceremonial monuments, the former for the ancestors and the latter for the living. This further helps to explain the process of 'lithicization' whereby certain of the timber monuments are reworked in stone, thereby acknowledging their passing from the realm of the living to the realm of the ancestors. Thus the changing of a monument from wood to stone is a marking of the movement of the living through death to ancestorhood, as the ceremonial places which were once associated with the living became places devoid of living people where the ancestors now reside. Late Neolithic Britain was essentially shared by two communities living side by side, the living and the spirits of the dead. Contrary to recent speculations by archaeologists, New Agers and other groups, the great stone monuments, once built, were largely the domain of the spirit world into which the living rarely entered.[25]

Acknowledgements. This paper came about as a result of collaboration in association with the making of a BBC documentary on Stonehenge. The working through of this idea and the realization that it is actually applicable to Stonehenge was captured on film on Tuesday 3 February 1998. We are particularly indebted to the programme's director, Jean-Claude Bragard, for arranging for Ramilisonina's visit to Britain and for helping us towards these conclusions through his acute and perceptive questions. Susan Crighton of the BBC is also to be thanked for her administrative support. We have also benefited from discussions with and advice from Mike Allen, John Barrett, Richard Bradley, Andrew David, Jane Downes, Mark Edmonds, Alex Gibson, Karen Godden, Georges Heurtebize, Dai Morgan-Evans, Colin Renfrew, Retsihisatse, Colin Richards, Niall Sharples, Geoffrey Wainwright and Alasdair Whittle. FIGURES 6 & 7 were drawn by Colin Merrony. The Androy project has been the basis of our own collaboration and resulted in this 'spin-off'. We thank its team members and the people of Androy who have helped us further to understand about living and working with stones. That project has been funded by the British Academy, the National Geographic Society, the Nuffield Foundation and the Society of Antiquaries of London.

25   We come full circle in remembering that the earliest surviving written interpretation of Stonehenge, that recorded by Geoffrey of Monmouth around 1136 (Chippindale 1983: 22), is that it was a cenotaph, a monument for the ancestors, commemorating 460 British lords massacred by the Saxon king Hengist at Mount Ambrius (Amesbury).

References

AHERN, E. 1973. *The cult of the dead in a Chinese village*. Stanford (CA): Stanford University Press.

ALLEN, M.J. 1995. Before Stonehenge, in Cleal *et al.*: 41–62.

1997. Environment and land-use; the economic development of the communities who built Stonehenge (an economy to support the stones), *Proceedings of the British Academy* 92: 115–44.

ALLEN, M.J. & A. BAYLISS. 1995. Appendix 2: the radiocarbon dating programme, in Cleal *et al.*: 511–35.

ATKINSON, R.J.C. 1979. *Stonehenge*. Revised edition. Harmondsworth: Penguin.

1987. *Stonehenge and neighbouring monuments*. London: English Heritage.

BARCLAY, A., M. GRAY & G. LAMBRICK. 1995. *Excavations at the Devil's Quoits, Stanton Harcourt, Oxfordshire, 1972–3 and 1988*. Oxford: Oxford University Committee for Archaeology.

BARRETT, J.C. 1997. Stonehenge, land, sky and the seasons, *British Archaeology* 29: 8–9.

BENDER, B. 1998. *Stonehenge: making space*. Oxford: Berg.

BLOCH, M. 1995a. People into places: Zafimaniry concepts of clarity, in E. Hirsch & M. O'Hanlon (ed.), *The anthropology of landscape: perspectives on place and space*: 63–77. Oxford: Clarendon Press.

1995b. Questions not to ask of Malagasy carvings, in I. Hodder, M. Shanks, A. Alexandri, V. Buchli, J. Carmen, J. Last & G. Lucas (ed.), *Interpreting archaeology: finding meaning in the past*: 212–15. London: Routledge.

BRADLEY, R. 1997. *Rock art and the prehistory of Atlantic Europe: signing the land*. London: Routledge.

BURL, A. 1979. *Prehistoric Avebury*. New Haven (CT): Yale University Press.

CHAMBERLAIN, A.C. 1996. More dating evidence for human remains in British caves, *Antiquity* 70: 950–53.

CHIDESTER, D. 1990. *Patterns of transcendence: religion, death, and dying*. Belmont (CA): Wadsworth.

CHIPPINDALE, C. 1983. *Stonehenge complete*. London: Thames & Hudson.

CHIPPINDALE, C., P. DEVEREUX, P. FOWLER, R. JONES & P. SEBASTIAN. 1990. *Who owns Stonehenge?* Cambridge: Cambridge University Press.

CLEAL, R.M.J. 1995. Pottery fabrics in Wessex in the fourth to second millennia BC, in Kinnes & Varndell (ed.): 185–94.

CLEAL, R.M.J., K.E. WALKER & R. MONTAGUE. 1995. *Stonehenge in its landscape: twentieth-century excavations*. London: English Heritage. Archaeological report 10.

CUNLIFFE, B.W. & A.C. RENFREW (ed.). 1997. Science and Stonehenge, *Proceedings of the British Academy* 92.

CUNNINGTON, M.E. 1929. *Woodhenge*. Devizes: Simpson.

1931. The 'Sanctuary' on Overton Hill, near Avebury, *Wiltshire Archaeological and Natural History Magazine* 45: 300–35.

DAMES, M. 1976. *The Silbury treasure: the great goddess rediscovered*. London: Thames & Hudson.

DARVILL, T. 1997. Ever increasing circles: the sacred geography of Stonehenge and its landscape, *Proceedings of the British Academy* 92: 167–202.

DAVID, A. & A. PAYNE. 1997. Geophysical surveying within the Stonehenge landscape: a review of past endeavour and future potential, *Proceedings of the British Academy* 92: 73-113.

EARLE, T. (ed.). 1991. *Chiefdoms: power, economy, and ideology*. Cambridge: Cambridge University Press.

EDMONDS, M. 1995. *Stone tools and society: working stone in Neolithic and Bronze Age Britain*. London: Batsford.

EVANS, J.G. 1984. Stonehenge — the environment in the Late Neolithic and Early Bronze Age and a Beaker-age burial, *Wiltshire Archaeological and Natural History Society Magazine* 78: 7–30.

EVANS-PRITCHARD, E.E. 1956. *Nuer religion*. Oxford: Oxford University Press.

GATHERCOLE, P. & D. LOWENTHAL (ed.). 1989. *The politics of the past*. London: Unwin Hyman.

GIBSON, A. 1994. Excavations at the Sarn-y-bryn-caled cursus complex, Welshpool, Powys, and the timber circles of Great Britain and Ireland, *Proceedings of the Prehistoric Society* 60: 143–223.

1995. First impressions: a review of Peterborough Ware in Wales, in Kinnes & Varndell (ed.): 23–39.

HAGGARTY, A. 1991. Machrie Moor, Arran: recent excavations at two stone circles, *Proceedings of the Society of Antiquaries of Scotland* 121: 51–94.

HAWKINS, G.S. 1966. *Stonehenge decoded*. London: Souvenir Press.

HODDER, I. 1982. *The present past: an introduction to anthropology for archaeologists*. London: Batsford.

HOYLE, F. 1966. Speculations on Stonehenge, *Antiquity* 40: 262–76.

JOHNSON, D.H. 1994. *Nuer prophets: a history of prophecy from the Upper Nile in the nineteenth and twentieth centuries*. Oxford: Clarendon Press.

JOUSSAUME, R. & V. RAHARIJAONA. 1985. Sépultures mégalithiques à Madagascar, *Bulletin de la Société Préhistorique Française* 82: 534–51.

KINNES, I. & G. VARNDELL (ed.). 1995. *'Unbaked urns of rudely shape': essays on British and Irish pottery for Ian Long-worth*. Oxford: Oxbow.

KUS, S. & V. RAHARIJAONA. In press. Between earth and sky there are only a few large boulders: sovereignty and monumentality in central Madagascar, *Journal of Anthropological Archaeology* 17.

LAYTON, R. (ed.). 1989a. *Conflict in the archaeology of living traditions*. London: Unwin Hyman.

1989b. *Who needs the past?: indigenous values and archaeology*. London: Unwin Hyman.

LEBRAS, J.-F. 1971. *Les transformations de l'architecture funéraire en Imerina*. Antananarivo: Musée d'Art et d'Archéologie.

LEHMANN, A.C. & J.C. MYERS. 1993. Ghosts, souls, and ancestors: power of the dead, in A.C. Lehmann & J.C. Myers (ed.), *Magic, witchcraft, and religion: an anthropological study of the supernatural*: 283–6. Palo Alto (CA): Mayfield.

MACK, J. 1986. *Madagascar: island of the ancestors*. London: British Museum.

MACKIE, E. 1977. *The megalith builders*. Oxford: Phaidon.

MALONE, C. 1989. *Avebury*. London: Batsford & English Heritage.

MERCER, R.J. 1981. The excavation of a Late Neolithic henge-type enclosure at Balfarg, Markinch, Fife, Scotland, 1977–8, *Proceedings of the Society of Antiquaries of Scotland* 111: 63–171.

MUSSON, C.R. 1971. A study of possible building forms at Durrington Walls, Woodhenge and the Sanctuary, in Wainwright & Longworth: 363–77.

NDEMA, J. 1973. *Fomba Antakay (Bezanozano)*. Fianarantsoa: Ambozontany.

PARKER PEARSON, M. 1992. Tombs and monumentality in southern Madagascar: preliminary results of the central Androy survey, *Antiquity* 66: 941–8.

1993. *Bronze Age Britain*. London: Batsford & English Heritage.

PARKER PEARSON, M., K. GODDEN, G. HEURTEBIZE, RAMILISONINA & RETSIHISATSE. 1996. The Central Androy Project: fourth report. Unpublished manuscript, Universities of Sheffield and Antananarivo.

PIGGOTT, S. 1947-48. Excavations at Cairnpapple Hill, West Lothian, 1947–8, *Proceedings of the Society of Antiquaries of Scotland* 82: 68–123.

PIGGOTT, S. & D.D.A. SIMPSON. 1971. Excavation of a stone circle at Croft Moraig, Perthshire, Scotland, *Proceedings of the Prehistoric Society* 37: 1–15.

PITTS, M. & A. WHITTLE. 1992. The development and date of Avebury, *Proceedings of the Prehistoric Society* 58: 203–12.

POLLARD, J. 1992. The Sanctuary, Overton Hill, Wiltshire: a re-examination, *Proceedings of the Prehistoric Society* 58: 213–26.

1995. Inscribing space: formal deposition at the later Neolithic monument of Woodhenge, Wiltshire, *Proceedings of the Prehistoric Society* 61: 137–56.

RENFREW, A.C. 1973. Monuments, mobilization and social organization in Neolithic Wessex, in A.C. Renfrew (ed.), *The explanation of culture change: models in prehistory*: 539–58. London: Duckworth.

RICHARDS, C. 1996. Henges and water: towards an elemental understanding of monumentality and landscape in Late Neolithic Britain, *Journal of Material Culture Studies* 1: 313-36.

RICHARDS, C. & J. THOMAS. 1984. Ritual activity and structured deposition in Later Neolithic Wessex, in R. Bradley & J. Gardiner (ed.), *Neolithic studies: a review of some current research*: 189–218. Oxford: British Archaeological Reports. British series 133.

RICHARDS, J.C. 1990. *The Stonehenge environs project*. London: English Heritage. Archaeological report 16.

1991. *Stonehenge*. London: Batsford & English Heritage.

RICHARDS, J.C. & M. WHITBY. 1997. The engineering of Stonehenge, *Proceedings of the British Academy* 92: 231–56.

RUGGLES, C. 1997. Astronomy and Stonehenge, *Proceedings of the British Academy* 92: 203–29.

SAHLINS, M. & E.R. SERVICE (ed.). 1960. *Evolution and culture*. Ann Arbor (MI): University of Michigan Press.

SCOTT, J.G. 1988–89. The stone circles at Temple Wood, Kilmartin, Argyll, *Glasgow Archaeological Journal* 15: 53–124.

SERVICE, E.R. 1962. Primitive social organization: an evolutionary perspective. New York (NY): Random House.

SMITH, I.F. 1965. *Windmill Hill and Avebury: excavations by Alexander Keiller 1925–1939*. Oxford: Clarendon Press.

SMITH, R.J.S., F. HEALY, M. ALLEN, E. MORRIS, I. BARNES & P. WOODWARD. 1997. *Excavations along the route of the Dorchester by-pass 1986–1988*. Salisbury: Wessex Archaeology.

STARTIN, D.W.A. & R. BRADLEY. 1981. Some notes on work organisation and society in prehistoric Wessex, in C. Ruggles & A. Whittle (ed.), *Astronomy and society in Britain during the period 4000–1500 BC*: 289–96. Oxford: British Archaeological Reports. British series 88.

STEADMAN, L.B., C.T. PALMER & C.F. TILLEY. 1996. The universality of ancestor worship, *Ethnology* 35: 63–76.

STEWART, M.E.C. 1985. The excavation of a henge, stone circles and metal working area at Moncrieffe, Perthshire, *Proceedings of the Society of Antiquaries of Scotland* 115: 125–50.

SWANSON, G.E. 1964. *The birth of the gods: the origin of primitive beliefs*. Ann Arbor (MI): University of Michigan Press.

TILLEY, C. 1996. The power of rocks: topography and monument construction on Bodmin Moor, *World Archaeology* 28: 161–76.

THOMAS, J. 1991. *Rethinking the Neolithic*. Cambridge: Cambridge University Press.

UCKO, P.J., M. HUNTER, A.J. CLARK & A. DAVID. 1991. *Avebury reconsidered: from the 1660s to the 1990s*. London: Unwin Hyman.

WAINWRIGHT, G.J. 1979. *Mount Pleasant, Dorset: excavations 1970–1971*. London: Society of Antiquaries.

1989. *The henge monuments: ceremony and society in prehistoric Britain*. London: Thames & Hudson.

WAINWRIGHT, G.J., J.G. EVANS & I.H. LONGWORTH. 1971. The excavation of a Late Neolithic enclosure at Marden, Wiltshire, *Antiquaries Journal* 51: 177–239.

WAINWRIGHT, G.J. & I.H. LONGWORTH. 1971. *Durrington Walls: excavations 1966–1968*. London: Society of Antiquaries.

WATSON, J. & E. RAWSKI (ed.). 1988. *Death ritual in late imperial and modern China*. Berkeley (CA): University of California Press.

WHITTLE, A. 1997a. *Sacred mound, holy rings: Silbury Hill and the West Kennet palisade enclosures: a Later Neolithic complex in north Wiltshire*. Oxford: Oxbow Monograph 74.

1997b. Remembered and imagined belongings: Stonehenge in its traditions and structures of meaning, *Proceedings of the British Academy* 92: 145–66.

WOODWARD, A.B. & P.J. WOODWARD. 1996. The topography of some barrow cemeteries in Bronze Age Wessex, *Proceedings of the Prehistoric Society* 62: 275–91.

Aerial reconnaissance of the Fen Basin
by F./Lt. D.N. RILEY

Antiquity 19 (75), 1945

AERIAL reconnaissance and photography are of great importance in the study of the early history of Fenland and the surrounding country, conditions often being very suitable for this method of investigation. A vast amount of information which can be recorded easily by air-photography, would only be obtained with the greatest difficulty, if at all, by field-work on the ground. The present paper is a brief record of observations made while flying over the fen basin during the course of duty. Unfortunately photography was not practicable, but systematic notes were kept of everything observed.* Further work should reveal much more.

Geology

The Fenland is bordered by chalk, limestone and clay country. Gravels are found along the edges of the fens and up the various river valleys in the area. The fens themselves are composed of fine silt on the seaward side and peat on the inland side.

The different subsoils affect air-archaeology in two ways, (A) by producing different types of country, some suitable, others unsuitable for occupation by early man, and (B) because on arable land soil-marks and crop-marks only appear on certain kinds of subsoil, others, particularly clay, being unfavourable. On old pastures which have not been ploughed since ancient times the second consideration is inoperative, as the ancient remains show as earthworks, whatever the subsoil may be. TABLE 1 summarizes the salient points of the different subsoils of the Fen Basin.

Clay, limestone and peat fen were unproductive of ancient sites and so need not be considered further in this paper. Chalk, gravel and silt fen were very rich and are described in detail.

The chalk hills

Chalk hills border the fen basin on the north, east and northeast. I saw very little of the Lincolnshire Wolds, which therefore must be omitted from this account, but quite often

subsoil	frequency of ancient sites seen from the air	earthworks in old pastures	soil-marks	crop-marks
chalk	fairly common	rare	very good	good
limestone	none	—	—	—
clay	rare	rare	very poor	very poor
gravel	common	occasional	poor	generally very good
silt fen	common	common	very good	good
peat fen	none	—	—	—

TABLE 1.

---

* Luckily the late Major G.W.G. Allen made several flights to this area and took a considerable number of photographs, two of which are here reproduced by courtesy of Mr E.T. Leeds, Keeper of the Ashmolean Museum, where all the Allen photographs are now preserved.

FIGURE 1. *Crop marks at Northborough, Northamptonshire (west of the Manor House).*

flew over the belt of chalk country which runs through west Norfolk, southern Cambridgeshire and northern Hertfordshire. Considerable areas of chalk are masked by boulder clay or gravel, but over large stretches of country the chalk lies immediately below the surface. Most of the land is arable and few ancient remains survive undamaged.

Considerable numbers of barrows have been destroyed, but they can still be traced by the circular ditches which once surrounded them which show up well as soil marks or crop marks (circles of this type are seen on FIGURE 1). In some cases remnants of the barrows still defy the plough. The concentration of barrows is not spectacular, as in some parts of England, but the total number must have been large. They are, for example, widely distributed in the fifteen-mile-long stretch of country from Baldock, through Royston to Duxford. Among discoveries made in 1944, may be mentioned a line of four barrows 850 yards east of Combe Farm, Therfield, Herts. and two double circles at Clothall, Herts., 2400 yards north-northwest of the church. O.G.S. Crawford[1] and the late Major G.W.G. Allen both worked on the Royston district and recorded much that is new, but a thorough air-survey is certainly needed for the whole chalk belt.

Ancient sites are less common on the chalk of west Norfolk, and the peculiar patterns of soil marks caused in many places by the hummocky surface of the chalk makes them difficult to spot. However, I saw several circles in the country round Marham and Narborough.

Remains of occupation sites were seldom seen on the chalk, the only one of interest being at Narborough, Norfolk, where soil marks east of Narborough Yards revealed a series of rectangular enclosures (compare the similar site shown on FIGURE 1). Romano-British pottery and animal bones were scattered over the surface. A few rectangular enclosures were noted in the parishes of Bygrave and Clothall, Herts.

No fresh information was obtained about the great linear earthworks and no new hill-forts were located.

Gravels

Gravels in parts of the Ouse and Nene valleys, in the Market Deeping area, and along the fen margin between Chatteris and Cambridge are rich in early sites. On the other hand, there is very little to be seen on the rest of the fen margin gravels or beside the smaller rivers, and the sands and gravels of Breckland are barren to the air-archaeologist. The explanation for these differences in the incidence of early sites visible from the air is probably that (A) only the wide spreads of gravel attracted early man, and (B) not all gravels are favourable to the development of crop-marks.

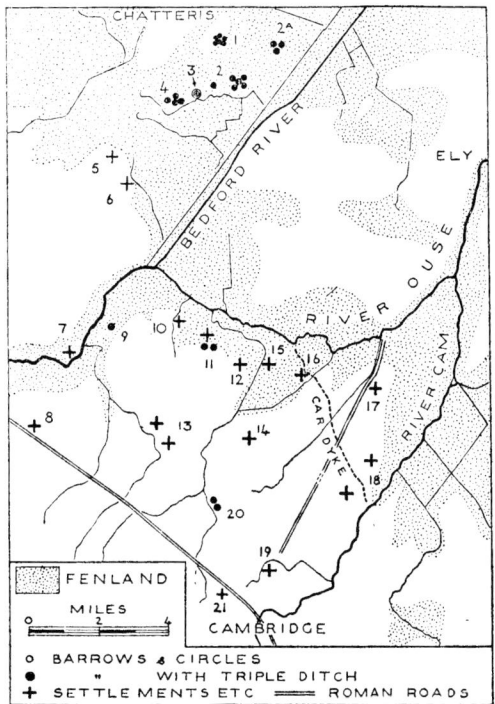

FIGURE 2.

1   The southern margin of the Fens

There were at least ten ditched round barrows (FIGURE 2, sites 2, 3), one with triple ditches, and four circles (site 4) visible in the fens southeast of Chatteris. The circles are no doubt the ditches of ploughed-out barrows. The land here is composed of gravel subsoil with a fairly thin covering of peaty soil, and for aerial study is much the same as ordinary gravel country, except that soil marks are much better, there being a greater contrast of colour between the soil (black and peaty) and subsoil (yellow gravel) than usual.

One barrow (site 9) and two circles (site 11) were seen near the Fen margin at Willingham and northwest of Histon were two circles (site 20) on gravels left by an old course of the Cam. In a pasture northeast of Wenny Farm, Chatteris (site 1) is an interesting group of small circular ditches about 30 ft in diameter and without mounds or banks; they may be compared to the groups of small circles shown by soil-marks in the silt fens.

Settlement sites are more prominent than the barrows and circles, which are relatively scarce compared with some areas. The sites all lie on gravel, except one on Lower Greensand at Cottenham (site 14). Owing to the low level of much of the land, there are many old pastures, and four sites (7, 10, 16,[2] 17) remain as earthworks. Site 5 is partly destroyed and the rest show only as soil-marks and/or crop marks. The majority (5–7, 10, 13, 15–19, 21) consist of groups of rectangular enclosures, often overlapping each other. Sites 8 and 14 include both round and rectangular enclosures.

There are two large enclosures near Willingham. Site 11 is a large double-ditched, four-sided enclosure, with round corners. Site 12 is similar, but larger (estimated 250 by 300 feet), with sharp corners and two or three ditches on all sides but the south.

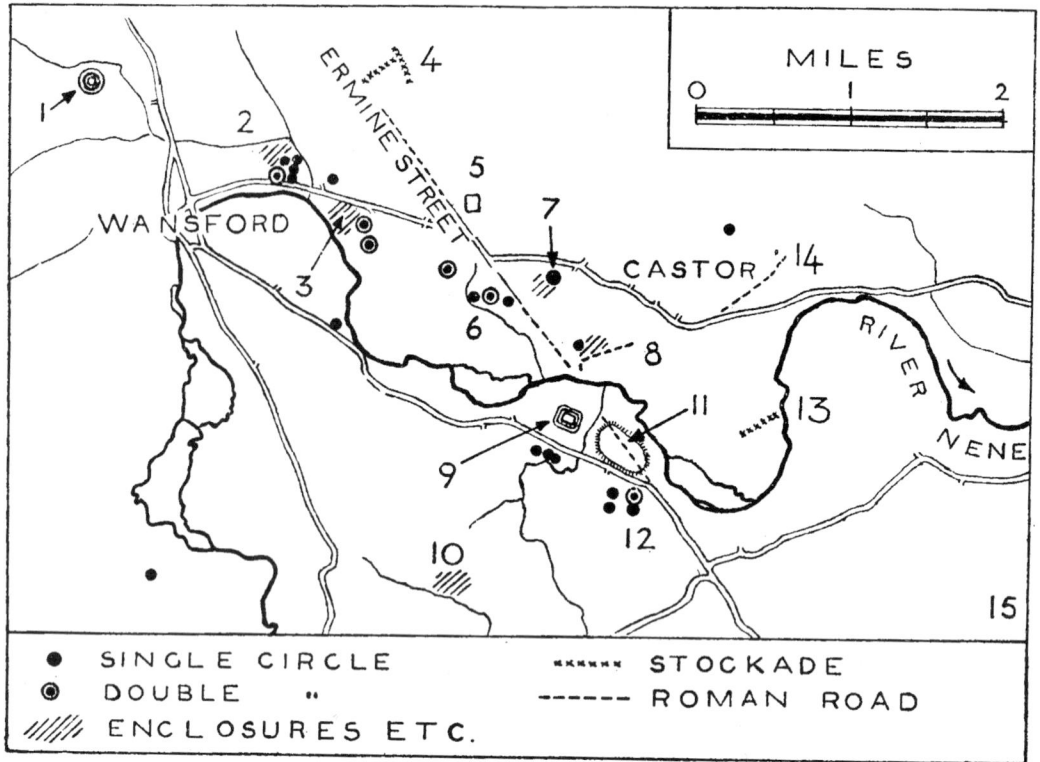

FIGURE 3.

2 The Ouse valley

Occasional crop-mark sites were seen as far up-stream as Newport Pagnell, though they were most frequent between St Neots and Huntingdon.

Circles appeared here and there, for example at Lathbury, Bucks. (one); Fenlake, southeast of Bedford (three); Buckden, Hunts. (three). Northwest of Moor End, Felmersham, Beds. was a fine double circle. There were settlement sites with many enclosures at Brampton, Hunts. (north of Grove Farm), south of Fen Drayton, Hunts. (FIGURE 2, site 8), and northeast of Godmanchester, Hunts.; the enclosures were respectively round, mixed round and rectangular, and all rectangular. Finally, at Little Paxton, Hunts. (1200 yards southwest of the church), and possibly also southwest of Brampton, Hunts. are traces of big stockades, indicated now by lines of large post-holes.[3]

3 The Nene valley

Flying down the Nene from Northampton to Peterborough nothing of archaeological interest was seen in 1944 except in the Wansford–Castor area. Here the valley widens and there are many signs of early occupation. I first examined the area at the suggestion of Dr J.K. St Joseph in the hope of rediscovering some of the numerous Roman houses shown on the map in Artis' '*Durobrivae*'. This was not realized, but disappointment was removed by the sight of many other interesting remains (FIGURE 3).

The earliest are presumably the circles, of which I noted 24 (18 single, 6 double), often in small groups. The diameter is normally of the order of 60 to 80 feet, similar to those seen in such numbers on gravels or chalk elsewhere, but there are two exceptions, a single (FIGURE 3, site 7) and a double circle (site 12), which are of exceptional size (estimated diameter approx. 300 feet) and have narrow and very accurately cut ditches.

The peculiar triple circle at Thornhaugh (site 1) may be mentioned here, though it actually lies off the gravel in a marshy valley. It has escaped ploughing. There are three ditches of different widths, approximate measurements (paced) being 12 feet for the outer, 30 feet for the second and 45 feet for the inner. The diameters are approximately 150 feet, 350 feet, and 500 feet. Between the second and inner ditches is a low bank; the central area also appears to have been embanked, but mutilation caused by a recent farm track makes it difficult to discern its original condition. There are narrow causeways across the inner ditch on the north and south of the central area.

Turning to the Roman sites, in which the Castor area is so rich, the most important is the camp (site 9) discovered by Crawford in 1930[4] and recently described by Hawkes.[5] The western end of this showed clearly, with gate and multiple ditches. Through the camp, running west-northwest–east-southeast, was a central road with ditch or gutter on either side. The eastern end did not show in 1944. On the other side of the river was seen the single-ditched camp (site 5) published by Margary.[6] On the site of the Roman town, 'The Castles', at Chesterton (site 11), the rampart, the streets and traces of build-ings were outlined in the crops. The usual chess-board town plan was absent and the streets were irregular, the only straight road being the Ermine Street, which bisects the town. The Roman roads of this district have been discussed already by Margary[7] and I am unable to add any new information. The Roman road called Lady Coneyburrow's Way by Artis (site 8) and its continuation (site 14) showed well.

Of uncertain date are four stockades (sites 2, 3, 4, 13) and several groups of small enclosures (sites 2,* 3, 7, 8, 10) presumably settlement sites.

4   The March gravels

On the fen islands at March and Stonea and on fen margin gravels between Eye and Thorney, are remains of settlements and fields similar to those of the silt fens, described below. Groups of small circles of the type seen on the silt fens occur north of March and at Stonea. These sites are included with the silt fen sites on FIGURE 4.

Earlier occupation is probably indicated by barrows at the Gores, Thorney and at Stonea (600 yards south of Daintree Farm) each with ditch and remains of central mound. Several circles west of Stonea probably remained from other barrows.

5   The Market Deeping area and the western margin of the Fens

At the edge of the 'highland' along the western margin of the fens from Peterborough to Heckington (nr. Sleaford) runs a strip of gravel, generally narrow, but broadening round Market Deeping to a width of up to six miles. The Car Dyke, the old canal which borders the fens, runs for almost all this part of its course along the strip of gravel. The rivers Welland and Glen flow through the Market Deeping area and it is traversed by King Street, a Roman road. When I flew down it last summer, the gravel country was devoid of any signs of early settlement except in the Market Deeping area, which was very rich in crop-mark sites, the positions of which were noted down from time to time and are here shown on FIGURES 5 & 6. Further work should add many more.

The circles (FIGURE 1) are generally of the usual sizes and types; 51 are single, 5 double and 2 triple. Much of the original barrow remains within a circle immediately

---

*   First seen by me July 1939 and photographed at once by Major Allen. — O.G.S.C.

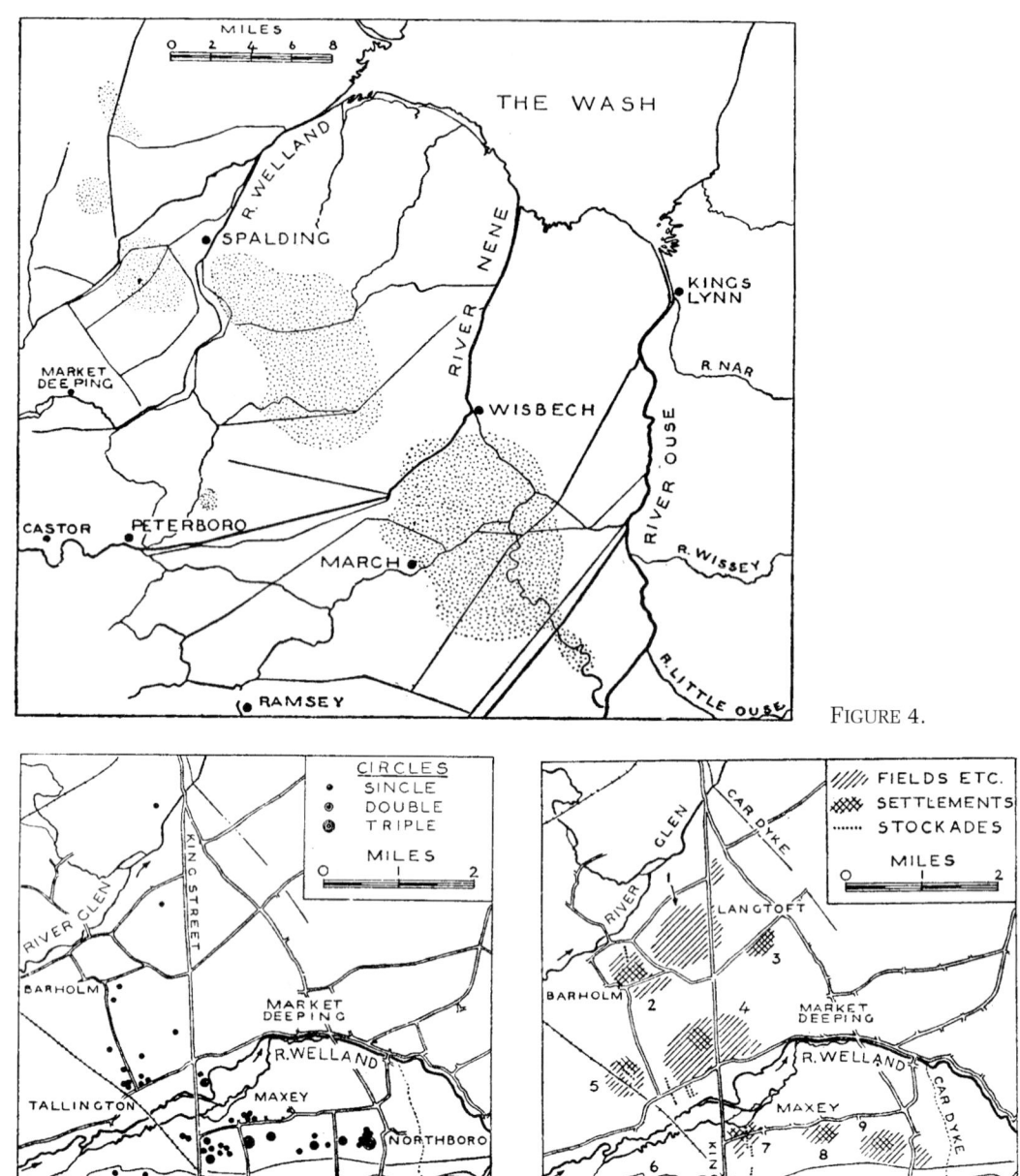

FIGURE 4.

FIGURE 5.

FIGURE 6.

northeast of Tallington railway station. Two of the double circles (below the 'A' of Maxey and 'N' of Northboro') (FIGURE 5) are exceptional in having a very large outer ditch and a comparatively small inner one (diameters approx. 250 feet and 70 feet respectively). A small ring (diam. approx. 2o feet) of post-holes showed in the western side of the former between the inner and outer circles.

A long rectangular enclosure near the group of circles north of Barnack has been published by C.W. Phillips[8] and compared with the similar but larger enclosures near the Upper Thames,[9] for which an early date has been suggested.

Large areas are covered by old fields (FIGURE 6), shown up by their boundary ditches, and there are many settlement sites, indicated by groups of rectangular enclosures. Lanes are seen in many places running between the fields or enclosures. FIGURE 1 shows what appear to be a settlement site and various field boundary ditches. It will be noticed that they are crossed by the furrows of later strip-cultivation. These remains are very similar to those in the silt fens, which were Roman.

Stockades, indicated by long lines of big post-holes, occur in surprising numbers. Near Bainton a whole series of them were seen (shown diagrammatically on FIGURE 6) and one end appeared to abut on to a ditch connected with a settlement or field-system. Southwest of Maxey, a stockade intersects a settlement site. In two places there are double stockades.

Nothing was seen in the upper parts of the valleys of the Welland and Glen. I did not examine the valleys of the Witham or of the small river Slea, near Sleaford.

6   Northern margin of the Fens and the Bain valley

The northern margin of the Fens, like the western, is fringed with gravel, which covers quite a considerable area round Coningsby and Woodhall Spa and extends up the valley of the Bain. I visited this area several times, and though occasional crop-marks were seen, all appeared to be due to ditches of recent origin, and no ancient sites were visible in 1944.

7   Eastern margin of the Fens, Breckland and the Lark, Little Ouse, Wissey and Nar valleys

These gravel areas were disappointing. Breckland is now largely tree-covered and its sands and gravels are probably not suitable for the production of crop marks, in any case. The river gravels showed very little. However, what may be an important discovery was made at Ixworth, Suffolk (northeast of Bury St. Edmunds), near a small stream, tributary to the Little Ouse. South of the village, crop-marks showed what appeared to be another Roman camp of the same type as that near Castor. It was diamond-shaped with rounded corners and defended by triple ditches. The site was partly obscured by modern roads and by an unsuitable crop in one field, so that the only gate which could be made out was one in the middle of the southeastern side.

Southeast of Ixworth a circle was seen, and west of Hockwold-cum-Wilton, Norfolk, on the edge of the fens, a large complex of rectangular enclosures resembling the silt fen sites.

The silt fens

The fen soils vary considerably in colour, and from the air the silt fens (yellowish soil), the peat fens (black soil) and the 'highlands' (brown soil) can easily be distinguished. Looking at the ground more closely, one sees innumerable old river and stream-beds, and in parts of the silt fens, very extensive systems of ditches dug in connexion with Romano-British settlements and fields. These early remains, which have been known for some years, are among the most important archaeological discoveries to have been made from the air in Great Britain.

The sites seen from the air sometimes remain as earthworks in pastures, but generally lie on arable land and show as soil marks and crop marks, due to the rich peaty soil which accumulated at the bottoms of the old ditches. In brief, the main features seen are (a) groups of small enclosures, often rectangular in shape, surrounded by (b) extensive

FIGURE 7. *Earthworks in a pasture at Gedney Hill, Lincs. (about 1 mile northwest of the railway station).*

systems of small fields, between which run (c) many droves or farm-tracks. The ditches are often very complicated. There are also (d) many groups of small circles.

One of Major Allen's air photographs is reproduced (FIGURE 7) showing a settlement site in a pasture near Gedney Hill, Lincs. Part of this land is now under plough and the ditches appear as soil marks (dark lines). I walked over the ground in 1944 and around A and B found it littered with animal bones and fragments of Roman pottery. There were several large fragments of rotary querns. The excavation of sites of this type, particularly in places where they have not been disturbed by modern ploughing, should yield new information. There are many points of resemblance between the sites on the silt fens and the settlements and occasional field systems seen on the gravels.

The approximate areas covered by these Romano-British remains is shown on FIGURE 4. It will be seen that I was unable to trace any near the modern coast-line on what is now good land.

The groups of small circles do not appear to have been noticed previously. They cannot be connected directly with the Roman sites, though they have a similar distribution. The circles show as rings of dark soil between 30 and 50 ft diameter (the circles on the gravels are usually 60–100 feet diameter) and must mark the positions of circular ditches in which peaty soil accumulated. Double circles and straight-sided ovals are seen occasionally. The circles may occur singly, but are generally in groups, often of as many as 20 or 30, and the total number in the silt fens must run into four figures.[10] They often intersect each other. I have walked over two groups of circles on ploughed land and saw no traces of any mounds or banks. Their origin cannot be settled without excavation; some agricultural operation may account for them, but the most likely explanation seems to be that they were small and low ditched round barrows. To judge from Major Allen's photograph, two small circles I noted at the Gedney Hill site were originally small barrows (C on FIGURE 7).

In Euximoor Fen, Upwell, Cambs. (south of Ivy House Farm), was seen a line of five larger circles, the diameters of which were estimated to be between 60 and 80 feet. These were presumably the ditches of barrows of normal size.

Finally, I should like to acknowledge the help received from Dr J. K. St. Joseph in the preparation of this article.

References

1 See *P.P.S.*, 1936, 97 ff.
2 This site, near the Car Dyke, at Cottenham, has been known for a long time, see Fox, *Archaeology of the Cambridge Region* (1923), p. 223.
3 Similar stockades near Castor, Northants. and Market Deeping, Lincs. are mentioned below. Others in the Upper Thames valley are described by the present writer in *Oxoniensia* VIII.
4 ANTIQUITY, 1930, IV, 274.
5 *ibid.* 1939, XIII, 178 ff. See also I.D. Margary, *ibid.* 455.
6 *Ant. Journ.*, XV, pl. XIII.
7 *ibid.* 113 ff.
8 *P.P.S.*, 1935, pl. XIX.
9 *Ant. Journ.*, XIV, 414 ff.
10 It is difficult to find similar groups of barrows or circles in England, but close parallels are seen in Dutch urnfields, for example those published in *Oudheid. Meded.*, XIV (1933), 26 ff. and XVII (1936), 38 ff, where numerous small circular ditches and occasional double circles and long ovals are seen. These are of Iron Age date.

The Fenland Project: from survey to management and beyond

by **JOHN COLES & DAVID HALL**

ANTIQUITY 71 (1997): 831–44

THE FENLAND PROJECT of eastern England has been one of Britain's largest wetland surveys, funded by the Department of the Environment/English Heritage over a period of nearly 20 years. An early note about the Project appeared in ANTIQUITY (Coles & Hall 1983) and an extensive treatment, forming a Special Section in ANTIQUITY for 1988, set out the discoveries in Cambridgeshire (Hall 1988), Lincolnshire (Lane 1988; Hayes 1988) and Norfolk (Silvester 1988a). The field surveys were associated with aerial photographic work (Palmer 1988) and a wide-ranging environmental programme (Waller 1988). These interim statements for ANTIQUITY readers were followed in 1992 by a short assessment of the survey results and an introduction to the next phase, the Fenland Evaluation Project (Hall 1992a). The thinking behind that Evaluation was non-controversial; what came afterwards has turned out less simple. To understand this, and to provide readers with the latest opinions, we will best turn back to the original concepts.

The Fenland Project began its major work in 1981 with a seven-year programme to examine as much of the drying/eroding/wasting Fenland in the three counties of Cambridgeshire, Lincolnshire and Norfolk as could be physically searched. The small piece of Fenland in Suffolk was also included in the survey but on a different time-frame, and David Hall had already started in Cambridgeshire in 1976. Over the survey period, about 60% of the entire Fenland, which in total covers 420,000 hectares (one million acres), was field-walked (FIGURE 1); the aim was to discover and identify sites of all periods that were being revealed by wastage of the peat and by erosion of the siltlands. It was known that sites, some of them waterlogged, had appeared, been ploughed away or otherwise lost, for many decades and the initial work of David Hall in the southern Fenland had clarified and demonstrated the losses. By 1988, the end of the survey period, over 2000 previously-unknown sites had been identified, ranging from the Late Glacial and Mesolithic to the medieval period. Responsibility for the control of the overall scheme lay in the hands of a Project committee; the surveys were county-based and the publication of the results, parish by parish, was the obligation of the individual field officers.

The results of the surveys have now appeared as seven monographs (Hall 1987; 1992b; 1996; Hayes & Lane 1992; Lane 1993; Silvester 1988b; 1991) with another book on the environmental work (Waller 1994). Through the goodwill of all concerned, and the close integration of results from all counties, a summary of the Fenland Project work was prepared (Hall & Coles 1994). Very much an overview, this book offered a broader, non-parish-based picture of Fenland settlement and activity. It also drew upon other Fenland work, not part of the Project and funded separately, to enhance the picture of the Fenland in ancient times. Among these other organizations, the work of the Fenland Archaeological Trust at Flag Fen and Fengate (Pryor 1991; 1992) as well as the Dyke Survey (French & Pryor 1993) and the Haddenham Project (Evans & Hodder 1985; 1986) are the most significant.

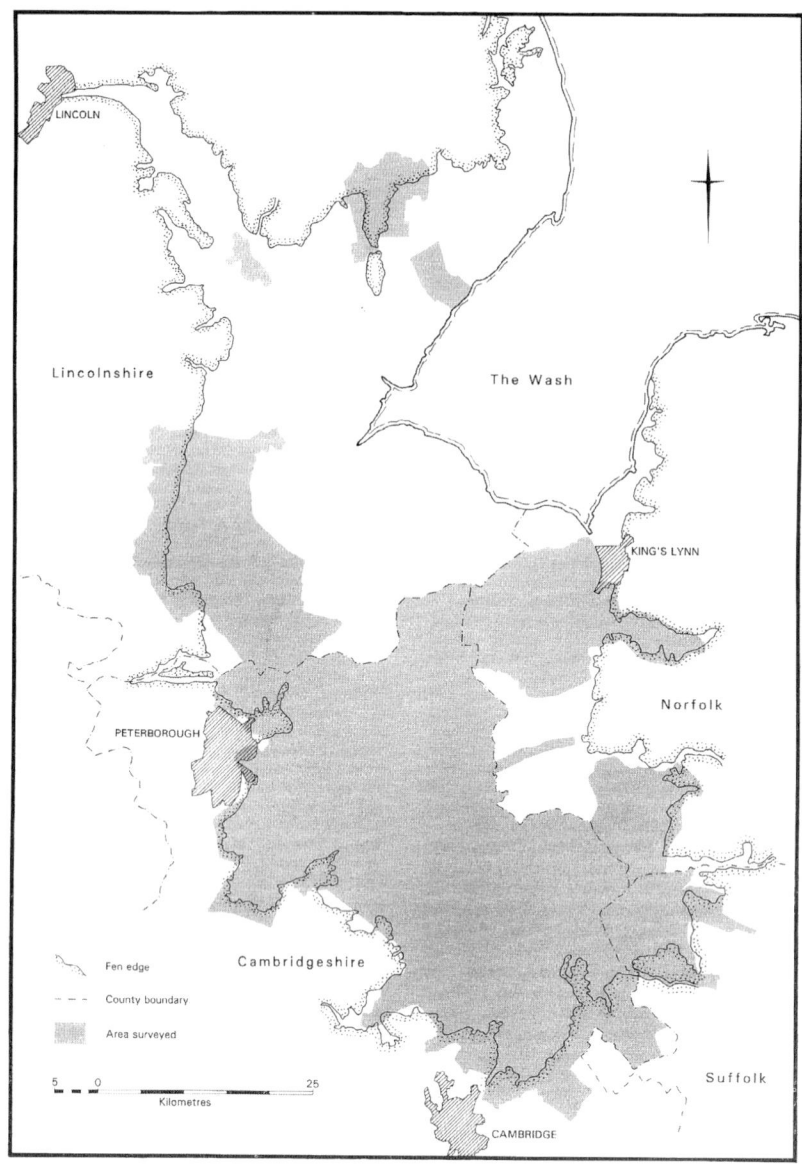

FIGURE 1. *The Fenland counties of England. The areas walked by the Fenland Field Officers. (Hall & Coles 1994: xii.)*

By 1988, the end of the Fenland (survey) Project, we could well appreciate that the Fenland was in serious trouble. There could have been an advantage here, for archaeology, if it had been possible to re-walk some of the black fens. The rate of peat wastage could be measured, and new sites identified; at its simplest and most obvious, an old land surface with wasting deposits upon and around it might reveal Bronze Age artefacts in a 1981 search but Neolithic debris in 1988, lower down on the shallow slopes. There is an interesting comparison, now published, of fen and fen-edge discoveries in Norfolk over a period of 30 years or more which show how the integrity and identification of sites are altered, diminished or destroyed by agriculture and drainage (Healy 1996). Drainage of the wet fens, deep ploughing and wind-blow are the major elements in the loss of the Fenland character, and in 1991 we 'humanized' the effects as follows (Coles 1991: 26):

> Today much of the Fenland lies like one of its bog bodies, a desiccated corpse, a thin skin of peat stretched to breaking point over the skeleton in some places, the bare bones of bedrock exposed in others. Its arteries, that once carried life to those limbs and organs, are detached now, and the water is dragged hurriedly along channels now raised above the dried body.

In 1988, the threat having been amply demonstrated yet again, a decision was made to evaluate some of the recently-discovered sites that seemed to warrant serious consideration for preservative action and management, or for partial or intensive examination in the future. The Fenland Evaluation Project, its selection of sites, and proposed actions, were outlined in ANTIQUITY (Hall 1992a). Dossiers were created for about 150 sites, and recommendations put forward to English Heritage (Coles *et al.* 1990). These ranged from earthwork sites which could be scheduled as Ancient Monuments (50 sites), to other sites less easily encompassed by the Act, hence for excavation (large- or small-scale, 44) or to abandonment (31 sites now shown to be wholly ploughed out or otherwise destroyed). Scheduling, to give legal protection, has now mostly been carried out on the first group of monuments. The excavation programme was institutionalized in a Fenland Management Project in 1991.

The Management Project was concerned to investigate sites already known to be of high potential, some of them probably suitable for Scheduling but whose precise character and state of preservation were not fully known. Because most were to be protected from future damage, the investigations were kept to a minimum, small trenches/sondages or small grid-square excavations, with appropriate boring and coring for site extent and especially for environmental sampling. A battery of specialists was made ready for analyses of pollen, seeds, beetles, soils, charcoal, bones, stones, pots and other minutiae. The work, again county-based, was undertaken from 1991 to 1995, closely monitored by English Heritage and by a small Management Committee. Commentaries on progress and discoveries appeared in *Fenland Research*, an in-house annual publication. Many surprises emerged from the peats and silts; a few are noted below. With a limited budget, hard choices had to be made about the sites. Some were so 'good' — good preservation, and/or more extensive than anticipated, more threatened than originally suspected, more elusive in identification — that permission was sought and often granted for more excavation. Other sites were so 'poor' — no structure remaining, and/or environmental conditions badly deteriorated, little hope of retrieval of useful information — that they could be abandoned rapidly. Several sites originally selected for this phase were removed from the programme with no excavation at all. In this way, the Committee could balance the books and keep on target over the five years. A few sites were extensively excavated.

In the event, 41 sites saw some work, always with the over-riding questions — in what way does this site possess evidence about the ancient Fenland that will add appreciably to our understanding of past human activities? And, can this evidence be somehow saved for the future, by devising management plans? If not, then should we investigate further, to retrieve what we can while we can? What are the questions for which we need answers, and how much work must we do to obtain this information? The Committee had to take advice, of course, from the excavation teams, and from the county-based archaeological managers, and from the regional specialists, and some difficult decisions had to be taken, not always to everyone's satisfaction.

In 1996, the various county-based team leaders and other specialists began to prepare reports on their work, which will appear in a series of Fenland volumes under the themes: Salterns; Saxons; Later prehistoric Lincolnshire; Later prehistoric Cambridgeshire; and a Site Summary. In addition, various papers on smaller sites or subjects will appear in regional or national journals. That will conclude the descriptive reports on the Fenland (survey) Project, and on the Fenland Management Project.

Management

But was it Management? We think that the name is an unfortunate choice — and were a part in its selection. What has been achieved is more than an evaluation exercise, but is well short of management. It is, in essence, a *preparation* for management decisions, an assessment of the potential, an acknowledgement of the unnecessary or undeserving, and an establishment of a scientific basis for future choices, in part building on an English Heritage project on wetland management (Coles 1995). The Fenland sample is, of course, ridiculously small; of 2500 known Fenland sites, we evaluated about 150. We expect about 50 to be scheduled, and we management-assessed about 40. We know that some of our evaluated 150, which were among our 'best' sites, are now damaged or destroyed by drainage and cultivation and wastage. What of the other 2350? Many are beyond hope; many identified 15 years ago are now almost certainly gone; but many remain, as sites with structure to them, with an integrity still intact in significant ways. Management of these high-potential sites is our next task, and can only be achieved by a landscape approach, not a site approach. We make further comment on this, our idealistic concept, in our closing paragraphs.

One interesting aspect of the Management Project was the opportunity to compare the overall results from the 40 investigated sites with the predictions made about them by the earlier Evaluation Project. This was also a test of the survey results which were the basis for the evaluation. A few conclusions could be made:

a   The pick-up of material from the survey and the evaluation had provided a general *chronological* position for the sites; in the management phase 24 of the sites could be dated with greater precision, a logical result.

b   The sites' *potential*, that is the potential for good structural and/or environmental evidence, was realized only in part. A majority of the 10 early prehistoric sites were in poorer condition than expected; in contrast, all 7 Roman sites proved in as good condition as expected.

c   *Waterlogging* of sites was anticipated for 5, and possible waterlogging for another 14; in the event, only 9 of these 19 sites had wet deposits of any significance, but 2 other sites yielded unexpected wet deposits.

d   In terms of *material culture* and *site structure*, a greater range of artefacts was, naturally enough, collected during excavation, particularly pottery (from 33 sites rather than the 28 previously identified), and 32 sites yielded traces of structure (ditch/pit/gully) rather than the 15 where aerial photographs of cropmarks or soilmarks indicated the presence of surviving features.

e   Site *identity* was another element clarified by the Management exercise. Depending on your interpretation of a 'settlement', highly debatable for the early prehistoric lithic scatters, 26 identifications were unaltered by the further work; the 14 with altered identifications tended to be more industrial than domestic.

Alongside these more detailed comparisons, early prehistoric sites show disappointing results, their condition much poorer than expected; sites in Lincolnshire were in much better condition than those of Cambridgeshire and slightly better than those of Norfolk. Of course, the sample is very small, but it must reflect drainage and cultivation intensity and effect on peatlands and siltlands.

Some results

Although late glacial flintwork was known from the region, exposures of contemporary land surfaces are very restricted and discoveries few. Early post-glacial sites are better known, although much of the Fenland basin was still dryland and many Mesolithic sites may lie under later silts and peats. Those several hundred found during the survey lie on the fen-edge, on promontories jutting into the lowland, and along stream and river banks where water flowed into the basin. Much of the Fenland was wooded, and only the river channels and some early-formed patches of waterlogged peats were free of woodland in the southern Fenland, although wider areas of open land may have existed to the north. By the 5th millennium BC, the picture becomes clearer, with a distinct concentration of lithic scatters along the southeastern fen-edge (Hall & Coles 1994: figure 15). Whether these represent permanent or seasonal settlements, kill sites or other specific-purpose sites is not yet known; those few sites examined in the Management Project did not clarify much because of their poor condition.

Lithic material of Neolithic character was recovered from many sites in the Fenland, with particular concentrations in the southeast. Farther north, much of the contemporary land surface is still sealed by silt but a scatter of sites was identified just north of the basin, in classic fen-edge positions. In the southeast, several hundred sites, spanning the period 3500–1500 BC, mark some presence and activity that is not clearly that of major settlement. The environmental evidence indicates a wooded landscape for the few sites examined in more depth. The survey found the long barrows at Haddenham all sealed by later peats; they had been constructed on a low hillock which subsequently became an island in the fen (FIGURE 2). One of the barrows was excavated in a separate project which has done much to elucidate the character of Neolithic and later exploitation of the Southern Fens (Hodder & Shand 1988; and see Evans & Hodder 1985; 1986). The results of the Fenland Survey were important in demonstrating a strong Neolithic interest and commitment to fen-edge and riverside occupation; mid-basin and mid-reach settlement is still unknown because sealed. Lithic scatter sites when excavated in the Management Project yielded little in terms of structure, but several gave us a taste of the possibilities. At Dogdike in south Lincolnshire, only the base of truncated pits had survived. At near-by Dowsby, however, an Iron Age occupation identified in the survey had masked the pits and post-holes of rectangular structures almost certainly of Neolithic date; this may be a powerful indicator of the potential for good survival of sites if early-sealed by natural silting or human debris.

By the late 3rd millennium BC, large areas of the southern Fenland were already waterlogged, or becoming so, and peats were forming over very wide expanses of the basin. Farther to the north and west, the influence of marine flooding was strong and silts as well as peats drowned the land. Matters deteriorated throughout much of the 2nd millennium BC. The survey recovered lithics, and some pottery, of Bronze Age character from numerous sites across the southern Fenland where the wastage of peat exposed ancient surfaces; many burial mounds, constructed on low ridges in the Fen basin, the whole submerged by water-borne sediments or by peat, began to emerge from the peatlands because of drainage and wastage. Whole cemeteries of barrows appeared (see FIGURE 2 for a sample). Farther north, where the siltland drainage was not so rewarding to the survey, numerous fen-edge sites were identified. To these records we could add the abundant finds of Bronze Age metalwork, mostly found long ago, and such splendid sites as Flag Fen/Fengate, all complementing the humble sites characterized by lithics, or the potentially rewarding burial mounds undamaged by our antiquarian ancestors.

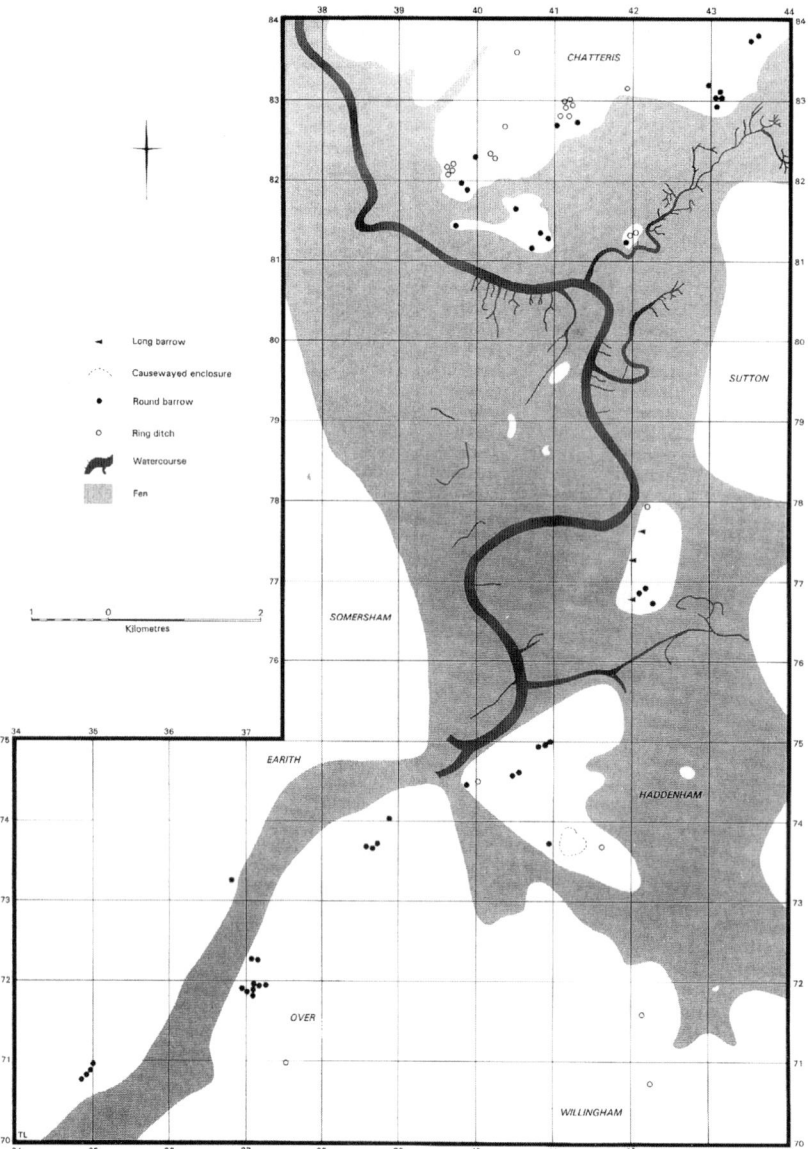

FIGURE 2. *The Chatteris–Haddenham area of the southern Fenland c. 2000 BC, with barrows (round and long), ring ditches and a causewayed enclosure set on fen-edge peninsulas and islands, and prehistoric watercourses flowing through the peat fens. (Drawn by S. Rouillard; Hall & Coles 1994: 83.)*

In advance of the Management phase, one of the barrows at Deeping St Nicholas in south Lincolnshire was fully excavated (French 1994); its history of early settlement — unmounded cenotaph for a child burial, and mounded monument for later ceremonial inhumations and cremations — reflects the complexity of traditions that can be understood only where such a monument is subsequently sealed (in this case by peat) and undisturbed by trenching or ploughing. But here, drainage had destroyed almost all organics, probably only 10 years before excavation, and ploughing had done its best to truncate the record; the nonetheless encouraging results emphasized the need to develop procedures to curtail and forestall further deterioration of many equally-valuable monuments in the Fenland.

A mound of burnt flint at Feltwell in Norfolk was examined by the Management Project, and again revealed a complex history unsuspected from the survey and evalua-

FIGURE 3. *Round houses at Deeping St James, Lincolnshire, part of a Bronze Age settlement preserved by river alluvium. Note the plough marks that have begun to damage the site; a grassland regime is proposed. (Photo Tom Lane, Heritage Lincolnshire.)*

tion. One of a series of such mounds in the southeastern Fenland, generally believed to be communal cooking sites, Feltwell contained a burial probably inserted through the mound after its industrial use; a waterlogged pit containing a wooden trough may well have been used as a hot-water bath, less likely as a cooking pit for non-humans according to environmental evidence. Were bath and burial related? A pit with withy lining from Swales Fen (Suffolk), examined by developer funding, appeared more likely to have been a cooking pit than a steam bath (Martin 1988).

Fenland Management work probably helped encourage other archaeological investigations to take place, and the Field Officers in particular were best placed to advise. In working on discoveries of the 1950s–1960s in the Norfolk Fenland, for example, as a complement to the Survey (Healy 1996), it was possible to assemble evidence for the deposition of human bodies in the fens, to carry out radiocarbon dating, to consider modern environmental analyses (Waller 1988; 1994), and to set the practice within a wider tradition of purposeful deposition in wetlands (Healy & Housley 1992).

In general, the Bronze Age sites selected for Management work turned out to be in good condition, in contrast to the earlier prehistoric sites. Settlement structure in the form of circular house gullies had survived at Deeping St James (FIGURE 3) along with a contemporary occupation surface with sherds and bones, and pits and wells with waterlogged material. Yet there were no surviving wooden elements of the buildings, and the waterlogged settlements remain elusive. A site at West Row Fen (Suffolk), examined outside the Fenland Management phase, had survived the plough sufficiently well to reveal round-house gully lines and post-holes, water-pits or wells, a flax-retting pit and antler soaks, and abundant pottery, flint, bone and antler tools, food bone debris and cereals; the settlement, near scrubland and wet woodland, presumably was overwhelmed after abandonment by swamping waters and eventual peat-beds (Martin & Murphy 1988; Olsen 1994). This site, and that of Flag Fen, are crucial to our understanding of Bronze Age settlement and exploitation in the southern Fenland; the full reports on each are eagerly awaited. They had the benefit of separation from the Fenland Management Project so that fuller and longer-term investigations could take place, rather than the short and intensive sampling procedures imposed by the Management phase. At Cottenham in Cambridgeshire, one of the small-scale investigations of a later Bronze Age site revealed again that although truncation of surfaces had occurred, waterlogged deep features survived; from one well came part of a wooden wheel. Drainage throughout the Fenland has in effect taken out almost all organics from old land surfaces, apart from bone, although in many places there are isolated pockets where preservation is still good. These also provide us with very useful information about environment and economy; both the separate excavation projects noted above and the Management Project investigations show that in the 2nd millennium BC the Fenland had been in effect opened up, the earlier crowding canopy of woodland now diminished in response to environmental change and human impact.

As late as 1978 it was believed that the Fenland had experienced no Iron Age settlement whatsoever (Godwin 1978). The major achievement of the Fenland survey was to identify over 100 sites quite clearly of Iron Age character, with the dense spread of sites most remarkable in the Lincolnshire siltlands (Hayes & Lane 1992); many of these were salterns on roddons, some more clearly settlements; they marked the first occupation of this Flandrian landscape. In the southern Fenland there was also ample evidence of Iron Age settlement on islands and fringes of the peatlands. On the Isle of Ely, for example, one solitary Iron Age artefact had been known before survey began; by the end, 7 occupation sites were identified. The Fenland was probably a wetland *par excellence*, with water tables higher than ever before, and the fen 'islands', occupied by ancestral Neolithic and Bronze Age people, and with contemporary cemeteries on the higher parts, were now mostly drowned. The environmental maps of the Fenland demonstrate the substantial waterlogging of the landscape (Hall & Coles 1994: figures 39 & 59; Waller 1994). Among major survey discoveries, allied with aerial reconnaissance work, several earthwork sites were identified, including 'hill-forts' except that they were not on hills; 'low-forts' in essence. Two scheduled monuments, long known, at Peakirk Moor and Willingham, were recognized as Iron Age ring-works. Salterns were more numerous, and settlements with paddock or drove alignments were situated on the fen-edge. In the south, where one island-defended site was already known, the survey added others. Undefended open sites of large size also emerged through the survey, their intensity of occupation still surviving for investigation.

At the Management phase, some high-potential sites were selected for partial or more extensive examination, and rewarded the county-based teams with outstanding results. A saltern at Cowbit had structural elements in good condition, and a large early settlement at Chatteris, covering 10 ha, yielded 13,000 artefacts and environmental evidence for arable cultivation. At Market Deeping, a late Iron Age and Roman occupation site was set beside a palaeochannel full of wood (some of it structural), cobbles, bone and pottery. The pottery, mostly of uncharacterized 'rustic' type, has been radiocarbon-dated to 185–95 BC. Iron Age structures were discovered at a multi-period site at Dowsby, where a ring gully had six separate phases. And then at Coveney another large-scale excavation exposed a double-ditched enclosure, with complex defended entrances and circular houses within. Environmental evidence indicated arable agriculture and hedge shrubbery along the defensive periphery of the 1-hectare settlement. The finds were prolific, with 6000 pottery sherds and 17,000 pieces of bone. Another camp, at Stonea, was already known; more recent work has demonstrated that it was never completed in its latest stage and it had little associated occupation (Malim 1992). It could be connected with the Boudiccan revolt or other military encounter of the mid 1st century AD (Jackson & Potter 1996: 42–4).

The Iron Age period saw a widespread extension of settlement around the fen-edge, on to the islands and on to Flandrian deposits. Arable cultivation of heavy clay at Coveney illustrates a wider range of soil types utilized than in previous periods. The sites were probably controlled by a hierarchy connected with the regularly spaced ring-works and defensive structures.

The Fenland is well known for its widespread Roman settlement (Phillips 1970), extensive activity occurring on the Flandrian silts. The survey revealed yet more sites on the silts, on islands and around the fen-edge. The most remarkable discovery was a large stone building and settlement at Stonea, near March, excavated by the British Museum in six seasons 1980–85. In the mid 2nd century AD a planned settlement was laid out, dominated by a large stone building, 60 x 40 m, using material from quarries in the Peterborough region 40 km distant. The building was richly decorated and had glazed windows. The rest of the site comprised buildings of timber and thatch, with a temple farther away, dedicated to Minerva and overlying an earlier shrine. The site is interpreted as an administrative and market centre of imperially-owned land (Jackson & Potter 1996: 678–94).

The large Iron Age site at Chatteris also had Roman activity; test pits made to determine the state of preservation revealed a stone building of three bays with lines of parallel post-holes forming aisles, dating to the 2nd–3rd century AD. Again the site must have had some importance to attract stone building material; its full elucidation lies in the future.

Several canals were identified, adding to those already known from the Fenland. They are referred to as 'canals' rather than drains because there is no evidence of Roman drainage, except possibly for the Lincolnshire Car Dyke which has been interpreted as a catchwater. Nearly all the channels link roddons that were active watercourses, forming a communication network. The excavation programme was limited to sectioning some and to investigating a few of the salterns.

The Fen Causeway is a well-known Roman road that began as a canal in places. Two sections were made in Norfolk. At Downham West the road was built first over an earlier saltern, followed by a canal in the late 1st century AD, using the early road for a retaining bank. Another section was made at Nordelph where the causeway was well preserved in a pasture paddock. It was the southern of the two separate routes in the locality. Again briquetage was found at the lowest level and the road was flanked by large contemporary wide ditches. Environmental analyses showed that peat fuel was used for the salterns and that the road was constructed over a saltmarsh.

In Lincolnshire, the Bourne-to-Morton canal, connecting the mainland with the siltland settlement, was sectioned at Morton. It had been 2 m deep and recut at least once because of silting. A nearby annular feature of 7 m diameter was one of the 'fen circles', commonly found on the silt and believed to be drainage gulleys for hay or corn stacks. An agricultural use is implied by the absence of finds and low phosphate levels.

The survey mapped a saltern industry more extensive than previously realised. Excavation of a well preserved example at Middleton (Norfolk), on the eastern fen-edge, revealed many features, including hearths, flues, channels and settling tanks. The regions of high saltern density are associated with numerous areas of parallel cuts that are interpreted as silt-filled turbaries, the largest groups lying at Christchurch.

The widespread saltern industry of the siltlands is closely associated with cropmarks of trackways, paddocks and more extensive planned fields, mainly visible on air photographs. The latest regional information for Cambridgeshire has been compiled in map form and related to the survey results (Palmer 1996). Southern Lincolnshire also has very intensive Roman settlement; selected areas have been mapped at 1:10,000 as part of the RCHM(E) National Mapping Programme (Palmer 1997).

The survey, supplemented by the excavations, has much extended knowledge about the Saxon period. On the siltlands, previous work had shown the presence of Middle Saxon sites: many more were discovered, forming a dispersed pattern of settlement lying away from the centres of medieval and modern villages. The extensive silts of Lincolnshire and Norfolk produced most sites; two were found on the small siltland area of Cambridgeshire. In some places occupation continued on Roman sites, as at Stonea (Jackson & Potter 1996: 692–3) and elsewhere. New sites were placed precariously on roddons open to tidal influence, many having to be abandoned by the end of the 9th century as the rising water-table began to reach its high medieval level.

The excavations found Middle Saxon sites better preserved than those of the Early Saxon period. Settlement-location in Norfolk Marshland seems to be ordered, six sites being spaced regularly on roddons between West Walton and Terrington St Clement; excavation at three revealed pits and buried ditches. No domestic structures were discovered of either Early or Middle Saxon date in Norfolk. Little metalwork was found, implying that the fen sites were of low status. Environmental remains showed that the sites were open to the sea, exposed to fast-moving tidal water.

In Lincolnshire, geophysical survey detected pits and ditches at a Gosberton Middle Saxon site. Excavation revealed many features, now very vulnerable to plough-damage. The earliest structures were deep, wet pits used for hemp-retting. Later linear ditches were filled with subtidal marine flooding layers and ash from possible salterns. The latest features were beam slots of rectangular buildings and circular gullies, one recut many times. The landscape was drier at this stage; arable crops were mainly barley with some wheat, rye, oats, peas and flax. Also present were bones of horse, cattle, sheep, poultry and fish.

Environmental evidence showed, surprisingly, that some arable agriculture was practised under tidal conditions in the Middle Saxon period, making use of salt-tolerant barley. In contrast, Late Saxon pits from several sites contained environmental deposits free of tidal influence showing that protective sea banks had been built. The banks were previously believed to be pre-1066 from the evidence of settlements and fields already well established by the early 12th century. This development led to intensive settlement of the silts in the Middle Ages.

The islands of the southern fen produced Early or Middle Saxon finds; it is likely that most early sites are concealed by the existing villages. On the fen-edge gravels, several sites were discovered by the survey. In the south, sites recently tested or excavated in advance of development have produced more early Saxon finds, and substantial sites have been found in the village centres of Cottenham and Willingham. Middle Saxon material, dated by Ipswich Ware, sherds, has come from Ely.

The survey of Cambridgeshire Fenland yielded abundant evidence of medieval settlement in a region dominated by the great southern peat fen (FIGURE 4). Most of the sites have been severely diminished by peat wastage, drainage and subsequent occupations; watertables have fallen to as much as 7·5 m below their original level in one well-documented case. The excavation programme was confined to four specialized sites, two receiving total excavation.

At Clenchwarton (Norfolk), a site near the Sea Bank had only 12th-century ditches and pits surviving. The Sea Bank, standing 1.7 m high, is made of sandy silt with occa-

FIGURE 4.
Distribution of medieval sites on a map of the fen landscape of Cambridgeshire, about 1500 AD. Dark tone peat, light tone meres. Triangles major settlements, circles minor settlements.

sional loamy slump bands, lying directly on convoluted silt containing 11th-century Thetford-type pottery. A landward east–west ditch is probably a quarry for bank material. Environmental data showed that the bank was constructed on an intertidal mudflat bordering a saltmarsh. There was no evidence of upper-marsh soil formation. The evidence confirms the late Saxon date of the siltland sea-defences.

Parson Drove, including part of a limited area of peat fen near Wisbech, has several sites lying on roddons that are associated with brick fragments. First interpreted as salterns, they were later considered 'settlements'. Excavation showed that one of the Parson Drove sites was a 14th-century saltern using pottery evaporation vessels supported by brick. It was abandoned when the fen was drained for cultivation by the 15th century. The group of sites is unique for operating a method of small-scale production similar to that used by the Romans. Most medieval salterns obtained salt from mudflats lying beyond the Sea Bank; the Parson Drove group may have been a landward response to the loss of mudflat salterns washed away by the sea in 1251 at Tydd St Gyles.

Holme Fen has sites lying on the edge of Whittlesey Mere identified during the survey as 'fishing stations' and characterized by mounded artefact spreads of pottery and lead fishing-line weights. Excavation of one site, making a full recovery of artefacts, showed that loss of peat and deflation was so great that piles from any wooden structure would have decayed long ago. Downham Hythe, a medieval 'port', lay at the end of a canal called the Oxlode, part of the fen-wide communication system. No structures survived in trial trenches, because desiccation had again caused decay of any wooden landing stage. We were too late.

Medieval pottery research has made considerable progress recently. Substantial quantities of sherds have been excavated at Ely and Cambridge as a result of development. Studies have also been helped by the identification of kiln sites at Ely and at Colne, 20 km west on the fen-edge. The kilns were working during the 14th–15th centuries and probably longer. A large-scale excavation at Ely medieval water-front provided a good series of waterlogged deposits now awaiting analysis. A complete sequence of pottery will form a standard series and identify when the local industry began. Other kilns have long been known at Grimston (Norfolk) and Bourne and Toynton All Saints (Lincs.). Products from all the fen kilns dominated the Fenland until the 15th century when, in the south, they were replaced by vessels from Essex.

Now what?

The results of these examinations and assessments during the Management phase are now available for further analysis in the difficult process ahead of us, namely, to decide which sites and areas must be protected from further damage. More difficult is the question of how they can be physically managed to ensure survival of the unique character of Fenland occupation and exploitation. It is quite clear that sites in isolation have little or no chance of preservation; and areas of former wetland once severely drained cannot be restored to their original condition either as natural wetlands or as repositories for ancient remains of human origin; once decayed, once ploughed, once desiccated — always so. It is only by identifying areas still in an acceptable state of preservation that actions may have a chance of success. Peatland moderately damp, organic soils not ploughed to destructive levels, siltlands equally surviving — all still protect to varying degrees a number of sites now identified by survey and evaluated by management. And other sites, identified by survey, remain for incorporation in any concentrated attempt to protect. As an example, take lithic sites. Lithic scatters, which do not fall within the parameters required to be considered for scheduling, are nevertheless important because they hold much information about the nature of the prehistoric activity and landscape. Many sites investigated during the management phase were poorly preserved and desiccated and were not selected as examples of prime sites; the latter were reserved for intended scheduling. Of the four major southern site complexes (possibly sub-regional centres), one at Soham was studied during the management on a wider remit than originally planned, partly because of serious artefact depletion by collectors. Two others, Isleham and the Swaffhams, are associated with waterlogged deposits immediately adjacent. The Swaffham sites have recently been under potential threat from drainage and farm-reservoir schemes. It is important to obtain information from these key sites, as well as taking steps to ensure their survival at least in part and in adequate holding conditions.

Sites examined in the management phase were not all under threat of the plough: grassed sites have a greater chance of survival so long as drainage is not allowed to desiccate the deposits unseen. But in most cases in the Fenland, a wide approach is necessary, with a buffer-zone to reduce the impact (short term) and to filter and supply the crucial area with water (long term). English Heritage commissioned a survey of such practices, and implementation of some procedures is now dependent on funding, goodwill and determination (Coles 1995).

It is essential, building on our original concept, to withdraw particular areas from the regimes that now pose threats to survival. Purchase of land, channelling and barrage work to introduce and retain sufficient water in the soil, and inducements to farmers and others to amend chemical and physical treatments would go some way towards the survival of both major and minor parts of the Fenland. Site manipulation alone is not adequate; a site's landscape has to be accepted as the minimum area. Can it be done? In a successful management scheme, Cambridgeshire County Council has grassed down many of the archaeological sites that occur on its extensive farmlands. These include a large Mesolithic site (10 ha) with near-by wet deposits at Somersham, and the Iron Age site at Stonea. Although not yet protected from desiccation, these sites are preserved from further destructive ploughing. The best of the earthwork sites (mostly medieval and Roman, but including a length of Neolithic ditch at Chatteris) have been protected as Scheduled Ancient Monuments, and further characterized and mapped at a large scale by RCHM(E). Other important sites survive as degraded earthworks in modern arable fields: many are also probably worth scheduling.

There is now some interest in a programme of re-creating areas of wet fenland, led by Cambridgeshire County Council, called 'Wet Fens for the Future', which will involve purchase of land and operations to flood it. This in theory should arrest the drying-out of adjacent as well as core sites but there are several uncertainties; it is not at all clear that wetting organic remains that have almost dried out will halt decay — there may well be harmful effects. On the practical side, there is danger that creation of a wetland might involve considerable earthmoving ('landscaping') to make deep pools and islands. The result may well suit plants and wildlife, but its making would be as destructive to archaeological remains as a builder's 'development'. Clearly there will need to be close liaison at the sites chosen about the scale of the civil engineering proposed. Work is in hand between English Heritage and Dr C. French of Cambridge to study the effects of dewatering and rewetting on waterlogged and partially dried archaeological remains. The programme also involves monitoring seasonal water-tables and studying the stability of modern organic samples deliberately buried in marginally waterlogged conditions.

All these actions and proposals are important to the archaeology of the Fenland. As we write, and as you read, Fenland sites and their landscapes continue to deteriorate; ploughing continues, drainage goes on, wastage occurs and delay feeds decay. Yet in all there are successes and achievements, as well as undoubted potential rewards.

a   Our understanding of the Fenland in ancient times has been hugely enhanced by the quantity and quality of the evidence.

b   Our attempts at management have resulted in the scheduling of a number of important sites and negotiating local agreements for others.

c   We recognize that the unwalked areas of Fenland, almost all in the north, probably contain new and perhaps unexpected types of information awaiting discovery.

d   We know that the walked black fens of the south have wasted still further since our survey, and land surfaces are now exposed. Re-walking these would also provide useful information about the rates of deterioration of organic soils.

English Heritage has now funded projects of survey and evaluation in four major wetlands of England (Somerset Levels, Fenland, Northwest and Humber wetlands); this indicates the importance placed on such landscapes by the agency concerned with the identification and protection of archaeological sites and areas. Much of the past funding of archaeology in England has gone to the drylands. Here in the Fens, as in the other wetlands, the opportunity has been taken to supplement that desiccated record. The interplay of action and reaction in dryland–wetland environments can now be seen to be complex and yet understandable. In an ideal world, preservation of the past would mean that future generations could see and study the wide landscape bands of eastern England, from coast to upland to lowland fen and silt, and thereby better understand how ancient people adapted, worked and managed their own territories.

In summary, what has been done in the Fenland has been substantial and important in national and international terms. The record could be enhanced by new work and the options for management have still to be refined. The Fenland has always been a dynamic landform; its future now lies outside natural processes and within the domain of human intervention. The continued support of English Heritage and other agencies is needed to ensure the survival of both the natural and human histories of this unique landscape.

Acknowledgements. The original and on-going support of English Heritage is the source of the Survey and Mananagement phases, and G.J. Wainwright and P.R. Walker have given unswerving encouragement. The work of the Field Officers (D. Hall for Cambridgeshire, P. Hayes and T. Lane for Lincolnshire and R. Silvester for Norfolk) and the Management team (C. Evans, T. Lane, M. Leah) have provided the basis for all the discoveries and developments noted here.

References

COLES, B. 1995. *Wetland Management: a survey for English Heritage*. Exeter: WAPP. Occasional paper 9.

COLES, J.M. 1991. *From the waters of oblivion*. Assen: Stichting voor de Nederlandse Archeologie. C.J. Reuvens Lezing 2.

COLES, J.M. & D. HALL. 1983. The Fenland Project, *Antiquity* 57: 51–2.

COLES, J.M., D. HALL & P. WALKER. 1990. Fenland Evaluation Project 1989–1990: summary of findings and recommendations. Report for English Heritage

EVANS, C. & I. HODDER. 1985. The Haddenham Project, *Fenland Research* 2: 18–23.

1986. The Haddenham Project, *Fenland Research* 3: 24–9.

FRENCH, C.A.I. 1994. *Excavation of the Deeping St Nicholas barrow complex, south Lincolnshire*. Heckington: Heritage Lincolnshire. Lincolnshire Archaeology and Heritage Report 1.

FRENCH, C.A.I. & F.M.M. PRYOR. 1993. *The South-West Fen Dyke Survey Project 1982–86*. East Anglian Archaeology 59.

GODWIN, H. 1978. *Fenland: its ancient past and uncertain future*. Cambridge: Cambridge University Press.

HALL, D. 1987. *The Fenland Project 2: Cambridgeshire survey, Peterborough to March*. East Anglian Archaeology 35.

1988. Survey results in the Cambridgeshire Fenland, *Antiquity* 62: 311–14.

1992a. The Fenland Project, *Antiquity* 66: 436–8.

1992b. *The Fenland Project 6: The south-western Cambridgeshire Fenlands*. East Anglian Archaeology 56.

1996. *The Fenland Project 10: Cambridgeshire survey, Isle of Ely and Wisbech*. East Anglian Archaeology 79.

HALL, D. & J.M. COLES. 1994. *Fenland Survey: an essay in landscape and persistence*. London: English Heritage. Archaeological Report 1.

HAYES, P.P. 1988. Roman to Saxon in the South Lincolnshire Fens, *Antiquity* 62: 321–6.

HAYES, P.P. & T.W. LANE. 1992. *The Fenland Project 5: Lincolnshire Survey, the South-Western Fens*. East Anglian Archaeology 55.

HEALY, F. 1996. *The Fenland Project 11: The Wissey Embayment: evidence for pre-Iron Age occupation prior to the Fenland Project*. East Anglian Archaeology 78.

HEALY, F. & R. HOUSLEY. 1992. Nancy was not alone: human skeletons of the Early Bronze Age from the Norfolk peat fen, *Antiquity* 66: 948–55.

HODDER, I. & P. SHAND. 1988. The Haddenham long barrow: an interim statement, *Antiquity* 62: 349–53.

JACKSON, R.P.J. & T.W. POTTER. 1996. *Excavations at Stonea Cambridgeshire 1980–85* . London: British Museum Press.

LANE, T.W. 1988. Pre-Roman origins for settlement on the Fens of south Lincolnshire, *Antiquity* 62: 314–21.

1993. *The Fenland Project 8: Lincolnshire Survey, the northern Fen-edge*. East Anglian Archaeology 66.

MALIM, T. 1992. *Stonea Camp, Wimblington*. Cambridge: Cambridgeshire County Council. Cambridgeshire Archaeology Report 71.

MARTIN, E. 1988. Swales Fen, Suffolk: a Bronze Age cooking pit?, *Antiquity* 62: 358–9.

MARTIN, E. & P. MURPHY. 1988. West Row Fen, Suffolk: a Bronze Age fen-edge settlement site, *Antiquity* 62: 353–8.

OLSEN, S.L. 1994. Exploitation of mammals at the Early Bronze Age site of West Row Fen (Mildenhall 165), Suffolk, England, *Annals of Carnegie Museum* 63: 115–53.

PALMER, R. 1988. Applications of air photo-archaeology to field-survey results from Thorney, Cambridgeshire, *Antiquity* 62: 331–5.

1996. The aerial evidence, in Hall (1996): 192–8.

1997. Air photo interpretation and the Lincolnshire Fenland, *Landscape History* 19: 5–16.

PHILLIPS, C.W. 1970. *The Fenland in Roman times*. London: Royal Geographical Society. Research series 5.

PRYOR, F. 1991. *Flag Fen prehistoric Fenland centre*. London: English Heritage.

1992. Current research at Flag Fen, Peterborough, *Antiquity* 66: 439–57.

SILVESTER, R.J. 1988a. The Norfolk Fens, *Antiquity* 62: 326–30.

1988b. *The Fenland Project 3: Norfolk Survey, Marshland and Nar Valley*. East Anglian Archaeology 45.

1991 *The Fenland Project 4: Norfolk Survey, the Wissey embayment and Fen Causeway*. East Anglian Archaeology 52.

WALLER, M. 1988. The Fenland Project's environmental programme, *Antiquity* 62: 336–43.

1994. *The Fenland Project 9: Flandrian environmental change in Fenland*. East Anglian Archaeology 70.

Siticulosa Apulia
by JOHN BRADFORD & P.R. WILLIAMS-HUNT

ANTIQUITY 20 (80), 1946

'PARCHED' APULIA* still describes the dominant characteristic of this region of southern Italy as aptly as when Horace wrote. The climate is one of sharp contrasts, especially apparent on the treeless plain round Foggia (the district known as the Capitanata). There, some midwinter snow and a few intermittent days of heavy rain between January and March are offset by almost continuous, and often pitiless, days of sunshine from April to the end of September, with the thermometer reaching 105° in the shade and scorching winds from the North[1] in late summer absorbing what little moisture remains. The average annual rainfall at Foggia is only 18–19 inches, or no more than in parts of lowland Tunisia; but the fertile soil is today intensively cultivated by dry farming, with immense open arable fields. Harvesting begins at the end of May and, as there is often little depth of cultivated soil above the absorbent subsoils, by early in July the dusty ground is baked as hard as iron.

Conditions were thus most favourable to the appearance of crop-marks indicating the presence and plan of archaeological sites beneath, following exactly the same logical principles as those conclusively demonstrated in England by O.G.S. Crawford, the late Major Allen and others. The crops on the *Tavoliere* (as the plain between the rivers Ofanto and Fortore is called) could not fail to provide a most sensitive and visible index of any artificially increased depth of soil caused by former enclosure ditches and the like, whose retained moisture would vitally affect and promote nourishment and growth. This retention makes for a slight but significant postponement of ripening and bleaching in the favoured vegetation, compared with the rest of the crop. When vertically seen from the air, in the plan view, the details of this difference in colour and texture assume a coherent form. But it was not until just after the Armistice in May 1945 that we had leisure enough to test our expectations experimentally, and then only a few weeks remained before harvesting virtually removed the evidence.

Most fortunately in the interval during training flights and routine camera tests, a number of air-photographs were taken, comprising both verticals and obliques; the former by R.A.F. units, the latter[†] by the present writers when Army officers. They resulted in

---

*   *Epodes, III,* i6.
'Nec tantus umquam siderum insedit vapor
Siticulosae Apuliae,
Nec munus humeris efficacis Herculis
Inarsit aestuosius'.
The subject of the poem is the strength of the garlic seasoning in a dish eaten at Maecenas' table.
†   The basis of our method was the same as that of the late Major Allen, i.e. a hand-held 8-inch focal length camera operating at 1000–1500 feet, but of course using roll-film. A light aircraft of the Fairchild high-wing monoplane type (economical, sufficiently slow and easily manoeuvred) proved very suitable; particularly as there is room for an observer–map reader (in addition to the pilot and camera-man) with the special task of plotting the exact position of the sites photographed. If these are numerous and the region has few distinguishing physical features in detail — as on the *Tavoliere* — this addition proves of the greatest value when the work of analysis later begins.

archaeological discoveries of no little importance on the *Tavoliere,* which was examined with some thoroughness. The accompanying illustrations are chosen from a selection of these photographs which received a Security clearance and was passed for reproduction.

The major discoveries can be summarised thus:—

1   150 to 200 crop-mark settlement sites, previously unsuspected, of a characteristic and homogeneous appearance which suggested parallels with the Neolithic ditch-enclosed sites at Matera in southern Apulia, and at Stentinello in Sicily, hitherto isolated examples of their kind. Trial excavation and field-work later provided pottery confirming a Neolithic–Chalcolithic *(Eneolitico)* date,* probably for the whole of our new group.

2   An extensive system, not hitherto known, of Roman field-partition by centuriation, covering the central and southern parts of the *Tavoliere.* This, too, was revealed by crop-marks caused by the boundary ditches between, and inside, the large square *insulae* of land marked out. Detailed analysis will give interesting social and economic evidence, for it is possible to study the internal subdivision of many of the *insulae.* Unlike the system of Roman centuriation still embodied and visible in the modern agricultural boundaries along the Via Emilia between Cesena and Bologna, this great Apulian field-system was, at some period, abandoned and was thus preserved (frozen, as it were) from the centuries of alterations in the internal partition of each *insula* that naturally befalls a living organism. The present field-pattern follows an entirely different course and gives no clue to the existence of the elaborate, regular, ' grid ' of ditched fields that now lies beneath the surface. Several Roman homestead sites ('villas'), associated with the centuriation, are also clearly visible.

3   More than two dozen assorted earthworks, most of them unrecorded and of medieval date. Some should throw fresh light on the activities of Normans and Hohenstaufen in this area. By good fortune the crop-marks of several abandoned medieval field-systems of a distinctive type, associated with earthworks, were also photographed. These will illuminate the obscure lot of the Apulian peasant.

4   Finally there exists a great mass of miscellaneous crop-mark sites. It is hoped that after careful comparative analysis other groups of sites will be recognised and found to be assignable to other periods, e.g. perhaps to the Early Iron Age.

It will be inevitably a little while before all this detail can be located on the map, measured, and studied with the care it deserves, but fair progress has already been made. In the meantime the present interim report on the sites of Neolithic–Chalcolithic character is put forward as a preliminary account[†] of that aspect of the discoveries.

Terrain, as always, is the decisive factor in determining the pattern of prehistoric settlement. It is important to distinguish between the three well-marked topographical zones into which Apulia falls (excluding the Salentine peninsula — the extremity of the 'Heel' — with which we are not concerned here).

These are, from north to south:

1   *The Gargano.* A wild rugged peninsula that juts far out into the Adriatic, and on the landward side presents a mountain-wall face to the *Tavoliere* below, with peaks reaching 3500 feet. Remote and isolated it has always retained a primitive economy and out-

---

*   This included sherds of thin-walled, evenly-fired black and brown bowls and basins highly burnished on both surfaces; smooth well-finished, buff-coloured ware painted 'a *fasce larghe*' in red, etc.

†   It is intended to deal next with the pottery of Neolithic–Chalcolithic type, from the selected test-site, near San Severo; followed by brief reports on the Roman centuriation of the *Tavoliere,* and on the earthworks. (J.S.P.B.)

look,* nor could it have ever had a prehistoric population of any size. Reconnaissance quickly confirmed that the broken ground and small terraced fields virtually ruled out any hopes of crop-mark sites.

2 *The Tavoliere.* A bare rolling plain, almost steppe, forming a roughly oval area some 60 miles in length from the Fortore to the Ofanto, and with a maximum width of up to 30 miles from the sea to the first serious foothills of the Apennines. Though it appears so flat there is now and then a gentle hillock (known locally as a *Coppa*) rising above the immediately surrounding country, in height varying from a few feet near the coast (e.g. Coppa Nevigata), to 150 feet or so, as one passes inland towards Lucera or Cerignola. These *Coppe* were much favoured in the Neolithic–Chalcolithic period. As they were also sought out by medieval and modern farmers, in order to raise their dwelling a little out of the malarial air it is by no means uncommon to see a *Masseria* neatly surrounded by the crop-mark of the enclosure-ditch of a Neolithic settlement. At the back of the plain a series of stream beds have cut steeply-sided, meandering, channels as they issue from the hills, and on low spurs along their banks† there are numerous Neolithic sites with single or multiple ditches on the exposed side (in one notable case with eight, arranged in two groups of four), generically similar to promontory forts.

The broad sandy beach 35 miles long from Manfredonia to Barletta which forms the sea frontage of the *Tavoliere* must have presented an easy environment to primitive fishing craft and would have been a very attractive feature on that account. Shell debris was found on our Neolithic–Chalcolithic test-site near San Severo, some way inland.

It is of special interest to observe that certain parts of this area have remained unploughed since the Roman period in spite of the great extension and alteration of the cultivated area fostered by the Fascist government. This explains the existence of an excellent series of grass-mark sites which are often just as clear as those seen in the crops. The physical destruction, together with the social and economic disruption wrought by the Lombards in the 5th century, and Islamic attacks in the 9th and 10th centuries, reduced this area (previously intensively and methodically cultivated, as the discovery of the centuriation shows) to a great open common or moorland covered with natural scrub on which Frederick II, 'Stupor Mundi', delighted to hunt.

3 *The Murge.* Bare undulating hills which form the south and southeast boundary of the *Tavoliere,* increasing gradually from 500 to 2000 feet and growing wilder and steeper as they rise towards the jagged backbone of the Apennines. These bleak stony downs, however, hold broad valleys and rolling plateaux which were attractive to Neolithic settlers. In general this region is far less suitable for the aerial photography of crop-mark sites than the *Tavoliere;* much of it is covered with small fields, bearing very mixed crops, all cultivated independently, though there are large open fields on the uplands round Matera which should give good results. But, having concentrated on the *Tavoliere,* it was not possible to examine the Murge until the first fortnight in July, when the harvest had been gathered for some weeks. Stubble-marks had proved quite effective in the identification of these Neolithic sites on the *Tavoliere* in early June, but on the sun-dried Murge little result was obtained in that way.

---

*   As one example of this it is of interest, anthropologically, to note that during the winter of 1943–4 when the plain of Foggia was crowded with the latest stream-lined aircraft that mid-20th century science could devise, inhabitants in the main street of S. Nicandro Garganico (a few miles into the hills) fled precipitately into their houses making the *Mano cornuta* sign to ward off the evil eye of the fair-haired stranger, possibly a *Jettatore,* when I first entered the village in an open car. (J.S.P.B.)

†   e.g. along the Triolo, Salsola, Vulgano, Celone, Cervaro, Carapelle, etc.

FIGURE 1. A. *Oblique. Typical circular enclosures of a 'homestead' site, etc.*
B. *Oblique. 'Hut-enclosure ditches' inside the domestic enclosure' of a 'homestead'.*
(All plates Crown Copyright reserved.)

On the coastal belt the nature of the cultivation changes quite suddenly south of the river Ofanto, giving way to a dense covering of vineyards and olive groves. The country is so cut up by these small holdings that virtually no crop-marks were identified. This alteration is chiefly due to the change in surface-geology, to a form of limestone reflected also in the shoreline where the sand gives place to dangerous, flat, rocky ledges with only an occasional cove.

We will now turn to a description of chosen illustrations.* Except where the development of the argument makes an expression of opinion necessary, the observed facts and measurements made from the photographs have been separated from the deductions ; the latter being assembled in a later section.

The fact of primary importance about these Neolithic–Chalcolithic sites is their remarkable homogeneity as a group ; a general uniformity that is especially impressive when one has studied the whole series of nearly 200. With a very few exceptions all are surrounded by one or more ditches. The larger type of site (big enough to be called a village) has multiple ditches set close together, while the smaller kind (units which, originally, may have been equivalent to a farm or a family) has usually only one or two but is like a smaller version of the former. However there are a few of the smaller and intermediate sites (noticeably in the southern part of the *Tavoliere)* which *are* surrounded by multiple ditches and this is also true of many of those (all sites of the smaller kind) which are sited like promontory forts, but are clearly only a variant, adapted to environment. There are no other crop-marks on the *Tavoliere* which resemble, even remotely, these here discussed.

FIGURE 1a (oblique) shows a typical example of the smaller, 'homestead', type of Neolithic–Chalcolithic site on the *Tavoliere,* of which about 100 have so far been identified from the air-photographs. Though there are a few variations in individual cases, they usually consist of (I) a roughly circular innermost enclosure ditch (on FIGURE 1a , *c.* 160 feet in diameter), which we shall provisionally call the 'domestic' enclosure, surrounded by, or adjacent to, (II) a larger oval or circular enclosure ditch (here *c.* 500 feet in diameter), experimentally termed the 'farmyard' and often by a third enclosure ditch, concentric with the 'farmyard' enclosure, but from *c.* 50 to 200 feet further out. In this particular example the outermost enclosure-ditch rejoins the second after the completion of only one half of the circumference, and seems to be a secondary extension. It is normal for the 'domestic' enclosure to be sited, not concentrically with, but towards one end of, the 'farmyard' enclosure surrounding it (as on FIGURE 1a).[2] The former is sometimes inserted into, and against one side of the latter, or occasionally is adjacent and semi-detached.[3] These 'homestead' sites, present in such numbers on the *Tavoliere* are clearly in the same class as those on the Murge close to Matera, 100 miles to the south, four of which have been recognised since the first investigations of Dr Domenico Ridola and Prof. Patroni just 50 years ago. None, however, has yet been fully excavated. Two of them (at Tirlecchia) were acutely identified early in June 1916 by Dr Ridola from their outline in the crop and the reason for the crop-mark was recognised by him. The enclosure ditches round the Matera sites, which are cut in the rock, ranged in width from 5 to

* During 1945, when in Rome on the staff of the Monuments, Fine Arts and Archives Sub-commission of the Allied Commission for Italy, I was most fortunate in having opportunities for the general discussion of these crop-mark sites with Professor Barocelli, Director of the Museo Preistorico-Etnografico, to whom I am particularly grateful, and with Professors Fraccaro, Lugli Mancini and Patroni all of whom kindly helped me in a number of ways, as did Lt.-Col. J.B. Ward Perkins, the Director of the Sub-Commission at that time. (J.S.P.B.)

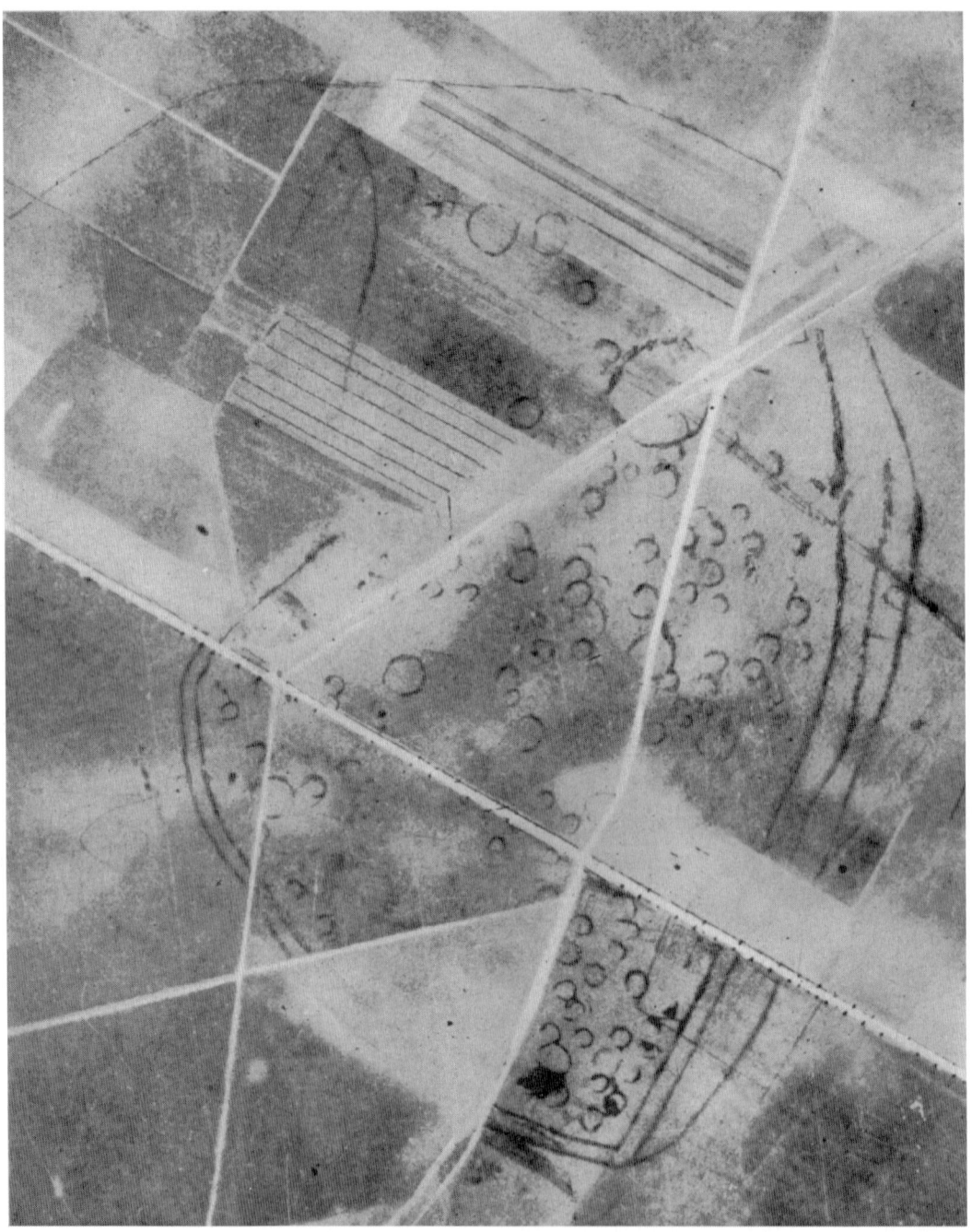

FIGURE 2. *Vertical. A 'village' enclosed by ditches. Compare oblique of same site on* FIGURE 3.

8 feet, and in depth from $3^1/_2$ to 8 feet. On FIGURE 1a, the width of the ditches (which does not vary between the different enclosures) is from 8 to 10 feet; this seems to be a fair average for many of our smaller sites. It should be observed that the measurements of the

FIGURE 3. A. *Low-level oblique of 'hut-enclosure ditches' with village ditches in fore-ground and background. (See lower half of FIGURE 2.)*

width of ditches made from vertical air-photographs proved very exact when checked by excavation on our test-site. The inner of the roughly circular ditches at Murgecchia, which measured *c.* 160 by 230 feet, corresponds to the 'domestic' enclosure of our site on FIGURE 1a, while the outer one, equivalent to our ' farmyard' enclosure, is *c.* 450 feet across. Thus the size of both enclosures at Murgecchia corresponds quite closely to our example.

Inside both the 'domestic' and the 'farmyard' enclosures of the 'homestead' sites on the *Tavoliere* (but more numerous in the former) are to be seen from four up to about a dozen circular, penannular, and semi-circular enclosure ditches of a much smaller kind. It is proposed to call these features 'hut-enclosure ditches', thus anticipating the later discussion of their significance. As it happens they do not show clearly on FIGURE 1a (though traces of several are visible on a vertical photograph) but are clearly shown on FIGURE 1b, inside the 'domestic' enclosure of that site. On these sites of 'homestead' type there is often a large, principal, 'hut-enclosure ditch' near the centre of the 'domestic' enclosure. Inside the sites of 'village' character they are of course much more numerous but do not seem to differ in any essential characteristics. In general, they vary from c. 50 to 110 feet in diameter, including the width of the ditch itself which (measured from vertical photographs) usually ranges from between 4 to 10 feet across, but sometimes has segments of its circumference widened (? by re-cutting) to 20 feet (see FIGURE 2). As far as can be seen, at present, the openings in these 'hut enclosure ditches' are always orientated in approximately the same direction within each particular site, and (though this can only be stated provisionally) they seem to be confined to points of the compass between ENE and WNW; that is in a northerly and not, as one might perhaps expect, in a southerly direction.

In the sites of 'homestead' character, and in some of the sites of an intermediate nature approaching the village-type, it is common to see the special form of entrance noted by Dr Ridola at Murgia Timone[4] and Tirlecchia,[5] and is characterized by a small external bulge in an otherwise continuous ditch; as seen, for example, on the nearer side of the 'farmyard' enclosure on FIGURE 1a.* At Murgia Timone and Tirlecchia it was found to belong to the circular ditch equivalent to our 'domestic' enclosure, and is frequently so found in our sites on the *Tavoliere*. We may therefore conclude that it is a standard and uniform feature in settlements of this period throughout Apulia.

FIGURE 2, which is an enlarged portion of a vertical air-photograph taken on 23 May 1945, and FIGURE 3 (an oblique view of part of the same site) illustrate one of the larger of the second class of Neolithic–Chalcolithic sites on the *Tavoliere* — those which may be termed 'villages' or 'kraals', circular in form and having multiple ditches. These settlements exhibit characteristics of the greatest interest. That shown on FIGURES 2–3 is unusual in that the enclosed area appears, from the distribution of the 'hut-enclosure ditches', to be sub-rectangular; but the crop-marks in the upper left-hand corner of the photograph are inadequately recorded by reason of the absence or unsuitability of the vegetation.

Another feature uncommon in these sites is the approximation to a *right-angled* change of direction in the enclosure ditches seen on the lower central part of FIGURE 2. It will be observed that the middle ditch of the three on the right-hand side is incomplete, and other photographs show unexcavated gaps in its length, on the further side of the road. These enclosure ditches measure from c. 12 to 25 feet across, and are shown in detail in the foreground of FIGURE 3.

This village has an overall measurement (i.e. including the surrounding ditches) of approximately 800 by 500 *yards*,[6] and lies in one corner of a very large, roughly oval, area (enclosed by a single ditch) between two and three times the extent of the village itself. The longer axis of this great enclosed annexe, clearly indicated by the crop-mark of the ditch, measures about 1500 yards. No 'hut-enclosure ditches' have yet been identified within it, and thus it must probably represent either (I) a kind of 'home-paddock' in which herds grazed under the villagers' protective eyes (at night or at certain sea-

---

*   The remaining crop-marks on this plate do not concern us now. They included a square enclosure (?Roman) overlapping the further side of the 'farmyard' enclosure; a track junction and fragment of field system (Medieval, by analogy with others associated with earthworks); a large square enclosure in the upper right-hand corner (partly obscured by cloud-shadow) adjoining the present farm-track; and a prominent-L-shaped crop-mark, the isolation of which a vertical photo confirms, probably connected with sheep-folding (thought to be post-Roman).

sons), or (II) the most valuable cultivated ground immediately adjoining the village. However these explanations are not mutually exclusive. A second definite example of a big village lying within, and at one end of, a ditch-enclosed area of greater size than itself, has also been established. The relationship, in position, of one to the other is reminiscent of that of the 'domestic' to the 'farmyard' enclosure on the 'homestead' sites.

Although at least one-third of the interior of this village, from this nature of cultivation at the time of photography, has not provided us with crop-marks, some 90 'hut-enclosure ditches', or fragments of them, have been counted in the remaining area. It will be seen (FIGURE 2) that all have their openings in the same general direction; in a few cases these ditches appear to have been re-cut, or the area demarcated by them subdivided internally.* It is not of course suggested that they were all inhabited simultaneously. Fifty-five were chosen as being sufficiently clear to give reasonably accurate data; and their mean overall diameters (including the ditch) range as follows

45 to 70 feet across	..	..	70 per cent	
70 to 90 ,,	..	..	20 ,,	
90 to 150 ,,	..	..	10 ,,	

The percentage of those less than 45 feet across is negligible. The three largest measure c. 120, 125 and 150 feet respectively. A very large circular enclosure, with an apparently funnel-shaped entrance, which dominates the village (FIGURE 2, near the junction of modern tracks) is here in a class by itself, being approximately 310 by 330 feet overall.

One might well have expected to see on FIGURE 3 the crop-marks of post-holes had there been any elaborate timber-structures, but they are not apparent. It might perhaps be argued that the severe parching of the ground would tend to iron out differences caused by such small features. At Murgia Timone, Ridola excavated several circular storage-pits from 1 foot 3 inches to 3 feet 6 inches deep, and 2 feet to 4 feet 3 inches across. It is believed that these can be seen on the air-photographs of the *Tavoliere,* but care has to be taken to distinguish them from similar marks made by plantations of olive-trees which have since disappeared. Crop-marks of later periods are also sometimes superimposed on these Neolithic–Chalcolithic settlements, but almost always they can be distinguished from them with fair ease. Thus, the roughly parallel lines which enter FIGURE 2 midway down the right-hand side, and those which cross the centre of FIGURE 3 diagonally belong to a complex of trackways probably of medieval date. The parallel cultivation-furrows (? former vineyards) and the rectangular enclosure ditch abutting on the road on FIGURE 3 may also be disregarded in the present context.

Another village is illustrated, for comparison, on FIGURE 4. This is an enlargement of part of a vertical photograph taken on 2 June 1945. The large field on the right-hand side has no crops on it and so presents a blank, but that on the left shows the crop-marks of a number of 'hut-enclosure ditches' (averaging 50–60 feet in diameter) surrounded by irregular multiple ditches, 15–20 feet across, which originally demarcated a roughly oval area. Part of this was later covered by a large kidney-shaped, medieval earthwork with a bank and ditch enclosing a kind of bailey with a species of motte (c. 160 feet across) in one corner, and another of similar size but detached, at the opposite end. The whole earthwork, excluding the ditch, measures c. 340 yards in overall length. This, and the other earthworks on the *Tavoliere* photographed from the air (most of which have scarcely any published documentation and some of which have none) will be discussed

---

*   Air-photographs of other sites show that sometimes the openings are closed by crop-marks resembling a palisade-trench; in other 'hut-enclosure ditches' there was evidently no intention of trying to close the gap with a ditch, and brush-wood or hurdles may have been partly employed.

FIGURE 4. *Vertical. Part of village site enclosed by ditches, having large earthwork with two mottes superimposed.*

on another occasion; the present purpose of this plate is to demonstrate the amount of detail which could be provided by vertical air-photographs to assist in the scientific excavation of one of these villages. But it must not be imagined that the majority of them have this rather disorderly appearance; indeed they are notable for a symmetry remarkable in such large sites. More commonly the villages, in their main features, resemble a greatly expanded version of the 'homestead', having multiple concentric ditches in the places where the smaller type of site normally has only one. We may take as a specimen (not illustrated here) a circular village measuring 530 yards across the inner area which is thickly covered with 'hut-enclosure ditches'; this is enclosed by two ditches each *c.* 15–20 feet wide placed 50 feet apart, and 220–260 feet beyond these is another pair of ditches of the same size and siting. The broad zone between the two pairs of ditches corresponds in position to the 'farmyard' enclosure on the' homestead' sites.

We can now turn to a brief discussion of some general conclusions that are suggested by the facts. In the first place, a comparative study of the whole series of 150–200 settlements makes us tend to the view that the group belongs to one homogeneous archaeological culture-phase. Pottery from a selected site of village character, and also from a 'homestead' indicates that both types of site were in existence by about 2300 BC. There still remains a great deal of work to be done on the internal chronology of Neolithic–Chalcolithic wares in Apulia, to say nothing of establishing their external relationships and derivations. All agree that an important element (particularly the *vasi dipinti),* though not the only one, has clear affinities with certain varieties of form and decoration found in the early Neolithic pottery of Thessaly (e.g. at Servia). This, however, will have to be discussed outside the present interim report on the crop-mark settlements, but the work of Miss Sylvia Benton on Neolithic sites from the coast of NW Greece has already opened the way to a fresh approach to the problem.

The number of settlements discovered on the *Tavoliere* confirms the long life of both types of site, which may well have extended over some five centuries. During this long period, villages and 'homesteads' would be rebuilt many times as they became too filthy to live in, or soil-exhaustion round them seriously increased. Villages with detailed similarities of plan are often to be seen in such close proximity that presumably they must be successive. It is not yet possible to say whether there is a break in the continuity of occupation of sites of this kind at the Bronze Age, and only systematic excavation can provide an answer. Some further comment must be made on the probable nature of the 'homesteads'. It has been observed that the outer ('farmyard')* enclosure, which does not seem primarily intended for habitation, nevertheless sometimes contains 'hut-enclosure ditches' of the sort found in the 'domestic' enclosure. But it should not be thought that the 'farmyard' must imply 'animals only', or their complete segregation. In this region, as in many parts of Europe, one may still see cattle and human beings huddled together in the same chamber, and in remote districts the belief dies hard that this is natural and desirable. Within the 'domestic' or inner enclosure of a homestead there is sometimes one 'hut-enclosure ditch'[7] of much larger size than the handful of others, but some intermediate settlements (transitional in plan to a small village) often contain a group (say 15) of approximately equal size. The relationship of the size of the 'hut-enclosure ditch' to that of the structure inside is not yet known; but it seems clear that essentially it is a form of compound and not structurally part of the

---

*   The average diameter of this enclosure is from 400–600 feet overall. These dimensions can be visualized by comparing the familiar ditch-enclosed farmyard of the Early Iron Age excavated at Little Woodbury, measuring *c.* 460 by 400 feet overall.

hut(s) within. If, as is very possible, these 'homesteads' were never a uniform agricultural unit, but primarily a social nucleus, i.e. a family group with sons and their wives,*
then variations in size would be expected. As a consequence of the discovery of these
sites one may naturally ask: are units corresponding to farms and villages functioning
side by side in this region by 2300 BC, or can it be that the larger sites evolved from the
smaller ones? The evidence provided by interpretation of the air-photographs inclines
one to the view that both types of community probably existed contemporaneously, and
that the plan of the village was only an expanded version of that of the 'homestead',
amplified and adapted for larger numbers.

A rough idea of the appearance presented by the *Tavoliere* when strewn with these
sites is given by air-photographs of the circular kraals of the Kavirondo[8] (agriculturalists
and dairymen of Kenya) crowding the plain east of Lake Victoria, where occupied and
extinct settlements of much the same size as ours are mixed together. One may perhaps
venture the comment that the general uniformity of plan, and the repetition of the practical,
functional sub-division internally, found throughout these Neolithic–Chalcolithic settlements
on the *Tavoliere* (executed with great regularity even in the largest villages) indicate a methodical, conservative, ingenious people, well knit-together both socially and economically.
Normally one would hesitate to speak thus of a group as yet scarcely examined by excavation; but never before has it been possible to view as a whole the detailed plans of such a
considerable number of sites of a uniform nature from so limited an area.

The value of air-photography as a means of archaeological research in suitable terrain is illustrated when we consider the effect of the addition of this new group of settlements on the existing distribution map of sites of this period, regionally and nationally.
Previously there were about ten known Neolithic–Chalcolithic sites (including occupied caves), strung out along the coast from the Gargano round as far as Taranto; together
with a scattered group on the Murge of which about ten sites can be identified definitely,
principally round Matera.† Only in a very few of these did the nature of the site or the
record of its discovery make it possible to reconstruct anything like a general site-plan,
to enable one to pass from the mere typological study of the pottery to a considered
appreciation of the economic and social organisation of the people. From the *Tavoliere*
itself there was only a small amount of mostly unlocalized occupation-material (chiefly
flint tools) originating in the Foggia area. But there is no wish to minimize the fieldwork
done by local archaeologists; for, although the outlines of these crop-marks sites are
visible on the plain at eye-level in a confused way, the only practicable method of dis-
covering and mapping with accuracy such large numbers is by air-photography. The
repercussions on the national distribution of Neolithic–Chalcolithic sites are also of interest. The most recent authoritative map[9] of this kind, based on Professor Patroni's researches, listed by name less than 150 sites in Italy, Sicily and Sardinia which had yielded
occupation-material (not always associated with any clearly defined type of settlement).

No one imagines that distribution maps can ever portray more than a small proportion of the total of existing sites, but the probable addition of 150–200 settlements from

---

*   Among the Masai a single 'patriarchal' household often has its own separate kraal of some 20 to 50
huts which will move as a unit.
†   The most southerly of the new Neolithic–Chalcolithic crop-mark settlements lies near the site of
Cannae, across the Ofanto midway between Barletta and Canosa. This site thus forms a link with the
contemporary ones on the Murge. Professor Drago, Soprintendente dell'Antichita, at Taranto, has kindly
informed me that enclosures similar to those at Murgia Timone (Matera) were seen by him near Vernole,
Province of Lecce (South Apulia).

one limited area — a number greater than all those recorded in the Peninsula and both islands — makes the overall pattern of distribution distinctly one-sided. Indeed one is tempted to suggest that when a recognisable type of site has been identified 'in the field' no map of the distribution can be made without the full employment of air-reconnaissance, which does not raise very considerable qualms about its use. Where conditions of terrain are suitable for air-photography the work of many years of unaided fieldwork on the ground can sometimes be done in a few days.* It is not a question of breaking records, but of quickly and accurately establishing that amount of material evidence needed to provide the numerical basis of the 'fair sample', required in all research conducted with scientific method. On the *Tavoliere* air-photography has provided a group of Neolithic–Chalcolithic settlements for which there exist extraordinary opportunities for comparative study. The photographs supply much data, and suggest many interpretations of the evidence, too complex to be brought into this brief summary. Taken in conjunction with the ditch-enclosed settlements reported as far south as the Province of Lecce, and the partially examined sites on the Murge which have produced Chalcolithic pottery and have proved to be of the same nature, the new evidence suggests that 'homesteads' and villages of the type described are numerously distributed all over Apulia. It should now be possible, with the precise and relatively complete site-plans available, to conduct excavations at selected points economically and with the minimum of difficulty; thus one could present a uniquely full picture of an important formative period in the prehistory of Italy, distinguished aesthetically by the technical excellence of its pottery and socially by the developed nature of its communities. It is greatly to be hoped that a planned scheme of excavation with limited but definite objectives can be put into effect.

References

1 See Semple, *The Geography of the Mediterranean Region: its relation to Ancient History*, p. 90.
2 Compare the closely similar plan given by Dr Ridola, of the Murgecchia site (op. cit. Tav. v) at Murgia Timone, near Matera. *Bulletino di Paletnologia Italiana*, XLIV, 1924, Tav. VI, one of the Matera group of homesteads.
3 This was also found by Ridola. See also Rellini, *Villaggi preistorici trincerati di Matera, Revista di Antropologia*, XXIII, 1919.
4 op. cit., Tav. V.
5 op. cit., p. 27, fig. 3.
6 This great size can be appreciated by comparing the main enclosure at the Neolithic village of Koln-Lindenthal which measured *c.* 200 by 240 yards overall (including the ditch); see *Germania* vol. 19 (April 1935), plan facing p. 112.
7 It is worthy of note that crop-marks generically somewhat similar to our 'hut-enclosure ditches' were photographed from the air, by the late Major Allen, inside Dyke Hills, Dorchester, Oxon. See *Oxoniensia*, III, plate xviii, or preferable *Luftbild und Vorgeschichte*, p. 46.
8 Soc. R.U. Light, *Focus on Africa*, American National Geographical Society's Special Publication, no. 25 (1941). This comprises a valuable series of air-photographs taken on a flight from the Cape to Cairo; there is a copy in the library of the Royal Geographical Society.
9 *Storia Politica d'Italia : La Preistoria* (1937); vol. I, map facing p. 455.

---

*   In Italy in 1938–9 aerial photography was being used to solve topographical problems in Roman archaeology and a report on the results obtained from the first planned flying-programme was published by Professor Lugli, who had long advocated the employment of this method of field work; see his *Saggi di Esplorazione Archeologica* a Mezzo Della Fotografia Aerea (Istito di Studi Romani).

Archaeology & the Etruscan countryside

by **GRAEME BARKER**

ANTIQUITY 62 (237), 1988

THE ETRUSCAN city states flourished in west-central Italy from the late 8th century BC until their conquest and absorption by the emergent state of Rome in the 4th century BC. In 1985 Italy celebrated the century or so of work on its oldest civilization with a series of major exhibitions under the slogan, *'Buongiorno Etruschi'* ('Good morning, Etruscans!'). There were eight major exhibitions in Tuscany displaying over 5000 objects from all the major collections in the region, designed to cover most aspects of Etruscan culture — settlement systems, domestic and religious architecture, religion, everyday life, crafts, and artistic achievement. As the sponsors FIAT wrote in their preface to the splendid catalogues produced for the project (e.g. Camporeale 1985; Carandini 1985; Cristofani 1985; Stopponi 1985), the intention of this massive undertaking was to convey to the Italian public that the Etruscans were not just a dead civilization known above all for the way of death of its élite, but 'a lively culture of ordinary people, merchants, and craftsmen'.

Yet as the *Year of the Etruscans* demonstrated very clearly, the cemetery archaeology which has dominated Etruscan studies for most of their history has inevitably produced a rich but fundamentally biased archaeology which tells us most about the aristocracy and their mortal concerns (Murray 1985). There has been little detailed information from archaeology on the layout and organization of the major settlements, the spatial variation in domestic and industrial areas visible from the surface remains at Doganella in the Albegna valley (Walker 1985) being a striking indication of the wealth of information waiting to be collected at other major settlements by survey and open-area excavation. The excavations by the Swedish Institute in Rome during the 1950s and 60s at Acquarossa and San Giovenale have provided critical information on the archaeology of medium-sized settlements, forming the basis of the two catalogues on settlement archaeology (Nylander 1986; Stopponi 1985). There has been far less research, however, on the lower part of the settlement hierarchy.

Until the last few years, the one project which had addressed this issue had been the British School at Rome's field survey in South Etruria during the 1950s and '60s, directed by John Ward-Perkins (Potter 1979; Ward-Perkins *et al.* 1968). This indicated an Etruscan countryside dotted with small sites in which the majority of Etruscans presumably lived. The purpose of this paper is to review current archaeological research investigating in more detail the nature of rural Etruscan settlement, the transformation in the countryside it represented in comparison with pre-Etruscan settlement, and the role of these Other Etruscans, so conspicuously silent when bid good morning three years ago, in the articulation of the state system.

The pre-Etruscan countryside

The survey evidence now available for South Etruria indicates discontinuous clusters of small Bronze Age sites by the later centuries of the 2nd millennium BC. In both the Fiora and Mignone valleys, for example, the settlement sites of this period are 4–6 km apart, invariably less than 2 ha in extent and often much smaller, with all sites very close to water (Maggiani & Pellegrini 1985; Pacciarelli 1982). Similar spacings have been indicated by survey in the environs of Rome (Bietti-Sestieri 1984; 1985). Survey on the coast has found numerous small occupation sites of the later Bronze Age, for example by the lagoons and marshes of the Piombino and Monte Argentario promontories (Bronson & Uggeri 1970; Fedeli & Galiberti 1979).

Excavations have in general found beaten earth floors, hearth areas of baked clay and a few postholes, suggesting collections of simple reed or thatch huts of the kind still used by shepherds and herdsmen in Etruria (Close-Brooks & Gibson 1966). There is no evidence in this period for significant variation amongst sites in terms of size and function. There is a unique example of substantial rock-cut houses at Luni in the Mignone valley (Östenberg 1967), but whilst the acropolis formed by the natural outcrop at the site measures 5 ha, the Apennine Bronze Age settlement was restricted to the area of the houses, an area very similar to the other settlements. This dispersed settlement system may in part have been a response to the trend to aridity that is fairly well documented for the later 2nd millennium BC in the Etrurian pollen diagrams (Bonatti 1961; 1963; 1970; Frank 1969; Hunt 1988). Underwater archaeology has shown that at this time, too, the volcanic lakes of South Etruria were ringed with small Apennine Bronze Age settlements (Fugazzola Delpino 1982).

The principal evidence for the agricultural base of these settlements has been provided by the Swedish Institute excavations of Luni (Östenberg 1967) and the British School at Rome excavations of Narce in the Treia valley (Potter 1976). Both communities cultivated a variety of cereals and legumes (Helbaek 1967; Jarman 1976) and practised mixed stock-keeping with sheep and goats (especially sheep) the principal stock, the age structure of the flocks suggesting an unspecialized system of animal husbandry for both secondary products and meat (Barker 1976). Settlements in the middle and upper Fiora valley have produced similar evidence for mixed farming with a strong pastoral component, the coastal Maremma sites in the lower Fiora perhaps being seasonal shepherding camps related to the larger settlements inland (Catacchio 1983; Maggiani & Pellegrini 1985). Thiessen polygon territories around the Mignone valley sites each measure about 1000 ha, of which 50–100 ha would have been cultivable alluvial soil near the settlements and the rest likely to have been natural grazing or woodland (Pacciarelli 1982).

There were major changes in settlement in South Etruria towards the end of the 2nd millennium BC. The coastal lagoons and inland lakes were no longer settled on the same scale, sites known are fewer in number but larger in size, and there are the first indications of hierarchical organization, both within certain settlements such as Luni and Sorgenti della Nova and within local settlement clusters, with the first evidence for defensive walling. More substantial domestic structures are known at sites such as Sorgenti della Nova compared with the preceding huts, with drystone walling increasingly common. At Narce, the huts of the initial phase of settlement were now replaced by buildings with stone footings and cobbled floors, which were probably surrounded by a wooden palisade (Potter 1976). The amount of metal in circulation increased dramatically, and new settlement clusters developed in the vicinity of the metal ores (Giardino 1984).

These developments coincide with evidence for agricultural diversification and expansion. Pacciarelli's locational analysis of the Mignone valley suggests increased areas of arable soil adjacent to most settlements (Pacciarelli 1982). The range of crops increased at Narce (Jarman 1976). An expansion of arable cultivation is registered in the pollen diagrams. There is some evidence in the faunal samples for an increasing importance of secondary products (Barker 1976).

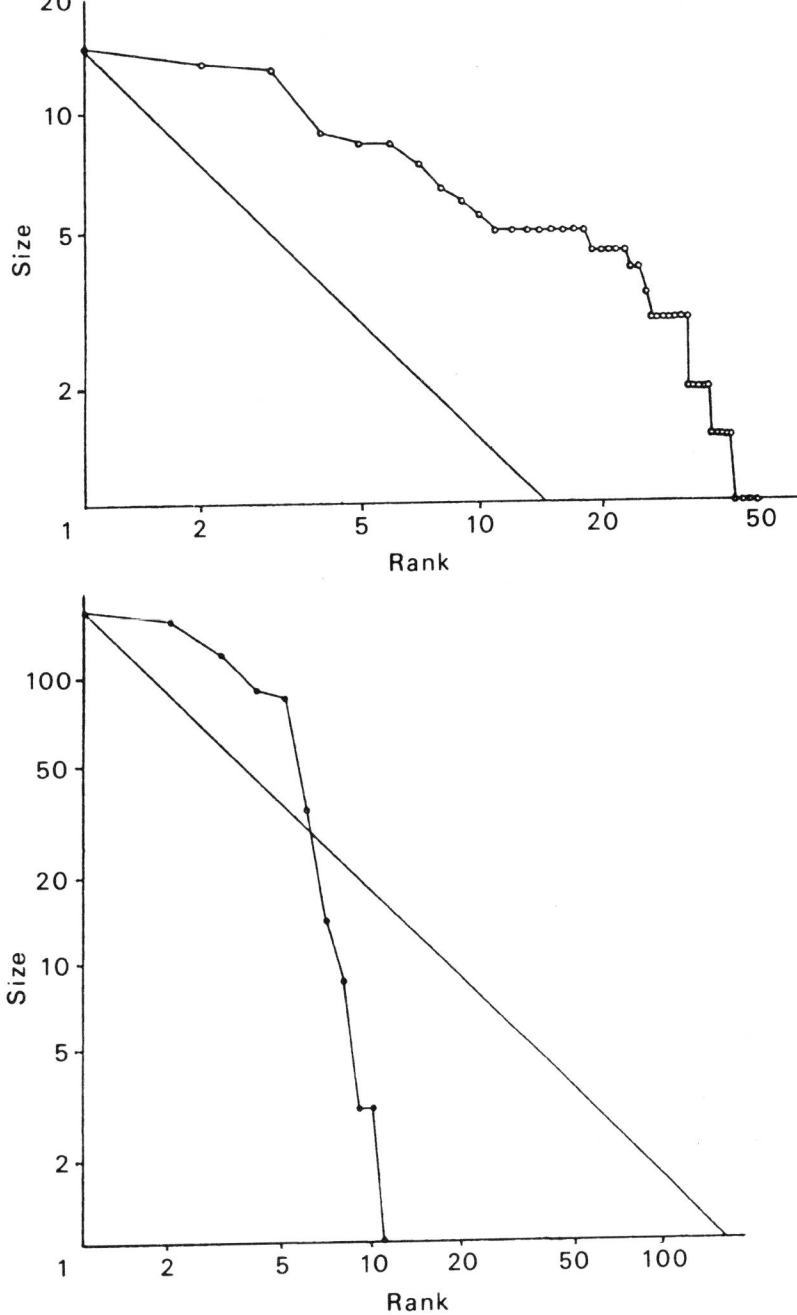

FIGURE 1. *Rank-size graphs for (above) 10th-century BC and (below) 9th-century BC settlements in South Etruria. (After Guidi 1985: figures 11.2, 11.4.)*

By the beginning of the 1st millennium BC there seem to have been distinct settlement enclaves in Etruria, suggesting a new degree of socio-political integration, but there is no evidence for the centralization of authority in a political sense that we can see a few centuries later with the emergence of the Etruscan state (Di Gennaro 1982). The 10th-century settlements form strongly convex curves in Guidi's (1985) rank size analy-

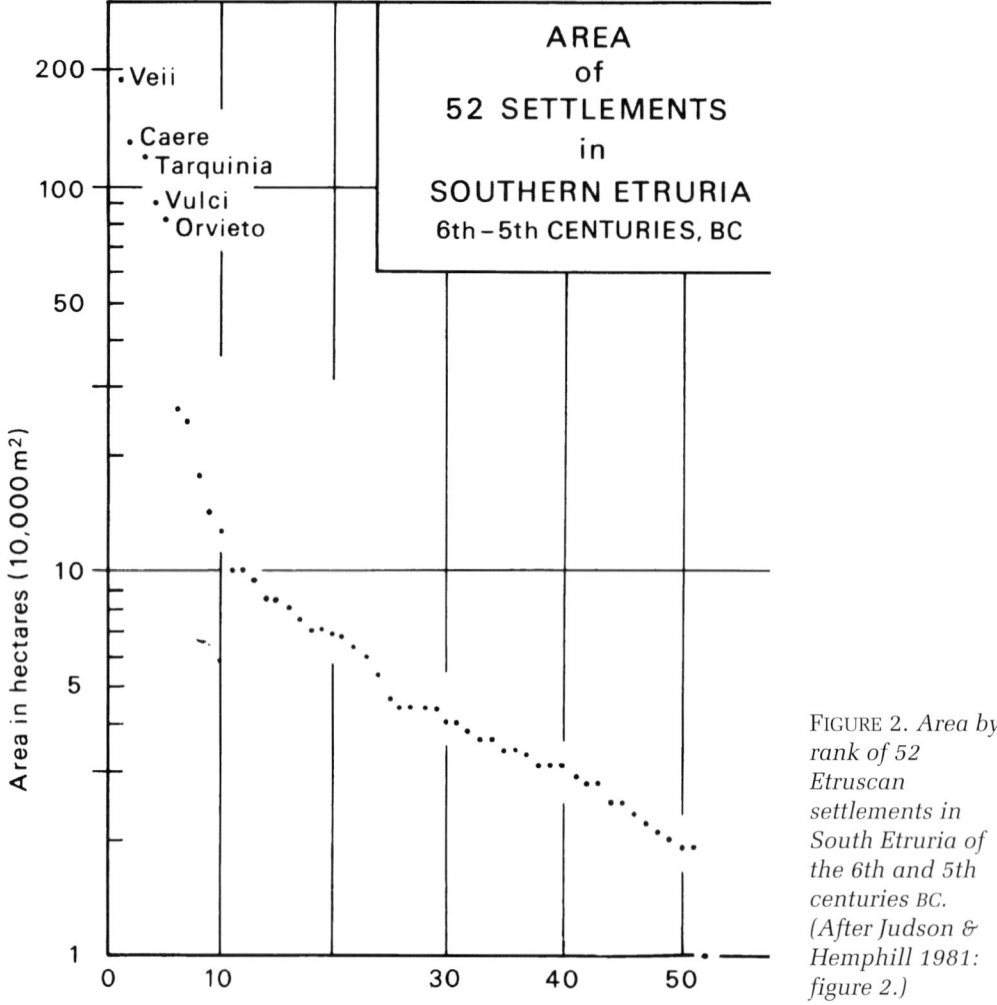

FIGURE 2. *Area by rank of 52 Etruscan settlements in South Etruria of the 6th and 5th centuries BC. (After Judson & Hemphill 1981: figure 2.)*

sis, a pattern of gradual change in site size normally taken to indicate a loosely developed level of articulation, stratification or interaction (FIGURE 1). In the countryside around Tuscania (FIGURE 3), the area of an intensive field survey in progress by the British School at Rome and the University of Manchester, the pre-Etruscan sites found by the survey form small clusters, particularly on terraces immediately adjacent to watercourses, and are in no particular relation to Tuscania, which became a medium-sized centre in the Etruscan period with a distinct territory (Barker & Rasmussen 1988).

Rural Etruscan settlement

During the course of the 9th century BC, there was an extraordinary transformation in settlement structure in South Etruria (Guidi 1985) and by the end of the century five major Villanovan centres had emerged which were to become the five major Etruscan cities of the region: Caere/Cerveteri, Veii, Tarquinia, Vulci, and Volsinii/Orvieto. There is some evidence for a transitional phase during the 9th century of competing centres within the territories where the five dominant centres then emerged at the end of the

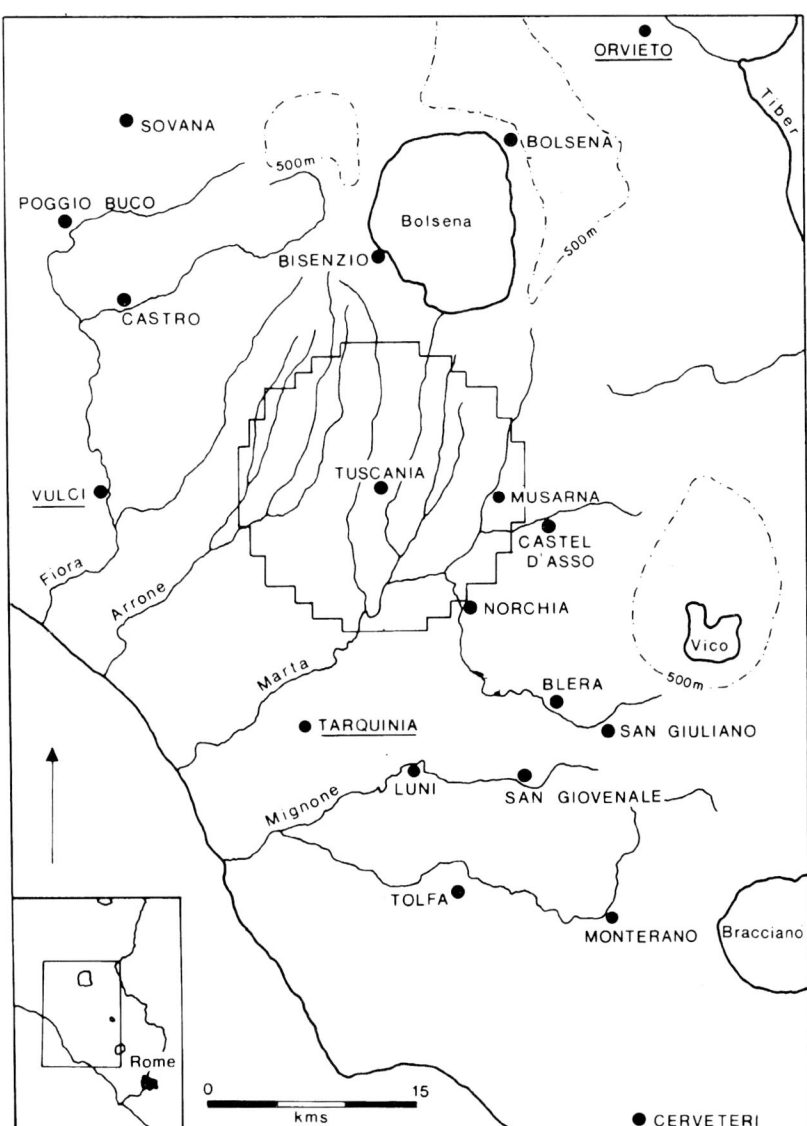

FIGURE 3.
*Etruscan centres
in South Etruria
(major centres
underlined). The
survey area
around Tuscania
is also shown
(see FIGURE 4).*

century (Di Gennaro 1982). In the rank size analysis there is an 'unbalanced primate pattern', with the five major centres each measuring between 100 and 200 ha followed by a succession of far smaller sites (FIGURE 1). The pattern of discrete cemeteries around the major centres underlines the impression of a dramatic process of nucleation in the 9th century of formerly distinct populations, perhaps enforced synoecism. The process of social stratification inferred from the Villanovan cemeteries seems to have been as rapid (Close-Brooks 1968; Toms 1986). In the following centuries a more graded system of site stratification gradually developed in South Etruria, but with the five centres always pre-eminent until they came under Roman control (Judson & Hemphill 1981: figure 2) (FIGURE 2).

Tuscania was a typical Etruscan centre of the minor category, the acropolis (Colle San Pietro) measuring some 8·5 ha. It was situated equidistant (15 km) from the two

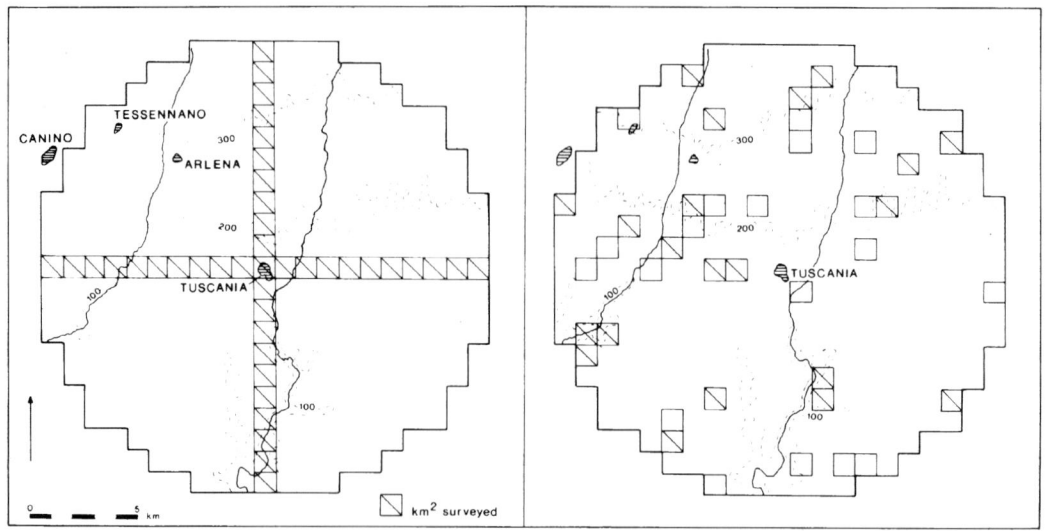

FIGURE 4. *The Tuscania Survey, showing the number of square kilometres studied between 1986 and 1988. The survey area has been defined as those square kilometres on the I.G.M. grid within a 10-km radius from the town.*
Left   *the cardinal transects of the first stage of the survey.*
Right   *the 10% random sample, showing those squares studied by the end of the 1988 season of fieldwork.*

major coastal centres of Tarquinia and Vulci, and 40 km from the major inland centre of Orvieto, with other minor centres 10–15 km away to the north, east, and south (FIGURE 3). On the basis of similarities in funerary material it is normally assumed that the town was within the territory of Tarquinia, although on occasion it may have been within Vulci's sphere of control (Colonna 1967; 1974; Sgubini Moretti 1982) — but it must be said that the precise nature of the control of a major centre such as Tarquinia over a minor centre such as Tuscania (whether in political, social, economic, or ideological terms) is extremely unclear.

The 1986 and 1987 seasons of field survey around Tuscania investigated four transects formed of the kilometre squares of the national Italian grid on the 1:25,000 I.G.M. maps, running north and south for 10 km from the town and west and east for 7 km (FIGURE 4). This sampling strategy was adopted for the first phase of the project as the simplest way to map the pattern of ancient settlement moving out from the town into its territory, given that there are no major natural biases in the area in terms of variations in topography or geology — the countryside consists of an undulating volcanic plateau dissected by the Marta stream and its territories. In the second phase of fieldwork, beginning in 1988, we have taken a 10% random sample of the kilometre squares in a 10-km radius from Tuscania to test the patterns which have emerged from the initial transects (FIGURE 4). The area is ideal for field walking given that it has not been subject to large scale alluviation and colluviation and is almost entirely cultivated. As a result, it has been possible to make detailed maps of both the 'site' and 'non-site' or 'off-site' archaeology from late prehistoric times onwards (Barker & Rasmussen 1988).

The survey has recorded almost 100 domestic Etruscan sites compared with about 20 late prehistoric (mostly Bronze Age) sites, documenting an extraordinary density of rural settlement (FIGURE 5). Little land is available for survey immediately north and

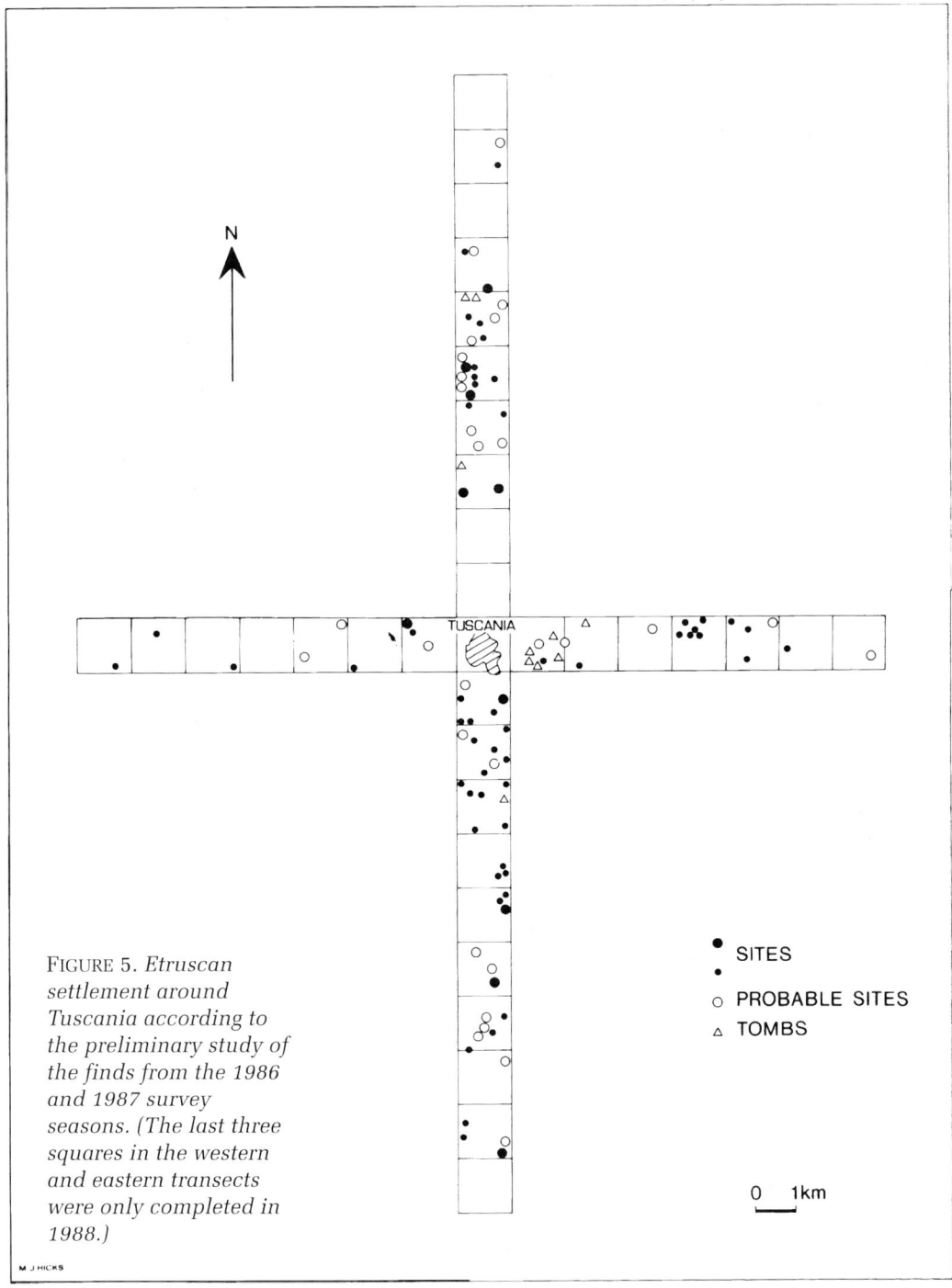

FIGURE 5. *Etruscan settlement around Tuscania according to the preliminary study of the finds from the 1986 and 1987 survey seasons. (The last three squares in the western and eastern transects were only completed in 1988.)*

● SITES
•
○ PROBABLE SITES
△ TOMBS

0   1km

M J HICKS

west of the town, resulting in the blank areas on the distribution map, and immediately east of Tuscania there were few domestic sites because this part of the territory, the Pian di Mola, was reserved for several major Etruscan cemeteries. On the southern plateau, however, the sites begin within the first kilometre of the Colle San Pietro acropolis. In general, there was a remarkably dense pattern of rural settlement within the first 5 or 6 km of the town. The sites found towards the far ends of the transects may belong to other settlement groupings, and it is noteworthy in this respect that the transects have crossed the Arrone river to the west (the assumed boundary between Vulci and Tarquinia), the Marta river to the south (a likely boundary with Norchia), and to the east and north are more than half way towards the next minor centres (Castel d'Asso and Bisenzio respectively).

The preliminary indications from the Tuscania survey are therefore that this minor centre was served by a discrete agricultural territory and controlled an economic unit of farms and smallholdings extending over about 12 sq. km. This pattern contrasts strikingly with those of the Roman Republican and imperial periods, for which the survey has revealed a landscape of substantial farms and villas fairly evenly distributed down the transects, components in an Italian and ultimately a Mediterranean-wide market system rather than a local network. The off-site data of tile debris, on the assumption that it reflects manuring, also demonstrates a transformation in the intensity of land use round the Roman farms compared with the amount of land cultivated round the Etruscan farms. Exactly the same phenomenon has been noted in the Montarrenti Survey in central Tuscany (Barker *et al.* 1986), though in this region, remote from an Etruscan centre, the densities of farms found were of the order of one per square kilometre, a third that of the densities around Tuscania.

Etruscan farms and farming

Until recently, most of our information on Etruscan rural buildings consisted of extrapolations from the domestic architecture of the excavated settlements, particularly Acquarossa. Here, the Swedish excavations revealed a variety of small rectangular houses with one, two, or less commonly three rooms, sometimes separated from the entrance by an anteroom. The foundations were in part excavated into the soft *tufo* bedrock, in part built up of *tufo* blocks. There was a sturdy timber frame supporting a heavy tile roof, external and partition walls of wattle and daub (sometimes painted), and a floor of beaten earth (Nylander 1986). Similar houses have been found at Ficana, Roselle, San Giovenale and Veio. The houses were generally grouped round a piazza, but were built to fit the local topography rather than to an orderly plan. At centres such as Acquarossa and Murlo (*Poggio Civitate* 1970), and south of Rome at Satricum (*Satricum* 1982), there were also much more substantial buildings, suites of rooms built of brick on stone foundations laid out to a rectangular or square plan round a central courtyard edged with a portico. The roofs of these buildings were lavishly decorated with figurative tiles and moulded clay antefixes. Their function has been much debated, particularly in the case of Murlo (Stopponi 1985 and references), with domestic, ritual and administrative roles variously postulated, but certainly they seem to have been the principal buildings used by the leading families who controlled the towns (Pianu 1985).

Surprisingly perhaps, the very few Etruscan rural sites excavated have all been far more similar in layout to the large 'villa' buildings of the major settlements than to their 'cottages'. At Podere Tartuchino, for example, one of the medium-sized surface sites with Etruscan pottery found by the Pisa and Siena Universities' survey in the Albegna Valley, excavations in 1985 and 1986 by Ida Attolini of the University of Pisa and Phil Perkins of the British School at Rome revealed a fairly large (30 x 30 m) farmstead of the 6th and 5th centuries BC with a substantial three-roomed building on one side of a courtyard and a narrower range, probably animal housing, on the other. The domestic building had a tile roof, external walls with stone footings, internal stone divisions, a beaten earth floor, and post-hole evidence for wooden room partitions and a portico. In structure and layout, clearly,

FIGURE 6. *An Etruscan ploughman and his oxen team: a bronze model from Arezzo dated to the 6th century* BC *in the Villa Giulia Museum, Rome. (Photograph kindly provided by the Soprintendenza Archeologica per l'Etruria Meridionale.)*

this farm was far removed from the hut clusters of the final prehistoric settlements and much more akin to the Roman villa farms that were to follow. The mining community of the Lago dell'Accesa settlement near Massa Marittima lived in houses rather similar in size and construction to those of Podere Tartucchino (Camporeale 1985).

Until recently there had been as little systematic research on Etruscan farming as on Etruscan farms. Our principal information has consisted of, on the one hand, what could be extrapolated backwards from the Roman literary sources and, on the other, the material evidence of the tomb paintings and tomb furniture, including objects such as the enchanting Arezzo Ploughman (FIGURE 6), a small bronze model of a ploughman and his ox team pulling a light plough that has been the essential illustration to virtually every discussion of Etruscan farming. To these data can now be added the evidence of the new excavations, and of associated studies of faunal and botanical residues. The importance of such material for Etruscan studies is only now being recognised. One of the research programmes I initiated at the British School at Rome when Director (1984–8) was to promote this approach to Etruscan farming, with faunal material being studied by Dr Gillian Clark and botanical sampling and analysis being undertaken by Jane Fitt and John Giorgi, whose preliminary results are summarized here. The botanical studies have been in collaboration with Dr Lorenzo Costantini, whose researches have been the only modern archaeobotanical work on Etruscan remains.

Though the data are very few, it is increasingly clear that the emergence of the Etruscan state system coincided with critical changes in the agricultural system just as much as in rural settlement patterns and farm organization. Whereas Bronze Age farming in Etruria had consisted of cereal/legume cultivation and generalized stock-keeping, there is widespread evidence for more intensified systems of land use in the Etruscan period in both plant and animal husbandry.

In terms of plant husbandry, Etruscan farming marked a clear break with the past in the systematic cultivation of tree crops as well as cereals and legumes. In the plant remains from Podere Tartuchino, for example, were large numbers of grape pips as well as cereals and associated weed seeds (Jane Fitt, pers. comm.). The residues from a late 4th-century BC pit at Blera (Le Pozze) included cereals, legumes, olives, and figs, but were dominated above all by grape pips (Costantini & Giorgi 1987). The quality of preserva-

FIGURE 7. *Wine drinking in the Etruscan banquet. (From The Banquet Frieze at Murlo, Small 1971: figure 1.)*

tion of the grape pips enabled Costantini to demonstrate their cultivated status from both morphological and metric criteria. Some of the amphorae found in the Etruscan ship wrecked off the island of Giglio contained olive stones (Bound 1985). Grapes and olives were also represented in late Etruscan deposits at the sanctuary of Pyrgi (Coccolini & Follieri 1980). In Rome, plant remains from two deposits of the Etruscan-period city on the Palatine are in course of study by John Giorgi, the first study of such material since Helbaek's pioneering work (Helbaek 1953; 1956). There is a surprisingly wide range of cereals (emmer, einkorn, bread wheat, barley, millet) and their harvesting debris, legumes and fruits, and quantities of olive stones, fig seeds, and grape pips.

The archaeobotanical evidence coincides with pictorial and artefactual evidence for the importance of tree crops in Etruscan farming. Perfume vases for oil were being manufactured by the end of the 7th century BC, and the classical sources place the beginnings of olive and vine cultivation around Rome in this period (Boardman 1976; Vallet 1962). The banquet played a critical role in the social interactions of the Etruscan nobility, and wine drinking, a fundamental component of the *symposion*, is commonly represented in Etruscan art — as for example in the famous Banquet Frieze from Murlo dated to about 580 BC (Small 1971: figure 1; FIGURE 7). Luxury table services for the preparation and drinking of the wine were being manufactured from the late 8th century BC onwards (Cristofani 1987). Wine was also an important item for trade, and Etruscan wine was widely exported around the western Mediterranean by the 6th century BC, together with the associated table services. The cargo of the Giglio shipwreck, dated to *c.* 600 BC, included Etruscan transport amphorae and fine *bucchero* pottery (Bound 1985). The numbers of fragments of wine amphorae at Podere Tartuchino confirm the importance of wine production at this substantial farm. A bronze sickle-like implement from the Lago dell'Accesa settlement has been identified as a tool for pruning vines (Camporeale 1985: 135). Direct evidence for vine cultivation has also been found in the recent emergency excavations by the Soprintendenza archeologica per l'Etruria Meridionale at Blera (Le Pozze), in the form of vine trenches of late Etruscan date; the first pressing equipment from an Etruscan site (whether for oil or wine or both is not certain) was also found here (Ricciardi 1987).

Animal husbandry also underwent significant changes. In the central room at Podere Tartuchino were a hearth, a sunken *dolium*, and an associated system of channels for liquids, at first thought to be for olive oil production but now identified more satisfactorily as a facility for the large scale processing of wool (Perkins, pers. comm.). The settlement excavations, both of the centres and of the farms, have invariably produced large numbers of spindle whorls. The faunal evidence discussed below confirms the importance of wool production. Like wine, the manufacture of high quality textiles in the Etruscan countryside was probably both to enhance the lifestyles of the élites in the centres (as clearly evidenced in their tomb paintings) and to provide them with prestige goods for trade.

Etruscan faunal material, so often discarded in past excavations, is still extremely limited, but there are indications of more specialized systems of meat production and distribution compared with the late prehistoric systems, and for the increased importance of secondary products. All of the faunal samples so far available are from major and minor centres rather than from farms, and so reflect patterns of urban consumption first and foremost. However, when butchery marks have been recorded, as in the case of the faunal material from Populonia studied by De Grossi Mazzorin (1985) and from Cerveteri (in course of study by Dr Gillian Clark), standardized systems of carcass processing have been found which are far more like those of the Roman period than the intensive but very variable systems of the later prehistoric settlements in Etruria. At Populonia, for example, in the case of cattle, sheep, and goats, the head was first removed from the trunk by a cut near the top of the cervical vertebrae, and the tongue removed by cracking open the lower jaw; the fore limb was removed at the base of the scapula, the hind limb at the top of the femur, and the main sections of the limbs were then separated at the articulations. Pig butchery was rather similar but the trotters were used as food, whereas the cattle, sheep and goat metapodials were set aside for tool manufacture. Clearly the needs of the craftsmen required standardized pieces of bone, but the main butchery served to produce standardized parcels of meat.

Most of the sheep and goats brought to Cerveteri and Populonia were relatively young animals, but the number of young adult and fully adult animals suggests that they came from flocks which were not for specialized meat production but a mixture of ewes, wethers and rams kept for breeding and for secondary products such as cheese and wool. The cattle brought to the centres for slaughter were mostly old animals, probably plough cattle beyond a useful working age. Pigs were useful only for the products of the carcass, those at Cerveteri normally being 2nd year males. The other faunal samples from Etruscan sites are all extremely small, but there are indications that the mix and age structures of the stock at Acquarossa (Gejvall 1982), Blera (Scali 1987a), Gran Carro (Scali 1987b) and San Giovenale (Sorrentino 1981a; 1981b) were rather similar to those of Cerveteri and Populonia.

Conclusion

As the foregoing discussion has shown, the emergence of the Etruscan state system marked a total transformation in the organization and appearance of the countryside. In South Etruria, within each 'early state module' (Renfrew 1975) or *polis*, apart from the major centre of population there was a series of smaller centres, each forming the focus (if Tuscania is typical) for an agricultural support system in a discrete territorial enclave. The principal Etruscan farm investigated seems to have been a substantial production unit, though it may well not have been the lowest level in the rural settlement hierarchy. The late prehistoric/protohistoric system of mixed farming (cereal/legume cultivation and generalized stock-keeping) was replaced by Mediterranean polyculture (cereals, legumes, olives, vines, figs) and more intensive stock-keeping, with perhaps a distinct emphasis on wool production.

The new crops have traditionally been regarded as Greek introductions, but in fact seem to have been indigenous, the wild vine certainly having been exploited in Italy since Neolithic times. There is some evidence for wine drinking amongst some Bronze Age communities in peninsular Italy in the later 2nd millennium BC, and for the use of olive oil by those people in southern Italy immediately adjacent to Mycenaean settlements (Peroni 1984). A simple explanation for the start of polyculture with the Etruscans could still be that the new technology came from contact with Greeks. However, it is surely significant that the development of systematic polyculture only began in Etruria within the context of state formation, at the time when a system of subsistence changed into a much more complex economic system and when society changed from one characterized by limited ranking to clearly stratified hierarchies. Just as Etruscan drainage systems allowed better use of heavier soils (Judson & Kahane 1963), and the new road system facilitated communications and the movement of goods, olives and vines certainly represented a more intensive use of the landscape (in particular a more effective use of valley sides). The system of plant and animal husbandry as a whole clearly supported far higher populations than hitherto both in the countryside and in the towns. At the same time, the products of the new agriculture served to emphasize the differences between élites and commoners and to provide the former with a marketable surplus.

There is very little agricultural data for the critical period of state formation in the 9th and 8th centuries, most of the evidence allowing us simply to characterize the nature of settlement and land use before and afterwards. However, it is noteworthy that the botanical residues from the 9th-century Villanovan settlement of Gran Carro on the shores of Lake Bolsena included grape pips and vine charcoal as well as cereals, legumes and fruits (Costantini & Costantini Biasini 1987), and that the important site of Cures in the Sabine Hills has produced, from an 8th-century BC context, cultivated grape pips and olive stones (Costantini & Biasini 1985) and a domestic fauna with butchery marks much like those of Cerveteri and Populonia and with similar age profiles (Ruffo 1985). None of this evidence of course is sufficient on its own to inform us about why and how the transformations in rural Etruscan settlement occurred, or about the priority or otherwise of demographic and agricultural change in the process of state formation. The range of disparate models proposed to account for the role of the earlier but rather comparable changes in rural settlement and agriculture in the Aegean in terms of the origins and functioning of the Minoan/Mycenaean state system (Bintliff 1977; Halstead 1981; Renfrew 1972) — where the archaeological and documentary evidence is singularly detailed — is a healthy reminder of how far we must progress in the archaeology of the Etruscan countryside before we can begin to construct any but the most simplistic models.

According to the Linear B tablets, the intensification in agricultural production marked by the development of systematic polyculture in the Aegean may have coincided with something of a decline in the quality of diet for many peasant farmers marked by increased quantities of bread and oil at the expense of meat. It can only be speculation at this stage, but it may well have been much the same story in Etruria, with the quality of life of many ordinary Etruscan farmers deteriorating as the quality of life of the new élites improved. Interestingly, a trace element analysis of Etruscan human skeletons has indicated a trend towards a diminution of animal products in the diet from the archaic to Hellenistic periods, compared with the opposite trend over the same period in Greece (Fornaciari & Mallegni 1987).

We cannot afford to dismiss this kind of archaeology as the unworthy pursuit of the everyday trivia of *Homo economicus*. In part, clearly, subsistence products were mobilized as economic resources. At the same time, however, at least some of the surplus animals (prime young stock for the most part) were consumed in feasting rituals in the sanctuaries (Colonna 1987), rituals which must have served to legitimate the authority of the élites amongst the peasantry who provided for them. Given the well known difficulties for classical farmers, according to the Roman agronomists, of maintaining even a plough team of oxen through the year given the inadequate feed available (White 1970: 283–4), killing prime cattle and small stock as part of the temple rituals must have been as conspicuous a form of consumption as any of the more permanent monuments of aristocratic display such as the great cemeteries, temples, and defence walls. To understand the full Etruscan achievement we need an integrated archaeology of town and country, of élite and commoners, of secular and ritual, if we are to bid good morning to the Etruscans next time with rather more familiarity than we had in 1985.

References

BARKER, G. 1976. Animal husbandry at Narce, in Potter (1976): 157–77.

BARKER, G. & T. RASMUSSEN. In press. The archaeology of an Etruscan polis: a preliminary report on the Tuscania project (1986 and 1987 seasons), *Papers of the British School at Rome* 56.

BARKER, G., S. COCCIA, D.A. JONES & J. SITZIA. 1986. The Montarrenti survey 1985: problems in integrating archaeological, environmental, and historical data, *Archeologia Medievale* 13: 291–320.

BIETTI-SESTIERI, A.-M. (ed.). 1984. *Preistoria e protostoria nel territorio di Roma*. Rome: De Luca.

   1985. (ed.). Preistoria e protostoria nel territorio di Roma: modelli di insediamento e vie di communicazione, in S. Quilici Gigli (ed.), *Il Tevere e le altre vie d'acqua del Lazio antico*: 30–70. Rome: Consiglio Nazionale delle Ricerche.

BINTLIFF, J.L. 1977. *Natural environment and human settlement in prehistoric Greece*. Oxford: British Archaeological Reports. International series 28.

BOARDMAN, J. 1976. The olive in the Mediterranean: its culture and use, *Philosophical Transactions of the Royal Society of London* series B, 275: 187–96.

BONATTI, E. 1961. I sedimenti del Lago di Monterosi, *Experientia* 17 (252): 1–4.

   1963. Stratigrafia pollinica dei sedimenti postglaciali di Baccano, lago craterico del Lazio, *Atti della Società Toscana di Scienze Naturali* series A, 70: 40–48.

   1970. Pollen sequence in the lake sediments, in G.E. Hutchinson (ed.), Ianula — an account of the history and development of the Lago di Monterosi, Latium, Italy, *Transactions of the American Philosophical Society* 60 (4): 26–31.

BOUND, M. 1985. Una nave mercantile di età arcaica all'Isola del Giglio, in *Il Commercio Etrusco Arcaico*: 65–70. Rome: Consiglio Nazionale delle Ricerche. Quaderni del Centro di Studio per l'Archeologia Etrusco-Italica 9.

BRONSON, R.G. & G. UGGERI. 1970. Isola del Giglio — Isola di Giannutri — Monte Argentario — Laguna di Orbetello, *Studi Etruschi* 38: 201–14.

CAMPOREALE, G. (ed.). 1985. *L'Etruria Mineraria*. Milan: Electa.

CARANDINI, A. (ed.). 1985. *La Romanizzazione dell'Etruria*. Milan: Electa.

CATACCHIO, N.N. (ed.). 1983. *Sorgenti della Nova: una comunità protostorica ed. il suo territorio nell'Etruria meridionale*. Rome: Vision.

CLOSE-BROOKS, J. 1968. Considerazioni sulla cronologia delle facies arcaiche dell'Etruria, *Studi Etruschi* 36: 323–9.

CLOSE-BROOKS, J. & S. GIBSON. 1966. A round hut near Rome, *Proceedings of the Prehistoric Society* 32: 349–52.

COCCOLINI, G. & M. FOLLIERI. 1980. I legni dai pozzi del Tempio A nel santuario etrusco di Pyrgi, *Studi Etruschi* 48: 277–91.

COLONNA, G. 1967. L'Etruria meridionale interna dal Villanoviano alle tombe rupestri, *Studi Etruschi* 35: 3–30.

   1974. La cultura dell'Etruria meridionale interna con particolare riguardo alle necropoli rupestre, *Atti VII Convegno Nazionale di Studi Etruschi ed Italici (Orvieto 1972)*: 253–65. Florence: Olschki.

   1987. Pyrgi, in *L'alimentazione...* (1987): 77–81.

COSTANTINI, L. & L. COSTANTINI BIASINI. 1985. Paleoetnobotanica — nota preliminare, pages 86–8 in A. Guidi (ed.), Cures Sabini, *Archeologia Laziale* 7: 77–92.

   1987. Bolsena — Gran Carro: i resti vegetali, in *L'alimentazione...* (1987): 61–7.

COSTANTINI, L. & J.A. GIORGI. 1987. Blera: i resti vegetali, in *L'alimentazione...* (1987): 83–6.

CRISTOFANI, M. (ed.). 1985 *Civiltà degli Etruschi*. Milan: Electa.

   1987. Il banchetto in Etruria, in *L'alimentazione...*(1987): 123–32.

DE GROSSI MAZZORIN, J. 1985. Reperti faunistici dall'acropoli di Populonia: testimonianze di allevamento e caccia nel III secolo a.C., *Rassegna di Archeologia* 5: 131–71.

DI GENNARO, F. 1982. Organizzazione del territorio nell'Etruria meridionale protostorica: applicazione di un modello grafico, *Dialoghi di Archeologia* 2: 102–12.

FEDELI, F. & A. GALIBERTI. 1979. Insediamenti dell'età del Bronzo nel comprensorio di Piombino (Livorno): nota preliminare, *Rassegna di Archeologia* 1: 147–238.

FORNACIARI, G. & F. MALLEGNI. 1987. Indagini paleonutrizionali su campioni di popolazioni a cultura etrusca, in *L'alimentazione...* (1987): 135–9.

FRANK, A.H.E. 1969. Pollen stratigraphy of the Lake of Vico (central Italy), *Palaeogeography, Palaeoclimatology, Palaeoecology* 6: 67–85.

FUGAZZOLA DELPINO, M.A. 1982. Rapporto preliminare sulle ricerche condotte dalla Soprintendenza Archeologica dell'Etruria Meridionale nei bacini lacustri del'Apparato vulcanico sabatino, *Bolletino d'Arte*, Supplemento 4: 123–49.

GEJVALL, N.-G. 1982. Animal remains from Zone A in Acquarossa, in M.-B. Lundgren & L. Wendt, *Acquarossa III: Zone A*: 68–70. Stockholm: Skrifter Utgivna av Svenska Institutet i Rom 4, 38 (3).

GIARDINO, C. 1984. Insediamenti e sfruttamento minerario del territorio durante la media e tarda età del bronze nel Lazio: ipotesi e considerazioni, *Nuovo Bullettino Archeologico Sardo* 1: 123–41.

GUIDI, A. 1985. An application of the rank size rule to protohistoric settlements in the middle Tyrrhenian area, in C. Malone & S. Stoddart (ed.), *Papers in Italian archaeology IV: volume 3: Patterns in protohistory*: 217–42. Oxford: British Archaeological Reports. International Series 245.

HALSTEAD, P. 1981. Counting sheep in neolithic and Bronze Age Greece, in I. Hodder, G. Isaac & N. Hammond (ed.), *Pattern in the past: studies in memory of David Clarke*: 307–39. Cambridge: Cambridge University Press.

HELBAEK, H. 1953. The plant remains, in E. Gjerstad, *Early Rome I*: 155–7. Lund: Skrifter Utgivna av Svenska Institutet i Rom 4, 17 (1).
    1956. Vegetables in the funeral meals of pre-urban Rome, in E. Gjerstad, *Early Rome II*: 286. Lund: Skrifter Utgivna av Svenska Institutet i Rom 4, 17 (2).
    1967. Agricoltura preistorica a Luni sul Mignone in Etruria. Appendice II, in C.E. Östenberg (1967): 277–9.

HUNT, C. In press. Environmental studies, in G. Barker & T. Rasmussen, The archaeology of an Etruscan polis: a preliminary report on the Tuscania project (1986 and 1987 seasons), *Papers of the British School at Rome* 56.

JARMAN, H.N. 1976. The plant remains, in Potter (1976): 308–10.

JUDSON, S. & P. HEMPHILL. 1981. Sizes of settlements in Southern Etruria, 6th–5th centuries BC, *Studi Etruschi* 49: 193–202.

JUDSON, S. & A. KAHANE. 1963. Underground drainageways in southern Etruria and northern Latium, *Papers of the British School at Rome* 31: 74–99.

L'Alimentazione del mondo antico: gli Etruschi. 1987. Rome: Istituto Poligrafico e Zecca dello Stato.

MAGGIANI, A. & E. PELLEGRINI. 1985. *La Media Valle del Fiora dalla Preistoria alla Romanizzazione*. Pitigliano: Comunità Montana Zona 'S', Colline del Fiora.

MURRAY, O. 1985. At the Etruscan banquet, *Times Literary Supplement* 30 August 1985: 948, 960.

NYLANDER, C. (ed.). 1986. *Architettura Etrusca nel Viterbese*. Rome: De Luca.

ÖSTENBERG, C.E. 1967. *Luni sul Mignone e Problemi della Preistoria d'Italia*. Lund: Skrifter Utgivna av Svenska Institutet i Rom 4, 25.

PACCIARELLI, M. 1982. Economia e organizzazione del territorio in Etruria Meridionale nell'età del Bronzo media e recente, *Dialoghi di Archeologia* 2: 69–79.

PERONI, R. (ed.). 1984. *Nuove Ricerche sulla Protostoria della Sibaritide*. Rome: Paleani.

PIANU, G. 1985. I luoghi della cultura figurativa, in M. Torelli, *L'arte degli Etruschi*: 269–335. Rome: Laterza.

POGGIO CIVITATE (MURLO, SIENA). 1970. Florence: Olschki.

POTTER, T.W. (ed.). 1976. *A Faliscan town in South Etruria: excavations at Narce 1966–71*. London: British School at Rome.
    1979. *The changing landscape of South Etruria*. London: Elek.

RENFREW, C. 1972. *The emergence of civilisation*. London: Methuen.
    1975. Trade as action at a distance: questions of integration and communication, in J.A. Sabloff & C.C. Lamberg-Karlovsky (ed.), *Ancient civilisation and trade*: 3–59. Albuquerque: University of New Mexico Press.

RICCIARDI, L. 1987. Blera: l'insediamento agricolo di Le Pozze, in *L'alimentazione...* (1987): 83.

RUFFO, G. 1985. Sintesi dei dati faunistici, page 84 in A. Guidi (ed.), Cures Sabini, *Archeologia Laziale* 7: 77–92.

Satricum. Una citta Latina. 1982. Florence: Alinari.

SCALI, S. 1987a. Bolsena — Gran Carro: i resti faunistici, in *L'alimentazione...* (1987): 67–70.
    1987b. Blera: i resti animali, in *L'alimentazione...* (1987): 86.

SGUBINI MORETTI, M. 1982. Tuscania. Necropoli in località Ara del Tufo. 1a campagna di scavo: relazione preliminare, in *Archeologia nella Tuscia*: 133–48. Rome: Consiglio Nazionale delle Ricerche (Istituti di Studi Etruschi ed. Italici).

SMALL, J.P. 1971. The Banquet Frieze from Poggio Civitate (Murlo), *Studi Etruschi* 39: 25–61.

SORRENTINO, C. 1981a. The fauna, in E. Berggren & K. Berggren, *San Giovenale II, 2: excavations in area B, 1957–1960*: 58–64. Stockholm: Skrifter Utgivna av Svenska Institutet i Rom 4, 36 (II, 2).
    1981b. La fauna, in B. Olinder & I. Pohl, *San Giovenale II, 4: the semi-subterranean building in area B*: 85–9. Stockholm: Skrifter Utgivna av Svenska Institutet i Rom 4, 36 (II, 4).

STOPPONI, S. (ed.).1985. *Case e Palazzi d'Etruria*. Milan: Electa.

TOMS, J. 1986. The relative chronology of the Villanovan cemetery of Quattro Fontanili at Veii, *Archeologia e Storia Antica* 8: 41–97.

VALLET, G. 1962. L'introduction de l'olivier en Italie centrale, in M. Renard (ed.), *Hommage à Albert Grenier*: 154–63. Brussels: Collection Latomus 58.

WALKER, S. 1985. Survey of a settlement: a strategy for the Etruscan site at Doganella in the Albegna valley, in C. Haselgrove, M. Millet & I. Smith (ed.), *Archaeology from the ploughsoil*: 87–94. Sheffield: Sheffield University (Department of Archaeology and Prehistory).

WARD-PERKINS, J.B., A. KAHANE & L. MURRAY-THREIPLAND. 1968. The Ager Veientanus north and east of Veii, *Papers of the British School at Rome* 36: 1–218.

WHITE, K.D. 1970. *Roman farming*. London: Thames & Hudson.

5 Physical landscapes

The modern archaeological study of landscapes too often concentrates exclusively on the cultural. The term 'natural', we are constantly reminded, is a relative term. At the very least, many Holocene natural landscapes are the product of a constant interrelationship between human activity and the physical landscape. In reality, the relative impact of the physical landscape on the cultural is strongly dependent on the timescale. The influential work of Braudel has stressed the *longue durée* of the physical landscape, but this is a simplification. Even in more recent times, there has been a constant negotiation of landscape crisis perceived by humans in the short term who develop different strategic options (Dincauze 2000: 73–9). Such crises are identified more prominently and visibly at some stages in the archaeological record than others, but only long-term archaeological hindsight can determine their relative importance. The short-term responses remain largely invisible unless cumulative. The longer-term responses are those where archaeology can have access. The key is to define detailed environmental context: the diversity of environmental conditions, scale, time, sequence, as well as mechanisms and potential equifinalities.

The first example tackles the longer time-scale and considers larger territorial scales of human landscapes. The article by Bailey and colleagues reprinted here interprets the frequent presence of Palaeolithic activity in tectonic basins. This is a global phenomenon not just restricted to the Mediterranean region which forms the focus of their study. Tectonics have a powerful effect on the rate of erosion and deposition of sediments. In dry regions such as the Mediterranean, traps of sediment may produce relatively stable regimes of topographic closure for hunter–gatherer populations and are additionally today preserved as relict land-surfaces. This pattern applied to Greece can probably also be transferred in modified form to the more open tectonic basins of central Italy which are also filled with Pleistocene deposits containing substantial Palaeolithic remains (Atti 1982; Bietti 1990; Piperno 1992; Reynolds 1994). Tectonic activity may not have had *archaeologically recognizable* transforming effects (e.g. earthquakes and consequent landslides) on the landscape at the time-scale of the memory of the individual hunter–gatherer; archaeoseismology is a new science which requires a reconciliation of disparate scales of evidence and time (McGuire *et al.* 2000). However, tectonics were very significant in defining those same individuals' and their descendants' hunting territories over millennia, providing paradoxically a medium-term stability (through sediment traps) which was positive and not the disruption normally associated with tectonic activity. Yet in the even longer geological time-scale (millions of years) those same hunting territories will be obliterated and completely transformed out of all recognition.

On the shorter time-scale of the Holocene (since 10,000 BP), any study of landscape should also take account of sedimentation and vegetation. In the light of recent research (Dincauze 2000: 198–201) it is at the small to medium spatial scale (1–10,000 sq. km) that archaeology can make a very real contribution to geomorphology, particularly in defining chronology. Detailed vegetational studies combining all sources of evidence are still relatively rare (Rackham & Moody 1996; Willis *et al.* 1998). More work has been undertaken on sediments. One debate has been the considerable controversy over the relative anthropogenic and climatic (and other natural) causes of erosion and sedimentation in the United States and Europe (Brown 1997). In the Mediterranean a fair number of case-studies have been explored to understand the long sequence of interrelated human activity, climatic change and sedimentary deposition (Dincauze 2000: 320–25).

The debate is centred around the seminal work of Vita-Finzi (1969). He identified two broad alluvial phases, a red Older Fill associated with Palaeolithic material and a Younger Fill associated with Late Classical. He considered both these to be the products of climatic change. These conclusions have subsequently been criticised on theoretical and empirical grounds. Further study of alluvial sequences in Greece (Jameson *et al.* 1994), Southern France, Spain (van der Leeuw 1994) and Italy (Malone & Stoddart 1994; Barker 1995; C. French pers. comm.) have reliably shown the complexity of alluvial sequences, particularly in the Holocene period, and thus that they cannot be attributed to broad climatic events. The balance of opinion is swinging towards localized processes strongly influenced by human activity. In these debates, there is no substitute for an array of detailed observations of relevant variables.

In the most sophisticated accounts, interdisciplinary techniques have been employed to reconstruct a palaeo-environment based on such an array of detailed observations. The work of Zangger and colleagues at Pylos (Zangger *et al.* 1997) and Troy (Zangger *et al.* 2000) has demonstrated that local communities employed developed engineering techniques in the construction of port facilities to affect profoundly the local environment. In other cases the human impact was more subtle. Study of the Étang de Berre in southern France (Trément 2000) has shown the stages of transformation of a 'natural environment'. By the Neolithic, the first farmers had greatly altered the vegetation and soils. During the Iron Age the destruction of the forest reached its peak, although the effects on erosion rates were less marked than in the Neolithic. By the Roman period, a new stability had been reached in spite of highest levels of deforestation. In both these cases, integration of diverse data contributed greatly to the understanding of geomorphological processes.

There is a basic need for archaeologists to understand the effects of these processes on their understanding of landscape. As Howard & Macklin (1999, reprinted here) explain through a classification based on fluvial energy, drawing on examples from northern Europe, landscape archaeologists should approach their research within a framework of appreciating the 'contrasting fluvial styles and sedimentation histories' of rivers. A thorough interdisciplinary integration following their guidance is an important way forward. Most modern landscape projects take good account of the physical environment, but there is always more that can be done through new techniques to establish clear sequences for deposits, to undertake dating and to comprehend causes through techniques such as micromorphology.

Active tectonics and land-use strategies: a Palaeolithic example from northwest Greece

by GEOFF BAILEY, GEOFF KING & DEREK STURDY

ANTIQUITY 67 (255), 1993

HUMANS live at the interface between the solid earth and the unstable atmosphere. The earth appears constant and safe, while the atmosphere is changeable and seems to have the greatest effect on environment. Droughts or floods, erosion or deposition of sediment and the consequent fertility or barrenness of soils are most readily explained by climate, or in recent millennia by human interference. Large-scale tectonic processes of mountain building or subsidence, driven by the motions of the continental plates, seem to operate too slowly, and to belong to a too far-distant geological past, to have any impact within the time span of human occupation. Even the most rapid changes — earthquakes and volcanic eruptions — appear disruptive and temporary in effect unless they seem to trigger some far-reaching social change.

Here we argue that this perspective is too simple. The inexorable changes in landscape geometry caused by deformation of the solid earth can determine the way in which climate affects the landscape, and the way in which the landscape in its turn affects, and is affected by, human activity. In many parts of the world, an appreciation of tectonics is needed to understand the distribution of agricultural soils or of animal herds. On the longer time-scales of prehistory, tectonically driven landscape change may become an active agent of selection, creating pressures or opportunities for changes in behaviour. It is easy to see that tectonic uplift can destroy an environment by triggering erosion, but active deformation is by no means always negative in effect. Tectonic subsidence can create well-watered sediment traps and the accumulation of fertile soils. Uplift and subsidence also create natural barriers to animal movement that can be exploited by humans. It is interesting to note that many early Palaeolithic sites are in regions of tectonic activity. The East African Rift Valley, North Africa, the Levant and Sub-Himalayan India are obvious examples. Undoubtedly the ease of site discovery can be assisted by tectonic changes. Tectonically active areas are those most likely to develop thick, rapidly formed sequences of terrestrial sediments favouring burial and fossilization of archaeological evidence, followed by rapid erosion and exposure to discovery. But the reverse is true and tectonically active regions can destroy or obscure human evidence within decades or centuries. In our discussion of Epirus, we discuss why ease of discovery is not the main reason why a correlation between early human settlement and tectonic activity is to be expected.

Active tectonics

Since the advent of Plate Tectonics, it has been evident that deformation of the Earth is a continuing process. Relative motions at major plate boundaries have rates that can approach 20 cm per year (Demets *et al.* 1990). In oceanic regions deformation can be localized to ridges, trenches or transform faults with widths of less than 100 km. Where plate boundaries cross continental crust, contraction, extension or sideways motion (strike-slip) can be spread over regions with widths exceeding 1000 km. The overall strike-slip motion of 5 cm per year between the Pacific and North American plates, commonly regarded as being accommodated by the San Andreas fault, actually extends from a short distance off the Californian coast to central Utah (Slemmons *et al.* 1991). At most, 50 % of the deformation (2·5 cm per year) occurs as strike-slip on the San Andreas, while the remainder is distributed on contractional, extensional and strike-slip structures which have lower rates. These lower rates can nonetheless result in substantial changes. The Coastal Ranges south of San Francisco, rising at 1 mm per year (Valansise 1992), are 1000 m high and less than 1 million years old, while the floor of Death Valley has dropped relative to its uplifting flanks by a similar amount in the same period of time (King & Ellis 1990).

By global standards, deformation of the western USA is not unusually rapid. Although overall deformation rates in the eastern Mediterranean are comparable, at >2 cm per year (Tapponier 1977), locally they are much higher: in the Aegean region >10 cm per year (King *et al.* in press), and from eastern Turkey to the Himalayas >7 cm per year (Demets *et al.* 1990; Tapponier & Molnar 1977). Again the zone of active deformation can be very wide. In the western zone of the Alpine–Himalayan belt, deformation extends for about 1500 km from the Maghreb to France and Germany; in the eastern zone from the Indus–Ganges basin to Lake Baikhal in Siberia, about 3000 km.

Deformation is not uniformly distributed within these zones. Death Valley or Lake Baikhal owe their present form to local extension and subsidence, while the Coastal Ranges in California, or the foothill folds of the Himalayas, are localizations of contraction. The rates in these regions accommodate only a part of the relative plate motions. Other active features create local uplift and subsidence in these deforming zones and even in the western USA not all have been identified, particularly features with annual rates of motion of less than 1 mm per year.

Deformation also occurs at a wide range of scales. Over long periods of time vast areas rise to form mountains such as the Alps or the Himalayas, or subside to form basins or valleys such as the Aegean trough or the Red Sea rift. These features result from the cumulative effect of motion on many smaller features which individually may have a shorter existence but nonetheless exhibit substantial rates of motion when active. At scales of 5 to 50 km, motion can be very rapid, and uplift or subsidence of 100 m is possible within historic times. In regions of contraction, not all motion is progressive uplift; in regions of extension, not all motion is progressive subsidence. Areas of local uplift and local subsidence can lie close together, only kilometres apart, or even hundreds of metres or less.

Temporal variability occurs and can cause activity to be overlooked, particularly on smaller features. Even features such as Death Valley and the associated Panamint Valley show little activity at present. But they are not dead. Ample morphological evidence exists that several major earthquakes have occurred in the last 10,000–15,000 years (Zhang *et al.* 1990). Similarly, historical data indicate that features between Turkey and Iran have had periods of major earthquakes lasting for tens of years separated by centuries of inactivity (Ambraseys 1989). In the absence of direct observations from instruments or historical reports, the best evidence for tectonic activity is commonly evidence for local disruption of rivers or evidence for local regions of erosion and deposition of sediment.

Human modes of land-use can be affected by modest amounts of uplift or subsidence. Even very small rates of movement can be significant in modifying water-table levels in the short term (100s or 1000s of years), or in creating substantial morphological features in the longer term. Overall, the effects of tectonic deformation may be expected to be widespread and not just restricted to regions where tectonic activity is widely acknowledged to be violent. Furthermore, understanding how tectonics influences human behaviour is not solely of use to the study of the past. Data collected for this purpose are also useful in understanding tectonic processes, and for addressing contemporary problems such as the vulnerability of critical engineering structures like chemical or nuclear facilities to earthquake hazard (Site Characterization Plan 1988; Wood & King 1991). Such information becomes particularly important in places like the British Isles, commonly but incorrectly thought to be inactive, where even a low probability of a major event poses a very serious hazard.

Sediment traps and climatic insensitivity

Local concentrations of sediment or water are almost self-evidently advantageous to a variety of plant and animal species and to a range of human subsistence economies under a diversity of climatic regimes. Local sediment traps are characteristically formed in river catchments on geological structures subject to normal faulting or compressional folding (FIGURE 1). Active structures produce a series of local folds or uplifted blocks separated by troughs, with river profiles which alternate between stretches of down-cutting of uplifted structures and aggradation in the subsiding region between them. Climatically induced cycles of incision and aggradation are superimposed on this pattern, but it is the tectonic processes that provide the underlying long-term determinants on the pattern of erosion and sedimentation in the landscape.

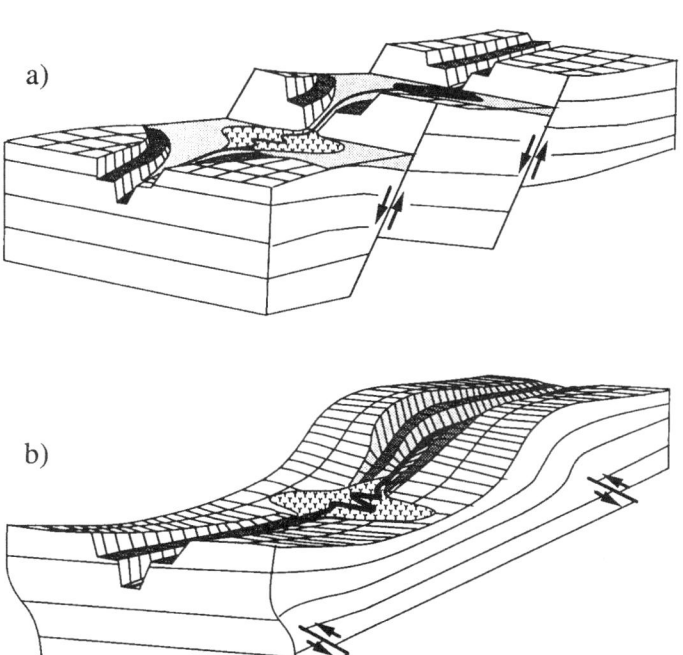

a)

b)

FIGURE 1. *Schematic illustration of the way in which active normal faulting (a) and reverse faulting (b) create rapid down-cutting and the formation of terraces plus local ponds of sediment. While the most straightforward conditions are produced when the drainage crosses dip-slip structures at 90°, similar effects can be found when rivers run sub-parallel to active features or are created by features that are largely strike-slip. Whatever the exact tectonic conditions, locally severe topography and local, fertile sediment traps are created and maintained by active tectonics. Such small-scale features do not persist for long when tectonic activity diminishes.*

Topographic change and sediment traps are not exclusively associated with regions of active tectonics. Vertical motion due to isostatic depression and rebound in regions of continental glaciation may have analogous effects, as can sea level change in coastal regions. Whether they result from glacial or tectonic causes, nearly all these features are associated with rates of vertical movement of metres or tens of metres per 1000 years (Slemmons *et al.* 1991). In regions of little activity, where the basic geometry of the landscape can be considered essentially static from the point of view of human land-use, climatically induced and humanly induced changes in erosional and sedimentary regimes may take prominence. Indeed, such regions can be said to be particularly vulnerable to such changes. Arid and semi-arid regions are especially fragile environments, where relatively small climatic or anthropogenic effects may have catastrophic consequences for economic viability and human survival. Conversely, in arid regions which are tectonically active, sedimentary traps will acquire an enhanced attraction through a degree of insensitivity to changes of climate and land-use, maintaining essentially stable environmental conditions for plant and animal life. The precise advantages of these sediment traps will vary depending on their size and other local factors, but will tend to become greater in conditions where soil and water are limiting factors and in regions which are otherwise environmentally fragile. Similar considerations apply at a much larger geographical scale, with regions of uplift providing rainfall catchment and a sediment supply which is concentrated in adjacent lowlands surrounded by an otherwise barren environment (FIGURE 2).

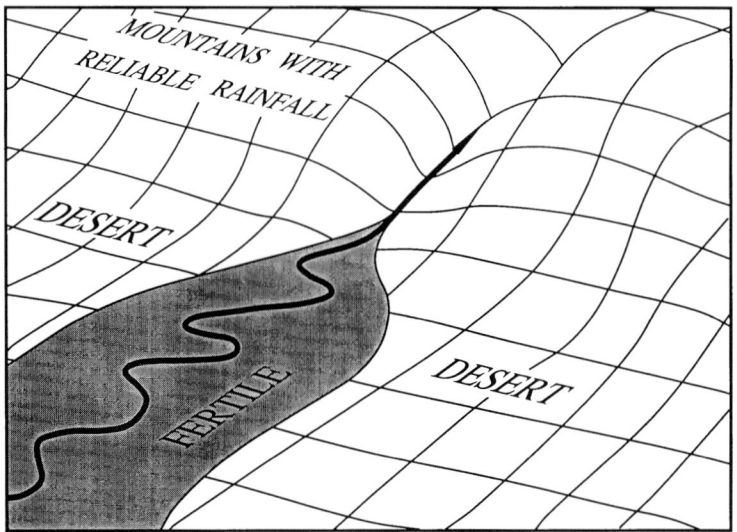

FIGURE 2. *Many areas of prehistoric settlement are associated with localization on a regional as well as a local scale. In the figure, a broader region of fertility is created from the outflow of water and sediment from a mountain range. The Nile Valley is one of the most dramatic examples of such an environment. Other examples are in East Africa (associated with the active rift valley), southern Siberia and Mongolia (associated with the active northern edge of the Himalayan system), the Middle East (associated with the Dead Sea rift, the Caucasus, Elborz or Zagros), or the Chilean valleys leaving the Himalayas. At these larger scales the role of rapid active tectonics is less obviously necessary. Mountains, once created, take many millions of years to disappear and hence the lag between activity and the disappearance of environments takes longer. Moreover, regional localization is created not by topographic barriers, but by desert. However, all of the above examples are associated with active tectonics, which can in some cases be shown to be important. For example, the active tectonics of Ethiopia are essential to create the heavy sediment load of the White Nile on which the lower valley depends for fertility.*

Topographic barriers and herd control
The notion of topographic barriers as ecologically advantageous features is not intuitively obvious, but follows from a consideration of humans as predators of medium and large sized mammals. One does not have to subscribe to a 'Man the Hunter' view of human origins, with its over-emphasis on meat-eating and male activities, to recognize that dependence on animals as a source of subsistence has been a significant selective factor in the course of human evolution, and in the survival and expansion of human populations up to the present day. Yet animal prey pose a double problem for the human predator: of accessibility; and of competition with other carnivores. This can be illustrated by taking the two extremes of the spectrum of 'man–animal' relationships. At one extreme is scavenging, where the human population relies on other carnivores to do the difficult work of immobilization and takes what is left over. At the other extreme is full domestication, in which the animal population is under permanent human control and protection. In between are a range of ill-defined relationships commonly labelled as 'hunting', which it is one of the main tasks of Pleistocene archaeology to explore and define.

Given that the initial reaction of a prey population to a predator is to flee, the hypothetically featureless plain offers a very poor chance of success to a technologically simple human hunter, unaided by efficient means of killing at a distance such as guns and horses, or by constraints on animal movement such as fences or other artificial barriers. Fertile local environments such as sediment traps and lake basins may help to 'tether' mobile prey to some extent, but do not solve the problem of their ability to resist capture by flight or defence, nor the problem of competition with other carnivores better adapted in body form to the needs of chase and attack. A complex topography with hill and mountain barriers, on the other hand, facilitates the monitoring, prediction and control of animal movements, creates bottlenecks where prey can be located and trapped and provides places to live or camp which are within easy access of the prey population, but hidden away so as to minimize disturbance of the animals — all features which an intelligent but otherwise unspecialized predator may be able to turn to advantage.

As in the discussion of sediment traps, tectonics plays a fundamental role in the creation of such landscape features, and these features may be advantageous both on a local scale — a matter of kilometres — where barriers are often juxtaposed with local sediment traps by the inherent nature of tectonic displacement and folding, and on a regional scale, where topographic barriers may circumscribe large blocks of favourable grazing terrain and confine the movements of animals within them (Sturdy 1975).

Palaeolithic Epirus
Investigation of the Palaeolithic archaeology of the Epirus region of northwest Greece over the past 30 years has been accompanied by an unusual emphasis on off-site archaeology and the reconstruction of local and regional palaeo-landscapes (Bailey 1992; Bailey & Gamble 1990; Bailey *et al.* 1983a; 1986a; 1990; Dakaris *et al.* 1964; Higgs 1978; Higgs & Vita-Finzi 1966; Higgs *et al.* 1967; Higgs & Webley 1971; King & Bailey 1985; Sturdy & Webley 1988; Vita-Finzi 1978). Northwest Greece is also one of the most seismically active areas of Eurasia (FIGURE 3) and may be expected to highlight the underlying effects of tectonically active structures on the prehistoric archaeology and land-use of a region.

Regional topography and seismicity
The topography of Epirus is rugged (FIGURE 4). A series of sharp ridges with elevations of 1000 m or more separate plateau regions that are in places deeply dissected by rivers. To

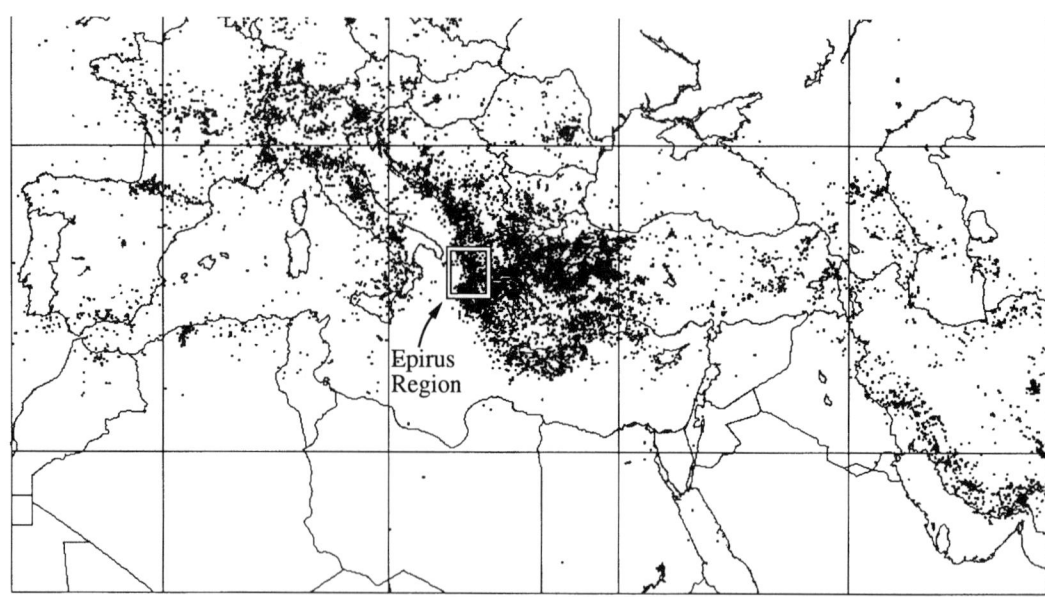

FIGURE 3. *Seismicity map of the Mediterranean–Himalayan region plotted from data compiled by the National Earthquake Information Center of the US Geological Survey, showing all events above magnitude 4 between 1970 and 1989. Since small earthquakes (indicated by the smallest dots) are only reliably located where there is a good network of local stations, the total number of epicentres does not necessarily reflect activity. Thus France, where a large number of small events are well located, is not more active than East Africa, where no small events are well recorded. Nevertheless, seismicity does indicate on-going tectonic deformation, and any region of the map where epicentres appear certainly experiences tectonic deformation with rates that may be archaeologically significant.*

the northwest in Albania and the northeast in the Pindus mountains, the terrain has higher elevations and even under the present interglacial conditions is relatively inaccessible. To the southwest the region is bounded by the Ionian Sea and to the south by the Gulf of Arta and the more subdued terrain of Akarnania.

The seismicity map (FIGURE 3) shows that Epirus is subject to earthquakes with a rate of activity comparable to regions such as Japan, New Zealand and parts of the Middle East, where uplift rates of between metres and tens of metres per millennium are well established. Both studies of earthquake mechanisms and the geology indicate a region subject to compression, and its broad features can be understood in such a context. However, more recent work indicates that strike-slip motion also plays a role and is important to a more complete understanding of recent evolution of the topography (King *et al.* in press). The deformation is concentrated on a series of structures oriented roughly 20° east (FIGURE 5). The structures shown must extend into Albania, and seismicity indicates that features parallel to those on land must be active offshore. Although the features south of the Gulf of Arta have a similar strike, net compression gives way to the net extension that is characteristic of the Aegean and Peloponnese. Compression and uplift does, however, restrict the mouth of the Gulf of Arta and extends down the coast of Levkas, where it becomes associated with the very active Hellenic arc subduction system.

Elements of the topography can be understood in terms of continuing tectonic evolution. The plateau-ridge system is associated with the telescoping of a series of fault-

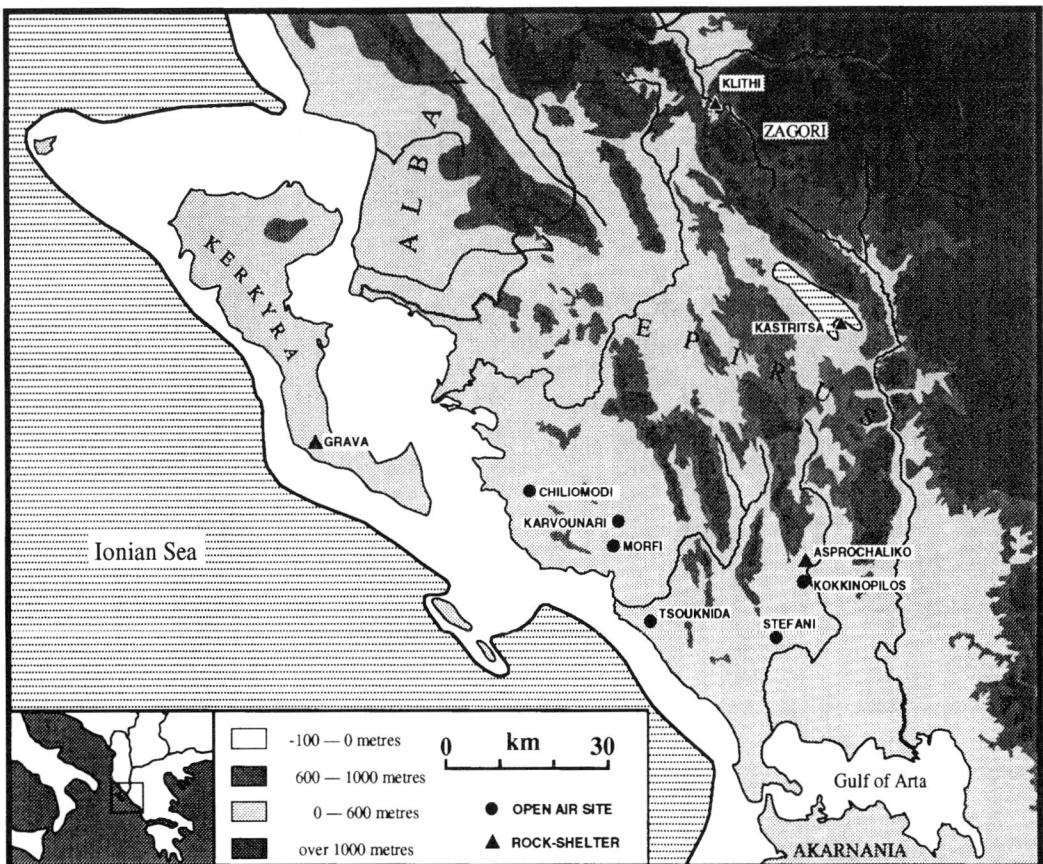

FIGURE 4. *Topography of the Epirus region, showing principal sites mentioned in the text.*

bounded limestone islands separated by sediment-filled marine basins. These basins are uplifted by progressive tectonic movements to form flysch and flysch-like rocks, which are the other dominant rock type alongside limestone. These are younger than the limestone, made from coarser and shallower sediments, and create softer, sandstone rocks, with varying proportions of clay, silt and siliceous material. They show spectacular folding and compression resulting from tectonic displacement. A schematic diagram of the mechanism is shown in FIGURE 6 and the main features of the geology in FIGURE 7. The limestone regions are separated from regions of flysch by narrow limestone ridges that are the topographic expression of the most active fault zones.

On a more local scale, features such as Lake Ioannina or the Gulf of Arta are associated with active relative depression and many more local regions of subsidence can be identified. Uplift has resulted in spectacular gorges in some places with river profiles that alternate between down-cutting and deposition over short distances.

The same processes continue offshore. Kerkyra (Corfu) is a limestone island, and rivers such as the Kalamas supply sediment that will become flysch when compacted and uplifted. The offshore tectonics is therefore a continuation of that seen on land. During the Last Glacial, when sea level receded, the land revealed would not have been a uniform plain, although the relief would have been more subdued than inland. Uplifted ridges would have been cut by valleys containing river terraces, with lakes and

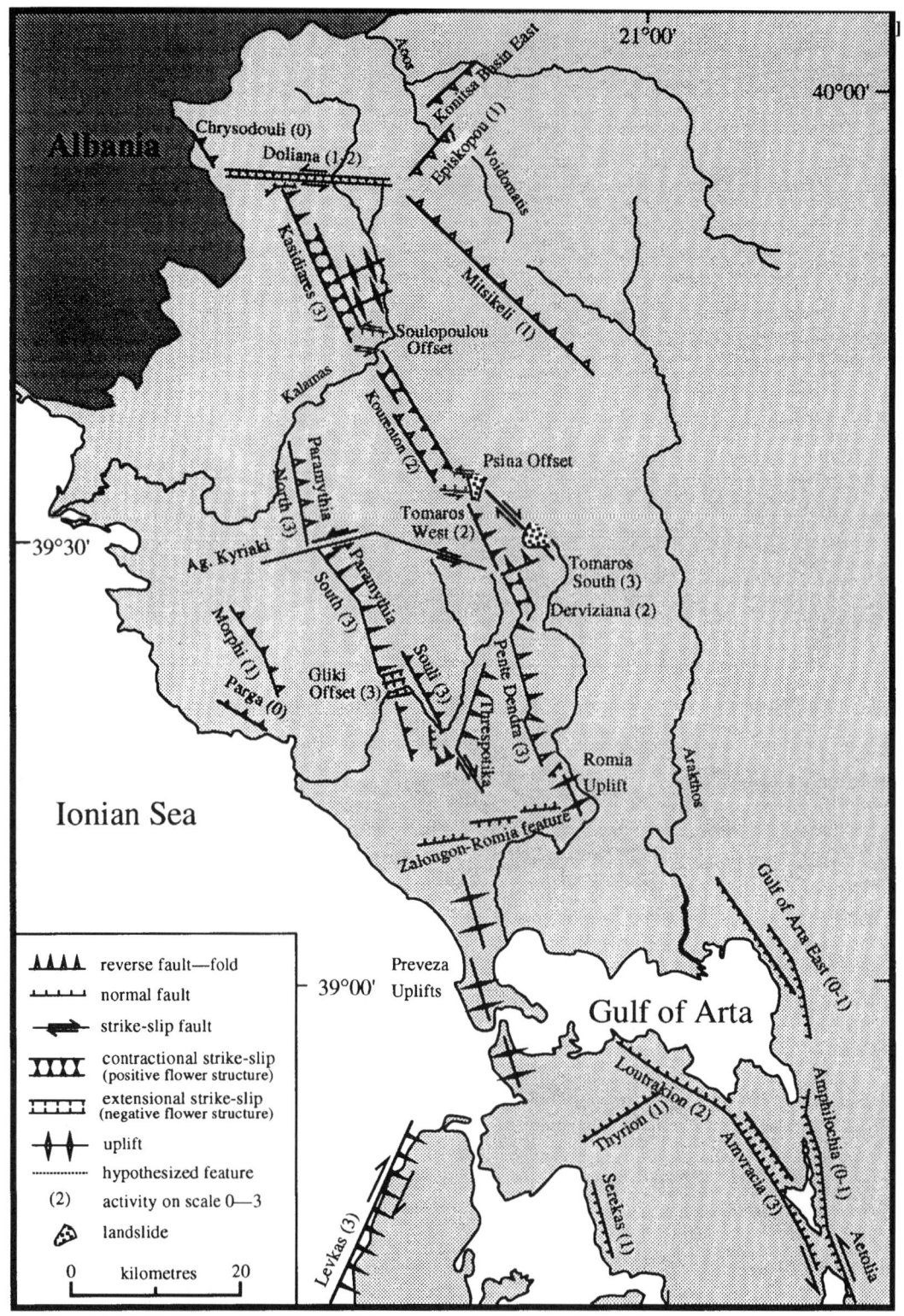

FIGURE 5. *Active structures of the Epirus region.*

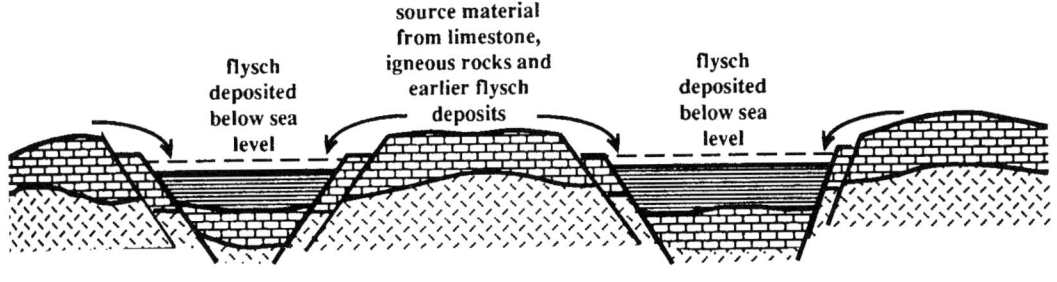

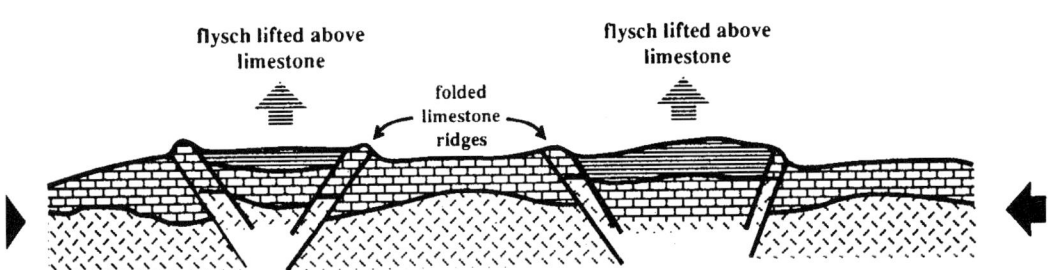

FIGURE 6. *Simplified illustration of geosynclinal processes, showing the way in which uplifting flysch basins are separated from limestone plateau areas by steeply folded limestone mountain ridges.*

ponded sediments occurring between these features. For example, the Gulf of Arta deposition could have continued throughout the glaciation as a result of the uplift at its mouth.

Different areas of the landscape thus have very different susceptibilities to tectonically induced surface disturbance. The limestone plateau regions are relatively undisturbed today while the flysch basins are tectonically very active. The flysch, being soft, erodes almost as fast as it deforms and the result is a heavily gullied 'badlands' landscape. Although it is tempting to attribute gullying and badlands of this kind to intensive pastoral and agricultural activity in the late Holocene and historical periods, this is a secondary factor in the geological circumstances of Epirus. The underlying primary cause of instability is tectonic.

This is demonstrated by a variety of indicators. Erosion of flysch is chronic in Epirus and extends well back into the Pleistocene. In the case of the river terraces of the Voïdomatis, some units are high in material derived from local flysch areas while others are dominated by glacial outwash materials (Bailey *et al.* 1990; Lewin *et al.* 1991). When glacial processes are not producing large amounts of removable material, it is the flysch erosion which supplies most of the sediment. River terraces dated to >150,000 years, *c.* 20,000 and *c.* 1000 years BP are all dominated by flysch-derived materials, and while human activities can be implicated in the most recent case, they can hardly be invoked for the earlier episodes.

To the west of Klithi in the Doliana basin, the terraces of the river Kalamas are of Holocene date and are largely composed of flysch-derived materials. The base of one terrace is dated to 9160±80 BP (OxA-3943), a higher unit to 6240±70 BP (OxA-3942), while sediments near the top are dated by TL to 4200±600 (BM lab ref. DOL6). This suggests a prolonged period during the early to mid Holocene, a period of climatically optimal conditions for vegetation growth and of less than intense agricultural activity,

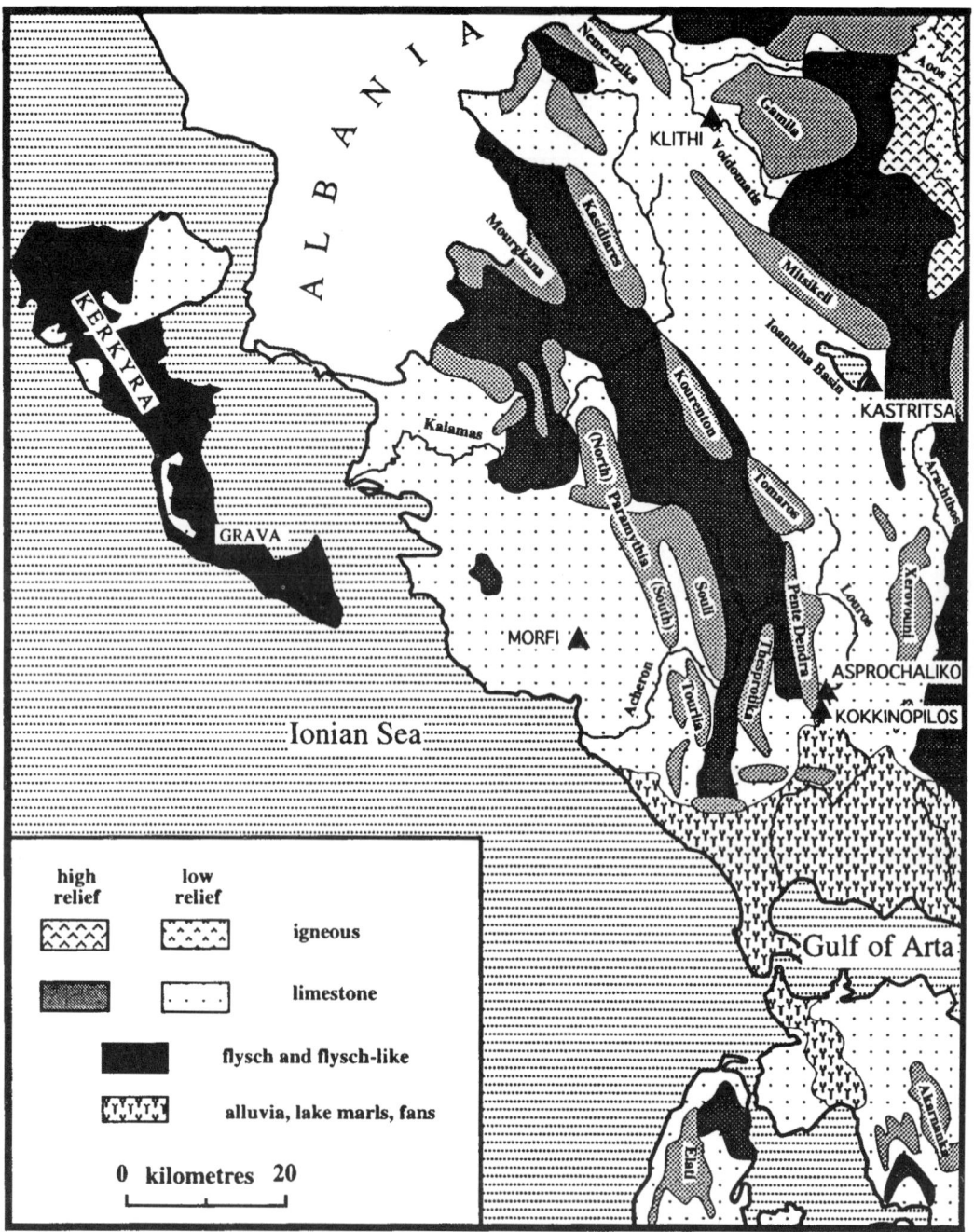

FIGURE 7. *Schematic geology of the Epirus region.*

during which flysch erosion in the river catchment maintained an apparently steady supply of sediment.

Finally, over the past 30 years there has been a substantial reduction in grazing pressure throughout Epirus, with consequent expansion of woodland and scrub vegetation, sometimes in the form of extensive and almost impenetrable thickets. Yet slope failure and gullying in the flysch basins continue unabated.

Palaeo-environment and palaeo-economy

Today Epirus is one of the wettest regions of Greece, with annual precipitation ranging from about 900 mm on the coast to 1300 mm inland, a pronounced dry summer season, and extensive winter snow cover in the hinterland and at higher altitude. Pollen studies indicate that, during the Last Glacial, cold and semi-arid conditions prevailed with a vegetation of *Artemisia* steppe and occasional stands of evergreen oak and pine, creating a predominantly open, or at best a parkland, landscape (Bottema 1974; Willis 1989). The combination of steppe landscapes with high lake levels, as recorded for example by beach deposits in the Kastritsa rock-shelter on the shores of Lake Ioannina, is best explained by a climate of cold winters, some 5°–6°C colder than at present, high winter precipitation, and summer aridity with temperatures 2°–3° C lower and less precipitation than today (Prentice *et al.* 1992). The Pindus mountains created locally wetter conditions, providing refuges for deciduous tree species, although the latter probably persisted only as isolated stands in protected localities, for example on the south-facing cliffs of the Vikos Gorge (Bennett *et al.* 1991; C. Turner pers. comm.; Willis 1989). Glacial moraines on the heights of the Pindus have been linked to valley-fill sediments which can be dated to between about 28,000 and 16,000 years BP, and the presence of local glaciation seems to have created conditions severe enough to inhibit any human use of the upland interior at the Last Glacial Maximum, i.e. from *c.* 20,000 to 16,000 years BP (Bailey *et al.* 1990. Lewin *et al.* 1991; Woodward 1990). Low plant biomass, snow cover in winter and water availability in summer would clearly have been important ecological limiting factors, with a major impact on regional population movements and individual settlement locations.

The Palaeolithic research conducted by Higgs in the 1960s culminated in the well-known hypothesis of seasonal transhumance, in which the rock-shelters of Asprochaliko and Kastritsa were interpreted as the winter and summer camps, respectively, of people who followed herds of red deer in their seasonal migrations between coast and hinterland (Higgs *et al.* 1967). The palaeo-environmental data that has become available since then has, if anything, reinforced the environmental basis for this hypothesis, emphasizing the low plant and animal biomass on a regional scale, and the seasonal contrast between summer and winter climates and between coast and hinterland.

Subsequent archaeological investigations, however, have refined this picture through new surveys, excavations, radiometric dates and faunal analyses, particularly at Klithi (FIGURE 4), demonstrating greater complexity and variability in the palaeoeconomy through time and space (Bailey 1992). Settlement on the coast is of long duration, extending back at least 100,000 years (Bailey *et al.* 1992; Huxtable *et al.* 1992). The hinterland was only visited sporadically or intermittently, if at all, until after the Last Glacial Maximum. The high density of artefacts and faunal remains in the upper levels of Kastritsa (Bailey *et al.* 1983b) and the thick, culturally sterile deposits at the base of the Klithi sequence (Bailey *et al.* 1986b; Bailey & Thomas 1987) suggest that intensive exploitation of the hinterland occurred only after about 16,000 years.

Faunal remains show a greater diversity than predicted by the original Higgs hypothesis. Ibex is at least as common in the Upper Palaeolithic levels at Asprochaliko as red deer (Bailey *et al.* 1983b); bovids and equids appear well represented at Grava (Sordinas 1969) and at Kastritsa; the large faunal collection from Klithi is dominated by remains of ibex and chamois (Bailey *et al.* 1986a), and suids are present in low frequency at several sites. In view of the environmental constraints discussed above, we think it likely that all these species would have made seasonal migratory movements of some degree, with deer and equids travelling over the longest distances, pig the shortest, and ibex and chamois shifting altitudinal range over relatively restricted distances. Hence we believe that seasonal mobility would have dominated land use strategies, although we do not now believe that this would have involved herd following in the strict sense, or have been shaped solely by the movements of red deer.

Carnivores are represented by bones of lion, lynx, wolf, fox and pine marten, which would have been potential competitors with human populations, although they appear to have made virtually no contribution to the accumulation of the archaeological bone assemblages, at least by the end of the Upper Palaeolithic period to judge from the Klithi assemblage, where evidence of carnivore bone chewing or modification is almost totally absent.

Although the possibility of substantial plant-food gathering is often raised, usually on the basis of inappropriate environmental and ethnographic analogies from other regions, we do not believe the local evidence justifies much attention to this. Pollen data for the Last Glacial indicate a regional environment with a generally low plant biomass and one that is poor in edible plant-foods. Even in refuge areas with more favourable microclimates and a higher plant biomass, as in the vicinity of Klithi, plant macrofossils and pollen data from local lake sediments indicate an environment which is unlikely to have supported any density of edible plant-food (K. Willis pers. comm.). At Klithi itself, full flotation and wet-sieving procedures were carried out during excavation to check for plant remains, but none were recovered in spite of favourable conditions for their preservation. Grinding equipment, found in late Palaeolithic sites in the Near East and North Africa, and putatively associated with processing of plant-foods, is absent from the Epirus sites. The backed bladelets which abound, and which Clarke (1976) in a famous piece of devil's advocacy suggested could have been used in slotted knives to cut and grate vegetable matter, have been shown at Klithi by microscopic study of edge damage to have been used as projectile tips or hide-working awls (E. Moss pers. comm.). We do not totally discount plant-foods. Chenopod seeds could have been collected in the Last Glacial environment, and perhaps the roots of plants growing on lake margins. To the extent that plant-foods were collected in the Palaeolithic period, we note that their exploitation would have benefited from the local tectonic features described below, no less than the exploitation of herd animals. But we doubt that plant foods could have contributed any more than they do to the modern Sarakatsani, who, notwithstanding the dominant pattern of animal transhumance in their lives, also scour the landscape for all available naturally occurring edible plant-foods as relishes and supplements to the staple diet (Campbell 1967). Even less of a case can be made for a significant contribution from sea-foods (Bailey 1982; Bailey *et al.* 1983a).

Regional barriers and animal distributions
Placing animals into the landscape is a matter of combining the known or inferred habitat preferences and behaviour of the various species with sub-divisions of the landscape based on their relative edaphic potential (i.e. their potential to provide food and essential nutrients for animals). For edaphic categories we rely on the underlying geology, soils where these are known to have existed during the Pleistocene, terrain, and general climatic and vegetational parameters supplied by pollen data. A fuller discussion of the method is given elsewhere (Sturdy & Webley 1988). Here we focus on the differences

between limestone and flysch geologies and the environmental and topographic barriers that they create.

Soils on the limestone plateaux are thin and patchy, except where sediments are concentrated in small basins, but they are much the most favourable for vegetation that is attractive to animals. Soluble phosphate, the principal vegetational contribution to the calcium compounds from which growing animals make bones, is between 2 and 4 times higher than in the flysch soils, and only the limestone soils have adequate trace elements for animal growth such as copper and cobalt (Sturdy & Webley 1988). In contrast, the flysch produces only thin and immature ranker soils and their edaphic quality remains low. It is important to emphasize that this characteristic of the flysch only applies to environments which are subject to repeated disturbance by tectonic factors. In stable environments productive soils eventually develop on the flysch, and this potential can be realized on a small scale in Epirus by terracing and intensive horticultural practices in the vicinity of villages. On a large scale, however, the extensive flysch basins have a poor grazing potential for animals, and have been treated as marginal for this purpose even in recent and historical times, whereas the limestone continues to be extensively grazed. The only advantage that flysch offers to grazing animals is that its soft sediments allow deep rooting plants to reach moisture, and hence may offer some browse of last resort on shrub and scrub vegetation during dry seasons in areas distant from well-watered lake and sedimentary basins.

Landscapes in a comparable geological and tectonic environment in North Island New Zealand have been used extensively for sheep and cattle since the early 1950s, but only as a result of aerial dressing with the trace elements the soils lack (Gibbs 1964). The withdrawal of government subsidies for appropriate aircraft in the 1980s is causing much of this land to become unproductive. The natural thick vegetation on these New Zealand soils or the flysch soils of Epirus superficially seems to be an ideal habitat for herbivorous mammals, compared to the thin vegetation on the Epirus limestone. We are, how-

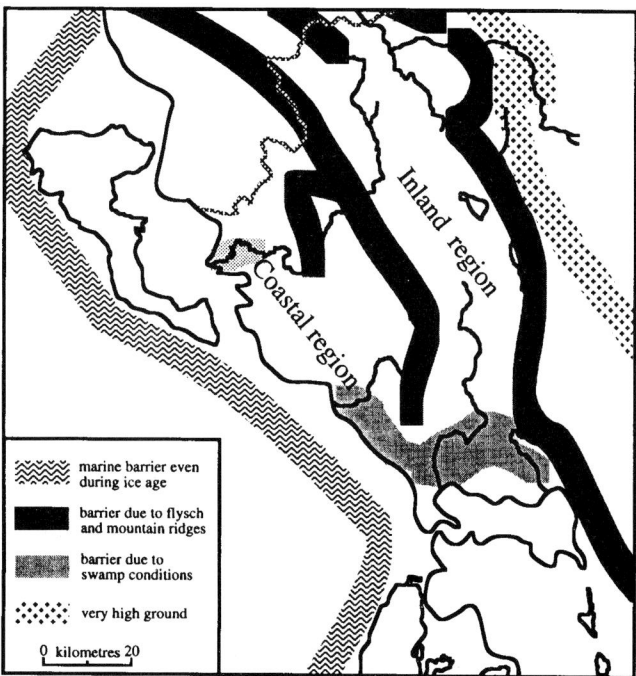

FIGURE 8. *Simplified physical barriers of the Epirus region.*

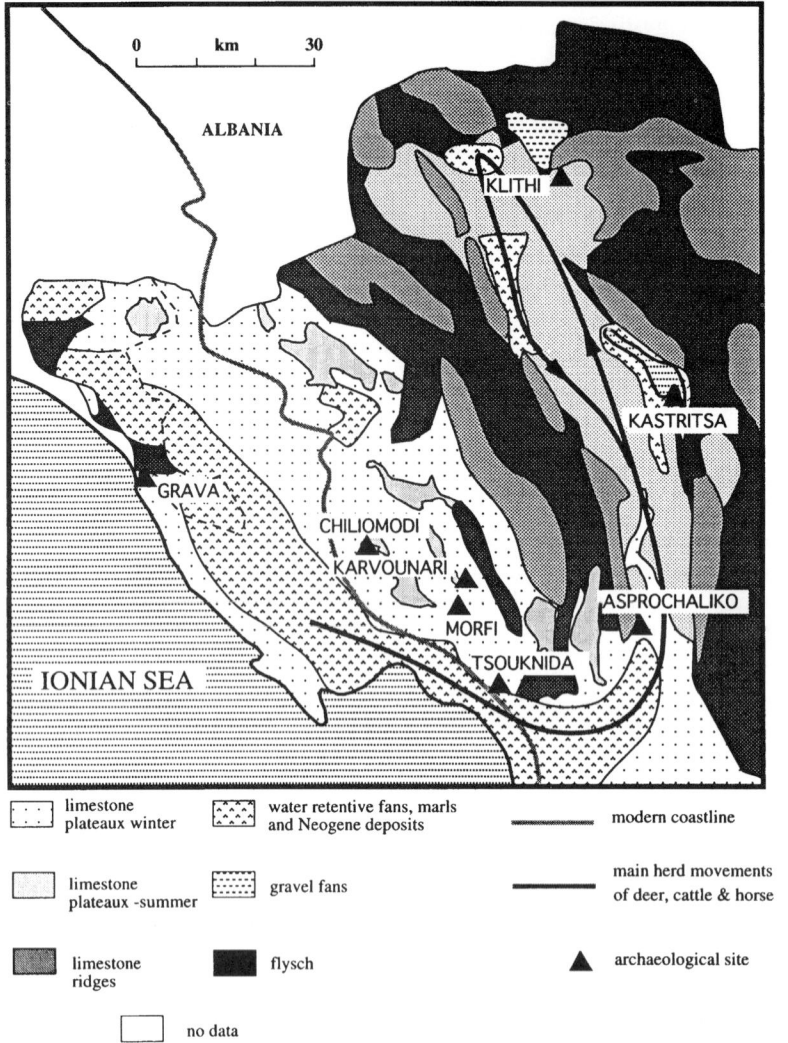

FIGURE 9. *Simplified map of regional terrain categories of Epirus, showing annual range of movements of main herd animals (deer, cattle and horse). Movements of ibex and chamois would have been more localized, with distinct annual ranges in the hinterland and nearer the coast. The water retentive areas shown for the coastal region comprise mostly terrestrial fan and marine Neogene sediments below present sea-level and on Kerkyra. The latter have edaphic characteristics similar to the flysch but tend to produce deeper and maturer soil profiles.*

ever, observing cause and effect. The limestone areas become heavily grazed because they are attractive to animals, while the adjacent flysch is relatively untouched.

Precipitation and temperatures were never such as to create a desert-bounded environment of the type indicated in FIGURE 2. However, topography and geology create analogous barriers (FIGURE 8). The narrow limestone ridges have very steep profiles and scree slopes and cliffs which act as formidable barriers to human and animal movement. The inadequacy of disturbed flysch to develop soils that produce satisfactory feedstock for herbivorous mammals could have inhibited animal movements as effectively as desert barriers in arid regions.

The effect of these barriers in combination with areas favourable for grazing reveals a large horseshoe-shaped area of grazing for the larger animals, enclosed by barriers of mountain, sea and flysch (FIGURE 9). The eastern arm of the horseshoe is an area of gentle limestone topography, forming an ideal grazing territory for the larger herbivores, bounded to the southwest by a flysch barrier and to the north and east by mountains and flysch, reinforced by permanent ice-fields at high elevation. These topographic features have the effect of making the eastern area of accessible grazing an effective cul-de-sac some 100 km long by 10–20 km wide, with important consequences for the control and prediction of animal movements. This is all the more significant given that deer, cattle and horse could only have used this area during summer because of the severity of the Last Glacial winters.

The western arm would have formed a similar large-scale enclosure of limestone plateaux, with optimal conditions for use in winter, enhanced by extensive areas of swampy ground in large basins like the area of the Gulf of Arta, where scrub and shrub vegetation would have provided important winter browse for deer and cattle, and insect infestation in summer would have powerfully stimulated seasonal herd dispersal. Some of the water-retentive soils could also have been important areas of summer grazing, and it is possible that this western coastal region formed an annual system of animal movements and economy at least partially independent of the eastern arm of the horseshoe (Bailey *et al.* 1986a). The eastern arm, however, would not have been viable without the complementary winter grazing of areas near the coast.

The Palaeolithic rock-shelters clearly have a patterned relationship to these regional features, controlling major points of entry and exit to the limestone plateaux. Many more Palaeolithic sites are known from extensive surveys throughout the region, including numerous open-air sites, but these are without exception found within the favoured areas of limestone terrain or around their edges. The absence of finds from the flysch basins is notable, if difficult to evaluate, given that any Palaeolithic artefacts deposited there are likely to have been removed or obscured by the intensive erosion to which the flysch is susceptible.

Local site environments
This phenomenon of topographic closure is reproduced at a smaller geographical scale in relation to the immediate surroundings of individual sites. Asprochaliko is in a small gorge hidden away to the west of the main deer migration routes, but well placed to intercept deer diverting from the main route into a small enclosed limestone plateau west of the site (FIGURE 10). This would have provided attractive spring grazing, especially for older stags and hinds, which are the animals most likely to leave the main herd at this season. The well-watered sediment trap to the northeast would also have been attractive towards the end of the summer, when dry conditions would have reduced grazing opportunities elsewhere, and lower temperatures were beginning to drive the herds back towards their winter territories nearer the coast. The site is also well placed to intercept ibex in local movements from high ground in the northwest to lower and more sheltered terrain in the southeast.

Kastritsa is on the northwest slope of a limestone 'island' protruding through lake sediments, and partly surrounded by the waters of the lake (FIGURE 11). Shallow gravel fans and water retentive lake sediments fringing the open water would have attracted horse and cattle respectively, with deer concentrating on the gentle limestone terrain to the south and west, feeding closer to the lake at the end of the summer. As at Asprochaliko, the site is well placed to one side of the main migration routes, but also controls a local enclosure formed by the eastern arm of the lake and steeper ground further to the east and north, while being secluded from it. Deer are most numerous amongst the bone remains, while cattle and horse are important secondary species, and the presence of all major anatomical elements suggests that the animals were killed near-by, rather than at more distant butchering locations (Kotzambopoulou 1988). The site location offers a

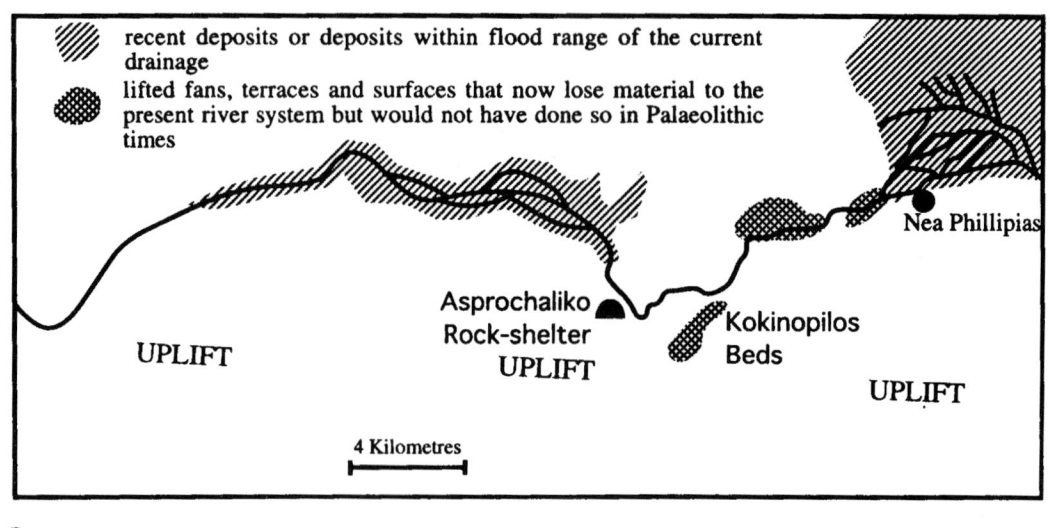

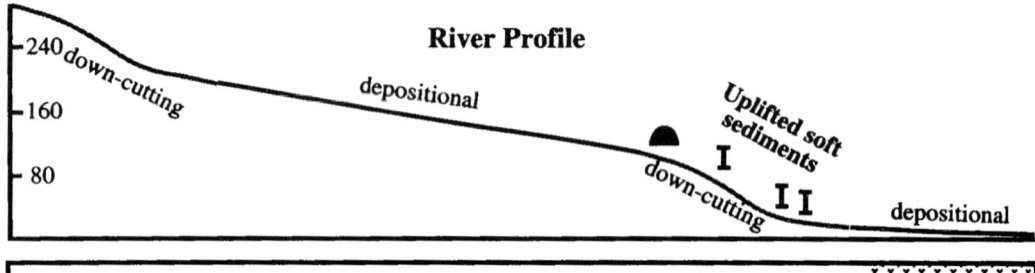

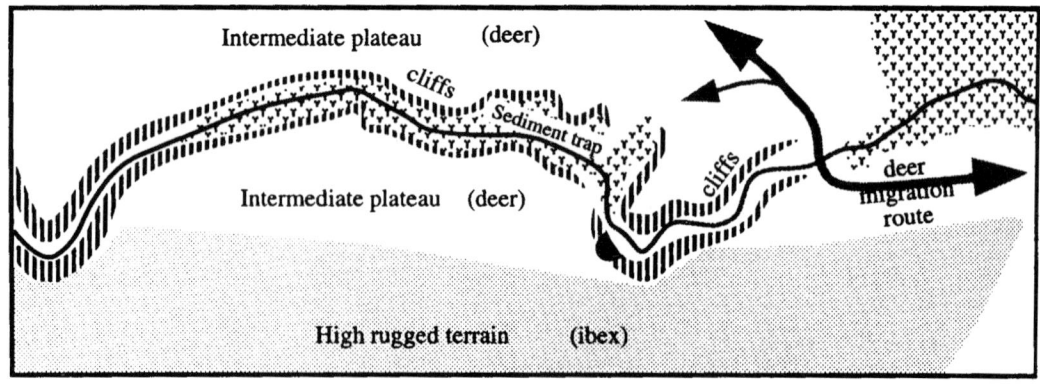

FIGURE 10a. *Localization of topographic features at Asprochaliko and their relationship to animal movements. The upper figure shows the course of the Louros river together with areas where active sedimentation is taking place. Areas of uplifted sediments that were earlier at or near river level are indicated. The central figure shows the profile of the river bed indicating regions of uplift and down-cutting. The similarity of these profiles to those found in regions where uplift is closely associated with recent earthquakes (King & Stein 1983; Stein & King 1984; King & Vita-Finzi 1981) should be noted. The lowest figure indicates an interpretation of how the environment was used.*

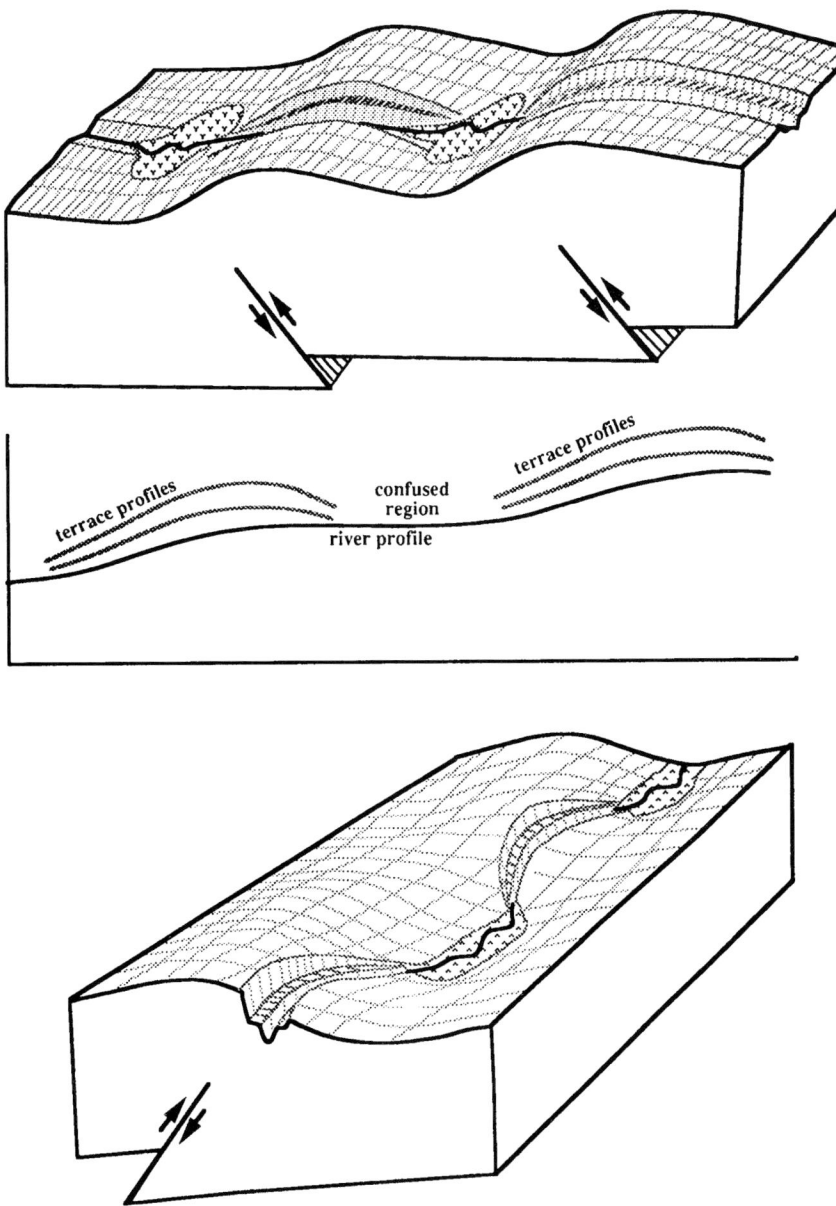

FIGURE 10b. *Two possible tectonic interpretations for the Asprochaliko–Kokkinopilos region are shown. In the upper figure, the river cuts directly across rising anticlines and in the lowest figure the river meanders towards and away from a single uplifting anticline. King & Bailey (1985) entertained both possibilities but favoured the former. However, a broader view of the tectonics of Epirus (King et al. in press) now favours the second. The first form of uplift, however, remains the most likely deformation associated with the Klithi site. It is important to appreciate that deformation of the form shown of the tectonics in these figures is superimposed on a pre-existing topography left by earlier tectonic processes. Thus, for example, the Louros river follows a valley inherited from much earlier times, and tectonic activity merely determines how it is currently being modified.*

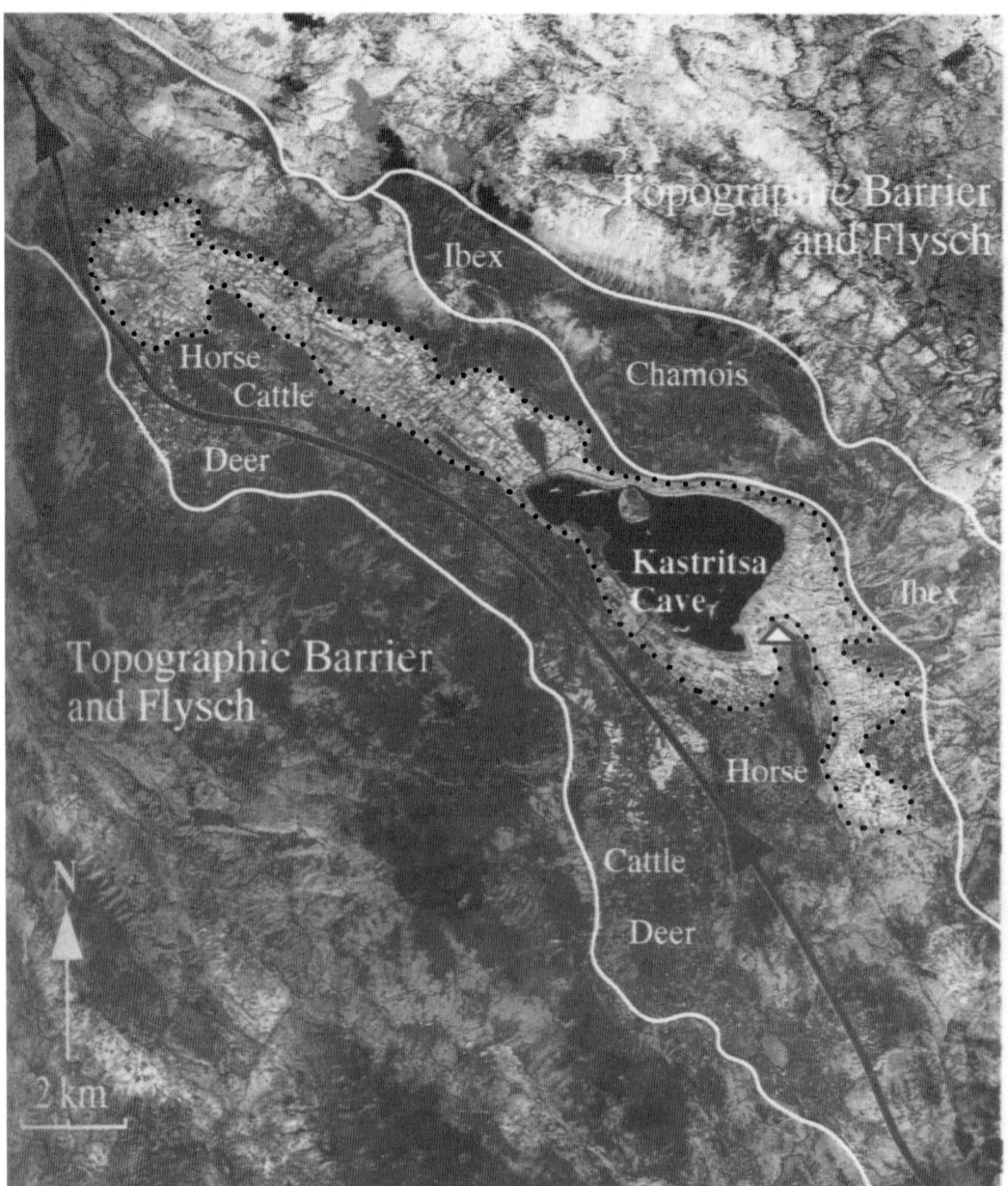

FIGURE 11. *Hypothesized animal distribution and movements near to the Kastritsa rockshelter (cave) site. A corridor suitable for deer, horse and cattle crosses the region from the southeast to the northwest. An outline of the Lake Ioannina that existed in Palaeolithic times is shown by a dotted line. The rockshelter is located near to the nose of an anticline that extended into the lake. Topographic barriers and flysch which represent areas that are difficult for animals to traverse or exploit appear to the west and northwest and to the southwest. Ibex and chamois terrain is restricted to hill slopes to the east and northeast.*

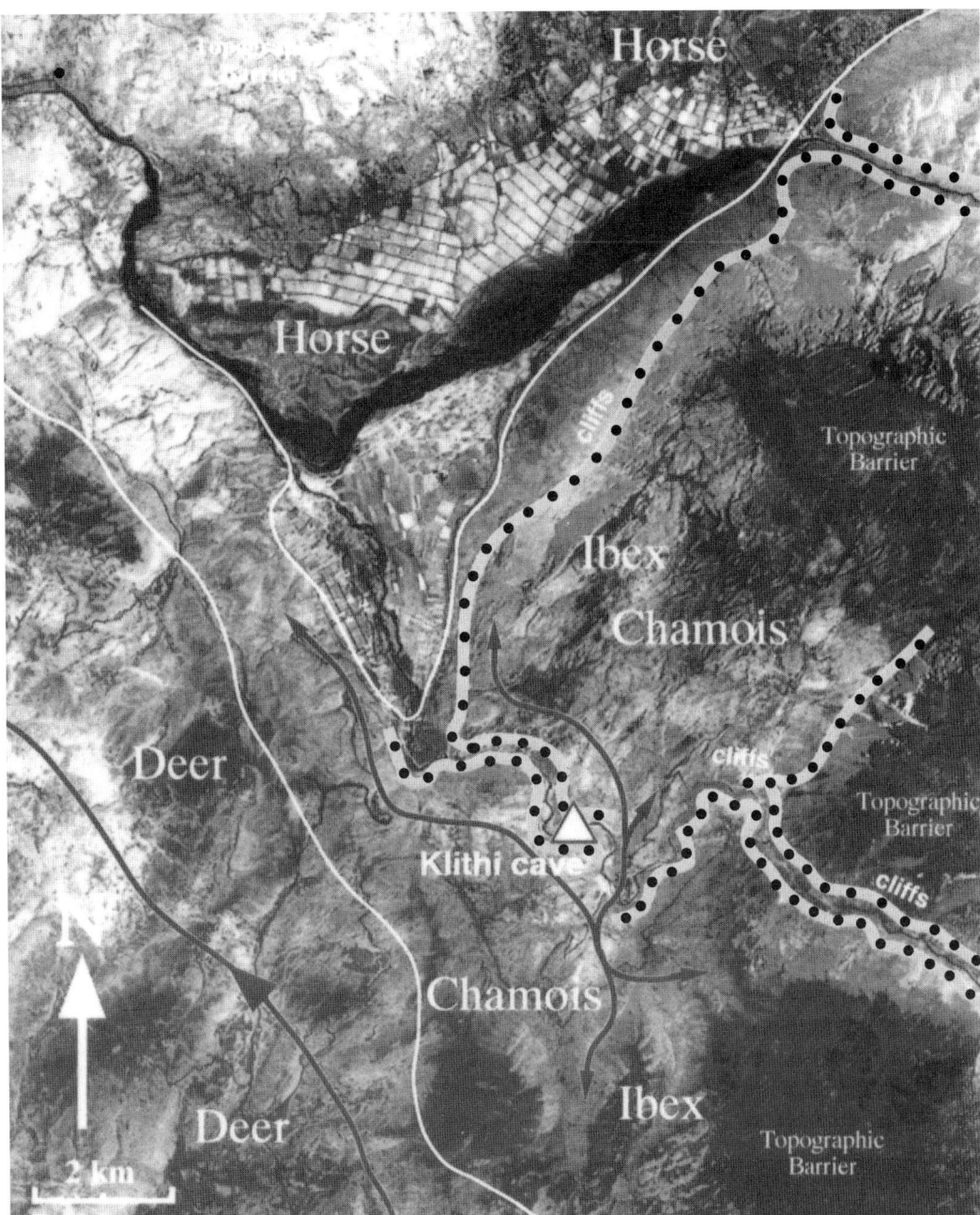

FIGURE 12. *Hypothesized animal distribution and movements near to the Klithi rockshelter (cave) site. Deer and horse terrains appear close to the site. The site itself is in a gorge surrounded by ibex and chamois country. Topographic barriers which represent areas that are difficult to traverse appear to the north and east. Cliffs are indicated separately from general topographic barriers and consist of slopes that are so extreme that, except for a few places they are totally impassable even to ibex or chamois.*

combination of attractions facilitating exploitation of all three species: local enclosure, a locally fertile and water retentive environment and strategic but secluded proximity to routes of animal movement.

Similarly, Klithi (FIGURE 12) is in a sheltered gorge, close to, but out of the way of, the main routes of seasonal movement of chamois and ibex, but well placed to control their movements into and out of an enclosed area of high summer grazing. The faunal remains suggest a very effective exploitation, with the introduction of whole carcasses into the site (Bailey *et al.* 1986a). In addition the occurrence of isolated deer bones associated with artefacts in the neighbouring rock-shelter of Megalakkos and at the mouth of the nearby plain suggests that the area may also have been important in monitoring deer movements at the extreme of their summer range to the west. The alluvial sediments that filled the valley in front of the site, and extended out over the large Konitsa basin to the northwest, appear to have consisted of active outwash gravels during the period when the site was occupied, between 16,000 and 10,000 years, and presented a bare and stony landscape with perhaps at best a light spring flush of fine grasses. The finer sediments and soils which provide a fertile basis for present-day agriculture are of late Holocene data (Lewin *et al.* 1991; Sturdy & Webley 1988). This represents an important difference from the other two sites, but is consistent with the emphasis on caprids in the site fauna, since these are animals which are less critically dependent on water supplies than the larger herbivores, and which could have mitigated any effects of summer aridity by moving to high altitude pastures.

Long-term dynamics
The above reconstructions describe the average conditions for the Last Glacial, and as such give a largely static picture of the landscape and of human economic activities within it. However, in assessing the long-term success of human and other populations in the regional environment, it is not so much the average conditions that are relevant as the shorter-term fluctuations, and especially the extremes in the range of such variability (King & Lindh in press). It is these extremes which are critical in defining the selective pressures which shape longer term trends, giving a competitive edge to those species and populations that are better equipped to cope with periods of environmental deterioration, and hence are better placed to respond rapidly when environmental conditions improve.

Winter cold and snow cover, especially in bad winters, is an obvious limiting factor of the Last Glacial environment, which would have placed a high premium on conditions of local shelter or at low altitude near the coast. The rock-shelter of Asprochaliko has long been recognized, with its south-facing aspect, as a favourable location for winter use (Legge 1972). The south-facing Klithi in its protected gorge offers a similar attraction, important even in the summer months for habitation near high altitude terrain in close proximity to a permanent ice-field. Recent palaeo-environmental data underline this point while also demonstrating that summer aridity would have been another powerful limiting factor, placing an equally high premium on areas of water-retentive sediments. The importance of tectonics in sustaining local areas of fertility under these circumstances cannot be overemphasized. The fact that the three sites discussed offer advantages of shelter, access to locally fertile and well-watered sediments, or both, is thus of great significance. By controlling those local areas of the landscape best protected against extremes of cold and aridity, the human population would have been well placed to cope with temporal variability in environmental conditions, both the large-scale changes associated with the Last Glacial Maximum, when aridity and cold would have been at their maximum, and smaller-scale fluctuations from year to year.

The hinterland region, being available for humans on only a seasonal basis, was probably always a marginal area for human exploitation. It certainly appears to have been visited only sporadically until quite late in the regional sequence of Palaeolithic occupation, and was therefore an area in which other carnivores could have competed successfully for prey. With climatic deterioration at the Last Glacial Maximum, all animal activity in the hinterland would have been severely restricted, and the carnivores would have been forced into the coastal lowlands into closer competition with humans who were already well established there. When conditions began to improve again, the human population, by virtue of their ability to control key topographic features in the landscape, would have been able to respond quickly, and thus to secure and maintain an increasingly effective control of the hinterland region and its seasonal population of herbivorous mammals. To the extent that tectonic processes have not simply created those features of the landscape that human populations have turned to their advantage, but have actively sustained and even accentuated them during the course of human occupation, tectonics needs to be considered as a far more active agent in human-environment interactions than has previously been the case, with further consequences for an understanding of other dynamics — climatic, vegetational, cultural and social.

The ecological and evolutionary 'drama' has traditionally been viewed in terms of ecological interactions between human populations and the biological organisms which provide food or act as predators, competitors and parasites. Quaternary climatic and vegetational change provide changes of scenery and sometime more active players. Changes in the solid earth, however, have been treated as external, adventitious and disruptive, causing a temporary halt in production or a change of venue, but not otherwise actively shaping the performance. This view is clearly over-simplified, and tectonics, like other environmental or biological processes, needs to be more actively incorporated as a variable shaping the long-term interactions which affect the course of human biological and socio-cultural change.

Conclusion

This case-study raises an issue of more general interest, and that is the nature of the different temporal scales at which landscape processes operate, the ways in which human groups perceive and interact with those processes, and the problem of how these different scales of phenomena are related. On very short time-scales of decades, essentially the time-scale of individual perception or living memory, the only visible impact of tectonic processes is the occasional earthquake, which must seem at best neutral, at worst disruptive. Obviously at this scale, the advantages of living in a tectonically active landscape are likely to be perceived in terms of superficial productivity of resources, rather than in terms of underlying tectonic processes, and the connection between the two may not be apparent.

On longer time-scales of thousands to tens of thousands of years tectonic processes in the Epirus context appear to have an essentially constructive impact on human land use, creating or sustaining local barriers and sediment traps and their concomitant advantages, resulting in human population stability in the face of adversely fluctuating climatic circumstances, or population growth at the expense of other ecological competitors. On longer time-scales again, hundreds of thousands to millions of years, tectonic processes may have a disruptive effect at the local scale, transforming local areas of subsidence into areas of uplift and erosion, as has happened with the Kokkinopilos red beds (Bailey *et al.* 1992), while on the longest time-scales of millions to tens of millions of years, whole regional landscapes are likely to be destroyed or transformed out of all recognition.

It is clearly important to be aware of the different effects that continuing tectonic evolution can have at different time-scales, the ways in which this can interrupt or modify other sorts of environmental processes and the ways in which these different scales of interaction can affect human behaviour at short and long time scales. For example, if our time perspective were confined solely to the Holocene, the principal cause of erosion on the flysch might be ascribed to agricultural practices, climatic changes or grazing pressures. All of these processes have been invoked as powerful agents of landscape change (and sometimes of landscape stability) at various times and places elsewhere in the Greek context (Davidson 1980; Pope & Van Andel 1984; Van Andel & Zangger 1990; Vita-Finzi 1969; Wagstaff 1981), and the controversy that surrounds the interpretation of, for example, Vita-Finzi's 'Younger Fill' is indicative of the difficulties of disentangling cause and effect. In the Epirus case, a longer time perspective reveals the underlying tectonic instability and the simple geological explanations for it, and many of the factors commonly invoked as causes of erosion may simply be triggers acting on the underlying instability. Without an appreciation of differential time-scales, we could easily draw the wrong conclusions, confusing proximate and ultimate causes, and playing havoc with decisions on future land-use policy.

At the longer end of the time-scale, tectonically induced landscape change may impose selection pressures resulting in evolutionary change. The location of archaeological sites in the complex landscape of Epirus has been discussed largely within the time scale of anatomically modern humans. But there is no reason why such an approach should not contribute a valuable understanding to much earlier periods and other parts of the world. Uplift can divert the course of rivers or cause them to create deeply incised channels. Fold and fault fronts produce local enclosure or natural fences. Such features lead to a complex topography, which, by channelling or concentrating nutrients and resources, offers much more potential than a featureless plain to a predator that must use its wits to be competitive. Given the complex topography of tectonically active areas, the human brain had additional material from which to fashion a unique technical competitiveness.

Acknowledgements. Fieldwork was supported by grants from the British Academy, the British School at Athens, the National Geographic Society and the Society of Antiquaries, and by permits issued through the good offices of the British School at Athens, the Ministry of Culture, Athens, the Institute of Geological and Mineralogical Research (IGME), Athens, the Ephoreia of Palaeoanthropology and Speleology, Athens and the Ephoreia of Prehistoric and Classical Archaeology, Ioannina. We are also grateful for financial support to the Archaeomedes Project on Desertification in Southern Europe, funded by Directorate XII of the European Economic Commission, and to the Oxford Radiocarbon Accelerator Unit and the British Museum Research Laboratory for radiometric dates.

References

AMBRASEYS, N.N. 1989. Temporary seismic quiescence: SE Turkey, *Geophysical Journal* 96: 311–31.
BAILEY, G.N. 1982. Coasts, lakes, and littorals, in M.R. Jarman, H.N. Jarman & G.N. Bailey (ed.), *Early European agriculture*: 72–107. Cambridge: Cambridge University Press.
     1992. The Palaeolithic of Klithi in its wider context, *Annual of the British School of Archaeology at Athens* 87: 1–28.
BAILEY, G.N., P.L. CARTER, C.S. GAMBLE & H.P. HIGGS. 1983a. Epirus revisited: seasonality and inter-site variation in the Upper Palaeolithic of north-west Greece, in G.N. Bailey (ed.), *Hunter-gatherer economy in prehistory: a European perspective:* 64–78. Cambridge: Cambridge University Press.

1983b. Asprochaliko and Kastritsa: further investigations of Palaeolithic settlement and economy in Epirus (north-west Greece), *Proceedings of the Prehistoric Society* 49: 15–42.

BAILEY, G.N., P.L. CARTER, C.S. GAMBLE, H.P. HIGGS & C. ROUBET. 1984. Palaeolithic investigations in Epirus: the results of the first season's excavations at Klithi, 1983, *Annual of the British School of Archaeology at Athens* 79: 7–22.

BAILEY, G.N. & C.S. GAMBLE. 1990. The Balkans at 18,000 BP: the view from Epirus, in C.S. Gamble & O. Soffer (ed.), *The world at 18,000 BP*: 148–67. London: Unwin Hyman.

BAILEY, G.N., C.S. GAMBLE, H.P. HIGGS, C. ROUBET, D.A. STURDY & D.P. WEBLEY. 1986a. Palaeolithic investigations at Klithi: preliminary results of the 1984–1985 field seasons, *Annual of the British School of Archaeology at Athens* 81: 7–35.

BAILEY, G.N., C.S. GAMBLE, H.P. HIGGS, C. ROUBET, D.P. WEBLEY, J.A.J. GOWLETT, D.A. STURDY & C. TURNER. 1986b. Dating results from Palaeolithic sites and palaeoenvironments in Epirus (north-west Greece), in J.A.J. Gowlett & R.E.M. Hedges (ed.), *Archaeological Results from Accelerator Dating*: 99–107. Oxford: Oxford University Committee for Archaeology.

BAILEY, G.N., J. LEWIN, M.G. MACKLIN & J.C. WOODWARD. 1990. The 'Older Fill' of Epirus, north-west Greece and its relationship to the Palaeolithic archaeology and glacial history of the region, *Journal of Archaeological Science* 17: 145–50.

BAILEY, G.N., V. PAPACONSTANTINOU & D.A. STURDY. 1992. Asprochaliko and Kokkinopilos: TL dating and reinterpretation of Middle Palaeolithic sites in Epirus, north-west Greece, *Cambridge Archaeological Journal* 2: 136–44.

BAILEY, G.N. & G. THOMAS. 1987. The use of percussion drilling to obtain core samples from rockshelter deposits, *Antiquity* 61: 430–39.

BENNETT, K.D., P.C. TZEDAKIS & K.J. WILLIS. 1991. Quaternary refugia of north European trees, *Journal of Biogeography* 18: 103–15.

BOTTEMA, S. 1974. *Late Quaternary vegetation history of northwestern Greece*. Groningen: Groningen University Press.

CAMPBELL, J.K. 1964. *Honour, family and patronage*. Oxford: Clarendon Press.

CLARKE, D.L. 1976. Mesolithic Europe: the economic basis, in G. de G. Sieveking, I.H. Longworth & K.E. Wilson (ed.), *Problems in economic and social archaeology*: 449–81. London: Duckworth.

DAKARIS, S.I., E.S. HIGGS & R.W. HEY. 1964. The climate, environment and industries of Stone Age Greece, part I, *Proceedings of the Prehistoric Society* 30: 199–244.

DAVIDSON, D.A. 1980. Erosion in Greece during the first and second millennia BC, in R.A. Cullingford, D.A. Davidson & J. Lewin (ed.), *Timescales in geomorphology*: 143–59. Chichester: Wiley.

DEMETS, C., R.G. GORDON, D.F. ARGUS & R.S. STEIN. 1990. Current plate motions, *International Geophysical Journal* 101: 425–78.

ELLIS, M. & G.C.P. KING. 1991. Structural control of flank volcanism in continental rifts, *Science* 254: 839–42.

GIBBS, H.S. 1964. Soils of Northland, in *National resources survey, Part III — Northland region*: 25–37. Wellington: Government Printer.

HIGGS, E.S. 1978. Environmental changes in northern Greece, in W.C. Brice (ed.), *The environmental history of the Near and Middle East since the last ice age*: 41–9. London: Academic Press.

HIGGS, E.S. & C. VITA-FINZI. 1966. The climate, environment and industries of Stone Age Greece, part II, *Proceedings of the Prehistoric Society* 32: 1–29.

HIGGS, E.S. & D.P. WEBLEY. 1971. Further information concerning the environment of Palaeolithic man in Epirus, *Proceedings of the Prehistoric Society* 37: 367–80.

HIGGS, E.S., C. VITA-FINZI, D.R. HARRIS & A.E. FAGG. 1967. The climate, environment and industries of Stone Age Greece, part III, *Proceedings of the Prehistoric Society* 33: 1–29.

HUXTABLE, J., J.A.J. GOWLETT, G.N. BAILEY, P.L. CARTER & V. PAPACONSTANTINOU. 1992. Thermoluminescence dates and a new analysis of the early Mousterian from Asprochaliko, *Current Anthropology* 33: 109–14.

KING, G.C.P. & G.N. BAILEY. 1985. The palaeoenvironment of some archaeological sites in Greece: the influence of accumulated uplift in a seismically active region, *Proceedings of the Prehistoric Society* 51: 273–82.

KING, G.C.P. & M. ELLIS. 1990. The origin of large local uplift in extensional regions, *Nature* 348: 20–27.

KING, G.C.P. & A.G. LINDH. In press. Predictability and the evolution of culture, in S. van der Leeuw (ed.), *Proceedings of the Cambridge conference on dynamical descriptions and human systems*. Edinburgh: Edinburgh University Press.

KING, G.C.P. & R.S. STEIN. 1983. Surface folding, river terrace deformation rate and earthquake repeat time in a reverse faulting environment: the Coalinga, California, earthquake of May 1983, in *The 1983 Coalinga, California, earthquake*: 61–9. Sacramento (CA): California Division of Mines and Geology. Special Publication 66.

KING, G.C.P. & C. VITA-FINZI. 1981. Active folding in the Algerian earthquake of 10 October, 1980, *Nature* 292: 22–6.

KING, G.C.P., D.A. STURDY & J. WHITNEY. In press. Landscape geometry and the active tectonics of northwest Greece, *Bulletin of the Geological Society of America*.

KOTZAMBOPOULOU, E. 1988. Faunal analysis of the Kastritsa Cave, Greece. Unpublished MPhil. thesis, Cambridge University.

LEGGE, A.J. 1972. Cave climates, in E.S. Higgs (ed.), *Papers in economic prehistory*: 97–103. Cambridge: Cambridge University Press.

LEWIN, J., M.G. MACKLIN & J.C. WOODWARD. 1991. Late Quaternary fluvial sedimentation in the Voïdomatis basin, Epirus, northwest Greece, *Quaternary Research* 35: 103–15.

POPE, K.O., & T.H. VAN ANDEL. 1984. Late Quaternary alluviation and soil formation in the Southern Argolid: its history, causes and archaeological implications. *Journal of Archaeological Science* 11: 281–306.

PRENTICE, I.C., J. GUIOT & S.P. HARRISON. 1992. Mediterranean vegetation, lake levels and palaeoclimate at the last glacial maximum, *Nature* 360: 658–60.

Site characterization plan. 1988. *Yucca Mountain Site, Nevada research and development area, Nevada*. Oak Ridge (TN): US Department of Energy, Office of Scientific and Technical Information.

SLEMMONS, D.B., E.R. ENGDAHL, M.D. ZOBACK & D.D. BLACKWELL (ed.). 1991. *The neotectonics of North America: Boulder Colorado, decade map* 1. Boulder (CO): Geological Society of America.

SORDINAS, A. 1969. Investigations of the prehistory of Corfu during 1964–1966, *Balkan Studies* 10: 393–424.

STEIN, R.S. & G.C.P. KING. 1984. Seismic potential revealed by surface folding: the 1983 Coalinga, California, earthquake, *Science* 224: 869–72.

STURDY, D.A. 1975. Some reindeer economies in prehistoric Europe, in E.S. Higgs (ed.), *Palaeoeconomy*: 55–95. Cambridge: Cambridge University Press.

STURDY, D.A. & D.P. WEBLEY. 1988. Palaeolithic geography: or where are the deer? *World Archaeology* 19: 262–80.

TAPPONIER, P. 1977. Evolution tectonique du système alpin en Mediterranée: poinconnément et écrasement rigide-plastique, *Bulletin de la Société Géologique de France* 19: 437–60.

TAPPONIER, P. & P. MOLNAR. 1977. Active faulting and tectonics in China, *Journal of Geophysical Research* 82: 2905–30.

VALANSISE, G. 1992. *Geological records of combined tectonic processes in the central Santa Cruz mountains*. Loma Prieta: United States Geological Survey.

VAN ANDEL, T.H. & E. ZANGGER. 1990. Landscape stability and destabilization in the prehistory of Greece, in S. Bottema, G. Entjes-Nieborg & W. Van Zeist (ed.), *Man's role in the shaping of the eastern Mediterranean landscape.*: 139–57. Rotterdam: Balkema.

VITA-FINZI, C. 1969. *The Mediterranean valleys: geological changes in historical times*. Cambridge: Cambridge University Press.

     1978. *Archaeological sites in their setting*. London: Thames & Hudson.

WAGSTAFF, J.M. 1981. Buried assumptions: some problems in the interpretation of the 'Younger Fill' raised by recent data from Greece, *Journal of Archaeological Science* 8: 247–64.

WILLIS, K.J. 1989. Late Quaternary vegetation history of Epirus northwest Greece. Unpublished Ph.D dissertation, Cambridge University.

WOODWARD, J. 1990. Late Quaternary sedimentary environments in the Voïdomatis Basin, northwest Greece. Unpublished Ph.D dissertation, Cambridge University.

ZHANG, P., M. ELLIS, D.B. SLEMMONS & F. MAO. 1990. Right-lateral displacements and the Holocene slip rate associated with prehistoric earthquakes along the southern Panamint Valley fault zone: implications for southern Basin and Range tectonics and coastal California deformation, *Journal of Geophysical Research* 95: 4857–72.

A guide for archaeologists investigating Holocene landscapes
by A.J. HOWARD & M.G. MACKLIN
ANTIQUITY 73 (281), 1999

ALLUVIAL LANDSCAPES offer some of the most attractive environments for human activity and settlement. Utilized since early prehistoric times, they have been the subject of intense world-wide archaeological and geoarchaeological research (e.g. Berendsen 1993; Bettis 1995; Brown 1997; Jing *et al.* 1997; Joyce & Mueller 1997; Martin-Consuegra *et al.* 1998; Needham & Macklin 1992). Their continued attraction for transportation networks, settlement and exploitation of resources such as minerals (Allen *et al.* 1997) and groundwater (Parker-Pearson & Sydes 1997), however, has put intense pressure on both cultural and environmental archaeological remains (Darvill & Fulton 1998). Destruction of archaeological sites in river valleys most commonly occurs because of construction and development and through drainage of valley floors resulting in lower water-tables and oxidation of alluvium.

Research on Holocene environmental change and archaeology within British river valleys over the last two decades has concentrated on a number of key themes. These include assessments of the potential attractiveness of river valley landscapes to human communities (Evans 1991) and analysis of the utilization of particular river zones (Robinson 1978), to excavation and recording of individual floodplain sites (Nayling & Caseldine 1997), through to identifying causal mechanisms of changing catchment hydrology and sedimentation styles (Robinson & Lambrick 1984; Macklin & Lewin 1993). Whilst a growing number of alluvial archaeological studies have demonstrated the wealth of the resource (Needham 1991), particularly where water-tables are high (Bell & Neumann 1997; Pryor *et al.* 1986; Parker-Pearson & Sydes 1997), geomorphological investigation has shown the complex evolution of these natural sedimentary systems and how river processes and channel dynamics influence archaeological site location and the quality of preservation (Lewin 1992; Passmore & Macklin 1997; Macklin 1999). In Britain, the Holocene fluvial stratigraphic record indicates that, prior to large-scale land drainage and channelization since the industrial revolution, there was a greater diversity of channel types and floodplain sedimentation styles than found today (Macklin & Needham 1992). These contrasting river patterns, included braided (laterally mobile multi-channelled rivers with wide and shallow, rapidly shifting channels, that divide and rejoin around sand and gravel bars, and vegetated islands) and anastomosed channel systems (inter-connected networks of low-gradient, relatively deep and narrow channels of variable sinuosity, characterized by stable, vegetated banks composed of fine-grained silt and clay; Smith & Smith 1983) which produce different alluvial sedimentary sequences (Brown & Keough 1992a; Passmore *et al.* 1993). Although many archaeologists and geomorphologists in Britain are increasingly aware of this, few have considered how temporal and spatial variability in river dynamics have affected the preservation and visibility of the cultural record in alluvial environments (for examples of those who have, see Brown & Keough 1992b; Lewin 1992; Macklin *et al.* 1992c; Macklin 1999). This paper considers

---

The original title of this paper was: A generic geomorphological approach to archaeological interpretation and prospectionin British river valleys: a guide for archaeologists investigating Holocene landscapes.

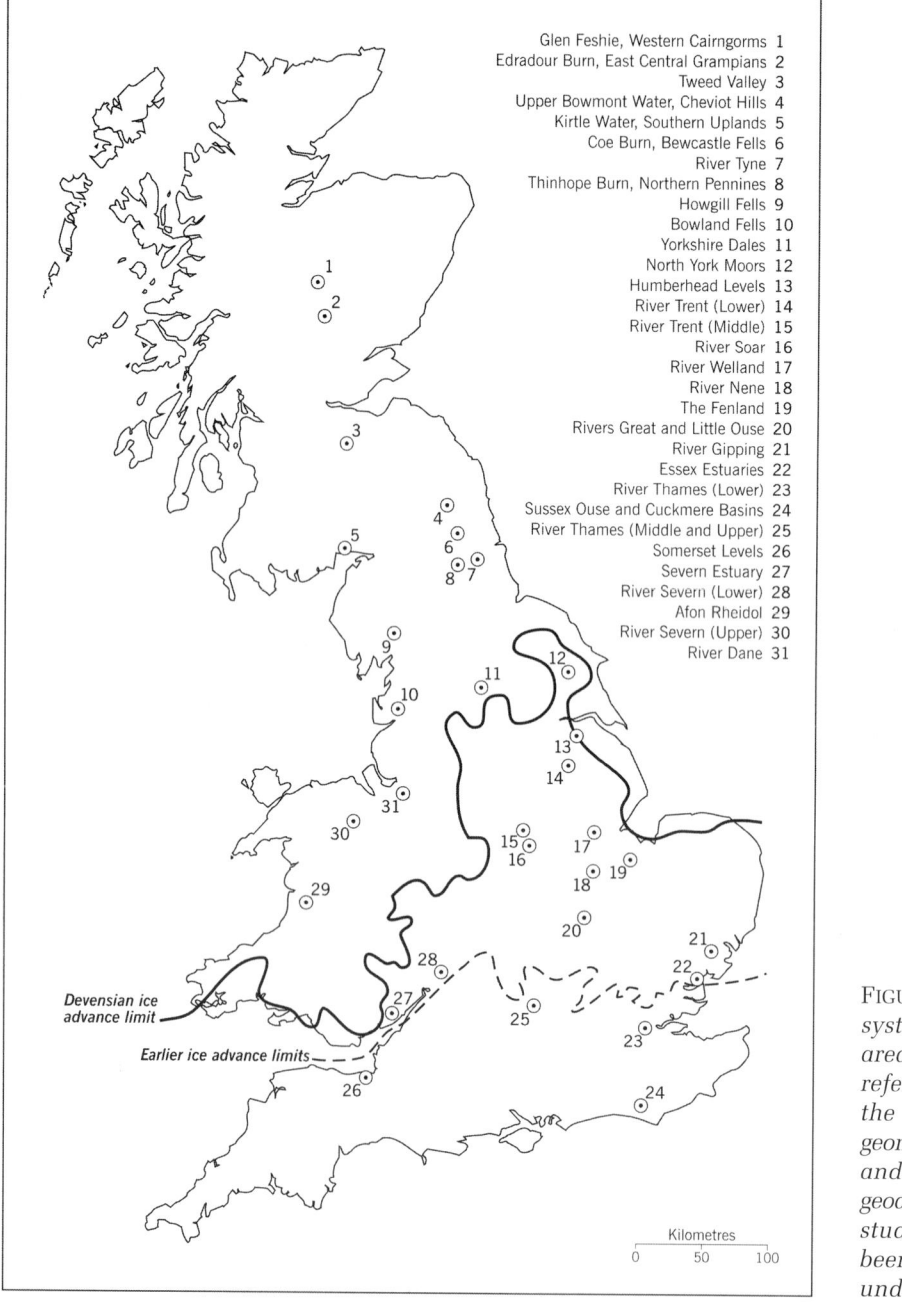

Glen Feshie, Western Cairngorms 1
Edradour Burn, East Central Grampians 2
Tweed Valley 3
Upper Bowmont Water, Cheviot Hills 4
Kirtle Water, Southern Uplands 5
Coe Burn, Bewcastle Fells 6
River Tyne 7
Thinhope Burn, Northern Pennines 8
Howgill Fells 9
Bowland Fells 10
Yorkshire Dales 11
North York Moors 12
Humberhead Levels 13
River Trent (Lower) 14
River Trent (Middle) 15
River Soar 16
River Welland 17
River Nene 18
The Fenland 19
Rivers Great and Little Ouse 20
River Gipping 21
Essex Estuaries 22
River Thames (Lower) 23
Sussex Ouse and Cuckmere Basins 24
River Thames (Middle and Upper) 25
Somerset Levels 26
Severn Estuary 27
River Severn (Lower) 28
Afon Rheidol 29
River Severn (Upper) 30
River Dane 31

Devensian ice advance limit

Earlier ice advance limits

Kilometres
0   50   100

FIGURE 1. *River systems and areas of Britain referred to in the text where geomorphological and geoarchaeological studies have been undertaken.*

the current state of research in this important area and presents an empirically-based model of Holocene river-valley evolution in Britain which highlights the impact that fluvial processes have had on the archaeological record.

River channel and floodplain classification
More than a century of study by fluvial geomorphologists has resulted in the classification of rivers and their floodplains on the basis of channel planform and sedimentation processes. Four styles of fluvial channel are commonly recognized; braided, meander-

ing, anastomosing and straight (Leopold & Wolman 1957; Leopold *et al.* 1964). All of these channel types have been identified in British Holocene fluvial sedimentary sequences, though divided multi-channel river systems (braided or anastomosing) are relatively rare in Britain today. Although these categories are useful, they must be considered as tendencies within a spectrum of channel types. British rivers have been further sub-divided into upland, piedmont, lowland and perimarine systems (Lewin 1981) on the basis of physiography and basin relief (Macklin & Lewin 1993).

In this paper we utilize a generic classification of floodplains developed by Nanson & Croke (1992) which is based upon stream power (the product of discharge and channel slope) and bank erodibility, within the geomorphic framework proposed for British rivers by Macklin & Lewin (1986; 1993). Such a classification is ideally suited to archaeological applications, since it can be used for the investigation of specific sites or short lengths of river valley.

High-energy river systems with non-cohesive channel banks
Holocene geomorphic development
These river systems are characteristic of the upland areas of northern and western Britain, having high river-channel gradients (>10 m km^{-1}) and bedload sediment transport rates, steep valley-side slopes which frequently merge into the channel without an intervening floodplain, and flow regimes in which large infrequent floods play an important role in valley-floor development (Newson & Macklin 1990; McEwen & Werritty 1988). Well-studied alluvial sequences of this type (FIGURE 1; TABLE 1) are present in the Howgill Fells (Harvey *et al.* 1981), the Bowland Fells (Harvey & Renwick 1987), the Northern Pennines (Macklin *et al.* 1992a; 1992b; Passmore *et al.* 1993), the Yorkshire Dales (Macklin 1997; Merrett & Macklin 1999), the North Yorkshire Moors (Richards *et al.* 1987) the Bewcastle Fells (Macklin *et al.* 1991), the Cheviots (Tipping 1994), the east-central Grampians (Tipping 1995a), the Cairngorms (Robertson-Rintoul 1986) and the Southern Uplands (Tipping & Halliday 1994).

All of these river systems flow through areas glaciated during the Late Devensian, which in many catchments has left a supply of sediment to the channel largely unrelated to contemporary geomorphic processes (*cf.* Church & Ryder 1972). High-energy upland rivers have responded to long-term glacio-isostatic uplift and declining sediment supply during the Holocene by progressive incision of their valley floors and entrenchment of tributary stream alluvial fans. Downcutting, however, has been episodic, interspersed with periods of valley-floor refilling resulting in well-developed flights of terraces (FIGURE 2; TABLE 1). For example, in the Northern Pennines, large-scale erosion of valley floors did not begin until 550–680 cal AD and coincided with a shift to colder, wetter climatic conditions preceded by vegetation disturbance (Macklin *et al.* 1992b). Similarly, in the Bowmont Valley, Cheviots, Tipping (1994) has demonstrated that, with the exception of the highest river terrace, all the lower terraces were formed within the last *c.* 250 years, primarily in response to increased flooding during the Little Ice Age (Rumsby & Macklin 1996). In other basins, accelerated sedimentation has been linked to human disturbance including the introduction of sheep farming in the Howgills by the Scandinavians in the 10th century AD (Harvey *et al.* 1981), overgrazing in the Scottish Highlands (Tipping 1995a) and coal and metal mining in northeast England (Macklin *et al.* 1991; Macklin & Lewin 1989).

Archaeological preservation and prospection potential
High-energy river systems in upland Britain have experienced considerable vertical and lateral movement during the Holocene (FIGURE 2). Whilst terraces would be attractive to

river type	geomorphic evolution	British examples	archaeological preservation issues
High-energy river systems with non-cohesive channel banks.	Episodic incision & aggradation with accelerated rates of change in the last 2000 years. Dominance of coarse-grained sedimentation in braided & meandering (wandering gravel bed) systems, resulting in stacked sequences of coarse-grained sediment members. Limited fine-grained sedimentation	The Howgill Fells (Harvey *et al.* 1981), the Bowland Fells (Harvey & Renwick 1987), the Northern Pennines (Macklin *et al.* 1992a; 1992b; Passmore *et al.* 1993), the Yorkshire Dales (Macklin 1997; Merrett & Macklin 1999), the North Yorkshire Moors (Richards *et al.* 1987), the Bewcastle Fells (Macklin *et al.* 1991), the Cheviots (Tipping 1994), the east-central Grampians (Tipping 1995a), the Cairngorms (Robertson-Rintoul 1986) & the Southern Uplands (Tipping & Halliday 1994).	• Preservation potential is greatest on the oldest terraces where multi-period archaeological remains may be present. • Narrow valley floors may prevent long-term terrace preservation. • High magnitude flood events are capable of flushing sediment fills from valleys. • Incision will result in the reworking of archaeological remains. • Incision will result in falling water-tables leading to dewatering & desiccation of cultural & environmental remains. • Aggradation may result in the burial of *in situ* remains. • Tributary stream alluvial fans may contain reworked remains & bury in situ archaeological material on terraces present in the trunk river valley floor. • Mass movement & colluviation may result in the erosion of archaeology on inclined slopes & burial on terrace & floodplain surfaces. • Organic remains may be preserved in palaeochannels and other water-logged depressions, or as buried soils on former land-surfaces. Organic clasts may be reworked into younger sedimentary units.

TABLE 1. *Examples of upland fluvial environments studied in Britain, Holocene evolution and issues of archaeological preservation.*

human use, especially following large-scale deforestation in the late Iron Age and Roman periods, since when channel entrenchment rates have been relatively high, preservation of features, structural remains, artefacts and ecofacts is reduced by falling water-tables and channel reworking of older alluvial deposits (TABLE 1). However, in Thinhope Burn, in the Northern Pennines (FIGURE 2), Macklin *et al.* (1992b) showed that valley-floor transformation in this upland region was relatively recent, with the first major period of channel entrenchment commencing between *c.* 250–530 and 660–980 AD. If this is typical of other high-energy river systems in the British Uplands, as seems to be the case (*cf.* Harvey *et al.* 1981; Tipping 1994), then the potential for preservation of earlier historic and prehistoric archaeology within such valleys is likely to be considerable.

Unfortunately, at present, the archaeological potential of high-energy upland river systems remains relatively unknown. With the exception of studies of historic mining landscapes such as those of the Yorkshire Dales (White 1998), systematic survey of these valley systems appears rare, with a continuing focus on the archaeological potential of

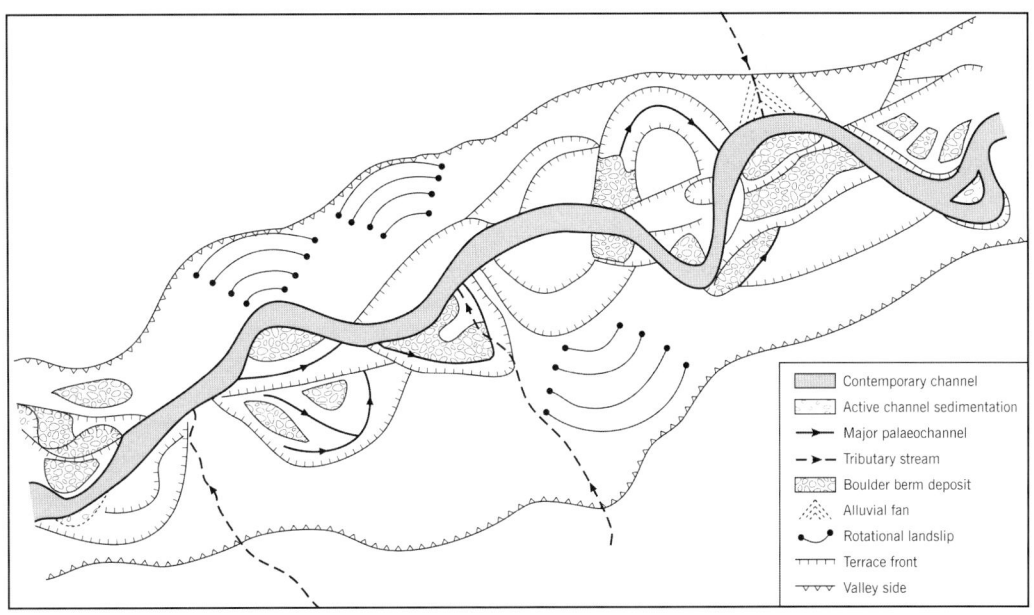

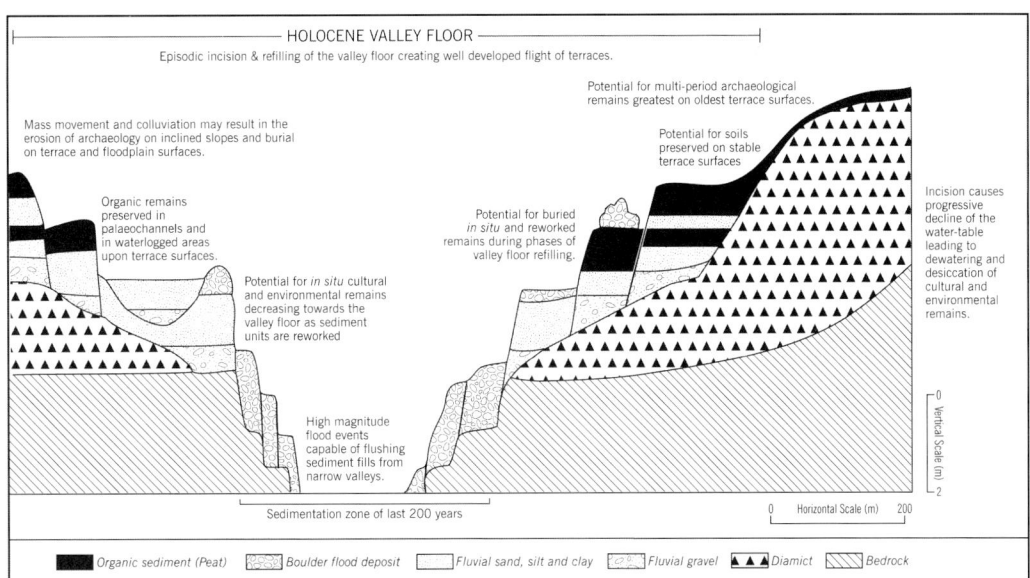

FIGURE 2. *Planform (2a) and cross-section (2b) of a high-energy river system with non-cohesive channel banks. Annotation on* 2b *refers to the potential for cultural and environmental archaeological remains and complements* TABLE 1 *(based upon Thinhope Burn, Northern Pennines, Macklin* et al. *1992b;* FIGURE 1, *area 8).*

moorland plateaux suffering blanket peat erosion (Howard-Davis 1996). However, the loss by fluvial erosion of robust building structures from metal mining sites (White 1998), particularly during high-magnitude events (Newson & Macklin 1990), attest to the problems facing archaeological preservation in these river systems.

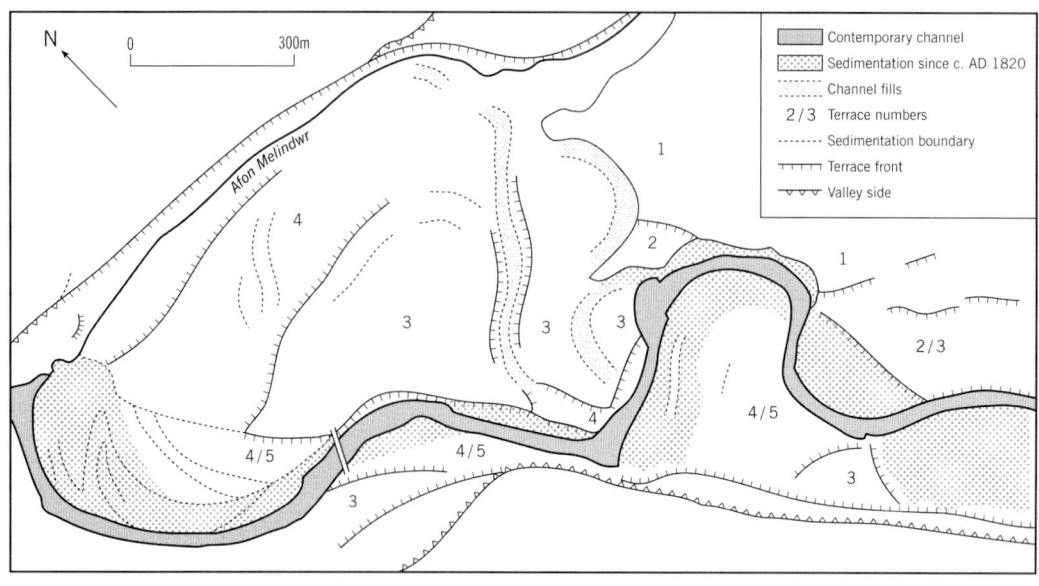

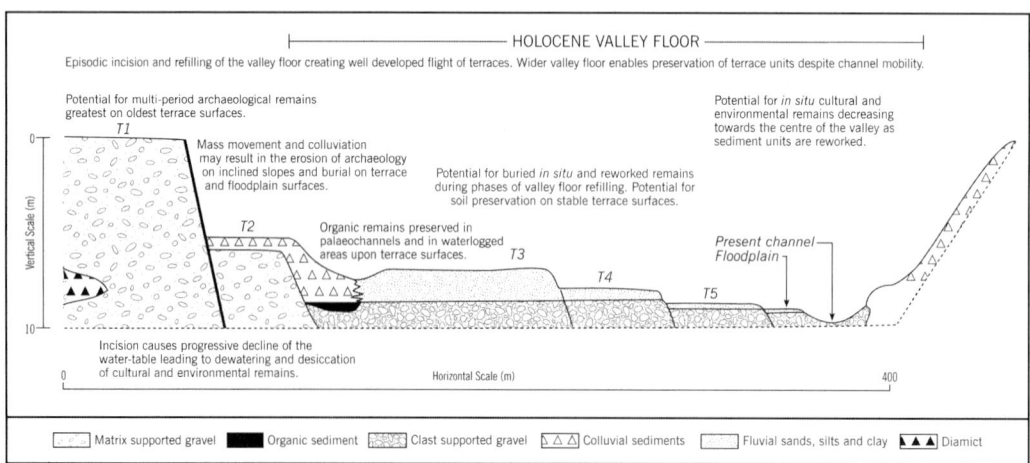

FIGURE 3. *Planform (3a) and cross-section (3b) of a medium-energy river system with non-cohesive channel banks. Annotation on 3b refers to the potential for cultural and environmental archaeological remains and complements* TABLE 2 *(based upon the Afon Rheidol, mid-Wales, Macklin & Lewin 1986;* FIGURE 1, *area 29).*

Organic deposits in the form of palaeochannel fills (Macklin *et al.* 1992b) and buried soils (Brazier *et al.* 1988) are common features in British upland environments and are highly suitable for palaeobiological 'off-site' archaeological study and radiometric dating (Long *et al.* 1998).

Medium-energy river systems with non-cohesive channel banks
Holocene geomorphic development
Medium-energy river systems tend to be located at the upland margins of northern and western Britain (FIGURE 1). The geomorphological attributes of these zones include: river-

river type	geomorphic evolution	British examples	archaeological preservation issues
Medium-energy river systems with non-cohesive channel banks.	Vertical & lateral instability, episodic incision & aggradation. Dominance of coarse grained sedimentation in braided, anasto-mosing & mean-dering (wandering gravel bed) systems. Fine grained accretion upon coarse sediment units during overbank 'flood' events.	The Cheshire basin (Hooke *et al.* 1990) the middle Trent Valley (Salisbury *et al.* 1984), the Northern Pennines (Macklin *et al.* 1992a; Passmore *et al.* 1993; Passmore & Macklin 1997), the Yorkshire Dales (Taylor & Macklin 1997) the Southern Uplands (Tipping 1995b), & in mid Wales (Macklin & Lewin 1986; Taylor & Lewin 1996).	• Preservation potential is greatest on oldest terrace surfaces where multi-period remains may be present. • Wider valley floors may allow for the preservation of terrace units & potentially longer archaeological records, despite channel mobility. • Incision may result in the reworking of archaeological remains. • Incision will result in falling water-tables leading to dewatering & desiccation of cultural & environ-mental remains. • Aggradation may result in the burial of *in situ* remains. • Tributary stream alluvial fans may contain reworked remains & bury in situ archaeological material on terraces present in the trunk river valley floor. • Mass movement & colluviation may result in the erosion of archaeology on inclined slopes & burial on terrace & floodplain surfaces. • Organic remains may be preserved in palaeochannels and other water-logged depressions, or as buried soils on former land-surfaces. Organic clasts may be reworked into younger sedimentary units.

TABLE 2. *Examples of upland margin fluvial environments studied in Britain, Holocene evolution and issues of archaeological preservation.*

channel gradients of between 2 and 10 m km^{-1}; steep valley-side slopes but with the development of a floodplain between the valley side and river channel; and transport of gravel bedload and deposition of fine-grained overbank material during flood events.

As with upland fluvial systems, many of these medium-energy rivers flow through areas glaciated during the Late Devensian, leaving a post-glacial supply of sediment to the channel, unrelated to contemporary geomorphic processes. This, combined with glacio-isostatic uplift, has resulted in vertical and lateral channel movement, very often creating flights of terraces (FIGURE 3; TABLE 2). Well studied systems of this type (FIGURE 1) are present to the west of the Peak District in the Cheshire basin (Hooke *et al.* 1990), to the south of the Peak District in the middle Trent Valley (Salisbury *et al.* 1984), the Northern Pennines (Macklin *et al.* 1992a; Passmore *et al.* 1993; Passmore & Macklin 1997), the Yorkshire Dales (Taylor & Macklin 1997), the Southern Uplands (Tipping 1995b) and in mid-Wales (Macklin & Lewin 1986; Taylor & Lewin 1996).

Higher terraces within these systems are generally of considerable antiquity with river channels having incised through glacial and periglacial sediments on the valley floor during the late Pleistocene and early Holocene. In contrast, aggradation of the lower, younger terraces have been influenced by changing climatic conditions and human activity, such as medieval soil erosion in the Dane valley of Cheshire (Hooke *et al.* 1990) and historic metal mining in mid-Wales (Macklin & Lewin 1986).

Archaeological preservation and prospection potential

Whilst vertical and lateral movement in medium-energy river systems would produce terrace surfaces attractive to human occupation, the potential for high-quality *in situ* preservation is reduced through time by channel reworking and falling water tables (Figure 3; Table 2). In contrast to higher-energy upland streams, this loss may be partially mitigated by wider valley floors enabling older terrace units to be preserved as higher facets within the landscape, usually along the valley side, that can be settled on a multi-period basis. Therefore, establishing a chronology of aggradation and incision in a study area is of paramount importance because the most favourable terraces for the preservation of multi-period archaeological remains are likely to be those of late Pleistocene/early Holocene age (Gibson 1994; Cardwell 1995; Cardwell & Speed 1996).

Although the quality of archaeological preservation is greatly reduced through channel incision and lateral migration across the valley floor, careful analysis of the alluvial record in these contexts can yield considerable amounts of information. In the Trent Valley for example, detailed mapping of uprooted tree trunks, *in situ* and reworked archaeological remains within coarse alluvial gravels combined with a programme of excavation and radiometric dating, has provided a unique insight into changing floodplain hydrology and human utilization of the river from the later prehistoric to post-medieval periods (Salisbury *et al.* 1984). The analysis of palaeoecological remains from a log-jam within sands and gravels also in the Trent Valley has shown the potential of even coarse grained deposits for preserving high-quality environmental information (Howard *et al.* 1999).

Wider valley floors increase the potential for the preservation of organic sediments in abandoned channels (Table 2). Palaeochannels, as well as providing important sediment traps for animal and plant environmental data (Tipping 1995c; 1995d), can also become the focus of human activity associated with the acquisition of natural resources such as fish and wildfowl, as well as providing raw materials for building. Furthermore, in later prehistoric periods, there is also the issue of the spiritual significance of rivers and wetlands (Bradley 1990). Human activity away from the contemporary channel could result in the preservation of artefacts either accidentally lost or deliberately placed in a watery context, or the preservation of *in situ* structural remains.

Low-energy river systems with cohesive channel banks

Holocene geomorphic development

Low-energy river systems are characteristic of the English Midlands, southern and eastern Britain (Figure 1). They possess low channel gradients (< 2 m km^{-1}), low-angle valley-side slopes, well-developed floodplains and transport predominantly fine-grained sediment. In Britain, these low-energy systems can be divided into those unaffected (here termed lowland) and those affected (here termed perimarine; Hageman 1969) directly by sea-level change. Well-studied lowland alluvial sequences include (Figure 1; Table 3) the major arterial rivers of the upper and middle Thames (Robinson & Lambrick 1984; Needham 1992; Robinson 1992), the lower Trent (Dinnin 1997) and lower Severn (Brown

river type	geomorphic evolution	British examples	archaeological preservation issues
Low energy 'lowland' river systems with cohesive channel banks.	Evolution from lateglacial braided to Holocene meandering/ anastomosing systems, with increased lateral stability & domi-nance of vertical accretion through time. Stratigraphy comprises fine-grained units of sand, silt, clay & peat.	The upper & middle Thames (Robinson & Lambrick 1984; Needham 1992; Robinson 1992), Lower Trent (Dinnin 1997) Lower Severn (Brown 1987), Gipping (Rose *et al.* 1980), Nene, Soar (Brown *et al.* 1994; French *et al.* 1992; Robinson 1992), Ouse & Welland (Robinson 1992).	• Stability of river systems & dominance of vertical accretion result in burial & preservation of *in situ* archaeology at multiple levels within the floodplain. • High water tables enhance waterlogging & preservation of organic materials & cultural remains. • Very high preservation potential for organic materials in palaeochannels, other waterlogged depressions & on former land-surfaces.
Low energy 'perimarine' river systems with cohesive banks.	Sea-level fluctua-tions result in flooding, peat development & overbank sedimen-tation in anastomo-sing & meandering channels. Stratigraphy comprises cyclical sequences of silt/ clay & peat.	The Humberhead Levels & Lower Trent Valley (Gaunt 1981; Parker Pearson & Sydes 1997; Van De Noort & Ellis 1997; 1998), the Welsh part of the Severn Estuary (Bell & Neumann 1997; Rippon 1996) the Somerset Levels (Coles 1978; Coles & Coles 1986), the Fens (Seale 1979; Pryor *et al.* 1985; Hall 1987; Hayes & Lane 1992; French *et al.* 1992; and Lane 1993); the lower Thames (Thomas & Rackham 1996); the Essex estuaries (Wilkinson *et al.* 1988); & Ouse & Cuckmere of the Sussex Weald (Burrin & Scaife 1984).	

TABLE 3. *Examples of lowland and perimarine fluvial environments studied in Britain, Holocene evolution and issues of archaeological preservation.*

1987); and regionally important rivers including the Gipping (Rose *et al.* 1980), Nene, Soar (Brown *et al.* 1994; French *et al.* 1992; Robinson 1992), Ouse and Welland (Robinson 1992).

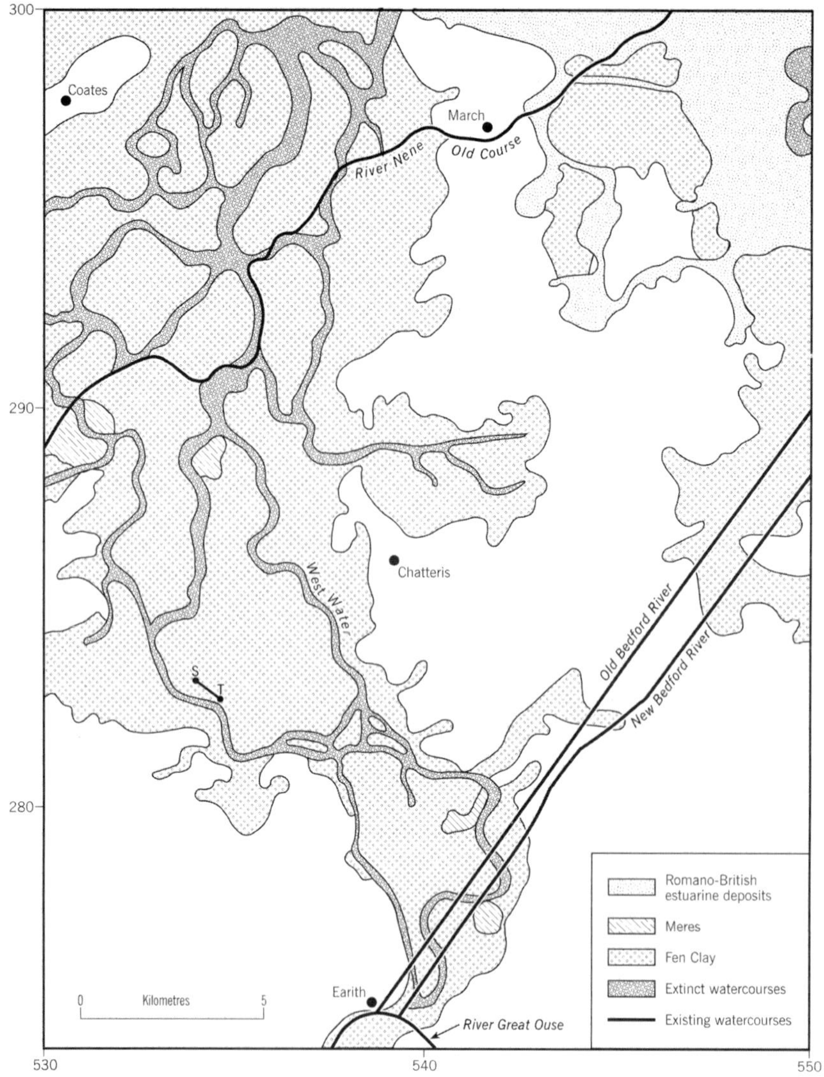

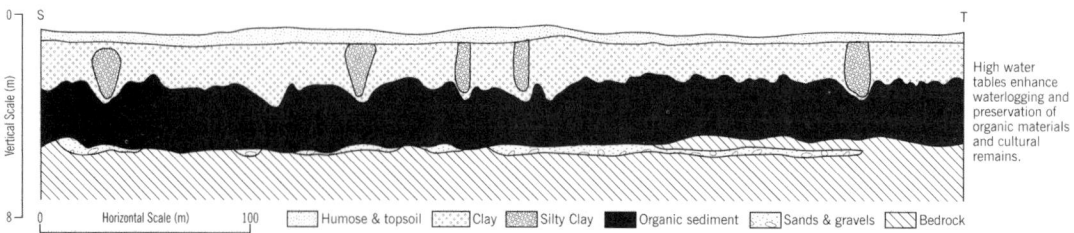

FIGURE 4. *Planform (4a) and cross-section (4b) of a lowland anastomosing river system with cohesive channel banks. Annotation on 4b refers to the potential for cultural and environmental archaeological remains and complements* TABLE 3 *(based upon the Great and Little Ouse, East Anglia, Seale 1979;* FIGURE 1, *area 20).*

Stable river system dominated by vertical accretion. Potential for the burial and preservation of *in situ* archaeology at multiple levels within the floodplain. High preservation potential for organic materials in palaeochannels, other waterlogged depressions and on former land-surfaces.

High water tables enhance waterlogging and preservation of organic materials and cultural remains.

In the Lateglacial, variable discharge and sediment supply created multi-channelled braided river systems. Climatic amelioration, especially in the early Holocene, reduced discharge and promoted vegetation growth which, in turn, decreased the erodibility of river banks, as well as reducing sediment availability to the channel (Brown *et al.* 1994).

Through the abandonment and infilling of secondary braid channels, meandering/anas-
tomosing channels with levées and backswamps developed. In the English Midlands,
the timing of floodplain metamorphosis has been put at *c.* 9500 BP with a further period
between *c.* 3500 and 2000 BP (Brown *et al.* 1994). In many systems, for example the
Gipping (Rose 1980), the contemporary channel is situated over the thickest sequence of
fine-grained sediments, suggesting a near stationary position of these low-energy systems throughout most of the Holocene. Vertical accretion of sediment has predominated
with significant backswamp sedimentation and frequent submergence of the floodplain
leading to the creation of extensive wetland areas.

In Britain, well-studied perimarine areas include (FIGURE 1; TABLE 3) the Humberhead
Levels (Gaunt 1981; Parker Pearson & Sydes 1997; Van De Noort & Ellis 1997) and Lower
Trent Valley (Van De Noort & Ellis 1998), the Welsh part of the Severn Estuary (Bell &
Neumann 1997; Rippon 1996), the Somerset Levels (Coles 1978; Coles & Coles 1986), the
Fens (Seale 1979; Pryor *et al.* 1985; Hall 1987; Hayes & Lane 1992; French *et al.* 1992; &
Lane 1993), the Lower Thames (Thomas & Rackham 1996), the Essex estuaries (Wilkinson
et al. 1988) and the Ouse and Cuckmere of the Sussex Weald (Burrin & Scaife 1984). River
base-level change in response to sea-level fluctuation has resulted in episodic flooding and
overbank sedimentation of silts and clays in anastomosing and meandering channel systems
(French *et al.* 1992), with peat development in waterlogged areas (FIGURE 4).

Archaeological preservation and prospection potential

The lateral stability of low-energy river systems and their accretionary nature frequently
results in the preservation of high-quality, *in situ,* multi-period cultural remains (FIGURE
4; TABLE 3), usually buried within or beneath thick sequences of fine-grained alluvium
(Thomas *et al.* 1986; Needham; 1992; Pollard 1996) or peat (Meddens 1996), or located
on gravel islands rising from beneath the alluvium (Woodfield & Johnson 1989). Until
recent pressures on groundwater resources, preservation quality has been further enhanced by high water tables, which increased between *c.* 5000–4000 BP (Brown *et al.*
1994) and around 2800 BP (Robinson & Lambrick 1984) as a result of climate-related
changes in catchment hydrology.

In the perimarine zone, flooding following long- or short-term sea-level rise is likely
to have resulted in settlement abandonment and movement to higher ground (Wilkinson
et al. 1988) and/or adaptation to allow continued exploitation of coastal resources, including the construction of trackways, jetties, platforms and enclosures, both within
and at the marshland edge (Meddens 1996; Thomas & Rackham 1996). In the port of
London, Roman and later waterfront archaeology including revetments and quays have
been buried over an area of *c.* 8 ha, beneath up to 10 m of alluvium (Hobley 1981), with
similar sequences known from other major ports in Northern Europe. Pryor *et al.* (1985)
have pointed out, however, that the relationship between waterlogging and abandonment may be far from simple, suggesting that causewayed enclosures at Etton, Barholm
and Uffington in the Welland Valley, and Tansor and Southwick in the Nene Valley,
indicate significant use of wet areas, possibly for ceremonial purposes, a point reinforced by the studies of Parker-Pearson & Sydes (1997) at Sutton Common in the
Humberhead Levels. In addition, work in the Severn Estuary has established little human response to sea-level rise in the later prehistoric, further indicating the complex
issues surrounding the use of wetlands (Bell & Neumann 1997). Nevertheless, whether
adaptation or abandonment followed waterlogging, the consequence for the archaeology
is eventual burial and preservation, as shown for example in the Fens (Pryor *et al.* 1986).

Organic sediments deposited in abandoned channels and flood basins in low-energy environments offer excellent environmental records and evidence of human activ-

procedure for establishing a geomorphic stratigraphic framework for assessing archaeological potential in river valleys	high-energy river systems with non-cohesive channel banks	medium-energy river systems with non-cohesive channel banks	low-energy 'lowland' river systems with cohesive channel banks	low-energy peri-marine river systems with cohesive banks
• Geomorphological mapping of alluvial valley floor to identify major fluvial landforms, terraces, alluvial fans, palaeochannels. Recording of artificial and natural exposures within the valley floor to establish chronology and environment of sediment deposition.	****	****	****	****
• Identify palaeochannels and other organic-rich sediment bodies.	***	****	****	****
• Identify palaeo-landsurfaces, higher terrace facets, gravel islands and levées.	*	**	****	****
• Recover suitable material for radiometric dating to provide a chronological framework.	****	****	****	****
• Identify the timing of major episodes of coarse grained aggradation.	****	****	**	*
• Identify the timing of fine-grained aggradation.	*	**	****	****
• Identify the timing of major episodes of incision.	****	****	**	**
• Zone valley floor according to age of alluvial units.	****	****	****	****
• Provenance fine-grained sediments from their geochemical (element) signature.	**	**	**	**
• Identify causal mechanisms of changing sedimentation styles by comparing alluvial sequences with local land-use & climatic records.	****	****	****	****
• Identify major zones of fine-grained sedimentation in which archaeology is unlikely to be located through conventional archaeological prospection techniques.	*	**	****	****
• In areas underlain by >2m of fine-grained alluvium, map the sub-surface topography through analysis of published boreholes, test-pitting and augering.	*	**	****	****
• Prospect for archaeology in areas where fine grained units are >2m thick through a combination of geophysical techniques, field-walking, test-pitting and trial-trenching.	*	**	****	****
• Input geomorphic dating and archaeological data into a GIS and produce maps of archaeological potential.	****	****	****	****

**** = most important   * = least important

ity (TABLE 3). In perimarine areas, the interbedding of peat with archaeological material provides not only excellent potential for palaeoenvironmental reconstruction, but also high-resolution dating control (Bell & Neumann 1997; Walker *et al.* 1998). In both lowland and perimarine zones, the vertical accretion of fine-grained sediment can, however, be both beneficial and detrimental for the archaeological remains. Although burial enhances the chances of preservation, it can mask the archaeological resource, preventing its identification through standard prospection methodologies such as aerial photography (*cf.* Whimster 1989).

Developing a geomorphic and stratigraphic framework for assessing and interpreting archaeological potential in river valleys

This review illustrates the contrasting fluvial styles and sedimentation histories which have shaped Britain's Holocene alluvial landscapes and the impact these contrasts have for the preservation of archaeological remains. It illustrates the need for archaeological studies to be underpinned by a geomorphological approach that provides a stratigraphic framework against which archaeological information can be assessed. To assist the archaeologist in construction of a geomorphological framework, a step by step 'task-list' is provided (TABLE 4) which should allow any given part of a British alluvial landscape (upland to perimarine) to be assessed for its archaeological potential.

Conclusions

Throughout history, rivers have provided a wide range of resources for human exploitation and have influenced the demarcation of physical, social and administrative landscapes. This review has elucidated the trends of river evolution in Britain and its effects on the development, preservation, and recovery of archaeology within the alluvial landscape. Its principal message is that riverine environments can only be effectively studied through a multi-disciplinary approach, with the elucidation of the geomorphological history and construction of empirically based models of landscape development forming a precursor to detailed archaeological survey (TABLES 1–4).

By integration of geomorphological and archaeological evidence, such models will serve as a guide to assessing important issues such as where cultural deposits are likely to be preserved or removed by subsequent erosion, buried and invisible to traditional methods of archaeological prospection; and how patterns in the sedimentary record might affect patterns in the archaeological record. It will form the basis not only for pragmatic risk assessment, but also for a critical analysis of human spatial behaviour in fluvial environments (*cf.* Bettis & Hajic 1995).

Acknowledgements. Many of the concepts on which this paper is based were initiated through the authors' combined experiences from over a decade of research in alluvial archaeology. AJH would like to thank all the staff of Trent & Peak Archaeological Trust (especially Keith Challis, Lee Elliott, Daryl Garton and Dr David Knight) who have provided discussion and support. In addition, Mike Bishop, Dr Dave Barrett and John Walker for putting alluvial archaeology on the agenda in the East Midlands, and to English Heritage, who together with Derbyshire and Nottinghamshire County Councils provided financial support for the Trent Valley Survey. MGM would like to thank NERC, Historic Scotland, English Heritage, the Leverhulme Trust and the Universities of Aberystwyth, Leeds and Newcastle-upon-Tyne for supporting his research into Holocene fluvial environments, and Professor John Lewin, Dr Dave Passmore and Dr Jamie Woodward for valued collaboration. Dr Roger Martlew and the two anonymous referees are thanked for their comments on a draft of this paper.

TABLE 4 (opposite). *Procedure for establishing a geomorphic and stratigraphic framework for assessing archaeological potential in river valleys.*

References

ALLEN, T., G. HEY & D. MILES. 1997. A line of time: approaches to archaeology in the Upper and Middle Thames Valley, England, *World Archaeology* 29: 114–29.

BELL, M. & H. NEUMANN. 1997. Prehistoric intertidal archaeology and environments in the Severn Estuary, Wales, *World Archaeology* 29: 95–113.

BERENDSEN, H.J.A. 1993. Holocene fluvial geomorphology of the floodplain of the rivers Rhine and Meuse in the Netherlands, in I. Douglas & J. Hagedorn (ed.), *Geomorphology and Geoecology, Fluvial Geomorphology*: 97–107. *Zeitschrift fur Geomorphologie* supplement 85.

BETTIS, E.A. 1995. *Archaeological geology of the Archaic Period in North America*. Boulder (CO): Geological Society of America. Special paper 297.

BETTIS, E.A. & HAJIC, E.R. 1995. Landscape development and the location of evidence of Archaic cultures in the Upper Midwest, in E.A. Bettis (ed.), *Archaeological geology of the Archaic Period in North America*: 87–113. Boulder (CO): Geological Society of America. Special paper 297.

BRADLEY, R. 1990. *The passage of arms: an archaeological analysis of prehistoric hoards and votive deposits*. Cambridge: Cambridge University Press.

BRAZIER, V.G. WHITTINGTON & C.K. BALLANTYNE. 1988. Holocene debris cone evolution in Glen Etive, Western Grampian Highlands, Scotland, *Earth Surface Processes and Landforms* 13: 525–31.

BROWN, A.G. 1987. Holocene floodplain sedimentation and channel response of the lower Severn, United Kingdom, *Zeitschrift fur Geomorphologie* 31: 293–310.

1997. *Alluvial geoarchaeology. Floodplain archaeology and environmental change*. Cambridge: Cambridge University Press.

BROWN, A.G. & M. KEOUGH. 1992a. Holocene floodplain metamorphosis in the Midlands, United Kingdom, *Geomorphology* 4: 433–45.

1992b. Palaeochannels, palaeo–landsurfaces and three dimensional reconstruction of floodplain environmental change, in P.A. Carling & G.E. Petts (ed.), *Lowland floodplain rivers: Geomorphological perspectives*: 185–202. Chichester: Wiley.

BROWN, A.G., M. KEOUGH & R.J. RICE. 1994. Floodplain evolution in the East Midlands, United Kingdom: the Lateglacial and Flandrian alluvial record from the Soar and Nene valleys, *Philosophical Transactions of the Royal Society of London* A348: 261–93.

BURRIN, P.J. & R.G. SCAIFE. 1984. Aspects of Holocene valley sedimentation and floodplain development in Southern England, *Proceedings of the Geologists Association* 95: 81–96.

CARDWELL, P. 1995. Excavation at the hospital of St Giles by Brompton Bridge, North Yorkshire, *Archaeological Journal* 152: 109–245.

CARDWELL, P. & G. SPEED. 1996. Prehistoric occupation at St. Giles by Brompton Bridge, North Yorkshire, *Durham Archaeological Journal* 12: 27–40.

CHURCH, M. & J.M. RYDER. 1972. Paraglacial sedimentation: A consideration of fluvial processes conditioned by glaciation, *Geological Society of America Bulletin* 83: 3059–72.

COLES, B. & J.M. COLES. 1986. *Sweet Track to Glastonbury. The Somerset Levels in Prehistory*. London: Thames & Hudson.

COLES, J.M. 1978. Man and landscape in the Somerset Levels, in S. Limbrey & J.G. Evans (ed.), *The effect of man on the landscape: the Lowland Zone*: 86–9. London: Council for British Archaeology. Research report 21.

DARVILL, T. & A.K. FULTON. 1998. *MARS: The Monuments at Risk Survey in England 1995. Main Report*. Bournemouth & London: Bournemouth University & English Heritage.

DINNIN, M. 1997. Holocene beetle assemblages from the Lower Trent floodplain at Bole Ings, Nottinghamshire, UK, in A.C. Ashworth, P.C. Buckland & J.P. Sadler (ed.), *Studies in Quaternary Entomology. An inordinate fondness for insects*: 83–104. London: Quaternary Research Association. Quaternary Proceedings 5.

EVANS, J.G. 1991. River valley bottoms and archaeology in the Holocene, in B. Coles (ed.), *The wetland revolution in prehistory*: 47–53. London: Prehistoric Society. WARP occasional paper 6.

FRENCH, C.A.I., M.G. MACKLIN & D.G. PASSMORE. 1992. Archaeology and palaeochannels in the Lower Welland and Nene valleys: alluvial archaeology at the fen-edge, Eastern England, in Needham & Macklin (ed.): 169–76.

GAUNT, G.D. 1981. Quaternary history of the southern part of the Vale of York, in J. Neale & J. Flenley (ed.), *The Quaternary in Britain: Essays, Reviews and Original Work on the Quaternary*: 82–97. Oxford: Pergamon Press.

GIBSON, A. 1994. Excavations at the Sarn-y-bryn-caled cursus complex, Welshpool, Powys, and the timber circles of Great Britain and Ireland, *Proceedings of the Prehistoric Society* 60: 143–223.

HAGEMAN, B.P. 1969. Development of the western part of the Netherlands during the Holocene, *Geol. Mijnbouw* 48: 373–88.

HALL, D. 1987. The Fenland Project, Number 2: Fenland Landscapes and Settlement between Peterborough and March, *East Anglian Archaeology* Report 35.

HALL, D., C. EVANS, I. HODDER & F. PRYOR. 1987. The Fenlands of East Anglia, England: Survey and Excavation, in J.M. Coles & A.J. Lawson (ed.), *European wetlands in prehistory*: 169–202. Oxford: Clarendon Press.

HARVEY, A.M., F. OLDFIELD, A.F. BARON & G.W. PEARSON. 1981. Dating of post-glacial landforms in the central Howgills, *Earth Surface Processes & Landforms* 6: 401–12.

HARVEY, A.M. & W.H. RENWICK. 1987. Holocene alluvial fan and terrace formation in the Bowland Fells, Northwest England, *Earth Surface Processes and Landforms* 12: 249–57.

HAYES, P.P. & T.W. LANE. 1992. The Fenland Project Number 5: Lincolnshire Survey, The South-West Fens, *East Anglian Archaeology* Report 55.

HOBLEY, B. 1981. The London waterfront — the exception or the rule, in G. Milne & B. Hobley. (ed.), *Waterfront archaeology in Britain and northern Europe*: 1–9. London: Council for British Archaeology. Research report 41.

HOOKE, J.M., A.M. HARVEY, S.Y. MILLER & C.E. REDMOND. 1990. The chronology and stratigraphy of the alluvial terraces of the River Dane valley, Cheshire, NW England, *Earth Surface Processes and Landforms* 15: 717–37.

HOWARD, A.J., D. GARTON, J. HILLAM, M. PEARCE & D.N. SMITH. 1999. Middle to Late Holocene environments in the Middle to Lower Trent Valley, in A.G. Brown & T.M. Quine (ed.), *Fluvial processes and environmental change*: 165–78. Chichester: Wiley.

HOWARD-DAVIS, C. 1996. Seeing the sites: survey and excavation on the Anglezarke Uplands, Lancashire, *Proceedings of the Prehistoric Society* 61: 133–66.

JING, Z., G. RAPP & T. GAO. 1997. Geoarchaeological aids in the investigation of early Shang civilisation on the floodplain of the lower Yellow River, China, *World Archaeology* 29: 36–50.

JOYCE, A.A. & R.G. MUELLER. 1997. Prehispanic human ecology of the Rio Verde drainage basin, Mexico, *World Archaeology* 29: 75–94.

LANE, T.W. 1993. The Fenland Project Number 8: Lincolnshire Survey, The Northern Fen-Edge, *East Anglian Archaeology* Report 66.

LEOPOLD, L.B. & M.G. WOLMAN. 1957. *River channel patterns — braided, meandering and straight*. U.S. Geological Survey. Professional paper 282B.

LEOPOLD, L.B, M.G. WOLMAN & J.P. MILLER. 1964. Fluvial processes in geomorphology. San Francisco (CA): W.H. Freeman.

LEWIN, J. 1981. *British rivers*. London: George Allen & Unwin.

1992. Alluvial sedimentation style and archaeological sites: the Lower Vyrnwy, Wales, in Needham & Macklin (ed.): 103–10.

LONG, D.J., F.M. CHAMBERS & J. BARNATT. 1998. The palaeoenvironment and the vegetation history of a Later Prehistoric Field System at Stoke Flat on the Gritstone Uplands of the Peak District, *Journal of Archaeological Science* 25: 505–19.

MACKLIN, M.G. 1997. Fluvial geomorphology of North-east England, in K.J. Gregory (ed.) *Fluvial geomorphology of Great Britain*: 202–38. London: Chapman & Hall.

1999. Holocene river environments in prehistoric Britain: human interaction and impact, *Journal of Quaternary Science (Quaternary Proceedings 7)*.

MACKLIN, M.G. & J. LEWIN. 1986. Terraced fills of Pleistocene and Holocene age in the Rheidol Valley, Wales, *Journal of Quaternary Science* 1: 21–34.

1989. Sediment transfer and transformation of an alluvial valley floor: the river South Tyne, Northumbria, UK, *Earth Surface Processes and Landforms* 14: 233–46.

1993. Holocene river alluviation in Britain, in I. Douglas & J. Hagedorn. (ed.), *Geomorphology and Geoecology, Fluvial Geomorphology*: 109–22. *Zeitschrift fur Geomorphologie* supplement 85.

MACKLIN, M.G. & S. NEEDHAM. 1992. Studies in British alluvial archaeology: potential and prospect, in Needham & Macklin (ed.): 9–23.

MACKLIN, M.G., D.G. PASSMORE, A.C. STEVENSON, D.C. COWLEY, D.N. EDWARDS & C.F. O'BRIEN. 1991. Holocene alluviation and land-use change on Callaly Moor, Northumberland, England, *Journal of Quaternary Science* 6: 225–32.

MACKLIN, M.G., D.G. PASSMORE & B.T. RUMSBY. 1992a. Climatic and cultural signals in Holocene alluvial sequences: the Tyne basin, northern England, in Needham & Macklin (ed.): 123–39.

MACKLIN, M.G., B.T. RUMSBY & T. HEAP. 1992b. Flood alluviation and entrenchment: Holocene valley floor development and transformation in the British uplands, *Geological Society of America Bulletin* 104: 631–43.

MACKLIN, M.G., D.G. PASSMORE, D.C. COWLEY, T.C. STEVENSON & C.F. O'BRIEN. 1992c. Geoarchaeological enhancement of river valley archaeology in North East England, in P. Spoerry. (ed.) *Geoprospection in the archaeological landscape*: 43–58. Oxford: Oxbow. Monograph 18.

MARTIN-CONSUEGRA, E., N. CHISVERT, L. CÀCERES & J.L. UBERA. 1998. Archaeological, palynological and geological contributions to landscape reconstruction in the alluvial plain of the Guadalquivir River at San Bernardo, Sevilla (Spain), *Journal of Archaeological Science* 25, 521–32.

MCEWEN, L.J. & A. WERRITTY. 1988. The hydrological and long-term geomorphic significance of a flash flood in the Cairngorm Mountains, Scotland, *Catena* 15: 361–77.

MEDDENS, F.M. 1996. Sites from the Thames estuary wetlands, and their Bronze Age use, *Antiquity* 70: 325–34.

MERRETT, S.P. & M.G. MACKLIN. 1999. Historic river response to extreme flooding in the Yorkshire Dales, Northern England, in A.G. Brown & T.M. Quine (ed.), *Fluvial processes and environmental change*: 345–60. Chichester: Wiley.

NANSON, G.C. & J.C. CROKE. 1992. A genetic classification of floodplains, *Geomorphology* 4: 459–86.

NAYLING, N. & A. CASELDINE. 1997. Excavations at Caldicot, Gwent: Bronze Age palaeochannels in the Lower Nedern Valley. London: Council for British Archaeology. Research report 108.

NEEDHAM, S.P. 1991. *Excavation and salvage at Runnymede Bridge 1978: The Late Bronze Age waterfront site*. London: British Museum Press.

1992. Holocene alluviation and interstratified settlement evidence in the Thames Valley at Runnymede Bridge, in Needham & Macklin (ed.): 249–60.

NEEDHAM, S. & M.G. MACKLIN (ed.). 1992. *Alluvial archaeology in Britain*. Oxford: Oxbow. Monograph 27.

NEWSON, M.D. & M.G. MACKLIN. 1990. The geomorphologically effective flood and vertical instability in river channels: a feedback mechanism in the flood series for gravel-bed rivers, in W.R. White (ed.), *International Conference on River Flood Hydraulics*: 123–41. Chichester: Wiley.

PARKER-PEARSON, M. & R.E. SYDES. 1997. The Iron Age enclosures and prehistoric landscape of Sutton Common, South Yorkshire, *Proceedings of the Prehistoric Society* 63: 221–59.

PASSMORE, D.G. & M.G. MACKLIN. 1997. Geoarchaeology of the Tyne Basin: Holocene River Valley Environments and the Archaeological Record, in C. Tolan-Smith (ed.), *Landscape archaeology in Tynedale*: 11–27. Newcastle: University of Newcastle upon Tyne, Tyne Solway Ancient and Historic Landscapes Research Programme. Monograph 1.

PASSMORE, D.G., M.G. MACKLIN, P.A. BREWER, J. LEWIN, B.T. RUMSBY & M.D. NEWSON. 1993. Variability of late Holocene braiding in Britain, in J.L. Best & C.S. Bristow (ed.), *Braided rivers*: 205–29. Bath: Geological Society. Special publication 75.

POLLARD, J. 1996. Iron Age riverside pit alignments at St Ives, Cambridgeshire, *Proceedings of the Prehistoric Society* 62: 93–115.

PRYOR, F., C. FRENCH, D. CROWTHER, D. GURNEY, G. SIMPSON & M. TAYLOR. 1985. The Fenland Project No. 1: Archaeology and Environment in the Lower Welland Valley Volume 1, *East Anglian Archaeology* Report 27(1).

PRYOR, F.M.M., C.A.I. FRENCH & M. TAYLOR. 1986. Flag Fen, Fengate, Peterborough I: discovery, reconnaissance and initial excavations (1982–85), *Proceedings of the Prehistoric Society* 52: 1–24.

RICHARDS, K.S., N.R. PETERS, M.S.E. ROBERTSON-RINTOUL & V.R. SWITSUR. 1987. Recent valley sediments in the North York Moors: Evidence and Interpretation, in V. Gardiner (ed.), *International Geomorphology* Part 1: 869–883. Chichester: Wiley.

RIPPON, S. 1996. *Gwent Levels: The evolution of a wetland landscape.* London: Council for British Archaeology. Research report 105.

ROBERTSON-RINTOUL, M.S.E. 1986. A quantitative soil-stratigraphic approach to the correlation and dating of post-glacial river terraces in Glen Feshie, western Cairngorms, *Earth Surface Processes and Landforms* 11: 605–17.

ROBINSON, M.A. 1978. A comparison between the effects of man on the environment of the first gravel terrace and floodplain of the Upper Thames Valley during the Iron Age and Roman periods, in S. Limbrey & J.G. Evans (ed.), *The effect of man on the landscape: the lowland zone*: 35–43. London: Council for British Archaeology. Research report 21.

1992. Environment, archaeology and alluvium on the river gravels of the South Midlands, in Needham & Macklin (ed.): 197–208.

ROBINSON, M.A. & G.H. LAMBRICK. 1984. Holocene alluviation and hydrology in the Upper Thames Basin, *Nature* 308: 809–14.

ROSE, J., C. TURNER, G.R. COOPE & M.D. BRYAN. 1980. Channel changes in a lowland river catchment over the last 13,000 years, in R.A. Cullingford, D.A. Davidson & J. Lewin. (ed.), *Timescales in Geomorphology*: 159–76. Chichester: Wiley.

RUMSBY, B.T. & M.G. MACKLIN. 1996. River response to the last Neoglacial cycle (the 'Little Ice Age') in northern, western and central Europe, in J. Branson, A.G. Brown & K.J. Gregory (ed.), *Global continental changes: the context of palaeohydrology*: 217–33. Bath: Geological Society. Special publication 115.

SALISBURY, C.R., P.J. WHITLEY, C.D. LITTON & J.L. FOX. 1984. Flandrian courses of the River Trent at Colwick, Nottingham, *Mercian Geologist* 9: 189–207.

SEALE, R.S. 1979. Ancient courses of the Great and Little Ouse in Fenland, *Proceedings of the Cambridgeshire Antiquarian Society* 69: 1–19.

SMITH, D.G. & N.D. SMITH. 1983. Sedimentation in anastomosed river systems: Examples from alluvial valleys near Banff, Alberta, *Journal of Sedimentary Petrology* 50: 157–64.

TAYLOR, M.P. & J. LEWIN. 1996. River behaviour and Holocene alluviation: The River Severn at Welshpool, Mid-Wales, U.K., *Earth Surface Processes and Landforms* 21: 77–91.

TAYLOR, M.P. & M.G. MACKLIN. 1997. Holocene alluvial sedimentation and valley floor development: the River Swale, Catterick, North Yorkshire, UK, *Proceedings of the Yorkshire Geological Society* 51: 317–27.

THOMAS, C. & J. RACKHAM. 1996. Bramcote Green, Bermondsey: a Bronze Age trackway and palaeo-environmental sequence, *Proceedings of the Prehistoric Society* 61: 221–53.

THOMAS, C., M. ROBINSON, J. BARRETT & B. WILSON. 1986. A Late Bronze Age riverside settlement at Wallingford, Oxfordshire, *Archaeological Journal* 143: 174–200.

TIPPING, R. 1994. Fluvial chronology and valley floor evolution of the Upper Bowmont Valley, Borders Region, Scotland, *Earth Surfaces Processes and Landforms* 19: 641–57.

1995a. Holocene landscape change at Carn Dubh, near Pitlochry, Perthshire, Scotland, *Journal of Quaternary Science* 10: 59–75.

1995b. Holocene evolution of a lowland Scottish landscape: Kirkpatrick Fleming. Part III, fluvial history, *The Holocene* 5: 184–95.

1995c. Holocene evolution of a lowland Scottish landscape: Kirkpatrick Fleming. Part I, peat and pollen-stratigraphic evidence for raised moss development and climatic change, *The Holocene* 5: 69–81.

1995d. Holocene evolution of a lowland Scottish landscape: Kirkpatrick Fleming. Part II, regional vegetation and land-use change, *The Holocene* 5: 83–96.

TIPPING, R. & S.P. HALLIDAY. 1994. The age of alluvial fan deposition at a site in the Southern Uplands of Scotland, *Earth Surfaces Processes and Landforms* 19: 333–48.

VAN DE NOORT, R. & S. ELLIS. 1997. *Wetland Heritage of the Humberhead Levels. An Archaeological Survey.* London: English Heritage.

1998. *Wetland Heritage of the Ancholme and Lower Trent Valleys. An Archaeological Survey.* London: English Heritage.

WALKER, M.J.C., M. BELL, A.E. CASELDINE, N.G. CAMERON, K.L. HUNTER, J.H. JAMES, S. JOHNSON & D.N. SMITH. 1998. Palaeoecological investigations of Middle & Late Flandrian buried peats on the Caldicot Levels, Severn Estuary, Wales, *Proceedings of the Geologists Association* 109: 51–78.

WHIMSTER, R. 1989. *The emerging past. Air photography and the buried landscape.* London: RCHME.

WHITE, R.F. 1998. The lead industry in the Yorkshire Dales, in A.J. Howard & M.G. Macklin (ed.), *The Quaternary of the eastern Yorkshire Dales. Field Guide*: 55–66. London: Quaternary Research Association.

WILKINSON, T.J., P. MURPHY, S. JUGGINS & K. MANSON. 1988. Wetland development and human activity in Essex estuaries during the Holocene transgression, in P. Murphy & C. French (ed.), *The exploitation of wetlands*: 213–38. Oxford: British Archaeological Reports. British series 186.

WOODFIELD, C. & C. JOHNSON. 1989. A Roman site at Stanton Low, on the Great Ouse, Buckinghamshire, *Archaeological Journal* 146: 135–278.

6 Industrial landscapes

Landscape is normally associated with countryside. It is scenery. Industrial archaeology started as a descriptive branch of archaeology, sheltering in the shadow of history and focusing on small-scale site-based or technological analyses (Palmer & Neaverson 1998). More recently, industrial archaeology has made immense theoretical strides, in particular through a focus on the study of landscapes and townscapes (Palmer & Neaverson 1998: 16–42). The same landscape approach is also now being applied to prehistoric phases of industrial production (Knapp 1998: 16–17). In the United Kingdom, the most comprehensive studies of a modern industrial landscape have been undertaken at the iconic origin of industrialization: Ironbridge Gorge (Alfrey & Clark 1993). The whole conception of this study is essentially archaeological since it starts with the material remains and then proceeds to the historical analysis. Too frequently, material remains in historical periods have been a footnote to documentary sources. A landscape approach contributes to this reworking of the historical past in a way that archival historians have not always perceived to be important.

The first article reprinted here (Clark 1987) reported on the survey of Ironbridge before full publication (Alfrey & Clark 1993). The rhetorical component of the article — the assertion of the isolated status of industrial archaeology epitomized by a contextless and landscape-poor approach of industrial archaeology — was immediately critiqued as doing an injustice to the rich study of context by industrial archaeologists (Palmer & Neaverson 1987). Clark replied that it was effectively the diachronic landscape that was missing from industrial archaeology. The remainder of Clark's article addresses the Ironbridge Gorge as landscape, as a system where sufficient scale is provided to understand supply and transport. In terms of methodology, a specific survey approach undertaken by plots of land was advocated.

The second reprinted article (Morris 1994) is a complementary approach to that of Clark (1987). Whereas Clark covered industrialization in a relatively concentrated area, Morris investigated the potentially more transitory buildings in the wider landscape, temporarily installed to construct linkage between the nodes of centralized industrial production. Railway and canal construction necessitated the housing of the workforce in the landscape, and archaeological work is now reconstructing the nature of such logistics, which are nowhere preserved in documentary records. Furthermore, this history of logistics is presented in a developmental perspective, where organization was at first devolved to the local industrial enterprise, and in time subject to increasing intervention from the state. Archaeology is powerful in the understanding of the lifestyle of marginal groups — 'navvies' — who are, in this case, fundamental to the whole industrial process.

Trouble at t'mill:
industrial archaeology in the 1980s
by **C.M. CLARK**

ANTIQUITY 61 (232), 1987

INDUSTRIAL ARCHAEOLOGY has often been the butt of savage criticism by geographers, archaeologists, economic and architectural historians. Even its practitioners have argued endlessly over the definition and proper field of enquiry of the subject. But there are signs of change. The techniques of traditional and landscape archaeology are bringing to the discipline a variety of new approaches, designed to put what has often just been technical history into a wider perspective.

Hitherto the study of industrial remains has been largely undertaken by non-archaeologists, with specialist skills in technical history. Engineers, metallurgists and geologists were among those in the forefront of the field. They founded the Newcomen Society in 1919, the Historical Metallurgy Group in 1962, and today continue a long and honourable tradition of studying the evolution of technology both practically and through surviving documentary evidence.

Some of these studies moved away from machines to looking at the landscape around them. Jespersen's pioneering study of the lades which supplied water to the Great Laxey wheel in the Isle of Man (1954) did much to explain many of the engineering anomalies of the site. This, the largest water wheel in Britain, only ever worked at a capacity of 60 h.p.; its water supply had been diverted elsewhere.

But by concentrating upon technical evolution, a concern for 'firsts' crept into the subject, recognizing innovation but often ignoring utilization. This is reflected in the official definition of an industrial monument — used as a means of identifying buildings for listing and scheduling — as something which 'illustrates or is significantly connected with the beginnings and evolution of industrial or technological process' (Falconer 1981). The literature is scattered with studies of the first beam engines, the first iron bridge, the first locomotive. The significance of a relic becomes suddenly devalued if an earlier example is unearthed, as happened when an iron bridge in Yorkshire was found to be earlier than the famous example in Shropshire — built in 1779 — which had been thought to be the earliest cast iron bridge in the world (Linsley 1980).

A second type of industrial archaeology developed in the 1950s through the efforts of amateur groups, involved in university extra-mural teaching and the Workers Educational Association. Practical fieldwork experience was needed, and tutors found an ideal source in local industrial remains. The term 'industrial archaeology' was used for these activities by one extra-mural tutor, Michael Rix, in 1955 (Rix 1967: 5). But the claim to have invented the subject was resented by technical historians, who saw nothing new (Hudson 1979: 1). Nonetheless the term caught on, a journal was founded, and a flood of books written. The movement coincided with what has been seen as a wave of nostalgia for Britain's industrial traditions in the face of burgeoning new towns (Cossons 1975: 30). Today the decline of Britain's world industrial supremacy gives added poignancy to the subject.

Industrial archaeology: aims and definitions

The 1960s were a period of unprecedented destruction of industrial remains. The demolition of the Euston Arch, the neoclassical portico of the London and North Western Railway's terminus, in 1962 was a watershed, and amateur enthusiasm was now kindled. The Council for British Archaeology set up a working party to co-ordinate the recording efforts initiated by growing numbers of local societies. Groups were sent out with cameras and pro-forma cards to record what was left. Eventually over 30,000 cards were filled in on a site-by-site basis for the National Register of Industrial Monuments, some of which were later used by the Ministry of Works (later the Department of the Environment) for listing and scheduling decisions. But this uncritical enthusiasm, which espoused a philosophy of 'record it, because it is there', led to serious shortcomings. The secretary of the working party himself admitted the very poor quality of the result (Falconer 1981: 2). This may not have been the fault of the amateur, but simply that complex sites cannot be described in terms of the same few questions.

More serious was the absence of an academic framework. Archaeology is little more than antiquarianism when there is no framework — whether behavioral, economic or social — on which to hang the evidence. Throughout the 1960s industrial antiquarianism seems to have been the principal activity of many industrial archaeologists; not a discipline, but an 'agreeable hobby' (Hudson 1963: 34).

The most pertinent illustration of the absence of a framework lies in the argument concerning the meaning of the very term 'industrial archaeology', a term almost unique to Britain. In Australia and America 'historical archaeology' is more generally used. Rix's 1955 definition was, 'recording, preserving in selected cases and interpreting the sites and structures of early industrial activity, particularly the monuments of the Industrial Revolution'. Other early practitioners concurred that the core of the subject was the study of the industrial remains of the Industrial Revolution in Britain, that is the 18th and 19th centuries (Buchanan 1972: 20–21; Rix 1967: 5). The historians of the 'pre-industrial archaeology era' objected to this narrow definition, and proposed the study of industry of all periods from the Neolithic to the Victorian, pushing 'back the starting point of industrial archaeology to the appearance of organized industry with special techniques' (Raistrick 1972: 9). Needless to say, when industry or craft activity are studied in isolation, divorced from the social context, naïve cultural generalizations can occur. Recent attempts, though technically very important, do not apply the same high standards to the interpretation of culture and cannot be called archaeology (Raistrick 1972: 99; Tylecote 1986: 10).

The thematic approach is based on the principle that practitioners of industrial archaeology rely on a 'special range of disciplines, which overlap with conventional archaeology, but which are not and cannot be identical with them' (Hudson 1979: 12). W.G. Hoskins, the founder of English landscape history, was clearly intimidated by the grease and engine-bearings of industrial archaeology, and suggested that it was, 'easier . . . for an engineer to pick up his history . . . than for an historian to acquire a sound knowledge of technology, and without this he cannot hope to write Industrial Archaeology as it needs to be written' (Hoskins 1967: 12). This disregard of industrial archaeology has been continued by his successors in landscape studies (Aston 1985). The result of this technical mystique is an isolation from the wider disciplines of archaeology or economic history. Excavation techniques are rudimentary and the concept of stratigraphy is rare. Rather than asking broad analytical questions there has been a tendency to produce a very specialist form of history.

An alternative definition, put forward by industrial archaeologist and museum director Neil Cossons, considers industrial archaeology to be a period rather than a thematic study (Cossons 1975: 16). The period in question is that of the Industrial Revolution and its aftermath, and the study of it is a logical follow-on from medieval and post-medieval archaeology. The term 'industrial' is used because industry was the prime mover of this period, just as Romans were in the Britain of AD 43 to 410. Of course, as with other archaeological periods, ante- and post-cedents must be carefully considered. Period definition allows a much wider field of study: houses as well as factories, footpaths as well as railways, rural as well as urban landscapes. By placing the physical evidence for industrialization within its wider landscape, and its social context, form of serious contribution might be made at last to economic and social history. This definition placed the subject firmly within the canons of more traditional archaeology.

Concern was voiced by the founding fathers that a period definition would exclude the amateurs, who remain the main practitioners: 'industrial archaeology belongs to them, just as much as it does to the economic historians' (Hudson 1979: 6). *Industrial Archaeology Review*, the leading journal, continues to reflect the dedication to plant rather than context — accounts of lime kilns without mention of the limestone quarries which supplied them (Bick 1984), water wheels without their water systems (Moore 1984). But there is a move towards the study of regions (Cleere & Crossley 1986), settlements (Jones 1982), social conditions (Trinder & Cox 1980) and archaeology (Hayman 1986). Even the technically excellent work of the Scottish Royal Commission tends to be oriented towards monument rather than context (Hay & Stell 1986).

Industry and its context as a system

One way of examining the context of industry is to look at the way in which it operates as a system. From the supply of raw materials through to the exploitation of a market, an industry is part of an operating system with many ramifications. Innovation cannot take place in the absence of capital, or expansion without new supplies of raw materials. However, the documentary evidence gives an often incomplete picture of the whole operation. The industrial archaeologist is in a unique position to combine field evidence, technical history and a critical view of the documentation. Such an approach requires the intensive study of a limited area, considering all its aspects, archaeological and architectural, within the framework of a landscape. Labour, capital, raw materials, transport, technology, ownership and power all had an impact upon the landscape, and provide the context of industrialization. Documentary history alone can only study some of these issues.

The Nuffield survey of the Ironbridge Gorge

In 1985 a comprehensive survey was commissioned by the Nuffield Foundation of the archaeology and architecture of the Ironbridge Gorge. The aim was to study the way in which industry operated in the landscape as a system. Three parishes, Benthall, Broseley and Madeley, were chosen as an area for intensive research along the slopes of the Gorge (FIGURE 1).

The Ironbridge Gorge is a small area of E Shropshire, a county located in the English West Midlands, which made a a major contribution to the extraordinary growth of industry during the opening, 18th-century phase of the British Industrial Revolution (Trinder 1981). Documentary evidence and extensive field remains make the Gorge an ideal place in which to test various methodologies in industrial archaeology. The River Severn, wind-

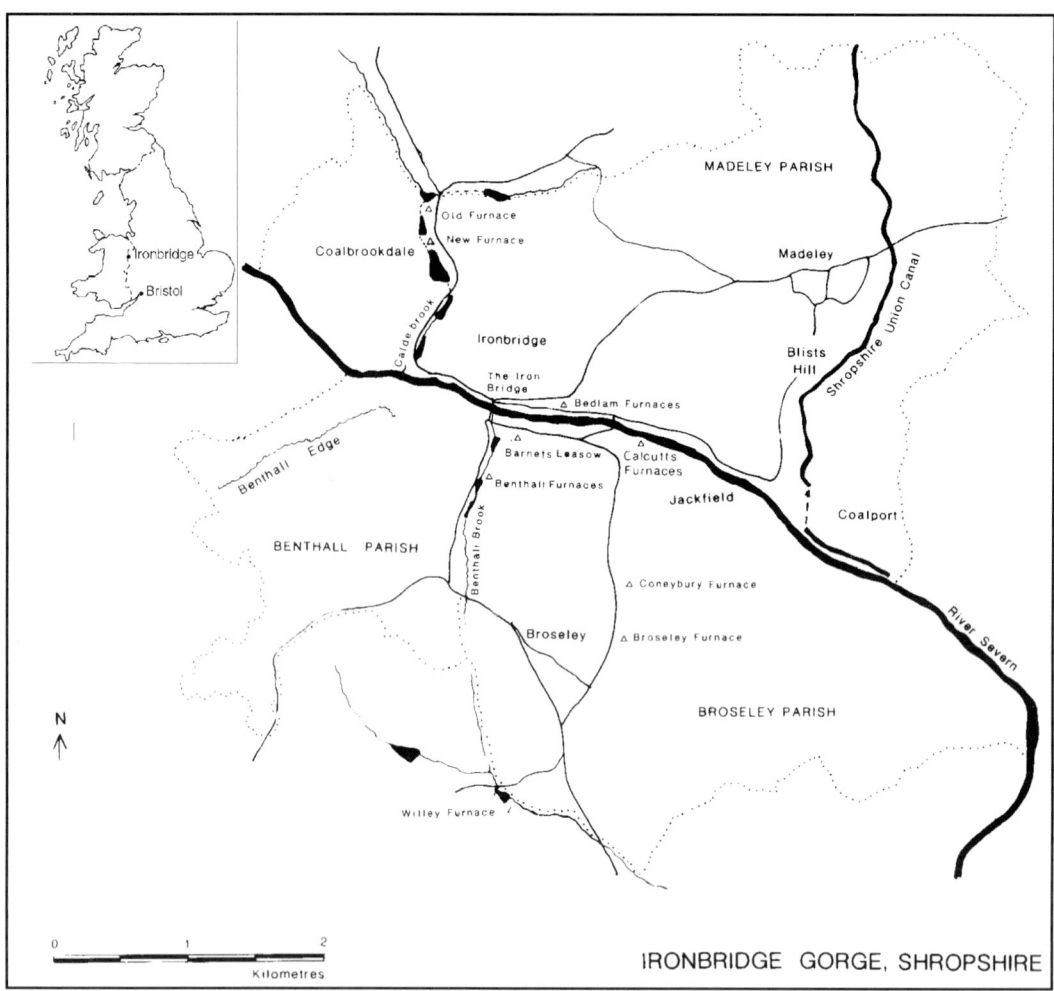

FIGURE 1. *Map of Ironbridge Gorge, Shropshire.*

ing S through the Midlands on its way to Bristol, has cut a gorge some 100 m deep and 4 km long, crossed by the Iron Bridge (FIGURE 2). A ridge of Silurian limestone runs diagonally across the gorge, and lapping up against it are the Carboniferous Coal Measures, with their productive coals, fire-clays and ironstones. It was these natural resources — a river transport network providing access to markets, water power and a local supply of minerals — which made the Ironbridge Gorge such an attractive location for early industry.

On one such stream — the Caldebrook — Abraham Darby first succeeded in smelting iron using coke instead of charcoal in 1709. This technique eventually ended the dependence of the iron industry upon wood supplies, which had previously restricted its development to areas such the Weald (Cleere & Crossley 1986). Another important innovation, patented by Darby, was the sand-casting of hollow-ware vessels using the iron produced by this process (Mott 1957).

By the 1750s, Shropshire was the largest producer of iron in Great Britain (Trinder 1981: 21), and in 1800 the Gorge, described by one contemporary traveller as 'the most extraordinary district in the world' (Trinder 1977), contained at least 12 iron furnaces, the largest concentration in Britain. The rapid success of the iron industry led to further innovation and industrialization. The Coalbrookdale company was involved in the early development of atmospheric and steam engines, iron railways, locomotives, iron-framed buildings, bridges and canal aqueducts (FIGURE 3). Local industries expanded during this period. Both pottery-making at Jackfield and the 16th-century clay-pipe industry at Broseley were transformed from individual activities to organized concerns. Entrepreneurs promoted a tar-processing industry, lead-smelting, engineering works, brick-making, glass-making, and an attempt to establish a chemical factory.

But high transport costs and the exhaustion of raw materials resulted in the Gorge's relative decline during the 19th century, while industry expanded in the rest of the country (Trinder 1981: 240). The Gorge continued to make specialist products — ornate iron castings, art pottery and decorative tiles — but could no longer compete in the larger mass-produced markets. Today the area is almost rural again. The artisan settlements of Ironbridge, Coalbrookdale and Broseley remain largely unchanged and their industrial buildings deserted. This preservation of the industrial landscape has enabled a group of museums, using the Iron Bridge as its symbol, to present the industries and way of life of the last two centuries (Cossons 1979).

Various explanations have been put forward for the extraordinary expansion of the Shropshire iron industry in the 18th century. Innovation, a fortuitous supply of suitable coking coal, an ideal location for both transport and raw materials, and the entrepreneurial abilities of the iron-founders themselves, have all been suggested. In turn the equally rapid decline of the area has been attributed to raw material shortages, the distance from the new communication systems and competition from other areas. Whilst each of these factors may have been important, archaeology has shown a very much

FIGURE 2. *A view of the Cast Iron Bridge near Coalbrookdale, by William Ellis after Michael Angelo Rooker, 1780 , showing Benthall Edge in background). (British Library.)*

FIGURE 3. *Coalbrookdale from Paradise Fields. Drawn by J.C.Bayliss, engraved by W. Bangham, c. 1856. (Ironbridge Gorge Museums Trust.)*

more complex situation at a local level. Innovation at Coalbrookdale was limited by an old-fashioned water system. Shortage of raw materials were as much a product of the pattern of ownership as exhaustion of supply. Despite the entrepreneurs, the river Severn was never made easily navigable, and river transport remained seasonal.

Economic historians have remained sceptical of the 'Ironbridge' phenomenon. Underlying this is a distrust of the technological determinism which occurs when industrial archaeologists place too much emphasis upon invention. The economic take-off after 1750 is more often seen in terms of national conditions of economy and society (Hobsbawn 1969: 38), than the discovery of the use of coke in iron-smelting or the design of the Spinning Jenny. It is hardly surprising that economic historians have little time for industrial archaeology.

Survey methods
Archaeology has developed a number of techniques for field survey, mainly based on the principle that the archaeological record is the sum of a definable number of individual sites (Mueller 1975). But it became obvious that a site based methodology, as used by the county Sites and Monuments Records for example, was inappropriate to the Ironbridge Gorge. The sheer complexity of the remains means it is not always possible to define where a site begins or ends, or to untangle its links with other landscape features. The method of landscape historians — investigating the landscape as a single site, often concentrating on single periods of activity, and invariably in a rural context (Taylor 1974) — also seemed inappropriate. The density of remains, the standing buildings, the area covered and the need to include much of what most archaeologists would classify as modern material, made it impossible to adopt a single site approach. Some means had to be found to divide up the landscape for study, without recourse to 'spot' sites.

The Nuffield survey chose to cover the whole landscape by examining individual plots of land. These plots are the units in which land has been described, conveyed and occupied since before the period of the Gorge's transformation. They were first mapped systematically in the enclosure awards and the later Tithe Commutation maps of the 1840s (Kain & Price 1985). The 1:2500 first-edition Ordnance Survey map shows in great detail these plots, still the basis of land division in the United Kingdom. Plot survey enables the study of buildings and archaeology to be integrated, and avoids the need to select buildings on architectural or aesthetic grounds. Housing and settlement are as important to the archaeological landscape as fields or industrial areas. Transport systems can also be adequately described.

This intensive treatment has proved a rapid, flexible and effective method. It forces the recording of the whole landscape, and because it uses defined parcels of land with relevance to the growth of settlement, makes an ideal framework on which to base statutory protection.

Two examples of the value of the wider approach can be suggested from the survey of the Gorge. The first concerns the development and the decline of water-powered iron-working in Coalbrookdale; the second, the supply of raw materials from Benthall Edge, on the south side of the river.

Water power in Coalbrookdale

Coalbrookdale provides a case study demonstrating a systemic approach to the industrial landscape (Clark & Alfrey 1986). One of the valleys leading down to the River Severn, it was the site of Darby's experiments in iron production in 1709 using an existing charcoal blast furnace, constructed around 1638. This 'Old Furnace', taken over by Darby, formed the nucleus of the Coalbrookdale Company. A second furnace was added lower down the valley in 1715. Other activities, on sites leased out to individuals, included forging, machine-tool making and puddling wrought iron. The whole complex was initially powered by water. A series of man-made pools was created to control the flow of water and to provide power (FIGURE 4).

The Coalbrookdale company has been well researched from documents, illustrating the operation of a family company as it grew from a small operation smelting iron and

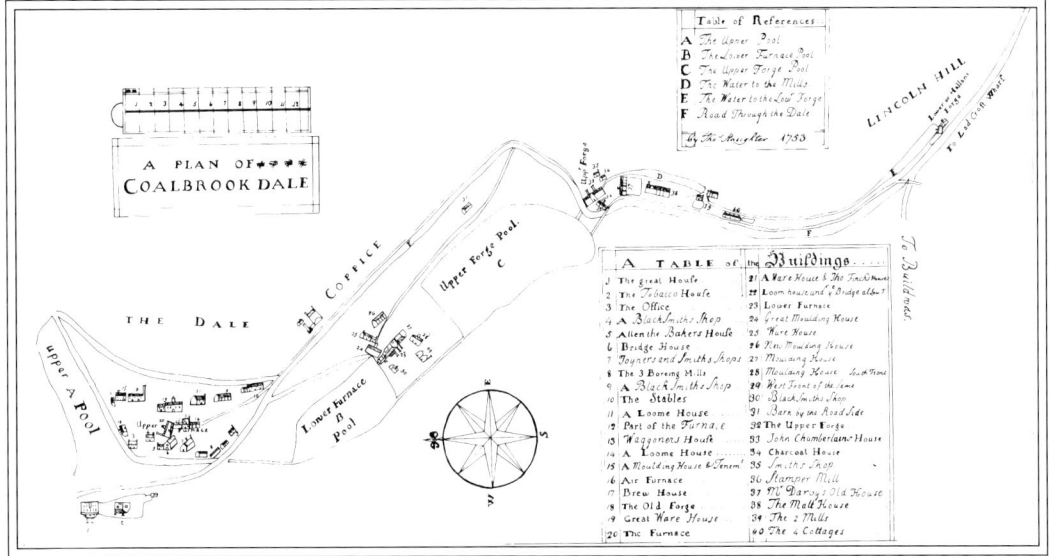

FIGURE 4. *A plan of Coalbrookdale by Thomas Slaughter, 1753 (tracing of original map held by Ironbridge Gorge Museums Trust).*

casting pots — taken by Darby himself to local markets — to a major producer of iron goods sold throughout the world (Raistrick 1953). But the company continued to rely on water-powered equipment well after the invention and use of steam engines, which they themselves helped to pioneer, for blowing the furnaces used for smelting iron. By the early 19th century its furnace operations were so expensive that it ceased smelting. Why did this happen?

Archaeological field survey in the Coalbrookdale valley gives a solution. The system of water power in the valley predates the arrival of Abraham Darby; a water-powered smithy existed in 1536, and iron was smelted before 1645 (VCH 1985: 48). The Upper Furnace pool was driving a large water wheel that provided air blast for the 17th-century 'Old Furnace'. The Upper Forge pool relates to a complex of small industrial buildings dating to the same period, part of which was used for steel-making (Wanklyn 1973). Below this pool the outlet respects Rose cottage — which may also have been an industrial building — dating to 1544. Another 17th-century cottage suggests early occupation at the bottom of the valley, and the dam creating the Lower Forge pool may date to this period.

Thus when Darby took over the Upper Furnace site, he inherited a complex and long-established water power system, dating back to at least the 16th century. His only addition to the system was the Lower Furnace pool in 1715 built to power his new furnace. The expansion of iron production in the 18th century meant there was insufficient water to work the wheel which operated the bellows for the furnaces. This was due to seasonal variation in the flow of the Caldebrook, a small stream with a limited catchment area. During the summer months, the furnaces were often shut down for lack of water (Raistrick 1953: 107). The manager of the works, Richard Ford, installed a 'machine for discharging a part of our water back into ye pool' to get round this problem. A horse-powered lifting pump at the new furnace took water from the Upper Forge pool into the Upper Furnace pool in 1735. This must have proved inadequate, as water shortages continued, and in 1742 the horse gin was replaced by a Newcomen atmospheric engine. Furnace figures show a marked improvement in output (Raistrick 1953: 109).

But even this new engine proved insufficient to recycle water during dry summers, so a drastic scheme was completed in 1781. This involved 'a subterraneous passage about half a mile in length to a pit at the top of the works 120 feet deep' (Anonymous 1801), linked to a new Boulton and Watt engine (called Resolution) of 102·6 h.p., the largest steam engine ever built at that time. This massive steam engine was employed in order to recycle water so as to keep old water-powered equipment in operation. The

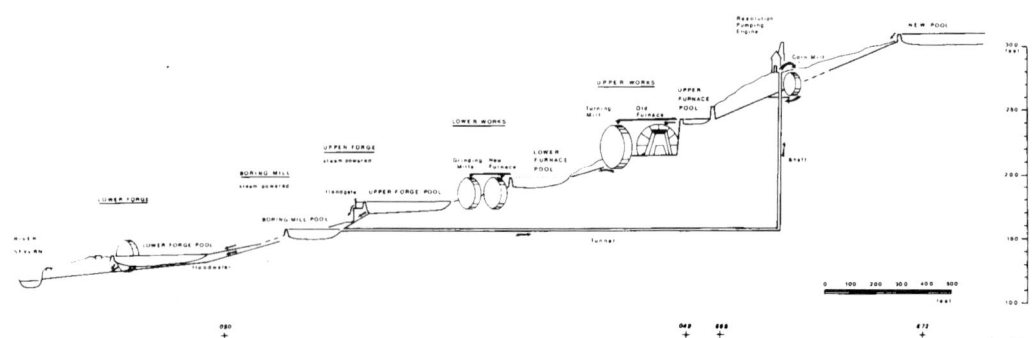

FIGURE 5. *Coalbrookdale — water power 1801–5, schematic section.*

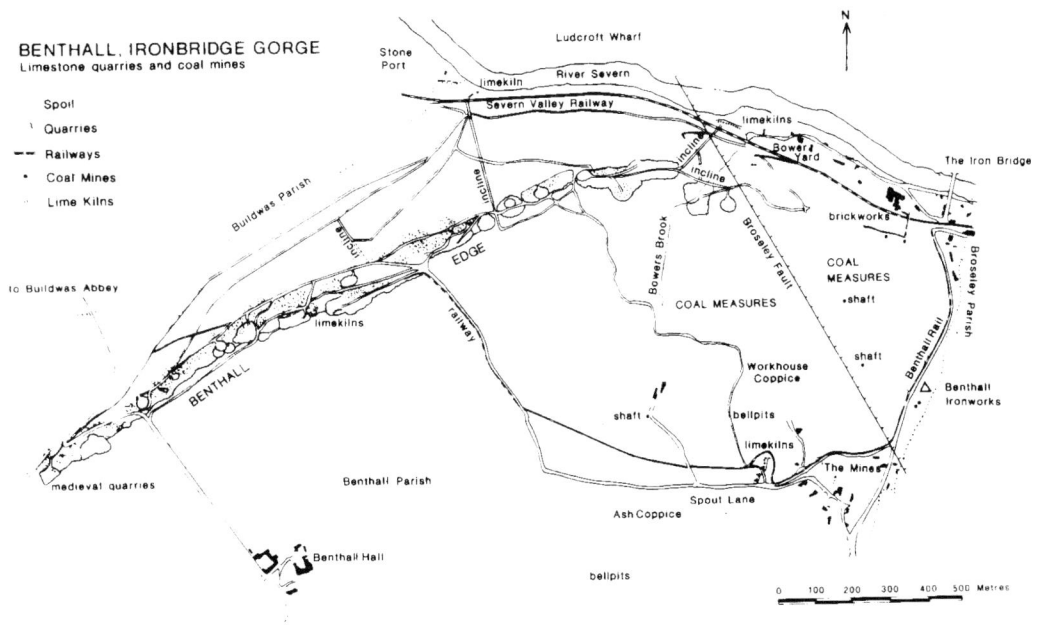

FIGURE 6. *Benthall, Ironbridge Gorge. Map showing limestone quarries and mines.*

investment is surprising in view of successful use of a much smaller Boulton and Watt engine directly to blow a furnace in 1776, at Willey on the other side of the Gorge (Trinder 1981: 273).

Clearly it was considered economic to make a large investment in recycling water, and keep old water-powered machinery in operation, than to replace existing plant, which included small and obsolete furnaces. In 1815 an observer remarked that the furnaces were 'blown by a water wheel, all the machinery old and clumsy and all the works seem to be conducted upon the old plans of forty years ago' (Trinder 1977). Soon after 1817, the Coalbrookdale furnaces went out of operation, and the company thereafter concentrated on castings. A company which had been in the forefront of innovation was, by the begining of the 19th century, hamstrung by the very water system that had made its early success possible.

Summer water shortages at Coalbrookdale had been identified through documents (Raistrick 1953), but until detailed field survey was undertaken it was not possible to place this information in the context of its landscape. The height of water head and the diameter of water wheels (calculated, for example, from scratches on the side of the Old Furnace) can be established with precision (FIGURE 5).

Field survey has demonstrated the scale of the system, and explains the company's reluctance to abandon an inefficient but massive investment.

Raw materials on Benthall Edge

The supply of coal, ironstone and limestone was another vital element of iron-smelting, while the clay obtained as a by-product supplied the large brick, tile, pottery and clay-pipe making industries. This pattern of exploitation led to integrated operations. Thus the Madeley Wood Company, mining coal and smelting iron, also operated brickworks. At a very much earlier date, it appears that the making of clay pipes, requiring white clays, was closely linked with the 16th century coal-mining in Benthall and Broseley.

Unfortunately almost no documentary evidence survives to explain the mechanics of this local supply network. Here again a systemic approach may be applicable.

Benthall Edge is a 100 m high scarp of limestone on the S bank of the river Severn (FIGURE 2). The cliff is capped with the best-quality limestone which is needed for fluxing. Lower deposits of poorer-quality stone could be burnt for lime and building mortar. At the E end, the Broseley fault upthrows coal measures, containing ironstone, fireclays and good-quality coal (FIGURE 6).

Archaeological survey of the network of limestone quarries, roads and railways along the scarp shows four phases of working.

To the W, medieval quarrying is linked with the very early road to the near-by Cistercian Abbey of Buildwas. The quarries that run along the top of the scarp provided the fluxing stone needed in the smelting of iron. This was removed via a group of roads which converge at a point on the river bank where a wharf was located. None of these quarries have associated lime kilns. This exploitation represented the transport of fluxing stone by river, probably for the early-18th-century iron industry at Coalbrookdale. Documentary evidence for this refers to barge owners shipping stone to Ludcroft Wharf, at the foot of Coalbrookdale, shortly after 1718.

Another series of long, open quarries is linked with a railway, leading in the opposite direction, towards Broseley. Twenty kilns are known from map and field evidence, all relating to this railway. Most of this stone was used for agricultural lime. One set of kilns was new in 1800, and the railway was still in use for lime-carrying in 1844. The railway was connected with Benthall Rail, a wooden horse-drawn railway in existence by 1686, which runs down to the river Severn. Finally at the eastern end of the scarp two inclines lead down to 10 lime kilns on the river bank (FIGURE 7). Initially the lime was taken out by river, but when the quarries were reopened c. 1920, another incline, crushing machinery and a railway siding were constructed.

The exploitation of coal and clay followed a similar pattern. Because the coal measures outcrop on the surface, the earliest exploitation was in surface workings. Later, shallow bell-pits and horizontal adits were dug into seams. In the 19th century the easily accessible coal was exhausted, and deeper shafts were dug. The bell-pits of Workhouse and Ash coppices date from the 17th centuries and were linked into the same wooden rail network as the limestone, one of the earliest in the country. Just as the shortage of summer water restricted the activities of the Coalbrookdale company, so the inability to secure adequate supplies of raw materials must have been one factor in the decline of iron-smelting in the Gorge. There seem to be two reasons for this, exhaustion and ownership.

Archaeological evidence suggests that the most easily exploited coal, ironstone and limestone was taken out before 1750s. What little remained was probably used by the Harries family, who owned the mineral rights, for their own iron-smelting operation close to the end of the Benthall Rail. The same railway system linked with the New Willey Furnaces, operated by John Wilkinson from 1757, and the Old Willey furnaces established in the early 17th century and rebuilt in the 1750s.

Benthall Edge was one of the closest sources of limestone for other furnaces of the Gorge, but most of the ironmasters were forced to obtain fluxing stone from more distant sources. The Coalbrookdale Company bought limestone from Much Wenlock and Gleeden Hill, 4 km beyond Benthall Edge. The partners in the railway to the Stone Port at Buildwas (who operated the furnaces at Bedlam, Calcutts and Wrens Nest) obtained stone from Wyke and Tickhill, and not from the near-by Edge. By 1835 the furnaces were using stone carried from Llanymynech on the Welsh border along the Shropshire Union Canal.

FIGURE 7. *Tykes Nest, Broseley, by Joseph Powell, c. 1816–18, showing limestone workings, railways and winding mechanism for inclined plane. (Reproduced with permission of Trustees of the Victoria and Albert Museum.)*

Although content to allow the quarrying of the poorer-quality shales for lime-burning, which took place on a very large scale in response to agricultural improvements in the late 18th century, it seems that the Harries family did not provide limestone for competing furnace-owners, however profitable this would have been.

Landscapes of industry

The Ironbridge Gorge shows how the development and decline of industry can best be understood within the fuller framework of the physical environment. This environment made possible the initial success of industry, by providing a minerals, water power and transport. In the same way it hamstrung long-term industrial development, through the exhaustion of raw materials and the inaccessibility of the Gorge to later transport networks. The early investment in equipment to harness and exploit this environment was on such a large scale that the operating companies were unwilling to replace it with more efficient manufacting systems. It was the rapid and early success of the Gorge which led to its long-term decline.

The process is very evident in the surviving landscape, which incorporates evidence for different factors of production: natural resources, capital, labour, patterns of ownership and networks of communication. The study of the changes in this landscape over time, using both documentary evidence and traditional methods of archaeological field survey enables long-term processes to be understood. An industrial landscape archaeology provides the overall view of the interaction of a variety of systems through space and time. The approach developed at Ironbridge extends beyond industrial archaeology to suggest a new tool for classical, economic and social historians as well as archaeologists. In history as well as archaeology, wider aspects of ancient society are being incorporated, town as well as countryside (Osborne 1987), the smith as well as the forge (Herbert 1984). Those developments are directly analogous to our approach to industrial archaeology, which considers the machines in a wider context. Perhaps the procedures of intensive survey based on the plot-by-plot analysis of land will be of more general applicability.

Acknowledgements. The Nuffield Foundation have most generously provided support for the work on which this article is based. The Ironbridge Institute, the Ironbridge Gorge Museums Trust and Telford Development Corporation have all provided facilities and assistance. I am very grateful to Judith Alfrey, Dr Ivor Brown, David de Haan, Dr Mark Horton, John Powell, Stuart Smith, Dr Michael Stratton, Dr Barrie Trinder and Michael Vanns for their comments and information.

References

ANONYMOUS. 1801 [1982]. *A description of Coalbrookdale in 1801.* Ironbridge: Ironbridge Gorge Museums Trust.
ASTON, M. 1985. *Interpreting the landscape.* London: Batsford.
BICK, A. 1984. Lime kilns on the Gloucestershire-Herefordshire border, *Industrial Archaeology Review* 7(1): 85–93.
BUCHANAN, A. 1972. *Industrial archaeology in Britain.* Harmondsworth: Penguin.
CLARK, C. & J. ALFREY. 1986. *Coalbrookdale: first interim report of the Nuffield Survey.* Ironbridge: Institute of Industrial
     Archaeology.
CLEERE, H. & D. CROSSLEY. 1986. *The iron industry in the Weald.* Leicester: Leicester University Press.
COSSONS, N. 1975. *BP book of industrial archaeology.* Newton Abbot: David & Charles.
     1979. Ironbridge — the first ten years, *Industrial Archaeology Review* 3(2): 179–89.
COUNCIL FOR BRITISH ARCHAEOLOGY. n.d. *Recording industrial sites: a review.* London: Council for British Archaeology.
FALCONER, K. 1981. Industrial monuments survey 1963–81. MS in Ironbridge Gorge Museums Trust Library.
HAY, G. & G. STELL. 1986. *Monuments of history.* Edinburgh: HMSO.
HAYMAN, R. 1986. Aberdulais Falls, *Industrial Archaeology Review* 8(2) : 147–65.
HERBERT, E. 1984. *Red gold of Africa.* Madison: University of Wisconsin Press.
HOBSBAWM, E. 1969. *Industry and empire.* Harmondsworth: Penguin.
HOSKINS, W. 1967. *Fieldwork in local history.* London: Faber.
HUDSON, K. 1963. *Industrial archaeology.* London: John Baker.
     1979. *World industrial archaeology.* Cambridge: Cambridge University Press.
JESPERSEN, A. 1954. *The Lady Isabella Wheel of the Great Laxey Mining Company,* Isle of Man. Privately published.
JONES, K., M. HUNT, J. MALAM & B. TRINDER. 1982. Holywell Lane: a squatter community in the Shropshire coalfield, *Indus-
     trial Archaeology Review* 6(3) : 163–85.
KAIN, R. & H. PRICE. 1985. *The tithe surveys of England and Wales.* Cambridge: Cambridge University Press.
LINSLEY, S. 1980. Editorial, *Industrial Archaeology Review* 4(3): 201.
MOORE, P. 1984. Waterpower on Bromwich Farm: an exercise in excavation, *Industrial Archaeology Review* 7(1) : 24–31.
MOTT, R.A. 1957. Coalbrookdale; the early years, *Transactions of the Shropshire Archaeological Society* 56: 68–81.
MUELLER, J. 1975. *Sampling in archaeology.* Tucson: University of Arizona Press.
OSBORNE, R. 1987. *Classical landscape with figures: the ancient Greek city and its countryside.* London: George Philip.
RAISTRICK, A. 1953. *Dynasty of ironfounders.* London: Longmans, Green.
     1972. *Industrial archaeology: an historical survey* London: Eyre Methuen.
RIX, M. 1967. *Industrial archaeology.* London: Historical Association.
SMITH, R. 1985. Issues in conservation: the Nottingham lace market, *Industrial Archaeology Review* 7(2): 139–53.
SMITH, S. 1979. *A view from the bridge.* Ironbridge: Ironbridge Gorge Museums Trust.
TAYLOR, C. 1974. *Fieldwork in medieval archaeology.* London: Batsford.
TRINDER, B. 1977. *The most extraordinary district in the world.* Chichester: Phillimore.
     1981. *The industrial revolution in Shropshire.* Chichester: Phillimore.
TRINDER B. & J. COX. 1980. *Yeoman and colliers in Telford.* Chichester: Phillimore.
TYLECOTE, R. 1986. *The prehistory of metallurgy in the British Isles.* London: Institute of Metals.
VCH (*Victoria history of the counties of England*). 1985. Shropshire 11. Oxford: Oxford University Press.
WANKLYN, M. 1973. Iron and steelworks in Coalbrookdale in 1645, *Shropshire News Letter* 44.

Towards an archaeology of navvy huts & settlements of the industrial revolution

by **MICHAEL MORRIS**

Antiquity 68 (260), 1994

UNTIL relatively recently the archaeology of the industrial revolution in Britain concentrated on the technology of industrialization (e.g. Buchanan 1972), but since the 1980s there has been increasing pressure to bring this area of study into the mainstream of British archaeological research, with an agenda focusing on broader changes in economy, landscape and society (Clark 1987: 169–71; Crossley 1990: 1–6; Palmer 1990). This note seeks to contribute towards this trend by highlighting the importance of a largely neglected class of site and its potential for gaining further insight into changing social conditions during this crucial period of British and world history.

The navvy (derived from the 'navigator' of the canal age) made up the specialized labour force which provided the muscle power and practical expertise for the great infrastructure projects of the industrial revolution from the later 18th to 20th centuries. As early as the 1790s, specialist contractors probably used established labour gangs for canal-digging (Burton 1972), although the archive sources for this period are poor. By the 1830s navvies had developed into a recognizable sub-culture within the working class, distinguishable from other, so-called unskilled labourers. With a special style of dress, particular forms of language and social and working codes, they tended to live outside mainstream society, moving from contract to contract and living in temporary but discrete communities.

Contrary to popular mythology, only a minority of navvies were Irish, the bulk being recruited from the poorest agricultural and industrial classes in England. They were regarded as folk devils by some contemporary commentators who emphasized their tendency towards violence, a high level of alcohol consumption, spendthrift attitudes and lack of conventional morality. Undoubtedly, their presence near often isolated local communities could be socially disruptive. Other accounts, however, lay stress on the appalling terms and conditions under which they laboured and the extraordinary work output which they achieved (and for which they were rewarded by relatively high wages) (Chesney 1970: 39–47; Coleman 1981; Sullivan 1983).

The sites of navvy camps and settlements, which ranged from isolated groups of huts to small towns housing several hundred people, lie scattered throughout the country, often in the bleaker and more inaccessible upland areas. In the broadest sense they form part of the history of lower-class housing (Burnett 1986). More specifically, however, they represent a rich and untapped source of information about the life-style, living conditions and material culture of the navvy.

Towards a settlement morphology

TABLE 1 presents a generalized model for the social analysis of navvy settlement morphology. It proposes a four-stage overlapping sequence which broadly coincides with the phases of great construction projects, the canals, railways, reservoirs and roads (Deane 1965: 75–80; Deane & Cole 1969: 229–33; Buchanan 1972: 331–3; Marwick 1990: 117–18). These stages can be outlined as follows:

period	dominant project	estimated navvy population	dominant settlement type	type site
1. 1760s–1830	canals	up to 25,000	mixed barracks	?
2. 1830s–?1880s	railways	1846 100,000 1875 40,000	unstructured/ large scale	Woodhead
3. 1880s–1930s	public works/ reservoirs	1889 90,000 c.1900 100–130,000	structured/ large scale	Manchester Ship Canal
4. 1930s–present	roads	?	local workforce caravans/portakabins	?

TABLE 1. *Proposed four-stage model for navvy settlement morphology (source for population, Sullivan 1983: 90–91).*

Period 1
The canal age: the prehistory of navvy settlements
1760s to 1830
Little is known about navvy living arrangements during this period; they were probably a combination of local lodgings, self-built huts and purpose-built dormitories. Huts are recorded on the Stroudwater canal in the 1770s and on the Gloucester & Berkeley canal in the 1790s (Sullivan 1983: 74). Some canal projects, especially tunnel construction, approached the scale of later railway contracts and, sometimes, the contractor provided purpose-built accommodation. The evidence we have suggests that barrack-type buildings were favoured, with their obvious connotations for the control and discipline of the workforce. In the 1780s, at the Sapperton tunnel on the Thames–Severn canal, 200–300 men were employed, many of whom were lodged in a special 3-storeyed building. The upper two floors were open dormitories, with the ground floor functioning as a communal dining- and tap-room. Outside was a water cistern, a bowling alley, stables and sheds (Household 1969: 60). Similarly, in 1792 the Worcester & Birmingham Canal Company resolved that the contractor should build a barracks for 100 men at Edgbaston (Sullivan 1983: 74).

Period 2
The railway age: unstructured settlements
1830s to c. 1880
In relatively densely settled areas, a significant proportion of navvies continued to be accommodated in rented property, lodgings or Inns. For example, a study of the labourforce on the Severn Valley Railway (opened in 1862), based mainly on the 1861 census, revealed that only 60 (8·1%) of the 741 recorded navvies lived in temporary accommodation. This consisted of a few scattered purpose-built huts, and more interestingly, *ad hoc* shelter in the form of a disused forge, an abandoned lime-kiln at Benthall Edge and an old windmill at Madeley Court (Harris 1984). Examples such as this, where squatter accommodation can be related to extant structures, offer good potential for archaeological study.

Where existing accommodation was lacking, large unstructured agglomerations appear to have been typical of this period. They reflect the *laissez faire* approach of the dominant 'entreprenurial ideal' of mid-19th-century England (see Perkin 1969: 271–339) and also the *floruit* of navvy sub-culture. The numerous major tunnel, embankment, cutting and viaduct projects demanded large numbers of resident workers but housing and welfare provision was left mainly to market forces. A wide variety of accommodation was used within these settlements, including wheeled vans and site outbuildings (Select Committee 1846: 66, 189). Suprisingly, given the need of the authorities to contain and control navvy society, barracks do not appear to have become common, perhaps because these would have required a significant capital outlay by the contractor. Instead, hut accommodation was the norm, within the tradition of the most basic form of single-storey rural cottage or squatter hut (*cf.* Brunskill 1982: 94–5; Trinder 1981: 188–90, plate 43). These huts comprised 2 main types, the 'shant' and the 'sod hut'.

The shant was a speculative property development built by the contractor, a specialist keeper or a ganger (foreman), which was then sub-let to a number of lodgers. A fairly standard pattern had emerged from the canal age, seemingly based on part, or all, of a working gang of perhaps a dozen men. TABLE 2 indicates that there was considerable variation in construction material and size. Those constructed of stone or brick may have left clear traces (see for example the Woodhead evidence cited below), whilst those of wood, turf, etc. may be detectable as platforms, earthworks or below-ground archaeological features.

It was within the locus of the shant that navvy sub-culture developed and flourished with little external constraint. Although a predominantly male society, women and children could form an accepted part of the social structure, albeit not in the context of the idealized family unit. For example, the Parliamentary Select Committee of 1846 records 'common prostitutes' resident within the shants on the North British and Harwick line, whilst on the London to Birmingham line, local women went to live with the navvies 'in habits that civilised language will scarcely allow description of' (Select Committee 1846: 26, 52).

Little is known in detail about the construction, use and frequency of the sod hut. It seems to have been used when no other accommodation was available or where the individual navvy was particularly independent (Coleman 1981: 80–85; Sullivan 1983: 73–80). It was a small, self-built dwelling constructed of locally available materials such as turf, timber and tarpaulin. Cutting back into a slope appears to have been a common means of creating a sheltered living space (and may be archaeologically discernible). Such huts would be scattered around the periphery of the works, often in small groups.

Shants and sod huts continued to be constructed into the first decade of the present century. On the Kinlochleven dam project in Scotland, *c.* 1908, there was a ring of shants surrounding a communal rubbish dump. Other examples are cited on the Water Orton to Kingsbury line, 1906, and at the construction of the one of the world's first purpose-built motor-racing circuits at Brooklands in Surrey, completed in 1907, where navvies lived in brushwood bivouacs which were destroyed by hostile locals (Sullivan 1983: 101–2, 80–81).

Woodhead: a site-type of the railway age
A classic site of this period is the Woodhead tunnel, constructed as part of the Sheffield to Manchester railway between 1839 and 1845. It was 3 miles 22 yards long and employed up to 1000 men (Holt 1978: 146–8). The living and working conditions on this project were made notorious by the social reformers Edwin Chadwick and John Roberton. Although the contractor supplied a number of 'comfortable cottage houses of good lime

site	construction	size	occupants
North British & Harwick line (1840s)	wood and turf walls, built into slope	8·5 x 3·7 m (31·4 sq. m)	20–30 inc. keeper & wife, female skivvies/prostitutes
village of Docker Garth, Lancashire & Carlisle Railway (1840s)	turf walls 1·5 m high, straw roofing	12·8 x 4·2 m (53·8 sq. m)	10–14 inc. keeper & wife total 84 (66 men, 9 women, 9 children) average per hut 6·5
Watford Tunnel, London & Birmingham Railway (1836–40) see FIGURE 4A	composite e.g. brick, stone, tile, wood, tarpaulin. earth floor	–	several + skivvy and female partners
Woodhead Tunnel (1840s) see FIGURE 2	stone, thatch or flag roof	9 x 5 m (45 sq. m)	up to 15, also women and children
Kettering–Manton line (1860s) see FIGURE 4B	timber, brick floor and chimney	–	lodgers + keeper & wife
Birchinlee, Derwent Valley (1903–15) see FIGURE 4D	corrugated iron walls and roof, board lining, brick or concrete foundations, brick chimney	11·3 x 4·9 m (55·4 sq. m)	8 lodgers + keeper & family

TABLE 2. *Sample descriptions of navvy huts.*

and stone, and slated' (Select Committee 1846: 192), these proved entirely inadequate for the numbers employed, and self-built huts abounded. John Roberton describes the scene (Chadwick & Roberton 1846: 9–10):

> At certain distances along the line of tunnel the moor is pierced by five shafts, averaging in depth about six hundred feet; and it is around these five shafts, and at each termination of the tunnel, that the huts of the workmen cluster.
> The huts are a curiosity. They are mostly of stones without mortar, the roof of thatch or of flags, erected by the men for their own temporary use, one workman building a hut in which he lives with his family, and lodges also a number of his fellow-workmen. In some instances as many as fourteen or fifteen men, we were told, lodged in the same hut; and this at best containing two apartments, an outer and an inner, the former alone having a fire-place. Many of the huts were filthy dens, while some were whitewashed and more cleanly; the difference, no doubt, depending on the turn and character of the inmates. In stormy weather, and in winter, this must be a most dreary situation to live in, even were the dwellings well-built and comfortable.

other details	no. of huts	source
usually 1 room, many with no windows	*c.* 47	Select Committee 1846: 56–7
2 rooms: kitchen/ dining room and bedroom	13	Select Committee 1846: 162–3
1 room with kitchen & sleeping areas	–	Sullivan 1983: 75-6 Select Committee 1846: 52
2 rooms, 1 with fireplace	–	Chadwick & Roberton 1846 recent field survey
3 rooms; central living room, dormitory + private bedroom for keeper & wife	–	Sullivan 1983: 76–7
6 rooms; central living room, dormitory, keeper's room & bedroom, attached scullery & pantry, coal-burning stove, paraffin lamps	50 +	Robinson 1993: 67, 130, 255–6

The area around the Woodhead airshafts is the author's choice for one of the most desolate and evocative groups of archaeological sites in Britain. Recent survey work has revealed evidence for construction debris, trackways and building foundations around four of the airshafts (FIGURE 1). The most visible remains lie around the remote airshaft, at SE135010, where the exposed foundations of several probable dry-stone dwellings have been recorded (FIGURE 2). Although some, or all, of these may belong to the construction of a second tunnel bore in the 1880s, they are, nevertheless, consistent with the written evidence for the 1840s phase.

Building 1, despite having a barrack-like appearance, is tentatively interpreted as a single-storey terrace of 6 units with 2 ground-floor rooms, in the tradition of miners' and quarrymen's dwellings (*cf.* Brunskill 1978: 176–7). The terrace was built along a steep slope close to the main access track, with the rear rooms *c.* 1·5 m higher than the front ones. These units are possible examples of the 'comfortable cottage houses' constructed by the contractor, referred to in the Select Committee Report (see above).

Four other structures appear compatible with Roberton's description of the Woodhead shants. Buildings 2 and 3 are especially convincing, with similar 2-room plans. The

FIGURE 1. *Woodhead. View from infilled airshaft at SK115000 above the Woodhead end of the tunnel. The airshaft is marked by the heap of rubble in the right foreground. The course of the railway, now converted to a roadway, is visible along the valley floor.*

outer, larger, room was perhaps the main lodging-room, with the keeper (?and family) residing in the inner room. Both huts are of similar size and fall within the general size range for such structures (see TABLE 2). The collapsed stone door frame of the main room of building 2 is visible *in situ* (FIGURE 3). The full plans of buildings 4 and 5 could not be established. They were partially built against earth banks and may have been of composite stone and turf construction. Indeed, they may be sod huts in type.

Building 6, less credible as a habitation, is perhaps associated with the site works. Alternatively, it may have been a large, contractor-built shant with a big central lodging room fronted by a corridor and separate quarters for the keeper on either side. Building 7 is an intact brick explosives store, probably relating to the 1880s works. Building 8 is an in-filled air-shaft.

The survey indicated that the area was not densely occupied but consisted of a relatively small number of habitations dispersed over at least 250 m. The larger structures (1 and 6) are sited close to the access track and the air-shafts, whilst the apparently self-built structures (2–5) are more random and isolated. The need for well-drained ground (buildings 2 and 3) or a sheltered location (buildings 4 and 5) may have influenced the actual siting of individual huts.

This limited evidence suggests centrally located contractor-built habitations with a scatter of randomly dispersed self-built huts further away, consistent with a cognitive distinction, respected by both employer and navvy, between officially sanctioned dwellings near the formal part of the site (air-shaft and communication route), and the peripheral self-built huts, which reflect the informality and independence of navvy culture.

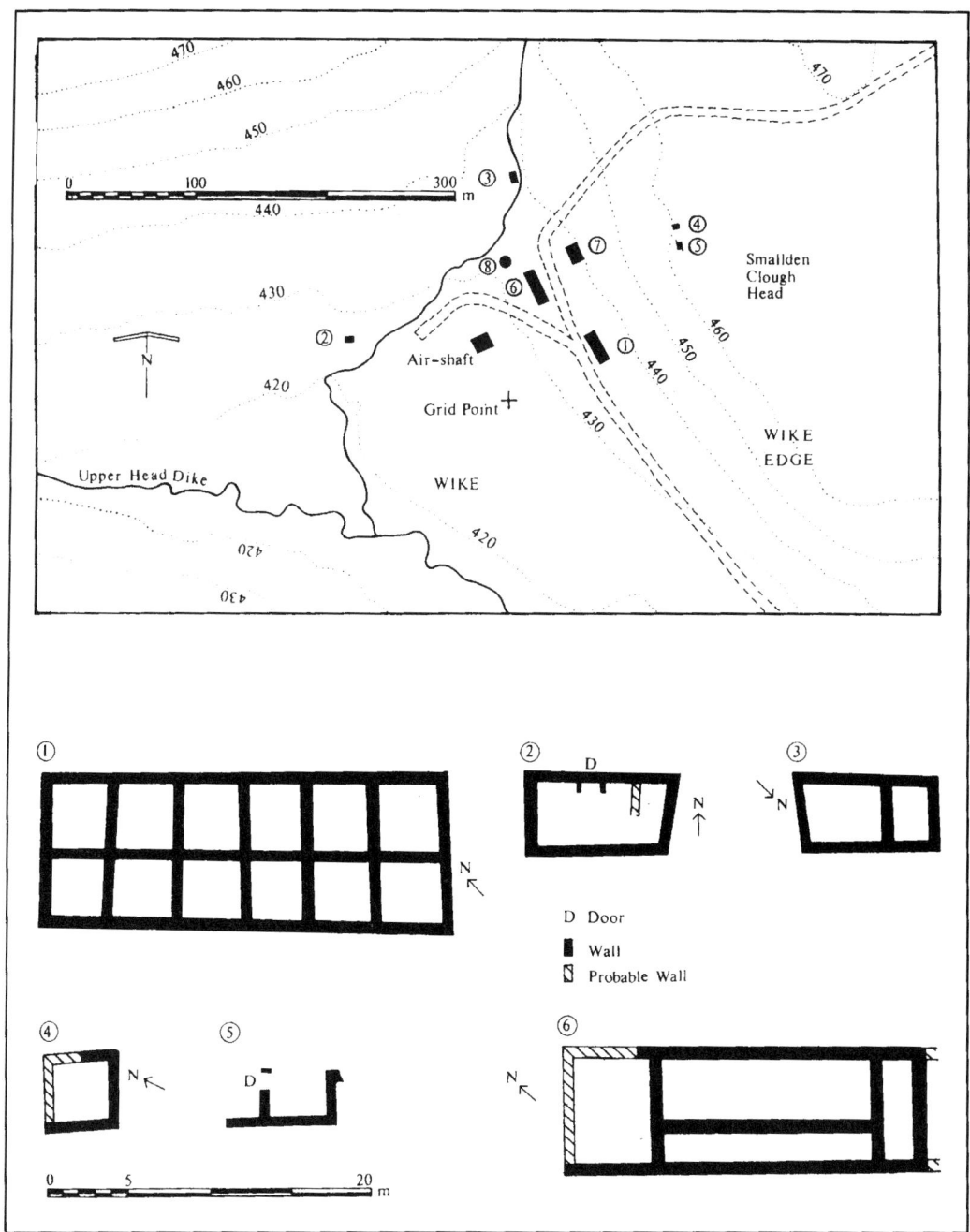

FIGURE 2. *Woodhead. Location plan and measured sketches of probable navvy dwellings and other remains at SE135010. Buildings 4 and 5 are shown in actual relationship to each other. (Surveyed by Keith Matthews 1994.)*

The sparseness of habitation at this location is, at first impression, suprising, especially given the evidence for a workforce of up to 1000 on the works as a whole. However, assuming 8 men per dwelling (a conservative estimate according to the contemporary sources (see TABLE 2)) and 10 dwellings (excluding building 6), a population of 80

FIGURE 3. *Woodhead. Remains of building 2 showing collapsed door frame.*

at this site is conceivable. Roberton's report, cited above, indicates settlements at four other airshafts, giving a population of up to 400 on the moor top. The main working sites may, in fact, have been around the tunnel mouths at Woodhead and Durnford where the workforce could have been accommodated in local lodgings or in temporary huts. Unfortunately, there has been extensive later activity at both these locations and no obvious navvy settlement evidence was observed.

Period 3
Municipal projects: structure and segregation
1880s to 1930s
The 3rd phase of navvy settlements was the widespread imposition of large-scale structured communities. The early attempts to intervene in the navvies' domestic sphere by the provision of barracks seems to have been undermined by the *laissez faire* approach of the railway companies and contractors. From the mid 19th century, however, there was increasing pressure for thorough-going reform in safety and working conditions, the abolition of the infamous truck system (paying wages in goods from the employer's shop) and the provision of appropriate accommodation. This manifestation of the mid-Victorian 'moral conscience' (Thomson 1950: 107–18) resulted partly from genuine humanitarian concern for the physical welfare of the workforce, as exemplified by Chadwick & Roberton (1846), and partly from the need for social, moral and spiritual control of the independent-minded workforce.

Isolated railway companies and contractors did accept a level of moral responsibility. On the Chester to Holyhead railway, in the 1840s, as well as requiring the construc-

tion of suitable housing, the company also
built a church and employed 6 missionaries to cater for the navvies' spiritual welfare. Another, more graphic insight into the
middle-class ethos, which opposed the open
navvy life-style, can be gained from the idealized accommodation schemes presented
as evidence to the 1846 Parliamentary Select Committee by Peter Thompson, a sup-
plier of temporary dwellings for the colo-
nies: Firstly there is a concern for individual
privacy, apparent in the inclusion of separate bedrooms in the designs for both hut
and barrack-style accommodation. Secondly, 'a moral plan for the separation of
the sexes' is realized by the requirement for
separate rooms for married couples and,
also, the distancing of children from their
parents' bedroom (FIGURE 4C) (Select Committee 1846: 144 and figures for question
2170).

Whilst the reformers could advocate improvements, it was not until the eclipse of
the entrepreneurial ideal by the ethos of col-
lectivism and centralization in the 1860s
(Perkin 1969: 437–54), that widespread
change could be contemplated. Municipal
authorities undertook more than 300 reservoir schemes during the later 19th and earlier 20th centuries, to supply clean water
for industry and the growing urban population (Sullivan 1983: 60–61). The paternal-
istic attitude of the local authorities resulted
in highly structured accommodation and
settlements with a proto-urban infrastructure. This gradually brought about greater
integration of the navvy within 'normal' society, with the recognition of the role of the
family unit and the need for education and
welfare. This process can perhaps be paralleled by the more recent attempts to restrict
gypsy society through the establishment of
permanent sites.

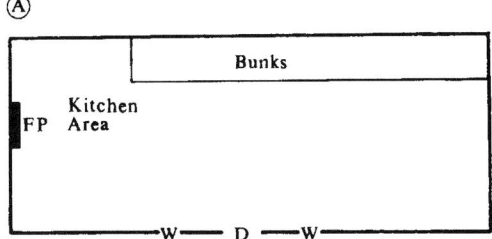

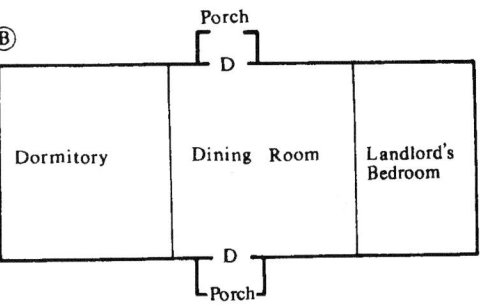

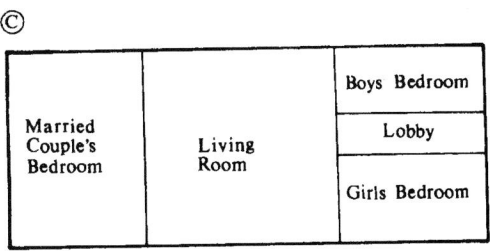

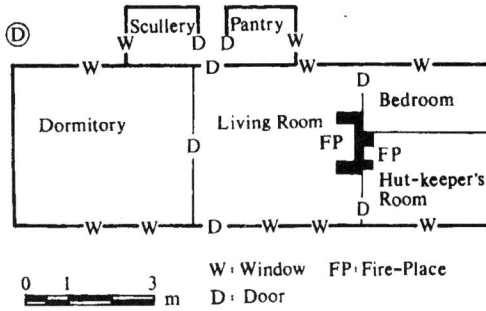

FIGURE 4. *Sketch plans of navvy huts. (A–C are taken from written descriptions and are not to scale.)*
A   *1830s, Watford tunnel, London and Birmingham line (Sullivan 1983: 75–6)*
B   *1860s, Kettering–Manton line (Select Committee 1846: 76)*
C   *1840s, idealized family hut (Select Committee 1846: 144)*
D   *1901–2, Birchinlee, Derwent Valley reservoirs, from an architect's plan (Robinson 1993: 130).*

FIGURE 5. *Single-storey terraced navvy housing at Acton Grange, Manchester Ship Canal, 1889. The buildings have weatherboarded walls and brick chimneys. The road and pavement are unsurfaced. The mixed age and sex of the occupants is clearly visible. (G.M.C.R.O. ref. 721204/ 199).*

The significant landmark during this period was the construction of the Manchester Ship Canal, between 1887 and 1894. It was one of the biggest construction projects in the world at that time, employing up to 16,000 men (Leech 1907 (ii): 37). The canal was built in sections; when close to established centres of population, such as Warrington or Runcorn, lodgings were the norm. On the more isolated sections large, purpose-built, settlements were established (FIGURE 5) (Owen 1983: 89*ff*). Where appropriate, the traditional shant system was allowed to operate, with a large hut rented to a ganger and his wife, and sub-let to a number of single men. Greater social segregation was created by the provision of plentiful accommodation for married couples and families. Equally importantly, communal facilities were also provided. This is illustrated by a contemporary account of the lost settlement on Frodsham marshes called, predictably, Marsh Ville (A.C.O.E.) 1889):

> Where was once a marsh, with not a single building upon it, are now neatly laid-out pastures, with a village containing a population of some hundred persons. In connection with it there is a church with a resident missionary, a school with a certified teacher, and a daily postal communication with the neighbouring township of Frodsham. Marsh Ville is a prettily laid-out place with two long rows of neatly white-washed huts and a large green patch of ground between them, which serves admirably for a playground for most of the younger end of the inhabitants.

FIGURE 6. *Navvy hut at Ewden village, Broomhead reservoir, 1993. Built to a standard pattern, probably in the 1920s or '30s, such units had weatherboarded walls with asbestos tile roofs, and measured* c. *20 m* x *5 m.*

A contemporary photo shows the 'neatly white-washed huts' to be dismal two-storey structures with a barrack-like external appearance (G.M.C.R.O. ref. 721204.194).

Although, by the turn of the century, there were more navvies employed than ever (TABLE 1) the heyday of their sub-culture was over, stifled by the order and control imposed on their daily lives by the new type of settlement. There can be little doubt that this external structuring and other general improvements were related to public sector involvement, rather than a change of heart by private contractors (see Robinson 1993: 58). Testimony from this time, which refers to the settlement at Birchinlee, which served the Upper Derwent Valley dam projects in Derbyshire, is unequivocal about this and its benefits (Quoted in Sullivan 1983: 80):

> Direct labour jobs were always best, not like these private enterprise gangsters. It was a proper little town at Birchinlee. Well, they called it Tin Town, anyhow. Two or three shops. One big grocery shop. A baker's. Barber shop. Baths as well. You never got that out of private contractors. They were robbers.

This particular settlement, built in 1901–2 and occupied from 1903 to 1915, reached a peak population of 967 in 1909. The buildings were timber-framed with corrugated-iron walls (hence the nickname Tin Town) and, in addition to the facilities described above, the site boasted a school and hospital (Coleman 1981: 73; Robinson 1993). There were 29 semi-detached lodging-houses (see TABLE 2 & FIGURE 4D), 20 married workmen's quarters and four foremen's huts. Although some structures were demolished when the settlement was vacated, many were sold and rebuilt elsewhere, including a number purchased by the War Office. The layout and building platforms are still visible at this site and one of the rebuilt structures survives in the nearby village of Hope (Robinson 1993: 100).

Another important 20th-century site is Ewden village at Broomhead reservoir, 20 km northwest of Sheffield. The now largely deserted site covers several acres and retains its street pattern, house plots and a handful of the original weather-boarded buildings, one of which is still (1993) occupied by the son of a navvy who worked on the construction of the reservoir (FIGURE 6).

Period 4
Motor transport infrastructure: the navvy as an endangered species?
1930s to present
Considerable road construction projects have continued to the present day, particularly since the 1960s, but improved transportation and mechanization have reduced the need for large encampments. Nevertheless, the niche persists in the form of groups of caravans and porta-kabins on motorway and other infrastructure projects, most notably, the Channel Tunnel works in Kent, 1986–93. It is at such locations that vestiges of the independent life-style of the navvy survive, as attested by Bob Geldof's (1986: 82–5) explicit account of his experiences working on the construction of the M25 in the 1970s.

Conclusion
This note has sought to draw attention to a marginalized social group which is poorly represented in the archaeological literature. The history of their settlements and living conditions reminds us of the reality of an unfettered free-market society and of the very real benefits which public intervention brought to the living and working conditions of the navvy. This is perhaps something which we should not undervalue, especially in the present-day climate of privatization and threatened welfare provision.

Investigation into sites of the canal age promises to be particularly fruitful due to the sparsity of archive material for this period. In contrast, the rich documentary and photographic evidence from some of the later projects such as the Manchester Ship Canal, 1887–94, the Great Central Railway from Nottingham to London, 1894–99, and the reservoir settlement at Birchinlee in Derbyshire, 1901–15, offers a broader context for the study of this subject (Ship Canal Archives; Rolt 1971; Robinson 1993; and see Crossley 1990; 2–3).

A basic pre-requisite for future archaeological analysis is the identification and entry into the sites and monuments record of navvy sites of all types and periods. Following on from this, field survey and excavation of type-sites should be considered in relation to the phases presented above. The following basic issues might perhaps be borne in mind:

- Evidence for an archaeologically distinctive navvy material culture.
- Spatial layout and use-patterns of individual structures and whole settlements.
- Archaeological indicators for social structure, hierarchy and the presence/absence of women and children.
- Supply, consumption, diet and refuse disposal.
- Cross-cultural comparisons with industrializing construction project settlements in other countries e.g. USA, Russia, Australia, China. Also with pre-industrial examples such as the 'workmen's village' at Deir el-Medina in Egypt (e.g. Romer 1984).

Additional research will undoubtedly modify and perhaps transform the morphological model presented in TABLE 1.

Acknowledgements. The seed for this paper was planted by John Walker in a conversation many years ago. I am grateful to Keith Matthews for leading the survey work at Woodhead, to Alison Jones for helping with the survey and for drawing the illustrations, and to both for their comments on the text. I would also like to thank Elizabeth Morris for tracking down references and primary source material, and Ken Smith (Peak National Park) for advice on the Peak District sites.

References

A.G.O.E. 1889. Ship canal rambles no. iii, *The Lancashire merchant and ship canal news* June 15 1889: 126.
BOWTELL, H.D. 1977. *Reservoir railways of Manchester and the Peak.* Blandford: Oakwood Press.
BRUNSKILL, R.W. 1978. *Illustrated handbook of vernacular architecture.* London: Faber & Faber.
    1982. Houses. London: Collins.
BUCHANAN, R.A. 1972. *Industrial archaeology in Britain.* Harmondsworth: Penguin.
BURNETT, J. 1986. *A social history of housing 1815–1985.* London: Methuen.
BURTON, A. 1972. *The canal builders.* London: Methuen
CHADWICK, E. & J. ROBERTON. 1846. *Papers read before the Statistical Society of Manchester on the demoralisation and injuries occasioned by the want of proper regulations of labourers engaged in the construction and working of railways.* Manchester: Statistical Society of Manchester.
CHESNEY, K. 1970. *The Victorian underworld.* Newton Abbot: Readers Union.
COLEMAN, T. 1981. *The railway navvies.* Harmondsworth: Penguin (1st edition 1965. London: Hutchinson.)
CROSSLEY, D. 1990. *Post-medieval archaeology in Britain.* Leicester: Leicester University Press.
CLARK, C 1987. Trouble at t'mill: industrial arcaeology in the 1980s, *Antiquity* 61: 169–79.
DEANE, P. 1965. The first industrial revolution. Cambridge: Cambridge University Press.
DEANE, P. & W.A. COLE. 1969. *British economic growth 1688–1959.* 2nd edition. Cambridge: Cambridge University Press.
GELDOF, B. 1986. *Is that it?* Harmondsworth: Penguin.
G.M.C.R.O. Greater Manchester County Record Office; Ship Canal Archives.
HARRIS, I. 1984. Shropshire navvies: the builders of the Severn Valley Railway, in B. Trinder (ed.), *Victorian Shrewsbury*: 97–104. Shrewsbury: Victorian Shrewsbury Research Group.
HOLT, G. 1978. *A regional history of the railways of Great Britain* 10: *The northwest.* Newton Abbot: David & Charles.
HOUSEHOLD, H. 1969. *The Thames and Severn Canal.* Newton Abbot: David & Charles.
LEECH, B. 1907. *History of the Manchester Ship Canal.* Manchester: Sherratt & Hughes.
MARWICK, A. 1990. *British society since 1945.* Harmondsworth: Penguin.
OWEN, D. 1983. *The Manchester Ship Canal.* Manchester: Manchester University Press.
PALMER, M. 1990. Industrial archaeology: a thematic or a period discipline?, *Antiquity* 64: 275–82.
PERKIN, H. 1969. *The origins of modern English society 1780–1880.* London: Routledge & Kegan Paul.
ROBINSON, B. 1993. *Walls across the valley: The building of the Howden and Derwent dams.* Cromford: Scarthin Books.
ROLT, L. 1971. *The making of a railway.* London: Hugh Evelyn.
ROMER, J. 1984. *Ancient lives: the story of the Pharaohs' tombmakers.* London: Weidenfeld & Nicholson.
SELECT COMMITTEE. 1846. Report from the select committee on railway labourers, House of Commons, 28 July 1846.
SHIP CANAL ARCHIVES. These are available at a variety of sources including Manchester Central Library, Greater Manchester Record Office and Ellesmere Port Boat Museum Library.
SULLIVAN, D. 1983. *Navvyman.* London: Coracle Books.
THOMSON, D. 1950. *England in the nineteenth century.* Harmondsworth: Penguin.
TRINDER, B. 1981. *The Industrial Revolution in Shropshire.* London: Phillimore.

7 Contested landscapes

One trend of 1990s archaeology, perhaps influenced by the then and continuing current political events, has been to see landscapes as an arena of the struggle of identity, allegiance and power. Identity is now multi-vocal (Jones 1997). These landscapes can be resolutely built landscapes of monuments and other imposing material culture, or more weighted towards control of symbols, embedded in the landscape itself. One influential approach has been Bender's analysis of Stonehenge (Bender 1993; 1998). For Bender, landscape is redolent of class and thus social division: landscape is appropriated. Her approach is to make a detailed historical contextualization of the Stonehenge landscape to uncover these contestations and appropriations, and the unevenness with which different voices are heard. As Jacquetta Hawkes (1967: 174) wrote in ANTIQUITY (and quoted by Bender): 'Every Age has the Stonehenge it deserves — or desires'.

The two papers reprinted here are drawn from more violent contestations of the last half of the 20th century. The first (Baker 1993) reminds us that the Berlin wall which divided Germany for 28 years is itself an archaeological monument that provided a focus of symbolic contestation of political rhetoric, as well as having a physical presence. In terms of symbolism the author explicitly links the Berlin Wall to Offa's Dyke, covered in the article by Fox. Both Fox and Baker emphasized the visual quality of defences: symbolic discouragement runs in parallel with physical discouragement. The wall was a complex of defences with a complex of meanings, some more deeply heard than others, difficult to arrange in a dichotomy of East and West, and difficult to translate from the German *Mauer*. On the one hand the wall was once physically large and latterly preserved as many fragments in individual curiosity cabinets; on the other it was open to a pluralism of interpretations, both at the time of the Cold War and now as historians work over the evidence. The wall had a process of construction, balancing central authority against the local variation provided by construction gangs. It later had a process of fall, its maintenance dependent on political will. Finally the wall had an aftermath, where its very fragments took on symbolic qualities related to differentially recorded and disputed memory.

The second paper relates to the power of symbols of the past contested in the present (Brown 1994, reprinted here). The dissolution of the former Yugoslavia has brought violent war to Europe and shocked European society. One aspect of this war has been systematically to destroy the material culture which might substantiate the historical presence of rival identities. Chapman (1994) has defined this situation as a cultural landscape at war. Another war is a struggle for control over symbols which may also have a presence in material form. The star (or sun) symbol has a deep-seated history that is contested in two different versions of Macedonia. The symbols have different meanings in different contexts, even within the same territorial borders, and are consequently ambiguous in their relationship to a 'real' landscape. Unfortunately, these disputes may continue to have an impact in the 21st century.

We can register these contested landscapes readily in the ethnographic present. We do not even have to rely on single ethnographic accounts. The varied sources of the media have carefully registered difference of opinion. Journalists have risked much to investigate alternative accounts which are at conflict with the umbrella propaganda of the state. However, as archaeologists we can readily ask how much this fragmented view of society is a product of our current industrial society and the curious processes of globalization and resistance to that very globalization. Our concepts of identity today are much influenced by what we have seen on the television screens of Indonesia, the Lebanon and the Balkans themselves. To what extent can contested landscapes be investigated in the more distant past? In this respect, it is very noticeable that Barbara Bender concentrates her attention on the medieval and later landscape of Stonehenge. What is needed for prehistoric contexts is a study of iconoclasm: evidence of deliberate slighting of earlier landscapes. This requires close study of context and explicit symbolic information from the prehistoric past. Deliberate destruction tends to appear only in state-organized societies, although evidence is being to appear in some prehistoric contexts such as those of Malta.

The Berlin Wall:
production, preservation &
consumption of a 20th-century monument
by **FREDERICK BAKER**

ANTIQUITY 67 (257), 1993

THOUGH IT was only built in 1961, the Berlin Wall is today an archaeological monument. Four years after its opening on 9 November 1989, less is left of the Berlin Wall than of Hadrian's Wall. To trace its former course through Germany's capital would now test the skills of many a field archaeologist. For archaeology, the study of material objects in a historical perspective, contemporary material objects, especially those of complex meaning and history like the Berlin Wall, are as valuable as the older border fortifications of China or of Northumberland.

The Wall is important for several reasons.

No single object better encapsulates the 20th-century European experience than the Berlin Wall. It was the central monument of the Cold War, 1945–89 in Europe, a conflict that had its roots in the European wars of 1914–18 and 1939–45. As the notorious part of the 'Iron Curtain', the petrified front-line of the Soviet empire from the Baltic to the Black Sea, it was also an emblem of the division of the late 20th-century world into two political spheres. The Wall's building was the symbol of the Cold War, its destruction a symbol of its end.

The Berlin Wall exemplifies features common to many monuments which carry special weights of symbol or meaning; the memory that has been preserved suffers from partiality, not just in how little physically remains, but also in its representation to the public today.

This article approaches the Berlin Wall in two stages: first it sets out the nature and development of the Wall up to its fall in 1989; then it examines the way in which parts of the Wall were preserved to be consumed by the tourist industry, and the distorted view of the Wall it offers.

The Berlin Walls

There was no such thing as 'the' Berlin Wall, there were several Berlin walls.

This is true at many levels, in time and in space. The 'border security system for the national frontier west', as it was officially known, went through several phases ('generations') of construction. And 'The Wall' was a set of in-depth border fortifications that consisted of *two* parallel walls: an interior and an exterior one enclosed a 'death strip' and watch-towers (FIGURE 1). But even these walls were not walls: the internal wall was often constituted of old boarded-up buildings, as at the Bernauer Straße, or by the banks of canals or rivers (FIGURES 2a, 2b). Only 37 km of the wall ran through areas of housing; 17 km ran through industrial areas, 30 km through woods, 24 km along waterways, and 55 km along rail embankments, fields and marshland (Rühle & Holzweißig 1988: 145). So in some places the Wall was made of wire fences not concrete, or was a line through a lake or a bridge, like the infamous Glienicker bridge, where spies were swapped between East and West.

FIGURE 1. *Official GDR border-guard photo 147 of the death strip, watch tower and both interior and exterior walls, from the Bethaniendamm in Kreuzberg/Friedrichshain. (Hagen Koch Archive.)*

The Wall's complexity goes beyond bricks and mortar, for its meaning was very different according to whether you lived on its East side or on its West side. This difference is best illustrated by the two German words that translate as the English word 'wall', *Mauer* and *Wand*. While *Mauer* means wall in the sense of a barrier, *Wand* means wall in the sense of the 'face' of a wall. According to Martin Walser, the novelist who predicted the fall of the Wall, 'The English can never fully understand what *"die Mauer"* meant for us Germans, because your word wall doesn't differentiate between *Wand* and *Mauer'* (1991, pers. comm.). When the Wall was built and all contact was broken off, the Wall was very much a *Mauer* for Westerners and Easterners alike. By the 1980s, when

FIGURE 2a. *Official GDR border-guard photo 95 of the death strip, looking from the Reichstagufer across the river Spree to the Schiffbauerdamm. (Hagen Koch Archive.)*

crossing from West into East had became easier for Westerners, the Wall was less *Mauer*, more *Wand*. For East Germans the Wall remained firmly a *Mauer*.

There had been a large city wall around Berlin, long before the Wall of 1961–89. The Brandenburg Gate's position, adjacent to the 1961 Wall, is no coincidence; it is the only survivor of the old Customs wall which was demolished in 1867 (Ribbe & Schmaedeke 1988: 107). That Prussian kings had built a customs wall which in places was followed by the exact course of the most recent Wall was often used to normalize the division of Berlin by another wall.

The Cold War and the construction of the Wall

The Wall was constructed in 1961, in the stalemate phase of the Cold War in Europe, before the focus of tensions turned to Cuba, Indo-China and Africa. The Soviets, having liberated Berlin during the Second World War, felt a moral right to its total occupation. Only with reluctance did they allow the Americans, British, and later the French, to take up an agreed four-power supervision of Berlin on 1 July 1945.

The frontier within the divided Germany that separated the Soviet zone (after 1949 the German Democratic Republic: East Germany) from the combined American/British/French zones (after 1949 the German Federal Republic: West Germany) ran about 200 km west of Berlin (Wagner 1990) (FIGURE 3). Berlin, as the old German capital, was divided between the Allies; the Soviet zone, East Berlin, was soon integrated into East Germany; the American, British and French zones, united as West Berlin, remained a Western island inside East Germany, closely linked to the West German Federal Republic and joined to it by air and surface access corridors through East Germany. The division line within Berlin, later the line of the Wall, followed the old boundaries of the historical local government boundaries, chopping across the old centre, through the middle of the Potsdamer Platz, the city's greatest square, and within a few yards of the *Reichstag*, united Germany's parliament building. The trains on some north–south underground railway lines went under East Berlin from the West, running non-stop through shut-down 'ghost stations' before reaching Western territory again.

FIGURE 2b. *Official GDR border-guard photo 96 of the watch-tower on the Reichstagufer, looking along the river Spree to the Marschall Brücke. (Hagen Koch Archive.)*

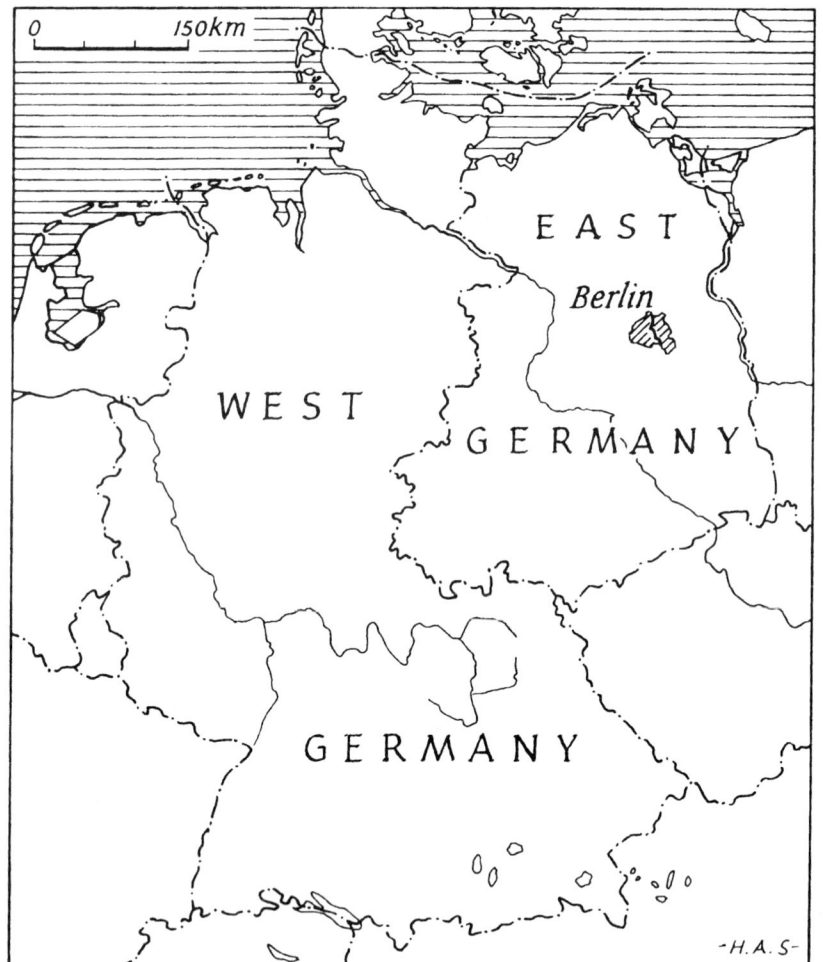

FIGURE 3. *Map of Germany, showing the Inner German border and the border through and around Berlin.*

The foundations of the Wall were laid in late 1945 when the USA changed its policy from attempted co-operation with the Soviet Union to 'containment', according to the new policy's progenitor George F. Kennan: 'if the West was not willing to "go the full hog" to block the USSR, the only alternative was to split Germany, partition Europe into two spheres and decide the "line beyond which we cannot afford to permit the Russians to exercise unchallenged power"' (McCauley 1983: 52). With two spheres of influence established, Berlin was the Western island of influence inside the Eastern zone that could become the 'the West's weakest spot' (McCauley 1983: 77). In 1948 Stalin block-aded surface access to West Berlin; the Western Allies kept Berlin provisioned by a massive air-lift. The episode hardened anti-Communist sentiment in West Berlin and proved to West Berliners that their half of the city was viable on its own.

The Wall was constructed in 1961 as a climax of the 'Berlin Crisis'. Its international dimension started with Khruschev's 1958 ultimatum to the Western Allies that they abrogate their right of residence under the four-powers status of Berlin (Rühle & Holzweißig 1981: 11), one of the several episodes of Soviet–American brinkmanship that culminated in the Cuba crisis of 1962.

In 1958 refugees told Western security services that the East German communist party had been preparing plans since 1951 for 'a hermetic and fixed border with West Berlin' (Rühle & Holzweißig 1982: 18).

A combination of economic difficulties in East Germany, the collectivization of agriculture, a hard-line phase of party policy, and Khruschev's threat to Berlin lead to a dramatic increase in the number of emigrants from East Germany, which reached 30,000 a month in July 1961 (Weber 1985: 321). In March 1961 the Warsaw Pact vetoed the plan of the East German leader, Walter Ulbricht, for a barbed-wire fence across the border to stem the flood.

In July US President Kennedy laid down the fundamentals of Western policy on Berlin: the presence of the Western powers, the right of free access to Berlin, and political self determination for the population of West Berlin (but not East Berlin) (Asmuss 1987: 103).

On 3 August 1961 a desperate East German leadership gave a Warsaw Pact meeting in Moscow three alternatives: closing the air routes to Berlin; building a wall; or the shutting the ring around greater Berlin (Weber 1982: 326). Ulbricht favoured the most radical course, 'a final blockade of Berlin'. As that prescription was too drastic for the Soviets, Ulbricht was authorised only to cut off the traffic between the Eastern and Western sectors of the city (Craig 1982: 52–3). The documents show that it was very much Erich Honecker's Wall. Later to lead the GDR, he was then the secretary of the national defence council and with three others planned the operation in secret. The archives reveal that the Central Committee of the Communist Party was only officially informed two days after the Wall was built (Möbius & Trotnow 1991).

The construction of the Wall allowed Ulbricht to stem the crippling flow of *c.* 2.7 million people who had left East Germany since 1949 (Weber 1982: 325), and to show the West a strong front, without infringing on Kennedy's fundamentals, which could have triggered a world war. In a message to the West German ambassador in Moscow, Khruschev said, 'I wouldn't want to conceal from you that it was I who in the last instance gave the order for it. . . . I know that the Wall is an ugly thing. It will also disappear. However only when the reasons for its construction have gone' (in Rühle & Holzweißig 1988: 18–19).

From the beginning the Wall had a second function. Beyond stopping mass emigration, it was given great symbolic significance from both sides. In the propaganda of the German Democratic Republic (GDR), the Wall was a contribution to world peace, 'a foundation stone for the success of our policy of relaxation and peaceful co-operation' (Honecker, 1973, quoted in Mehls & Mehls 1979: 43). In Party rhetoric, the Wall was an 'anti-fascist protection wall' (Honecker 1980: 205) not to keep Easterners in, but to keep the Western influence out. It was anti-fascist, because Honecker saw West Germany's capitalist economy and the formation of an army within Nato (which included some ex-*Wehrmacht* military men) as putting the Federal Republic on a par with Nazi Germany. On the first anniversary of its construction, the Party paper said, 'Now that a year has passed, we can establish that the protection wall that we built against the aggressors has proved itself to be tenable and has secured the peace' (*Neues Deutschland* 1962, in Rühle & Holzweißig 1988: 156). Just as rhetorically, American President Kennedy said on his famous visit in 1963, 'The Wall is the most repulsive and strongest demonstration of the failure of the Communist system' (in Möbius & Trotnow 1990: 14). For West as well as East, the Wall was a useful visual short-hand. It showed each side who they were, by creating a clear enemy, a clear image of what they were not. As Edelmann (1985) has pointed out, for most people politics today is nothing more than a sequence of pictures

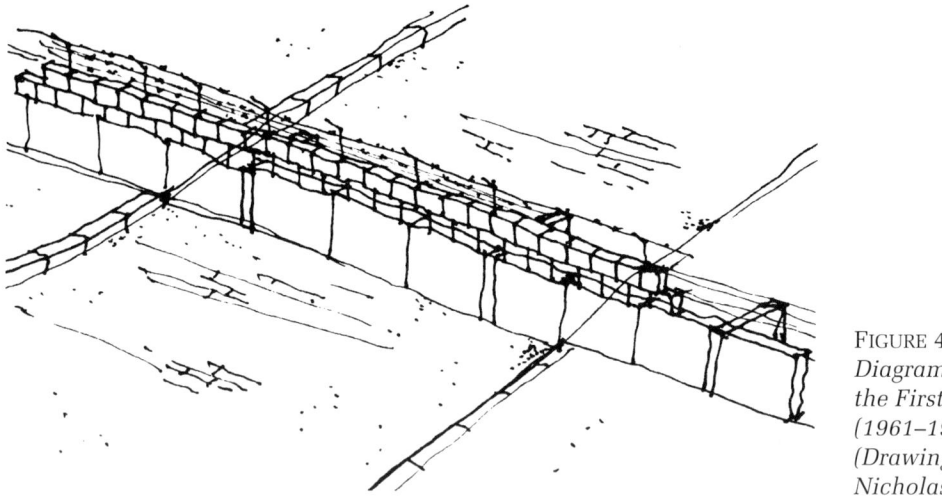

FIGURE 4.
*Diagram showing
the First Wall
(1961–1964).
(Drawing:
Nicholas Baker.)*

from the TV, newspapers magazines; the Wall provided the perfect image to sum up the
Cold War world, the picture-bite to go with the sound bite. This was the basis of the
power of the Wall, and the aura that each fragment carries.

The first Wall, 13 August 1961 to 1964

The construction of the Berlin Wall started at 2.15 a.m. on 13 August 1961, when members of the East German security forces started to break up the pavements at the Friedrich-
Ebert Straße with pneumatic drills. At the Potsdamer Platz concrete posts were put up
along with rolls of barbed wire. By the afternoon the border was complete, West Berlin
was surrounded. Simultaneously, a few hundred kilometres to the west, a double row of
barbed wire fences was being put up from the Baltic to Bohemia, along the East Germany's border with West Germany (Gerig 1986). Then, 'When no effective Western retalia-
tion materialised they replaced the temporary barrier with a cement wall' (Craig 1982:
53). This barrier of earth, breeze blocks, concrete, Spanish riders and barbed wire formed
the first phase of the Wall (FIGURE 4). Round the outskirts of the city, multi-layered barbed
wire fences formed the Wall (Hildebrandt 1988a: 9). This 'ring around Berlin' consisted
of '12 km of wall, 137 km of barbed wire fortifications (made up of 8000–10,000 km of
barbed wire) and 450,000–500,000 square metres of no-man's land'. Before the Wall was
built, 10,000 West Berliners had allotments or holiday homes in East Berlin, 53,000 East
Berliners had jobs in the West, and 1100 schoolchildren commuted from the East to the
West. The Wall cut across eight overground (*S-Bahn*) and four underground (*U-Bahn*)
railway lines, and 193 roads. Before, there were 81 crossing points into the Soviet sector;
after there were only 7 (Rühle & Holzweißig 1988: 145–7).

This initial phase saw the forced evacuation of buildings on the border, infamously
the moving of almost 2000 people from their flats on the Bernauer Straße (Möbius &
Trotnow 1990). Many people jumped into the Western sector from high windows. Four
died (Petschull 1990, Rühle & Holzweißig 1988: 146).

Mander (1962: 10) described this first-generation Wall:

> It does not look very impressive, even in photographs. Close up, it is even
> less so. When I first saw it I was impressed by its flimsiness. It was the sort of wall
> that asked to be pushed over — a tank or a bulldozer could flatten it.

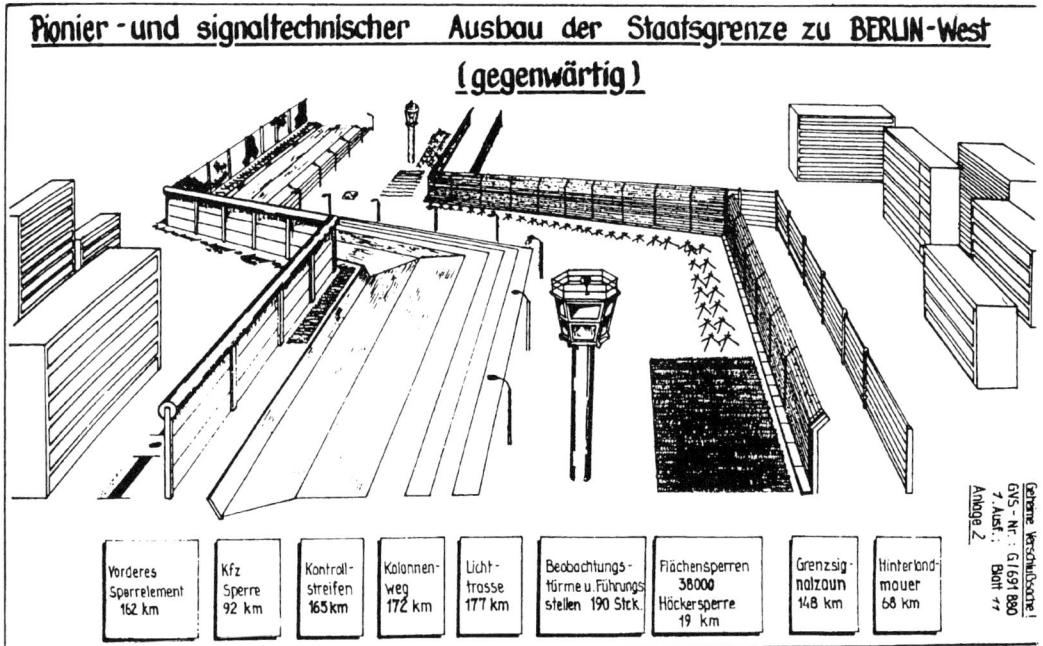

Pionier - und signaltechnischer   Ausbau der   Staatsgrenze zu BERLIN-West
(gegenwärtig)

| Vorderes Sperrelement 162 km | Kfz Sperre 92 km | Kontroll- streifen 165 km | Kolonnen- weg 172 km | Licht- trasse 177 km | Beobachtungs- türme u. Führungs stellen 190 Stck. | Flächensperren 38000 Höckersperre 19 km | Grenzsig- nalzaun 148 km | Hinterland- mauer 68 km |

FIGURE 5. *Official GDR border-guard diagram of the second Wall (1964–1976) for the border with West Berlin. Marked as 'Classified Information'. (Hagen Koch archive.)*

The point was not lost on the Americans who planned to dynamite the Wall on New Year's Eve 1961, a project vetoed by the British. Some Berliners took things into their own hands; in the first two years 23 violent attacks were recorded on the Wall. On 2 December 1962, a big bomb did rip a hole in the Wall, but for the politicians the Wall was already part of the *status quo*. West Berlin's mayor Willy Brandt, criticized the bomb, saying: 'Explosives are not just no argument, explosives damage Berlin' (*Berliner Zeitung* 1992a). From then on, words were the only dynamite to be flung against the Wall. However flimsy, the first Wall did its job for Honecker: the number of emigrants dropped from 14,821 in September to 2420 in December 1961 (Rühle & Holzweißig 1988: 154).

East Germany then felt secure enough to allow the first contact between East and West Berliners. The first visits by relatives took place between 19 December 1963 and 5 January 1964 (Möbius & Trotnow 1990: 56).

The second Wall, 1964–1976: 'The modern border'

Exact phasing of the Wall's construction is difficult, because the Wall was organized in local sections, each with different commanders, terrain and resources; detailed investigations reveal local idiosyncrasies in construction, in the timing of changes and the way modernizations were carried out (Trotnow pers. comm.) — the same local differences one can see in other great walls of history. What makes this second Wall stand out is its pre-calculated nature. Gone were the improvised materials of the first Wall. This second Wall was made of standard, pre-fabricated parts and for the first time had the typical smooth pipe along the top, replacing the barbed wire (Hildebrandt 1988a: 12) (FIGURE 5). Peter Schneider describes it (1983: 52–3):

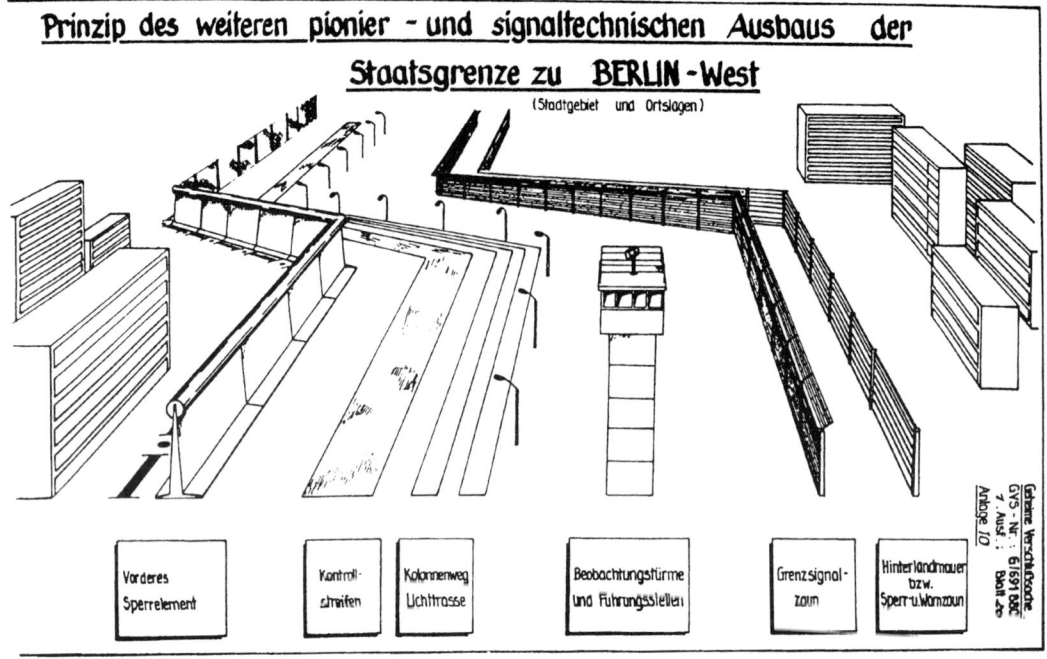

FIGURE 6. *Official GDR border regiment diagram of the Final Wall (1976–1989) for the border with urban areas of West Berlin. Marked as 'Classified Information'. (Hagen Koch archive.)*

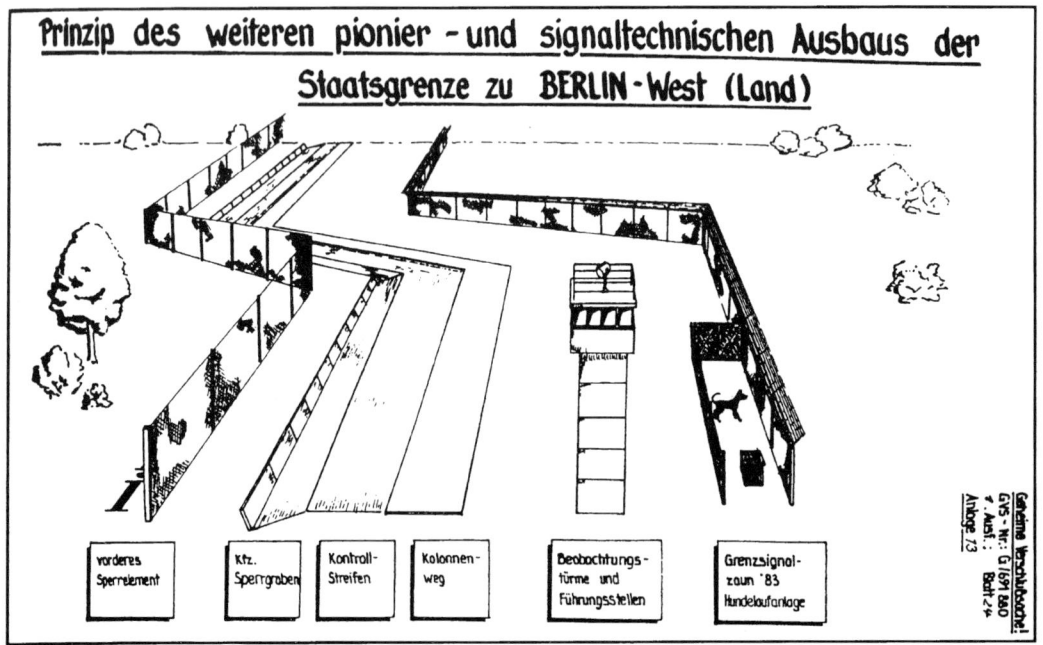

FIGURE 7. *Official GDR border regiment diagram of the Final Wall (1976–1989) 'for the border with rural parts of West Berlin'. Marked as 'Classified Information'. (Hagen Koch archive.)*

The ring around West Berlin is 102.5 miles long. Of this, 65.8 miles consist of concrete slabs topped with a pipe; another 34 miles is constructed of stamped-metal fencing. 260 watch-towers stand along the border, manned day and night by twice that many border guards. The towers are linked by a tarred military road, which runs along the border strip. To the right and left of the road, a carefully raked stretch of sand conceals trip wires: flares go off if anything touches them. Should this happen, jeeps stand ready for border troops, and dogs are stationed at 267 dog runs along the way. Access to the strip from the east is further prevented by an inner wall at the foot of which are spikes which can literally nail a jumper to the ground, spiking him on 5-inch prongs. Long stretches of the inner wall still consist of the façades of houses situated along the border, but their doors and windows have been bricked up. Underground in the sewers, the border is secured by electrified fences, which grant free passage only to the excretions from both parts of the city.

The third and final Wall, 1976 to 9 November 1989

With the boast was that this was 'the best security system in the world' (Hildebrandt 1988a: 73), the third Wall was started in 1976, intended as the final version. It was final, not as Honecker had hoped in the sense of permanent, but in the other sense of last. The huge L-profile prefabricated blocks of this third Wall are what we see in all the TV pictures being toppled to the great cheers of the crowd; it is these portions of the late Wall which have gone down in the public imagination as *the* Berlin Wall.

On 28 October 1969, West German Chancellor Willy Brandt said he was prepared to deal on equal terms with the GDR, in a Germany that was 'two states, but . . . one nation' (Diemer 1990: 83). Against the background of Brandt's *Ostpolitik*, a new 'Four-powers agreement over Berlin' in 1971 stabilized West Berlin's position and eased the number of visits possible to East Berlin (Diemer 1990: 88). By 1973 the GDR, accepted into UNESCO, had established diplomatic relations with Great Britain and France. It could think of the third-generation Wall as the final Wall, firm in belief; 'The Berlin Wall will also be standing in 50 and also in 100 years. . . . The Wall protects us from robbers', said Erich Honecker in early 1989 — just seven months before he and his Wall were destroyed (*Berliner Zeitung*, 20 January 1989).

The Western, outer barrier of this 'final' Wall had a height of 3·6 m; it was built of pre-cast slabs set side by side (FIGURES 6, 7). The sections were of a steel-reinforced concrete of high density (Möbius & Trotnow 1990: figure 71), which included large amounts of asbestos, reaching levels of up to 75% (Malzahn 1989). This form and the smooth flat surface it offered was to have a big impact on the graffiti art of the Wall's Western face. According to Lapp (1987: 139), 111·6 km of the border around Berlin were by then walled; there was 124·9 km of electric fence, a 124-km road along the death strip for patrol cars and bikes, 258 dog runs, 298 watch-towers and 52 bunkers (FIGURES 8, 9). Although it had more wall, the politically more sensitive Berlin border was not the most brutal. In Berlin there were no tripwire-activated gun systems as there were on the inner German border to the west until 1985, when under pressure from the West these were dismantled (Lapp 1987: 140).

This new Wall was more efficient as a barrier. Its visual strength and force bore a symbolism as well — to heighten the crime of fleeing the republic. Samson (1992: 32) says of Offa's Dyke, a frontier defence that was immense in the technology of its own era: 'if Offa's Dyke appears to have involved an unnecessary amount of effort in erection, so the "illegal" crossing of it would have been seen as more serious.' The symbolic discouragement should not be exaggerated in comparison with the physical: the order to shoot,

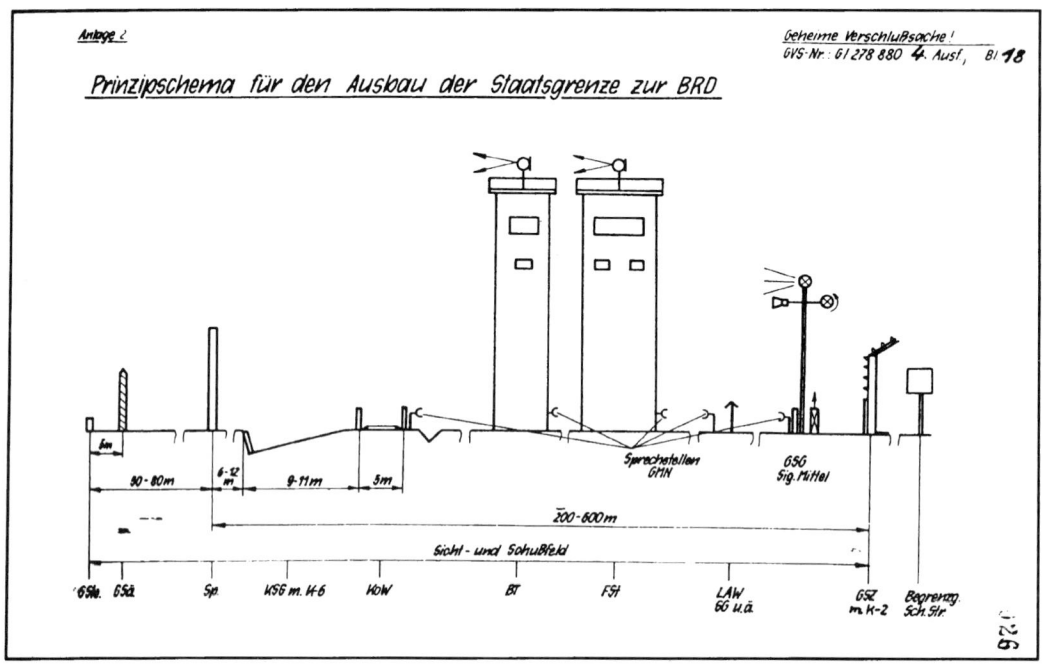

FIGURE 8. *Official GDR border regiment section-drawing of the Final Wall (1976–1989) 'for the border with the Federal Republic of Germany'. Marked as 'Classified Information'. (Hagen Koch archive.)*

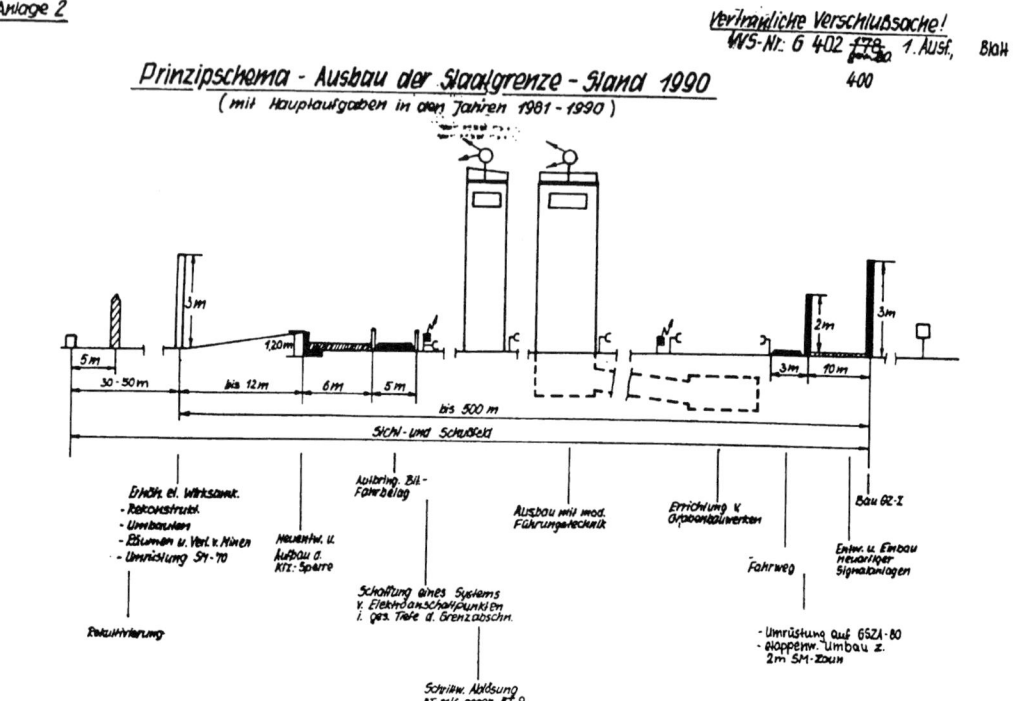

FIGURE 9. *Official GDR border regiment section-drawing of the planned expansion of the Final Wall to be completed by 1990. Marked as 'Classified Information'. (Hagen Koch archive.)*

in operation on the border since the 1950s, became a part of the official constitution in May 1982. Latest figures put the fatalities since the building of the Wall in Berlin at 122, on the Inner German border 144, and in the Baltic 81 Twenty-five East German border guards were shot by Western agents, by escapees and by colleagues while attempting to flee (Hildebrandt 1993).

The fall of the Wall

A factor in creating the limbo after the Wall opened was a Western inertia, the shock from an event which a whole generation had been convinced was impossible. Among the very few to predict the fall of the Wall was novelist Martin Walser (1989: 100), who said on 3 October 1988: 'The majority of the opinion makers, left and right, work at making the division rational. . . . One would like to think that . . . the Germans would vote in both their states for a way to unity.' In 1989, architects at Darmstadt University analysing Berlin's urban structure concluded that social, cultural and economic barriers in both halves of the city 'influence the development of both half cities much more than the Wall' (Drosdeck *et al.* 1989: 34).

By the late 1980s the standing Wall had already been run through by the new media, which no medieval city wall had to cope with: 'The broadcast frequencies reach well over it. Policies of political relaxation have created the possibility to travel across — all be it that these are unequally divided. . . . The Wall is undermined by a natural gas pipeline from the Soviet Union and an optic cable leading to the Federal Republic' (Eckardt 1987: 39).

The late 1980s were also witness to a bizarre manifestation of a slow thaw in the Cold War. East German border guards helped West Berlin ecological radicals to flee across the Wall when the Western police cleared the Linné triangle (Smith 1991). Once over the Wall, they were given a cup of coffee and taken back to the West when the demo had died down.

The *Zeitgeist* of this suppressed longing to overcome the division is captured brilliantly in Wim Wenders & Peter Handke's (1989) film *Wings of desire*; its heroes are two angels with wings to fly and invisible to the human eye, who can traverse the Wall at will and even stroll along the death strip. It is an amazing premonition of today when the former no-man's land is the largest cycle path and promenade in the city.

Power relations in the GDR were crucial, since the control of the Wall became a symbol for a larger debate; as Samson (1992: 32) says, 'Without the authority and power to make them function, walls cannot act as barriers, far less as serious fences, they are neutral without the social relations necessary to make them work.' He continues (1992: 36): 'The symbolic function of town walls is reflected by Gregory of Tour's belief that their collapse was an unmistakable sign that the king would die.' As the king of East Berlin's city Wall, Erich Honecker fell, so did his handiwork a few days later. History had now overtaken him; the decade demanded not the hero of the Wall's construction but a 'real hero of deconstruction', 'a hero of a new kind, representing not victory, conquest and triumph, but renunciation, reduction and dismantling' (Enzensberger 1989: 136). As in the construction of the Wall local factors in East Germany combined with international factors in the Soviet Union. Crucial to the fall of the Wall locally was successor Honecker's Egon Krenz; however the real architect of demolition was Khruschev's successor in the Kremlin, Mikhail Gorbachev. As early as 1987 Gorbachev recalls feeling 'the archaic nature of the "Iron Curtain"' (1988: 194). When he came to the celebrations of the 40th birthday of East Germany, a few weeks before the Wall fell, Gorbachev made it publicly clear he saw no future for a GDR which did not recognize the changing times.

Krenz soon suffered the archetypal fate of the historical demolition man: 'in doing his job he ended up undermining his own position. The dynamics he set in motion hurled him aside, and he was buried by his own successes' (Enzensberger 1989: 138).

The Wall started to fall not in Berlin but in Hungary, where on 11 September 1989 the government chose to let the 6500 East German tourists cross the iron curtain to Austria (Aanderud & Knopp 1991). The pressure of the New Forum movement and the numbers fleeing via Prague, Warsaw and Budapest built up. On 6 November, Klaus Hartung could already title an editorial commentary 'The fall of the Wall' (1989). Three days later, on the evening of 9 November, the East German government spokesman Günter Schabowski announced that citizens of the GDR could 'cross the border' (Geisler 1992: 262). With this event the East German revolution had changed gear; the ordered stride of the autumns demos now became a rush (Warnecken 1992: 21). As word spread, crowds pushing forward to the border crossings were to their astonishment let through to the West.

With hindsight, we see this was the end of the Wall (Darnton 1991: 51):

> On 9 November it still cut the heart of Berlin, a jagged wound in the centre of a great city, the great division of the cold war. But on the 10th it was a dance floor, a picture gallery, a black board, a cinema screen, a video cassette, a museum and as the cleaning lady in my office said 'just a pile of stones'. Like the storming of the Bastille the breaching of the Wall changed the world.

One must remember that the Wall only *opened* on 9 November. No one knew whether it would close again or whether it would crumble, as it did not just at the Potsdamer Platz, but also along its whole length. The whole city was in a state of limbo. All East German institutions, the border forces included, were paralysed by a crisis of authority. A state of anarchy activated and empowered individuals to take the political and physical future of the Wall upon themselves, a champagne bottle in one hand, a chisel in the other. The next day, 10 November, the West Berlin paper *Volksblatt* carried two headlines next to each other: 'The Wall has fallen,' and 'Bonn calls for the demolition of the Wall.' Darnton (1991: 51) comments: 'Both were correct. The Wall was there and no longer existed.'

According to Gottfried Korff (1990: 156): 'it was a situation in which the past was negated, erased, cast aside, but the future hadn't begun yet'. It is in light of this tension that the attempts at preserving, as well as consuming the Berlin Wall must be understood.

Consuming the Wall

The fall of the Wall gripped the world (Smith 1990: 75–6):

> As the news from Berlin rippled outward, dousing everyone in instant history, tourists began pouring in, from the rest of Germany, and from Europe and America and Japan, just to see, pick up a souvenir, take pictures, live briefly in a moment of significance. 1989 was a boom year for Berlin tourism, and in the first week after the opening, British Airways carried 30% more passengers to Berlin, than at the same time a year before. By the Wall there was a good deal of strutting by those who felt their system vindicated.

For the tourist industry the Wall was the defining feature of Berlin. The Wall had become the eighth wonder of the world in the West. TV showed the world within seconds the Berliners' instant reaction — to take physical possession of it, first climbing on it, and then hacking at it. Characteristic of 1980s tourism is the consumption of goods, a means to prove attendance at the history that one is consuming: 'One day, maybe, stores and museums will become the same . . . with everything for display, inspection and sale' (Bayley 1989: 7). That day came with 9 November 1989. Within hours, pieces of Wall were on sale in West Berlin's premier shopping street.

Why did people buy a bit of the Wall? The skilful marketing of the heritage industry cannot be responsible, since this souvenir trade was not directed by professional merchandising. In a world where history is kept in the hands of professionals and its physical artefacts are locked away in Museums, the collapse of political authority over the Wall left a vacuum which allowed everyone access to fragments of a historical object imbued with historical significance. The Wall belonged to anyone with time on their hands.

At the Wall, more was at work. Television played a crucial role in the events of autumn 1989 (Garton Ash 1990: 23), its clearest images the joy and the destruction of the physical substance of the Wall with pick-axes or crow-bars. The personal pleasure of meeting was mixed with the *Schadenfreude* of climbing on to the forbidden Wall and smashing it. These images went into the home of the world. When tourists later made it to Berlin, the joy had gone, but the *Schadenfreude*, the central passion of our reaction, remained; you could yourself attack the Wall or just take a piece of it. You could buy a piece, or pay 5 DM to hire a hammer and chisel for 20 minutes and get your own pieces. If as Michel Butor said (in Hildebrandt 1988a: 64), 'you have to touch the Wall to believe it is reality', then you have to strike the Wall to believe its destruction. Even Ronald Reagan had a go at Wall-pecking when he visited Berlin on 12 September 1990 (Aanderud & Knopp 1991: 24). A crowd of 'Wall-peckers' made a profession of chipping pieces off the Berlin Wall and selling them to tourists (Baker 1992a). It was the marginals of German society (students, pensioners, and Polish, Italian or Turkish *Gastarbeiter*), who most frequently tried to make some quick money from this symbol of German history.

Mass consumption demands mass production. When the supply of Wall-fragments carrying genuine graffiti stopped, the demand did not. One evening in February 1990 I met a man in no-man's land. He was smashing pieces out of the east side of the Wall, carefully following the line of a chaotic band of colour he had sprayed on to the grey surface. At his feet lay a bag full of spray-paint cans of every colour. I asked him what he was doing. He answered: 'I'm producing Wall fragments for my stall by the *Reichstag*. I'm getting a pneumatic drill next week. That will give me a year's supply.' But why did he have to spray the grey east face of the Wall first? 'Because fragments with graffiti sell better, and otherwise people wouldn't believe that the fragments were real. Anyway the Wall-peckers have chiselled off all the graffiti on the West side.' Mr De Carolis, an Italian labourer in Berlin for 15 years, was forging history, with genuine materials. The small flakes of Wall that the tourists bought at his stall by the *Reichstag*, were genuine pieces of Berlin Wall, but these originally grey pieces of a *Mauer* which 189 people died trying to cross, had been converted into the harmless *Wand,* West Berlin's colourful scribble-pad and wonder of the post-modern world. The impact of tourism was again to distort: 'The local and "exotic" are torn out of place and time to be repackaged for the world bazaar' (Robins 1991: 31). The Berlin Wall was consumed by our little purchases at the souvenir stalls in a post-modern era when we are 'condemned to seek history by way of our own pop images and *simulacra* of that history, which itself remains forever out of reach' (Jameson 1984: 71), and seems best explained by Daniel Miller (1987) who has described how the desire to personalize, to appropriate and finally to re-contextualize objects is a prime motivation for consuming them.

FIGURE 10. *Wall-peckers at work on the Wall's western face; seen from the Tiergarten, looking across the death-strip to the as-yet graffiti-free internal Wall in the East, 1990. (Photo Gerlind Klemens.)*

Graffiti art: just one of the Wall's four faces

At the heart of this paradox is the opposition that Walser summarized between *Wand* and *Mauer*. And the story shows that the florescence against the absence of graffiti is the direct visual corollary (FIGURE 10).

The image the final Wall presented to the East was of an absolute, insurmountable barrier, painted with military order in pale grey-green-coloured panels. The image to the west that is remembered of the same physical barrier is a surface wildly coloured with graffiti. The graffiti became a crucial hallmark of the Wall in the popular imagination, and now provides the dominant European memory of what the Wall was like.

The graffiti of the Wall have their own structure and their own history.

Most of the graffiti starts with the second of the Wall's three generations when 'at the end of the 60s the students movement discovered the Wall as the perfect medium for visual protest' (Kuzdas 1990: 10). 'In the early years this was paint brush work, often done at night. There were some arrests by the East German border guards for defacing People's property' (Smith 1990: 20–21). The rough slatted surface of the early Wall was not conducive to proper painting; when Frank Liefeoghe wanted to paint the Wall on the Wilhelm Straße he had to attach plywood boards to make the Wall a usable surface (Hildebrandt 1988a: 22).

As the GDR tried finally to turn its back on the west, it created the final form of the Wall with a beautifully polished, pristine surface that just begged to be defiled. The panel of the Final Wall provided such perfect frames that 'each single panel of the Wall ironically obeys the law of the classical column, with a "base", "pillar" and "capital"' (Kuzdas 1990: 10). The Wall provided a frame as well as a surface. Artists even used to sign their works on the round concrete tube that ran along the top and made an upper 'frame' for the picture.

According to Hildebrandt (1988a: 48), Lew Nussberg of the 1962 Moscow non-conformist 'Movement Group' who emigrated with his followers in 1976 was the first internationally known artist to express a wish to paint on the Berlin Wall. There followed Boucher & Noir's 'Statues of Liberty' and Keith Haring's 100-m long chain of human figures (Kuzdas 1990: 12); Haring, it will be remembered, was a New York graffiti artist whose street style became fashionable fine art.

'Overcoming the Wall by painting the wall' was the crucial ambition of much of the art on the Wall, summarized in the title of an exhibition organized by Dr Rainer Hildebrandt's (1988a) private Checkpoint Charlie Museum in 1984. The 3000-mark prize went to East German dissident Mattias Hohl-Stein.

By the mid 1980s, with the arrival of the spray can, the Wall's paintwork had become a permanently changing exhibition proclaiming the slogans of every struggle in Europe. Some of its graffiti was passionate and witty. The bulk wasn't. Much was in English, the work of non-Berliners.

In late 1986 a group of expelled East German dissidents from Weimar painted a broad white line at eye level along the whole length of the by-then colourful Wall between Mariannen Platz and the Potsdamer Platz: 'The Wall must be seen again for what it is. It is not a tourist attraction.' Their white line symbolically wiped out Wall art. They opposed the Wall being considered the 'eighth wonder of the world' (Kuzdas 1990: 55). Their act shows how, even before the Wall fell, there was a struggle and a difference in the perception of the Wall and its graffiti between Easterners for whom it was a wall, a barrier and the Westerners for whom it was a canvas, a wonder of the world.

The word *graffiti* was first used by classical archaeologists to distinguish between officially sanctioned inscriptions and unofficial texts (Stahl 1989: 12). Even after the fall

FIGURE 11. *Section of Wall awaiting to be recycled at the Wall 'graveyard' in Pankow, 1990. (Photo Gerlind Klemens).*

of the Wall this official/unofficial defined the graffiti. Lieutenant Colonel Karsch, who served with the border regiment for 25 years from the age of 18 recalls (Fischer & Von der Schulenburg 1990: 27):

> Well, all of a sudden our artists from East Berlin began to paint the Wall at this point, without asking the border guards for permission. So we had to give the guards a pot of paint and a brush and order them to paint over it. If they had asked for permission, then they would have got it, straight away, no problem. But as it was we had no choice but to order the guards to paint over it. I'm sure you understand.

The reaction is understandable. It was soldiers who built, manned, maintained and therefore *defined* the Wall. Till now they had been the sole Eastern wall artists, the only ones able to paint it. Even when it was breached, they tried to control who could paint on it and what they painted. It was a military structure, the product of the orderly military mind.

Censorship had not been confined to the East. The Wall was built a metre or two to the east of the exact frontier line, so even its Western, painted face was on the territory of East Berlin. Smith (1990: 108) notes:

> For years and years they fought against graffiti, the Western police discouraged it, there was so much uncertainty what the other side might do, could do. In some points such as the Potsdamer Platz, which were very sensitive points, they tried to keep it white, continually whitewashing. When Jimmy Carter came to West Berlin the West whited out anti-American slogans there. But eventually they gave up in the mid eighties.

In early 1990 a long section of Eastern Wall near the Oberbaumbrücke was given over panel by panel to an international collection of artists. Dubbed the 'East Side Gallery', the signed and copyrighted panels were to be removed and sent round the world as a travelling exhibition to art museums, transferring the Western tradition of high art on the Wall to the East. The East Side Gallery remains in place along the Mühlen Straße, saved from removal by its local popularity.

The last chapter in the artistic history of the Wall was reached by the sale of complete concrete segments with fine pieces of Western Wall art. In January 1990 the East German government, estimating the value of the total Wall at DM800,000,000 (about £3.7 million), set to marketing segments to museums, companies and rich individuals (Grant 1992: 150). Some of the best pieces went to art galleries like the Museum of Modern Art in New York (Aanderud & Knopp 1992: 124). Others of what was now a sculpture were sold at auction in Monte Carlo to the Vatican (Escaut-Marquet 1990), and to the Expo in Seville (*Berliner Zeitung* 1992b; Grant 1992; Gow 1991). After German reunification on 3 October 1990, the Defence Ministry in Bonn, as the Wall's new owner, staked its claim on the money raised from the art sales to help pay for the Wall's removal. 'Artistic' sections of the Wall are now spread between 18 countries, from Fatima to Japan (Koch in Hildebrandt 1993: 47). The other parts are in 'graveyards' (FIGURE 11) awaiting recycling into 0·54 mm granules for road-building at DM23 (£9.20) per ton. Metal fence posts go to gardeners, farmers and steelworks (Wedow 1992).

The dialectical nature of art's relationship with the military structure which was the Berlin Wall had reached its conclusion; the art had the effect on the Wall of *Aufheben* in the Hegelian sense of the word. *Aufheben* has two meanings: raising or lifting as well as preserving or keeping (Gonzsalez-Marcen & Risch 1990: 102). Art had been a symptom of relaxing East–West tensions. It so captured the public and political imagination as a metaphor for a pluralistic open democratic society, that it became a force in finally lifting and removing the Wall. But Art had also the power to preserve the Wall; the art painted on the west face of the Wall as an attempt to overcome the Wall came to save some pieces from destruction.

The Berlin Wall and the Bastille

So while everyone from labourers to the Defence Minister are busy consuming the Wall, a comparison with the treatment of the Bastille after its revolutionary fall in 1789 reminds us of the Wall's symbolic function; which gives fragments a special national aura, affects both their consumption and preservation.

Commentators have reached back to the French Revolution of 1789 as an analogy for the events of 1989 (Biermann 1991: 9; Darnton 1991: 51). Chippindale (1990a) noted a specific analogy. The collapse of the Berlin Wall was the great symbolic event in the revolutions of the late 1980's in Eastern Bloc Europe, just as the storming of the Bastille was the great symbolic event in the French revolution of 1789. There are telling similarities in what happened to each: the rage of the people that was let loose on the monument, its rapid demolition and the turning of fragments into souvenirs, touchstones of the revolution's reality and meaning.

On the evening of 14 July 1789 Pierre-François Palloy started the job of demolishing the Bastille. He had helped storm the old fortress earlier that day. Within a year only foundations and a pile of rubble remained. Palloy, more than a demolition contractor, was a self-professed 'Apostle of liberty' (Lüsebrink & Reichardt 1990: 136). Presenting a piece of the Bastille to the *département* of Calvados, he wrote: 'It was not enough for me to have been there and contributing to the destruction of the walls of this, I also have the urge to immortalize the memory of its horror' (Lüsebrink & Reichardt 1990: 137).

In October and November 1790 Palloy sent miniatures of the Bastille, carved from the dismantled blocks of that 'Temple of Despair' to each of the 83 French *départements* at his own cost, accompanied by 'Apostles of freedom' to give public readings of Palloy's tracts. The new *départements* were new land divisions sweeping away the old 'intendencies', each new entity launched with a physical part of the Revolution.

Palloy did not see the Bastille stones purely as 'reliquaries' of a new patriotic cult, but also as 'emblems' or 'dead pledge of Liberty, which irreparably unite the regenerated body of the nation and give it new energy (Lüsebrink & Reichardt 1990: 139–40). Dubbed 'destroyer of the Bastille' by the press in March 1792, Palloy produced medals for the 900 members of the French parliament, made from the iron bars and chains of the Bastille (1990: 141). Bastille stones were even used as settings in patriotic jewellery of liberty.

Ken Smith (1990: 189) reports of Wall fragments: 'Some mount their chips as badges, brooches, earrings, sculpture, assemblages of wire and glazed surfaces. Others are set in PVC resin. Others are authenticated by various sorts of certificate'. Stall-holders equip themselves with rubber stamps, which they print on fragments as 'proof' of authenticity. Again the paint is important as a talisman; at the stalls round the *Reichstag* in 1990, every one of the many hundred fragments of Wall on sale was painted; the pattern of paint on a big, expensive chunk showed it had been painted *after* it had been broken off.

On the first anniversary of the storming, Palloy threw a 'revolutionary party, 'Here there will be dancing, there will always be dancing'. The dance-floor was erected on stones from the Bastille. Palloy's workers gave tours of the Bastille cellars, which they had rebuilt and fitted out as a horror and torture chamber. At Palloy's house a *papier-maché* copy of the Bastille was stormed to the cheers of the crowd, who freed a heavily chained white-haired 'prisoner', and then all processed in triumph through the streets (Lüsebrink & Reichardt 1990: 143).

Berlin's equivalent to Palloy may be Hagen Koch, the Stasi officer who left his commission in 1985 and who collects representative elements of the Wall for the Checkpoint Charlie Museum (Dobberke 1993). But typically his case is more complex; it was he who drew the line across the road at Checkpoint Charlie where the Wall-builders had started on the night of 13 August 1961. The destroyer-cum-recorder-cum-preserver had himself been the builder. Interviewed in 1990, he made clear the political purpose behind his collection of Wall sections for the museum (Thames 1990) was '. . . to confront people walking passed with the former defence systems of the border, and to remind the people of this topic because it cannot be that many countries will receive parts of the wall via me . . . and in Berlin there is nothing left for future generations'.

Palloy understood the need to make abstract ideas — tyranny, freedom, liberty — physically tangible and accessible for the general public; like the Bastille, the Berlin Wall is a 'collective symbol' (Drews *et al.* 1985), an easily identifiable, emotionally charged, physical embodiment of the political system which made it — both symbol of tyranny and symbol of liberation from tyranny.

In Catholic France in 1789, the politics followed religious metaphors. A tract of 1792 declares (Lüsebrink & Reichardt 1990: 138–9): 'France is a new world, and in order to maintain this achievement, it is necessary, to sow out the fragments of our old enslavement, just as when Leviticus in the Book of Moses distributed the limbs of his wife in all directions of the wind, to wreak revenge.' In secular Berlin in 1989, metaphors were mixed; the Wall fragments went with travel souvenirs, rock concerts, art or 'history'.

In Berlin the rock concert became one of the experiences through which people collectively expressed themselves in those first heady weeks, in which there were more

Berliners than tourists. They danced three times on the Wall: at the opening of the Wall on 9 November, at the opening of the Brandenburg Gate on 21 December, and at New Year on 31 December 1989. In the Berlin 'Wall dance', there was neither music nor dance steps, people shouted and gesticulated like they do at rock concerts (Darnton 1990: 79). But there was also carnival, fireworks, bottles opened. 'The dancers wore jeans and anoraks. Many of them were young, almost all of them under 30 . . . most of them born after 1961 the year of the Wall's construction' (Darnton 1991: 82). At these rock concerts, the folk dances of our age, the merchandising led on the commodification of Wall memorabilia, particularly T-shirts; one said thank you to Gorbachev as 'GorBATchev Man' smashing through the Wall in the figure of Batman.

Large concerts were staged on the West side of the Wall near the Reichstag. One can be seen (Darnton 1991: 83) as

> the key event, which gave the East Berlin demonstrations lots of impulses. It took place on 19 June at a Michael Jackson concert. While Jackson filled the air with sound near the Reichstag on the Western side of the Wall, a group of young people gathered on the Eastern side to listen. The police tried to drive them away, but the crowd defended itself . . . Rock on one side of the Wall, riots on the other. At the big Wall dance at New Year 1990 they came together.

Rock came back the following summer, 1990, as a medium for consuming the Wall and echoing Palloy's re-enactment of the storming of the Bastille. A huge wall of polystyrene blocks was smashed down as the climax to Pink Floyd's performance of their concept album and film *The Wall* (*Spiegel* 1990).

A final collective medium for the appreciation of the Wall was the modern chronological concept of history. As Hermann Bausinger has noted, the collective concept of history in the 18th century had a very close horizon of two to three generations; the days when grand-dad was a child were as distant as the Romans. In 1989, 'However imprecise the historical comprehension of the people, consciousness of history and the historical is no longer foreign for them, and the "limited horizon" . . . has finally fallen for ordinary people' (Bausinger 1986: 134). Souvenirs quickly appeared in which fragments of graffiti-ed Wall were mounted in a case of clear plastic, along with the Wall's chronology 1961–89: instant scientifically fixed and chronologically fixed history ready for the museum. And the idea of a historical record, remains for which one was responsible to future generations, led to attempts to preserve Wall sections *in situ* in a pristine condition.

Some graffiti pleaded. 'Don't disturb History.' *'Prière de ne pas toucher au mur pour ne pas toucher à histoire.* MERCI.' 'This part — only this part(!!) is for you! but please take care for the other pieces of these' (Kegel pers. comm. — original emphasis). That these messages at the Potsdamer Platz should be in English and French as well as German, shows the Wall as a world monument, not just a Berliner's or even a German's concern. The considerable tension between local and international perceptions of the Wall has many manifestations.

Preserving the Wall

Wall nostalgia combined with 1980s heritage awareness of conservation (Assion 1986: 353; Lübbe 1990: 41; Bausinger 1986: 98) in a complex conservation debate, which ran both in parallel with and in reaction to the consumption of the Wall.

'It is typical for us Germans that at the end of an historical era we want to rip everything down and forget it ever happened. It occurred with the Nazi sites, now it's happen-

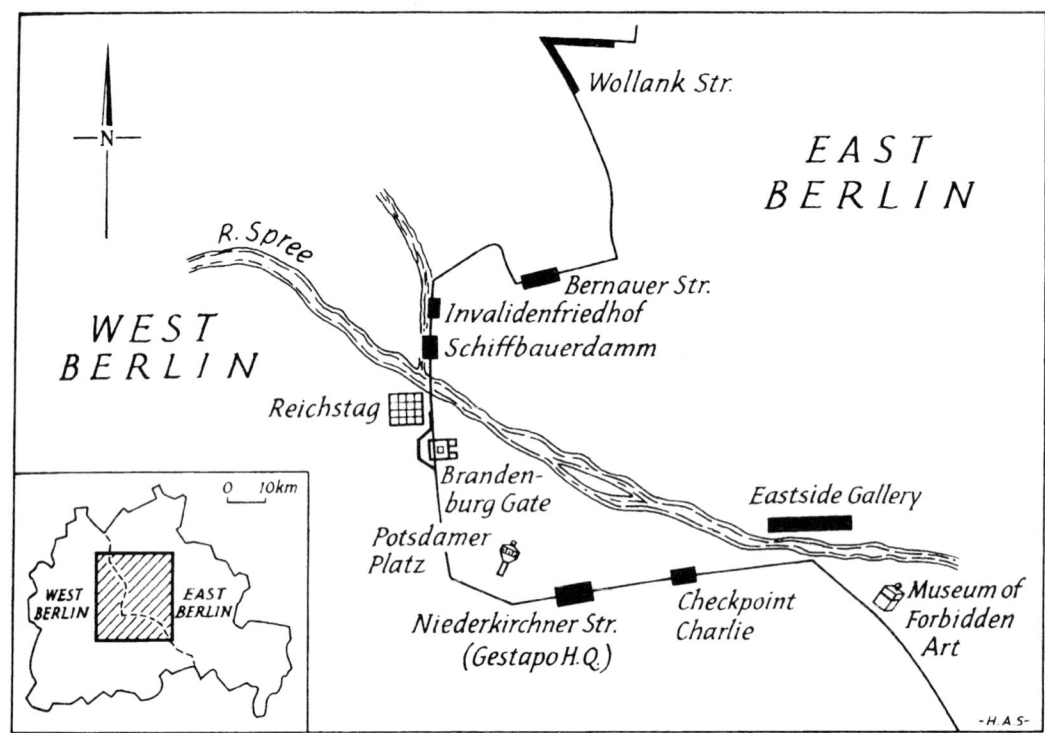

FIGURE 12. *Map of Berlin showing the location of the Niederkirchner Straße, Invaliden Friedhof, the Bernauer Straße, Checkpoint Charlie and East Side Gallery, Museum of Forbidden Art.*

ing with the Berlin Wall,' said Dr Alfred Kernd'l, Berlin's chief archaeologist (pers. comm.). He continued, 'It is indicative that I as an archaeologist have responsibility for 20th-century sites, which were first demolished and then had to be re-excavated, like the former Gestapo-SS HQ on the Niederkirchner Straße' (pers. comm.). The Active Museum of Berlin, who initiated that excavation (Baker 1988a; 1990a; 1990b) warned, 'The destruction of the Berlin Wall is taking place with unparalleled ferocity. There is a danger that no section of the Wall is going to be preserved as an historical document.' 'Save the Wall!' said Sabine Weissler, cultural spokesperson of Berlin's Green Party. 'The Wall did not just divide Berlin, it also made it an island. The Wall is the key to understanding the past 30 years of the city. Where parts of the Wall remain they should be kept' (Weissler 1990).

In 1990 Chippindale (Thames 1990b) warned, 'The Berlin Wall is the central symbol of the Cold War. It is the most significant monument of the 20th century, and there is a danger that like the Bastille which is the central monument of the 18th century, the Wall will all be sold off to tourists leaving nothing for future generations.'

According to Sabine Weissler, 'The Wall must remain where it is part of the historic context' (pers. comm.). Her colleague Eberhard Elfert has proposed a history trail, like the 'freedom trails' in Boston (Massachusetts), along the strip of no-man's land from the Oberbaumbrücke in Kreuzberg to the Bernauer Straße so as 'to show the layeredness of history' (in Scheub 1992). But which bit of history, relevant to whom? Three major sections remain standing under conservation orders: at the Niederkirchner Straße, Bernauer Straße and the Invaliden Friedhof (FIGURE 12). Controversy centres on the first two locations.

FIGURE 13. *The section of Wall at the Bernauer Straße to be restored by the Deutsches Historisches Museum (1990). (Photo Frederick Baker).*

Niederkirchner Straße

Halfway between Checkpoint Charlie and the Potsdamer Platz, the Wall runs for 200 m alongside what was in its time the most feared address in Berlin, the former Gestapo and SS HQ of Himmler and Heydrich. On the other side of the road, in former East Berlin, is the Luftwaffe ministry (1938), from where Goering planned the Blitz. Completing the historical landscape is the Kaiser's 19th-century Prussian Parliament building.

'We have to keep the Wall here, because the Wall is a result of Hitler's War and the Nazi terror which was planned and administered from this site,' argues Silvia Lange of the Active Museum (pers. comm.). 'It is crucial to preserve this physical relationship, so as to confront visitors with the interrelationships of German History.'

Dr Kernd'l (pers. comm.) disagrees: 'If you leave the Wall standing here, then everyone will come and say: "Oh look there is the Wall next to the Gestapo headquarters, they were just as bad as each other, the Gestapo and the Stasi were just the same," and they were not. The danger is that leaving the Wall standing here will relativize and therefore dilute the crimes of the Nazis.'

'People already compare the Nazis and the Stasi,' counters Silvia Lange, 'and keeping the Wall here will provoke debate. It all depends on how the site is presented.'

Kernd'l replies (Thames 1990), 'With the Wall there you can't understand the Gestapo-SS site. We've still got remains of the old pavement there, and we ought to concentrate on presenting the Nazi period here properly and deal with the Wall properly elsewhere, the Bernauer Straße for instance.'

In the latest architectural competition for presenting the site (1993), the winning design has left the Wall exactly where it is. Dr Kernd'l seems to have lost.

Bernauer Straße

The Bernauer Straße is the other centre of present controversy (FIGURE 13). For Berliners this is the most notorious and tragic part of the Wall (Hildebrandt 1988b). In

August 1990 a sign appeared on the Wall at the Bernauer Straße addressed to the 'Wall-peckers':

> Dear Wall-peckers, please don't peck at this part of the Wall. The area of border between the Acker and Garten Straße is, with the support of the East and West German governments to become a memorial to the Berlin Wall. Join in conserving an authentic and worthy memorial to the victims of the Wall.

The notice was signed by Pastor Manfred Fischer, a young Protestant minister, whose old church — isolated in no-man's land by the Bernauer Straße — had been dynamited by East German border troops five years before.

Pastor Fischer's neighbours are 200 old people in the Lazarus Nursing Home (Möbius & Trotnow 1990: 31). Interviewed in 1990 (Thames 1990), its matron Sister Christa Heckel took a different view:

> The Wall on the Bernauer Straße has to go as fast and as completely as possible. I speak not only for myself, but for 200 old people, who live in the Nursing home overlooking the proposed museum. They experienced the terror of this Wall being built, had to live with it for 29 years and are now suffering psychologically from still seeing it outside their window long after the border has opened. When this place was a hospital, this was where they brought all the injured escapees. Part of the Wall should be kept, but not opposite 200 old people. Tourists can go, these old people can't. The Wall should also go, so we can have direct access to the graves of our Diakonissen order, which we were previously unable to visit, because they were in no-man's land.

Among Pastor Fischer's powerful allies are Hagen Koch and the German Chancellor Helmut Kohl's new Museum for German History (Baker & Korff 1992a; 1992b). Koch remembers the Fall as a dream from which he was afraid to wake up from and find out it wasn't true. The Berlin Wall was not just a wall, but a whole military system with an interior wall, watch towers, water patrols and minefields. In order to show this, he thinks (pers. comm.), we need an authentic Wall Museum.

'What they want is a chamber of horrors. You can't get authenticity. The Wall is an ambiguous object and it would be more appropriate to get artists to interpret it,' says Sabine Weissler (pers. comm. 1990).

For Dieter Havichek, the local Mayor, the plans for the museum on the Bernauer Straße run counter to the stated popular sentiment in the boroughs of Mitte and Wedding:

> There is no space for Walls in Berlin any more. The legacy of the Wall's victims demands that divisions be irrevocably removed. The Bernauer Straße must become a normal street where people live and go shopping again. The division must be overcome. Moreover, the Wall is causing the old people in the Lazarus Nursing home psychological stress, that too, has got to be understood.

Pastor Fischer believes Havichek has less altruistic reasons for opposing the Wall museum. 'It is all part of the preparations for an Olympic bid. The two stadia would be near here and they want to build a ring road and link the two. The Bernauer Straße is a key link in such a plan' (pers. comm. 1990).

Challenged, Havichek defends himself. 'It would be perverse if a Wall museum, held up plans for a new ring road. I am not against a Wall memorial, but not here. There should be one central memorial perhaps on the Niederkirchner Straße' (pers. comm. 1992).

In the end the view of the Deutsches Historisches Museum has been followed; in 1992 it launched an architectural competition to design a memorial and museum to go with the section of Wall (Trotnow pers. comm.).

Although the preservers moved to save the Wall here, and it was fenced off, they were already too late. The watch-tower had been cut down, the concrete segments of the outer Wall had been hammered through to the reinforcing bars, and much of the inner Wall had been torn down. 'Preserving' the Wall at the Bernauer Straße will be more a work of reconstruction than of preserving what is presently there. Now the discovery of World War II graves under the site is delaying these plans.

Invaliden Friedhof

North of the former crossing-point Invaliden Straße, a stretch of the Wall still runs between the Berlin–Spandauer-Schiffahrtskanal and the Invaliden cemetery, where many of the former Prussian military leadership are buried. the most famous is Scharnhorst, who is buried under an imposing monumental grave designed by the famous Berlin architect Karl-Friedrich Schinkel. In contrast, Gestapo boss Reinhard Heydrich's grave is today unmarked. The Nazis buried him there after his Prague 1942 assassination, aware of its links with Prussia's military tradition: the same links which prompted conservationists to argue that the Wall should be left here, precisely because the graveyard so visibly showed the Wall's historical roots in German militarism. Apart from murmurs that Heydrich's grave should be marked, this site has been uncontroversial.

In addition to the East Side Gallery on the Mühlen Straße that has already been described, differing fragments of the Wall of varying status are still extant as this article goes to press (September 1993).

Checkpoint Charlie

At the private Checkpoint Charlie Museum the collection, 'Topography of the German–German border', consists of individual segments of wall and representative examples of bunkers and border-posts, mixed in with sculptures inspired by the Cold War. Each artefact is displayed like a work of art with a blue-and-white plaque of the Haag Convention for the protection of world cultural heritage, prominently displayed to replace the artist's signature as a guarantee of authenticity. The problem with Koch's collection is that his exhibits are not warnings (see above), but just larger versions of the rubber-stamped wall fragments sold to the tourists on the street outside. By reducing the wall to the museum equivalent of the sound bite it may be more easily consumable for passers-by, but it is also more forgettable. A lapse of memory definitely seems to have occurred with the developers of the planned American Business Centre at Checkpoint Charlie. Their plans threaten to destroy the very 24 m of wall at which US Sergeant Pool threw a line to an escapee and dragged him to the west (Kugler 1991).

Kapelle Ufer

The stump of a watch tower stands next to five relocated segments of Wall with the word 'ART' painted on them. Highly visible from the train, this has been the site of frequent freelance artworks such as the recycling artist's 'Mutoid Waste' arch made from three abandoned armoured personnel carriers (APCs).

Oberer Freiarchenbrücke
A command tower has been saved from demolition at the former crossing point Puschkin Allee next to the lock where the Landwehr canal enters the river Spree. Ironically, amongst the group who saved it are young East Germans who themselves fled across another part of the Iron Curtain in Hungary in the spring of 1989. Now called *Museum der Verbotenen Kunst* (Museum of Forbidden Art), it has a very libertarian anti-censorship agenda. It has exhibited censored Stasi files and the border guards' own Wall photos, including FIG-URES 1, 2a & 2b (Nürnberger 1992).

Schiffbauerdamm
The stretch of the inner wall that can be seen on the right-hand side of FIGURE 2a is still extant. Today it has a double function. The eastern face encloses the car park of a Toyota repair workshop. The western face is now a 'Memorial for the Victims of Violence and War'. Clearly visible from the crosses of the Wall dead next to the Reichstag on the other river bank, a stark black-and-white mural chronicles the Wall's victims. Starting at 1961, each of the Wall's 29 years gets one segment with that year's death toll painted on it (Cleven 1993). The death strip has been planted with a so-called 'Parliament of trees' and three relocated wall segments form a sign for a 'Europe memorial', which consists of earth banks arranged to form the words 'EUROPA ERDE WIEDER' (Europe Earth Again), so that they are clearly visible to passengers in the passing trains.

Pankow
A very long stretch of western outside wall has been preserved as a factory wall parallel to the railway line between Wilhelmsruh and the Nordgraben.

Potsdamer Platz
A guard tower along with some little graffiti-ed segments of back wall still standing between the Leipziger and Stresemann Straße in the coalyard next to the offices of the archaeological section of the former East Berlin Academy of Sciences.

Nostalgia for the Wall?
Tourists, fed on the TV images of November 1989, could scarcely imagine an opinion poll amongst Berliners asking 'Do you want the Wall back?' in which 1 in 4 West Berliners, and 1 in 5 East Berliners said they were nostalgic about the Wall. But that is exactly what the GEWIS poll (1990: 26) found in May 1990. One in four said they had thought back to the period before the fall of the Wall with nostalgia, Westerners more nostalgic for the time of the Wall than Easterners (27% to 17%). When they put the same question in October 1990, the number of nostalgic West Berliners had grown to one in three. Particularly prone were West Berliners under 30 years old, 39% of whom 'had shed a tear for the passing of the Wall' (Gewis 1990: 26).

In 1961 the Wall was experienced as a noose around the Western part of the city, which threatened to kill it, but in 1989 one saw the Wall in West Berlin as a source of support. The Bonn government made billions of marks available to the city thanks to this monument.

The special status of Berlin also freed men from having to do military service. For those who lived opposite the Wall, it provided silence and seclusion (Smith 1990), a seclusion much missed once the Wall opened. The Wall, protecting the east from crime, AIDS, pornography, drugs, etc., also protected West Berliners, from military service and recession. Western subventions to this 'front-line' city protected, culture and the arts from the cold winds of recession when blew throughout Europe. This may be a reason why the degree of Wall nostalgia is particularly strong amongst young West Berliners. (Gewis 1990); it is an argument for preserving the large and *in situ* section of the Wall which will be needed to explain to future generations how East and West Germans are, paradoxically, 'two totally different generations of the same age' (Kutter in Pokatsky 1990).

Conclusion

In the end the archaeologist stands before the question, What is the Berlin Wall?

As is true of the Roman walls, the Berlin Wall which is now available for preservation is the last phase and as ruined, atypical of the monument's original purpose and life-span. For example: the Berlin Wall has the image of the Iron Curtain, but no! — the Iron Curtain ran mostly through countryside, as a fence not a wall, and far to the west of Berlin. The Wall was typical of Berlin, but no! — much of the city border was fenced instead and ran through fields. The Wall was massive and flat surfaced, but no! — only in its last phase. The Wall was unprecedented, but no! — a wall had existed on the very same border 100 years before. The Wall was the biggest graffiti art gallery in the world, but no! — the graffiti only really came with the last phase of Wall and only on one of the Wall's four faces. The Wall was an impenetrable barrier, but no! — it wasn't impenetrable to Westerners.

Security system. Sculpture. Art canvas. Historical monument. The Berlin Wall, in its construction, consumption and preservation, has been all of these things. For the Cold War warriors and the TV audience, it stood for the binary world of opposing systems; a Wall flake or one Wall segment is enough to be 'The Wall' as long as it has only two sides. For the relatives of Easterners who died crossing the Wall the military aspect is important; the Museum on the Bernauer Straße the security system, is the Wall. The Wall had effect and visual force from its going on for ever. Preserving a section of Wall even 50 or 100 metres long misses the point if you can see it ending; it ought to look endless. Fragments as large as a single cast segment or as small as a painted crumb gives a visitor a fundamentally different experience and interpretation of what the Wall was (Chippindale 1990a).

The role of art and graffiti shows the paradoxical, mutually dependent relationship between the consuming and the preserving of monuments. The Wall was painted in order to overcome it. It is those painted sections which are preserved. At the East Side Gallery a grey Eastern *Mauer* has been turned into a coloured Western *Wand*. The key question is: If a public which sees politics as a succession of images is shown the Eastern *Mauer* visually transformed (reduced) into the Western *Wand*, then what becomes of the memory of those who died at the Wall and of the perspective of Easterners who were locked behind the Wall?

If the Wall shows that monuments are diverse in their forms and meanings, than the only way to do justice to their preservation is to demand and to tolerate an equally diverse spectrum of preservation.

Since the first piece of Wall was hacked out under the fire of water cannon on 9 November 1989, the historical memory of the Berlin Wall has been atomized into a million fragments. The relationship between consumption and preservation is more a dialectical than a simple opposition. The Wall-peckers destroy segments of the Wall but also preserve the Wall as a folk memory in the atomized global 'museums without walls' of individual mantelpieces, curiosity cabinet, and shoe-boxes. Fragments of the Wall will be heirlooms passed down through family genealogies, an unofficial personal alternative to public museums. Very few monuments are as physically large as the Berlin Wall, so few allow such a pluralism of preservation and interpretations; it is atypical. It is exactly this exceptional magnitude which allows such insight into the complexity of people's interaction with and use of the material culture they perceive to be part of the past: a complexity not exclusive to the Wall.

Acknowledgements. I am grateful to Dr Alfred Kernd'l, Hagen Koch, Prof. Dr Gottfried Korff and Dr Helmut Trotnow for their historical advice. I am grateful to Nicholas Baker, Waltraut Kegel, Astrid Möller, Frau Rosenthal, Mojca Tiar, Alex West, David Wilson and all at Channel 4's series *Down to Earth* for their help in realizing this research. Special thanks to Gerling Klemens and Hagen Koch for the photographic material. All translations by author unless otherwise stated.

References

AANDERUD, K.-A. & G. KNOPP. 1991. *Die Eingemauerte Stadt: die Geschichte der Berliner Mauer.* Recklinghausen: Georg Bitter.

ASMUSS, B. 1987. *Berlin, Berlin: Materialien zur Geschichte der Stadt.* Berlin (West): Berliner Festspiele.

ASSION, P. 1986. Historismus, Traditionalismus, Folklorismus: zur musealisiereden Tendenz der Gegenwartskultur, in Utz Jeggle *et al.* (ed.), *Volkskultur in der Moderne*: 351–62. Reinbek bei Hamburg: Rowohlt Taschenbuch.

BAKER, F. 1988a. History that hurts: excavating 1933–45, *Archaeological Review from Cambridge* 7: 93–109.

     1988b. Museums without walls. Unpublished MPhil. dissertation, Department of Archaeology, University of Cambridge.

     1990a. Archaeology, Habermas and the pathologies of modernity, in Baker & Thomas 1990: 54–62.

     1990b. The problems of conservation in a unifying Berlin, *Archaeological Review from Cambridge* 9: 167–9.

     1992a. Mauerspechte, in *Wörter, Sachen, Sinne, eine kleine volkskundliche Enzyklopädie Studien und Materialien* 9: 113–15. Tübingen: Tübinger Vereinigung für Volkskunde.

BAKER, F. & G. KORFF. 1992a. National, Heimat and Active museums: an outline of the development of the German museums into the 1990s, in *New Research in Museum Studies* 3: *Museums in Europe.* London: Athlone Press.

     1992b. Nacionalni, domozanski in aktivni muzeji: oris razvoja nemskih muzejev na poti v devetdeseta leta, *Ethnolog, Glasnik Slovenskega Ethnografskega Muzeja* 2(2).53. Ljubljana.

BAKER, F & J. THOMAS (ed.). 1990. *Writing the past in the present.* Lampeter: St David's University College.

BALFOUR, A. 1990. *Berlin, the politics of order.* New York (NY): Rizzoli.

BAUSINGER, H. 1986. *Volkskultur in der technischen Welt.* Frankfurt am Main: Campus Verlag. (First edition 1961.)

BAYLEY, S. 1989. *Commerce and culture: from pre-industrial art to Post-industrial value.* London: Design Museum.

Berliner Zeitung. 1989. Erich Honecker, *Berliner Zeitung* (20 January).

     1992a. Geheimplan: Berliner Mauer sollte schon 1961 wieder gesprengt werden, *Berliner Zeitung* (2 January).

     1992b. Mauer-Rest als Expo-Stück, *Berliner Zeitung* (22 April).

BIERMANN, W. 1991. *Über das Geld und andere Herzensdinge: Prosaische Versuche über Deutschland.* Köln: Kiepenheuer & Witsch.

BOHN, R, K. HICKETHIER & E. MÜLLER (ed.). 1992. *Mauer-Show: Das Ende der DDR, die deutsche Einheit und die Medien.* Berlin: Sigma Medienwissenschaft Rainer Bohn.

BREDOW, J. 1992. Wall Hawkers say 'Buyer Beware!', *Checkpoint* 11.

BUFORD, B. (ed.). 1989. *New Europe.* Cambridge: Granta Publications. *Granta* 30.

CHIPPINDALE, C. 1990a. Editorial. *Antiquity* 64: 705–7.

     1990b. Contributions to Thames 1990.

CLEVEN, T. 1993. Es gibt keinene Grund, die Mauer zu vergessen, *Ostsee-Zeitung* (13 August).

CORNER, J. & S. HARVEY (ed.). 1991. *Enterprise and heritage: crosscurrents of the national culture.* London: Routledge.

CRAIG, G.A. 1982. *The Germans.* Harmondsworth: Penguin.

DARNTON, R. 1991. *Der letzte Tanz auf der Mauer: Berliner Journal 1989–1990.* München: Carl Hanser.

DIEMER, G. (ed.). 1990. *Kurze Chronik der Deutschen Frage.* München: Olzog. Geschichte und Staat Band 288.

DOBBERKE, C. 1992. Die Mauer läßt ihn nicht los, *Die Welt* (2 August).

DRAECKER, J. 1990. 2 Millionen aus dem Mauer-verkauf für Denkmalpflege und Gesundheit, *Berliner Morgenpost* (18 October).

DREWS, A., U. GERHARD & J. LINK. 1985. Moderne Kollektivsymbolik: eine diskurstheoritisch orientierte Einführung, *Internationales Archiv für Sozialgeschichte der deutschen Literatur*, Sonderheft 1. Tübingen: Niemeyer.

DROSDECK, A. *et al.* 1989. *Grenze als Städtebauliche Aufgabe: Berlin.* Darmstadt: Technische Hochschule Darmstadt– Fachbereich Architektur.

ECKHARDT, U. 1987. *Der Moses Mendelssohn Pfad.* Berlin (West): Berliner Festspiele.

EDELMANN, M. 1975. Die symbolische Seite der Politik, in W.-D. Narr & C. Offe (ed.), *Wohlfahrtsstaat und Massenloyalität*: 307–22. Köln: WestDeutscher Verlag.

ENZENSBERGER, H.M. 1989. The state of Europe, in Buford 1989: 136–42.

ESCAUT-MARQUET, M.T. 1990. *Die Mauer. The Berlin Wall Special Auction*. Monte Carlo: Galerie Park Palace.

FISCHER, G. & F. VON DER SCHULENBURG. 1990. *Die Mauer: monument of the century*. Berlin: Ernst & Sohn.

GARTON ASH, T. 1990. *We the people: the revolution of 89 witnessed in Warsaw, Budapest, Berlin and Prague*. Cambridge: Granta Books.

GEISLER, M.E. 1992. Mehrfach gebrochene Mauerschau: 1989–1990 in den US-Medien, in Bohn *et al.* 1992: 257–75.

GERIG, U. 1986 *Barrieren aus Eisen und Beton: in Berlin und quer durch Deutschland*. Krefeld: Röhr.

GEWIS. 1990. Wollen die Berliner die Mauer wieder? Trauer um die Mauer, *Prinz* (8 November): 20–26.

GONSZALEZ-MARCEN, P. & R. RISCH. 1990. Archaeology and historical materialism, in Baker & Thomas 1990: 94–104.

GORBACHEV, M. 1988. *Perestroika: new thinking for our country and the world*. London: Fontana/Collins.

GOW, D. 1991. Wall artists help to fill state coffers, *Guardian* (6 February).

GRANT, R.G. 1991. *The rise and fall of the Berlin Wall*. Leicester: Magna Books.

HARTUNG, K. 1989. Der Fall der Mauer, *Tageszeitung* (6 November).

HILDEBRANDT, R. 1988a. *The Wall speaks/Die Mauer Spricht*. Berlin: Haus am Checkpoint Charlie.

1988b. *It happened at the Wall*. Berlin: Haus am Checkpoint Charlie.

1993. *Die Deutsche Teilung: Tödlichegrenzfälle und Schwerverletzte*. Berlin: Haus am Checkpoint Charlie.

HILDEBRANDT, R. *et al.* 1990. Grenzen durch Berlin und durch Deutschland. Zablein-material. Berlin, *Arbeitsgemeinschaft* (13 August). Berlin: Haus am Checkpoint Charlie.

HONECKER, E. 1980. *Aus meinem Leben*. Berlin (East): Dietz.

JAMESON, F. 1984. Post-modernism, or the cultural logic of late Capitalism, *New Left Review* 146.

KORFF, G. 1990. Rote Fahnen und Bananen: Notizen zur politischen Symbolik im Prozess der Vereinigung von DDR und DDR, *Schweizerischen Archiv für Volkskunde* 3/4: 130–60. Basel.

KORNGIEBEL, W. & J. LINK. 1992. Von einstürzenden Mauern, europäischen Zügen und deutschen Autos in Bildern und Sprachbildern der Medien, in Bohn *et al.* 1992: 31–53.

KUGLER, A. 1991. Später Sieg des Dollars, *Tageszeitung* (9 December).

KUZDAS, H.J. 1990. *Berliner Mauer Kunst*. Berlin: Elephanten Presse.

LAPP, P.J. 1987. *Frontdienst im Frieden: Die Grenztruppen der DDR*. Koblenz: Bernard & Graefe.

LÜBBE, H. 1990. Zeit-Verhältnisse: über die veränderte Gegenwart von Zukunft und Vergangenheit, in W. Zacharias (ed.), *Der Verschwinden der Gegenwart und die Konstruktion der Errinerung*: 40–49. Essen: Klartext .

LÜSEBRINK, H.-J. & R. REICHARDT. 1990. *Die. Bastille: zur Symbolgeschichte von Herrschaft und Freiheit*. Frankfurt am Main: Fischer Taschenbuch.

MCCAULEY, M. 1983. *The origins of the Cold War*. London: Longmans.

MALZAHN, C.C. 1988. Asbest-Alarm: Die Mauer unter Glas!, *Tageszeitung* (2 December).

MANDER, J. 1962. *Berlin the hostage of the West*. Harmondsworth: Penguin.

MEHLS, E. & H. MEHLS. 1979. 1*3 August: illustrierte historische Hefte 17*. Berlin (East): VEB Deutscher Verlag der Wissenschaften.

MILLER, D. 1987. *Material culture and mass consumption*. Oxford: Basil Blackwell.

MÖBIUS, P. & H. TROTNOW. 1990. *Mauern sind nicht für ewig gebaut: zur Geschichte der Berliner Mauer*. Berlin & Frankfurt am Main: Propyläen.

1991. Das Mauer-Komplott, *Die Zeit* (Hamburg) (9 August).

NÜRNBERGER, D. 1992. Der letzte Wachtturm Passender Ausstellungsort, *Berliner Zeitung* (14 August).

PETSCHULL, J. 1990. *Die Mauer*. Hamburg: Stern Bücher.

POKATZY, K. 1990. Ostler gegen Wessie-sicht, (Hamburg) *Die Zeit* (29 June).

RIBBE, W. & J. SCHMAEDEKE. 1988. *Kleine Berlin Geschichte*. Berlin (West): Landeszentrale für politische Bildungsarbeit.

ROBINS, K. 1991. Tradition and translation: national culture in its global context, in Corner & Harvey 1991: 21–45.

RÜHLE, J. & G. HOLZWEISSIG. 1988. 1*3 August 1961. Die Mauer von Berlin*. Köln: Verlag Wissenschaft und Politik.

RÜRUP, R. (ed.). 1989. *Topography of terror*. Berlin (West): Verlag Willmuth Arenhövel.

SAMSON, R. 1992. Knowledge, constraint and power in inaction: the defenceless medieval wall, in P. Schackel & B. Little (ed.), *Historical Archaeology* 26: 26–44.

SCHEUB, U. 1992. Geschichte auf der Straße, *Tageszeitung* (29 February).

SCHNEIDER, P. 1983. *The Wall jumper*. New York (NY): Pantheon.

SMITH, K. 1990. *Berlin: coming in from the cold*. Harmondsworth: Penguin.

SPIEGEL. 1990. Auch das noch!, *Spiegel* 28: 156–8.

STAHL, J. 1989. *An der Wand: Grafitti zwischen Grafiti und Anarchie*. Köln: DuMont.

THAMES TELEVISION. 1990. In search of the Berlin Wall, film in series *Down to Earth*, broadcast on Channel 4, London, 8 November.

WAGNER, H. 1990. Die Innendeutsche Grenzen, in A. Demandt (ed.), *Deutschlands Grenzen in der Geschichte* : 235–76. München: C.H. Beck.

WALSER, M. 1989. *Über Deutschland Reden*. Frankfurt am Main: Edition Suhrkamp 1553.

WARNECKEN, B.J. 1992. 'Aufrechter Gang' Metamorphosen einer Parole des DDR-Umbruchs, in Bohn *et al.* 1992: 17–29.

WEBER, H. 1985. *Geschichte der DDR*. München: DTV-Wissenschaft 4430.

1990. *Kleine Geschichte der DDR*. Köln: Edition Deutschland Archiv.

WEDOW, J. 1992. What happened to the Wall?, *Checkpoint* 11.

WEISSLER, S. 1990. *Rettet die Mauer!* Berlin: Presseerklärung der Al-Fraktion im Abgeordneten Haus (10 October).

WENDERS, W. & P. HANDKE. 1989. *Der Himmel über Berlin: ein Filmbuch*. Frankfurt am Main: Suhrkamp.

Seeing stars: character and identity in the landscapes of modern Macedonia

by **KEITH BROWN**

ANTIQUITY 68 (261), 1994

THIS PAPER explores the meeting-point of symbolic and material landscapes in the Former Yugoslav Republic of Macedonia (henceforth FYR Macedonia), the only Republic so far largely to have avoided involvement in the fighting which marked the break-up of former Yugoslavia (FIGURE 1). The paper opens with a consideration of the new Macedonian flag, and the issues that it has raised. The paper then considers the ways in which an internal crisis of legitimation underlies this most visible dispute. The flag is just one example of the way that symbols of various kinds link people and territory together in the Balkans, and how escalating tensions between groups drive the deployment of such symbols, which then contribute further to focus ideological dispute. The question of the flag has been noted and largely dismissed as two Balkan states squabbling over an empty symbol: much less attention has been paid to its significance in the complex and on-going struggle to re-shape the contours of the past, present and future Macedonian landscape.

In this respect, this paper seeks to extend to FYR Macedonia the kind of analysis suggested by Mitchell (1994) in a consideration of the Israeli landscape, and by Chapman (1994) in an analysis of the destruction of buildings of national and religious significance in Bosnia. Like both these territories, Macedonia is and has been a home to different groups, all of which have claims on the ground. In Israel and now in Bosnia these claims resulted in policies which aim to erase other elements from the landscape. In FYR Macedonia, though, still in train are various constructive processes by which differences are being expressed and made significant. It thereby still offers an opportunity to examine the different ways in which territory comes to be imbued with exclusive identity, and symbols come to matter.

History

Until 1944, the meanings of Macedonia existed in different time zones. Ancient Macedonia was acknowledged as belonging to the classical and Hellenistic world: modern Macedonia was a battleground of Slavic and Greek national movements in the late 19th century, divided between Serbia, Bulgaria and Greece after the Balkan Wars of 1912–13. In 1944, though, a new federal Yugoslavia was created, the southernmost republic of which was called Macedonia, and the slavic inhabitants of that region acknowledged as a nation in their own right. Greece always disputed the application of the name to this territory and these inhabitants, but her objections have only been highlighted in the wider world since the declaration of autonomy by the Republic of Macedonia in late 1991.

In 1994, both sides are trying to bring together the past and present of Macedonia, to impose a single unambiguous meaning on the word that currently means so much to both of them. Greeks privilege the ancient world, and emphasize the Hellenic connections and aspirations of Philip II and Alexander III; today, they argue, Macedonia is wholly Greek. The former Yugoslav Macedonians point to evidence that ancient Mac-

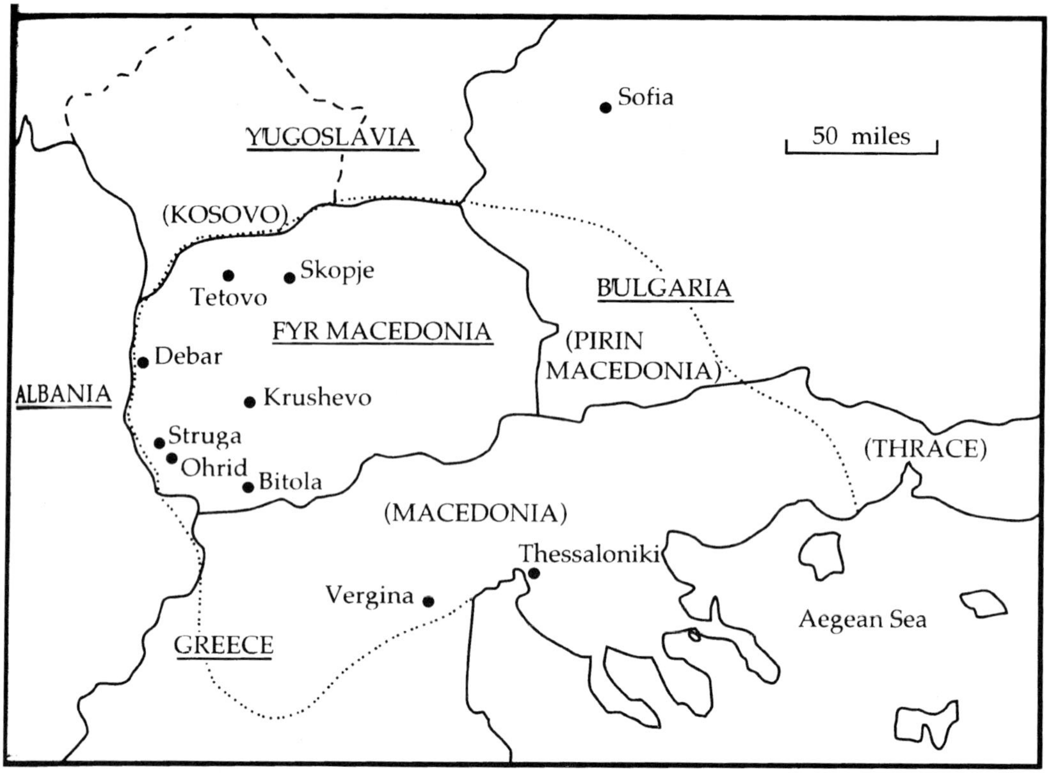

FIGURE 1. *Macedonia's meanings. State names are underlined. Regional names are in brackets. The dotted line marks the approximate extent of geographical Macedonia.*

FIGURE 2. *Emblems of the two flags: the five-pointed star of the Yugoslav period, and the 16-pointed sun/star of FYR Macedonia.*

edonians were not Greeks in their bid to carve out a heritage for themselves and their
very young state. In the confrontation, a single symbol has taken centre-stage: the 16-
pointed sun or star. This was established as the emblem of the royal house of ancient Macedonia by Manolis Andronicos, when he discovered the royal tombs at Vergina in 1978. In
1992, the democratically-elected Parliament of FYR Macedonia adopted it as the device on
the new state flag. A symbol empowered by archaeology is today a token by which present
regimes claim stewardship of the past and thus gain legitimacy and authority.

The passing of the *petokratka*: a crisis of succession

The 16-pointed star has come into prominence with the passing of the dominant symbol
of Macedonian solidarity in the Yugoslav period, the five-pointed star or *petokratka*
(FIGURE 2). It used to feature in all kinds of mundane contexts: on grave-stones and car
number-plates, and in the names of small businesses as well as on monuments. In these
sites its replacement is going on gradually, and without attracting considerable attention. But the star also appeared in symbolic sites where it was highly visible, and in
these cases its replacement has provoked controversy. The period from the declaration
of Macedonian autonomy until August 1992, when the new flag was officially adopted,
was marked by a protracted debate in the newspapers and other public fora of FYR
Macedonia over the new state's symbols. While it was agreed that a decisive break with
the socialist era should be made, it was also felt that any new state symbols should
capture the spirit of an older past and thus demonstrate again the historical existence of
the Macedonian people, which with the demise of federal Yugoslavia came under renewed scrutiny. Anthem, crest and flag were examined, and disagreements immediately
arose over the form that new variants should take. The anthem, ultimately, remained
unaltered; the new flag was officially ratified in August 1992; at the time of writing,
September 1994, the Republic has no official crest.

The debate was underscored by the problem of re-integrating the period of the Republic's membership of Federal Yugoslavia, formerly presented as the final realization
of Macedonian aspirations, into the broader canvas of a newly configured national history. Where symbols and rhetoric had woven together socialist and national ideals, the
new political reality called for the first to be downplayed and the second emphasized.
The debate over the flag quickly confronted this issue. As early as May 1992 Spase
Šuplinovski, in the FYR Macedonian daily newspaper, *Nova Makedonija*, argued that
the socialist symbols had 'really' been Macedonian all along. Although the *petokratka*
and the red flag might appear as pre-eminent markers of a socialist state, he argued, the
mode of their deployment on the old flag was uniquely Macedonian. He traced the motif
of a golden device on a red background through four named armed uprisings to King
Samuil and the Ohrid Archepiscopate of the 11th century, thereby making each of these
events distinctively Macedonian, by virtue of the banners they waved. Whether the golden
device was a five-pointed star, a lion, a cross, or two hands gripping a lighted torch (as in
the flag of the Krushevo Republic set up during the 1903 Ilinden Rising), it was, in his
argument, a marker of territorial and ethnic continuity (Šuplinovski 1992).

This argument effectively presented Macedonian history as wholly independent of
Yugoslavia, and its premiss seemed to be accepted. Although a number of emblems were
proposed for the flag, the basic format of gold on red was broadly adhered to in the
submissions entered in competition to a committee to select the new symbols of state.
Proposals came from all kinds of sources: from ordinary citizens with strong opinions
and from professional designers, as well as from political parties. There was considerable support from the Macedonian nationalist party, VMRO-DPMNE, for a golden lion

FIGURE 3. Gold casket from Vergina, on its lid the 'Star of Vergina'.

on a red background. But eventually the commission put before parliament the proposal of a 16-pointed sun, and this was passed unanimously in mid August 1992: on 20 August it was hung outside the parliament building in Skopje. The proposal of the same design for the crest did not pass, and at time of writing remains unresolved.

However, the new 16-pointed sun provoked a rather stronger reaction in Greece, where the selection was seen as an implicit claim to the territory of northern Greece which is a part of the geographical area called Macedonia until the Balkan Wars of 1912–13. Professor Andronicos' discovery at Vergina (FIGURE 3) in the late 1970s had been extensively marketed as proof of the Greek character of Macedonia generally and Alexander the Great in particular (Green 1989). Following the FYR Macedonian adoption of the new flag, the 'Star of Vergina' quickly became even more widespread in northern Greece, and its alleged usurpation became one more sign that Greek heritage and territory were under threat from the ex-communist state. The Greeks do not dispute that it is a Macedonian symbol: what they dispute is the right of the former Yugoslavs of the Republic of Macedonia to call themselves Macedonians. 'Macedonia is Greek. Study History!' is the phrase that rings out across posters, the bottom of receipts, and in response to queries in Thessaloniki (Karakasidou 1994).

In contrast, initial reaction in FYR Macedonia to the new flag was less unanimous (FIGURE 4). However, it quickly became important to the citizens of the new state, who came to take this debate as an infringement on their sovereignty. By the end of November 1992, according to a survey published in *Nova Makedonija* on 9 December, only 6% of those questioned would be willing to change the flag, even if it would mean Macedonia's immediate recognition. This compared with an even smaller proportion, 2%, who said that they would accept a change in the national anthem. The united front on these

FIGURE 4. The new Macedonia: cut off by blockade from winter fuel, its people vainly seek warmth from the sun of the new flag. Cartoon from the cover of Osten, Skopje's satirical weekly, winter 1993.

two issues contrasted with the relatively high proportion of respondents (25%) who were willing to accept amendment in the constitution. The survey was of 1147 citizens, of whom 788 were Macedonians and 219 were Albanians; constitutional change was considered viable by a high proportion of Albanians, who seek parity as a people (as opposed to equality as individuals) in the state (Kočovska 1992).

The flag as totem
What the new flag in Macedonia seems to represent is a phenomenon of the kind explored by Durkheim in *The elementary forms of the religious life* (1915). What preoccupied him in this work were precisely the mechanisms by which a society maintains or establishes a sense of collective identity in periods of apparent dispersal: this, he argued, is achieved by the sacralization of particular places which derive their sacred quality less by what is in them, than by illuminating the solidarity of those who view them. In this respect Durkheim paid particular attention to the notion of the tattoo, a single, apparently arbitrary device which is nonetheless invested with a collective force which makes it sacred (1915 [1965]: 265):

> it does not seek to reproduce the aspect of the thing that it is supposed to represent. It is made up of lines and points to which a wholly conventional significance is attributed. Its object is not to represent or bring to mind a determined object, but to bear witness to the fact that a certain number of individuals participate in the same moral life.

As Herzfeld (1992: 34) has suggested, Durkheim's model of societal solidarity appears particularly appropriate as a description of the working of the nation-state, which Benedict Anderson persuasively defined as primarily an *imagined* community (1983).

Drawing more explicitly on Durkheim than Anderson, Kapferer (1989) has argued this 'wholly conventional significance' is never arbitrary: in terms that recall Durkheim's own, he notes that the symbol may amplify and focus a collective feeling, but does not create. In the case of the flag of this new state, the representational continuity lay in the frame — gold on red. But the contested symbol which lay within that frame was by the act of incorporation transfigured and endowed with a particular meaning that had not, until this crisis, exhausted its significance. The name of 'Macedonia', and this most visible symbol associated with that name, had until 1992 retained its various meanings. But a world of autonomous states does not permit such ambiguity: and so Greece and FYR Macedonia are now vying for exclusive rights to the symbol, the name, and thereby, it appears, to the legacy of a historical figure in whose time the meanings of 'Greek' and 'Macedonian' had wholly different resonances (Badian 1982).

Change and crisis: total symbols

In a recent review of Fernand Braudel's *The identity of France* ([1980]*)*, Perry Anderson (1992) gives a model of how to conceptualize this total investment in a single symbol. Noting the polarity that Braudel most famously set up in his work on the Mediterranean, between the *longue durée* and the *événementielle* in history, Anderson maps a cognate distinction in the discourse of national solidarity. Increasingly, he argues, theorists discuss national *identity* where they used to focus on national *character*. He notes the effect on the register of debate — where character *changes*, identity has *crisis* — and then considers the wider implications of this shift (1992: 268):

> If national character was thought to be a settled disposition, national identity is a self-conscious projection. It always involves a process of selection, in which the empirical mass of collective living is distilled into armorial form. Subjectivity is here inseparable from symbolization. The symbols capture the past and announce the future.

Not surprisingly, given Anderson's own intellectual heritage, this way of considering the distinction overlaps with certain time-honoured structural distinctions of Marxian thought. Most striking, perhaps, is the sense in which character appears as a realm of hegemony, impermeable because it includes everything and therefore beyond question. Any selection from it, then, can be viewed as ideological in its self-conscious assertion, and, as Anderson goes on to indicate, thereby inherently more sharp-edged and fragile (1992: 269–70):

> Identity might be the deeper concept, but it is also — for nations as for persons — the more brittle. The very rigidity of its social projection, into a few cherished images, made it prey to a kind of structural anxiety.

Central in the dispute between Greece and FYR Macedonia is the fact that compromise on the flag seems impossible. Despite the somewhat ironical point that the symbol has different names in the two countries — for Greece it is a star, for Macedonia a sun — it cannot be shared: one or the other must give up all claims to possession. In this respect it is qualitatively different from the Macedonian constitution, which could be modified and yet remain in character the same constitution. The flag, then, seems the kind of 'self-conscious projection' that because of its totalizing nature cannot endure change.

Anderson reads Braudel's own work as an artefact in the construction of French identity; not merely documenting the phenomenon, but serving to give it contours and thereby to mould it. As such, he argues, it plays its own part in a whole set of practices which highlight the 'few, cherished images'. The stress which Anderson places on image-making is in line with recent scholarship on nationalism, where the inventive processes associated with it are frequently emphasized (Hobsbawm & Ranger 1983: Handler 1988). What Anderson offers is a way of distinguishing between these inventions by virtue of their different bases. They may either invoke discrete markers of identity and thereby occupy a place in the foreground of the imagination, or they may serve to point to more diffuse but still characteristic practices. These differences become apparent in the case of FYR Macedonia, when we move from the realm of the flag to the material landscape of the land over which it is waved.

Symbols in collision: neighbouring complaints

Most commentators on the Greek–Macedonian dispute appear to consider both sides irrational. More appear puzzled by FYR Macedonia's intransigence than by Greece's. This is in part a result of the success of the Greek state's publicity campaign to establish control of the ancient Macedonian past, though it could also be viewed, more cynically, as a measure of the reputation for chauvinist extremism that Greece has established. Puzzlement at the FYR Macedonian position can also be traced to a commitment to *realpolitik*. Without the internal market that Federal Yugoslavia used to provide, say the realists, FYR Macedonia is economically unviable. It must therefore gain access to the sea via Thessaloniki by establishing friendly relations with Greece: consequently, its government should capitulate to any and all Greek demands.

The argument is readily comprehensible: a weaker power should recognize its weakness and surrender unconditionally when there can be only one winner. In this case, though, it ignores two factors: Greece's foreign policy agenda, and the internal identity politics of the Republic of Macedonia. If the *realpolitik* argument is followed further it reveals that the choice facing Macedonia is not straightforward. If Greece is as well-disposed to Serbia as many indications suggest, then Greece's continuing blockade of FYR Macedonia could be seen as linked less to the question of the flag than to assisting Serbia to beat the UN sanctions. While the border with Greece is kept closed, FYR Macedonia is forced to continue to trade with Serbia: and — because the UN is unwilling to take punitive measures against FYR Macedonia — the UN blockade of Serbia is by this route circumvented. The flag, in this light, appears merely as a useful pretext to disguise the Greek–Serbian axis: if the Macedonians were to yield, another would be easily found.

The identity politics within FYR Macedonia are complex, but they centre around a single issue: what kind of state will the Republic of Macedonia be? Nationalist politicians of VMRO-DPMNE call for greater rights for ethnic Macedonians (the slavic-speaking majority in the Republic), while some Albanian politicians call for regional autonomy for areas around Debar, Struga and Tetovo, where Albanians outnumber Macedonians. The ruling coalition seeks to preserve a unified and multi-cultural state. The consensus on the 16-pointed sun, a rare marker of solidarity across the internal boundaries of ethnic group and religion that dominate most discussions, makes clear the reluctance of the government to abandon the flag: especially as that government has faced three no-confidence motions since its formation in summer 1992.

Beyond that, the issue of the flag's replacement immediately calls attention to the fact that no other symbol could unify public opinion in the same way. The Macedonian sun/star of Vergina has historical resonances for a variety of increasingly vocal ethnic groups in FYR Macedonia: Vlachs, for example, now fly an eight-pointed star and claim descent from Philip II by various dubious arguments, one being that the Greek name for their people — *Koutsovlachs* — arose because Philip II was lame — *koutsos*. Albanian parties, by contrast, claim Alexander because he was the son of Olympias, the Illyrian queen, and they claim descent from the Illyrians. Alexander's Macedonia, according to Greek historians as well as to the *Oxford English Dictionary* in its account of how *macédoine* came to mean fruit salad, was an empire of mixed traditions and heritages. The spirit of the selection of the 16-pointed star by a parliament drawn from different ethnic groups seems to evoke this past diversity. Although in the Greek view the flag appears to make exclusive claims about identity, within FYR Macedonia it remains one of the more inclusive symbols from the past.

Symbols in collision: domestic rivals

The sun's inclusive quality is particularly striking when it is compared with other images that have come into view in the last two years. The lion, annexed by VMRO-DPMNE, the Macedonian nationalist party, is displayed at gatherings where the government's policies of conciliation toward other ethnic groups are under attack. The replacement of the *petokratka* of communist days by a Christian cross on a prominent clock-tower in Bitola in 1992 provoked enough reaction from Moslem Albanian circles to merit a mention in the Report on Human Rights in Macedonia for 1994.

Like the lion, which has come to represent the Slavic character of Macedonia, the cross draws attention to fault-lines within the new Macedonian state. Its emplacement in Bitola fits into a framework of activism by the Macedonian Orthodox Church, which has actively sought to take the place of the socialist state as the guardian of Macedonian tradition, which it thereby defines as being exclusively Christian in character. Churches are being renovated or built all over Macedonia, and the church is increasingly visible at state holidays and festivals: so too, its links with VMRO-DPMNE are becoming more apparent. The political party was formed in 1989, the modern Macedonian church dates only from 1967, yet both look beyond the time of communist rule for spiritual continuity with figures and events of the Middle Ages.

This investment in the creation of a distinctively Macedonian past by both church and VMRO arises in part from further external pressures that each face. The Macedonian Orthodox Church, only recognized within Yugoslavia in 1967, remains outside the Orthodox world community (Alexander 1976). Since the break-up of Yugoslavia the Serbian church has repeatedly claimed that 1967 represented a communist-inspired schism. Consequently, the Macedonian dioceses should come under the authority of the Belgrade-based Serbian Orthodox Church and all churches and monasteries built prior to 1967 are the property of the Serbian church, which thus lays claim to the very same ecclesiastical history which the Macedonian church celebrates (Poulton 1993). VMRO, by contrast, was the name of an organization founded in 1893, when the Slavic inhabitants of Macedonia were considered by external observers to be Bulgarian. Between the two World Wars it was taken as the name of a terrorist organization based in Bulgaria which sought the unification of Macedonia with Bulgaria. Even today, the official Bulgarian position is that the Macedonian people do not exist as a separate ethnic group, and that VMRO has always been a Bulgarian organization (Perry 1988).

The symbols of both organizations — lion and cross — do not distinguish them from the larger organizations — Bulgarian state and Serbian church — that deploy the same symbols. It is this fact that appears to drive the commitment of both the Macedonian church and VMRO to embed their disputed symbols in a uniquely Macedonian landscape. Yet this presents them with a further problem: for no such landscape exists and must itself be imagined. As the Albanian reaction to the replacement of the *petokratka* in Bitola demonstrated, the visible steps in this process of imagination are being resisted, by parties who pursue their own visions of Macedonia's past and future. The historical trajectory of development in FYR Macedonia has produced a situation in which two parties each consider themselves victimized by outside forces and by the other, and thereby privilege common elements in what each considers to be their heritage.

The national imagination: the rural past

Henry Brailsford, one of the few western travellers to Macedonia at the turn of the century who spent time in the countryside, wrote (1906: 87):

> [T]he real Macedonia is the rural Macedonia, a land of village communities, where we may ride for weeks without encountering so much as a hamlet whose native language is other than Bulgarian or Albanian.

What he called Bulgarian was probably a dialect of Macedonian, which was only codified in 1944 (Friedman 1975). But this source of confusion does not alter the force of Brailsford's central point; the Vlachs, Gypsies, Turks, Greeks, Jews and Serbs who could be seen in the market-places of the larger towns were characters only of the urban social world. The main groups of the countryside, and the country as a whole, were Slavs and Albanians. In his time, as now, this divide was also a religious one: the Albanians of Macedonia are virtually all Muslims, while Slavs are mostly Orthodox Christian.

In the histories of both peoples, researched extensively only since the Second World War, rural culture and life-ways have been important in the construction of historical and cultural continuity. This can be viewed as a result of the relatively late articulation of national projects, as both peoples were largely rural and lacked intelligentsia until the late nineteenth century. Both also lacked literature from earlier periods, and folklore thus became vital in the process of documenting their longevity. The connection of folklore with nationalism has of course been well-established and documented in various cases (Herzfeld 1982: Fernandez 1985). The particular elevation of the peasant as a 'national signifier' is less common, but has been treated in depth by Swedenburg (1990) in the Palestinian case, as well as more generally in eastern Europe by various authors (Winner & Winner 1984).

Macedonians in FYR Macedonia see their past, and their national 'essence', as firmly rooted in the countryside. The heroes of the national struggles in Macedonia in the late 19th and early 20th centuries are mostly associated with villages or small towns. Although the term *selanec* — villager — is used in some cases as a term of abuse, there is still, as Allcock reports in the Serbian case, a sense that the hard-working peasant is the backbone of the nation, while city-folk are slick, manipulative and treacherous (Allcock 1992; *cf.* Simić 1977). Tied in with this way of life was a whole world-view concerning property and ownership of the material and the spiritual heritage of the land. Apostolov's (1962: 58–9) account of Serbian colonization between the wars represents conservatism and faith in the enduring nature of property rights as characteristic of the Macedonian peasantry — features which appear also to explain the refusal of Christian peasants in the earlier part of the century to abandon their villages for a better life abroad. When Brailsford questioned villagers in 1903, they reported that they had to stay to conserve the local church or monastery and, more particularly, the graveyard (Brailsford 1906: 59–60). Theirs was a very local patriotism, rooted in the symbolic spaces of their own village and its history, without wider extension. It was expressed then, and still through traditional practices and in modern literature, in the maintenance of ancestors' remains, and rituals of respect towards them (Nedelkovski 1974; Solev 1974; Ford 1982: 117, 121; Bicevski 1993).

The socialist government sought to inherit the legacy of these lifeways in turning the Macedonian people into a *rabotnićki narod,* a working people. The industriousness of rural Macedonia was emphasized and attempts were made to map new socialist values on to those of the rural small-holder. The state also introduced rituals which mirrored local practices, duplicating the mass of individual celebrations of the ancestors with ceremonies of re-interment of specific national heroes. So in 1948 the bones of Goce Delchev, a leader in the Macedonian Revolutionary Organization until his death in 1903, were brought from Sofia to Skopje, while in 1989 Dimitrija Šuplinovski's bones made the trip from Russia.

Such repetition of local rural customs at the central urban level is more often than not a conscious evocation of tradition, aimed at infusing solidarity in the nation as a whole (Hobsbawm & Ranger 1983). However, as Allcock (1992: 293) observes in the case of Slobodan Milošević's leadership of Serbia, a populist may use this evocation in rhetoric which emphasizes a distance between the calculating, manipulative administrators of the city and the honest, natural people of the soil. Although over a quarter of the population of FYR Macedonia now lives in the capital, the countryside and its values have retained a formidable hold over the imagination of these urbanites, who continue to value a 'Macedonian' over a 'Skopjean' history. This phenomenon, undoubtedly encouraged by image-making political opportunists, has roots in the particular conditions of the city's growth in the last 50 years.

Skopje: socialist vision, nationalist's nightmare

H.R. Wilkinson, visiting in the early 1950s, noted the diversity in the physical landscape of Skopje (1952: 399). This seems to mirror Brailsford's claims concerning the character of Macedonian cities from half a century earlier. In fact, Wilkinson saw a city where the mode of that diversity was already very different. For his description is not just of different communities with different languages and faiths: he juxtaposes official buildings with private homes, and the remains of past régimes with the work-places of the new, closing his word-picture by recording (1952: 399):

> Skopje's present role is eloquently expressed in the new gleaming building with its hammer and sickle in neon lights, in which the Macedonian Communist Party has its headquarters. Oddly enough this building adjoins the Turkish fortress. The emblems of the old masters and the new stand side-by-side.

This juxtaposition of the visible markers of secular power was swept away in July 1963, when an earthquake destroyed Skopje. A state of natural disaster was declared, assistance came from all over the world, and the United Nations stepped in to assist in the making of a new city that was to stand as a symbol of international peace and under-

standing. An overall city plan incorporated elements from Japanese and Slovenian proposals. Most standing remains were bulldozed and levelled, and new, earthquake-proof
and self-consciously modern buildings in reinforced concrete took their place.

The issues that arose around this process in some sense foreshadowed those described by Holston's anthropological critique of Brasilia (1990). Holston documents the
planners' agenda of modernization, which re-configured domestic space and household
practices, as well as public space and sociability. In Brasilia, the enforced change in the
practices of everyday life, defined by Bourdieu (1982) as the *habitus*, was most apparent
in the elimination from the apartment layout of the *copa*, an intermediate space between
kitchen and dining-room which in traditional households served as a focus for everyday
social life. The inhabitants of these new apartments found them 'cold' (Holston 1990:
177–8). The same criticism was extended to the city as a whole, from which streets and
their intersections were abolished, and the concept of meeting in 'the bar on the corner'
was stripped of its meaning.

Apartment living similarly became the norm for the residents of the south bank of
the Vardar in Skopje, where the destruction had been greatest. Mostly from villages and
smaller towns, these newcomers faced the task of adapting themselves to an alien environment, in which domestic space was limited and its uses planned by architects with
different ideas of ways of life. The UN report on the project notes the resistance of some
inhabitants to the projected 'rational' use of their new homes. Some families insisted on
reserving one room, the 'white room', only for guests, even though that entailed living
day-by-day under what the UN outsiders considered unnecessarily cramped conditions
(UNDP 1970: 266). The spaces between and around the new apartment blocks are generally unkempt and swept only by dusty winds created by the restructuring of the local
topography; the new neighbourhoods are described as lacking any soul. The modern
city appears to negate the tie to the land so integral to Macedonian national sentiment,
and some ethnic Macedonians thus feel they have been robbed of a part of their authentic character.

In the midst of this restructuring, two quite different sets of physical structures were
spared by the planners. On both banks of the river, certain sites and buildings marked as
historically significant were not destroyed. Churches and mosques and Turkish *hans*
(travellers' rest-houses which also housed shops) survived, as did the stone bridge, a
pedestrian bridge across the Vardar. The *Kale*, the old Turkish citadel on the hill, was
left in its ruined state: so too was the old railway station, with its clock that stopped at
the time of the earthquake. These markers of the past were complemented by a programme of new monuments to the particular past that socialist Macedonia celebrated:
the Second World War struggles of the partisans, and cases of individual heroism, were
marked in many squares. As a result of all this, the nature of both private and social
space and memories were transformed: instead of living in a city with its own history,
the residents of the new Skopje were presented with a modern urban landscape into
which the past was written only at various, discrete points: a landscape from which
character had been effaced, but which was pregnant with identity.

On the north bank a very different Skopje endures today (FIGURE 5). In the old arija,
or market area, domestic buildings survived as well as public ones. Although building
was carried out in this area — new theatres, museums, department stores — the district
was largely left as it had been, with cobblestone streets and single- or double-storey
houses and shops. Much has changed in the economic activity of the area: where different trades once congregated on particular streets, the only legacy of this spatial division

FIGURE 5. *Streets of old and of new Skopje.*

of labour is 'Wall Street' where the currency-dealers ply their trade. But the history of this section of Skopje is written in the busy street corners and not through abstract and socialist-realist art at the centres of deserted squares.

These different social worlds are a part of the same city and the same country, and their existence has always provoked comment from residents as well as foreign visitors. Now, though, their contrast is being freighted with tensions, as the Macedonian population finds its return to its roots blocked. For each world — the one modern and self-conscious, the other older, more 'natural' — has taken on the character of one of the two dominant ethnic groups in the Republic: the two worlds, in Skopje and throughout the country, increasingly encroach on one another.

Macedonian residents of Skopje are disturbed by the growth of what are termed *divi gradbi* — 'wild settlements', the shanty towns in the shadows of the tower blocks, which are themselves degrading along with much of the city's infrastructure, strained by a population that certainly exceeds official statistics. Macedonians ascribe this to an influx of Albanians from Kosovo in the 1980s, and fault the authorities of the Yugoslav period for not taking stronger measures to prevent this migration, which they now see as part of a long-term and stealthy Albanian plan to alter the demographics of FYR Macedonia. They point to the increasing number of mosques — whose minarets they dub 'Pershings' — that dot the rural landscape, and the contrasting derelict status of once-populous Macedonian villages, whose natives now live in the tower-blocks of Skopje.

Albanians, by contrast, have protested the Macedonian state's intervention in sites which they consider invested with Albanian character, as well as recent initiatives of the Macedonian church. Elez Biberaj, for example, records as anti-Albanian the activities of the Macedonian state in the early 1980s when what Biberaj call the 'traditional' walls surrounding Albanian houses were apparently being systematically destroyed (1993: 5, 16). In Skopje, over the last two years, there has been a marked increase in religiously-charged practices and buildings that could be argued to be self-conscious expressions of Macedonian Orthodox Christian identity. Religious rituals, as opposed to those of the old regime, are now performed in the public spaces of Skopje. In both 1991 and 1992, the ritual of throwing a cross into the water on Vodici (12 January) was conducted on the stone bridge, at the heart of the city, and accompanied by a politically charged sermon. Easter, too, is now celebrated in the centre, at the newly-finished cathedral, while it used to be celebrated only on the margins of Skopje. The University of Kiril & Methodi is now the University of Saints Kiril & Methodi: religion is increasingly foregrounded as a part of Macedonian identity, and interwoven with state rituals. What took place on the clock-tower in Bitola, then, is no isolated incident, but part of a wider re-inscription of Macedonian identity in a new set of markers that are explicitly religious.

The local and the national

Goulbourne (1991) has stressed that national movements, utilizing local patriotism, take on the same idioms of attachment to a 'home' that is extended, in the imagination, to the borders of the nation state. Confino (1993) has demonstrated the mechanics of this operation in 19th-century Germany, arguing that the idea of *Heimat* served to unite village, region and nation, such that 'the nation resembled the Russian Matryoshka doll, as it accommodated and integrated smaller versions of itself' (1993: 58). Reproductions of a generic church tower were a central element in this imagined nation, as a symbol of the 'manageable and intimate community' (1993: 64). Such symbols, at once national and local, territorialize the abstract cross, and universalize the local landscape.

Swedenburg (1990) noted similar impulses in the modern Palestinian movement in Israel, where postcard reproductions of West-Bank artists' paintings show Arab villages filled with people in traditional dress and carrying out traditional practices, inhabiting what he called 'a mythical rural past which is at the same time continuous with the present' (1990: 21). He acknowledged that these representations contribute to the making of myth and the essentialization of cultural authenticity, but argued that they must be read against 'the backdrop of the colonial reality' (1990: 21) in which Arab villages and inhabitants have been cleared by Israeli occupation (cf. Kidron 1988).

The complexity of that backdrop is made apparent by W.J.T. Mitchell (1994), whose account of Palestine includes a picture juxtaposing a fortified Israeli camp on a hill-top and a Palestinian village in the valley. Exploring the questions of ownership at stake in any landscape where, for one reason or another, human agency has failed to establish the 'Russian doll' model, he concludes (1994: 29):

> [N]o one 'owns' this landscape in the sense of having clear, unquestionable title to it — contestation and struggle are inscribed indelibly on it. But everyone 'owns' (or ought to own) this landscape in the sense that everyone must acknowledge or own up to some responsibility for it, some complicity in it. This is not just a question of geopolitics and the question of Israel as the site of big-power imperialist maneuvering; it is also a matter of a global poetics in which the Holy Land plays a historical and mythic role as the imaginary landscape where Eastern and Western cultures encounter one another in a struggle that refuses to confine itself to the Imaginary.

The self-identified ethnic Macedonians who constitute a majority in the FYR Macedonia have in the last two years been tossed on the horns of a dilemma. Individual markers of their national identity — the symbols of statehood, an autonomous church, and a coherent narrative history in which state and nation constitute decisive agents — are all contested by neighbouring states. The response among a range of organizations within the Republic — political parties, church leaders, local councils — has been to seek to invest these markers with territorial dimensions; to emphasize, in other words, the material context of these images within a whole set of features which together make up Macedonian character. With respect to the world of nation-states, they could be argued to be in the position of the Palestinians as described by Swedenburg, compelled to project into their national imagination a local and material dimension in order to establish any sense of collectivity.

Yet in so doing, they may find themselves condemned as cultural aggressors. For in seeking to imbue symbols with local sentiment, they simultaneously re-shape the contours of a material landscape that is inhabited by different groups with different histories. The *petokratka* on the clock-tower, standing visibly on the Bitola skyline among mosque minarets and church towers, sought to unify the town and its inhabitants as Yugoslavs of Macedonia. Its replacement with a cross aspires to identify the tower and the town not merely as Macedonian, but as Christian. It thereby paints the ethnic Orthodox Macedonians as the inheritors of the Macedonian state: a symbol under which the different traditions could be united has been superseded by one under which they cannot.

The current government has continually sought to grant cultural autonomy to the minorities of FYR Macedonia, while maintaining the Republic's territorial integrity. In such a charged internal political climate, the selection of a flag acceptable to all parties was a remarkable achievement. But external pressures such as that exerted by Greece have reduced the credibility of the government and thereby increased the intensity with which it is attacked by Albanian and Macedonian nationalist parties. Its attempts to assert control over a part of Skopje which had become a virtual no-go area for state authorities led to accusations of anti-Albanian bias after four people died in gunfire when police tried to prevent illegal cigarette-dealing in November 1992. The problems over the new state's symbols, and the financial weakness that has accompanied international non-recognition, have left the church in a strong position to take on the role of representative of the Macedonian people through ritual and through the remaking of the symbolic landscape.

The increased polarization of the parties within the Republic is visible in the changing patterns of construction of religious buildings and the reinscription of particular meanings on public and private space. Should the multinational government fail, as did its peer in Bosnia, the stage is set for an Macedonian ethnoarchaeology of destruction that will undoubtedly, as in Bosnia, consume this landscape, and make it still more symbolically charged in the process. These attempts to 'build character' cannot be considered as based on false images of the past, or as driven by the propaganda of political élites. In FYR Macedonia, sentiments are being mobilized that are recognizably similar to those integral to the making of national collectivities in other parts of the world. It is their context, in a landscape whose ownership is disputed not just by its inhabitants but by a variety of external interests, that imbues these sentiments and their symbols with destructive agency.

Acknowledgements. The research on which this paper is based was assisted by a grant from the Joint Committee on Western Europe of the American Council of Learned Societies and the Social Science Research Council, with funds provided by the Ford and Mellon Foundations. I would like to thank ANTIQUITY's anonymous reviewer for constructive comments.

References

ALEXANDER, S. 1979. *Church and state in Yugoslavia since 1945.* Cambridge: Cambridge University Press.

ALLCOCK, J.B. 1992. Rhetorics of nationalism in Yugoslav Politics, in J.B. Allcock, J.J. Horton & M. Milivojevic (ed.), *Yugoslavia in transition: choices and constraints: essays in honour of Fred Singleton.* New York (NY): Berg.

ANDERSON, B. 1983. *Imagined communities.* London: Verso.

ANDERSON, P. 1992. Fernand Braudel and national identity, in *A zone of engagement.* London: Verso.

APOSTOLOV, A. 1962. *Kolonizacijata na Makedonija bo Stara Jugoslavija.* Skopje: Misla.

BADIAN E. 1982. Greeks and Macedonians, in B. Barr Sherrar & E.N. Borza (ed.), *Macedonia and Greece in Late Classical and Early Hellenistic Times* (Studies in the History of Art 10): 33–51.

BICEVSKI, P. 1993. *Našite Koski.* Skopje: Matica Makedonska.

BOURDIEU, P. 1982. *Outline of a theory of practice.* Cambridge: Cambridge University Press.

BRAILSFORD, H.N. 1906. *Macedonia: its races and their future.* London: Methuen.

CHAPMAN, J. 1994. Destruction of a common heritage: the archaeology of war in Croatia, Bosnia and Hercegovina, *Antiquity* 68: 120–26.

CONFINO, A. 1993. The nation as a local metaphor: Heimat, national memory and the German Empire, 1871–1918, *Memory and History* 5(1): 42–86.

DURKHEIM, E. 1915 [1965]. *The elementary forms of the religious life.* New York (NY): Free Press.

FERNANDEZ, J. 1985. Folklorists as agents of nationalism, *New York Folklore* 11(1–4): 135–47.

FORD, G. 1982. Networks, ritual and 'Vrski': a study of urban adjustment in Macedonia. Unpublished Ph.D dissertation, Tempe (AZ): Arizona State University.

FRIEDMAN, V. 1975. Macedonian language and nationalism during the nineteenth and early twentieth centuries, *Balkanistica* 2: 83–98.

GOULBOURNE, H. 1991. *Ethnicity and nationalism in post-imperial Britain.* Cambridge: Cambridge University Press.

GREEN, P. 1989. The Macedonian connection, in *Classical bearings: interpreting ancient history and culture*: 151–64. New York (NY): Thames and Hudson.

HANDLER, R. 1988. *Nationalism and the politics of culture in Quebec.* Madison (WI): University of Wisconsin.

HERZFELD, M. 1982. *Ours once more: folklore, ideology and the making of modern Greece.* New York (NY): Pella.
    1992. *The social production of indifference.* Chicago (IL): University of Chicago Press.

HOBSBAWM, E.J. & T.O. RANGER (ed.). 1983. *The invention of tradition.* Cambridge: Cambridge Univesity Press.

HOLTON, M. (ed.). 1974. *The big horse and other stories of modern Macedonia.* Columbia (MO): University of Missouri Press.

HOLSTON, J. 1988. *The modernist city.* Chicago (IL): University of Chicago Press.

KAPFERER, B. 1989. *Legends of people, myths of state.* Washington (DC): Smithsonian Institute Press.

KARAKASIDOU, A. 1994. Sacred scholars, profane advocates: intellectuals molding national consciousness in Greece, *Identities* 1(1): 35–62.

KIDRON, P. 1988. Truth whereby nations live, in E.W. Said & C. Hitchens (ed.), *Blaming the victims: spurious scholarship and the Palestinian question.* New York (NY): Verso.

KOČOVSKA, J. 1992. Mnoz̆instvoto — protiv promena na imeto, *Nova Makedonija* (9 December): 4.

MITCHELL, W.J.T. 1994. Imperial landscape, in W.J.T. Mitchell (ed.), *Landscape and power.* Chicago (IL): University of Chicago Press.

NEDELKOVSKI, M. 1974. The body that belonged to no one, in Holton (ed.).

PERRY, D. 1988. *The politics of terror: the Macedonian liberation movements 1893–1903.* Durham (NC): Duke University Press.

POULTON, H. 1993. The Republic of Macedonia after UN Recognition, *RFE/RL Research Report* 2/23.

St ERLICH, V. 1984. Historical awareness and the peasant, in Winner & Winner (ed.).

SIMIĆ, A. 1973. *The peasant urbanites: a study of rural–urban mobility in Serbia.* London: Seminar Press.

SOLEV, D. 1974. The round trip of a shadow in Holton (ed.).

SWEDENBURG, T. 1990. The Palestinian peasant as national signifier, *Anthropological Quarterly* 63(1): 18–30.

ŠUPLINOVSKI, S. 1992. Zname: zamena ili izmena? *Nova Makedonija* (5 May): 4.

WILKINSON, H.R. 1952. Jugoslav Macedonia in transition, *Geographical Journal* 118(4): 390–405.

UNDP (UNITED NATIONS DEVELOPMENT PROGRAMME). 1970. *Skopje resurgent: the story of a United Nations Special Fund town planning project.* New York (NY): United Nations.

WINNER, I.P. & T.G. WINNER. 1984. *The peasant and the city in eastern Europe: interpenetrating structures.* Cambridge (MA): Schenkmann.

8 Experienced landscapes

'The reader will suffer me here to recall to his mind the shapes of the valleys
. . . He will people the valleys with lakes and rivers . . . He will conceive that from
the point on which he stood, he looks down upon this scene before the country had
been penetrated by any inhabitants: — to vary his sensations, and to break upon
their stillness, he form to himself an image of the tide visiting and revisiting the
friths . . . He may see or hear in fancy the winds sweeping over the lakes or piping
with a loud voice among the primaeval woods shedding and renewing their leaves
. . .

(WORDSWORTH [1810] 1951: 85–6)

A further trend of modern studies of landscape is to introduce experience of those landscapes. In some ways this is not a new trend, but one much apparent in any literary
approach to landscape (Piggott 1937). The challenge is that although we can reconstruct
physically an ancient landscape and even make attempts individually to experience
that landscape, it is a different matter to have an experience of that landscape as a prehistoric individual. Different routes to prehistoric experience have been attempted. Barrett
(1994) has explored the processional ways of the monumental landscapes of Wessex,
within the physical and cultural constraints they still leave us. Tilley (1994) is interested in exploring the paths, movements and narratives which link locales or places, but
he is ultimately still an individual from the age of capitalism exploring landscapes which
once contained prehistoric individuals. Edmonds (1999) has interspersed fictional narrative with archaeological theory. Tilley (1999) constructs one metaphorical hypothesis
on another; metaphors are key to understanding early landscapes, but metaphors are
deeply embedded in an individual culture. Modern archaeologists are right to address
this challenge, but the boundary with more or less good fiction is marginal. Fleming
(1999) has been particularly critical of the interpretations of one experiential reconstruction, partly on grounds of sampling, but also on the grounds that many other alternative reconstuctions are possible, many of which are more securely based on the archaeological evidence.

The first article reprinted here (McMann 1994) employs the constraints of space to
guide access to prehistoric experience. Yet this author still manages to remain analyti-
cally distant from the prehistoric past (and for me this is praise rather than criticism) by
providing an architectural framework through which to address the dimension of
cosmological experience. The second article is the only New World landscape reprinted
in this selection of papers from ANTIQUITY (Gartner 1999). A seemingly agricultural landscape is transformed into a landscape where meaning is experienced, through the close
reading of ethnography. At the same time, the importance of the physical landscape is
not lost.

Forms of power: dimensions of an Irish megalithic landscape

by JEAN MCMANN

ANTIQUITY 68 (260), 1994

'WHAT MUST it have been like to *be* here in ancient times?' — where 'here' is inside one of the Great Zimbabwe enclosures or a Mesoamerican ball-court. An architectural approach to built spaces may make coherent that felt experience, here applied to the Loughcrew chamber-tombs, classic built spaces of Irish prehistory.

Nature, culture and ancient architecture

To construct a space is to create a world, a built environment connecting 'nature' and 'culture'. Architects appropriate nature in order to write culture, and in the process they rewrite nature as well.[1] Where prehistoric architectural spaces survive, as in the 'Neolithic passage-tomb cemeteries' of Ireland, we can situate ourselves within ancient, if approximate, spatial boundaries (e.g. FIGURES 1–5).[2] Despite their temporal collapse, physical depletion and mistaken reconstructions, these ruins allow our anatomically prehistoric bodies to experience a kind of 'virtual reality', the wordless reiteration of ancient spatial themes and variations. At the same time, we participate in the contemporary play of forms, meanings and sensations.

Abstract plans provide a cryptic counterpoint to this flow of sensation and imagination. A plan's 'flatland' is nothing like our world, with its geomorphological, historical and psychological 'placeness'. However, ancient maps and plans testify to the longevity of these flawed but serviceable conceptual tools; I use them as an architectural shorthand to explore limited aspects of a landscape we cannot situate precisely in time and space. Loosely adapting Henry Glassie's version of the structuralism of Lévi-Strauss, I discuss floor- and site-plans from the megalithic cemetery at Loughcrew in terms of paired structural concepts (Glassie 1975). These are conceived less as contrasts or oppositions than as fused dualities, or single concepts with a twofold nature. Further, I view design structure at Loughcrew as changeable, and passage-tomb cemeteries as 'landscapes in motion' (Upton 1990; see also Sahlins 1985). Changing social processes and practices generate changing symbolic meanings; structure changes over time.

---

1   I use 'nature' and 'culture' as makeshift devices for discussing the relationships between human constructions (including architecture and other objects, ideas, actions, feelings and so on) and the physical environment. To draw firm boundaries between the natural and the cultural, for example to make a clean separation between humans and other animals, is impossible (Ingold 1987). My approach to 'reading' material culture is generally based on Hodder (e.g. 1982; 1988), Ricoeur (e.g. 1981) and Kus (1983), as well as Leone's (1986) and Patrik's (1985) discussions of archaeological approaches to interpretation.

2   These terms, of course, are too limited or too broad. 'Neolithic' is necessary but ambiguous for the time period in Irish prehistory (roughly before *c.* 4000 BC until *c.* 2000 BC) when megalithic tombs were built and first used, and during which subsistence strategies changed from primarily hunting–gathering to primarily hunting–cultivating. The monuments held human remains, yet they were (and are) quite different from our tombs and cemeteries. Perhaps they were more like sacred parks or civic centres, with functions similar not only to our burial grounds, but to such spaces as theatres, churches, museums, schools and sports arenas.

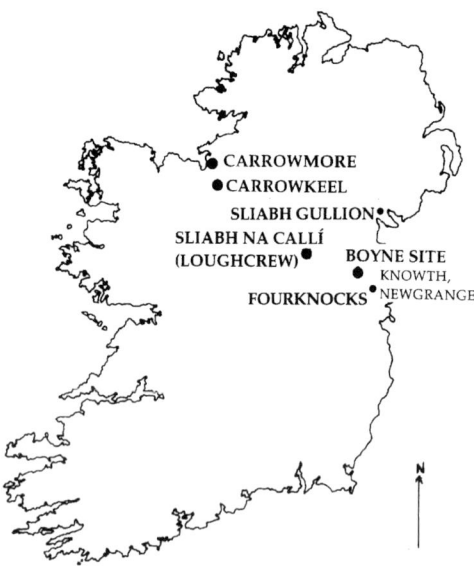

● Sites with 9 or more passage tombs
● Sites with 1-8 passage tombs

FIGURE 1. *Location of sites mentioned in the text.*

Recent scholars have viewed the monumental architecture of western European passage tombs as both expressing and imposing concepts involving 'taming', 'owning' or otherwise controlling nature (e.g. Renfrew 1976; Miller & Tilley 1984; Criado Boado & Fábregas Valcarce 1989; Hodder 1990; Thomas 1991). In my view, rather than simply expressing the 'triumph of the cultural over the natural' (Hodder 1990: 200), design structure at Loughcrew ameliorates and softens cultural elements by including natural ones (McMann 1991). In a similar vein, Julian Thomas (1991: 184) has interpreted British Neolithic deposition practices as an effort 'simultaneously to include and exclude the wild'. The architecture at Loughcrew may reflect and perpetuate two conflicting and/or coexisting belief systems, the first characteristic of a 'wild', primarily hunting–gathering society, and the second of a 'tame', hunting–cultivating

LOUGHCREW Site Map

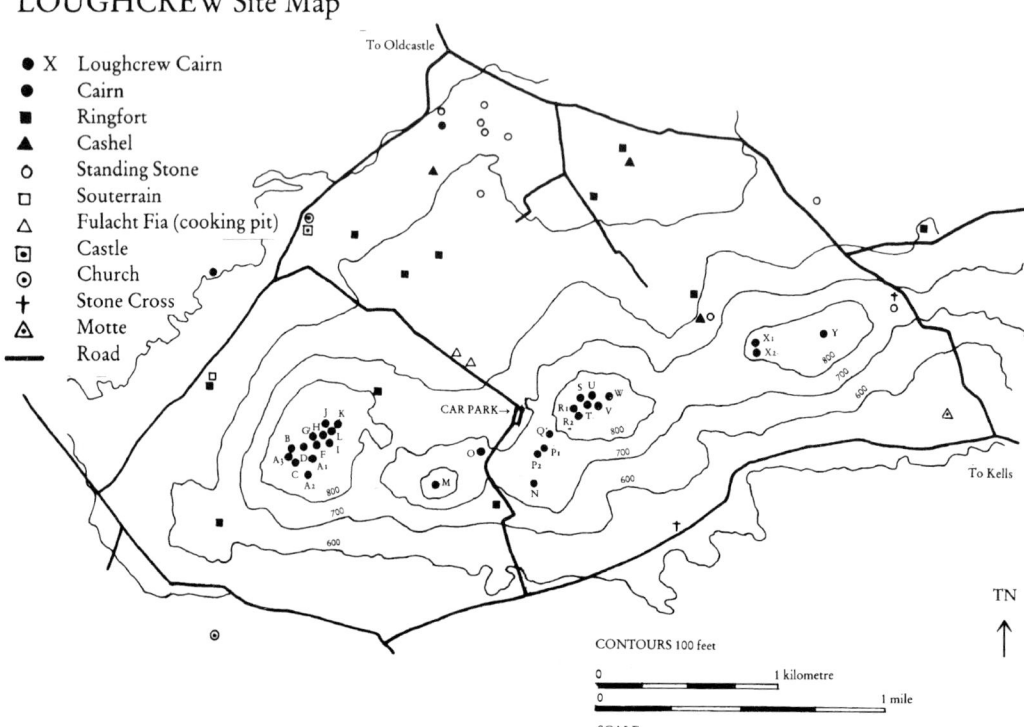

FIGURE 2. *Loughcrew site map. (Based on the Ordnance Survey by permission of the government (permit No. 5872), and on Moore 1987.)*

or primarily cultivating society. Rather than emphasizing structural boundaries between these two systems, I stress their fluid inter-relationship, and find evidence for this in spatial patterns.

Loughcrew

A brief history of the site

Of Ireland's four large passage tomb cemeteries (FIGURE 1), Loughcrew has been the least published. On early maps it is written both as Loughcrew (probably for a small local lake) and as *Sliabh na Caillighe* (hill of the witch or hag). A 15th-century will calls it *Tri Choiscem na Callighe* (the three footprints of the hag), referring to its etiological legend (McMann 1991). In that legend, the ancient hag Cailleach Bhéarra leapt from hill to hill, forming cairns by dropping stones from her apron in a supernatural but ultimately unsuccessful bid for power (see Ó Crualaoich 1988 on the hag and McMann 1991 on links between passage tombs and legendary Irish females).

In the 19th century, the excavations of School Inspector Eugene Conwell (Conwell 1866; 1873 etc.) aroused some antiquarian interest in the site. Although the finds and architecture still have not been scientifically dated, Irish archaeologists place the chambered cairns there within the range of radiocarbon dates for the other three large cemeteries. Although a strongly disputed date, *c.* 4840–4370 BC, was obtained from Carrowmore, generally accepted dates range from *c.* 4000 BC to 2800 BC.

Remains

Remains of approximately thirty cairns are visible at Loughcrew today, set along a ridge running roughly southwest/northeast, with four summits more than 244 m (800 ft) above sea level. Most cluster on the two highest hills, usually called Carnbane East and Carnbane West. The rubble outline or 'footprint' (as architects call the imprint of a building) of at least one large cairn is found on each of the two other summits, as well as a few remains of smaller cairns, mostly along the crest of the ridge (FIGURES 2–3). All of the 30 cairns now visible at the site have left at least traces of their footprints. Seven have near-intact plans, while interior fragments remain of 21 others. Seventeen of the cairns have partial or complete kerbs. These varied remains — plans, kerbs and footprints — comprise the basis for the following observations regarding design structure.

Site plan

Cairn remains can be seen from various vantage points to the north and south below the Loughcrew ridge. With a few exceptions, they are positioned on knolls and subtle rises, continuing and extending these natural landforms (see FIGURE 3). Cairn H, which the late Joseph Raftery suggested might be an Iron Age addition, is one of the few cairns on Carnbane West sited in a comparatively low, flat area.[3]

The site plan shows the cairns distributed asymmetrically along an axis passing through the highest points on the four hills. On Carnbane East and Carnbane West, smaller cairns cluster around two of the three remaining large ones. In contrast, Cairn D, the largest on Carnbane West, is ringed by a 12-m-wide empty zone. The spacing of Cairns J, K and L on Carnbane West is nearly identical to that of Cairns S, T and U on Carnbane East; at both Loughcrew and the Boyne site, there are more remains on the westernmost hill (Cooney 1990). Cairn form and siting conform closely to particular geomorphological

---

3   Raftery, an Irish archaeologist, excavated the cairn in 1943; no excavation report has been published. Finding Iron Age material at 'foundation level', he suggested that the Neolithic-style cairn was remodelled and/ or re-used, or perhaps originally built, during the Iron Age (*c.* 100 AD) (Raftery 1953 and pers. comm. 1990).

FIGURE 3. Aerial view of Carnbane West. (Cambridge University Collection; copyright reserved.)

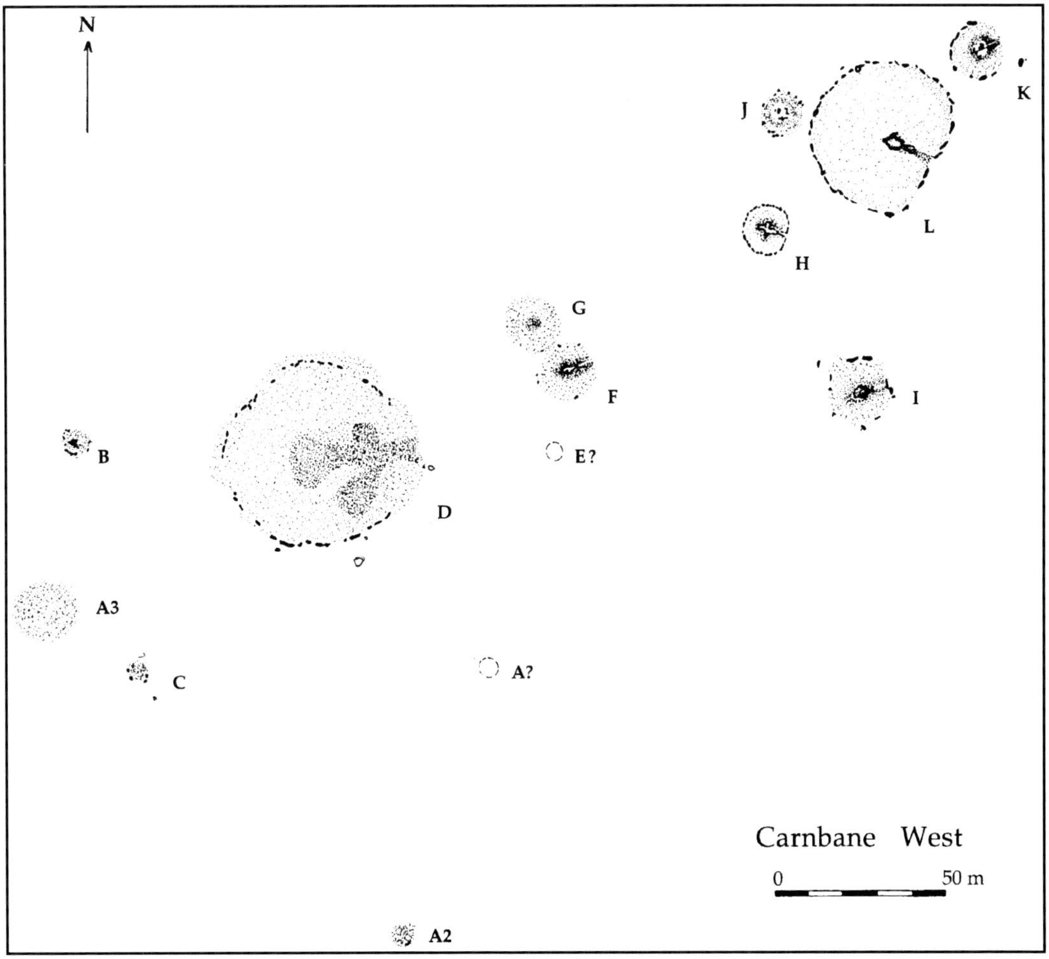

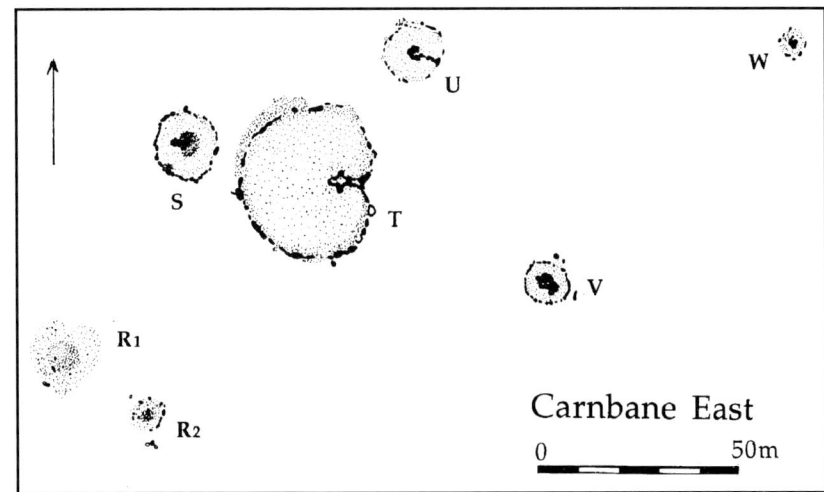

FIGURE 4. *Cairns on Carnbane West (includes areas of Carnbane, Loughcrew and Newtown townlands).*

FIGURE 5. *Cairns on Carnbane East (includes areas in Corstown, Balrath and Ballinvalley townlands).*

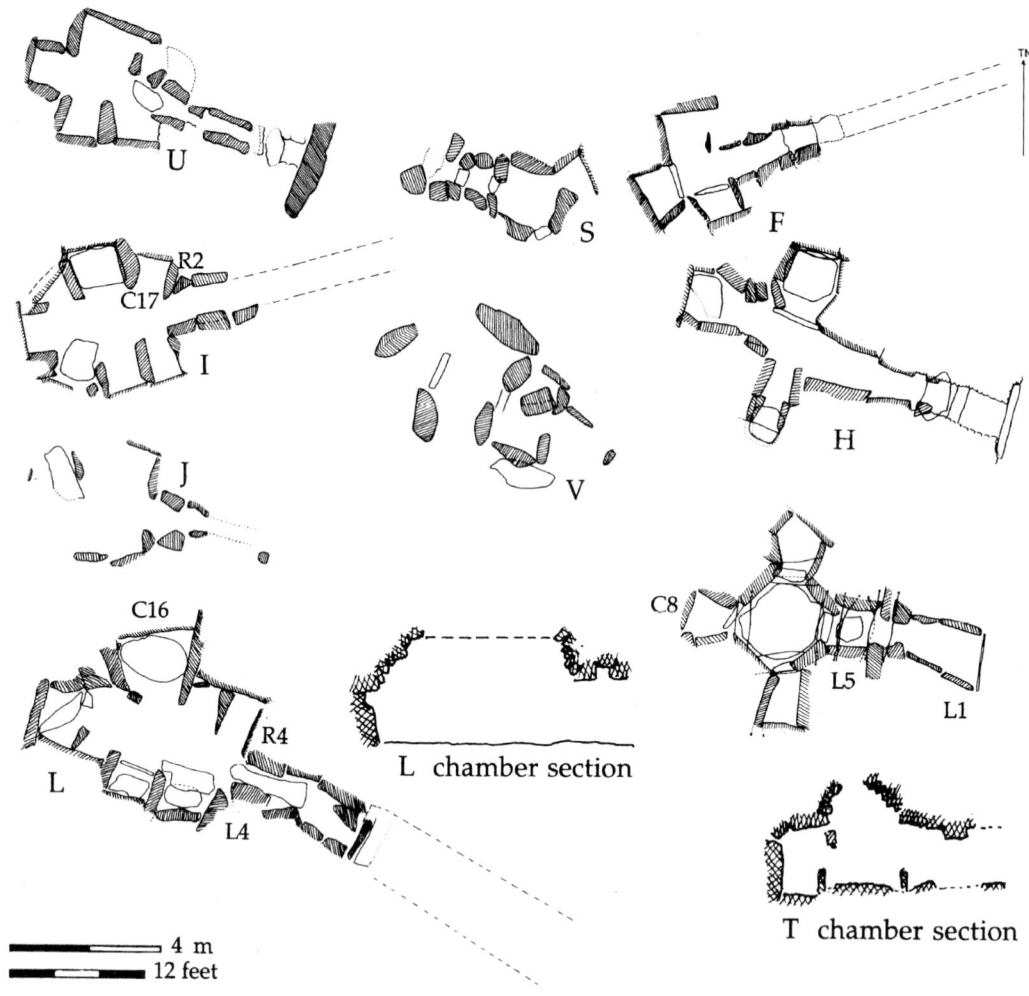

FIGURE 6. *Plans of cairn interiors, drawn from field measurements in 1990, 1992, and 1993.*

features at Loughcrew (FIGURES 2 & 3). This aspect of passage tomb architecture deserves more attention; most studies have focussed on interior plans at the expense of siting and exterior design (but see Cooney 1983; 1990).

Exterior design
Despite destruction and attrition, the Loughcrew cairns still reveal much of their exterior form (including shape, materials, and kerbs), as well as the technology of their construction. From this evidence, it seems that the mounds were nearly without directionality. Although entrances of the larger cairns are marked by a flattening or inward curve of the kerb, we see no such indication in the few smaller cairns where sufficient evidence remains. Certainly the sharp directional differentiation of, for example, a pyramid or conventional rectangular monument is absent from these subtle articulations of volume,

FIGURE 7 (opposite). *Interior plans drawn by William Frazer (1893: plate VIII), after George du Noyer and Eugene Conwell. Note the contrasts in style and information between these earlier and my later plans. Both sets have the virtue (and flaw) of making space intelligible to a particular audience.*

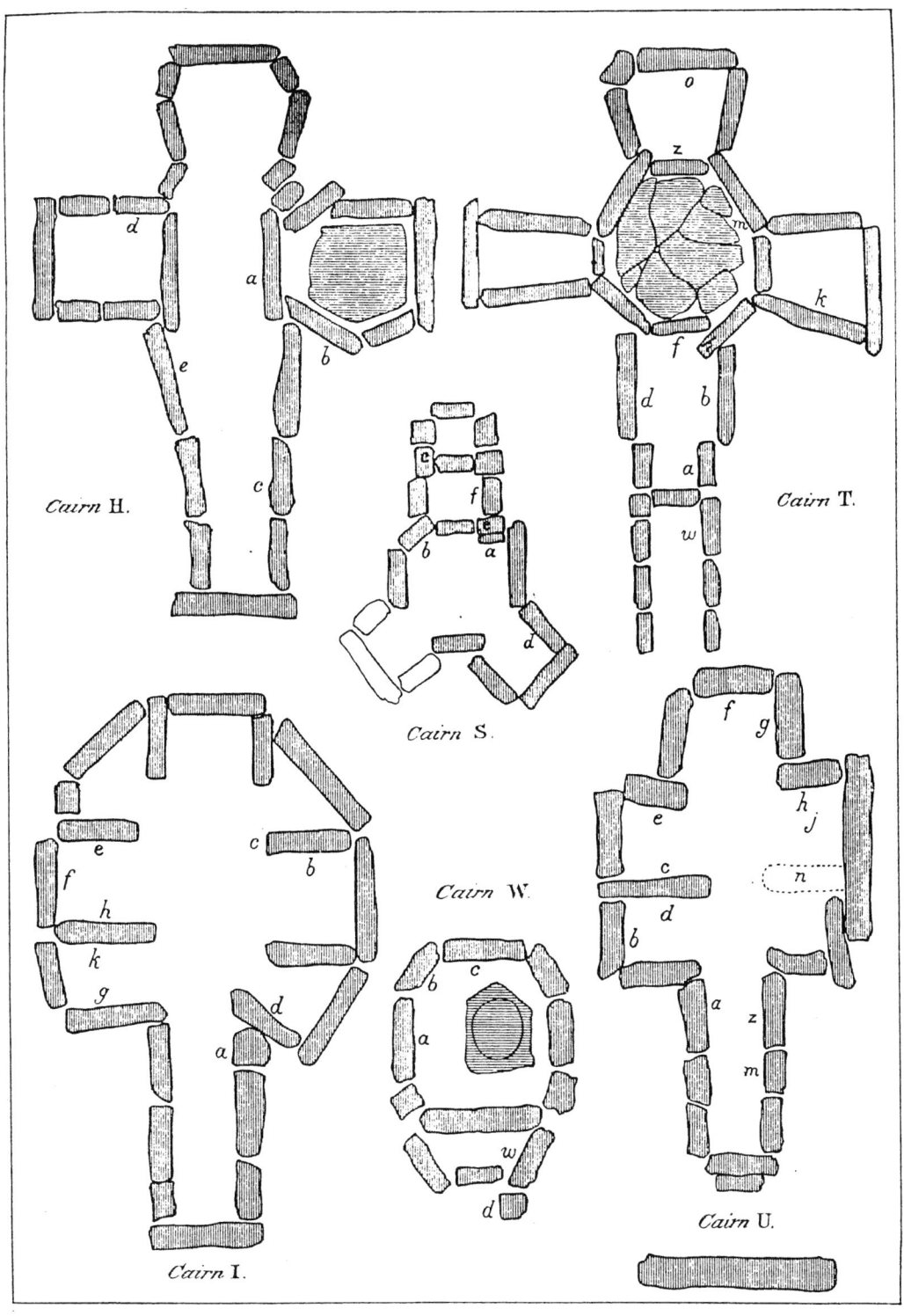

GROUND PLANS OF CHAMBERS OF CAIRNS AT SLIEVE-NA-CALLIAGHE.

(Scale, 8 feet to an inch.)

which follow the forms of the hillocks and rises they are situated upon. However, as at the Boyne, white quartz, stone pavings and other materials and features probably marked entrance façades and may have differentiated one cairn from another. A local landowner, E.C. Rotheram (1985: 311), uncovered three 'circles' or pavings of white quartz outside the entrance of Cairn T, and another 'lying to the south-west' of the cairn. At Loughcrew, there are no traces of the entry-blocking stones found at Knowth and Newgrange. However, such desirable, relatively accessible stones could have been removed or re-used; the re-use of inscribed stones has been documented at other megalithic sites (L'Helgouach 1983; Bradley 1989). Despite the possibility of such accents, both siting and exterior design seem to echo existing landforms rather than to impose bold new shapes. The bold forms are found within.

Interior design

Interior plans of the surviving cairns at Loughcrew are mostly either cruciform or elaborations on a kind of keyhole shape, in which a round or oval chamber is subdivided into cells (see FIGURE 6). Examples of each of these two plan types are found on both Carnbane West and Carnbane East. Neither type bears any resemblance to the exterior forms of the cairns.

In contrast to the informal flow of the siting, cairn interiors at Loughcrew are separated into distinct segments, or modules (see Kinnes 1975). Sills, lintels and variations in the height and angle of structural elements define roughly rectangular areas, generating a staccato spatial rhythm. Symmetry is maintained in various ways, for example by approximately matching the sizes of opposed orthostats and other structural stones in passages and side cells, and by balancing the size and location of the cells. However, the differing shapes of the stones, the placement of carved designs and the consistently larger size of the right-hand cells provide subtle variations in this balance. Larger right-hand side-cells also have been noted at Knowth, Dowth and Newgrange (O'Kelly 1982; Eogan 1984). The position of the largest cell in multi-celled cairns like L, I and U at Loughcrew might best be described as located at 'three o'clock', with the passage entry as 'six o'clock' and the end cell opposite as 'twelve o'clock'. In these three cairns, smaller cells are located to the right between the passage and the largest cell (see McMann 1991 for a more extensive analysis).

The corbelled domes are the most daring feature of the interiors. Although extensive corbelling has survived only in the largest cairns at the site, many (if not all) were probably roofed by this means. In Cairn T each of the side cells is corbelled separately, so that its roof rises up behind the lintel. The corbels are invisible from eye level in the central chamber. A much larger corbelled dome once spanned the chamber of Cairn L (see sections, FIGURE 6). Now restored to a height of about 3 m, the dome probably rose at least 4 m originally. Although more skill and effort were required to span this greater diameter, the result was a much more flexible plan, in which the chamber could be subdivided or remodelled without structural change.

In both designs, the transition from entry to inner chamber is breathtaking. Just after the low passage from the outer world narrows, the space explodes. Shadowy side cells, curtained by sills, lintels and orthostats, expand the chamber boundaries. Huge corbels circle high overhead. Although the vertical emphasis of this kiln-like space strongly evokes the idea of 'centre', it is rarely placed at the central point of the cairn, one of many disjunctions between exterior and interior form. The design of such radically innovative spaces has been little discussed in architectural histories; yet megalithic tombs are milestones in the history of building, and, indeed, the history of art.

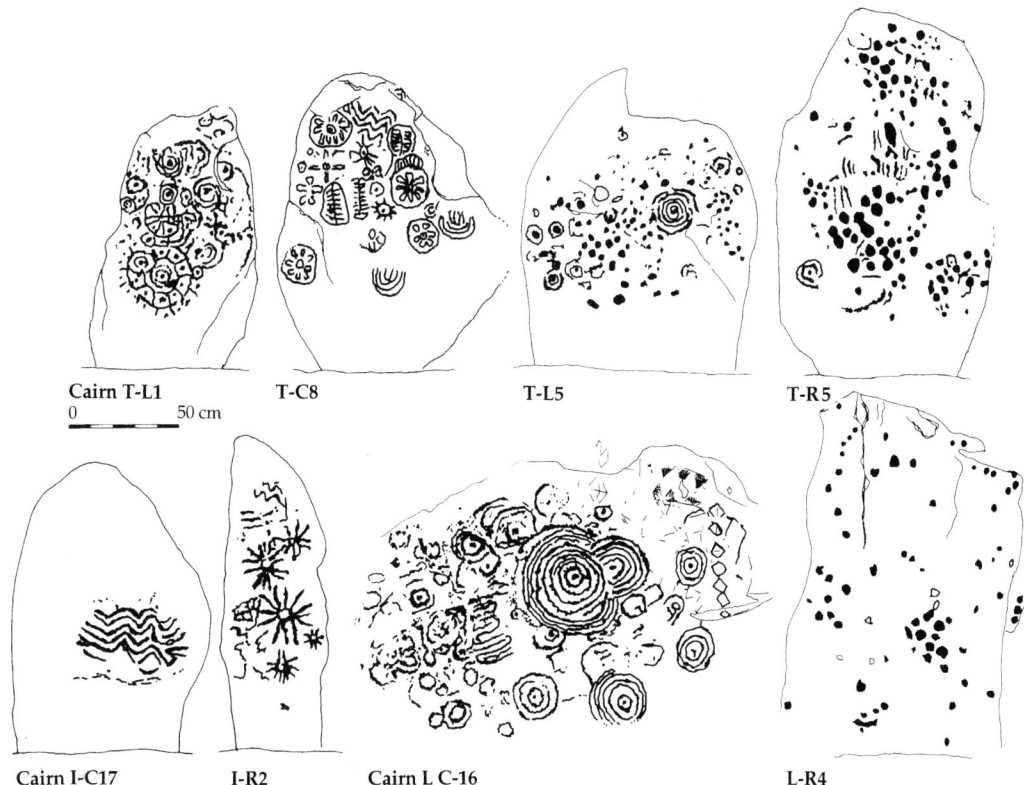

Cairn T-L1   T-C8   T-L5   T-R5
0   50 cm

Cairn I-C17   I-R2   Cairn L C-16   L-R4

FIGURE 8. *Carved motifs and pitting at Loughcrew, after Shee Twohig 1981.*

Megalithic 'art'

In addition to the site plan and the plans of the individual cairns, the motifs carved on
the interior stones at Loughcrew provide a third instance of spatial patterning that I
assume to be roughly contemporary. These designs are often referred to as 'megalithic
art'. Although strong arguments may be made against using the term, I think of the entire
passage tomb, and indeed all architecture, as a form of art. Passage tombs may have little
in common with the contemporary commodity we call art, yet they too functioned as a
means of visual communication. They also share properties, such as style and probably
iconography, distinctive to art as a medium (Layton 1991).

The carved designs, then, are one aspect of the larger works of art at Loughcrew.
Elizabeth Shee Twohig (1981) has recorded designs on 108 interior stones there. The
vocabulary of graphic elements is limited and apparently abstract, mostly circles and
lines combined or repeated to form discrete, unconnected motifs (see FIGURE 8). The
loose organization of these elements, in a field seemingly bounded only by the edges of
the stone, contrasts with the regular, symmetrical interior structure of most of the individual designs. Their placement seems cumulative, often radiating out from an apparent
focal point near the centre of the stone. The contrast between this informal placement
and the rigid interior divisions of individual designs recalls that between the asymmetrical siting of the architecture and its orderly, symmetrical interior structure. However, although the designs often seem to take advantage of natural pits in the stone, they
do not obviously follow its form as the cairn siting does the form of the ridge. Design

structure in this layered evidence suggests tantalizing congruencies, yet its ambiguities and contradictions subvert one-dimensional interpretations.

Interpreting passage tombs

I use 'interpreting' here in the sense developed by Paul Ricoeur (e.g. 1981: 152; see also Moore 1990: 112). All too briefly, interpretation for Ricoeur involves a dialectic of sense (structure) and reference (social process, involving social actors in social contexts). Material culture embodies meaning, in fact ambiguous meanings, as does any text. The ambiguity of these meanings may be reduced (but never eliminated) by interpretation, which also expands meaning through metaphor.

Of course, all interpretations may be criticized not only as moral and political acts, but (and simultaneously) as pure subjectivity. It is also true that material culture is not simply a symbol or a written text to be 'read'. To think of it in this way is only to employ a metaphor. Yet 'pragmatic metaphors' are a primary means not only through which past humans understood their lives, but by which we understand our own, and attempt to understand aspects of the lives of Others (see Bird-David 1992 and Gudeman 1986; also Turner 1967; Upton 1986; Lakoff & Johnson 1980).

Since Colin Renfrew (e.g. 1976) developed his model of relatively egalitarian, 'segmentary' societies with megaliths as 'territorial markers', scholars have focussed on the ideological, legitimizing powers of the tombs (e.g. Bradley 1989; Hodder 1990; Barrett 1991; Thomas 1992). Some, of course, have also discussed alternatives to conceiving of monument building purely as a power base. Nonetheless, most recent archaeological interpretations propose or imply 'progressive' models in which societies develop increasing control over social sub-groups, subsistence and their environment. Such studies address functional meanings, how monuments 'work' as elements in social, technological and ideological systems. Susan Kus refers to this as the 'quotidian' element of meaning, concerning the pragmatic and adaptive aspects of human life. Yet the 'human use of space and time' not only orders the quotidian, but also 'maps the cosmological' (Kus 1983b: 286).

During any design process, responses to pragmatic social and ideological agendas underlie and are intertwined with cosmological ideas, beliefs and metaphors. The latter, reductively considered as means to ideological ends, are much less discussed. As M.L. West commented, each generation shuns areas 'in which its immediate predecessors most obviously made idiots [or monsters] of themselves' (Goodison 1989: xiii). Yet cosmological concepts are intrinsic to historical and ethnographic accounts of architecture (e.g. Isbell 1976; Fritz 1978; Kus 1983b; Moore 1986; Upton 1986; Blier 1987; Goodison 1989; Dillehay 1991; Skeates 1991). To imagine such concepts and the part they played in generating spatial arrangements enriches our understanding of the passage tombs.

In the measurable remains at Loughcrew, there are traces of a dynamic dialectic that might be interpreted and fictionally dramatized as an ongoing exchange between designers/users/culture and materials/environment/nature. (See Criado Boado & Fábregas Valcarce 1989b for a structural dialectic of passage tomb design.) In modern practice, architects often refer to the design process as a dialogue between *programme* (or functional requirements) and *site*. There is no reason to suppose that designing the cairns was anything like our modern process of balancing practical, economic and ideological considerations, with an isolated 'client's list' of functional requirements. Still, some process generated these particular forms for these particular locations. Plans and siting at

Loughcrew strongly suggest that concepts of 'place', as phenomenologists have described it, played a powerful role in such a process (see Tuan 1974; Relph 1976; Casey 1979).

Powers of place

At the onset of Neolithic building, a dramatic landmark such as the Loughcrew ridge might already have been seen as 'commissioning' or 'demanding' a monument, recalling Strabo's *genius loci*. Relph (1993: 32) characterizes such places in myth as 'value-laden localities in which the powers of nature reside'. Neolithic cemeteries may have been sited as part of a process of inserting monumental built form into a long-standing Mesolithic system of paths and significant locations based on perceived sacred powers of place.

The continuity of place manifested in the re-use and remodelling of ritual sites has been well documented in the European Neolithic. Thomas (1988: 551) suggests that cairns in the Cotswold–Severn area were built where feasting and exchange transactions had already taken place. In many cases, multi-phase 'cumulicity', including dismantling and reconstruction, continued through long successive periods (e.g. Kinnes 1982; Bradley 1988). At Carrowmore, 'ritual activity' may have occurred before the first passage tombs were built *c.* 4000 BC (Woodman 1992: 304; Burenhult 1984). Finds in the Loughcrew area also indicate a Mesolithic presence there (Cooney 1987: 145).

Indigenous Mesolithic hunter–gatherers in Ireland may not have settled and taken up farming in the Early Neolithic, but continued to be scattered and highly mobile. Some scholars suggest that Neolithic populations in general may have been less sedentary than has been assumed (Zvelebil & Rowly-Conwy 1984; Armit & Finlayson 1992; see also Woodman 1992). Barbara Bender (1983) proposed that early passage tombs in Brittany might have been constructed before farming developed there, citing monumental mound-building by hunter-gatherers in North America. Building monuments, she argued, does not necessarily require a sedentary, agrarian community. In Bender's view, such constructions provided 'monumental permanence' for an otherwise transient population that might have returned periodically to ceremonial sites.

At Loughcrew in particular and in Irish passage tomb cemeteries in general, a transitional, Mesolithic/Neolithic phase may have persisted for centuries. During this period, cosmological beliefs associated with an 'immediate-return', hunting–gathering economy may have continued into the Neolithic, with its developing 'delayed-return' economy. Expanding Marshall Sahlins' ideas regarding their 'affluence', Nurit Bird-David (1990) characterizes hunter–gatherers' relationship with their environment as a 'cosmic economy of sharing'. She contrasts the metaphoric model of a giving environment with that of a delayed-return economy involving cultivation, in which nature is seen not as a giving parent, but as a reciprocating ancestor.

Differences in subsistence strategies, then, imply differing relationships between humans and their environments. I see the contrasts in design structure at Loughcrew as reflecting dual relations between nature and culture, during or after a lengthy transition from hunting–gathering to hunting–cultivation. In the plans, 'natural' exteriors, apparently based on forms in the environment, enclose 'unnatural' interiors, spaces which introduce right angles, redundant boundaries and enclosures, and other divisions that call culture to mind. In each cairn, these contrasting orders are held in tension, without resolution or unification. The formal element that seems to mediate, although not to resolve, this tension is the axis of roughly bilateral symmetry shared by chamber, passage and cairn.

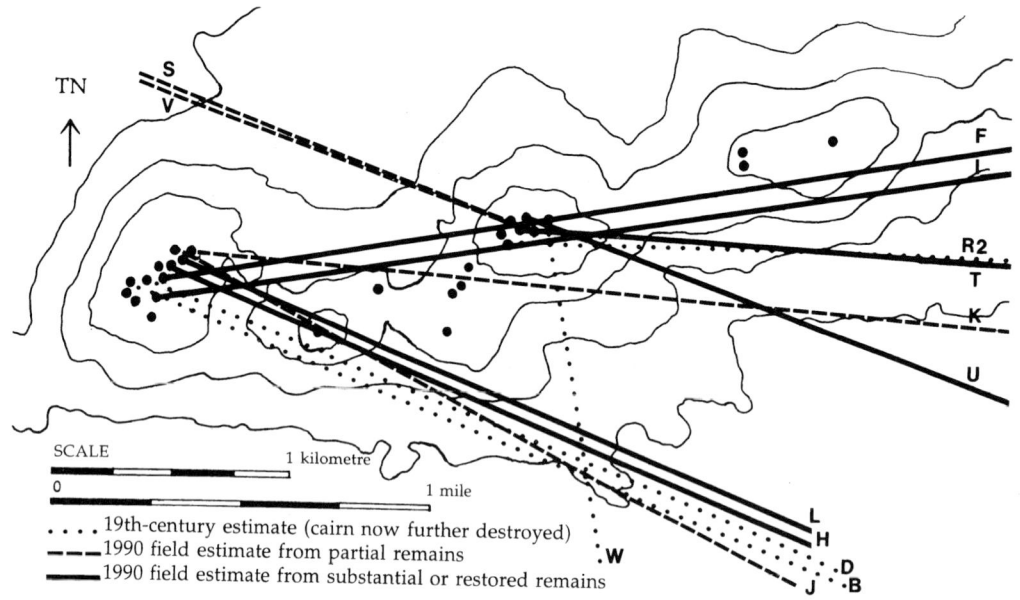

SCALE   1 kilometre

0   1 mile

. . . . 19th-century estimate (cairn now further destroyed)
— — —1990 field estimate from partial remains
———1990 field estimate from substantial or restored remains

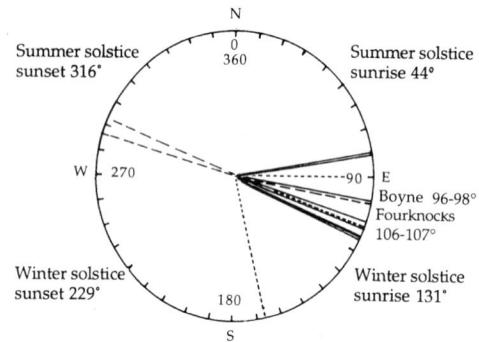

Azimuths at Loughcrew
(Sun positions for c. 3400 BC, first and last flash)

FIGURE 9. *Approximate orientations of Loughcrew cairns.*

The axis

Cairn and site plans at Loughcrew show two types of axial alignment. One is their distribution along the axis formed by the curving spine of the ridge. At oblique angles to this topological line are the cairn axes, defining a rough bilateral symmetry (FIGURE 9). Although plans of the cairns show their mass as an overtly circular, 'containing' motif, distribution of cairns over the site suggests that linear axes of the large cairns L, T and D extend beyond their containers into the landscape. Similarly, Bradley & Chambers (1988) note persisting axial extensions at the Dorset Cursus Complex.

Where cairn remains permitted, I have established these 'axial' lines by extending a point at the approximate centre of the chamber through a point midway between the stones forming the entrance, or, if the entrance has been destroyed, midway between characteristic opposed orthostats in the passage. The lines may be deceptive: the choice of points is somewhat arbitrary, and passages are not straight but flexible, often bending southward. Still, axes obtained from the three largest cairns at the site follow or establish what seem to be unobstructed sightlines or paths to the east. Two, Cairns L and T, are complete enough to be certain that they were oriented eastward. By Conwell's (1866: 361) account, the third, Cairn D, once curved inward at a point implying an axis of 110°. Extending this axis forms an eastward sightline roughly parallel to the axes of Cairns U, L, H and J (and possibly Cairn B).

At Knowth and Newgrange, kerbstones at each end of the axes bisecting the cairns are marked with a pronounced vertical stroke (FIGURE 10). To me, this stroke implies that

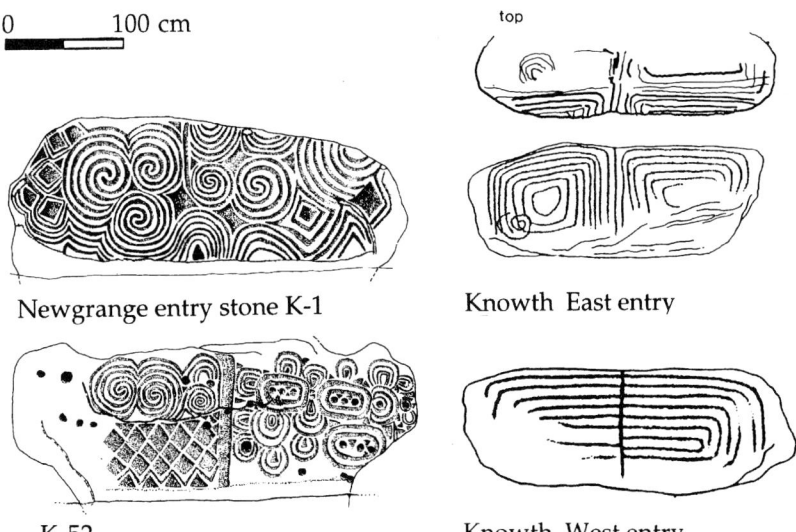

0 100 cm

top

Newgrange entry stone K-1

Knowth East entry

K-52

Knowth West entry

FIGURE 10. Entry stones at Newgrange (after O'Kelly 1982: 154, 158) and Knowth (after Eogan 1986: 194, 195, plate 16).

the axis extends through the solid cairn onward into the landscape (or *vice versa*). The axial line continues informally on the backs of Kerb 11, the east-facing entry stone at Knowth East, and Kerb 52, directly opposite the entry at Newgrange. At Newgrange the cairn perimeter bulges just behind Kerb 52, perhaps following a previous cairn or other feature on the same axis (O'Kelly 1982: 92). Although the kerbstones at Loughcrew are too worn to determine whether they had similar markings, the axis serves as a strong organizing principle in all remaining reconstructible interior plans (FIGURES 4–6).[4]

Except for three with atypical plans, all the measurable cairns at Loughcrew are aligned eastward, within a very approximate range of 32° (see FIGURE 9). In the five cairns with what seem unequivocal remains, axial lines as defined above fall at azimuths between 80° and 112°, clustering near the Equinoxes (88°). Three other cairns, with partial remains including traces of passages, seem to face between 90° and 112°. Another, Cairn W, may have faced due south, as Conwell (1873: 67) thought. The remaining two, Cairns S and V, may both be oriented northwest, although Conwell (1873: 67) thought that Cairn V faced southeast. Cairns W, S and V are atypical at Loughcrew not only in orientation but in form (FIGURE 6).

Standing stones are presently scattered singly and in clusters of two to four along the ridge and in fields to the north. They may have marked axial paths or sightlines other than those I have proposed, although their placement is questionable. Many are recumbent — of these, some may have been dragged down from the cairns. Some of the standing stones may have been re-erected, or, as at Newgrange (Sweetman 1985), erected centuries later. Whether they are earlier or (as seems likely) later than the cairns, these stones appear to extend the 'boundaries' of the site. The structures and traces we see today may be remnants of what was once an expanded, interconnected network of features related to myth and the cosmos as well as to geography.

4   Much weathering has taken place since Conwell commissioned drawings of the art at the site. He described traces of motifs on one kerbstone, the huge 'Hag's Chair' at Cairn T (1973: 27–8); a few faint lines remain. However, most of the kerbstones at Loughcrew are such soft calcareous sandstone that any exposed carvings would have disappeared long ago. Tombstones of the same material with dates of 1600 and earlier in the old Loughcrew Church graveyard have worn nearly smooth.

Astronomical sightlines

Archaeologists, astronomers and enthusiastic others have proposed many interesting ways in which European passage tombs might relate to celestial phenomena. I believe that the sun, and probably the stars and planets as well, played an important role in the design and siting of the cairns. The orientation of Newgrange toward the winter solstice sunrise is a famous corroboration of this idea. Sunlight was important at Loughcrew as well, but its east-facing cairns do not seem carefully aligned to obvious solar or lunar events. In a few, notably the large, restored Cairn T, direct sunlight would have entered the chamber shortly after dawn at the equinoxes, as it does today. Much has been made of this 'equinoctial alignment', where sunlight shaped by the entrance of Cairn T now illuminates particular engraved motifs on the backstone of the chamber (Brennan 1983; O'Brien *et al.* 1987; O'Brien 1993). However, as with the other 'restored' cairns at Loughcrew, the shape of the rebuilt entrance and most of the passage is derived from OPW decisions of which no written records can be found.[5]

In any case, the wide variation in azimuths of the east-facing entrances at Loughcrew casts considerable doubt on the popular idea that the cairns were constructed for 'scientific' astronomical investigations or served primarily calendrical purposes. Many cultures orient houses and religious buildings east- or westward, from Navajo hogans to Gothic cathedrals; none of these is an observatory. Rather, the design at Loughcrew may be based on a custom similar to that of the Batammaliba of Togo and Benin, who orient their houses along an east–west axis so that the setting sun's rays fall upon west-facing shrines to their elders and wild game. When this happens, the sun god is communicating with the deceased elders (Blier 1987: 85). Standing stones or other markers such as those outside the cairn entrances at Knowth and Newgrange, perhaps associated with the pavings found at all three sites, may have served to receive light, cast significant shadows or otherwise interact with the sun. Perhaps the orientation of the Loughcrew cairns allowed light to become a conduit, a line of cosmic connection.

Intervisibility and other forms of communication

The Loughcrew cairns probably established some general connection with solar or other astronomical phenomena. At the same time they may well have been oriented, like beacons, toward other features in the landscape, including megalithic sites. In many instances, intra- and inter-site visibility seem to have been a consideration in siting Neolithic chambered cairns (Cooney 1990). David Fraser (1983) has determined that intervisibility was an important aspect of cairn siting in Orkney. In Ireland, a passage tomb on Sliabh Gullion faces southeast toward Loughcrew. At the passage-tomb cemetery of Carrowmore/Knocknarea, most of the cairns seem to be oriented toward Maeve's

---

5   Although OPW records are missing for the largest cairns, metal lintels and concrete at the entrance and along the passage in Cairn T are clear evidence of restoration. Cairn T was filled with stones and rubble and had undergone considerable destruction before Conwell first documented it (1864: 46, see also 1873: 29–45). According to Benny Tobin, a neighbouring farmer who worked on the OPW restoration in the 1940s, the slab that now serves as lintel over the entrance was found toward the end of the passage (Tobin pers. comm. 1992). His account is consistent with that of Conwell (1873: 30), who found only one passage roofing stone, about six feet from the entrance, in place. At the entry the lintel does not rest on the passage orthostats but is supported by concrete at a level well above their height. In fact, no passage at the site has survived intact to adjoin the kerb. Since none of the entrances has retained its original shape, patterns formed by sunlight in the interior of Cairn T or other 'restored' cairns at Loughcrew cannot be relied upon. However, O'Brien's (1993: 50) observed correlation between the sun's daily movement and spatial increments in some of the designs is interesting.

Cairn, the largest mound in the vicinity. The smaller cairns at Knowth are generally oriented toward the main mound (Eogan 1986). At Loughcrew, surveyor Jon Patrick calculated that six cairns bore within 10·5° of Newgrange (Patrick 1975: 12). By my calculations, six cairns face points within 8° of the passage tomb site at Fourknocks, which, unlike Newgrange, is intervisible with Loughcrew.

We might imagine axial sightlines or corridors at Loughcrew to extend outward to terrestrial landmarks as well as inward to receive light from sun, moon or stars. These landmarks might have been marked or located not only by such permanently visible monuments as quartz-faced cairns, but also by temporary, even evanescent, means. Bonfires, wooden posts, banners or arrangements of pebbles would leave few traces in the archaeological record.

A ceremonial environment also may temporarily be created or enlarged by human (and animal) events and components. The *Annals of the Four Masters,* a compilation of early Irish texts, describes such an assembly in early historic times. The Fair of Tailten, which may have been held for many centuries not far to the east of the Loughcrew ridge, included 'horses and cavalry' from the northern half of Ireland 'spread out' for a great distance on the plain (O'Donovan 1851: AD 1168). In a similar manner, earlier monumental displays and performances may have added an important, if transitory, dimension to the architecture of a place.

In addition to establishing visual or other sensory lines of connection, architecture at Loughcrew may have created or manifested further intangible links. Mycenean tholos tombs, according to Emily Vermeule (1979: 42), may have expressed the Greek idea that a 'spiritual tunnel' linked the body of the deceased to the new home of the soul. Vermeule (1979: 51) notes that the classical Greek words for the architectural elements of the tomb are used for parts of the underworld, and that in myth and poetry the tomb represents some stage between the archaic tradition of 'forms' (ideal entities) and classical thought. Frances Lynch (1969) has proposed a communicative or oracular function for some apertures in Neolithic chambered cairns, such as the 'roofbox' opening above the entrance at Newgrange (Lynch 1969). These proposals suggest an idea that is missing from the usual accounts of dominance and social territories: the concept of 'immanent' power.

Dominance and immanence
Immanent power is always present, not only in ethnographic accounts of traditional societies, but in our contemporary, dominance-based Western culture. Although relationships of immanence may complement and reinforce those involving dominance, the former emphasize capabilities rather than action and control. We still conceive of certain powers as inherent or in-dwelling: the regenerative or reproductive powers of plants and animals (including humans, particularly females); innate, supernatural powers bestowed on 'sacred' landscape features such as mountains, stones and bodies of water; and the personal powers of such figures as healers, shamans and spiritual leaders. In describing a typical relationship between human actors and their natural environment in hunter–gatherer societies, Tim Ingold (1992: 42) refers to the 'nonhuman constituents' of the environment as 'imbued with personal powers'.

These personal powers can also be political, and employed in relations of domination and control. As cultural projections, concepts of immanence as well as dominance may be incorporated into oppressive ideologies. Yet to distinguish between the two allows us to imagine some additional metaphors in relation to the design process at Loughcrew. As Ingold (1992: 42) describes them, hunter–gatherers often consider their environment not as two separate worlds, one natural, one social or cultural, but rather as one whole, 'saturated' with the powers of humans, plants, animals and landscape.

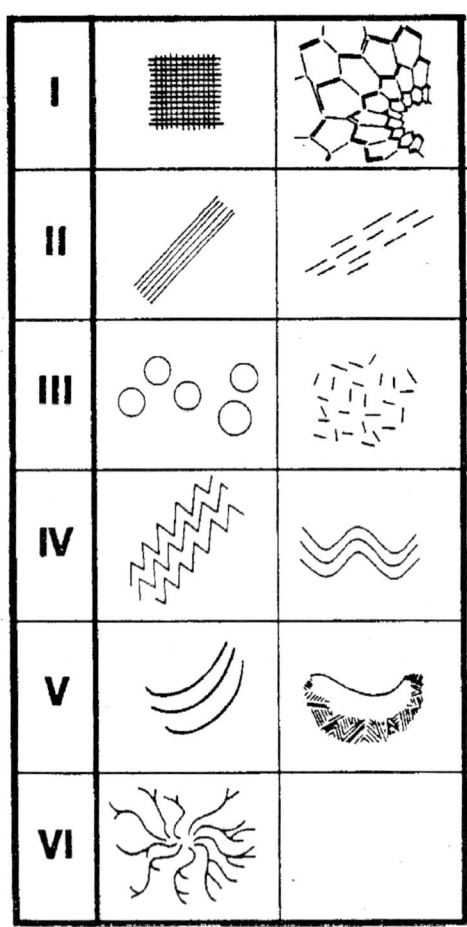

FIGURE 11. Entoptic motifs, after Lewis-Williams & Dowson 1988.

For example, many societies have seen stone as having supernatural powers, using it as what Victor Turner (1967) called an 'instrumental symbol'. The careful selection and use of stone in megalithic monuments, as well as the re-use of inscribed stones in new structures, testifies to the power and significance of this material. At a time of changing relations with nature, a deference to geomorphological forms and a reverence for stone might represent either an immanent relation of 'belonging' to nature, or the response to a threat to that relation. A longing for union or reconciliation with the natural world may have led to the design of events or performances intended to link humans with the supernatural.

Rituals of connection

J.D. Lewis-Williams & T.A. Dowson (1988) have developed a neurophysical model describing the generation, elaboration and interpretation of trance-induced, entoptic designs in shamanistic art, based on ethnographic data from the southern African San (see FIGURE 11). The symmetrical, repeated elements that comprise most of the motifs at Loughcrew may be related to these entoptic configurations (Bradley 1991; Lewis-Williams & Dowson 1993). Lewis-Williams & Dowson agree with Bradley's suggestion that motifs found in Neolithic passage tombs may be based on images generated in trance. They propose broad, cross-cultural applications for their neuropsychological models, including not only passage tomb art but motifs in Palaeolithic caves. In keeping with current preoccupations, these archaeologists consider the production of entoptic images on these rock surfaces in functional terms: as one means for an élite to appropriate and control knowledge and/or religious experience (Bradley 1989b: 72; Lewis-Williams & Dowson 1993: 21, 22).

Whether or not these motifs are unequivocally 'entoptic', trance-generated visions as one source of inspiration for megalithic art seems a valid concept (see Sherratt 1991). The informal, seemingly spontaneous designs at Loughcrew and in some Boyne locations may have been created in trance-related, 'participatory' ceremonies connecting living humans with the supernatural powers or beings (perhaps ancestors) immanent in stones. At Loughcrew, stone might have been seen as an interactive participant in ceremonies associated with the cairns, and the act of carving as a record or instrument of this interaction. The repetition of such acts could result in the apparently haphazard arrangement of motifs characteristic of Loughcrew. The present-day location of some designs in inaccessible places (on the backs of stones at Newgrange, for example, and on the roofstone of Cell 2 in Cairn T at Loughcrew) does not contradict this idea. Stones were often inscribed before they were used in construction (e.g. O'Kelly 1982) as well as

FIGURE 12. Chalk balls found in Cairns L and T at Loughcrew.

moved and reincorporated in new settings; ritually inscribed stones would have had particular significance for relocation.

Permeable boundaries

Some interior stones at Loughcrew also may bear traces of interactive performances. In both Cairn T and Cairn L, orthostats at a similar point in the passage just outside the chamber (R5 and L5 in Cairn T, R4 in Cairn L) have pits that seem deepened by repeated contact. Worn pits are also found in Cairn L on stone C16 (the right cell backstone) and in Cairn T on C3 (the left cell backstone; see FIGURES 6, 8 & 14). Surface diameters of these pits range from approximately 1 cm to 8·5 cm. In Cairn L, Conwell (1873: 61) found three polished stone balls (diameters 1·9, 2·5, 7 cm) and eight chalk balls (diameters 1·9–4·6 cm) under the basin in the right cell (Conwell 1873: 61). He found one stone ball and six chalk balls of similar dimensions in Cairn H (1873: 52). While the stone balls are smooth and highly polished, the roughly-shaped chalk balls show signs of abrasion (FIGURE 12). Conwell (1873) also found hundreds of water-rounded pebbles in cairns at the site.

These objects may have been used in ritual performances both inside and outside the cairns, perhaps for tracing over or inserting into previously-carved designs. Replicas of the chalk balls from Loughcrew fit neatly into most of the worn indentations on the pitted orthostats outside the chamber in Cairns L and T, and on C3 in Cairn T and C16 in Cairn L (McMann 1993; FIGURES 8, 13 & 14).

Similar stone and chalk balls have been found at many Irish passage-tomb sites, including Carrowmore, Fourknocks, Newgrange and Knowth (Herity 1974). At Newgrange

FIGURE 13. Replica of chalk ball, inserted into pit in orthostat L5, Cairn T (1992).

and Knowth there are also kerb and interior stones with worn depressions. Near the entrance to the chamber at Newgrange, orthostats R20 and R21 bear what Claire O'Kelly (1982: 73, 74) calls 'deepened pits'. On Kerbstone K52, at the north end of the axis at Newgrange, 25 pronounced, worn hollows have been incorporated as important elements in the pecked design (FIGURE 10). Repeated performances utilizing 'natural' designs visualized in trance might have been another way to penetrate or dissolve boundaries between humans and stone, or between this world and the Otherworld.

As architectural elements or as representing supernatural (perhaps ancestral) 'beings' (or both), the stones may have had heightened, cumulative powers, during a period characterized by changing interactions with natural forces in the environment. Whether or not they were evoked in trance states, designs used during earlier phases at both Loughcrew and the Boyne might have been refined and elaborated at Newgrange and Knowth during a later, less spontaneous and less performance-oriented phase. In a stylistic chronology of Irish megalithic carvings, Muiris O'Sullivan (1989) contrasts an earlier, informal 'depictive' style (as at Loughcrew, FIGURE 8) with a later, 'plastic' style (as at Newgrange and Knowth, FIGURE 10). During the later, 'plastic' phase, stone may no longer have been consulted as part of a performance or dialogue, but rather utilized as a passive ground. Carved motifs on the entrance stone at Newgrange, for example, seem carefully planned and executed rather than accumulated in the informal style of the Loughcrew designs. As additional evidence of design structure, the carved motifs at Loughcrew add another dimension to our interpretation of that structure.

FIGURE 14.
*Orthostat R5,
viewed from the
chamber of Cairn
T (1977).*

Conclusions

From plans and carved motifs, I have inferred some aspects of the complex, changing interrelationships between ancient builders and their environment at Longhcrew. Like all such sites, the place is a unique overlay of architectural form in a particular, if shifting, historical context. As P.L. Travers would say, it 'overflows with meaning'. Always both undergoing and resisting change, the Loughcrew tombs are not now and never were signifiers with constant meanings, but rather symbolic 'bundles' of themes and variations loosely related to persisting preoccupations, both cosmological and quotidian. To study their plans today is to imagine echoes and transformations of metaphors that may first have been expressed in impermanent spatial arrangements far longer than 5000 years ago.

The monuments do not signal an advance (or Fall), from one socio-economic system to another. Rather, they may express a dual, transitional relationship with the environment, incorporating cosmological concepts springing from both Mesolithic and Neolithic subsistence. Unlike modern buildings, their interior and exterior design structure were not unified or synthesized, but held in tension. Instead of representing a one-sided appropriation of space and materials, the passage tombs may have functioned as symbolic bridges, serving both to connect and to separate the natural and the cultural.

This is not to deny that design at Loughcrew could have been an instrument of territoriality, domination and social control. To explore such power relations expands our understanding of 'past pasts' and illuminates the archaeological–historical enterprise in the present. However, in emphasizing the powers of male authority figures, weapons, and territorial boundaries that dominate contemporary discourse, conventional interpretations slight the innate powers of Others, including women, underclasses, non-human forms of life and 'non-living' things. We may describe the architecture not only in such metaphors of dominance as a 'machine for the reproduction of a uniform ideology' or a 'weapon in the struggle to assert and maintain a sectional interpretation of reality', (Thomas 1992: 154), but also, and simultaneously, in metaphors of immanence. At Loughcrew, animals, hills, lakes and springs, glacial boulders, quartz pebbles and ancestral spirits may have been taken as powerful, immanent forces interconnected with designers and other human actors engaged with their world. A sense that people belonged to nature, more characteristic of hunter–gatherers than farmers, may have continued into the Irish Neolithic even after different views had arisen, such as the idea that nature belonged to people.

The power of an interpretation lies in the strength of the connection it makes between the material evidence and a narrative imagination based on contemporary needs and realities. Wild interpretations, (those that seem outdated or outlandish, or lack the reassuring falsifiability of scientific fact) are often considered to obscure some single truth, past or present. Yet, like a solitary thread from an elaborately woven textile, a one-dimensional model falsely unifies the past. No one approach, whether scientific, sociological, metaphysical or other, can come to terms with the multiple, shifting realities of the passage tombs.

In a process as powerful as myth and as mysterious as metaphor, varied, even contradictory, interpretations may combine and coalesce to form new insights. Rather than reducing the meaning of the passage tombs at Loughcrew to the single common denominator of social function, I have proposed an additional, cosmological interpretation. It is not intended to disclose 'the past', but rather to move the question of meaning in this prehistoric architecture toward the diverse new visions essential to resolving our modern dilemmas.

Acknowledgements. I am grateful to Richard Bradley for suggesting that I explore the work of Nurit Bird-David and Tim Ingold. My interpretative framework owes much to all three, although I have not cited Bradley's *Altering the earth* (1992), as it became available to me only after I had completed this paper. Archaeologists Margaret Conkey, Gabriel Cooney, Margaret Ronayne, Elizabeth Shee Twohig and Ruth Tringham, architects Cary James and Elizabeth Macdonald, my colleaugues Jean-Pierre Protzen and Dell Upton and my field and research assistant Emily Payne made useful comments on drafts; I retain responsibility for any remaining flaws. Thanks are also due to the National Museum of Ireland, which kindly provided access to its collections, to the University of California at Berkeley for a number of grants and fellowships, to the US National Endowment for the Humanities for a Travel to Collections Grant, and to Douglas Muir and Emily T. Robertson for special funding to allow me to carry out my research in Ireland.

References

ARMIT, I. & B. FINLAYSON. 1992. The transition to agriculture in northern and western Europe, *Antiquity* 66: 664–76.

BARRETT, J. 1991. Towards an archaeology of ritual, in Garwood *et al.* (ed.): 1–9.

BENDER, B. 1985. Prehistoric developments in the American midcontinent and in Brittany, north-west France, in D. Price & J. Brown (ed.), *Prehistoric hunter gatherers*: 21–57. New York (NY): Academic Press.

BIRD-DAVID, N. 1990. The giving environment: Another perspective on the economic system of gatherer–hunters, *Current Anthropology* 31(2): 25–47.

1992. Beyond 'the original affluent society': a culturalist reformulation, *Current Anthropology* 33(1): 189–95.

BLIER, S. 1987. *The anatomy of architecture: ontology and metaphor in Batammaliba architectural expression*. Cambridge: Cambridge University Press.

BRADLEY, R. & R. CHAMBERS. 1988. A new study of the cursus complex at Dorchester on Thames, *Oxford Journal of Archaeology* 7(3): 271–89.

1989. Deaths and entrances: a contextual analysis of megalithic art, *Current Anthropology* 30: 68–76.

1991. Rock art and the perception of landscape, *Cambridge Archaeological Journal* 1(1): 77.

BRENNAN, M. 1983. *The stars and the stones*. London: Thames & Hudson.

BURENULT, G. 1984. *The archaeology of Carrowmore, County Sligo* Stockholm: G. Burenhults Förlag. Theses and Papers in North European Archaeology 14.

CASEY, E. 1979. *Remembering: a phenomenological study*. Bloomington (IN): Indiana University Press.

CONWELL, E.A. 1866. Examination of the ancient sephulcral cairns on the Loughcrew Hills, County of Meath, *Proceedings of the Royal Irish Academy* 9: 355–79.

1873. *Discovery of the tomb of Ollamh Fodhla*. Dublin: McGlashan & Gill.

COONEY, G. 1983. Megalithic tombs in their environmental setting: a settlement perspective, in T. Reeves-Smyth & F. Hammond (ed.), *Landscape archaeology in Ireland*: 179–94. Oxford: British Archaeological Reports. British series 116.

1987. North Leinster in the earlier prehistoric period (7000–1400 BC): a settlement and environmental perspective on foragers, farmers and early metallurgists 1. Unpublished Ph.D thesis, University College, Dublin.

1990. The place of megalithic tomb cemeteries in Ireland, *Antiquity* 64: 741–53.

CRIADO BOADO, F. & R. FÁBREGAS VALCARCE. 1989a. The megalithic phenomenon of northwest Spain: main trends, *Antiquity* 63: 682–96.

1989b. Aspectos generales del megalitismo Galaico, *Arqueologia* 19: 48–62.

DILLEHAY, T.D. 1991. Mapuche ceremonial landscape, Social recruitment and resource rights, *World Archaeology* 22(2): 223–41.

EOGAN, G. 1974. Report on the excavations of some passage graves, unprotected inhumation burials and a settlement site at Knowth, Co. Meath, *Proceedings of the Royal Irish Academy* 74C(2): 11–112.

1984. *Knowth and the passage tombs of Ireland*. London: Thames & Hudson.

1986. *Excavations at Knowth*. Dublin: Royal Irish Academy.

FRASER, D. 1983. *Land and society in Neolithic Orkney*. Oxford: British Archaeological Reports. British Series 117(i), (ii).

FRAZER, W. 1893. Notes on incised sculpturings of stones in the cairns of Sliabh-na-Calliaghe, near Loughcrew, County Meath, Ireland. With illustrations from a series of groundplans and water-colour sketches, by the late G.V. du Noyer of the Geological Survey of Ireland, *Proceedings of the Society of Antiquaries of Scotland* 27: 294–340.

FRITZ, J. 1978. Paleopsychology today: ideational systems and human adaptation in prehistory, in C. Redman (ed.), *Social archaeology: beyond subsistence and dating*: 37–59. New York (NY): Academic Press.

GARWOOD, P. *et al.* (ed.). 1991. *Sacred and profane: proceedings of a conference on archaeology, ritual and religion: Oxford, 1989*. Oxford: Oxford University Committee for Archaeology.

GLASSIE, H. 1975. *Folk housing in middle Virginia*. Knoxville (TN): University of Tennessee Press.

GOODISON, L. 1989. *Death, women and the sun: symbolism of regeneration in early Aegean religion*. London: Institute of Classical Studies. Bulletin Supplement 53.

GUDEMAN, E.S. 1986. *Economics as culture: models and metaphors of livelihood*. London: Routledge & Kegan Paul.

HERITY, M. 1974. *Irish passage graves*. Dublin: Irish University Press.

HODDER, I. 1982. *Symbolic and structural archaeology*. Cambridge: Cambridge University Press.

1988. Material culture texts and social change: a theoretical discussion and some archaeological examples, *Proceedings of the Prehistoric Society* 54: 67–75.

1990. *The domestication of Europe*. Oxford: Basil Blackwell.

INGOLD, T. 1987. *The appropriation of nature*. Manchester: Manchester University Press.

1992. Comment, *Current Anthropology* 33(1): 41–2.

ISBELL, W. 1976. Cosmological order expressed in prehistoric ceremonial centers, *XLIIe Congres Internacional des Americanistes*, volume 4. Paris.

KINNES, I. 1982. Les Fouillages and megalithic origins, *Antiquity* 56: 24–30.

1975. Monumental function in British Neolithic burial practices, *World Archaeology* 7(1): 16–29.

KUS, S.M. 1983. The social representation of space: dimensioning the cosmological and the quotidian, in J.A. Moore & A.S. Keene (ed.), *Archaeological hammers and theories*: 277–305. New York (NY): Academic Press.

LAKOFF, G. & R. JOHNSON. 1980. *Metaphors we live by*. Chicago (IL): University of Chicago Press.

LAYTON, R. 1991. *The anthropology of art*. 2nd edition. Cambridge: Cambridge University Press.

LEWIS-WILLIAMS, J.D. & T.A. DOWSON. 1988. The signs of all times: entoptic phenomena in Upper Paleolithic art, *Current Anthropology* 29: 201–45.

1993. On vision and power in the Neolithic: evidence from the decorated monuments, *Current Anthropology* 34: 55–65.

LEONE, M. 1986. Symbolic, structural and critical archaeology, in D. Meltzer *et al.* (ed.), *American archaeology, past and future*: 415–38. Washington (DC): Smithsonian Institution Press.

L'HELGOUACH, J. 1983. Les idoles qu'on abat, où les vissicitudes des grands stèles de Locmariaquer, *Bulletin Société Polymathique du Morbihan* 110: 57–68.

LYNCH, F. 1973. The use of the passage in certain passage graves as a means of communication rather than access, in G.E. Daniel & P.J. Kjaerum (ed.), *Megalithic graves and ritual: papers presented at the III Atlantic Colloquium, Moesgard, 1969*: 141–61. Copenhagen: Jutland Archaeological Society.

McMANN, J. 1991. Loughcrew: form, history and meaning in an Irish megalithic landscape. Ph.D dissertation, University of California, Berkeley. Ann Arbor (MI): University Microfilms.

     1993. *Loughcrew: the Cairns. A guide to an ancient Irish landscape*. Oldcastle, Co. Meath: After Hours Books.

MILLER, D. & C. TILLEY (ed.). 1984. *Ideology, power and prehistory*. Cambridge: Cambridge University Press.

MOORE, H. 1986. *Space, text and gender*. Cambridge: Cambridge University Press.

     1990. Paul Ricoeur: action, meaning and text, in C. Tilley (ed.), *Reading material culture*: 85–120. Oxford: Basil Blackwell.

MOORE, M. 1987. *Archaeological inventory of County Meath*. Dublin: Stationery Office.

O'BRIEN, T. *et al.* 1987. The equinox cycle as recorded at Cairn T Loughcrew. *Ríocht na Midhe* 8: 3–15.

     1993. *Light years ago: a study of the cairns of Newgrange and Cairn T Loughcrew Co. Meath Ireland*. Dublin: Black Cat Press.

Ó CRUALAOICH, G. 1988. Continuity and adaptation in legends of Cailleach Bhéarra, *Bealoideas* 56: 153–78.

O'DONOVAN, J. 1851. *Annals of the Kingdom of Ireland by the four masters from the earliest period to the year 1616*. Dublin: Hodges & Smith.

O'KELLY, B. 1982. *Newgrange: archaeology, art and legend*. London: Thames & Hudson.

O'SULLIVAN, M. 1989. A stylistic evolution in the megalithic art of the Boyne Valley, *Archaeology Ireland* 3(9): 138–42.

PATRICK, J. 1975. Megalithic exegesis, *Irish Archaeological Research Forum* 2: 9–14.

PATRIK, L. 1985. Is there an archaeological record?, in M.B. Shiffer (ed.), *Advances in archaeological method and theory*, volume 8: 27–62. New York (NY): Academic Press.

RAFTERY, J. 1950. Loughcrew, Co. Meath: ein Megalithgrab der La-Tene-Zeit, in E. Vogt (ed.), *Congrés International des Sciences Préhistoriques et Protohistoriques, Actes de la IIIe Session*: 284–7. Zurich.

RELPH, E. 1976. *Place and placelessness*. London: Pion.

     1993. The reclamation of place, *Orion* (Winter): 32–6.

RENFREW, C. 1976. Megaliths, territories and populations, in S. deLaet (ed.), *Acculturation, and continuity in Atlantic Europe*: 198–220. Bruges: de Tempel.

RICOEUR, P. 1981. *Hermeneutics and the human sciences*. Edited and translated by John B. Thompson. Cambridge: Cambridge University Press.

ROTHERAM, E.C. 1895. On the excavation of a cairn of Slieve-na-Caillighe, *Journal of the Royal Society of Antiquaries of Ireland* 5: 311–16.

SAHLINS, M. 1968. Notes on the original affluent society, in R.B. Lee & I. DeVore (ed.), *Man the hunter*: 85–9. Chicago (IL): Aldine.

     1985. *Islands in history*. Chicago (IL): Chicago University Press.

SHEE TWOHIG, E. 1981. *The megalithic art of western Europe*. Oxford: Oxford University Press.

     1993. Megalithic tombs and megalithic art in Atlantic Europe, in C. Scarre & F. Healy (ed.), *Trade and exchange in prehistoric Europe: proceedings of a Conference held at the University of Bristol, April 1992*: 87–99. Oxford: Oxbow Books.

SHERRATT, A. 1991. Sacred and profane substances: the ritual use of narcotics in later Neolithic Europe, in Garwood *et al.* (ed.): 50–64.

SKEATES, R. 1991. Caves, cult and children in Neolithic Abruzzo, Central Italy, in Garwood *et al.* (ed.): 122–34.

SWEETMAN, D. 1985. A late Neolithic/Early Bronze Age pit circle at Newgrange, Co. Meath, *Proceedings of the Royal Irish Academy* 85C: 195–221.

THOMAS, J. 1988. The social significance of Cotswold–Severn Burial Practices, *Man* 23: 540–59.

     1991. *Rethinking the Neolithic*. Cambridge: Cambridge University Press.

     1992. Monuments, movement and the context of megalithic art, in N. Sharples & A. Sheridan (ed.), *Vessels for the ancestors: essays on the Neolithic of Britain and Ireland*: 143–155. Edinburgh: Edinburgh University Press.

TUAN, YI-FU. 1974. *Topophilia: a study of environmental perceptions, attitudes and values*. New York (NY): Columbia University Press.

TURNER, V. 1967. *The forest of symbols: aspects of Ndembu ritual*. Ithaca (NY): Cornell University Press.

UPTON, D. 1986. *Holy things and profane: Anglican parish churches in colonial Virginia*. Cambridge (MA) & London: MIT Press.

     1990. The tradition of change. Paper delivered at the International Association for the Study of Traditional Environments conference, Berkeley (CA).

VERMEULE, E. 1979. *Aspects of death in Early Greek art and poetry*. Berkeley (CA): University of California Press.

WOODMAN, P. 1992. Filling in the spaces in Irish prehistory, *Antiquity* 66: 295–314.

ZVELEBIL, M. & P. ROWLEY-CONWY. 1984. Transition to farming in northern Europe: a hunter–gatherer perspective, *Norwegian Archaeological Review* 17(2): 104–27.

Late woodland landscapes of Wisconsin: ridged fields, effigy mounds and territoriality

by WILLIAM GUSTAV GARTNER

ANTIQUITY 73 (1999): 671–83

SAUER (1925) saw the terrestrial scene as more than a natural arena for human action. He recognized the repeated human impact on a living earth which created an ever-changing stage of landscape. Geographical conceptions of landscape have changed in the intervening 75 years. Today, geographers acknowledge the historically contingent qualities of nature and society and their inter-relationships (Zimmerer 1994). Many also recognize the critical roles of architecture and material culture for experiencing landscapes, both monumental and mundane (Tuan 1977; Wheatley 1971). Moreover, people create and comprehend landscapes by constantly manipulating symbols and reinterpreting architectural spaces that are embedded in a larger social world (Baker 1992). Individuals often have disparate experiences within the same landscape (Bender 1993).

The cast of characters

The later half of the Late Woodland Period in Wisconsin witnessed three landscape innovations: effigy mounds, palisades and ridged fields. Raised fields are 'any prepared land involving the transfer and elevation of soil above the natural surface of the earth in order to improve cultivating conditions' (Denevan & Turner 1974: 24). The two basic forms in North America are small, individually set conical hillocks (corn hills) and long linear/curvilinear features (ridged fields). Corn hills are common in eastern North America (Doolittle in press), but Wisconsin has the most ridged fields (FIGURE 1).

By 1000 AD, effigy mounds had long been conspicuous in the Wisconsin landscape. These mounds are dated by radiocarbon to AD 700–1050 and are associated with Madison Ware ceramics — grit-tempered, cord-impressed, sometimes elaborately decorated pottery. By 1000 AD, the makers of Madison Ware ceramics lived varied lifestyles (Stevenson *et al.* 1997: 170–79). In Eastern Wisconsin, some built effigy mounds, lived in oval semi-subterranean houses and were hunter–gatherers (Horicon phase, *c.* AD 700–1050). Others also made collared pottery, lived in keyhole-shaped houses and farmed maize, beans and squash in fields (Kekoskee phase, *c.* AD 900–1150). In unglaciated southwestern Wisconsin, some built effigy mounds, hunted, gathered and planted maize, sunflowers and presumably older domesticates such as squash and sumpweed in gardens (Eastman phase, AD 750–1050).

An emerging Oneota tradition was well established by 1000 AD in the Lake Koshkonong area and perhaps elsewhere in the state (Overstreet 1997: 255–66; but see Stoltman 1986). Oneota peoples eventually became the main practioners of ridged-field agriculture and their rise to prominence after 1150 AD correlates with the cessation of mound construction in Wisconsin. Various types of culture contact between Middle Mississippian and Late Woodland peoples were also extant by 1000 AD and intensified over the next century (Stoltman 1986; FIGURE 2).

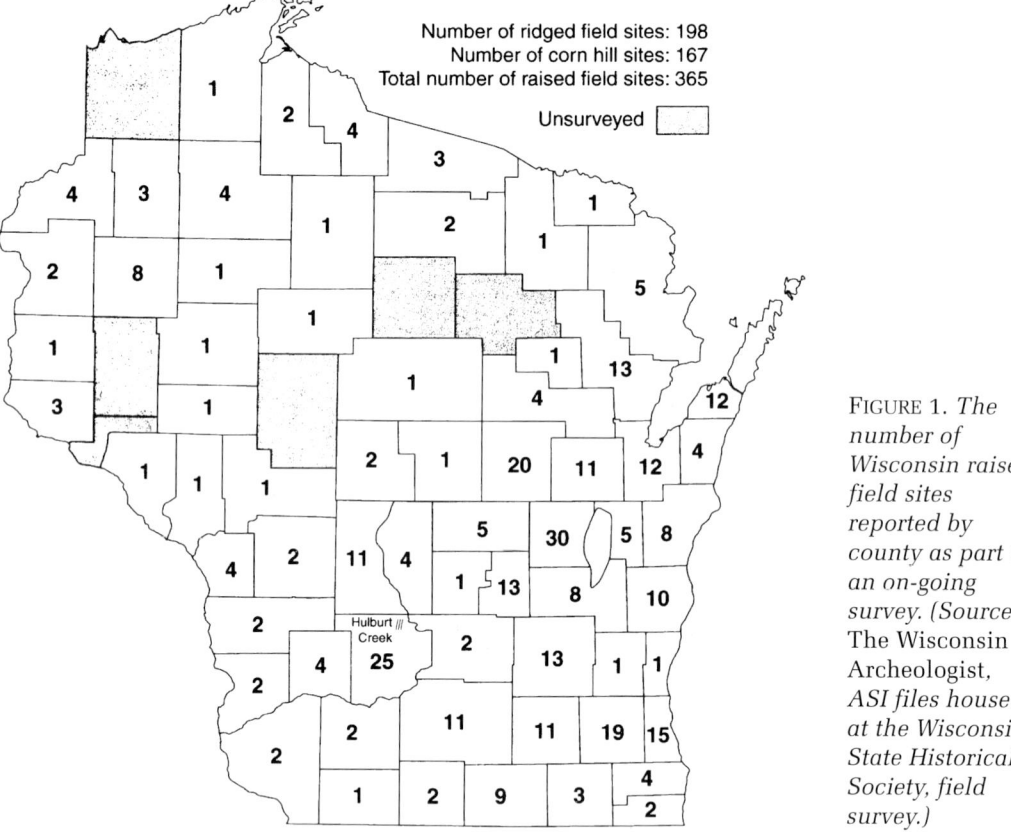

Number of ridged field sites: 198
Number of corn hill sites: 167
Total number of raised field sites: 365

Unsurveyed

FIGURE 1. *The number of Wisconsin raised field sites reported by county as part of an on-going survey. (Source: The Wisconsin Archeologist, ASI files housed at the Wisconsin State Historical Society, field survey.)*

A landscape narrative centred on territoriality

Effigy mounds, palisades and ridged fields represent long-term social strategies of territoriality as defined by Sack (1986). They embody concepts of classified area, boundary, enforced control and conflict at local and regional scales. Moreover, they conveyed such messages within and across generations. Pre-capitalist societies often reify myth, ritual and symbol to create specialized spaces that encode such enduring cultural messages (Sack 1986: 38; Tuan 1977: 85–135; Wheatley 1971: 416).

The link between territoriality and the origins of ridged-field agriculture is essentially one of social circumscription. In short, some Late Woodland groups could no longer follow their traditional subsistence round due to the rigid control of particular geographical areas by other Late Woodlanders. Unfettered access to dispersed geographic areas are critical for a mixed subsistence economy based on gathering, hunting, fishing and cultivation (Theler 1987; Arzigian 1987; Steventon *et al* 1997). Seasons of plenty may become periods of hunger and landscapes of degradation when territories are contested. Restricted access induced innovation, culminating with the practice of ridged-field agriculture at 1000 AD.

The Hulburt Creek ridged fields

The Hulburt Creek ridged fields are located near Wisconsin Dells (FIGURE 1), within the uplands of a small, deeply dissected tributary of the Wisconsin river. They appear as sinuously shaped parallel ridges generally aligned on the long axes 10°E of N. Planting surfaces

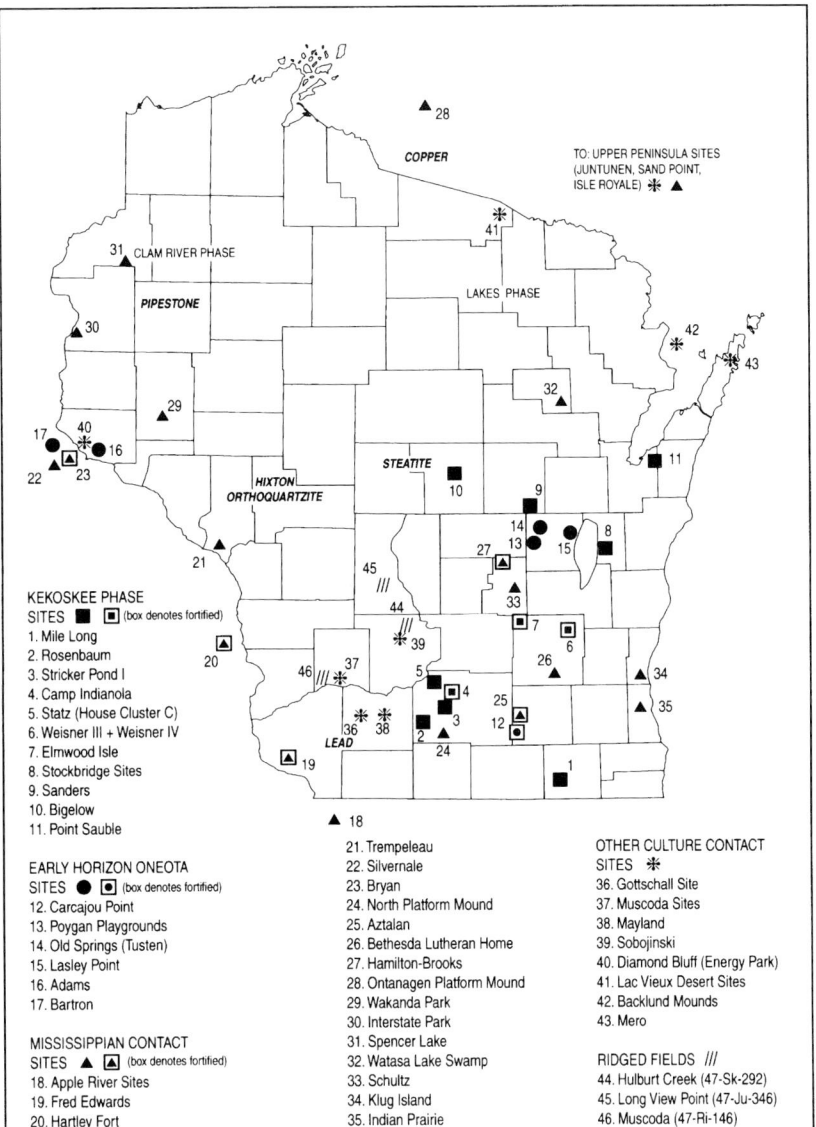

FIGURE 2. *The cultural and political landscape of Wisconsin (900–1150 AD).*

Within the figure:

28

COPPER

TO: UPPER PENINSULA SITES (JUNTUNEN, SAND POINT, ISLE ROYALE) ❋ ▲

41

31 CLAM RIVER PHASE

PIPESTONE

LAKES PHASE

30

42

29

32

17 40
22 23 ● 16

STEATITE

43

HIXTON ORTHOQUARTZITE

11

21

STEATITE
10

9

14
13 15 8
27
45
///

44

33

7
6

KEKOSKEE PHASE
SITES ■ ▣ (box denotes fortified)
1. Mile Long
2. Rosenbaum
3. Stricker Pond I
4. Camp Indianola
5. Statz (House Cluster C)
6. Weisner III + Weisner IV
7. Elmwood Isle
8. Stockbridge Sites
9. Sanders
10. Bigelow
11. Point Sauble

20

46

37
38 ///

39

5
4

26
34

25
12 35

36
LEAD

2
3

24

19

1

18

EARLY HORIZON ONEOTA
SITES ● ▣ (box denotes fortified)
12. Carcajou Point
13. Poygan Playgrounds
14. Old Springs (Tusten)
15. Lasley Point
16. Adams
17. Bartron

MISSISSIPPIAN CONTACT
SITES ▲ ▣ (box denotes fortified)
18. Apple River Sites
19. Fred Edwards
20. Hartley Fort

21. Trempeleau
22. Silvernale
23. Bryan
24. North Platform Mound
25. Aztalan
26. Bethesda Lutheran Home
27. Hamilton-Brooks
28. Ontanagon Platform Mound
29. Wakanda Park
30. Interstate Park
31. Spencer Lake
32. Watasa Lake Swamp
33. Schultz
34. Klug Island
35. Indian Prairie

OTHER CULTURE CONTACT
SITES ❋
36. Gottschall Site
37. Muscoda Sites
38. Mayland
39. Sobojinski
40. Diamond Bluff (Energy Park)
41. Lac Vieux Desert Sites
42. Backlund Mounds
43. Mero

RIDGED FIELDS ///
44. Hulburt Creek (47-Sk-292)
45. Long View Point (47-Ju-346)
46. Muscoda (47-Ri-146)

are typically 10 m long, 1–2 m wide and 40 cm high. Mere remnants of a possible 80-ha system survive today. Native peoples slashed and burned a large area. Finely textured deposits eroded down gentle slopes and buried the pre-agricultural surface (2Ab in FIGURE 3). This newly formed surface was then ditched, with the excavated deposits placed into the bed. The operation created a more fertile planting surface by concentrating silts, clays, charcoal and ash in an otherwise sandy and nutrient-poor parent material. Planting surfaces were rebuilt with sediments trapped in the ditches (zones 1, 2 and 4 in FIGURE 3), which, coupled with the burning of crop residues, maintained fertility. The Hulburt Creek fields simultaneously provided drainage and water storage, aerating the planting surface for the 'oxygen roots' of crops and storing moisture at the base of the bed for 'water roots' (indicated by waterlogged deposits near the base of the bed).

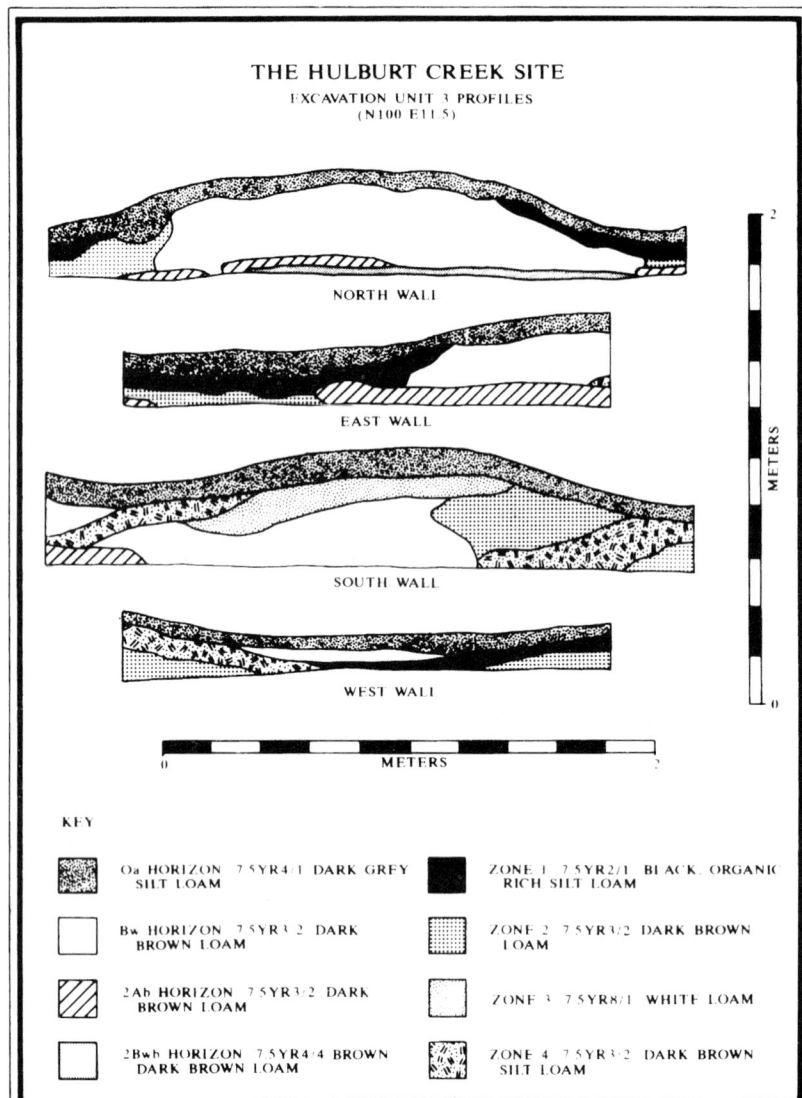

FIGURE 3. Excavation Unit 3 profiles from the Hulburt Creek site illustrating the pre-agricultural surface (2Ab) of the ground and rebuilding episodes (Zone 4). (Drawing by Richard L. Green & William G. Gartner.)

Experiments show that the Hulburt Creek fields ameliorated microclimate in important ways. Wisconsin's short growing season was improved by the cold-air drainage function of ridged fields (Riley & Freimuth 1979). Temperature experiments indicate that the Hulburt Creek fields effectively drain radiation frosts, caused by the near-surface heat loss on still, clear nights, documenting four more frost-free days during a five-week period of October/November 1991 than in adjacent areas. Furthermore, the north–south orientation of the beds maximizes planting surface solar radiation receipt and minimizes the shading of tall crops, like maize, over short ones, such as squash. The net result is a warmer soil. Hulburt Creek's well-drained and loamy planting surfaces warm up quickly in the spring, the critical first 30 days of crop growth (Aly *et al* . 1987: 9–10).

The fields probably improved cultivating conditions in other ways. Non-contiguous planting surfaces and root masses often slow the spread of many crop diseases and certain insect pests (Thurston 1990). Cultivation techniques associated with raised-field agriculture improve crop habitat, providing effective weed control as well as producing a loose, well-aerated and fertile planting surface (Gallagher & Sasso 1987: 147–8; Heidenreich 1971: 168–200). The combination of raised fields and intercropping enhances space management (Wilken 1987: 240–61). Raised fields provide low-risk yields over a sustained period, thereby promoting long-term labour flexibility (Siemens 1990). Indeed, the long-term labour costs of flat cultivation might be higher than those for raised fields, given the inefficiency of land clearance with a stone axe (Denevan 1992) and the effort required to relocate agricultural villages on a more frequent basis (Heidenreich 1971: 180–82, 213–16).[1]

We obtained radiocarbon ages of AD 984 (980±50 BP; WIS-2214) from the pre-agricultural ground surface and AD 1002 (950±50 BP; WIS-2215) from an earth oven truncating the ridged fields. These ages are compatible with an Effigy Mound occupation, a speculation supported by isolated finds of Madison Ware pottery from sites adjacent to and near the Hulburt Creek fields.

Excavations at the Hulburt Creek site raise many questions, the most important one being Why here? Oneota peoples, who eventually became the main practitioners of ridged-field agriculture, lived elsewhere in the state. The Hulburt Creek site, with its shallow soils, is a peculiar choice for cultivation as more fertile soils are near-by. And, except for the substantial Effigy Mound villages in the Muscoda region (Gartner 1997: 342–4), few other large Effigy Mound settlements have been reported.

The dense network of Indian trails that link the Hulburt Creek site with other ridged-field sites, as well as effigy mounds, earthen enclosures and Late Woodland hamlets (FIGURE 4) is of paramount importance in resolving such issues. The Hulburt Creek and other nearby ridged-field sites are one type of focal place networked together in an extant humanized world (Gartner 1997). This network facilitated the social and spatial integration of Late Woodland peoples and their descendants. Issues of site selection relate to multiple factors forged from the realms of nature, social relations and meaning.

Ridged fields and the realm of nature

Ridged fields cannot simply be explained as a response to the constraints of nature on maize production. Wisconsin is not located in a peripheral area for maize agriculture. Vickers Focus peoples grew maize in Manitoba at a latitude of nearly 51°N (Deck & Shay 1992), a practice that continued into historic times there (Moody & Kaye 1969). Historic evidence for maize agriculture exists for Quebec province during the Little Ice Age (Morissoneau 1978; Cartier 1993: 25, 49; Champlain 1878: 276). Native peoples practised maize agriculture in areas with growing seasons of 80 frost-free days or less, and did so without ridged fields.

The cold-air drainage function of Upper Midwestern ridged fields is proportionate to relief. Despite the unique height of the Hulburt Creek fields, the autumnal growing season was only extended by four days. Moreover, the date of the first frost for both the Hulburt Creek fields and the adjacent control site was the same. This first freeze was the result of advection, the importation of a cold-air mass, followed by conditions favourable for a radiation frost. Upper Midwestern ridged fields do not exhibit enough relief to

---

1   However, such labour costs are debatable. Historical accounts indicate that many native North Americans girdled trees and then burned the trunks rather than felling them outright. Periodic village relocation counterbalances the diminishing returns of resource depletion.

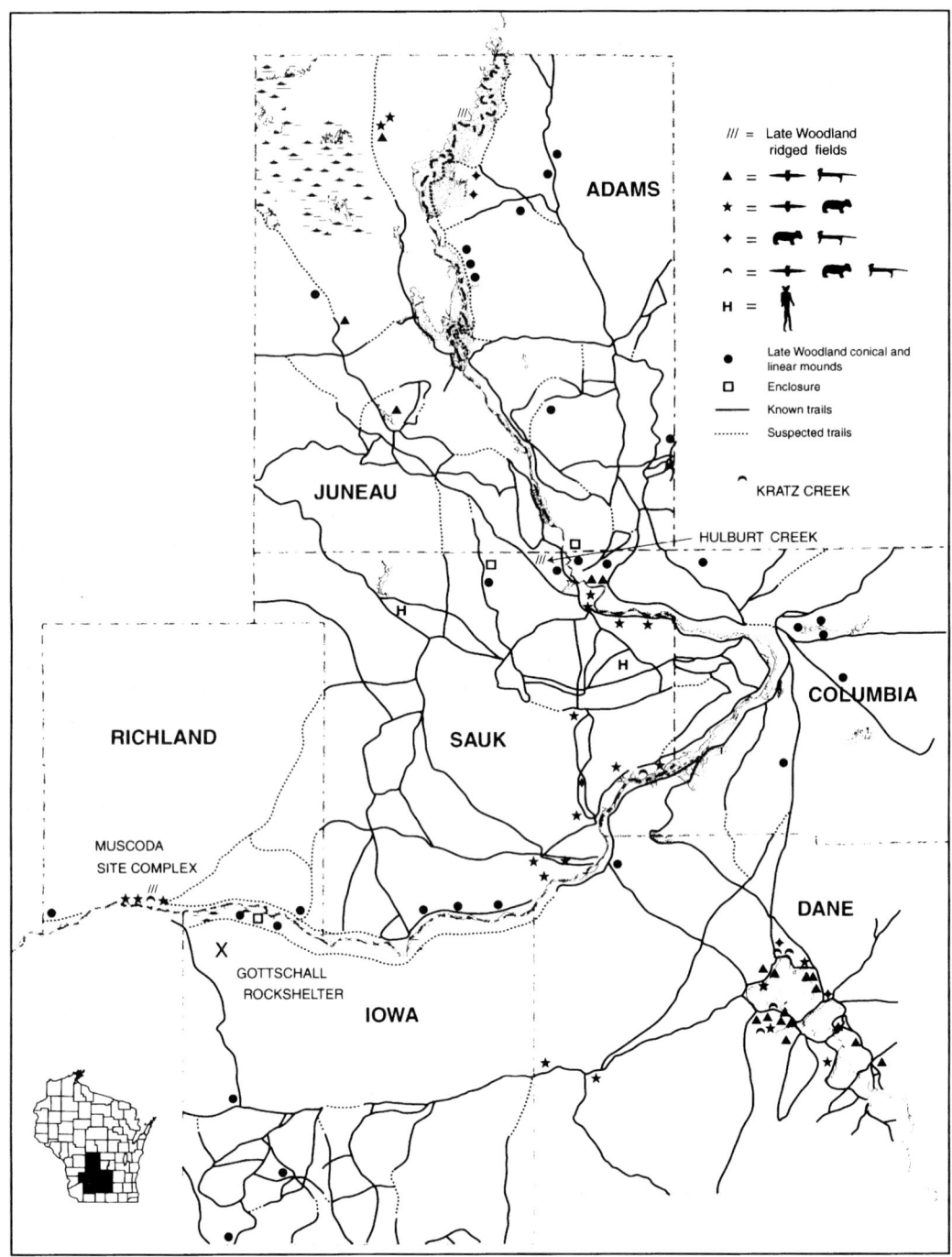

FIGURE 4. *Effigy Mound landscapes (700–1050 AD) consist of trails, villages, mounds, ridged fields and other focal places. Note the spatial segregation of bear and panther mounds. (Source: The Charles E. Brown archaeological atlas housed at the Wisconsin State Historical Society,* The Wisconsin Archeologist, *survey.)*

drain cold air associated with most frosts. Many Wisconsin ridged fields are located where both advective and radiative processes cause crop-killing frosts.

Adjacent land forms in Wisconsin have frost-free growing seasons that differ by up-wards of 30 days. Given the Hulburt Creek temperature experiments, site selection rather than ridging is a more effective way of coping with growing-season variability. My own on-going surveys indicate that Wisconsin's ridged fields are usually found in areas with 150 consecutive frost-free days or more (N=65). Thus far, I have tallied 24 sites at locales that have between 90 and 110 consecutive frost-free days. Interestingly, spring frost-depth ap-pears to be more important for ridged-field site selection than the number of frost-free days. Nearly all sites with an average 15 March frost-depth of at least 30 cm (N=71) are found on sites with a sandy soil and a southern exposure, settings that warm quickly in the spring. However, this is less than half the total number of ridged fields mapped in FIGURE 1.

There are many different definitions of a growing season, and the importance of 120 consecutive frost-free days for native maize agriculture is probably overstated. Growing degree days and soil temperatures during the first 30 days of germination and growth are the critical climatic factors for maize production, an assertion supported by ridged-field site selection in areas with deep spring frost-depth. Also, growing degree days can be negatively correlated with the number of consecutive frost-free days (Brinkmann 1979).

Upper Midwestern and Northern Plains Indians possessed no fewer than 23 varie-ties of maize that fully ripened in 120 days or less (Will & Hyde 1917). Several varieties fully ripened in about 70 days. Many tribes favoured green corn, maize in its milky immature stage, typically harvested 45 to 60 days after sowing. Native peoples also prac-tised intercropping. Every variety of bean, squash, gourd and starchy or oily seed has differ-ent climate sensitivities. Many native peoples selected and planted individual plants by hand — a clear advantage for coping with bad weather. For example, the Huron soaked and germinated maize in their warm long houses during a late spring (Heidenreich 1971: 175–6).

Finally, the coupling of ridged-field form and function is itself problematic. Follow-ing Flannery's (1986) amusing *A visit to the master* parable, explanation must separate the final cause, or that for the sake of which something is made, from efficient, formal and material causes. Historic accounts of corn-hill agriculture indicate that raised-field relief often results from the gradual and successive additions of soil (the material cause) over extended periods of time (Doolittle in press). The rebuilding episodes at the Hulburt Creek site suggest that this is true for some ridged-field sites as well.[2] Thus, the general benefits of ridged-field agriculture may be indistinguishable from Indian tillage prac-tices (the efficient cause), so long as those practices culminate in an elevated planting surface (the formal cause). It is difficult to couple ridged-field form and function if the shape is the end result of farming.

Climate is undeniably important for maize agriculture. And agricultural harvests did occasionally fail. Famine and disease were powerful agents of acculturation during the early history of Wisconsin, as noted in the *Jesuit relations* (Alloues in Thwaites 1901 (60): 199):

> During the following summer [1675], their [Fox] corn was frozen; they gathered
> but little of it, and that little rotted in the autumn in the places for storage where
> they had concealed it.

---

2   The short interval between burial episodes at the Sand Lake site suggests that final ridged-field form was intentional there.

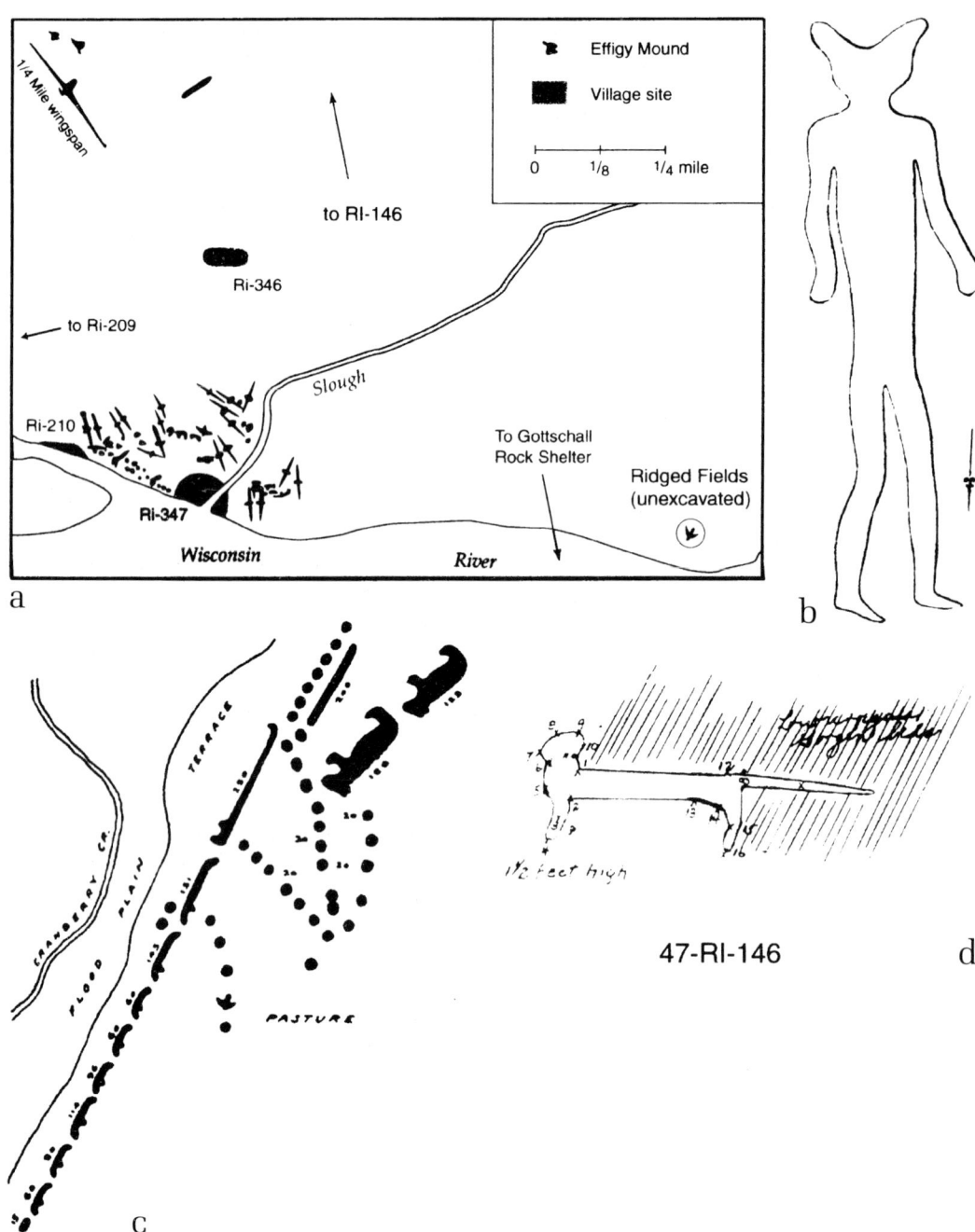

FIGURE 5. *Effigy Mound site plans.* a *the central group in the Muscoda complex (after Gartner 1997: 342);* b *a Bear impersonator (after Radin 1990: 47);* c *portion of the Cranberry Creek group (after Buell 1918: plate 3);* d *a panther effigy mound superimposed on ridged fields in the Muscoda complex (after T.H. Lewis, Northwestern Archaeological Survey, Field Notebook 25: 9, entry of 6 April 1886. Courtesy of G. Christensen and A. Rosebrough). Effigy Mounds commemorating Bear and Raptor impersonators are respectively most abundant in northeast Sauk County, near the Hulburt Creek fields, and in Richland County as part of the greater Muscoda complex.*

However, the misfortunes of the Fox were not due solely to the miserable growing season of 1675, since neighbouring tribes had an adequate, if diminished, agricultural harvest. Rather, winter warfare with the Sioux delayed the spring planting, while warfare with the Illinois plus an epidemic hampered late fall food collection. As is so often the case in the history of famine, nature and social relations combine to produce human misery.

Nature and social relations also combine to produce bounty. Maize agriculture supplemented millennia-old traditions of gathering, hunting and fishing — it did not supplant them. The seasonal abundance of greens, seeds, tubers, nuts, fruits, migrating waterfowl, anadromous fish and periods of large-game congregation all potentially conflict with the labour-intensive sowing and harvesting of maize in Wisconsin. Ridged fields, which warm up quickly in the spring and decrease long-term field relocation frequencies, minimize labour conflicts in native subsistence calendars. It is the seasonal availability of these other resources — not the number of frost-free days — that influence ridged-field geographies.

Effigy mounds, ridged fields and the realm of social relations

The reasons for effigy-mound construction are not readily apparent from the archaeological record. Few effigy mounds contain multiple burials or abundant grave goods. All ages and both sexes were interred in primary fashion, as secondary or bundle reburials, or cremated. Evidence for precious and exotic items is virtually non-existent. Some effigy mounds are apparently 'empty' as they do not contain artefacts or burials. Why, then, build effigy mounds?

Effigy Mound peoples were seasonally mobile over large expanses of the landscape, exploiting both upland food resources during cooler months and aquatic resources during warmer months (Theler 1987; Arzigian 1987; Steventon *et al* 1997). A periodic gathering of disparate mobile bands at a particular locale for feasting, gift-giving, marriage and to mourn the passing of a loved one reaffirmed larger constellations of social relationships. However, such gatherings are also exclusive, since not all Effigy Mound peoples congregated in one locale. Thus, the construction of effigy mounds not only commemorated and reaffirmed social bonds, it also legitimated territorial boundaries.

Totems as a social definition of territory: an ethnographic model

Winnebago, or Ho-Chunk, tribal organization provides an excellent model showing how effigy mounds potentially embody the social definitions of territory. The Winnebago exhibit dual social organization, comprising 'those who are above' and 'those who are below'. Moieties are composed of multiple clans, each with animal appellations. The social and territorial position of the clan depends exclusively on the nature of its clan animal (Radin 1990: 137-138, 140-141, 155). Older informants indicated that dual social organization once regulated reciprocal burial rites; residence rules; clan-specific oral traditions; and calendrically timed, place-specific feasts (Radin 1990: 139-144, 159–205, 270–301).

Winnebago dual social organization also had political manifestations. The Thunderbird clan ruled the upper phratry, and often the entire tribe. The bear clan ruled the land-animal clans of the lower phratry. The water-spirit clan ruled the aquatic clans of the lower phratry, though in past times it ruled the entire lower phratry and perhaps the entire tribe (Radin 1990: 193). Significantly, the animal totems representing these clans — the bird, the bear, and the panther — are the most common effigy mound types (Radin 1990: 50; Hall 1993: 42–4).

Given the past importance of moieties to Winnebago life — including where one lives, who one marries, one's membership in a ceremonial organization and where and how one is buried — the notion that totemic effigy mounds embody social definitions of territory is not far-fetched.

Effigy Mounds, a classification of landscape, and maize

Effigy mound groups exhibit many spatial patterns. Some effigy-mound groups segregate celestial from terrestrial animals. Others, however, do not. Some effigy-mound groups, such as those along the western shores of Glacial Lake Wisconsin, show distinct design alignments with local landscape features and topography. Others proclaim spatial chaos. But nearly all effigy-mound groups reference dual division as both celestial and terestrial animals are present in a single mound group (Hall 1993: 44).

Individual effigy-mound groups tend to be dominated by either birds or terrestrial animals such as bears or panthers (Radin 1990: 50). This probably signifies areas where reciprocal relations are respectively controlled by clans or lineages belonging to 'those who are above' or 'those who are on earth'. However, animals from the opposite grouping are usually present (Radin 1990: 54). The Necedah mounds, for example, consist of several lines of marching bears and conical mounds. However, among the 55 mounds there is one small bird (FIGURE 5c). Conversely, several bears appear among the many raptor effigies in the Muscoda complex (FIGURE 5a).

Bird forms are found in nearly all effigy-mound groups, an appropriate distribution for the political power ascribed to 'those who are above'. However, the totems of 'those who are on earth' exhibit a regional classification of area.

A literature review suggests that about 80% of all bear effigies are found in the Driftless Area and within Glacial Lake Wisconsin's shorelines. Pleistocene-aged till deposits are absent from these areas. Most exceptions to the bear-area rule are located in Marquette and Dane counties, near the western margins of the Green Bay lobe. More than 90% of all panther effigies are found in areas underlain by glacial till or outwash. Most exceptions to the panther-area rule are found in Sauk, Juneau, Richland and Grant counties.

The segregation of panther and bear effigy mounds, though not absolute (FIGURE 5a), exemplifies a regional classification and control of area. This spatial differentiation had political and territorial importance for 'those who are on earth'. The clustering of exceptions along the Wisconsin River and its adjacent environments suggests that social and territorial boundaries were contested in those regions where ridged-field agriculture first developed.

This is well-exemplified by the Kratz Creek site. ^{13}C analyses suggest that some Effigy Mound peoples at the Kratz Creek site ate maize. Moreover, graphic and unambiguous evidence for violent death (read warfare) is evident there (Barrett & Hawkes 1919: plate XIX). Most intriguingly, Late Woodlanders removed special sediments from an 'out of place' bear mound at the Kratz Creek site and then built a panther mound on top of the older effigy (Barrett & Hawkes 1919: 54–9, plate VIII). This superpositioning arguably provides a dramatic example of a contested territorial discourse among 'those who are below' and a reappropriation of place by the builders of the panther mound.

Effigy Mound Peoples practised maize agriculture in the Muscoda region. At the Gottschall Rockshelter, maize kernels, panicoid phytoliths and d^{13}C values of −13·2 (ppt) on a human patella have all been found with Madison-ware ceramics in secure stratigraphic contexts dated to AD 850. An out-of-place panther effigy mound superimposes ridged fields at the Muscoda complex (FIGURE 5d), a suite of mound groups and villages otherwise dominated by birds and bears.

Effigy mounds and the reification of myth, ritual and symbol

If Late Woodland peoples built effigy mounds as part of a strategy of territoriality, than the mounds must convey notions of social and geographic boundary within and across generations. Pre-capitalist societies often utilize myth, ritual and symbol in conjunction with architecture to convey such enduring messages. The existence of 'empty' effigy mounds strongly suggests that it is the actual construction of mounds that was important to Late Woodlanders, not their contents. Acordingly, we may look to mound stratigraphy for the embodiment of cultural ideals, particularly when specially selected and prepared deposits are present (Gartner 1993: 99–102, 116–19).

The use of special earths is clearly present at the Kratz Creek site, where exotic 'golden sands' and 'yellow sandy loams' and oxidized 'brick red sand' and 'red clay' were all delicately inter-layered with local deposits to construct some mounds. Strata of fire-blackened earth, charcoal, ashes and decomposed organic matter often define earthen architectural features such as altars and internments. These special deposits 'point to the celebration of elaborate ceremonies' (Barrett & Hawkes 1919: 15–16), rituals that must have taken place over time given the stratigraphic separation of fire features within a mound.

The ritual use of fire is evident in most effigy mounds. McKern (1930: 456, 518–19) noted the importance of prolonged fires when he described the numerous hearths and limestone pavements 'reduced to the consistency of chalk' in the Kleitzen and Nitschke effigy mounds. Some mound deposits here contained water-logged sediments taken from distant areas (McKern 1930: 461–2). Such deposits are surely a tangible reference to the earth-diver world creation myth, an oral tradition with many archaeological manifestations (Hall 1997: 17–23).

Geoarchaeological analyses at the Gottschall Rockshelter demonstrate that Late Woodland peoples crushed limestone, clam shell, bone, exotic minerals such as hornblende and galena, and then added these materials to the ashes of coniferous trees and grasses. After heating this mixture, native peoples placed this manufactured sediment within a platform. Late Woodland peoples followed the same recipe, more or less, and prescribed mode of deposition for 700 years (Gartner 1993). Near the end of the sequence, native peoples painted an elaborate composition on the rock-shelter wall that portrays the main characters of the Winnebago and Ioway legend of Red Horn (Salzer 1987: 456–67). A reincarnation rite at the end of this oral tradition takes place on a specially prepared earthen platform constructed from ash and crushed bone, two of the main ingredients at the Gottschall site.

As the preceeding examples illustrate, some earthen deposits clearly have meaning. In terms of Late Woodland territoriality, myths, rituals and symbols associated with special sediments conveyed information within and across generations. Social boundaries are enforced by unequal access rites. Territorial boundaries are communicated by effigy-mound location. Most effigy-mound groups overlook streams and lakes or, when located on interfluves, are adjacent to trails. Whether travelling by foot or canoe, effigy mounds are an enduring reminder of 'who is where'.

In sum, effigy mounds classify area, communicate boundary and enforce control. At first, Effigy Mound territoriality was a strategy between social groups comprising 'those who are below' and between moieties. Between 900 and 1050 AD, after the appearance of fortified Kekoskee-phase villages, Late Woodland territoriality took on new dimensions. Some Late Woodland peoples changed their lifestyles and/or adopted new webs of alliance and trade (Steventon *et al.* 1997; Stoltman 1986). However, others apparently tried to maintain their traditional ways. Two strategies for maintaining some semblance of autonomy and identity in a differentiated cultural landscape are intensifying food production and reifying cultural symbols. Ridged fields do both.

Ridged fields and the realm of meaning

A strong association between fertility and mortuary symbolism exists in the mound stratigraphy and art of both Middle Mississippian and Late Woodland societies (Prentice 1986; Swanton 1928: 503–6; Brose 1985: 85–9). However, Oneota art divorces mortuary and fertility symbolism. The proliferation of Oneota ridged-field agriculture is coincident with the cessation of mound building in Wisconsin.

Ridged fields exhibit a great diversity of field patterns, a plethora, and at times a collage, of forms whose meanings have long been debated (Gallagher 1992). In Oneota contexts, ridged fields also represent the greatest input of communal labour upon the landscape. Agriculture necessitates a commitment to place. This combination of attributes suggests to me that ridged fields constitute the symbolic successor for mounds in Oneota societies. Perhaps this is why ridged-field patterns appear as designs on both Oneota and terminal Late Woodland ceramics.

I am not suggesting that the ceramic designs discussed below are maps of ridged fields *per se*. Rather, I believe that some ridged-field forms and their corresponding ceramic designs are icons of country. That is, both reference a geographic concept important to cultural cohesion and discourse. As I shall argue by means of analogy with the Winnebago Mid-Winter's feast, this concept may represent underworld forces present at world creation that are important to 'those who are on earth'.

The Winnebago Mid-Winter's feast

Winnebago war-bundle holders host calendrically timed, place-specific feasts (Radin 1990: 393–7). During the course of such feasts, they offer painted deer hides mounted on frames to honour the forces present at world creation. The buckskin frames are carefully arranged with respect to an east–west orientated lodge. In effect, they together produce an architectural map of the primordial world. The purpose of the ceremony is to influence and guide the forces of creation in order to bring the Winnebago victory in war. Except for the painted buckskins, there is little material evidence of this cartographic performance due to purification rites. However, some Midwinter's Feast symbols also apear on world ritual artefacts like Winnebago calendar sticks.

Many of the painted buckskin symbols from the historic war-bundle feasts are found as trailed designs on Pre-Columbian Oneota pottery (Salzer 1994). Most prominent are symbols representing the forces of Sun, Moon, Earthmaker and Earth. Except for the block of parallel lines representing Earth, which look suspiciously like ridged fields, the other symbols are rare in Oneota contexts.

The resemblance of certain sets of parallel trailed lines to plan view projections of ridged fields is more than coincidental. One of the few Oneota mound sites (but see Overstreet 1997: 283) is Lasley Point, which also has ridged fields. In Mound 42, a pot with trailed designs duplicates the topological sequence of the adjacent ridged fields (compare Overstreet (1997: 285) with Griffin (1960: 859 H)). I am not suggesting that all trailed or punctate designs on Oneota ceramics represent raised fields. Many chevron and triangular designs represent raptor tails, a reference to warrior societies (Hall 1991: 27–30). However, all symbols have multiple meanings. The Winnebago, for example, reference warfare and agriculture when dedicating a deer hide with parallel lines to Earth (Radin 1990: 488).

A symbolic discourse centred on warfare has a long history, as the Oneota raptor theme has Late Woodland roots (Benn 1995). So too, do representations of ridged fields. At Aztalan, a grit-tempered Late Woodland sherd has blocks of lines that may duplicate the topological sequence of ridged fields (compare Gallagher (1992: 118) with Barrett (1970: 557)). An unusual cord-marked design on a rim sherd collected from a field adjacent to the Hulburt Creek site may show a plan-view projection of the fields.

Perhaps the presence of the similar symbols on Oneota and Late Woodland pots underscore cultural continuity in a way that vessel form and tempering agent can not. Late Woodland cultural landscapes exemplify a narrative of territoriality — of warfare and agriculture. After the cessation of mound building and Late Woodland lifestyles, Oneota peoples commemorated those historic successes when decorating their pots and building ridged fields.

Conclusions

A landscape approach shows that Wisconsin's Late Woodland Stage is not simply a dull archaeological interlude between Hopewell and Mississippian. Rather, effigy mounds, trails, palisades and ridged fields shaped a dynamic and differentiated Late Woodland world between 700 and 1150 AD.

Excavations at the Hulburt Creek site demonstrate that native peoples practised ridged-field agriculture around 1000 AD. Geoarchaeological and experimental analyses suggest that the Hulburt Creek fields improved fertility, simultaneously provided drainage and water storage and ameliorated microclimate. Ridged fields improve crop habitats in multiple ways related to construction sequences and landscape placement. Hence, it is unlikely that any single cultural or ecological variable could explain the distribution of Upper Midwestern ridged fields.

Effigy Mound peoples of the central and lower Wisconsin River drainage initiated ridged-field agriculture around 1000 AD. They did so as part of a social strategy of territoriality. The multiplication of territories — signified by effigy-mound construction between 700 and 1050 AD, exacerbated by the appearance of fortified settlements after 900 AD and regional trade and alliance networks after 1000 AD — restricted access to dispersed geographical areas. Seasonal migration was critical for the mixed susbsistence economies of Late Woodland peoples. Within Wisconsin's diverse environments, ridged fields were a method of intensifying food production while minimizing risk, subsistence calendar conflicts and land degradation. Ridged fields served as a means of maintaining local identity and regional control.

Future research will probably unravel aspects of this landscape narrative. Few sites have been adequately surveyed, excavated and numerically dated. Ethnographic analogies do not have the explanatory strength of historic homologies. But, as Sauer (1925: 53) notes,

> In the colourful reality of life there is a continuous resistance of fact to confinement within any simplistic theory. Our naively selected selection of reality, the landscape, is undergoing manifold change. Human contact with a changeful home, as expressed through the cultural landscape, is our field of work.

With respect to Late Woodland landscapes and ridged fields there is still much work to do.

Acknowledgements. Financial, intellectual and moral support for the Hulburt Creek site investigations and my regional surveys came from the Wisconsin Alumni Research Foundation through a grant to William M. Denevan, the Southwest Wisconsin Regional Archaeology Program through James B. Stoltman, and William Sawyer Gartner and Astrid Renskoug (my parents). The Center for Climatic Research paid for the Hulburt Creek radiocarbon ages through the Climate Dynamics program, National Science Foundation grant no. ATM90-02849. This research would not have been possible without the generosity and insights of the Sauk Trails chapter of the IAAA, Robert J. Salzer of Beloit College and Robert A. Birmingham of the Wisconsin State Historical Society. A special thanks to Richard Worthington and Onno Brouwer of the UW-Madison Cartography Lab. I am also indebted to Tina Thurston and Chris Fisher for all of our stimulating discussions about archaeology and landscape.

References

ALLY, L., J.E. RAMEY & C.D. SPENCER. 1987. *Wisconsin crops and Wisconsin weather*. Madison (WI): Wisconsin Agricultural Statistics Service.

ARZIGIAN, C.M. 1987. The emergence of horticultural economies in Southwestern Wisconsin, in W.F. Keegan (ed.), *Emergent horticultural economies of the eastern woodlands*: 217–42. Carbondale (IL): Southern Illinois University.

BAKER, A.R. 1992. Introduction: on ideology and landscape, in A.R. Baker & G. Biger (ed.), *Ideology and landscape in historical perspective*: 1–14. Cambridge: Cambridge University Press.

BARRETT, S.A. 1970. *Ancient Aztalan*. Westport (CT): Greenwood Press.

BARRETT, S.A. & E.W. HAWKES. 1919. The Kratz Creek mound group, *Bulletin of the Public Museum of the City of Milwaukee* 3: 1–100.

BENDER, B. 1993. Landscape-meaning and action, in B. Bender (ed.), *Landscapes politics and perspectives*: 1–17. Providence (RI): Berg.

BENN, D. 1995. Woodland people and the roots of Oneota, in W. Green (ed.), *Oneota archaeology: past, present, and future*: 91–139. Iowa City (IA): Office of the State Archaeologist.

BROSE, D.S. 1985. The woodland period in D. Penney (ed.), *Ancient art of the American Woodland Indians*: 43–91. New York (NY): Harry N. Abrams.

BRINKMANN, W. 1979. Growing season length as an indicator of climatic variations? *Climatic Change* 2: 127–38.

CARTIER, J. 1993. *The voyages of Jacques Cartier*. Toronto: University of Toronto Press.

CHAMPLAIN, S. DE. 1878. *Voyages of Samuel de Champlain* II. (Translated by C.P. Otis.) New York (NY: Burt Franklin.

DECK, D.A. & T. SHAY. 1992. A preliminary report on plant remains from the Lockport site (EaLf-1), *Manitoba Archaeology Journal* 2: 36–49.

DENEVAN, W.M. 1992. Stone *vs* metal axes: the ambiguity of shifting cultivation in prehistoric Amazonia, *Journal of Steward Anthropological Society* 20: 153–65.

DENEVAN, W.M. & B.L. TURNER II. 1974. Forms, functions, and associations of raised fields in the old world tropics, *The Journal of Tropical Geography* 39: 24–33.

DOOLITTLE, W.E. In press. *Cultivated landscapes of native North America*. Oxford: Oxford University Press.

FLANNERY, K.V. 1986. A visit to the master, in, K. Flannery (ed.), *Guilá Naquitz*: 511–19. New York (NY): Academic Press.

GALLAGHER, J.P. 1992. Prehistoric field systems in the Upper Midwest, in W.I. Woods (ed.), *Late prehistoric agriculture: observations from the Midwest*: 95–135. Springfield (IL): Illinois Historic Preservation Agency.

GALLAGHER, J.P. & R.F. SASSO. 1987. Investigaions into Oneota ridged field agriculture on the northern margin of the prairie peninsula, *Plains Anthropologist* 32: 141–52.

GARTNER, W.G. 1993. The geoarchaeology of sediment renewal ceremonies at the Gottschall rockshelter, Wisconsin. Unpublished Masters thesis, Department of Geography, University of Wisconsin-Madison.

1997. Four worlds without an Eden: pre-Columbian peoples and the Wisconsin landscape, in R.C. Ostergren & T.R. Vale (ed.), *Wisconsin land and life*: 331–50. Madison (WI): University of Wisconsin Press.

GRIFFIN, J.B. 1960. A hypothesis for the prehistory of the Winnebago, in S. Diamond (ed.), *Culture in history: essays in honor of Paul Radin*: 809–68. New York (NY): Columbia University Press.

HALL, R.L. 1991. Cahokia identity and interaction models of Cahokia Mississippian, in T. Emerson & R. Lewis (ed.), *Cahokia and the hinterlands*: 3–34. Urbana (IL): University of Illinois Press.

1993. Red Banks, Oneota, and the Winnebago: views from a distant rock, *Wisconsin Archeologist* 74: 10–79.

1997. *An archaeology of the soul: North American indian belief and ritual*. Urbana (IL): University of Illinois Press.

HEIDENREICH, C. 1971. *Huronia: a history and geography of the Huron Indians, 1600–1650*. Toronto: McClelland & Steward.

McKERN, W.C. 1930. The Kleitzien and Nitschke Mound Groups, *Bulletin of the Public Museum of the City of Milwaukee* 3: 426–96.

MOODIE, D. & B. KAYE. 1969. The northern limit of indian agriculture in North America, *The Geographical Review* 59: 513–29.

MORISSONNEAU, C. 1978. Huron of Lorette, in B.G. Trigger, (ed.), *Handbook of North American Indians: Northeast*: 389–92. Washington (DC): Smithsonian Institution.

OVERSTREET, D. 1997. Oneota prehistory and history, *The Wisconsin Archeologist*: 78: 250–96.

PRENTICE, G. 1986. An analysis of the symbolism expressed by the Birger Figurine, *American Antiquity* 51: 239–66.

RADIN, P. 1990. *The Winnebago tribe*. Lincoln (NB): University of Nebraska Press.

RILEY, T.J. & G. FREIMUTH. 1979. Field systems and frost drainage in the prehistoric agriculture of the Upper Great lakes, *American Antiquity* 44: 271–85.

SACK, R. 1986. *Human territoriality: its theory and history*. Cambridge: Cambridge University Press.

SALZER, R.J. 1987. Preliminary report on the Gottschall site (47Ia80), *Wisconsin Archeologist* 68: 419–72.

    1994. Archaeology and the Winnebago Midwinter Feast. Presentation at Oneota Roundtable, Midwest Archaeology Conference, 4–5 March, Iowa City.

SAUER, C.O. 1925. The morphology of landscape, *University of California Publications in Geography* 2: 19–54.

SIEMENS, A.H. 1990. Reducing the risk: some indications regarding pre-Hispanic wetland agricultural intensification from contemporary use of a wetland/terra firma boundary zone in central Vera Cruz, in S. Gliessman (ed.), *Agroecology*: 233–50. New York (NY): Springer-Verlag.

STEVENSON, K.P., R. BOSZHARDT, C. MOFFAT, P. SALKIN, T. PLEGER, J. THELER & C. ARZIGIAN. 1997. The Woodland Tradition, *The Wisconsin Archeologist* 78: 140–201.

STOLTMAN, J.B. 1986. The appearance of the Mississippian cultural tradition in the Upper Mississippi valley in J.B. Stoltman (ed.), *Prehistoric mound builders of the Mississippi Valley*: 26–34. Davenport (IA): Putnam Museum.

SWANTON, J. R. 1928. The interpretation of aboriginal mounds by means of Creek indian customs, *Annual Report of the Board of Regents of the Smithsonian Institution, Publication 2927*: 495–506, plates 1–7.

THELER, J.L. 1987. *Woodland tradition economic strategies: animal resource utilization in Southwestern Wisconsin and Northeastern Iowa*. Iowa City (IA): Office of the State Archaeologist.

THURSTON, H.D. 1990. Plant disease management practices of traditional farmers, *Plant Diseases* 74: 96–102.

THWAITES, R.G. (ed.). 1901. *Jesuit relations and allied documents*. Cleaveland (OH): Burrows Brothers.

TUAN, Y. 1977. *Space and place*. Minneapolis (MN): University of Minnesota Press.

WHEATLEY, P. 1971. *The pivot of the four quarters*. Chicago (IL): Aldine.

WILKEN, G.C. 1987. *Good farmers: traditional agricultural resource management in Mexico and Cental America*. Berkeley (CA): University of California Press.

WILL, G.F. & G.E. HYDE. 1917. *Corn among the indians of the Upper Missouri*. Lincoln (NB): University of Nebraska Press.

ZIMMERER, K.S. 1994. Human geography and the new ecology: the prospect and promise of integration, *Annals of the Association of American Geographers* 84: 108–25.

Changing places — revisited

> Rummidge and Euphoria are places on the map of a comic world which
> resembles the one we are standing on without corresponding exactly to it, and which
> is peopled by figments of the imagination
>
> (LODGE 1983: 6)

A CODA to a recent special section on landscape was provocatively headed by this quotation (Stoddart & Zubrow 1999). Novels and films customarily start with a careful disclaimer of any association with reality. The risk is very real for the author of fiction. Some living individual might be offended. Should archaeological reconstructions of landscapes also be accompanied by similar disclosures? The risk is different since archaeologists are not assessing the living. Umbrage is only taken at the low level of acceptance of a personal academic theory, or by the accompanying personalized attack. However, at least some archaeologists are aiming to correspond as exactly as possible to a past reality, and as a profession we need to address how close we can come to understanding landscapes.

What is clear is that landscape is a major industry of intellectual production. The very diversity of approaches is part of the success of landscape studies today. The diversity is, in part, based on the scale of the landscape considered. The scale ranges from the household to the region. However, the diversity is more fundamentally based on the conceptual approach to landscape. The strength of landscape studies would be enhanced by greater interaction between these increasingly disparate approaches. It is rare for a phenomenological study to start with clear understanding of the physical changes in a landscape since the archaeological phase that is being re-experienced. It is rare for a Geographical Information System project to produce concrete results on questions of landscape experience or perception. Some attempt should be made to provide a sense of both the natural and cultural landscape, even if such clear dichotomies are not accepted by all. At a more fundamental level there needs to be good methodology in collecting data (even if the purity of the term is controversial for some) whatever the theoretical position of the practioner.

Archaeology is the only sound means of penetrating the landscapes of the past. It is relatively easy to outline the assumptions of our understanding when we take a quantitative approach. The workings of tricky formulae such as demographic density can be explained and assumptions expressed (Perkins 1999; Stoddart 1999). The assumptions may often appear to be wild, but they are readily stated. However, qualitative analyses are much more difficult to outline in such terms. Our experience of a landscape is tightly knit to our personal memory, drawn from a broader cultural memory. We cannot express effectively the assumptions of transfering such experience to a prehistoric past.

The ultimate test of all these alternative views of landscape will be time itself. Seventy-five years is longish for the archaeological profession. It is possible to have some measure of the importance of the impact of Crawford, Curwen and Fox. We cannot yet determine the future weight of the later authors whose work is reprinted here. Obituaries are rarely written about living scholars, except in informal oral discourse. What is certain is that the well-researched landscapes — Wessex, the Fens, part of the Mediterranean — will recur in the theories of past landscapes, in much the same way as the well-researched sites — Glastonbury, Star Carr and Danebury. There is much to be said for the empirical tradition, even if it is only that it provides the *sine qua non* for assessing successful theory.

References

AGACHE, R. 1964. Aerial reconnaissance in Picardy, *Antiquity* 38: 113–19.

 1978. *La Somme pré-romaine et Romaine d'après les prospections à basse altitude*. Amiens: Société des Antiquaires de Picardie/Musée de Picardie.

 1999. *L'archéologie aérienne en France: le passé vu du ciel*. Paris: Errance.

AGACHE, R. & B. BRÉART. 1975. *Atlas d'archéologie aérienne de Picardie*. Amiens: Société des Antiquaires de Picardie/Musée de Picardie.

ALFREY, J. & C. CLARK. 1993. *The landscape of industry. Patterns of change in the Ironbridge gorge*. London: Routledge.

ALLEN, K.M., S.W. GREEN & E.B. ZUBROW. 1990. *Interpreting space. GIS and archaeology*. London: Taylor & Francis.

ALLEN, M.J. & A. LEWISON. 1987. Reconstructing an agrarian system in the Alpes-Maritimes, France, *Antiquity* 61: 364–9.

AMMERMAN, A.J. 1981. Surveys and archaeological research, *Annual Review of Anthropology* 10: 63–8.

ALVISI, G. 1970. *La viabilità romana della Daunia*. Bari: Tipografia del Sud.

APPLETON, J. 1996. *The experience of landscape*. Chichester: John Wiley.

ASHMORE, W. & A.B. KNAPP. 1999. *Archaeologies of landscape. Contemporary perspectives*. Oxford: Blackwell.

Atti 1982 = *Atti della XXIII Riunione Scientifica* 1982. *Il paleolitico inferiore in Italia*. Firenze: Istituto Italiano di Preistoria e Protostoria.

BAILEY, G., G. KING & D. STURDY. 1993. Active tectonics and land-use strategies: a Palaeolithic example from northwest Greece, *Antiquity* 67: 292–312.

BAKER, F. 1993. The Berlin wall: production, preservation and consumption of a 20th century monument, *Antiquity* 67: 709–33.

BARKER, G. 1977. The archaeology of Samnite settlement in Molise, *Antiquity* 51: 20–24.

 1988. Archaeology and the Etruscan countryside, *Antiquity* 62: 772–85.

 1995a. *A Mediterranean valley: landscape archaeology and* Annales *history in the Biferno valley*. London: Leicester University Press.

 1995b. *The Biferno valley: the archaeological and geomorphological record*. London: Leicester University Press.

BARKER, G. & T. RASMUSSEN. 1998. *The Etruscans*. Oxford: Blackwell.

BARRETT, J. 1994. *Fragments from antiquity*. Oxford: Blackwell.

BARRETT, J.C., M. BRADLEY & M. GREEN. 1991. *Landscape, monuments and society: the prehistory of Cranbourne Chase*. Cambridge: Cambridge University Press.

BARRETT, J.C. & K.J. FEWSTER. 1998. Stonehenge: is the medium the message?, *Antiquity* 72: 847–52.

BASSO, K.H. 1996. *Wisdom sits in places. Landscape and language among the Western Apache*. Albuquerque (NM): University of New Mexico Press.

BELCHER, M., A. HARRISON & S. STODDART. 1999. Analysing Rome's hinterland, in M. Gillings, D. Mattingly & J. van Dalen (ed.), *Geographical information systems and landscape archaeology*: 95–101. Oxford: Oxbow. The archaeology of Mediterranean landscapes 3.

BENDER, B. 1992. Theorizing landscapes, and the prehistoric landscape of Stonehenge, *Man* 27: 735–55.

 (Ed.). 1993a. *Landscape. Politics and perspectives*. Oxford: Berg.

 1993b. Stonehenge — contested landscapes (medieval to the present day), in Bender (ed.): 245–79.

 1998. *Stonehenge. Making space*. Oxford: Berg.

BENDER, B., S. HAMILTON & C. TILLEY. 1997. Leskernick: Stone worlds; alternative narratives; nested landscapes, *Proceedings of the Prehistoric Society* 63: 147–78.

BERESFORD, M. & J.K.S. ST JOSEPH. 1979. *Medieval England: an aerial survey*. Cambridge: Cambridge University Press.

BERSU, G. 1938. The excavation at Woodbury, Wiltshire, during 1938, *Proceedings of the Prehistoric Society* 4: 308–13.

 1940. Excavations at Little Woodbury, Wiltshire, *Proceedings of the Prehistoric Society* 6: 30–111.

BEVAN, B. (ed) 1999. *Northern exposure: interpretative devolution and the Iron Ages in Britain*. Leicester: Leicester University. Leicester Archaeology Monograph 4.

BEWLEY, R., O. BRAASCH & R. PALMER. 1996. An aerial archaeology training week, 15–22 June 1996, held near Siófok, Lake Balaton, Hungary, *Antiquity* 70: 745–50.

BIETTI, A. 1990. The late upper palaeolithic in Italy: an overview, *Journal of World Prehistory* 4(1): 95–155.

BINTLIFF, J.L. & A.M. SNODGRASS. 1985. The Cambridge/Bradford Expedition: the first four years, *Journal of Field Archaeology* 12: 123–61.

 1988a. Mediterranean survey and the city, *Antiquity* 62: 57–71.

 1988b. Off site pottery distributions: a regional and interregional perspective. *Current Anthropology* 29(3): 506–13.

BONANNO, A. 1997. *Malta. An archaeological paradise*. Valletta: M.J. Publications.

BRADFORD, J. 1947. Etruria from the air, *Antiquity* 21: 74–83.

 1949. Buried landscapes in Southern Italy, *Antiquity* 23: 58–72.

 1950. The Apulia expedition: an interim report, *Antiquity* 24: 84–94.

1957. *Ancient landscapes. Studies in field archaeology.* London: G. Bell & Sons.

BRADFORD, J. & P.R. WILLIAMS-HUNT. 1946. Siticulosa Apulia, *Antiquity* 20: 191–200.

BRADLEY, R. 1993. *Altering the earth. The origins of monuments in Britain and Continental Europe.* Edinburgh: Society of Antiquaries of Scotland.

1998. *The significance of monuments.* London: Routledge.

2000. *The archaeology of natural places.* London: Routledge.

BRIGGS, S. 1981. A.H.A. Hogg — an appreciation, in G. Guilbert (ed.), *Hill-fort studies. Essays for A.H.A. Hogg*: 15–18. Leicester: Leicester University Press.

BROWN, A.G. 1997. *Alluvial geoarchaeology. Floodplain archaeology and environmental change.* Cambridge: Cambridge University Press.

BROWN, K.S. 1994. Seeing stars: character and identity in the landscapes of modern Macedonia, *Antiquity* 68: 784–96.

BROWN, N. & J. GLAZEBROOK (ed.). 2000. *Research and archaeology: a framework for the Eastern counties* 2. *Research agenda and strategy.* Norwich: Scole Archaeological Committee. East Anglian Archaeology Occasional Paper 8.

BRÜCK, J. & M. GOODMAN (ed.). 1999. *Making places in the prehistoric world. Themes in settlement archaeology.* London: UCL Press.

BÜCHSENSCHÜTZ, O. & L. OLIVIER (ed.). 1989. *Les Viereckschanzen et les enceintes quadrilaterales en Europe Celtique.* Paris: Errance. Actes du IXe Colloque de l'A.F.E.A.F., Chateaudun, 16–19 mai 1985.

BURGESS, C. 1984. The prehistoric settlement of Northumberland: a speculative survey, in R. Miket & C. Burgess (ed.), *Between and beyond the walls. Essays on the prehistory and history of north Britain in honour of George Jobey*: 126–75. Edinburgh: John Donald.

CAMBI, F. & N. TERRENATO. 1994. *Introduzione all'archeologia dei paesaggi.* Roma: La Nuova Italia Scientifica.

CARMICHAEL, D.L., J. HUBERT, B. REEVES & A. SCHANCHE (ed.). 1994. *Sacred sites, sacred places.* London: Routledge.

CHAPMAN, J. 1994. Destruction of a common heritage: the a;rchaeology of war in Croatia, Bosnia and Hercegovina, *Antiquity* 68: 120–26.

CHERRY, J. 1983. Frogs around the pond: perspectives on current archaeological survey projects in the Mediterranean region, in D.R. Keller & D.L. Rupp (ed.), *Archaeological survey in the Mediterranean area*: 375–416. Oxford: British Archaeological Reports. International series S155.

CHERRY, J.F., J.L. DAVIS & E. MANTZOURANI. 1991. *Landscape archaeology as long-term history. Northern Keos in the Cycladic Islands from earliest times until Modern times.* Los Angeles (CA): University of California Press.

CHILDE, V.G. 1956. *Piecing together the past. The interpretation of archaeological data.* London: Routledge & Kegan Paul.

CLARK, C.M. 1987. Trouble at t'mill: industrial archaeology in the 1980s, *Antiquity* 61: 169–79.

CLARKE, D.L. 1968. *Analytical archaeology.* London: Methuen.

1972. A provisional model of an Iron Age society and its settlement system, in D.L. Clarke (ed.), *Models in archaeology*: 801–69. London: Methuen.

CLEAL, R.M.J., K.E. WALKER & R. MONTAGUE (ed.). 1995. *Stonehenge and its landscape. Twentieth century excavations.* London: English Heritage.

COLES, J. & D. HALL. 1997. The Fenland project: from survey to management and beyond, *Antiquity* 71: 831–44.

1998. *Changing landscapes: the ancient fenland.* Cambridge: Cambridgeshire County Council. Wetland Archaeology Research Project 13.

COSGROVE, D. & S. DANIELS (ed.). 1988. *The iconography of landscape. Essays on the symbolic representation, design and use of past environments.* Cambridge: Cambridge University Press.

CRANDELL, G. 1993. *Nature pictorialized. 'The view' in landscape history.* London: John Hopkins University Press.

CRAWFORD, O.G.S. 1929. Woodbury. Two marvellous air-photographs, *Antiquity* 3: 452–5.

1939. Air reconnaissance of Roman Scotland, *Antiquity* 13: 280–92.

CRAWFORD, O.G.S. & A. KEILLER. 1928. *Wessex from the air.* Oxford: Clarendon Press.

CUNLIFFE, B. & A.C. RENFREW. 1997. *Science and Stonehenge.* Oxford: Oxford University Press.

CURWEN, E. 1927. Prehistoric agriculture in Britain, *Antiquity* 1: 261–89.

1928. Ancient cultivations at Grassington, Yorkshire. *Antiquity* 2: 168–72.

1929. *Prehistoric Sussex.* London: The Homeland Association.

1930. Neolithic Camps, *Antiquity* 4: 22–54.

1932. Ancient cultivations, *Antiquity* 6: 389–406.

1938. The Hebrides: a cultural backwater, *Antiquity* 12: 261–89.

DANIEL, G. 1986. *Some small harvest. The memoirs of Glyn Daniel.* London: Thames & Hudson.

DANIELS, S. & D. COSGROVE. 1988. Introduction: iconography and landscape, in D. Cosgrove & S. Daniels (ed.), *The iconography of landscape. Essays on the symbolic representation, design and use of past environments*: 1–10. Cambridge: Cambridge University Press.

DARVILL, T. 1996. *Prehistoric Britain from the air: a study of space time and society.* Cambridge: Cambridge University Press.

DECKER, K.V. 1968. Die jüngere Latènezeit im Neuwieder Becken, *Jahrbuch für Geschichte und Kunst des Mittelrheins* 1: 7–180.

DECKER, K.V. & I. SCOLLAR. 1962. Iron Age square enclosures in Rhineland, *Antiquity* 36: 175–8.

DINCAUZE, D.F. 2000.*Environmental archaeology. Principles and practice.* Cambridge: Cambridge University Press.

DOBINSON, C.S., J. LAKE & A.J. SCHOFIELD. 1997. Monuments of war: defining England's 20th-century defence heritage, *Antiquity* 71: 288–99.

EDMONDS, M. 1999. *Ancestral geographies of the Neolithic. Landscapes, monuments and memory*. London: Routledge.

EDIS, J., D. MACLEOD & R. BEWLEY. 1989. An archaeologist's guide to classification of cropmarks and soilmarks, *Antiquity* 63: 112–26.

ENEI, F. 1993. *Cerveteri. Ricognizioni archeologiche nel territorio di una città etrusca*. Ladispoli: Gruppo Archeologico Romano.

EVANS, C. 1989. Archaeology and modern times: Bersu's Woodbury 1938 and 1939, *Antiquity* 63: 436–50.

2000. Archaeological distribution. The problem of dots, in Kirby & Oosthuizen (ed.): 3.

EVANS, J.G., S. LIMBREY, I. MATÉ & R. MOUNT. 1993. An environmental history of the upper Kennet valley, Wiltshire, for the last 10,000 years, *Proceedings of the Prehistoric Society* 59: 139–95.

EVERSON, P. 1999. Preface, in P. Pattison, D. Field & S. Ainsworth. 1999. *Patterns of the past. Essays in landscape archaeology for Christopher Taylor*: xi–xii. Oxford: Oxbow.

FLANNERY, K.V. 1976. (ed.). *The Early Mesoamerican village*. New York (NY): Academic Press.

FLEMING, A. 1999. Phenomenology and the megaliths of Wales: a dreaming too far?, *Oxford Journal of Archaeology* 18(2): 119–25.

FOLEY, R. 1981. *Offsite archaeology and human adaptation in eastern Africa*. Oxford: British Archaeological Reports. Cambridge Monographs in African Archaeology 3/BAR International series 97.

FOX, A. 2000. *Aileen — a pioneering archaeologist. The autobiography of Aileen Fox*. Leominster: Gracewing.

FOX, C. 1923. *The archaeology of the Cambridge region: a topographical study of the Bronze, early Iron, Roman and Anglo-Saxon ages, with an introductory note on the Neolithic age*. Cambridge: Cambridge University Press.

1929. Dykes, *Antiquity* 3: 135–54.

1937. Peasant crofts in north Pembrokeshire, *Antiquity* 11: 427–30.

1952. *The personality of Britain. Its influence on inhabitant and invader in prehistoric and early historic times*. Cardiff: National Museum of Wales.

FOX, C. & A. FOX. 1934. Forts and farms on Margam Mountain, Glamorgan, *Antiquity* 8: 395–413.

FRANCOVICH, R. & H. PATTERSON (ed.). 2000. *Extracting meaning from ploughsoil assemblages*. Oxford: Oxbow.

FRERE, S.S. & J.K.S. ST JOSEPH. 1983. *Roman Britain from the air*. Cambridge: Cambridge University Press.

GAFFNEY, C., V. GAFFNEY & M. TINGLE. 1985. Settlement, economy or behaviour? Micro-regional land use models and the interpretation of surface artefact patterns, in C. Haselgrove, M. Millett & I. Smith (ed.), *Archaeology from the ploughsoil. Studies in the collection and interpretation of Field Survey data*: 95–107. Sheffield: University of Sheffield, Department of Archaeology & Prehistory.

GAFFNEY, V. & Z. STANČIĆ. 1991. *GIS approaches to regional analysis. A case study from the island of Hvar*. Ljubljana: Znanstveni institut Filozofske facultete.

GAFFNEY, V. & M. VAN LEUSEN. 1995. Post-script — GIS, environmental determinism and archaeology: a parallel text, in Lock & Stančič (ed.): 367–82.

GARTNER, W.G. 1999. Late Woodland landscapes of Wisconsin: ridged fields, effigy mounds and territoriality, *Antiquity* 73: 671–83.

GILLINGS, M., D. MATTINGLY & J. VAN DALEN (ed.). 1999. *Geographical information systems and landscape archaeology*. Oxford: Oxbow.

GILLINGS, M., J. POLLARD & D. WHEATLEY. 2000. Avebury and the Beckhampton Avenue, *Current Archaeology* 167: 428–33.

GOJDA, M. 1993. Bohemia from the air: seven decades after Crawford, *Antiquity* 67: 869–75.

GRACIE, H.S. 1954. The ancient cart-tracks of Malta, *Antiquity* 28: 91–9.

GREENE, K. 1986. *The archaeology of the Roman economy*. London: Batsford.

GRIMA, R. 2000. Naxxar: An archaeological profile, in P. Catania & L.J. Scerri (ed.), *Naxxar. A village and its people*: 27–64. Hal Tarxien: Gutenberg Press.

GUIDI, A. 1985. An application of the rank size rule to protohistoric settlements in the middle Tyrrhenian area, in C.A.T. Malone & S.K.F. Stoddart (ed.), *Papers in Italian Archaeology* IV(3): *Patterns in Protohistory*: 217–42. Oxford: British Archaeological Reports. International series S245.

HAFFNER, A. 1989. Das Gräberfeld von Wederath-Belginum vom 4. Jahrhundert vor bis 4. Jahrhundert nach Christi Geburt, in A. Haffner (ed.), *Gräber — Spiegel des Lebens zum Totenbrauchtum der Kelten und Römer am Beispiel des Treverer-Gräberfeldes Wederath-Belginum*: 37–128. Mainz am Rhein: Verlag Philipp von Zabern.

HALL, D. & J. COLES. 1994. *Fenland survey: an essay in landscape and persistence*. London: English heritage.

HALL, M. 2000. *Archaeology and the modern world. Colonial transcripts in South Africa and the Chesapeake*. London: Routledge.

HAMPTON, J.N. 1972. RCHM (England): NMR: the Air Photographs Unit, *Antiquity* 46: 59–61.

HASELGROVE, C. (ed.). N.d. Understanding the British Iron Age. An agenda for action. Unpublished discussion document.

HAWKES, J. 1967. God in the machine, *Antiquity* 41: 174–80.

HIRSCH, E. & M. O'HANLON (ed.). 1995. *The anthropology of landscape: perspectives on place andspace*. Oxford: Clarendon Press.

HODDER, I. & C.A.T. MALONE. 1984. An intensive survey of the Stilo region, Calabria, *Proceedings of the Prehistoric Society* 50: 121–50.

HOGG, A.H.A. 1943. Native settlements of Northumberland, *Antiquity* 17: 136–47.

HOLGATE, R. 1987. Neolithic settlement patterns at Avebury, Wiltshire, *Antiquity* 61: 259–63.

HOLLEYMAN, G.A. 1935. The Celtic Field-System in South Britain: a survey of the Brighton District, *Antiquity* 9: 443–54.

HOSKINS, W.C. 1955. *The making of the English landscape*. Harmondsworth: Penguin.
  1977. *The making of the English landscape*. London: Hodder & Stoughton.
HOWARD, A.J. & M.G. MACKLIN. 1999. A generic geomorphological approach to archaeological interpretation and prospection in British river valleys: a guide for archaeologists investigating Holocene landscapes, *Antiquity* 73: 527–41.
HUGHES, K.J. 1999. Persistent features in a palaeolandscape: the ancient tracks of the Maltese islands, *The Geographical Journal* 165(1): 62–78.
JAMESON, M.H., C.N. RUNNELS & T.H. VAN ANDEL (ed.). 1994. *A Greek countryside. The Southern Argolid from prehistory to the present day*. Stanford (CA): Stanford University Press.
JOHNSON, M. 1996. *An archaeology of capitalism*. Oxford: Blackwell.
JONES, G.D.B. 1987. *Apulia I. Neolithic settlement in the Tavoliere*. London: Society of Antiquaries/Thames & Hudson.
JONES, S. 1997. *The archaeology of ethnicity. Constructing identities in the past and present*. London: Routledge.
KENNEDY, D. 1996. A Mediterranean landscape, *Antiquity* 70: 694–9.
KENNEDY, D. & D. RILEY. 1990. *Rome's desert frontier from the air*. London: Batsford.
KIRBY, A. & S. OOSTHUIZEN (ed.). 2000. *An atlas of Cambridgeshire and Huntingdonshire history*. Cambridge: Anglia Polytechnic University.
KNAPP, A.B. 1998. Social approaches to the archaeology and anthropology of mining, in A.B. Knapp, V.C. Pigott & E.W. Herbert (ed.), *Social approaches to an industrial past. The archaeology and anthropology of mining*: 1–23. London: Routledge.
LAST, J. 1999. Out of line: cursuses and monument typology in eastern England, in G. Barclay & J. Harding (ed.), *Pathways and ceremonies. The cursus monuments of Britain and Ireland*: 86–97. Oxford: Oxbow. Neolithic Studies Papers 4.
LLOBERA, M. 1996. Exploring the topography of mind: GIS, social space and archaeology, *Antiquity* 70: 612–22.
LOCK, G. & Z. STANČIČ. 1995. (ed.) *Archaeology and Geographical Information Systems: a European perspective*. London: Taylor & Francis.
LODGE, D. 1983. *Changing places. A tale of two campuses*. Harmondsworth: Penguin.
MAITLAND, F.L. 1927. The 'works of the Old Men' in Arabia, *Antiquity* 1: 197–203.
MALIM, T. 2000. The Anglo-Saxon dykes, in Kirby & Oosthuizen (ed.): 27.
MALLORY, J. 1984–7. Lagnano da Piede: an early Neolithic village in the Tavoliere, *Origini* 13: 193–290.
MALONE, C. 1989. *Avebury*. London: Batsford.
MALONE, C. & S. STODDART. 1994. *Time, territory and state. The archaeological develop;ment of the Gubbio Valley*. Cambridge: Cambridge University Press.
MANDOLESI, A. 1999. *La Prima Tarquinia. L'insediamento protostorico sulla civita e nel territorio circostante*. Firenze: All'Insegna del Giglio. Grandi Contesti e Problemi della Protostoria Italiana 2.
MCGUIRE, W.J., D.R. GRIFFITHS, P.L. HANCOCK & I.S. STEWART. 2000. *The archaeology of geological catastrophes*. London: Geological Society. Special Publication 171.
MCMANN, J. 1994. Forms of power: dimensions of an Irish megalithic landscape, *Antiquity* 68: 525–44.
MEE, C. & H. FORBES (ed.). 1997. *A rough and rocky place*. Liverpool: Liverpool University Press.
MORRIS, M. 1994. Towards an archaeology of navvy huts and settlements of the industrial revolution, *Antiquity* 68: 573–84.
MUIR, R. 1999. *Approaches to landscape*. London: Macmillan.
NORMAN, E.R. & J.K.S. ST JOSEPH. 1969. *The early development of Irish Society: the evidence of aerial photography*. Cambridge: Cambridge University Press.
PACCIARELLI, M. 1991. Ricerche topografiche a Vulci: dati e problemi relativi all'origine delle citta medio-tirreniche, *Studi Etruschi* 56: 11–48.
PALMER, M. & P.A. NEAVERSON. 1987. Industrial archaeology: the reality, *Antiquity* 61: 459–61.
  1998. *Industrial archaeology. Principles and practice*. London: Routledge.
PALMER, R. 1984. *Danebury. An Iron Age hillfort in Hampshire. An aerial photographic interpretation of its environs*. London: Royal Commission on Historical Monuments (England). Supplementary Series 6.
PARKER, R. & M. RUBINSTEIN. 1984. *The cart-ruts on Malta and Gozo*. Malta: Gozo Press.
PARKER PEARSON, M. AND RAMILISONINA. 1998a. Stonehenge for the ancestors: the stones pass on the message, *Antiquity* 72: 308–26.
  1998b. Stonehenge for the ancestors: part two, *Antiquity* 72: 855–6.
PARSONS, J.R. 1972. Archaeological settlement patterns, *Annual Review of Anthropology* 1: 127–50.
PATTERSON, H., F. DI GENNARO, H. DI GIUSEPPE, S. FONTANA, V. GAFFNEY, A. HARRISON, S.J. KEAY, M. MILLETT, M. RENDELI, P. ROBERTS, S. STODDART & R. WITCHER. 2000. The Tiber Valley Project: the Tiber and Rome through two millennia, *Antiquity* 74: 395–403.
PIGGOTT, S. 1937. Prehistory and the Romantic movement, *Antiquity* 11: 31–8.
PIPERNO, M. 1992. Il palaeolitico inferiore, in A. Guidi & M. Piperno (ed.), *Italia preistorica*: 139–69. Roma: Editori Laterza.
PERKINS, P. 1999. Reconstructing the population history of the Albegna valley and Ager Cosanus, Tuscany, Italy, in the Etruscan period, in Gillings *et al.*: 103–11.
PERKINS, P. & I. ATTOLINI. 1992. An Etruscan farm at Podere Tartucchino, *Papers of the British School at Rome* 60: 71–134.
PIGGOTT, S. 1965. Archaeological draughtsmanship: principles and practice. Part I: principles and retrospect, *Antiquity* 39: 165–76.
POLLARD, J. 1999. 'These places have their moments': thoughts on settlement practices in the British Neolithic, in J. Brück & M. Goodman (ed.), *Making places in the prehistoric world. Themes in settlement archaeology*: 76–93. London: UCL Press.

POTTER, T. 1979. *The changing landscape of south Etruria*. London: Elek.

RACKHAM, O. & J. MOODY. 1996. *The making of the Cretan landscape*. Manchester: Manchester University Press.

RALSTON, I. 1988. Central Gaul at the Roman conquest: conceptions and misconceptions, *Antiquity* 62: 786–94.

RENDELI, M. 1993. *Città aperte*. Rome: Gruppi Editoriali Internazionali.

REYNOLDS, T. 1994. The evidence of lithics, in C. Malone & S. Stoddart (ed.), *Time, territory and state. The archaeological development of the Gubbio valley*: 59–67. Cambridge: Cambridge University Press.

RICHARDS, J. 1990. *The Stonehenge environs project*. London: English Heritage. Historic Buildings & Monuments Commission for England Archaeological Report 16.

RILEY, D.N. 1945. Aerial reconnaissance of the Fen Basin, *Antiquity* 19: 145–53.

1992. New aerial reconnaissance in Apulia, *Papers of the British School at Rome* 60: 291–307.

RIVA, C. & S. STODDART. 1996. Ritual landscapes in Archaic Etruria, in J.B. Wilkins (ed.), *Approaches to the study of ritual. Italy and the ancient Mediterranean*: 91–109. London: Accordia Research Centre. Accordia Specialist Studies on the Mediterranean 2.

ROBERTS, B.K. 1996. *Landscapes of settlement. Prehistory to the present*. London: Routledge.

ROYMANS, N. 1990. *Tribal societies in Northern Gaul. An anthropological perspective*. Amsterdam: Universiteit van Amsterdam. Cingula 12.

ST JOSEPH, J.K. 1967. Air reconnaissance: recent results 11, *Antiquity* 41: 216–18.

1972. Air reconnaissance: recent results 28, *Antiquity* 46: 224–6.

ST JOSEPH, J.K. & D.R. WILSON. 1976. Air reconnaissance: recent results 41, *Antiquity* 50: 237–9.

SHACKEL, P. 1993. *Personal discipline and material culture: an archaeology of Annapolis, Maryland, 1695–1870*. Knoxville (TN): University of Tennessee Press.

SCHAMA, S. 1995. *Landscape and memory*. London: HarperCollins.

SCHOFIELD, A.J. 1987. Putting lithics to the test. Non site analysis and the Neolithic settlement of Southern England, *Oxford Journal of Archaeology* 6(3): 269–86.

1989. Understanding early medieval pottery distributions: cautionary tales and their implications for future research, *Antiquity* 63: 460–70.

(Ed.) 1990. *Interpreting artefact scatters. Contributions to ploughzone archaeology*. Oxford: Oxbow. Monograph 4.

SHENNAN, S. 1985. *Experiments in the collection and analysis of archaeological survey data: the east Hampshire survey*. Sheffield: University of Sheffield, Department of Archaeology & Prehistory.

SPIRN, A.W. 1998. *The language of landscape*. New Haven (CT): Yale University Press.

SPIVEY, N. & S. STODDART. 1990. *Etruscan Italy*. London: Batsford.

STODDART, S. 1987. Complex polity formation in North Etruria and Umbria. 1200–500 BC. Unpublished Ph.D thesis, University of Cambridge.

1990. The political landscape of Etruria, *Journal of the Accordia Research Centre* 1: 39–51.

1999. Beyond historical demography: the contribution of archaeological survey, in J. Bintliff & K. Sbonias (ed.), *Reconstructing past population trends in Mediterranean Europe*: 129–31. Oxford: Oxbow. The archaeology of Mediterranean landscapes 1.

STODDART, S. & E. ZUBROW. 1999. Changing places, *Antiquity* 73: 686–8.

THOMAS, J. 1991. *Rethinking the Neolithic*. Cambridge: Cambridge University Press.

1993. The politics of vision and the archaeologies of landscape, in Bender (ed.): 19–48.

TILLEY, C. 1994. *A phenomenology of landscape: places, paths and monuments*. Oxford: Berg.

1996. The power of rocks: topography and monument construction on Bodmin Moor, *World Archaeology* 28(2): 161–76.

1999. Landscapes and a sense of place, in C. Tilley (ed.), *Metaphor and material culture*: 175–273. Oxford: Blackwell.

TINÉ, S. 1983. *Passo di Corvo e la civiltà neolitica del Tavoliere*. Genova: Sagep.

TOWNSEND, R.F. 1992. *The ancient Americas: Art from sacred landscapes*. Chicago (IL): Art Institute of Chicago/Munich: Prestel Verlag.

TOZZI, C. & M. VEROLA. 1990. La campagna di scavo 1990 a Ripatetta (Lucera, FG), *Atti del 12 convegno di Preistoria, Protostoria e Storia della Daunia*: 37–48.

TRÉMENT, F. 2000. The integration of historical, archaeological and palaeoenvironmental data at the regional scale: the Étang de Berre, Southern France, in P. Leveau, F. Trément, K. Walsh & K. Barker (ed.), *Environmental reconstruction in Mediterranean landscape archaeology*: 193–205. Oxford: Oxbow. The archaeology of Mediterranean landscapes 2.

TRUMP, D. 1998. The cart ruts of Malta, *Treasures of Malta* 4(2): 33–7.

UCKO, P.J., M. HUNTER, A.J. CLARK & A. DAVID. 1991. *Avebury reconsidered: from the 1960s to the 1990s*. London: Unwin Hyman.

UCKO, P.J. & R. LAYTON (ed.). 1999. *The archaeology and anthropology of landscape. Shaping your landscape*. London: Routledge.

VAN DER LEEUW, S.E. 1994. *Understanding the natural and anthropogenic causes of soil degradation and desertification in the Mediterranean Basin 2: temporalities and desertification in the Vera basin*. Cambridge: Directorate General XII of the Commission of the European Union.

VENTURA, F. & T. TANTI. 1994. The cart tracks at San Pawl tat-targa, Naxxar, *Melita Historica* 11(3): 219–40.

VITA-FINZI, C. 1969. *The Mediterranean valleys. The Mediterranean valleys: geological change in historical time*. Cambridge: Cambridge University Press.

WAGSTAFF, J.M. (ed.). 1987. *Landscape and culture. Geographical and archaeological perspectives*. Oxford: Blackwell.

WANSLEEBEN, M. & L. VERHART. 1997. Geographical systems. Methodological progress and theoretical decline? *Archaeological Dialogues* 4(1): 53–70.

WEBSTER, D.S. 1999. The concept of affordance and GIS: a note on Llobera (1996), *Antiquity* 73: 915–17.

WHEATLEY, D. 1995. Cumulative viewshed analysis: a GIS-based method for investigating intervisibility, and its archaeological application, in Lock & Stančič (ed.): 171–85.

WHITTLE, A. 1997. *Sacred mound, holy rings. Silbury hill and the West Kennett palisade enclosures: a later Neolithic complex in North Wiltshire.* Oxford: Oxbow.

1998. People and the diverse past: two comments on Stonehenge for the ancestors, *Antiquity* 72: 852–4.

WHITTLE, A., J. POLLARD & C. GRIGSON (ed.). 1999. *The harmony of symbols. The Windmill Hill causewayed enclosure.* Oxford: Oxbow.

WILLIS, K.J., P. SÜMEGI, M. BRAUN, K.D. BENNETT & A.TOTH. 1998. Prehistoric land degradation in Hungary: who, how and why?, *Antiquity* 72: 101–13.

WIGHTMAN, E.M. 1970 Rhineland 'Grabgärten' and their context, *Bonner Jahrbucher* 170: 211–32.

1985. *Gallia Belgica.* London: Batsford.

WILSON, D.R. 1982. *Air photo interpretation for archaeologists.* London: Batsford.

WITCHER, R. 1999. GIS and landscapes of perception, in Gillings *et al.* (ed.): 13–22.

WORDSWORTH, W. [1810] 1951. *A Guide through the District of the Lakes in the North of England with a Description of the Scenery, &c. for the use of Tourists and Residents.* London: Rupert Hart Davis.

YOUNG, G. 1987. Pioneer settlement patterns in the Onkaparinga District Council of South Australia, *Antiquity* 61: 297–310.

ZAMMIT, T. 1928. Prehistoric cart-tracks in Malta, *Antiquity* 2: 18–25.

ZANGGER, E., M.E. TIMPSON, S.B. YAZVENKO & H. LEIERMANN. 2000. Searching for the ports of Troy, in P. Leveau, F. Trément, K. Walsh & K. Barker (ed.), *Environmental reconstruction in Mediterranean landscape archaeology*: 89–103. Oxford: Oxbow. The archaeology of Mediterranean landscapes 2.

ZANGGER, E., S.B. YAZVENKO, M.E. TIMPSON, F. KUHNKE & J. KNAUSS. 1997. The Pylos regional archaeological project part II: Landscape evolution and site preservation, *Hesperia* 66(4): 549–641.